That's Not The Way I Remember It!

by

Bernard F. Barcio, L.H.D.

Barcio, Bernard F., L.H.D.
That's Not the Way I Remember It
Second Edition
ISBN 978-0-9849159-7-2

Copyright © 2014, Bernard F. Barcio, L.H.D.

All Rights Reserved.

No part of this book may be reproduced, stored in a retrieval system, or transmitted by any means, electronic, mechanical, photocopying, recording or otherwise, without written permission from the author.

Originally published by
Bookman Publishing and Marketing in 2004
ISBN: 1-59453-516-7

Republished with some additions and minor revisions by the author in 2014 by The Constance Book Project
Las Vegas, Nevada, U.S.A.
Constancebookproject@gmail.com

This book preserves a collection of more than a century and a quarter of family stories passed on by two Italian immigrant families, the Barcios and the Nudis.

These stories will amaze, inspire, entertain, shock, inform and move the reader to tears. They are retold through the eyes and imagination of a grandson, Bernard F. Barcio, L.H.D., the stories of whose own life and family (also included) will, at times, challenge believability.

As the title clearly states, every family member or friend familiar with any of these stories will, no doubt, remark, "That's not the way I remember it." And this is perfectly fine with the author who has made every effort to include as many accurate facts, correct dates and details as could be reliably researched or inferred from family photos, documents and oral histories. The presentation of the stories has been embossed, occasionally, with fictitious situations and dialog.

Several standard and colloquial Italian conversations and phrases are included without translations. The standard Italian can easily be translated using an Italian/English dictionary. Many of the colloquial Italian phrases unfortunately are literally untranslatable. In fact, they were usually not intended to be understood by those at whom they were directed. Their meaning was to be inferred from the tone of voice and body language of the speaker.

    Some dates are approximate when no precise records or reliable memories were available.

    Parents with young children should be advised that the content of this family history is to be considered PG-13.

    Names of immediate family members have not been changed. No one is innocent.

Dedication

To my wife, Lillian, whose determination, stamina and courage in confronting incredible challenges throughout her life are an ongoing inspiration to me and to all those privileged to have known and worked with her;

To Theodore J. Barcio who fantasized about having his life story celebrated in a Johnny Cash ballad (hope this will be even better, Dad!);

To all those ancestors, family members, friends and acquaintances whose stories have enriched all our lives;

To all those descendants who will have the opportunity to share and preserve these stories and the memory of those who lived them.

Special thanks to my son, Phillip, for his encouragement, his contributions, his editorial and proofreading expertise and his invaluable technical assistance in preparing the many photos included in this publication. I also owe Phillip my sincere thanks for his encouragement and help with the correcting, updating, expanding and publishing of this second edition.

Thanks also to Joe Barcio for his story contributions, his editorial and proofreading expertise, and for continuing to share our life together as Italian brothers even after he read this entire book.

Author's Preface to the 2nd Edition

When, in December of 2013, I found myself with only one copy of the 1st edition of **That's Not the Way I Remember It**, I attempted to return to Bookman Publishing to inquire about another press run. Bookman Publishing, however, after receiving negative publicity for its questionable book promotion tactics, had first changed its name to Airleaf Publishing, and then, on December 21, 2007, was finally driven out of business.

I subsequently decided to republish the book under the auspices of The Constance Book Project.

It is hoped that the corrections, updates, and additions (both text and photo) made in this second edition have resulted in an even more appreciated record of the wonderful stories of the Barcio and Nudi families.

Bernard F. Barcio, L.H.D.
April 15, 2014

PART I

February 1877 – October 1927

Getting off the Boat and Settling in

February 27, 1877
Cervicati, Italy

Chiara Canatara, the daughter of Pietro Canatara, wife of Angelo Nudi, had just given birth to her son, Antonio. Chiara and Angelo also had a son named Domenico, but their family was not destined to be very large. Chiara passed away six years later. All Tony Nudi could remember about his mother in his old age was that she had been buried at a convent in La Rigniana at Madona di Catina in Italy.

Tony Nudi's uncle, Michael Nudi (b. a. 1850), had a son named Francesco (b. ca. 1880). After his wife gave birth to two children in Italy (Flora & Batistina), they emigrated to Argentina, where they had three more children: Rafaelo (b. ca. 1910), Mario and Jose. Rafaelo had two children, Abél (b. 1933) and Francesco Oscar (b. 1937/8).

Tony Nudi never heard anything more about his Cousin Francesco until Francesco's son Abél sent him a postcard from Argentina in April of 1962 advertising his musical group called *Los Callejeros*.

It was with the help of this postcard that Tony's granddaughter, Kathy, (daughter of his son Gusty) was able to locate and meet Abél in Buenos Aires when she travelled to Argentina in 2011. Unfortunately, she was not able to meet any other members of Abél's family.

As fate would have it, Tony's future wife, Filomena, would have a cousin (Caesare Comprechioli, son of Filomena's sister, Josephine) whose first son would also move to Argentina. His name would be Francino Comprechioli. In 1965, his address—as provided to Bernie Barcio who visited the Comprechioli's in Agnino, Provincia di Campobasso, Reggio di Abruzzi, Italy—was Colle Gabotto 1925, Hurlingham, Buenos Aires, Argentina. During that visit, Bernie also learned that among the twelve other children in Filomena's family—two brothers, Vincenzo and Antonio, and a sister named Stafana—had also moved to Argentina although no one knew their addresses.

Tony Nudi recalled that he had been born and lived for a while in Cervicati in Calabria before he and his father moved "to the farm country" in nearby Marinello. It was there that Tony had been sent to school—for two days only. After that, his dad decided that Tony had learned enough and that he needed him to work on the farm instead. Later in life, Tony taught himself to sign his name which he could still do in July of 1970 when he was 93 years old. This is attested to by a napkin bearing his signature, dated and preserved by his daughter Stella.

When Tony had turned 18, he joined the Italian army, serving for two years. After he was discharged from the army, Tony returned to the Provincia di Cosenza in southern Italy.

October, 1891
La Mattina, Italy

It was Sunday morning. As Vincenzo Barci loaded his wife Rachela and their five children, Angelina, Violanda, Raffaelli, Bernardo and Giuseppe into the family wagon, he looked across the hills and saw the *Torre Normanna*. San Marco Argentano was just a few miles distant from the village of La Mattina, near which lay the farm that he rented from his *Padrone*, Longarre Valentoni.

The whole family was dressed in their best clothing since they would be attending the Mass of All Souls in the *Chiesa di Santa Maria Della Matina* (in contrast with the name of the town, the name of the church is spelled with only one "t" on its literature) that occupied the ground floor of the *Palazzo* owned by Longarre Valentoni, a *Palazzo* that had been built in A.D. 1002, some fifty years before the Normans built their tower in San Marco Argentano.

In addition to farming land rented from his *Padrone*, Vincenzo also kept sheep, the care of which was shared by his five-year old son, Giuseppe.

When the family had ridden about a quarter mile from their farmhouse, Vincenzo looked down at his son, Giuseppe, and noticed that his son did not have his good hat with him.

"*Giuseppe, dovè tua capella buona?*"

"*Eh, mannagia,*" said little Giuseppe letting a slang expression slip that he had heard his father use, "*ho dimenticato la mia capella buona a la casa.*"

"*Scende subito. Prende tua capella e torne subito! Vai, Vai! Affretarsi!*"

Giuseppe immediately jumped down from the wagon and began running back to his house to get his good hat.

"*MEMORIA BREVE, GAMBE LONGE!*" called his father after him.

This little bit of local Italian wisdom, "Short memory, long legs," would be one that Giuseppe would pass on to his own children, and they on to theirs.

When the Barci family arrived outside the *Palazzo*, Vincenzo secured the horse and then with rural dignity led his family into the *Chiesa*, nodding his respects to his *Padrone* before he and his family took their places.

After his eyes adjusted to the dim light in the small church, little Giuseppe began to look around, stopping only when he saw little two-year-old Vrigita Verta staring back at him from across the aisle. Next to her was her brother, Giovanni. At five years old, Giuseppe had little interest in this girl who would end up being his wife in fifteen years.

The Verta family stood with stiff-backed nobility. *Signora* Verta's maiden name was Caruso, a family distantly related to a young tenor, Enrico Caruso, who, at age 18, was already making a name for himself in the taverns of *Napoli,* Italy.

Also in the chapel on this special feast day were the Paraino family and a family named Bruno. The Paraino family had a son, Jacomo, who was an occasional playmate of little Giuseppe Barci.

October, 1897
Cosenza, Italy

It was a beautiful fall day in Southern Italy, and Raffaele Bruno was resting with his five-year old son, also named Raffaele, in the vineyard they rented from their *Padrone*. The grapes had all been harvested, and the wine was in the first stages of fermentation. This was the time when vines needed to be pruned before winter set in.

As they snacked on bread, cheese and oil-cured olives, father and son looked out over the hills that lay quietly under the warm midday sun. It was one of those clear fall days when they could see the *Torre Normanna* miles away in San Marco Angentano.

"Do you think anyone will ever find it, Pa?" asked little Raffaele.

"Find what, *figghio mio*?"

"The buried silver that the Normans hid in the river when they fled from *San Marco*."

"Nobody has found any treasure in eight hundred years. I think maybe it's just a story."

"Guido told me that his father says there is a tunnel under the Tower. Do you think it could lead to the treasure?"

"Guido who?"

"Guido Malatesta."

"*Signor* Malatesta may be a very smart man, Raffaele, but sometimes people don't know everything."

"Do you know the *Torre Normanna*?"

"Of course I know the *Torre Normanna*. We used to play there when we were little."

"Did you ever find the tunnel?"

"*Come no? Ma* sure we found the tunnel. We even went in with candles one day to see where it would lead."

"Did you find a treasure?"

"The tunnel is all walled up inside. It doesn't lead anywhere, and there's no treasure. Do you want to find a treasure, *figghio mio*?"

"Where should I look?"

"Well, some people are looking in America."

"Can we move to America, too?"

"Who knows? Maybe someday when you get older, you can go."

"Wouldn't you and Ma want to come too?"

"I tell you what," said the elder Raffaele, smiling, "you go first and make your fortune. Then maybe you can send for your Mamma and me."

The next day was All Souls Day. After church, Raffaele Bruno happened to strike up a conversation with a stranger who was still wearing a soldier's uniform. The stranger's name turned out to be Antonio Nudi. Antonio was a 5 foot 4 inch tall, sturdily built young man, 20 years old, who had the bravado of a quick-witted farmer and the confidence of a soldier. He prided himself on being tough. The two men hit it off so well that Raffaele invited Tony to stop at the house for *un' bicchière di vino*.

After the usual introductions to his family, and the setting out of a tray of meats, cheese and olives, the rest of the family was dismissed as Antonio and Raffaele got down to some serious wine drinking and conversation. Unnoticed by his father and their visitor, little five-year-old Raffaele sat quietly in a corner to listen.

"So," asked Raffaele, "what are your plans now that you have been discharged from the army?"

"I think I'm gonna move to America," said Antonio.

"Who do you know in America?"

"I don't have to know anyone. I tell you, my new friend, my cousin, Francesco Nudi, is thinking about leaving his home in Castel Liba and sailing with his wife and two daughters, Flora and Batistina, to Argentina in South America. He's not afraid, and I'm not afraid either. In America, they say, the streets are paved with gold!"

"What can you do? How will you support yourself in America?"

By now, the effect of several water glasses full of wine was beginning to be noticeable, and the conversation took on a more personal and intense tone.

"What can I do? I got two hands and a head on my shoulders. What else does a man need? I can use my head to learn any job that my hands need to do."

"America is a big place, you know. Where will you live?"

"*Qui sacia*? Maybe New York. Maybe Chicago"

"You're a brave man, Antonio. Do you have family that you're leaving behind?"

"*Si, mio padre e mio fratello*," replied Antonio.

"*Come si chiamano?*"

"*Mio padre si chiama Angelo, e mio fratello è Domenico.*"

"Don't your father and your brother want to go with you?"

"No. They don't believe in America. But who knows? Maybe some day I'll come back and see them again. Don't you have anyone in your family that wants to move to America?" asked Antonio.

"Well, my brother's son, whose name is also Domenico, told his father he wants to move to America when he grows up. And, of course, my little son, Raffaele, wants to do the same thing. But you know how kids are. One day they have an idea, and the next day they forget all about it. And talking about kids, Antonio, what about you? I don't see a ring on your finger. Surely, you want to have a son some day. How are you going to find a wife in America when you won't know anyone?"

"I keep my eyes open and use my head. God will do the rest. I'm going to *Napoli* in March. From there I will sail on a ship called *La Plata* for New York. Now, I gotta go. *Tante mille grazie per la vostra ospitalità.*"

"*Buona fortuna*! Who knows what the future may bring?" said Raffaele.

It wasn't until his guest had left that Raffaele saw his little son sitting in the corner.

"*Figghio mio*, what are you doing sitting in the corner?"

"I was just listening, Pa. Do you really think that I can go to America, too, someday?"

"We'll see. No one knows what God has planned. Now, *Vai, vai*! Go to bed. It's late. *Buona notte*."

March 31, 1898
Ellis Island, New York

So, leaving his father, Angelo, and his brother, Domenico, in the town of Castel Liba in Calabria, Italy, Antonio Nudi boarded a train for *Napoli* to travel to America. The trip from Naples to New York was not pleasant. Twenty-one-year old Antonio Nudi had days when it was all he could do to keep from losing what little food he ate. Luckily, he had brought enough cheese and sopressada with him so that he could have a little each day. Others who had not prepared were forced to beg or go hungry. The sickness of many passengers turned out to be more than motion sickness, and, upon reaching Ellis Island they were confined immediately in the hospital facilities. Those that did not recover quickly either died or were shipped back to Italy.

Not only had Antonio thought to bring enough food with him for the boat trip, but he had also brought enough money to purchase a railroad ticket from New York to Chicago.

When he arrived at the station in downtown Chicago, Antonio set about trying to find work and a place to live. Things did not go well, however, and Tony finally decided that maybe he would have better luck in New York. So, before he completely ran out of money, Tony returned to the train station in downtown Chicago and bought a return ticket to New York City.

New York, however, proved no more promising than Chicago. Besides, Antonio, or "Tony" as he was now being called by some in America, did not really take to any of the fellow Italians that he met there. He reconsidered his decision, and, as soon as he had saved up enough for train fare, he returned to Chicago to make a life for himself.

The first job that Tony Nudi found was with the Chicago and Northwestern Railroad in Huntley, Illinois. Working out of this town, located about 12 miles northwest of Elgin, Tony earned $1.13 per day as a section laborer.

This job, however, lasted only a few months. Tony next worked for the Pennsylvania Railroad where he once again hired on as a section laborer. This job would last—as he remembered in his old age—two or three years.

During this time, Tony would save up enough money to buy a horse and wagon. With these he later applied for a job with the City of Chicago as a lamplighter—a job he would hold for about 18 years.

Easter Sunday, 1900
Santo Stefano di Camastra, Sicily

"*Buona Pasqua!*" said *Signor* Mingari as his sister-in-law Lucia (whose maiden name was Rampola) and her husband, *Signor* Galati, entered his house for the traditional Easter visit.

Members of both the Mingari and Rampola families were destined to marry into the Barci(o) family in later years.

"*Buona Pasqua, Padrone!*" returned *Signor* Galati as his wife hurried into the kitchen to help her sister Sabastiana (whom her family preferred to call "Lizabéth") with the food.

While the two sisters were busy in the *cucina*, the two men sat down at a small table pleasantly located under a low hanging olive tree to enjoy some *vino rosso* and discuss future plans. Of the two, *Signor* Mingari was the more wealthy. He owned several pieces of land which he leased to tenants who all paid him the respect owed a *padrone*.

"So," began *Signor* Mingari, "have you decided where you are going to live when you and your wife go to America?"

"*Si*, we have decided to travel to Milwaukee. We have heard it is a nice clean city with many opportunities for work. How about you?"

"I've decided to go to Pennsylvania. There is a city there called Nazareth. They have coal mines and steel mills in that part of America, and there should be many opportunities to make money," said *Signor* Mingari.

"What about your land here? Are you going to sell it?"

"No," replied *Signor* Mingari. "I'll put one of my tenants in charge. You never know. Things might not work out in America, and we may want to come back to Sicily."

"*Hai raggione*," said *Signor* Galati.

"*Allora, mangiamo*," invited *Signor* Mingari, and the two men headed for the dinner table and the beautiful Easter meal that their wives had prepared.

February 18, 1902
Cosenza, Italy

Young Raffaele Bruno had turned twenty. He had never forgotten the visit of the young soldier on the evening of All Souls Day those many years ago. Since then, his constant dream was to go to America, a dream he was now about to realize.

Although young Raffaele's father was reluctant to pull up roots and move his whole family to America with his son, his brother's son, Domenico Bruno, had decided to try his luck by moving to a city called Milwaukee.

"Now, Raffaele, remember. When you get to America, you must travel to Milwaukee, in the state of Wisconsin. I've heard that that city is a safe place to find good work."

"*Si*, Pa, I know. I have all the information written down. I don't think I'll have any trouble. I will write a letter to you and Mama when I am settled in. And maybe someday I can go to Chicago and visit Jacomo Paraino. His father said that he moved to Chicago in America."

"That's right. Remember Jacomo. And don't forget your *cugino*, Domenico. He's also living in Milwaukee, in a little place called Bay View. That's your blood. You can rely on him, and you should never turn him down if he ever comes to you for help."

Raffaele Bruno disembarked from the Kaeserin Maria Theresa on Ellis Island on February 18, 1902. As soon as he was processed, he crossed over to the dock in New York City.

After landing on the New York docks, Raffaele looked around for an Italian face that looked like it hadn't just got off the boat.

"Scusi, come si trova la statazzione ferroviaria?"

At the railroad station, the same approach was used.

"Scusi, signor. Dovè posso comprare un biglietto?"

The ticket seller recognized the look as Raffaele shuffled up to the counter.

"O.K., *paisano*, where do you want to go? Philadelphia? Chicago? Milwaukee?"

"*Si*, Milwaukee," stammered Raffaele trying out his first English.

The ticket seller stamped out a series of tickets that would deposit Raffaele Bruno in Milwaukee, Wisconsin, to look for his own pot of gold.

July, 1903
Agnone, Provincia di Campbasso, Regio di Abruzzi, Italy
"Mama, perche dobbiamo andare in America. Io non voglio!"

"Citta," said Fididuccia using the colloquial pronunciation of *"Zitta."* *"Tu e tue sorelle saranno piu meglio li!"*

Twelve-year old Filomena Comprechioli—who was destined to marry Antonio Nudi in just a couple years—really did not understand why she and her sisters were being sent to live in America. The truth of the matter was, however, that her mother and father, Fididuccia and Nunzio Pasquale, welcomed the opportunity to send three of their daughters to live with relatives in America. Nunzio Pasquale and Fididuccia (Orlando) Comprechioli had had twelve children, two of which had died when they were small. The surviving children were named Marchucci, Giuseppena, Vincenzo, Rosina, Stefana, Papinella, Carminuccio, Michalino, Antonio and Filomena.

"If you and Pa can't take care of all us here, why can't I live with Pa's brother, *Zio* Marchucci."

"Because you will do what your Mamma and I tell you to do, Filomena," ordered her father. "*Capisce*?"

"*Ma*," began Filomena.

"*Basta! Stai citta!*" commanded Filomena's mom.

And that pretty much settled it.

Filomena and her sisters Rosina and Giuseppena (whose Americanized name was Josephina) were sent by their parents to America. When they got to Philadelphia, they were met by their father's relatives.

Fididuccia, whose maiden name was Orlando, had a brother living in Chicago who had agreed to take Filomena, and her husband, Nunzio Pasquale, had relatives living in Philadelphia who had agreed to take Giuseppena and Rosina.

Before long, each of these sisters would be married to husbands that were found for them. Josephina became Josephina Bariglio, and Rosina became Rosina Di Ciacco. Although both Josephina and Rosina would have several children, by 2013, the only surviving member of the two families turned out to be Giuseppena's grandson Harry Marone, son of Giuseppena's daughter, Fanny, who passed away in 2012 in her mid 90's. Harry and his wife Norma have no children.

February 20, 1905
South Chicago, Illinois

When Filomena arrived in Philadelphia, she was met by a stern looking Italian sporting a bushy mustache. He was *Signor* Orlando, her uncle on her mother's side, who was living with his wife and his daughter, Johanna, in South Chicago. Once *Signor* Orlando identified his *nipota*, he picked up one of her bags and told her to carry her remaining luggage while he roughly grabbed her by her well-padded arm. In addition to her coat, Filomena was wearing three dresses and two sweaters—a human closet. The two then headed for the Philadelphia train station where her stern *Zio* bought two one-way tickets to Chicago.

When Antonio Nudi had first met Filomena, she was thirteen years old and was being held in virtual slavery by her Aunt and Uncle Orlando, who lived in a house near 95th and Commercial Ave. in South Chicago. Not only was she forced to work hard, but she was also cruelly abused. This was something Antonio couldn't stand to see happening to such a beautiful young red-haired girl from the province of Campobasso in the stylish region of Abruzzi in Central Italy.

After obtaining the permission of her *Zio* Orlando, Antonio and Filomena began to spend time together.

"Why do you stay with your *Zio* and *Zia* who mistreat you?" Antonio asked her one Sunday after church.

"What can I do, Antonio? My parents washed their hands of my sisters and me when they sent us to America. We were told to behave and not cause any trouble so we could have a better life."

"But your life is not better. Your *Zia* and *Zio* yell at you, make you do all their dirty work and hit you. I don't want to make you feel embarrassed, but just look at what they make you wear. Aren't you ashamed?"

"Of course, I'm ashamed, Antonio," Filomena said with a warning flash in her eyes that Antonio would learn to avoid at all costs. "What can I do? I'm a 13-year-old immigrant in a strange country. Who's gonna help me?"

"Somebody!" said Antonio definitively.

"Who? The priest?" Filomena turned her head and spit. "He would just tell me to be thankful that I have a roof over my head."

"Filomena, I want to help you."

"What can you do? Do you know another family I can live with?"

"No, but if you will let me marry you, I promise I will never treat you bad. That is how I can help."

This is how it came about that on February 20, 1905, Filomena's cousin, Johanna Orlando, and an employee of the court, James Frey, stood before a Justice of the Peace in Chicago to witness the wedding of Antonio, age 28, and

Filomena Camprechioli (or, as incorrectly transcribed on their marriage certificate, "Carpietrole"), age 14, a young girl who was then the same height as Antonio, 5 feet 4 inches tall.

One of their houses would be a small one-story cottage house on the east side of South Chicago. A photo of this house exists with his daughter, Stella, standing before it as a teenager wearing a traditional Italian dress.

Later, when Filomena grew into an impressive red-haired northern Italian woman, she stood a good 6 inches taller than her husband, Antonio.

When the author visited St. Mary's Cemetery in Chicago in 2010, he was able to locate the grave of Johanna Orlando who had played an important role in his Grandmother Filomena's life. Johanna is buried in Grave 285, Block 2, Section J, not far from where Filomena and Antonio Nudi are buried along with the author's parents.

1906
San Marco alla Mattina, Italy

Longarre Valentoni was the *Padrone* who owned all of the farmland surrounding his *Palazzo* in San Marco alla Mattina. Several of the farms were leased to members of the Barci family, descendents of Bernardo Barci. Since the *Chiesa di Santa Maria Della Matina* occupied the ground floor of the *Palazzo*, this seemed to give divine sanction to the power held by the *Padrone* over his tenants.

Similar to the role played by an ancient Roman *patronus*, *Padrone* Longarre Valentoni looked after the interests of his tenants. He provided farming, marketing, legal, personal and financial advice to his tenants, and they, in turn, turned over a portion of their crops, paid rent and treated him with great respect. He was a guest of honor at baptisms, confirmations, weddings and funerals. Tenants visited by guests staying more than one night at their homes were expected to make arrangements to "present" their guests to the *Padrone*.

As Giuseppe left the church with his bride Vrigita, it was Longarre Valentoni who greeted the new bride with *"Benediga! Felicitazione, carissima!"* and placed the first congratulatory kisses on her blushing cheeks.

Also present for the wedding were Vrigita's only sister, Maria (who would later marry Salvatore Bufano and have a son named Frank), Vrigita's oldest brother, Giovanni, her middle brother (whose name her daughter Angeline could not recall when interviewed by the author) and her youngest brother, Michael. (Both Michael and Vrigita's middle brother would later be killed while serving in the military.)

Vrigita's parents also raised two foster sons whom she considered to be brothers. One was named Luigi, and the other was named Benedetto Riccio, the father of Emil Riccio whom Ted Barcio referred to as his cousin.

The wedding was a wonderful family event.

Later Longarre Valentoni would have to be stern with Giuseppe as he informed him that there were no more tracts of land available to be rented to him and his new wife.

"But, *Padrone*, my whole family is here in La Mattina. I need to have work to do here."

"You can find plenty of work here, Giuseppe."

"But how can I do that if there is no land to rent."

"You can support your family by working for me, if you like."

"What could I do, *Padrone*?"

"I need a good shepherd. I have a large flock that needs another shepherd to watch them at night. Are you a good shepherd?"

"I have been a shepherd since I was a little boy. But where will we live?"

"There is a small apartment on the second floor of the large house across the square. I can rent it to you."

After Giuseppe's first child, Tirigi (Theodore) was born on August 6, 1907, in that small apartment, his mother Vrigita would sing him to sleep at night with the soft Italian luluby, "Sleep, baby, sleep. Your Daddy's watching the sheep."

Twelve days later, Longarre Valentoni was a guest of honor at the small baptismal party given by Giuseppe and Vrigita in their apartment when they returned from the Cathedral of *Santo Nicola di Mira* in San Marco Argentano where little Tirigi was baptized on August 18, 1907. Like the *Palazzo* owned by the *Padrone*, the Cathedral also dated back to the 11th century, having been built on the ruins of an ancient Greek temple to Poseidon in 1048.

When a second child, Angelina, was born, Giuseppe realized that he would have to look elsewhere to house and support his growing family.

September 17, 1908
Nazareth, Pennsylvania

"*Signor* Mingari," announced the midwife as she came out of the bedroom, "you have a beautiful son. Have you and your wife decided what you will name him?"

"*Si*. His name will be Giuseppe," announced *Signor* Mingari. "*Come sta* Sabastiana?"

"You're wife is doing fine."

As nice a city as Nazareth, Pennsylvania, was, and as many opportunities as there were there for immigrants, *Signor* Mingari was not really content living there. In Sicily, he had been a well-respected *padrone*. In America, he was just another immigrant trying to make a life for his wife and his son, Giuseppe.

So it was that about five years later, *Signor* Mingari moved his small family back to *Santo Stefano di Camastra*.

His son, Giuseppe, however, would retain his American citizenship and sail back to America when he turned 18. This time to settle in Milwaukee.

April 26, 1910
Ellis Island, New York

Having left his wife and children in their small apartment in La Mattina (Vrigitta would have to support herself and the children by doing odd jobs for others and depending on the generosity of the other Barci families), Giuseppe Barci had boarded the Duca di Genova in Naples, Italy, on April 13 and set out with great determination to find a place for himself and his family in America. He disembarked in New York on April 26. Since he could not read or write, he had told his wife Vrigita not to worry if she did not hear from him for a while. As soon as he saved up enough money he would send it to her so she and Tirigi and Angelina could join him.

Giuseppe knew that a young man named Raffaele, the son of the Bruno family he knew in Cosenza, and a cousin of Raffaele, named Domenico, had also immigrated to Milwaukee, Wisconsin. He would travel to Milwaukee since he had heard that there were a lot of opportunities in that city for Italian immigrants, many of whom had settled on the south side of Milwaukee.

1911
Czechoslovakia

Mrs. Pozanska had no choice in the matter. It was either accept the position of wet nurse in Austria or starve to death trying to keep her last child, Helen, with her in Czechoslovakia. She had already managed to send her two older sons on their way to make lives for themselves in America.

A future granddaughter (Rose) of Mrs. Posanka was destined to marry into the Nudi family.

"But, Ma, why can't I come to Austria with you?" asked 12-year-old Helen Pozanska.

"Because you can't! This is what is best for both of us, Helen. You will live here with Mr. & Mrs. Fusic, and I will go to Austria. I will send money to Mr. Fusic so he can care for you."

"Why can't I go to America like my brothers?"

"Because we have no money for you to travel! Besides, there is no way for a young lady to go to America by herself. Now, be good and do what you are told. When you get older, you will understand why this is necessary."

So it was that Helen Pozanska came to be known as Helen Pozanska Fusic. She did try to be good and to understand what her mother had to do, but it didn't take her long to realize that, if her mother was indeed sending money to Mr. Fusic for her care, very little of it was being spent on her.

March 7, 1911
Milwaukee, Wisconsin

"*Signor* Galati," announced the midwife as she came out of the bedroom, "congratulations! You have a beautiful daughter. Do you know what you are going to name her?"

"*Si*," replied *Signor* Galati, "we decided that if we had a *bambina*, we would call her Sarafina. *Come sta* Lucia?"

"Your wife is just fine," replied the midwife.

Like her sister Sabastiana, Lucia and her husband would return to Sicily. There, their daughter Sarafina, called Sara or "Sally" for short, would grow into a beautiful Italian young lady.

When Sarafina turned sixteen, however, she was brought back to America to live, once again, in Milwaukee.

1912
St. Francis, Wisconsin

As it turned out, both Raffaele Bruno, his cousin Domenico Bruno and Giuseppe Barci all ended up being hired by Joe Savaglia, the foreman of the St. Francis section of the Chicago & North Western Railroad. One day as they were tamping ties together, they heard the Angelus being sounded by the bells of a nearby Catholic Church. The two men straightened out to say a prayer while they listened.

"Giuseppe," asked Raffaele, as they returned to work. "Why don't you come and live in Bay View by me and my *cugino*, Domenico. There are a lot of Italian families there, and you would feel right at home."

"You hear those church bells, Raffaele?" asked Giuseppe.

"*Si.*"

"Well, to me that's the most beautiful sound in the world," said Giuseppe.

"What church is that?" asked Raffaele.

"Those are the bells of the Sacred Heart of Jesus in St. Francis. The first time I heard those bells, I knew that this was where I was going to live. I think I'll stay here in St. Francis."

So, even though they lived in different suburbs, the friendship formed between these friends who had come from Cosenza, Italy, would continue to grow through several generations.

1912
Czechoslovakia

By the time Helen Pozanska Fusic had turned 13, she had made up her mind. If her brothers had been able to go to America, she was also going to go.

"Helen, be sure to come right home after you give this money we owe to the grocer. Here, hide it deeper in your coat, and don't stop to talk to anyone along the way. If you lose it or come home late, you'll go without dinner again tonight."

"I'll be careful, Mrs. Fusic. I'm not a little kid anymore, you know. I'm 13 years old. I can take care of myself."

And this is exactly what Helen Pozanska Fusic had been planning to do for several months now. She was going to take care of herself all the way to America.

When Helen didn't come home that evening, Mr. Fusic went to look for her. No, she had never arrived at the grocery. No, she had not been seen talking to other children in the streets during the day. Helen had disappeared.

It had taken her a while, and she had to use all her cleverness and strength of character, but 13-year-old Helen Pozanska Fusic was on a boat headed for America. She was cold. She was hungry. She was a stowaway, and if she were to survive the journey and disembark successfully, she would have to be very careful and very lucky.

1914
St. Francis, Wisconsin

Giuseppe Barci had changed the spelling of his name slightly by adding an "o" on the end of Barci. He was now Giuseppe (Joe) Barcio, and he had just been promoted to foreman of the St. Francis section crew on the Chicago and North Western Railroad. Even though he was illiterate, Joe had a fantastic memory and simply memorized everything he needed to know as a foreman. In fact, Joe Barcio would continue to work as a foreman for the Chicago & Northwestern Railroad for the next 45 years and 10 months before being forced into retirement (at age 70) by a stroke that would leave his right arm paralyzed.

It was Friday night, and tomorrow he would be paying Raffaele Bruno and the other members of his section crew in cash that he was on his way to pick up from the paymaster at the station. Raffaele's cousin, Domenico, had decided to leave the Milwaukee area and try his luck in South Chicago where he married a cousin of a young girl named Filomena Comprechioli.

"Joe, how is it going, my friend? When am I going to taste your new wine?"

"Well, she's not quite ready yet. But don't worry! I'll let you know when to stop by the house."

"Here's your payroll envelope. Sign your mark on this line right here."

"O.K., that's a-my mark. I'll see you next week."

"Hey, Joe. Be careful. I heard a foreman up the line was held up a couple weeks ago."

"Don't worry about me," said Joe as he checked his back pocket for the revolver he carried with him on paydays. "And don't worry about the wine either. When she's-a ready, I'll have you over for *una bella piata di pasta*."

Joe placed the thick envelope of bills in his inside coat pocket with his right hand as he closed the door behind him with his left. Then his right hand checked his back pocket once more just to be sure.

He was only a few blocks from the station when he heard the voice behind him.

"O.K., Dago. Don't turn around. Just reach in that pocket of yours and throw the money on the ground."

"*Ma tu sei pazzo*," said Joe.

As soon as the man behind him saw that Joe was reaching, not for the envelope of money he had watched him put in his coat pocket, but into his back pocket, he fired.

The bullet hit Joe in the back of his neck, but he didn't go down. He finished pulling his gun as he turned, yelling in broken English, "You sum a bitch!" and shot his assailant dead.

At the hospital, Joe was told that the bullet had lodged in such a position at the back of his neck that it would be more dangerous to remove it than it would be to simply leave it in. Which they did. Joe Barcio carried that bullet in the back of his neck until he died from a heart attack fifty-one years later. The gun that he had used to defend himself had its handle damaged in a house fire several years later, but it was still in the possession of his son, Eugene Barcio, who showed it to the author during a 2005 visit.

April, 1916
San Marco alla Mattina, Italy

Living in Italy without their father was a challenging and sometimes frightening situation for both Tirigi and Angelina.

"Here they come again, Tirigi!" whispered Angelina when she felt the familiar rumble grow closer.

"*Citta*!" snapped Tirigi, using the Calabrese colloquial pronunciation of "*Zitta*." "Just be quiet and they won't see us."

As the two children watched, a convoy of military trucks rumbled through their village square just below their second floor apartment.

"What's in the trucks?" asked Angelina in a hoarse whisper.

"Prisoners," answered her brother.

It was WWI, and German forces were transporting prisoners through San Marco alla Mattina on their way to a nearby concentration camp. The frightening images of those trucks were still vivid as Angelina recalled the event to the author in June, 2004.

February 9, 1920
Chicago, Illinois

Like so many other immigrants, Helen Pozanska Fusic had successfully found her way to Chicago, Illinois, where she applied for citizenship. To provide her with the legitimacy needed, she was "assigned" a ship with no embarrassing probe as to her true method of transportation to America. Before long she had met and married a young Croatian named David Klobuchar. On February 9, Helen gave birth to a baby girl who was named Rose Klobuchar, the future wife of Gusty Nudi, son of Antonio.

April, 1920
South Chicago, Illinois

Tony "Nudo," as he had recently come to call himself, and his wife, Filomena, were raising five children, Margaret, Stella, Gusty, Angelo and Lucy. He had achieved his dream of owning a bar that advertised "Fine Beer." Filomena had become a woman and was now a good six inches taller than Tony. She worked side by side with him in their bar. In addition to running the bar, Tony and his son, Angelo, continued to work as lamplighters for the City of Chicago.

Gloria Leo recounts the story that when her Aunt Maggie was born, she weighed a good 16 lbs. Gloria's mother, Lucy, also had told her that her Aunt Maggie had to be withdrawn from her first year in school because she was too large to fit in the standard classroom student seats. Margaret would continue to have a problem with her weight for most of the rest of her life.

There is a photo taken in front of Tony Nudo's bar, located at 2711 93rd Street in South Chicago that shows him posing with his much taller wife, his daughters Stella and Maggie and his young son, Gusty. Tony's older son, Angelo, who was seven at this time, is not in the photo since he had lamp lighting responsibilities that kept him busy. He had started lighting lamps with his father when he was six years old, and he would quit school after the seventh grade to work full time at the job. Kerosene streetlights had to be lit each night and extinguished each morning by placing a small cap over the jet so rainwater would not get into the fixture.

Tony was seriously burned one evening when kerosene he had tried to pour into a lamp that had become filled with rainwater poured down on him and was ignited by the torch he carried. In agony, Tony climbed back into the wagon and slumped down in the seat while the horse, well used to the routine of the route, completed his rounds and returned home where Tony was discovered and treated.

After the lamps were extinguished, Angelo had to unhitch the horse, rub it down and put it out to pasture before refilling the supplies in the wagon so it would be ready for the evening.

Tony's daughter, Stella, used to enjoy telling the story about how her father and a friend of his got drunk one night after Tony had finished his lamp lighting route. Since neither wanted to allow the other to go home alone in their condition, they simply continued driving the horse, first to one of their houses and then to the other, apparently until Tony was finally sober enough to return home alone.

When customers in the bar, attracted by Filomena's features and red hair, insisted on buying her a drink, she always obliged them, pouring hers from a special bottle of colored water she kept behind the bar. If customers took liberties, kicked over spittoons, or simply got out of hand, Filomena, now impressively strong, would personally throw them.

March 28, 1921
South Chicago, Illinois

Filomena Nudi gave birth to her last child, and named him Nunzio Pasquale after her father. Like many other Italians named Pasquale, her son would later be called "Charles." Her father's name Pasquale turned out to be very appropriate for her son in view of the fact that he was born near the feast of Easter, *La Pasqua* in Italian. Nunzio Pasquale Comprechioli lived to be 93 years old and Filomena's mother Fididuccia lived to be 103.

Filomena's daughter, Stella, was now 11 years old and had been taken downtown Chicago along Lakeshore Drive with the rest of her fifth grade class at Phillip Sheridan Grade School, located at 90th and Escanaba Ave. There they joined students from other schools for a patriotic rally. When Stella was in her 90's, she still recalled that the children were all made to chant, "One, two, three, four, who are we for? Wilson! Wilson! Five, six, seven, eight, who do we hate? Kaiser! Kaiser!" It was at this time that President Woodrow Wilson, along with the leaders of the other Allied Forces were still trying to enforce post-World War I conditions that had been imposed on Germany, led by Kaiser Wilhelm II, following their defeat.

April, 1921
San Marco alla Mattina, Italy

"Tirigi," suddenly snapped his mother, Vrigitta. "Did you do what I told you?"

"Yes, Ma, we did it."

"You better be sure you did, or your *Zio* Bernardo is going to twist your ear off."

"Ma, it wasn't my fault that my cat had her kittens under his bed."

"Did you kill them, like he told you."

"Yes, they're all dead."

"What happened to your hand? Why is it all bloody?"

"We put the cats in a bag and were taking them to the river to throw them in, like *Zio* told me to do. But when I got ready to throw the bag in, the mother cat bit me right through the bag."

"So, did you throw the bag in the river?"

"Of course I did. Then I got real mad because she bit my hand. So when the bag landed in the water, me and my friends threw rocks at it until it sunk. It never came up again. They're all dead."

These were tough times, and, being the "man of the house," Tirigi had to grow up tough. That didn't mean, however, that he didn't have his playful moments. In the winter when it was time to prepare the Christmas chestnuts for roasting, he always made sure one or two nuts didn't get slit to let the air escape as they were heated. These un-slit chestnuts would then explode, frightening his mother and sister while giving him a moment of great glee.

Later in life, Tirigi would relate to his own children how he was often sent outside after a fresh snow to gather a plate full over which his mother would pour honey—as close as he and his sister, Angelina, would come to a dish of ice cream for many years.

"Angelina!" commanded Vrigitta.

"Si, Mamma, che vuole?"

"Isn't it time for you to go to the Padrone's *palazzo* to watch the *bambina*?"

"*Si*," replied Angelina. "*Vado presto!*"

The Padrone's wife had had a baby, and after the *bambina* had been fed by its wet nurse—wealthy women, like ancient Roman *matronae*, often spent little time caring for their infants—it would be put to sleep in its room where Angelina was to watch it until it awoke.

Angelina was getting herself organized to descend the stairs from their apartment when she was distracted by someone running up them.

"Vrigitta, Vrigitta. Where are you?" called the voice from the stairs.

"Tirigi, go see what's the matter."

But before Tirigi could turn and head for the door, in came running *Zia* Giuseppina, the wife of Tirigi's Uncle Bernardo.

"Vrigitta, it's your m*arito*, Giuseppe."

Before anyone knew what happened, Vrigitta fainted into a chair since she had not received any news at all from her husband in ten years.

"Get a *mappina* and make it wet with cold water," Giuseppina told Tirigi.

"Angelina, come here and rub your Mamma's hands so she will wake up."

When Vrigitta woke up from a fainting spell that would become her very predictable reaction to any upsetting events during the rest of her long life, she asked, "Is he dead?"

"No, Vrigitta, he's fine. And look. He has sent you money so you can travel to America to be with him."

"But we don't even know where he is in America."

"Vrigitta, it's all written down here. The letter was sent to the *Padrone*, and he read it to me. Giuseppe is in Milwaukee. And, look, *Padrone* said that these papers here will make it possible for you to travel directly to Philadelphia instead of having to be processed like the other immigrants. He wants you to leave as quickly as possible and travel to Naples to sail to America. And when you get to Philadelphia, he wants you to get a train ticket to Milwaukee where he will be waiting to pick you up."

Although all the other Barci wanted Vrigitta to wait until they could attend mass together on *Mezz' Augusto*, she was determined to be on her way by the end of April.

May 9, 1921
Philadelphia, Pennsylvania

When Vrigitta got to the train station in Philadelphia along with Louis and Raffalina Nardi with whom she had traveled from Cosenza, Louis explained that although they were going to Milwaukee to live, they were going to be met at the train station in Chicago. Rather than let Vrigitta travel unaccompanied to Milwaukee with her two children, he encouraged her to buy her ticket for Chicago only. One of his relatives could then accompany her to Milwaukee. When the tickets were all purchased, Vrigitta and her two children, Tirigi and Angelina, boarded the train along with Louis and Raffalina.

On the appointed day, Joe Barcio and Raffaele Bruno stood on the Chicago and North Western train station platform in St. Francis and watched the passengers step down from the cars. There were many Italians, some with small children, but he saw no one that resembled Vrigitta. They quickly went to another train station to see if, by chance, they had ridden on the Milwaukee Road. Still no luck. There would be trains later that night, but, in the end, Joe and Raffaele were forced to admit that something had gone wrong. They thought it best to go home and wait for news.

Meanwhile, on a bench on the train platform in Chicago, sat Vrigitta with Angelina curled up on one of her arms while 14-year-old Tirigi sat on the luggage and tried to be brave for his mother. With them were Louis and Raffalina who were waiting for Louis' brother, Jim Nardi, to come and pick them up. When Jim arrived, Louis and Raffalina introduced him to Vrigitta with her two children and explained the situation.

"Come home with us, Vrigitta," said Jim once he knew what was going on. "Someone will drive you to Milwaukee tomorrow."

The next day, Jim Nardi got a friend of his, Jacomo (Jim) Paraino, who had known Giuseppe Barci in Cosenza, and they drove Vrigita and her two children to Milwaukee so they could be with her husband whom she had not seen for ten years.

Joseph Barcio, the grandson of Giuseppe, has suggested that the ten-year separation was, no doubt, contributed to by the fact that WWI broke out in Europe in 1914, four years after Giuseppe had emigrated to America, and had only ended three years earlier at the close of 1918, thereby clearing the way for the resumption of emigration from Italy.

September, 1921
St. Francis, Wisconsin

In September of 1921 Theodore (the English version of Tirigi) and Angeline Barcio were enrolled in Sacred Heart of Jesus School, 3641 S. Kinnickinnic Ave., in Milwaukee where they would attend school until 1925. At this time, the Barcio family lived at 1841 E. St. Francis Ave. in St. Francis.

Giuseppe and Vrigita went on to have four more children, Ida, Esther, Eugene and Yolanda.

This house was damaged by a fire in 1934, a fire which also melted the grip on the Beretta Giuseppe had used to defend himself during the robbery that left a bullet imbedded in his neck.

After the fire, Giuseppe rented a house at 1802 E. Cora Ave., in St. Francis for a few months until he purchased a building at 1934 St. Francis Ave. that had been a hardware store. He remodeled it and lived there with his family before moving his family into a house at 3777 S. Ahmedi Ave., in St. Francis that he also remodeled.

Giuseppe would later move his family into a home at 3545 S. Iowa Ave. in St. Francis and install a yard swing that was still in use on the property when visited by the author in 2005.

In 1953, Giuseppe would make a final move, this time into a home he built with the help of his son Eugene at 627 Elm Ave. in South Milwaukee.

In July of 2005, the author, with the help of his uncle Eugene, was able to visit and photograph all the homes Giuseppe had owned and rented in St. Francis.

Christmas Eve, 1921
Singuaglossa, Sicily

"Francesco, you are a sword in your mother's heart. She lives in constant fear for you."

Francesco was involved with the Sicilian Mafia, and his life was destined to become fatally involved with that of Antonio Nudi.

"And what about you, Pa? Is she proud of you? Look at this place you call our home. We have nothing. This is the real sword in my mother's heart!"

"And what about you? I don't see gold rings on your fingers! I don't see you bringing food to our table. All we do is watch you go in and out of jail."

"At least I'm trying to better myself. And I'm not in jail tonight, am I?"

"Right, *Buon Natale!*"

"I'll *Buon Natale* you, old man. You don't even have a good suit of clothes to wear to Midnight Mass, and you've got the nerve to tell me that I'm no good?"

"OK, big shot. You're so good, what do you have for your mother and me as a gift for Christmas? Maybe some little thing to show how grateful your are for us feeding you, giving you a place to live and putting clothes on your back for the past 24 years!"

"I got a good gift for you. Hey, Ma, you want to know what gift your son has for you this year?"

"*Figghio mio, figghio mio*, why do you want to hurt your mother?"

"Here's your gift. Your son is being given a chance to join the *Mano Nero!*" said Frank, hushing his voice as he mentioned the term *Mano Nero*. "That's right. Now you can hold your heads up high. I'm gonna be an enforcer for the Mafia," again hushing his voice when he spoke the name of the secret organization.

"Oh, *figghio mio*, why do you push that knife in your mother's heart?"

"Wait, here's the best part. You won't have to worry about me any more because I'm moving to Palermo and who knows where from there? *Buon Natale!*"

That same night, Francesco Strano, age 24, left for Palermo, Sicily, where members of the Mafia would give him a chance to be a member of the *Mano Nero* in America. After getting their blessing, he traveled to Naples in April, 1921, and boarded the ship Canada for New York. Also heading for America on the same ship were Leonardo Leo, who had come from a small town in southern Italy called Cariati Marina, and Antonio Miresso, who had left his mother, Felomena Disantis, in Sansevero in Foggia in central Italy to travel to America. On April 19, 1921, Francesco was processed through Ellis Island, crossed over to Grand Central Station in New York City and bought a ticket for Chicago

Although, according to his daughter Gloria, Leonard Leo's Ellis Island record indicates that he was married when he entered America, there is no record of what ever happened to his first wife.

When the author visited Felomena Disantis in 1965, she was living at Via Incanto #98 in Sansevero. He also met six other relatives of hers: Alessandro Renna, Santina Manna, Francesca Renna, Domenico Malizia, Filomena Renna and Socorso Malizia.

October 24, 1922
South Chicago, Illinois

On October 24, 1922, Tony Nudi's daughter, Estelle (later called Stella), received her first City of Chicago Department of Health physical check up. She was in the sixth grade at Phillip Sheridan School; however, because of events that would occur two years later, in July of 1924, Stella would not graduate from the eighth grade until the spring of 1926.

April 23, 1923
Saint Francis, Wisconsin

"*Tirigi, dovè tuo fiore?*" asked his mom after Tirigi and his folks were already on their way to church for the First Communion ceremony.

Each first communicant had been given a flower attached to a ribbon that was supposed to be worn pinned to the communicant's left lapel. Tirigi did not have his on.

"Eh, *mannagia*," said Tirigi repeating an expression he had often heard his mother use, "I left it on the the table in the house."

"*Curre subito. Lo prende!*"

As Tirigi began hurrying back to the house to get his floral ribbon, his dad called after him.

"*Memoria breve, gambe longe!*"

Tirigi was still 15 years old, and would not turn 16 until August 5. He had been carefully prepared by the Nuns at Sacred Heart of Jesus Church in St. Francis, and he was now making his first communion with the pastor, Reverend Philip J. Klein. Later he would pose for a formal photo wearing high-laced shoes, long stockings and knickers—his floral ribbon neatly pinned to his left lapel.

Two months later, on June 24, Tirigi would be confirmed at Sacred Heart of Jesus Church by the Most Reverend Sebastian Messner, Bishop of Milwaukee.

September 30, 1923
South Chicago, Illinois

Francesco Strano, having befriended Antonio Nudo (as he had changed the spelling of his name from "Nudi" at this time) and having requested the hand of his 16 year old daughter, Michelina (later called Margaret or Maggie), in marriage, was married in St. Francis di Paula Church in South Chicago.

Francesco Strano was a very short young man. When posing for the one photo of him that has survived, he sat with one leg resting on a stool while facing the camera.

Sunday, July 13, 1924
South Chicago, Illinois

Francesco Strano proved to be a true professional who let nothing stand in the way of his duty to the Mafia, not even family ties. Thus, when a contract for death was issued on his father-in-law, Francesco accepted the job since he was closest to the target. He did, however, have to work himself into the mood.

He began by not allowing himself to become too attached to his new bride. In fact, he was down right abusive to her. When she complained to her father, she was told that she had to listen to her husband and try not to make him mad.

"But, Pa. He gets mad at me over everything. He yells and hits me. He's a son of a bitch *Sigiliano*," complained Maggie to her father in their second floor apartment above the bar he owned at 2711 93rd St. in South Chicago.

"*Figghia mia*, it's your job to make him love you. If he gets mad, just go in another room for awhile."

"Pa, I'm not sure I can take living with him."

"What do you want to do, *figghia mia*? Get a divorce and live with that sin in your life?"

"Can't you do anything to help me, Pa?"

"You try your best and we'll see. Go."

It wasn't long, however, before Tony Nudo realized that his son-in-law really was the son-of-bitch that his daughter said he was.

It was a Sunday afternoon and Francesco Strano was driving his father-in-law in the front seat of his brand new black convertible while his bride, Michelina, sat in the back. They were on their way back home from having attended an Italian *festa* at a nearby church of St. Januarius, as Lucy Leo later told her daughter, Gloria. Both men wore their fedoras tilted slightly to one side. Both were clean shaven, something Tony, by principal, did only on Sundays. Anyone giving him the traditional double-cheek kiss during the week got their face scraped. How badly depended on how far into the week it was. Francesco had told his wife Margaret to open her own door and climb into the back seat even though he knew that his wife was pregnant.

"Francesco," said Margaret from the back seat, "could you please slow down. My hat is going to fly off."

"What the hell, Michelina! When I'm driving, you shut up. If you're worried about your stupid hat, take it off."

"Francesco," said Tony in a confidential, friendly voice from the passenger seat, "Francesco, slow down just a little bit."

"What the hell is this business? It's just a Goddamn hat!" yelled Francesco losing his temper.

At that point Francesco turned around and pulled Margaret's hat from her head and threw it out of the car.

"There," he said. "Now maybe we can have some peace."

"You son of a bitch, *Sigiliano*," said Tony. "You're not gonna have any peace if I can help it."

"Oh yah, old man? Let me tell you. You're going down like cut wheat. You won't even see the sickle coming. What do you think about that?"

When they got home, Tony and Francesco went their separate ways but the argument continued.

Sunday, July 20, 1924
South Chicago, Illinois

There are two versions of the following story. This first version was the "official" family version that was passed down for years in the family to any of Tony's grandchildren who asked about it.

On Sunday morning, July 20, Francesco told his wife Margaret that her father was going to see just what kind of a *Sigiliano* he was that night.

"Pa," Michelina confided to her father as he prepared to leave the house to light lamps with his son Angelo that evening, "I think Francesco is going to try and kill you tonight. Don't go. Stay home. Let Angelo light the lamps by himself tonight."

"Who the hell do you think you are to tell me what to do, *figghia mia*."

As was his usual Sunday custom, Tony Nudo had shared several bottles of *vino rosso* with his friends during the day, but he was a good drinker and still very much in control. Tony owned a little black Beretta with a bullet clip in its handle and a heavy six-shooter revolver. He was an excellent shot. The Beretta he carried with him on his lamp lighting route and the revolver he left home locked in his dresser in the bedroom, the same dresser that his grandson, the author, now uses as his own. That was the revolver his wife, Filomena, also knew how to use. She loved to fire it into the air from the back porch of their house at 95th and Commercial on New Year's Eve. If Tony felt especially festive on New Year's Eve, he would get the double-barreled shotgun that he kept loaded leaning behind the bedroom door and fire a couple of shells off to welcome in the new year.

Tony checked to be sure his pistol was loaded and tucked into his jacket pocket. He then headed for the railroad tracks a few blocks from his house on the other side of which the lamp lighting wagon was kept. Angelo had gone ahead to get the horse from the pasture.

As Tony approached the gate that would lead into the pasture, he glanced behind him and saw Francesco approaching in the distance. His son-in-law obviously planned to attack him as he and his son were hitching the wagon and getting ready to start filling and lighting the lamps. At the last minute, Tony decided not to turn into the pasture. Instead, he quickened his pace and headed for a small grove of trees that lay before him.

Angelo looked up and wondered why his father hadn't come into the pasture. Then he saw Francesco Strano hurrying after his father toward the grove of trees. Francesco had rolled the cuffs of his nice pants up so they wouldn't get dirty as he walked along the tracks. He would, however, have to clean his shoes afterwards before joining his friends later that night. His jacket collar was turned up, and, despite the fact that it was the middle of July, he wore his fedora cocked slightly to one side as usual. He kept his right hand on his gun in his jacket pocket. Angelo dropped what he was doing and began hurrying after the two men.

As soon as Tony reached the grove of trees, he found a secure hiding place and dropped out of sight. Before long, his son-in-law approached and continued right on by. When Francesco had gotten about ten yards past Tony's hiding place, Tony stepped out.

Francesco's right hand tightened on his gun in his pocket. Something was wrong. As Angelo, unnoticed, quickly and quietly approached the two men from the rear, he saw his father come out of hiding, take his Beretta from his jacket pocket, hold it straight before him and shoot Francesco Strano square in the back.

On his death certificate it is recorded that Francesco Strano was 25 years old.

As vividly as these events were handed down as the family's "official" version of the shooting of Frank Strano, Sr., his son, Frank "Rudy" Strano, Jr., discovered the true version when he did some research on his own following his service with the Marines during WWII.

After years of Rudy encouraging the author to find the original newspaper reporting of the shooting, in September, 2010 the author finally made a trip to Chicago to do the research.

"It's all there, Bernie," Rudy had told him. "**The Daily Calumet**, July 29, 1924."

Although **The Daily Calumet** ceased publication in 1980, a complete set of its issues is preserved on microfilm at the Chicago History Museum. After scrolling to the July 29, 1924, issue, the author read Page 1, on which the Police Beat articles were published, but saw no reference to the shooting. So he began to workhisy way backwards until he came to the Monday Evening July 21st issue. And there it was! The lead half-column article on the top left.

KILLS SON – IN - LAW IN ARGUMENT OVER BUYING DAUGHTER A NEW HAT

FATHER-IN-LAW FIRES TWO SHOTS INTO BODY OF DAUGHTER'S HUSBAND AND THEN MAKES ESCAPE

POLICE SEEK ASSAILANT

"Incensed because his son-in-law had thrown his wife's hat from a truck during a truck party, and then refused to buy a new one, Tony Nuddi [*sic*], 2711 Ninety-third street, last night shot and killed his son-in-law, Frank Strano, age 25, 2711 East Ninety-third street.

"The father-in-law fired two shots into his victim's body, as they were standing and arguing on the sidewalk, in front of 9325 Marquette avenue. One bullet penetrated his back, and the other his right arm. Strano fell dead on the walk. Nuddi, seeing his son-in-law fall, ran from the scene, revolver in hand, and disappeared. The police are making diligent efforts to apprehend him.

"According to police, Nuddi, his wife, and their daughter and her husband, left early in the morning for a family picnic at Sixty-Ninth Street and Hermitage Avenue. They were gone most of the day. On the way home, the daughter, Mrs. Marie Strano, and her husband, became engaged in an argument, while the father-in-law looked on. Suddenly Strano, in a fit of anger, grabbed his wife's hat from her head and threw it into the street. The vehicle was stopped and the hat was recovered, after it had rolled in the mud.

"The father-in-law remonstrated, and told the son-in-law that he ought to buy her a new hat. The two men began to argue. After they left the truck, the quarrel was continued on the sidewalk. Nuddi suddenly whipped out a revolver and fired the fatal shots.

"Strano's body was removed to the Brown undertaking parlors where an inquest will be held tomorrow at 2 o'clock p.m. Meanwhile the police are searching for the father-in-law."

To make two things the author's Mom insisted on fit with this report, Frank would have had to threaten Nonno, saying, "Old man, you're going down like cut wheat," and Aunt Maggie would have had to yell, noticing her husband's hand go into his pocket, "Pa, he's going to shoot you." Such a warning would, no doubt, have prompted Nonno to shoot first. But only the transcript of Nonno's trial would be able to verify the family lore that Frank Strano was a *Mano Nero* (Black Hand) assassin working for the South Chicago Mafia. The author's Mom insisted that these three things are what acquitted her dad with a verdict of "Self Defense."

Since none of the details of the author's Uncle Angelo's story match the account of Frank's death reported in the **Daily Calumet**, it could well be that what Uncle Angelo witnessed was a completely separate never-reported shooting, the details of which simply got blended together with the publically-recorded shooting of Frank Strano.

Curiously, on the bottom of the front page of the July 23, 1924, issue the author also came across the following short Police Beat article:

GETS BLACK HAND LETTER
REPORTS TO POLICE

"Vincent Marbelle, 9229 Commercial Avenue, reported to the South Chicago police that he had obtained a Black Hand letter which requested him to place a certain amount of money under a can and leave it at One Hundred and Twelfth Street and Torrence Avenue. The matter is being investigated."

And so, to follow the story through to the end, the author next sent a letter to the Historical Records Office of the Circuit Court of Cook County, requesting a search for a transcript of the trial, "The State of Illinois vs. Antonio Nudi/Nudo," which he guessed would have taken place sometime between 1925 and 1928.

Imagine his surprise on October 8, 2010, when he received from the Office of the Clerk of the Circuit Court "...the best possible copies of the documents you requested concerning the above matter," and learned that the trial had taken place on October 27, 1924.

Tony Nudi had made his first court appearance on September 19, 1924, when the following charges were filed:

"The Grand Jurors ...present that one Tony Nudi...on the 20th day of July in the year of our Lord one thousand nine hundred and twenty four in said County of Cook, in the State of Illinois...did discharge and shott [sic] off, to, against and upon the said Frank Strano...three leaden bullets aforesaid out of the pistol aforesaid...[which] did strike, penetrate and wound him...in and upon the chest throax [sic] abdomen, back and body...divers mortal wounds of the depth of five inches, and of the breadth of half an inch, of which mortal wounds the said Frank Strano...did languish, languishing did live...and...of the said mortal wounds died.

"The Grand Jurors aforesaid...do further present that one Tony Nudi late of the County of Cook, on the twentieth day of July in the year of our Lord, one thousand nine hundred and twenty four...did unlawfully with malice aforethought by shooting kill and murder Frank Strano contrary to the Statute, and against the peace and dignity of the same People of the State of Illinois."

Robert E. Crowe
State's Attorney

According to the copies of the records the author received from the Office of the Clerk (Case #34252, Nudi, Anthony, Vol. 299, Pg. 53; Dkt. 57, Pg. 467), Tony Nudi next appeared in court on September 24, 1924, when a motion to fix bail was continued to "10:00 a.m. to-morrow."

On September 25, 1924, the States Attorney recommended that bail be set at $15,000.

On October 10, 1924, a defense motion was accepted to continue the case to October 22, 1924.

The next court appearance, however, did not take place until October 27, 1924, when a defense motion "to Quash Indictment" was overruled, leading to the arraignment of Tony Nudi and a "PLEA OF NOT GUILTY ENTERED." This led to an immediate "Jury Trial" which is summarized as follows on the only court records preserved:

"Jury sworn. Testimony heard. Arguments heard. Instruction given. Jury retires, etc. Jury returns Verdict of Not Guilty."

The witnesses whose testimony was received were Margaret Strano, Elsie Faroni, Mary Citi, James Riley and Patsy Scopillite. And that, as the saying goes, is apparently that, leaving us only with the traditional family-lore evidence that led to the acquittal, to wit, that Frank Strano had threatened Nonno, saying, "Old man, you're going down like cut wheat," and that Aunt Maggie, noticing her husband's hand go into his pocket, yelled, "Pa, he's going to shoot you," thereby prompting Nonno to shoot first, and—something that Rudy repeatedly affirmed—that Frank Strano was a *Mano Nero* (Black Hand) assassin working for the South Chicago Mafia, and that he had been given a contract to kill Nonno.

After growing up with this pivotal family incident ever present in the shadows of our South Chicago past, the author was relieved to have followed it through, even if not all his questions were answered. In his mind, at least, Uncle Frank Strano and Nonno can finally rest in peace.

After Rudy grew up and could afford it, he identified the grave of his father, Frank Strano, Sr., at St. Mary's Cemetery in Chicago (Grave 53, Block 2, Section EI) and had a proper tombstone set in place bearing the inscription:

BELOVED FATHER
FRANCIS STRANO
1894—1924

Friday, July 25, 1924
South Chicago, Illinois
After Tony was found hiding in their apartment and arrested, he knew that his family would have to "disappear" for a while to protect them from friends that his son-in-law had in the Mafia.

"Antonio," suggested Filomena, "I can ask my Uncle Orlando to find me a place to stay with relatives here in South Chicago. Nobody will know where we are."

September 19, 1924
South Chicago, Illinois
Tony Nudi made his first court appearance. After he was indicted for the murder of Frank Strano, he was remanded to the Cook County Jail for five days until, on September 25, his bail was set at $15,000. Once free on bail, Tony knew he would have to leave town for a while.

"Where will you go?" asked Filomena.

"I don't know yet. I'll need to go somewhere where nobody knows me," said Tony.

"Antonio, go see Dominic Bruno," said Filomena. "He's married to my cousin."

"What can he do?" asked Tony.

"He's got a *cugino* in Milwaukee. Maybe he can take you there to stay until it's safe to come back."

So Tony Nudi and Dominic Bruno headed north to Milwaukee.

Once they got there, Dominic introduced Tony to his cousin from Cosenza, Raffaele Bruno, who lived near many other Italian families in the Bay View area.

When the two men met, they looked carefully at each other. Each saw something familiar in the other, but neither could put their finger on it. Neither would ever realize that Raffaele Bruno was, in fact, the five-year old son of the man that Tony had met after mass on All Souls Day in Cosenza in 1897.

Tony stayed with Raffaele for a short while, but soon decided that it would not be wise to stay in Bay View with so many other Italian families. Someone might get word back to Chicago.

"Raffale," said Tony, "I think I need to live somewhere else where there aren't so many *paisani*. Do you have any friends who live somewhere else in Milwaukee?"

"Well, Antonio, I work with Joe Barcio. He lives in St. Francis. Would you like to go see him?"

So Raffaele, introduced Tony Nudi to Joe Barcio and his family.

Since Joe Barcio had also come from Cosenza, his bond with Tony was quick and natural. By now, Joe had a wine cellar lined with 50-gallon barrels of *vino rosso,* and he knew how to share. As an added bonus, Joe had a handsome eighteen-year old son who was on his way up with the Chicago & Northwestern Railroad after having started as a water boy just a few years earlier. This was of particular interest to Tony who, after all, had two daughters, besides the recently widowed Maggie, sequestered away in South Chicago for whom he needed to find husbands.

Joe invited Tony to live with him and his family as long as he needed, which he did.

"Antonio," asked Joe after Tony Nudi had settled in, "do you want to come to work with me on the railroad?"

"*Grazie, Giuseppe, ma no*," replied Tony. "I don't want to work with a bunch of other guys right now. I think it's better if I just keep to myself for a while."

"How will you support yourself?" asked Joe Barcio.

"I've seen a lot of willow trees here," said Tony.

Tony Nudi intended to support himself by weaving willow baskets, a skill he had acquired as a boy in Italy.

September, 1924
St. Francis, Wisconsin

So, there was a new willow basket weaver in town, Tony Nudi (he had decided to change the spelling of his name from Nudo back to its original spelling in case anyone came from South Chicago to look for him), and every Italian family was eager to have him replenish their entire supply—everything from small, one-handled gallon sized baskets to large two-handled laundry baskets. This little basket weaver could be seen early in the morning walking along the shore of Lake Michigan harvesting branches from low-hanging weeping willow trees. When he had all he could carry, he would head for home, seat himself near a small cement pond and strip and soak the branches. Then out would come his keen-edged pocketknife and he would go to work on the framework for the bottom of a basket.

He was a skilled weaver. He could turn out enough baskets in a week to support himself, and send money to his secretly cloistered family in South Chicago.

December 19, 1924
South Chicago, Illinois

On December 19, 1924, Michelina gave birth to a son whom she named Frank after his deceased father. Because Michelina was totally enamored with Rudolph Valentino, however, she nicknamed her son Rudy.

Rudy was born in the flat in which she and her ill-fated husband had lived in above Tony Nudo's Bar.

January 29, 1926
South Chicago, Illinois

Stella Nudi was finally graduating from the eighth grade at Phillip Sheridan School. Luckily, at Phillip Sheridan, Stella was not surrounded by a lot of other Italians who might be asking embarrassing questions.

The fourteen teachers whose names are inscribed in her Girl Graduate's Journal were all women, none of whom had an Italian surname: Morse, Blanks, Keller, Imler, Matthews, Galligan, Pimpton, Lutton, Dowling, Brandon, Christy, Muenich, Hardy and Neville. This battery of teachers taught Stella and her classmates Geography, History, Reading, Arithmetic, Writing, Spelling, Drawing, Singing, Sewing, Cooking, Gymnasium and Physiology.

The majority of her forty-five classmates sported such Polish surnames as Androszkiewicz, Augustynski, Wojciehowski and Sulski. There were a few Jewish classmates such a Rose Goldman and Minnie Levin, and a few Germans such as Bessie Weinberg, Jacob Hamburg, Harry Van Hiel and Herbert Kraus. Only three of her forty-five classmates had identifiably Italian surnames: James Perone, Peter Cigura and Joe Giza.

Before the girls went their separate ways, they took time to sign each other's Girl Graduate's Journals using their nicknames. Boys were not expected to sign the girls' books.

"Roses are red,
Violets are blue.
Wish you good luck
And a good looking Jew."
Madge

"There is a Miss Nudi for sale as a wife.
Does anyone want a treasure for life?
She's very good looking and neat as a pin.
For further information enquire within."
Rosie

"Our eyes have met,
Our lips not yet,
But Oh, you kid,
I'll get you yet."
Minn

"Little Miss Muffet
Sat on a tuffet
Rolling down her hose.
Along came a shiek
And took a peek,
So she bust him in the nose"
Wosie

"When you are dead
and in the ground,
phone me up
and I'll come down."
Mirie

"Love many,
trust few,
Always paddle your own canoe."
Skinny

"When you are married
and live by the lake,
don't forget to send me
a piece of your wedding cake."
An

"May your life be as bright
as Edison's electric light."
Dimples

"When you are at the tub
think of me at every rub.
And if the water proves too hot,
Think of me and forget me not."
Clara

Other nickname signatures included Banany, Blonde, Shiek, Daddy, Toodles, Midget, and Fat.

Stella was happy. When she got home, she would pose for pictures in a traditional Italian dress, and she would get to operate the brand new Story and Clark player piano that she had asked for and received from her father as a graduation present. Her son Bernie (the author) and his wife Lillian later had the piano refitted to play old-fashioned rolls electronically as well as by pedal power, and then refinished its exterior. As of 2014, the piano is still in the possession of the author.

October, 1927
South Chicago, Illinois

Tony Nudi had moved back to South Chicago. He bought another horse he was once again pasturing in a nearby field.

"Pa, the horse is gone," said Angelo who had been sent ahead to harness the horse.

By this time, Angelo was working at Devco in Crown Point, Indiana. He was about to elope and marry a young girl named Helen, but in the meantime he still made himself available to help his father on occasion.

"What are you talking about? Did you look good for it?" asked his father.

"Yes, Pa. It's not there," confirmed Angelo.

And he was right. Toni Nudi's horse had been stolen. It wasn't long, however, before Tony was able to find someone who had witnessed the theft.

"It was that Mosacchio boy," Tony was told.

Tony knew exactly who the Mosacchio boy was. The sister of Tony's mother, Chiara, had married a Mosacchio, and she and her husband were now living in South Chicago. The horse thief, Fred, was their son, Tony's cousin.

So, when Tony paid a visit to his Uncle and Aunt who reminded him a little of his mother, he tried to be as polite as possible.

"Fred," asked his father, "did you steal your cousin's horse from the pasture?"

"Who says I did?" asked Fred defiantly.

"I've got a witness who saw you take the horse," said Tony. "If you just give it back, we can have a glass of wine and forget the whole thing."

"I don't have your horse," gruffed Fred.

"What did you do with it?" demanded his father.

"I sold it," said Fred.

Fred no longer had the money, and his parents weren't in any position to pay Tony. Since Tony really couldn't have his cousin arrested, the matter was pretty much settled.

It must be added, however, that when the author was recounting this part of the story to Angeline Santostefano and Ralph Mallo in June of 2004, they both insisted that Fred Mosacchio was also, as they remembered it, related to Giuseppe Barcio, perhaps on his father's side. Fred does, in fact, have two surviving daughters, one named Barbara and the other Judy Stajak. Neither, however, could be located by the author for corroboration when this book was first published in 2004.

When the author did locate his cousin Judy by phone in 2007, they had so many other things to catch up on that he never got around to asking if their dad was related to Giuseppe Barci. The author finally got to reconnect with both Judy and Barbara, whom he had not seen for more than 40 years, when he was invited in August 2009 to attend the retirement party for Judy's husband, Ted Stojak, at their farm, called The Knot Yet Ranch, located near Montague, Michigan. Unfortunately, they could not corroborate what Angeline and Ralph had told the author.

May 21, 1931
Chicago, Illinois

Tony Nudi's oldest son, Angelo, had eloped in 1927 to marry a Croatian girl, Helen Radalia in Crown Point, Indiana. Although they went on to have three more children (Anthony—called "Sonny," Raymond and Evelyn), their first daughter, Jean, passed away on May 21, 1931. She was buried in Grave 50, Block 12, Section EI of St. Mary's Cemetery in Chicago.

Her sister Evelyn (Evy) says that Jean was six years old when she died. As of 2013, there was no head stone on the grave of Jean Nudi.

Cluster of homes of San Marco Alla Matina, including the Palazzo, built in 1002 A.D., and originally owned by the family of Michele Valentoni.
The entire cluster now belongs to the Barci Family.

Interior of the Church of
Santa Maria Della Matina
La Mattina, Cosenza, Italy

House at San Marco Alla Matina in which Tirigi Barci was born

Tirigi (Ted) Barcio's 1st Communion
April 23, 1923

Family of Raffaeli Barci [1937 photo]
FRONT (L/R): Giovanni (b.1905), Maria, Raffaeli Barci, Ricardo (b. 1920). BACK (L/R): Silvio (b. 1918), Domenico (b. 1912), Antonio (b. 1914), Ernesto (b. 1916)

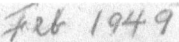

Section Crew—1912

This was a section crew at St. Francis, Wis., in April 1912, foreman for which was Joe Savaglia. Others in the crew were Ralph and Dominic Bruno, Tony and Matt Palladino and Joseph Barcio, (extreme right) who submitted this photo to The Newsliner. Barcio started with the North Western as a section laborer in May 1910 and was promoted to foreman in 1914, which position he still holds. His son, Ted, is roadmaster at Norfolk.

Angelo Nudi
Born ca. 1820

Filomena and Antonio Nudi
Wedding February 20, 1905

Filomena & Antonio Nudi
With Michelina (Maggie)

Tony Nudo's bar in 2005 Photo by Frank (Rudy) Strano, Jr.

NONO (L) AS S. CHICAGO LAMPLIGHTER

CHARLE   MAGIE   MA   RUDOLPH
1928

Frank Strano, Sr., Maggie's first husband, Frank (Rudolph) Strano's father. He was shot in the back and arm three times by Nono in a dispute over Aunt Maggie's hat. According to Stella Barcio, It was ruled self-defense because Frank had a hand on a gun in his pocket.

East Chicago First Cottage House

Stella Nudi wearing traditional Italian dress

Ted Barcio, 21 years old in 1928

Stella Nudi, 8th Grade Graduation
January 29, 1926 (age 16?)

Charles Nudi and Fanny Marone in Philadelphia, July 2005

Vrigita and Giuseppe Barcio's family showing the
age difference Between Tirigi (Ted) and Angeline born in
Italy, and (L to R) Esther, Yolanda, Ida and Eugene born in
St. Francis, Wisconsin.

Rafaelo Nudi, Wife, son Abél & Mother-in-law. He Is holding Francesco.

Abél Nudi with Kathi Nudi
Buenos Aires, Argentina, 2011

PART II

July 1931 – October 1948

The Cudahy, Wisconsin, Years

July 2, 1931
Carrollvile, Wisconsin

Ted Barcio had begun his career with the Chicago and Northwestern Railroad as a waterboy working for his father on the St. Francis section. Now, at age 23, he was hired as a section laborer for the Chicago and Northwestern Railroad at Carrollville, Wisconsin. Two years later he would be promoted to assistant foreman at Racine. Not long afterwards, Ted would spend several years as assistant foreman on a maintenance crew.

Ted had an amazing work ethic. Throughout his entire career on the railroad, he never used an alarm clock. No matter how tired he was or how little sleep he was going to be able to get, Ted simply told himself what time he needed to be up, and he would automatically wake up at that time.

When Ted worked in Carrollville, he naturally spent time at the home of his sister Angeline and her husband Henry Santostefano who had purchased a home on South 5th Avenue in Carrollville. In the house just south of his sister lived a family who had a teenage daughter named Irene. Although Irene was only 15 years old, Ted found himself strongly attracted to her and began to court her. When, however, he presented Irene with an expensive inlaid jewelry box, Irene's parents decided to put an end to the relationship.

"Please," said Irene's mother when she called on Angeline, "give this gift back to your brother."

"But," replied Angeline, "my brother really likes your daughter, and he wanted her to have it as a present."

"Our daughter is too young to be accepting such expensive gifts," countered Irene's mother. "Please tell your brother that we do not want him to see her anymore."

So this put an end to Ted's first love. He never would forget Irene, however, and in later years he loved to tease his wife Stella—who was well aware of his early interest in the young girl—by singing along with the song "Good night, Irene," whenever it would be playing on the car radio and he was feeling a little devilish.

Ironically, when the author hosted a funeral luncheon for his mother, who died in 2003, the marquee of the restaurant was advertising a special party for a lady named "Irene."

December, 1932
South Chicago, Illinois

Tony Nudi, now 55 years old, was currently working in the Yard at International Harvester Co. (Badge # 5043), a division of Wisconsin Steel. He and Filomena were dressed in their Sunday best, as were daughters Lucille (generally called Lucy) and Estelle (generally called Stella). They were waiting to welcome Joe and Vrigitta Barcio and their son Theodore from Wisconsin.

"Ma," said Stella. "Tell Lucy not to embarrass us by standing on her head when they get here."

"Oh, Stell, I haven't done that for years. You just don't want me to have any fun."

"And no funny tricks."

"Ma, tell Stella not to be such a stick in the mud."

After the Barcios arrived and made their way up the front stairs, everyone was seated around the kitchen table. Wine was served and plates of traditional Italian cookies were set out along with plates of sliced cheese and cured Italian meats and pickles. After a while, Lucy decided to liven things up a little.

"Ted," she said, "would you like to hear a tune on our player piano. Well, actually it belongs to my sister, Stella, but I'm sure she won't mind."

Ted looked at his parents, and his dad said, "Go ahead, Tirigi. Go see the piano."

Lucy got up and took Ted by the hand to lead him into the dining room where a next-to-new player piano sat against the wall. Its top was graced with a lace covering on which were arranged an assortment of formal family photos. Lucy pulled back the stool, bent over and opened the door located in the center of the bottom of the piano.

"Ted," she said, "could you please reach in there and pull down the pedals."

Ted gracefully knelt on one knee and pulled the pedal unit out.

"See, Stell," Lucy joked, "I told you I would have him on his knee as soon as he got here."

Lucy arranged herself on the stool, opened the door above the keyboard and looped the tiny metal ring on the end of a piano roll over a small brass hook on the take-up spool. Thus the holes punched into the roll would pass over the brass tube in the middle, and the air admitted would activate the keys. Then she started pumping to build up an air supply in the billows. When it was ready, the roll began to turn and the keys slowly began to play themselves as the music for "K' Kitty Katie," filled the room.

Lucy immediately broke into song, reading the words that were printed on the right side of the scroll: "K' Kitty Katie, K' Kitty Katie, I'll be waiting by the K' Kitty Kitchen door."

And then with no warning, Lucy put her fingers to her nose and began to accompany the music by playing "nose harp," one of her favorite attention getters.

Ted was honestly amused and flashed one of his pearly white smiles that were his trademark.

"And see this lever, Ted? By sliding it over you can change the key of the music."

Ted reached his hand out and Lucy guided it to the brass key-changing mechanism. Just as suddenly, Lucy scooted her stool back and moved Ted's hand down toward her lap. He was relieved when she stopped and opened a small door at the base of the keyboard.

"Watch this, Ted," she said.

Sliding a brass lever to the right, the tempo of the music suddenly increased, and then, just as suddenly, decreased when she slid the lever back again.

"Here," she said, again taking his hand. "You move the lever while I pump."

Ted was truly fascinated both by the wonderful mechanism of the player piano and by the relaxed playfulness of Lucy. He was taken with her.

"Do you want to pump the piano now?" Lucy asked.

"Tirigi, *veni ca*," his father called from the kitchen, using the colloquial pronunciation of "*Veni qui*."

Ted walked to the kitchen while Stella moved in behind Lucy at the piano and roughly ran her hands down her sister's sides, ending with a pinch on her waist.

"Ouch!" cried Lucy.

"Lucia," called her father from the kitchen. "*State citta*! Go sit nice in the front room with your sister."

When Ted returned to the kitchen, Tony Nudi, his Mom and his Dad all looked very serious.

"Tirigi," said his dad. "Do you like *Signor* Nudi's daughters?"

Ted looked at Signor Nudi and smiled.

"*Si. Sono belissime*."

"Would you like to come back to visit one of them again some time?"

"*Si*. That would be very nice."

Signor Nudi wants to know which daughter you would like to see again."

Ted gave the question some slow, serious thought before replying.

"Well, *Signor* Nudi, I think your daughter Lucy certainly seems like a very nice young lady. I think I would like to get to know her a little better."

As Ted's sister Angeline recalled in June of 2004, Joe and Vrigitta Barcio were hoping that Tirigi would choose Stella. They were impressed by the way she waited on them during their visit, making sure they were served special snacks and drinks.

March, 1933
South Chicago, Illinois

"Pa, it's not right," Stella was insisting as she sat at the kitchen table with her mom and dad and her sister Lucy.

"I'm older than Lucy, and I should get married before she does."

"Stella," interrupted her sister, "you already have the shoemaker who's got his eye on you. You can't have everyone, you know."

"*Citta, Lucille*," said Filomena as the back of her hand rapped Lucy's upper lip against her teeth.

"Stella," said her father, "Tirigi likes Lucille and says he wants to see her again."

"I don't care. I'm older. You'll just have to tell him that he has to see me when he comes to visit again. I'm the one who needs to be married first, and the shoemaker is all front and no back. He will never talk to you about me unless you get rich on the ponies. All he does is sit in his back room and collect bets."

December 21, 1933
South Chicago, Illinois

"Dear Theodore,

"I am taking great pleasure in droping (*sic*) you these few lines to let you know we are all feeling fine and hoping to hear the same from you all out there.

"Dear Theodore I received your Card and was very glad to get it. I was waiting for your letter but I did not get any. I was expecting it iether (*sic*) yesterday or Early (*sic*) this morning but I didn't hear from you so I thought I would write. I know you are always saying you never have time so I will keep you busy reading mine.

"Ted tell your mother the pickles she brought us are sure swell. Every time my mother opens a jar I'm always there to get the first one. Not only one. I stay near that jar till it's gone. Dose (*sic*) my mother get a kick out of me. She's always afraid I will get sick from them. My mother said she's going to tell your mother not to bring any more because I eat them all. Ha Ha. Well, are you going to have a Christmas tree? If I was living close by, I would help you trim it. Too bad I can't come out to see it. I know you won't let Christmas pass by without having a Christmas tree. Well, Ted, don't forget to hang your stocking by the fireside or Santa won't be good to you. Ha. Ha.

"Tell Emil not to forget to hang his. Ha. Ha.

"Well, this is all I have to say. Regards to all from all. Regards to Angeline and family.

"Good by (*sic*). Good news.

"Answer soon.

"Yours truly,

"Stella"

April 30, 1934
South Chicago, Illinois

Stella's hair was done up in waves pressed close to the side of her head, and she was wearing a new blue dress decorated with rows of white dots. The bodice was decorated with a flounce accentuated by a floral attachment in the center. She held hands with Ted as they posed in the back yard behind her house in South Chicago on the day they were engaged.

It was at this time that Ted's dad was remodeling and repairing the damage to the house at 1841 E. St. Francis Avenue that had been caused by a fire. When he finished, he intended to move back in with his family and their little dog, Brownie (a name forgotten by the author but recalled by his cousin Jeannie Mallo in June of 2004).

June, 1934
South Chicago, Illinois

Augusto (generally called Gusty), the second son of Tony Nudi, was sixteen years old, and he was taller than his father. As he stood by the window of the bathroom looking into the narrow passageway between their house and the one south of it near the corner of 95th and Commercial Ave., he knew it was unfair. Here he was, locked in by his father who didn't want him to go out with his friends. His brother Angelo was already married when he was 18. Of course, he had to elope and get married by a Justice of the Peace at the courthouse in Crown Point, Indiana, across the street from the Devco where he worked.

Finally, Gusty couldn't take the humiliation any more. He opened the window and climbed into the small opening. The passageway between the two houses was no more than two feet wide and he had little trouble pressing his feet against the far wall while carefully sliding his back down the wall of his own house. Little by little, he made his way to the ground, checked to be sure he had not been spotted and went off to join his friends.

In all fairness, it must be said that Tony Nudi was not, at heart, a mean person. He loved his wife and children, but he demanded unquestioning obedience from them. He was proud of his wine cellar in the basement stocked with six 50-gallon wine barrels, three on each wall resting on their sides on wooden frames. From the ceiling hung a variety of Italian cheeses, home made sausages, pepperoni, salami and drying herbs. The basement was also equipped with a sink and a gas stove, as well as a sewer drain where the gore could be washed when an occasional pig was slaughtered in-house. The basement was not well lit, and one had to be careful not to run into several posts that supported the floor above.

If Tony Nudi were crossed, however, his temper—fueled by several *bicchièri di vino rosso*—could be violent. And Tony Nudi had been crossed.

When Gusty tried to sneak back into the house after his forbidden evening spent with friends, his dad whistled at him. And could his dad whistle! It was one of those shrieking whistles that could resonate through an entire house or wake a neighborhood. Gusty froze in his tracks.

As his dad approached, Gusty knew he could put up a fight, but somehow he just couldn't bring himself to strike his dad. So he allowed himself to be dragged down into the basement and chained to one of the posts. Tony then went into one of the dark corners and came out with a horsewhip.

"Who the hell, do you think you are? When I tell you not to do something, you better…"

The wine-breathed lecture was emphasized with effectively delivered lashings of the whip that Tony well knew how to use.

"…you better by God do it! I don't care how big and tough you think you are, I'm still your father, and you're by God gonna do what I tell you to do."

Years later, Gusty had successfully managed to block the memory of this ordeal from his head, but his older sister, Stella, still remembered it vividly when she was in her nineties. Along with her mother and the other children, Stella had been waiting nervously up in their 2nd floor flat to see what their father was going to do when Gusty got home.

July 22, 1934
Chicago, Illinois

John Dillinger was celebrating his 31st birthday by attending a movie in downtown Chicago. The color of his date's dress had been pre-arranged with the FBI. The movie let out at 10:20 p.m., and by 10:30 p.m. Dillinger lay dead on the sidewalk, gunned down by a battery of FBI agents who had just that year been empowered by Congress to carry weapons.

Several days later, John's body was laid out for viewing in the living room of his sister, Mrs. Hancock, in Maywood, Indiana. Attending the viewing was little Lillian Hacker who had just turned three. She lay sleeping on the arm of her Grandma Nelli Hacker, whose mother, Nancy Jane (Ozmunt), was an aunt of John Dillinger's stepmother, Lizzie Fields Dillinger.

Little Lillian Hacker was destined to become a part of the Barcio family by marrying the author.

A crowd of people visited Mrs. Hancock's house to view the body of this notorious bank robber, including Alva and Marie Ellis who had driven to Maywood from nearby Mars Hill in Indianapolis with their three-and-half year old daughter, Pat. Years later, after being married to Bill Robinson, Pat would become one of Lillian's close friends.

Lillian's dad, Eugene Hacker, had grown up on a farm that was right next to that owned by John Dillinger's father in Mooresville, Indiana. Eugene's mom and dad, Nellie (Bunnell) Hacker and Winfred Ellsworth Hacker, had seven children. Two boys died as infants. The five that survived were Charlotte, Robert, Eugene, James and Helen (nicknamed "Dood" by her dad who had a special nickname for each of his children). Eugene's older brother, Robert, used to go over to the Dillinger farm and hang out with John when they were younger.

Lillian's Grandma Nellie Hacker always said that John Dillinger, Jr., was a good boy. He just got mixed up with a bad crowd. Nelli had occasion to get to know John personally as she was a first cousin of his stepmother.

Nelli also recalled how John had been furloughed from prison to visit his dying stepmother, Lizzie. Unfortunately, by the time the car in which he was being escorted home got to their farm in Mooresville, it had to follow the hearse into the driveway. Lizzie Ozmunt Dillinger had passed away about a half hour earlier.

Although Robert Hacker never got involved with John Dillinger's gang later in life, he did have a rough streak in him that he may have picked up from hanging around the same "bad crowd" that John hung with.

Both Robert and his brother, Eugene, (Lillian's dad) were scrappers. They never walked away from a fight and managed to start quite a few on their own. Lillian recalls being in constant fear whenever she rode in a car with her dad because he would inevitably get out of his car to challenge someone to a fight at a stoplight before the trip would end.

Robert, unfortunately, was destined to die from injuries he would receive in a bar fight. The men who beat Robert to death stomped his groin into a bloody pulp before dumping his body on his mother's front lawn.

Lillian's cousin, Jack Hacker, son of her Uncle Robert and Aunt Mary Hacker, joined the Indianapolis Police Force later in life and was able to check on his own dad's rap sheet, which turned out to be considerable. Not only had Jack's dad gone AWOL from the military, but he had also escaped from the Pendleton Penitentiary twice and once from the prison in Michigan City, Indiana.

When the author was attending the funeral of Jack Hacker on January 10, 2008, he learned surreptitiously that Jack had also made a point of finding out the names of the men who killed his dad, and that "he had taken care of them."

August, 1934
Chicago, Illinois

This was the summer of the Chicago World's Fair. Ted and Stella attended the fair prior to their wedding and had their photos taken in one of the amazing instant photo boxes that were featured at the Fair. As is attested to by a family photo that survives, Ted and Stella were accompanied at the Fair by Stella's mom and dad and her sister, Lucy. Amazingly, standing off to the side in the photo is Leonard Leo, the young man who would later build the back porch for Tony Nudi and be given his daughter Lucy in marriage as a reward. A big feature at the Fair was a group of midgets who posed for photos with the visitors. Ted and Stella had their picture taken with a very short 35-year-old young lady midget and took photos of a 45-year-old midget barber and a midget policeman.

September 2, 1934
St. Francis, Wisconsin

"Here comes their car, everybody!"

All those in the hall rose to their feet, and accordionist Henry Mastronardi broke into a festive Italian melody.

It was not a small wedding party. In addition to her Maid of Honor, Stella had four other bridesmaids and two flower girls. One of the flower girls, Rose, (destined to marry the ring bearer, Rudy Aloia) was the daughter of Ted's sister, Angeline. In addition to his Best Man, three other young men stood up with Ted in the wedding party, one of whom was Stella's brother, Gusty.

After they had worked their way through the initial reception line, Tony and Filomena Nudi stood to the right of their daughter Stella next to the cake, and Ted stood with his Mom and Dad on the left for a formal picture. This, their second wedding cake of the day, stood on a table and was only four feet high. The one that Stella's father had ordered for the South Chicago reception held earlier during the day had been a full six-feet in height and had to be placed directly on the floor for the formal "cake picture." Since it would have been a hardship for many of the friends of Joe and Vrigitta to travel to South Chicago for the wedding—and since South Chicago was not a preferred destination at this time of intense gangster activity in that area—not to mention the fact that John Dillinger had been gunned down by the FBI in a bloody Chicago street shooting earlier in July—a second ceremony and reception were being held in St. Francis.

Stella looked very pleasant in her white gown and thin veil, but Ted was having a hard time settling in. He still occasionally pressed his hand against his pocket where a small caliber pistol was concealed. The shoemaker had put the word on the street in South Chicago that Tirigi Barcio would never get Stella out of South Chicago alive, and Ted had felt it would be prudent to take precautions.

Nothing had happened, perhaps because of the rain that put a damper on things, and perhaps because of the last minute decision not to hold the ceremony in St. Patrick's Church (the name of which is formally recorded on their Memorial of Marriage) across the street from Tony Nudi's house, but in a different church a few blocks away. Following the traditional pelting of rice, *cumbitte* (Jordan almonds) and coins, the new couple was whisked away to a reception featuring the six-foot tall wedding cake. After toasting their guests with shot glasses full of 110 proof liqueurs, the newlyweds were hurried to a convoy of cars waiting to drive them to Wisconsin.

September 17, 1935
St. Francis, Wisconsin

"Ma, what do you want me to do?" asked Ted when he returned home where he and his wife were living with his parents at 3777 S. Ahmedi St. in St. Francis Heights.

"You go bowling tonight, like you're supposed to," said Vrigitta. "There's nothing for you to do here. This is women's work."

This was Ted's bowling night, and he really didn't want to miss it, although he would if he had a responsibility to be present. Ted was highly motivated by his sense of responsibility. He bowled for the St. Joseph League, a league sponsored by Anderson Grocers whose ad was proudly embroidered on the back of the league's bowling shirts. And Ted was a great bowler, one whose absence would be noticed and missed. During the 1930-1931 bowling season Ted earned an Individual Champion medal with a High Single Game Score of 247 and a High Three Game Score of 653.

Ted needed to go bowling.

Later that night, Stella was lying on her bed in the bedroom. She was in labor with her first child.

"I want my husband! Ted! Where are you?"

"Stella, *state citta* and push," said Vrigitta who stood at the foot of the bed wearing a bib apron. As Stella's mother-in-law, it was her duty to serve as midwife.

"Where's Ted?" asked Stella as she lay in bed, her face covered with sweat.

"Your husband's not here," said Angeline who was present to help her mother, as was her younger sister, Yolanda.

"But I want Ted to be here!"

"Stella," said Vrigitta, "this is Ted's bowling night. You know he had to go bowling."

"To hell with bowling," cried Stella, gritting her teeth. "Get me my husband!"

"Angelina," said Vrigitta, "grab Ted's pants from that chair over there and give them to me."

Angeline gathered the pants up into a ball and handed them to her mother.

As Stella was just beginning to call out "Ted!" once more, Vrigitta threw his pants into her face.

"Here," said Vrigitta. "You want your husband? Here, have his pants!"

"Ma," said Yolanda who came running into the room at that moment. "Ma, there's an owl hooting in the tree in the front of the house. Isn't that a bad sign?"

Stella couldn't take it anymore and let out a scream, pushed with all her might and gave birth to her first son, Joseph.

In November of 1935 Ted would be promoted to section foreman on the Chicago & Northwestern Railroad in Cudahy, Wisconsin.

July, 1936
South Chicago, Illinois

Tony Nudi really was not in any mood to deal with his two sons who seemed to become more rebellious every year. He had other problems.

Luckily, Tony Miresso, who had travelled with Frank Strano on the ship Canada from Italy, agreed to marry his daughter Michelina even though she came complete with her son, Frank, Jr. (Rudy).

Tony Nudi had next put the word out in the Italian community that he needed a two-story porch built on the backside of his house and that he was willing to give the hand of his daughter Lucy to an Italian carpenter up to the job.

Before long, a young craftsman named Leonard Leo, who had also accompanied Frank Strano on the ship Canada, accepted the offer. Besides, he had already had his eye on Lucy since he had attended the World's Fair in 1934 with her and other members of her family.

The author's mother, Stella Barcio, always referred to Frank Strano, Tony Miresso and Leonard Leo as the "Canada guys." For years the author thought this meant that they had all come to South Chicago from Canada. Only later did he learn that The Canada was the name of the ship on which they had travelled to America.

Leonard turned out to be an excellent craftsman. He finished the porch easily, and, as well as can be determined, on or about July 28, 1936, he married Tony's daughter, Lucy, and settled in to raise a small family while moving into the front bedroom in Tony Nudi's second floor flat. Leonard was a highly skilled cabinetmaker who commanded good wages for very professional work, work he always insisted be paid for in cash. Years later, at Leonard's funeral, mourners would recall that through skill and luck, Leonard had avoided paying any income tax throughout his entire life. Leonard's daughter, Mary Leo, seems to recall a story about her father being hired to build a garage for famed Chicago mobster, Al Capone—another infamous tax-evader. Leonard, however, was not always employed, and when he had money, he gambled heavily on the ponies, consistently losing. Plus, like many of his South Chicago friends, Leonard loved to drink, and spent many afternoons at the corner saloon in his favorite booth, often in the company of his father-in-law.

When, in the 1960s, a runaway car crashed into the corner bar, injuring Leonard, his father-in-law and several of their drinking buddies, the cash settlement slipped quickly through his fingers.

Since both of their husbands were addicted to gambling, Lucy and Maggie were sometimes forced to rely on food stamps to feed their children over the years—this according to the author's mom. Lucy's daughter, Mary Leo, however, adamantly denies that her mom ever used food stamps to feed her family.

Maggie lived with her new husband in the first floor flat, leaving the front showroom available for possible rental to a merchant willing to pay the rent—something that happened infrequently. Maggie and Tony Miresso were busy starting their family that would eventually number four daughters (Carmella, Florence, Rose and Mary Ann) and four more sons of their own (Dickie, Andrew, Anthony and Jimmie).

It needs to be recorded here that Mary Leo believes Dickie's given name was actually Leonard.

By Christmas, 1937, Lucy's sister, Stella, had already had one child, named Joseph after his paternal grandfather, and she was about to become pregnant with her second to be named Bernard. Lucy was pregnant with her first child.

"Hi, Ma. How are you?" asked Stella as she entered the second story flat after having climbed the stairs up the new back porch built by Leonard. "Where's Lucy?"

"Stella, Tirigi, *Buona venuta! Sto bene.*"

"*Buona truata!*" said Ted giving the traditional reply.

"Ma," repeated Stella, "where's my sister?"

"I think she's in the front bedroom trying to get something down from the shelf in the closet. I told her not to climb on a chair because she's pregnant, but she's such a *capo tosto!*"

Ted sat down at the table to sample one of the *piscia lite* that were his mother-in-law's signature bread snacks. Stella went quietly toward the front of the house, always kept dark during the day, to sneak up on her sister. When she peaked through the doorway of the front bedroom, she saw her sister standing on her tiptoes on a chair in the closet. Stella went up behind her quietly and quickly ran her hands down her sister's sides to scare her.

Lucy's reaction was totally unexpected and fatal for her unborn child. She screamed and became so frightened that she always believed that this was what caused her to lose her first baby.

Although Lucy did lose her first baby, two years later she gave birth to a daughter, Gloria, to be followed later by their second and final child, Mary.

Lucy's husband, Leonard, was actually a very talented and fun loving guy. He was both a skilled carpenter and cabinetmaker and an excellent mandolin player. Leonard loved pet birds and always had a canary or two in a small cage in the kitchen of the South Chicago flat. He would lovingly care for his birds, pet them, talk to them and let them eat from his mouth.

Leonard loved children, and children were naturally drawn to him, although Stella always discouraged her boys from hanging around with him too much. She considered Leonard a negative influence since he was a free-lance carpenter and did not hold a salaried position. Nonetheless, whenever he had an opportunity, he enjoyed taking Bernie and Joe for rides in his truck.

In fact, Joe Barcio has clear memories of riding with his Uncle Leonard when he was 12 or 13 years old. Joe had just been taught how to shift gears by his dad.

"Uncle Leonard, can I shift the gears?" asked Joe who was seated beside his uncle in the front seat of his truck.

"Why sure, Joe. Here, grab hold of this big knob. When I push the clutch in with my foot, you shift the gears," said his uncle.

So Joe got to shift from 1st, to 2nd, and to 3rd. It was a really big stick shift, almost three feet long, and it protruded from the middle of the floor just in front of the seat.

Leonard also loved his beer. He frequently began his day by pouring himself a tall glass of beer and then breaking a fresh egg into it.

"There," he would say, "Now I've got my breakfast in my beer!"

He would then down the entire mixture.

Leonard's other home entertainment included the use of horseracing cards. These were cards that had four or five "tracks" on them on which bets could be placed. Once all bets were placed, a tiny fuse would be lit at one end of the card. Whichever "track" burned the fastest and got to the finish line first won.

September 18, 1937
Milwaukee, Wisconsin

Giuseppe (Joe) Mingari had come to Milwaukee after he had decided to claim his American citizenship. There, he stayed with an aunt, a sister of his mother, who was married to a Mr. Dovi. The Dovi's lived on Holmes Ave. and had a daughter named Mary (whose mother's maiden name was Rampola) who would later marry Eugene Barcio.

While living with the Dovi's, Joe looked up his *Zio* and *Zia* Galati and there he once again saw his first cousin, Sarafina Galati, whom he had known when they were little in the small town of Santo Stefano in Sicily.

The two fell in love and wanted dearly to be married, but were concerned that first-cousin marriages were not legal in Wisconsin. Their solution—as true love always does find a solution—was to travel to Louisville, Kentucky, where they found a Justice of the Peace who was not restricted by Wisconsin's laws.

Later, when they returned to Milwaukee with a valid marriage license, they were formally remarried in St. Rita's Church on Cass Street on September 18, 1937.

Within a couple of years, Joe and Sally (her familiar name) would have their first child, a boy whom they would name Giuseppe Santo. Unfortunately, little Giuseppe would be a breech baby destined to live only seventeen days.

October 10, 1938
Cudahy, Wisconsin

Ted and Stella had moved. They now rented a second story flat in a house located at 3673 E. Holmes Ave. in Cudahy. Ted was making quite a name for himself, both on the railroad—where he let it be known that he would personally take care of any section hand that bad mouthed their foreman, his father—and also in Cudahy politics. Ted even served on the Library Board. He was active in the Italian American League, for which he and Stella frequently cooked lavish spaghetti dinners. And his bowling arm was as good as ever.

This time, as Stella lay in bed attended by her midwife mother-in-law, Vrigitta, she knew better than to call for her husband. She had adjusted to his life style and had resigned herself to dealing with his family.

She was giving birth to her second son, Bernard, in their home on Holmes Ave.

Shortly after that, Angeline began coming over to help Stella with the housework and laundry. But when a neighbor, named Antonia, offered to hold the author as a baby and help with the housework, Angeline was told she would not have to make the trip from Carrollville any more.

Antonia lived with her family across the street from Stella and Ted. She had befriended Stella and frequently went across the street to help her new "friend" with her washing and ironing and housekeeping. Antonia soon became Stella's "best friend" and was even driven by Ted and Stella to South Chicago where she was introduced to Stella's brother, Gusty.

November, 1938
Cudahy, Wisconsin

"Protect our husbands! Fire Antonia! Protect our husbands! Fire Antonia!" chanted a small group of ladies marching back and forth on a Packard Ave. sidewalk outside Ladish Drop Forge.

During the war many women had joined the workforce in factories. Although this flew in the face of the tradition of stay-at-home Moms (such as Stella Barcio prided herself on being), women were needed in the workplace, and their presence was more or less accepted.

Antonia, however, had crossed the line, apparently with several married men. After her involvement with a married man at Ladish had forced him to move his family to California to escape her, she began to play the field. She started frequenting Cudahy's bowling alley where she now focused her attention on her "best friend's" husband, Ted Barcio.

After Angeline had been told not to come and help Stella with the housework any more, Angeline began to suspect that something funny was going on between her brother and Antonia, but decided not to interfere. Ted, however, had confided his indiscretions with Antonia to his brother-in-law, Charlie, asking him to keep the matter secret. This Charlie did until June of 2004 when he finally shared the secret with the author.

Rumors, however, soon flew through the network of families that were friends of Joe Barcio. Things finally reached a climax when Antonia discovered she was pregnant and looked around for someone she could single out as the most promising father. Her quest finally took her back across the street to 3673 E. Holmes Ave.

"Is Ted here?" asked Antonia when Stella answered the door.

"No, he's not. Come in and sit for a minute."

"Stella, we need to talk," said Antonia as she patted her bulging stomach.

Stella couldn't believe her ears as she listened to her "best friend" accuse her husband of fathering her baby. Finally, she could take it no more, best friend or no best friend.

"*Puttana!*" yelled Stella as she glared at Antonia in disbelief.

"Look, Stella, I think that your husband is the father of my child, and I need to know what he's going to do about it."

"Get the hell out of my house, *puttana*," yelled Stella as she shoved Antonia toward the door. Stella then put her hands to the sides of her head and, poking her index fingers into the air, gave Antonia the double *cornuta* while letting lose a string of carefully worded Italian curses.

When Ted did get home, all hell broke lose. After hours of accusations and denials, Ted finally left and went to his folks' house in St. Francis. He explained the whole situation.

Now Joe Barcio had never been one to walk away from any problem, and he was not about to ignore this one. He had arranged this marriage of his son with the daughter of Tony Nudi and, by God, it was a marriage that was going to work if he had anything to do about it.

At a meeting of the two families that was later assembled at her father-in-laws house, Stella was told how it was going to be. As far as Joe and Vrigitta Barcio were concerned, their son was innocent. Furthermore, if Stella would only pay more attention to her husband at home, he wouldn't need to be spending time with women outside the house. In other words, whatever the problem was, it was Stella's. They would remain married, and that would be the end of it.

This, of course, brought Tony and Filomena Nudi to the rescue of their daughter.

"Tirigi," shouted Tony Nudi. "Are you gonna let them say that stuff about your wife?"

When Ted refused to antagonize his parents in their anger, a vicious argument followed. As remembered by Charlie Nudi, this created a rift between the Nudis and the Barcios that took years to heal. In fact, according to Charlie, things were never quite the same again between the two families.

Two days later, according to Ted's sister-in-law, Mary Barcio, Ted and Stella moved from their home on Holmes Ave. into a rented flat where they would stay until Ted would purchase a house on E. Hammond Ave., next door to the Stankowskis.

Later, when Antonia decided to abort her baby, she ended up in the hospital where she was even visited by both Stella and Ted.

"Stella," said Angeline when she heard of the visit, "why did you go visit her when you knew she had done wrong with your husband?"

Angeline was nearly 95 years old when she shared this conversation with the author, adding that while she loved her brother, she had to say the truth and admit that she thought he had done wrong.

"We're friends with her family," Stella had replied, "and we had to go to show our respect."

Go figure!

December, 1938
Cudahy, Wisconsin

Ted Barcio bought the house at 3626 Hammond Ave. The house had previously belonged to a bootlegger who ran a still in the back bedroom. The original toilet was in the basement under the stairs. Eventually, the still had blown up, leaving all the interior walls black with soot when Ted purchased it. In addition to cleaning the inside, Ted also built a bathroom on the main floor and raised the roof to build a second-floor bedroom for his two young sons.

Behind the house there was an alley onto which opened a line of garages the whole block long. It was rumored that in one of these garages John Dillinger had once kept one of his cars for use during his frequent getaway trips to Wisconsin.

As mentioned earlier, the house was next door to the Stankowskis. In this home a Polish gentleman named Ojciec Ignacy (nicknamed "Ignots") Stankowski lived with his eight children, Vera, Regina, Jean, Carrie, Martha, Helen, Stanley and Frank.

Ignots was generally addressed as *JaJa* (Polish for "Pappa").

In 1939, Charlie Nudi decided it was time to escape from increasingly intolerable living conditions in South Chicago. He thus came to Cudahy to live with his sister and brother-in-law. Ted would hire him as a waterboy on the Chicago & North Western Railroad, and he would get to meet his future wife, Martha Stankowski.

Ignots died in 1947, and by 2014 the only surviving Stankowski child was Carrie, who continued to share her father's house with her brother-in-law Charlie, even though his wife, Martha, had passed away in 1993.

March, 1940
Cudahy, Wisconsin

As might have been expected, Charlie was not finding it easy to get along with his sister. He was interested in the girl next door, Martha Stankowski, and Stella wasn't about to stand for it.

Stella's neighbor, Mrs. Grzeca, was an older woman who lived at 3648 E. Hammond Ave. For Stella, Mrs. Grzeca was a mother figure and someone for whom she had a lot of respect. Mrs. Grzeca collected all the little bars of used soap from her neighbors that she would melt down to make new soap for her family. This impressed Stella. Mrs. Grzeca also had two daughters named Gertrude and Hattie and a 20-year old son named Bernard who worked at the Scherer Leather Co. and was very active at Holy Family Church where he had many friends. Hattie was engaged to be married to Pvt. Edward Racewicz who was stationed in Seattle, Washington. To Stella's mind, this was definitely a very respectable family.

Mrs. Grzeca had filled Stella in on the wayward ways of the Stankowski girls, and Stella had made it her personal crusade to put down all of the Stankowski girls whenever any one of them happened to be on their front porch when Stella was on hers. When Stella learned that Vera Stankowski had given birth to a daughter, Donna Mae, while unmarried and still living at home, she simply classed all the Stankowski girls as *puttane* and spared no invectives from her porch whenever she saw one of them on their porch, the railings of which were only about two feet apart.

August 20, 1940
Cudahy, Wisconsin

Bernard Grzeca decided to join the Coast Artillery. In 1941 he would be shipped overseas to the Philippines where he would earn the rating of corporal. In a letter Bernard wrote to his parents on November 23, 1941, he stated that he had become good friends with the Filipinos. He also wrote that while walking down a street in Manila, he passed a soldier who looked very familiar. On going back, he discovered that the soldier was an old school mate of his, Frank Dertz. Bernard wrote that they talked for about two hours, mostly about the good times they had back in Cudahy.

November 21, 1940
Rochester, Minnesota

"Congratulations, Mr. Mingari," said the nurse who came into the waiting room of the Mayo Clinic where Joe Mingari was waiting. "You have a beautiful daughter. Do you know what you are going to name her?"

"Yes," said Joe Mingari. "We decided that if we had a daughter, we would name her Elizabeth after her Grandmother."

Since Sally Mingari had lost her first child, her Milwaukee doctor had recommended that she travel to the Mayo Clinic in Rochester to deliver her second child. Their facilities were excellent, and should she be once again faced with a difficult delivery, they would be able to offer her the most modern medical help available. And it worked.

Elizabeth Mingari was a healthy *bambina* who would grow up into a beautiful Italian young lady destined to be introduced by her cousin Mary (Rampola Dovi) Barcio, wife of Eugene Barcio, to Joseph Anthony Barcio, the son of Eugene's brother and sister-in-law, Ted and Stella.

December, 1940
Carrollville, Wisconsin

As already mentioned, Angeline Barcio was married to Henry Santostefano, a short and stocky young Italian. Like so many of Joe Barcio's friends and family, Henry worked for the Chicago & Northwestern Railroad, on a section of track just south of that over which Joe Barcio served as foreman. Henry had bought a home on Fifth Ave. in Carrollville, opposite a glue factory that stood about a quarter mile behind his house on the shore of Lake Michigan. The location made the cost of the house very reasonable.

By this time Ted and Stella had two boys, Joe and Bernard, and Stella was pregnant a third time.

"Stella," said Angeline, "please go upstairs and get a stack of clean *mappine* from the hall closet so we can put the noodles on them to dry."

"But, Angie, I'm pregnant. Send one of the kids."

"The kids are all playing nice outside. Don't be a *capo tosto*, Stella. It won't hurt you. Hurry up or we'll never get dinner ready for everyone."

As it turned out, it did hurt Stella to go upstairs to get the clean *mappine;* for as she was starting back down, she tripped and fell head over heals to the bottom of the staircase. It was now her turn to have a miscarriage.

January, 1941
Cudahy, Wisconsin

This was destined not to be a very pleasant winter for Stella Barcio. She had just suffered a miscarriage and now, despite her objections, her oldest son, Joe, had been given a sled.

"But those things are dangerous, Ted!"

"He'll be alright. Just don't let him sled on Hammond Ave."

"So where should he be allowed to use it?"

"Well, he could slide down our own driveway. It slopes into the backyard."

So Joe got his first sled. After a while, however, sliding down the driveway lost some of its appeal. Besides, he had seen other neighborhood kids sliding down a hill just across the alley from the Stankowski house.

"Ma, can I go slide down the hill in the alley?"

"No. Slide in your own yard!"

"But, Ma, all the other kids slide on their sleds there. It's safe. And you can even watch me from the back door window!"

Even though it was against her better judgment, Stella finally agreed and moved into position by the back door to watch her son.

Joe pulled his sled out the back gate and along the alley, until he reached the hill that sloped down from Packard Avenue toward the alley that ran to the east behind his own house. At the west end of this alley, running along the bottom of the hill, was another short alley that ran north and south and formed the top of a T-formation in the layout of the two allies. As his mother watched, Joe got to the cross alley, looked both ways to be sure no cars were using it, and began pulling his sled to the top of the hill.

The snow on the hill had been well packed by other sledders, and the alleys below were covered with enough snow and ice that Joe hoped to be able to slide all the way back to his own alley gate.

He checked to be sure his mom was watching, gave a little wave, and then lay down on his belly on the sled. With his right foot off the sled, he shoved off and headed down the hill.

Stella watched in horror as a car suddenly appeared going north in the cross alley. It was an older model car that had a high wheelbase and running boards on each side. Both sled and car reached the center of the T in the alley at the same time.

"Oh, my God!" screamed Stella as she closed her eyes to spare herself the shock.

The driver quickly realized that his back wheel had bounced over some obstruction and stopped as soon as he was able. He was horrified to see Joe lying on top his crushed sled.

As Joe himself remembers the incident:

"What happened was that I missed the front wheel, went under the car, and the right rear wheel went over me and my sled. Mom says she saw the car coming. She shut her eyes and heard me scream. Naturally, the sled was smashed, and my left leg was broken. (A foot or two either way could have put my head in contact with one of the wheels.)"

"But I have to reach my husband. It's an emergency!" screamed Stella into the phone.

"O.K., Mrs. Barcio, we'll try to locate him. What should we tell him?"

"Tell him his son was hit by a car, and we've got to take him to the doctor right away!"

"*Che successo?*" asked Ted when he hurried into the house.

Once Stella explained what had happened, he carefully loaded Joe into the back seat of his car and they drove to the doctor's office.

"What seems to be the problem?" asked the doctor as Ted stood in the doctor's office holding his injured son in his arms.

"He was sledding in the alley, and his leg was run over by a car. It may be broken," answered Stella.

"Hmmm," said the doctor. "Put him down, and let him try to walk."

It was a primitive diagnosis, but when Joe let out a blood-curdling yell, the doctor decided that his leg was indeed broken and set about preparing a cast.

"So," as Joe recalled some 60 years later, "I remember walking around the house for some time with a cast on my leg. I do not ever remember having another sled."

Christmas, 1941
South Chicago, Illinois

"*Buono Venuto! Buon Natale*," chimed Tony Nudi and his wife Filomena.

"*Buono Truato! Buon Natale*," replied their guest who had made his way up to the second floor flat of their South Chicago home.

It was Christmas, and true to his custom, Antonio Imperio was stopping in to present Filomena Nudi with a special Christmas gift. Antonio had been selected to serve as their daughter, Stella's, godfather, and he was so honored that he felt eternally grateful to Filomena for the privilege.

Antonio had spent a number of years in prison for having killed a policeman, and after he was released, he made it a point to bring a special Christmas gift to Filomena every year.

Stella and Ted later received the following note from Antonio:

> "Dear *Compare* and *Commare*,
> "I'm in Florida and I got your card. Thanks, I'm O.K. Hope you are all well. If your father is with you, say hello to him. I send you this card to remember me. My best regards to you and all.
> *Compare* Antonio"

February, 1942
South Chicago, Illinois

After working for a while at Youngstown Sheet and Tool in Indiana (he and his son-in-law, Tony Miresso, used to ride the bus to work together each morning), Tony Nudi concluded his formal working years by spending two or three years at Republic Steel in South Chicago. He had now turned 65. It had only been seven years since the Supreme Court of the United States had upheld the provisions and operations of the Social Security Act signed into law on August 14, 1935. Although Tony Nudi had only paid into the program during his final few years of employment, he qualified to join some 24 million other workers who were already receiving the old age insurance provided for wage earners in the original Act.

When Tony was in his 90's, his daughter Stella made the following list of his monthly incomes:

Social Security: $65.00
Steel Mill Retirement: $61.00
Railroad Retirement: $38.00
Rent (when paid): $40.00

This gave Tony Nudi, in his 90's, an annual income of $2,448.00. With this he paid $232 a year in property taxes on his home at 9506 Commercial Ave. in South Chicago, $144.00 a year for house fire insurance on the same property and $30 a year for a special insurance policy on the plate glass windows of the store front located on the first floor of the house. Much to the chagrin of his daughter Stella, Tony also seemed to pay most of the fuel and utility bills for his daughters Lucy and Maggie who lived in the house.

If, however, Tony was generous with these two daughters, they still had to face many challenges while living in their father's house.

"Ma, guess where your cat is?" said one of Maggie's children.

"It's probably outside. Nonno doesn't like it to be in the house."

"Oh, it's in the house, all right."

"Where?"

"In the basement."

"Well, you better go down and take it outside before Nonno sees it."

"Nonno already saw it, Ma. He killed it."

"No, he wouldn't kill my cat!"

"He and the broom maker are down there right now cleaning it. They're going to put it in the spaghetti sauce!"

When Tony wasn't having a drink with his son-in-laws Leonard Leo or Tony Miresso, he liked to spend time with the broom maker or the shoemaker, who was also the local bookie. These two would come over to play an Italian card game called *Briscola* while they all enjoyed a big bowl of spaghetti and drank *vino rosso*.

Gloria Leo recalls times when Nonno would accuse one or the other of his friends of cheating and simply tip the game table over on them, spaghetti, wine and all.

Of course, a couple days later, they would be back and a new game would be started.

March 1, 1942
Cudahy, Wisconsin

Now that Tony Nudi had retired, he and Filomena came to Cudahy and were staying with Stella and Ted in their house at 3626 E. Hammond Ave. Their son Charlie was also living with Ted and Stella since he had been hired as a section hand on the Chicago and Northwestern Railroad by his brother-in-law. Charlie was earning about $40 a week on the railroad, and his sister Stella made him pay her $10 a week room and board to stay with them.

Next door, living at 3624 E. Hammond Ave., were Ignots Stankowski and his family.

"Pa," said Stella one evening, "Charlie is hanging around with one of the Stankowski girls next door."

"It's not the one with the *bambina*, is it?" asked her father.

"No, it's not Vera. It's the younger one, Martha. It doesn't look good for him to be seen with one of those girls. You should talk to him, Pa," insisted Stella.

So, Tony Nudi decided, once more, to try and influence the love life of one of his sons.

"Nunzio Pasquale, *veni ca!*" commanded Tony after his son had returned from work the next day.

"*Che successo?*" asked Charlie, whose proper name, Nunzio Pasquale (after his grandfather on his mother's side), was still used by his dad.

"Stella says you are seeing Martha from next door. Is that right?" asked Tony.

"Yeah, that's right," said Charlie. "She's a nice girl, and I like her."

"She's a Polak, and her sister is a *puttana*. I don't want you to go over there any more!" commanded Tony.

"Look, Pa," said Charlie sharply, "I didn't tell you who to marry, and you're not gonna tell me who I'm gonna marry!"

SLAP!

Tony gave his son a good one across the face for his disrespect, knowing full well that Charlie would not dare hit him back. And Charlie didn't. He simply went upstairs to his room, gathered up his belongings and left.

March 10, 1942
Cudahy, Wisconsin

"Filomena, you're sick. You gotta stop crying all the time. You'll just get worse," said Tony Nudi to his wife.

"Where's Nunzio? What did you do to Nunzio? Why did he leave? I want to see my son!" demanded Filomena.

No one had any idea what had happened to Charlie. Unbeknownst to them, however, he had simply moved into the basement of the Stankowski home next door. He quit his job on the railroad and got a job at Ladish Drop Forge located just a half block away. Each morning he would get up early and walk to work through the back alley. At night he would return the same way.

Because his wife was making herself sick over his absence, Tony finally asked around and found out where his son was now working. He then began waiting for him about a block away from the factory exit. Charlie spotted him the very first day and simply walked in the other direction. This went on for several days until Tony finally decided to wait right outside the factory door for his son.

"Nunzio!" commanded Tony.

"Pa, what do you want with me?" asked Charlie.

"Nunzio, you come home with me right now!" said Tony.

"Pa, I'm not a kid anymore. You can't tell me what to do."

Charlie knew he was risking another slap from his father, but he had made his break, and he wasn't about to put himself back under his dad's control.

"Nunzio, your Mamma she's sick with worry. At least come home and talk to her. Then you can go back where you want."

And so Charlie had earned his freedom and a little respect from his dad. His dad had asked nicely, and Charlie agreed to visit his mom in the hopes of making her feel better.

As it turned out, however, Charlie's mom was actually suffering from breast cancer. She had been unaware that anything was wrong until one day, as she was shopping in a Chicago department store, a woman jammed her elbow into Filomena's breast as she struggled through the crowd. When the pain did not subside, it was discovered that Filomena had a well-developed cancer in her breast that she had not been aware of.

June, 1942
Cudahy, Wisconsin

Tony Nudi may have been able to arrange marriages for his three daughters, but his sons definitely had minds of their own. Angelo had eloped to marry sixteen-year old Helen Radelia in 1927.

Gusty Nudi had married Rose, the daughter of Helen Posanka Fusic and Dave Klobuchar, a Croation, on June 1st, 1940, shortly before he joined the 39th Infantry Training Battalion at Camp Croft, South Carolina, from where he was shipped to Europe to spend months in the water-filled trenches at Anzio.

Rose was, in fact, the daughter of the Helen Pozanska Fusic who had come to America as a stowaway in 1911, as recounted earlier.

Gusty's war experience in that theater was so traumatic that he seldom ever spoke of it to anyone afterwards. On one occasion, however, he did confide to his brother Charlie that he had spent 72 hours standing in a foxhole at Anzio with water up to his hips. He couldn't crouch down, and he didn't dare stick his head up over the top lest he draw enemy fire. Gusty was lucky and managed to come out of the situation with both his feet. Many of his foxhole mates got gangrene and had to have feet and legs amputated. While Gusty was serving in Italy, his wife Rose was home having their first son, Don Aaron.

Now it was time for the youngest Nudi boy, Nunzio Pasquale, or Charles, to make his move. He had fallen in love with the girl next door, Martha Stankowski, and had been earning good money working in Ladish Drop Forge at the end of the street for the past two years.

"Pa, I know she's a Polak, but I love her, and we're gonna be married."

"Nunzio, why don't you let me find a nice Italian girl for you to marry?"

"Pa, let's not get into that again. I'm picking my own wife, and it's going to be Martha Stankowski."

"*Va bene, figghio mio.* When do you want to marry this girl?"

"We want to get married on July 4, before I get drafted."

"Well then, *figghio mio*, we better get started this Sunday."

"Get started doing what?"

"We need to visit all of my friends here and invite them to your wedding in person."

When Stella learned that her father had agreed to Charlie marrying Martha Stankowski, she hit the roof.

"Pa, why are you letting Charlie marry that girl? Don't you know she's a Polak?"

"*Citta, figghia mia*. What I do is my business."

"So now it's your business to have a *puttana* in the family?"

SLAP!

Before she knew what was happening, her dad had gotten up from his place at the table, grabbed her right arm from behind with his left arm, spun her around and smacked her in the face with the open palm of his right hand.

"Don't think you're too old to be slapped! I don't care how old you are. I'm still your father and I deserve your respect!"

Years later, when she was in her nineties, Stella took great satisfaction in recalling her father's statement that parents retain the right to slap their children no matter their age.

So, the next day, Tony Nudi shaved—always a special event for him—and he and his son, wearing their nicest clothes, began their walk around Cudahy, calling on each of Tony Nudi's friends and extending a personal invitation to attend the wedding of his son. At each house they were, of course, offered the traditional glass of *vino rosso* and a little something to eat. Since it would have been rude to refuse either, Charles and his father were stuffed and more than a little tipsy by the time the final invitation had been delivered.

July 5, 1942
Cudahy, Wisconsin

Charlie Nudi and Martha Stankowski were married on the 4th of July—an easy anniversary to remember. The next day Charlie went next door to get the keys for the 1941 Plymouth he and his brother-in-law had pooled their money to buy.

"But, Ted, we had an agreement. We each chipped in to buy this car. The deal was that I would use it on my honeymoon, and then we would take turns."

"I know, Charlie. But Stella says she's sick. She wants the car left here so that I can take her to the hospital if she has to go. You know your sister."

"Sure, I know my sister, Ted. She's sick when she wants to be sick. She just doesn't want me and Martha to use the car."

"I'm sorry, Charlie, but there's nothing I can do. You can try to talk to her if you like."

"She can just go to hell. We'll walk to our honeymoon if we have to."

Their honeymoon plans thus had to be put on hold. Then, in August, Charles Nudi was drafted into the army. He reported for duty on September 21, 1942 and was assigned to the 28th Division of the 112th Infantry.

By this time, Tony Nudi and his wife, Filomena, had returned to South Chicago.

Wednesday, December 30, 1942
South Chicago, Illinois

Filomena's breast cancer had gotten progressively worse, and there was no doubt that she was dying. After having lived for a year in Cudahy with her daughter, she spent the last several months of her life with her husband in South Chicago. Stella had come to South Chicago with her two sons to be at her dying mother's bedside. The second floor flat was darker than usual because, following the tradition, *mappine* had been draped over any lamp that was turned on. Charlie had been notified of his mother's impending death, and had been granted a furlough to attend her funeral. He was already on his way back to Illinois. All three daughters were dressed in black and were talking in hushed tones out of respect for their mother, who lay dying in the bedroom off the kitchen.

"Who's gonna tie the *mappina* around Ma's head?," asked Maggie.

"Why do we have to do that to Ma?" asked Lucy. "That's cruel. What if she wants to breathe some more?"

"If someone doesn't tie the *mappina* around her head," said Maggie, "her jaw will fall open, and the undertaker won't be able to get it closed again."

"*Musa tu!* She won't want to breathe," said Stella, assuming command. "Whoever bends down to catch her last breath will tie the *mappina*."

"Pa should do it," said Maggie.

"Pa's been drinking too much," said Stella.

"Maggie, you're the oldest. You do it," whispered Lucy in desperation.

"I'm not bending down to get the last breath. I don't believe in that stuff, so I'm not gonna tie the *mappina*."

"Both of you go in the front room and sit down," said Stella finally. "I'll stay with her and listen for her last words. Then I'll take care of the *mappina*."

January 4, 1943
Chicago, Illinois

At 9 a.m. on Monday, January 4, Filomena Nudi was laid to rest in Lot 216, Section I in St. Mary's Cemetery. Tony purchased a quadrant of four lots and had an Italian headstone set in the center. On the right side of the north face of the headstone, above the work NUDI, was engraved the name FILOMENA and the dates 1890—1942. Filomena's birthday, July 8, was not included.

Tony Nudi himself would later be interred to her left, and in the two lots on the south side of the headstone both his son-in-law, Ted Barcio, and his daughter Stella would eventually round out the quartet.

On the anniversary of Filomena's death, her family ran the following notice in the newspaper:

"To the beautiful and loving memory of our proudest possession—wife, mother and grandmother—Felomena (*sic*) Nudi who passed away 1 year ago, Dec. 30, 1942: / A year has passed since that sad day / we lost our proudest possession; / a precious one from us has gone, / a place is vacant in our home; / which never can be filled; / there's many a lonely heartache, / there's many a silent tear, / as we walk through life alone; / for all of us you did your best, / loving and kind in all your ways; / your willing hands will toil no more. / One who was better, God never made. / You had a nature you could not help loving, / a heart purer than gold. / Just when your life was brightest, / just when your years were best, / the one we could not hold. / 'Twas a finished life with work done well. / One in a million that mother, was you; / friends may think the wound is healed, / but we know the sorrow lies within our hearts concealed. / Friend to all with a smile sincere, / our proudest possession that mother was you. / Nothing can ever take away / the love a heart holds dear today, / as we visit your precious grave. / You're in God's beautiful garden, / it ends this first sad year.

"Sadly missed by
Tony Nudi and Children,
Sons and Daughters, Daughters-in-law
and Sons-in-law and Grandchildren."

Similar "In Memoriam" clippings were preserved for two subsequent years.

September, 1943
Indianapolis, Indiana
"Aunt Dood, Aunt Charlotte is calling me "Micky" again," complained twelve-year old Lillian Hacker, who, as was frequently the case, was spending time living with her Grandma Nelli while her Mom was off on one of her various adventures.

"Charlotte," snapped Aunt Dood whose real name was Helen, "quite picking on Ridgin."

"Ridgin" was another nickname that Lillian detested.

"But she has those big ol' Mickey Mouse ears! I can't help it."

"I'll smack you if you do it again!" threatened Lillian's Aunt Dood.

(In June of 2004, Aunt Dood confided to the author that, in fact, she also used to enjoy teasing Lillian by calling her Mickey.)

"You do and I'll tell Mom," countered Helen's sister.

But that threat wouldn't have stopped Helen. She was known for her physical solutions to problems. When it came to disciplining her own sons, she would hold on to them with one arm while applying the "strap" smartly with the other.

"Are you conquered?" Aunt Dood would yell as a recalcitrant son would squirm beneath her blows.

"No, I'm not," would answer her youngest, a particularly rebellious boy.

"Then you'll just get more!"

Since her youngest son never would admit to "being conquered," Aunt Dood would finally tire and eventually send him on his way with all the proper threats.

Luckily, Lillian never had to endure the wrath of her Aunt Dood or her Grandma Nelli. She was a meek and humble child who was just glad to get through each day without too much hassle.

Unfortunately, however, as Lillian entered the Eighth Grade, she was about to become the victim of even more teasing.

In those days, the Indianapolis Public Grade Schools taught music appreciation by having each student practice an instrument.

Lillian's cousin, Jack Hacker, remembers that he was first given a trumpet with which he had absolutely no luck. When his teacher finally realized that there was no way Jack would ever get any worthwhile sound to come out of the bell of the trumpet, he switched Jack to drums. Jack recalls, however, that he had no luck with them either.

Poor Lillian was introduced to the cello. She did well enough on it, but it was just that the cello—in the eyes of other Eighth Graders, at least—is not the most ladylike of instruments. This, of course, led to even more teasing.

When things began to get more than she could bear, Lillian's only recourse was to recite to herself a short healing prayer she had learned as part of her Christian Science upbringing. This was a prayer that she could still recite in her 70's when she was suffering from fatal kidney cancer. Even though she had long since converted to Catholicism, this prayer still provided some comfort to her.

February 18, 1943
Cudahy, Wisconsin

The author, Bernie Barcio, was only four years old, but he remembers the day that Mrs. Grzeca came to visit his mother with the sad news that would later be reported in the newspaper. He remembers standing on the front porch of his house, crying along with everyone else.

Later a headline would proclaim,

"Corp. Grzeca Dies While a Jap Prisoner."

First reported missing in action at Corregidor in April, 1942, Corporal Bernard W. Grzeca, son of Mr. And Mrs. Paul Grzeca, 3648 E. Hammond Ave., was now listed as dead from wounds suffered in that last ditch effort made by the American troops before Corregidor fell. It was believed that he died while a prisoner of the Japanese. Bernard's last letter to his parents was dated November 23, 1941.

The dreaded telegram that his parents received read as follows:

> "The Secretary of War desires me to express his deep regret that report is now received from Japanese government through International Red Cross that your son, Corp. Bernard W. Grzeca, died of wounds received in action in defense of his country in Philippine Island."

Joseph Barcio, the author's brother, remembers a visit Bernard Grzeca made to the house when on furlough to thank Stella Barcio for the cookies which she had sent him at camp. Joe was especially impressed by the young soldier's long trench coat.

Frank Dertz, Sr., the father of the school chum that Bernard had met on the streets of Manila, had received word in May, 1942, that his son was also missing in action in the Philippines. His son's last letter home had been in November of 1941.

The front doors of both families' homes were now hung with the small banners decorated with gold stars indicating that they had lost sons in the war. Other homes that had family members in any branch of the service displayed small banners decorated with a blue star for each person serving.

Joseph Barcio also distinctly remembers when his Uncle Gene left for the service about 1942. Joe was about 7 years old and was very excited because he had been given the privilege of hanging the little banner with one blue star in the window.

Later, during the war, Uncle Gene would write v-mail letters home to Joe's Nanna and Pappa. Inevitably, Nanna would faint. Her fainting spells became so routine, in fact, that even Joe would be given the pungent smelling salts to revive her.

"Joey, just hold it under Nanna's nose," someone would instruct.

He did, and eventually, she would revive.

August, 1943
Cudahy, Wisconsin

Having a stuffed and mounted pheasant on display in the living room epitomized a household headed by a "real" Italian man.

Joe Barcio had such a pheasant that he had shot on display. He also took great pride in the fact that his first-born son, Ted, was also a competent hunter. Ted not only had the correct shotgun, he also cut a very dashing figure in his entire hunting outfit, as is attested by a photo of him posing with his shotgun. At this time, Joe had sold his home at 3777 S. Ahmedi Ave., in St. Francis Heights, and he was now living at 3573 S. Iowa Ave., in St. Francis. He would live at this address until he built a new home from scratch on a lot he would buy at 918 Elm Ave., in South Milwaukee in 1952.

Since Ted, as his son Bernard, had apparently begun life as a "lefty" before being "straightened out" by his mother, he always shouldered his shotguns and rifles as a left-handed shooter. Nevertheless, true to his dad's training, he was still an excellent shot.

By nature, Ted was a fun-loving guy. He enjoyed amusing his nieces and nephews by taking a simple kitchen towel (*mappina*) and, by tying its corners and twisting its middle, creating a little cloth animal. He would then cuddle his creation in his arms and begin to talk to it. When a child would draw near for a closer look, Ted, with a flick of a finger on the hand that was holding the bottom of his cloth animal, would make his creation leap half way out of his arms to the delight of all.

Ted also enjoyed scaring his wife and any other passengers who might be riding with him on one of his night time drives through Grant Park in South Milwaukee near Lake Michigan. To get down to the beach level, one had to follow a very steep and curvy road. Half way down that road, without slowing down or stopping, Ted delighted in turning off his headlights, thereby evoking screams of terror and delight from his passengers.

On those rare occasions when Ted had time to "play" with his family, he enjoyed taking them to the beach in the park where they would all remove their shoes and socks and walk barefoot through the waves that gently lapped the shore.

At Italian-American Fourth of July picnics held in Sheridan Park in Cudahy, Ted enjoyed taking part in such competitions as running and horseshoe pitching. He also loved to scare the dickens out of ladies he knew by exploding very small firecrackers—called Lady Fingers—behind them unexpectedly.

September 21, 1943
Cudahy, Wisconsin
Charles Nudi was back from the army in record time. Having received a medical disability discharge, he celebrated his honeymoon with his wife Martha who had come to be with him in Florida before returning to live with his wife's father, next door to his sister, Stella.

August 12, 1944
Cudahy, Wisconsin
Ted Barcio was making his way toward the lake on Hammond Ave., checking to be sure no lights were visible from any of the homes. Around the left upper arm of his jacket was wrapped a six-inch wide coil of paper that read "BLACK OUT WARDEN, August 12." In his left hand he carried a small pad and in his right a special pen that had a tiny battery operated light at its tip so he could see to make notes in the dark. It was his job to note any houses who were breaking the "light's out" curfew and record their addresses.

Ted had been exempted from the draft because he worked for the railroad—a war-critical industry. He did his duty for his country by helping with Italian recordings that could be used as propaganda in Italy and by serving as a Blackout Official and an Air Raid Warden.

Since Ladish Drop Forge, located right in the middle of Cudahy, made the posts for airplane landing wheels, it was considered to be a prime target. When the air raid sirens would sound signaling a drill, all air raid captains, including Ted Barcio, would don their armbands and go on immediate patrol.

The author's brother, Joe Barcio, recalls that "black-outs" were always scary for him. His classmates had told him that an enemy plane overhead could see even the smallest light and its crew was trained to drop its bombs on the light. Sirens were sounded to start a black-out, and Joe can still remember sitting in the window of his house on Hammond Ave. and watching for enemy bombers in the sky—and never seeing any. It was always a tense time as he waited for the all-clear siren to be sounded.

Whenever the sirens went off and his Dad would go out on patrol, Joe just knew that his Dad had to make sure that everyone turned off their lights. He remembers one incident when his Dad came home from his black-out patrol and explained to Joe's Mom how he had come across a house with a light in the window. Although the window had a blanket hanging over it, the light was still visible. When he knocked on the door, a lady answered who explained that she needed to have the light on because she was nursing her baby. Joe's Dad, however, insisted that the light be put out.

"There's a war on, and this is an air raid practice!" insisted Ted.

The light was turned off.

Ted Barcio also served his country by buying war bonds. His two sons, like all the other school children in Cudahy, helped by taking part in rag drives and newspaper drives in support of the war effort. Cudahy school children also competed to create the largest tin foil balls possible by searching for gum and cigarette wrappers on the street, separating the paper from the foil and carefully wrapping the foil around their foil balls. These would be turned in at school for small prizes and recognition.

Cudahy school children also wrapped their schoolbooks in brown paper book covers distributed in the interest of the national wartime nutrition program by Jimmy Baxter Enriched Bread.

The fronts of these book covers portrayed line drawings of American heroes in each of the four services. A lower caption read: HOW BOYS AND GIRLS ARE HELPING TO WIN THE WAR. Below this caption were line drawings of children.

> "Alice says: I buy War Stamps regularly.
> Jim: Eddie and I collect scrap metal and rubber.
> Bill: I work after school and put my money in War Bonds.
> Jane: My Victory Garden saves food for Our Heroes."

The backs of the book covers promoted the seven basic food groups needed daily for good nutrition and explained how *Enriched* Bread was helping to win the war:

> "GOOD WHITE BREAD...all the more nutritious now that it is enriched with essential vitamins and minerals, is helping win the war. There is no shortage of *enriched* bread. Plenty for our boys in the service...plenty for your mother's table...plenty for your school lunch...plenty for the men and women who need lots of bread for strength to build tanks, planes and guns. For health and strength eat more *enriched* bread every day."

September, 1944
Cudahy, Wisconsin

Bernie Barcio just seemed to have gotten off on the wrong foot. To start with, he insisted on doing things with his left hand. Since no good Italian mother was ever going to let her child be branded as a "lefty" all his life, Bernie's little spirit would have to be broken. Early.

Every time he tried to write or draw with his left hand, he would be smacked. His left hand would be tied behind his back and he would be forced to learn to use his right hand. If he cried and seemed determined to let others know how he was being tortured by rubbing his tear-filled eyes until they turned red, his free hand would be dipped into cayenne pepper. That would put a stop to the eye rubbing in a hurry.

Of course, this constant frustration soon led to the development of a bad stuttering habit that would take Bernie years of hard work to correct. Not to mention the associated bedwetting problem. But, no matter. He would not be allowed to grow up left-handed.

Seemingly frustrated on all sides, Bernie soon began to express himself in other ways. He began to get in trouble whenever he was away from the repression he endured at home.

His history of getting into trouble started when he was in kindergarten and got kicked out of the Snow White and the Seven Dwarfs skit that his class was putting on for their parents. Rather than tell his folks that he had been kicked out of the skit, Bernie had simply gone on singing "Whistle While You Work" around the house. The night of the performance he reported back stage and hid. After the skit was finished, he returned to the audience to meet his parents.

"Where were you?" asked his mother. "We couldn't see you on stage."

"Oh, I was on stage. You just couldn't see me."

And, of course, he had been on stage. Back stage.

When his school antics would result in the good Nuns sending notes home with him intended to get him into trouble for his misbehavior, he quickly figured out that such notes could simply be deposited in the large wooden garbage box that sat behind his house next to the alley.

Seeing no change in his behavior, the good Nuns finally decided to send home notes that would need to be returned with a signature so they could be sure that the wrath of God had properly visited Bernie on the home front.

When the to-be-signed notes were not returned (since they, too, found their final resting places in the garbage box), the good Nuns followed up with a phone call.

"Bernard, come in here!" called his mom.

He could tell by the tone that some doom awaited him.

"Bernard, do you have something you're supposed to give us?" asked his mom.

"Not that I remember," lied the little left-hander being turned into a right-hander.

"Sister called and said she gave you a note to bring home. Where is it?"

Bernie was nailed. Who knew Nuns had telephones?

"I threw it away."

"*Musa tu!* Where did you throw it?" pressed his mother.

"In the garbage box."

"Go climb in there and find it."

Of course, once the incriminating note had been handed over, there would have to be some form of in-house punishment. One of the spookier forms administered would be to require Bernie to go down into the basement and kneel in the dark coal bin with his nose pressed to the wall.

The noose of control was definitely beginning to tighten around his little life.

November 22, 1944
Somewhere in the Pacific

Eugene Barcio returned a letter to his nephew Joseph living in Cudahy, Wisconsin:

> "Dear Joe,
>
> "It sure was good to receive a letter from you again. I'm glad to learn you are in the best of health. I am feeling just fine myself.
>
> "Say Joe, you'd better quit telling me about the pumpkin pies & pineapple upside down cakes that your mother makes because it sure makes me hungry and lonesome for home. My mouth waters just thinking about it. Your mother always did make good pies & cakes & you tell her I sure miss them out here.
>
> "So Bernard wants to know how many stripes I have. Well you tell him I have one stripe & that stripe is the same thing as a sergeant has in the army. Only we don't call them sergeants & so on. I am a petty officer 3rd class.
>
> "Well Joe I can't think of much more to say so I'd better close for now. Give my love to your daddy & mother & [Bernie]. Be good Joe & write again soon. Love, Uncle Gene"

March, 1945
Cudahy, Wisconsin

The war in Europe was winding down, and family members were beginning to return home. Gusty Nudi, having been one of the few in his unit to survive the disastrous Allied landing at Anzio, would soon be returning to his wife, Rose, in Chicago. Charlie Nudi, after completing his training in Florida as a bi-pod machine gunner, had been given a medical discharge, and was never shipped overseas. He had returned earlier to Cudahy to move in with his wife and father-in-law next door to his sister Stella.

Charlie's nephew, Rudy Strano, had entered the marines. In 1943 he was a part of the 379th Platoon that was stationed in San Diego. Rudy had also been recently discharged from the military and had decided to visit his Aunt Stella in Cudahy and maybe try to find work there.

Now, in those days, Rudy, as the spark in his eyes still indicated in 2004, was definitely full of piss and vinegar. He cut a handsome figure in his uniform and considered himself quite a lady's man.

One day, while his Aunt Stella—this is her story related when she was in her 90's—was bending over the bathtub as she prepared the water to bathe her boys, Rudy sneaked up behind her and put his arms around her waist. He was just about to plant a "tease" kiss on the back of his aunt's neck when she spun him around and flipped him into the tub full of water.

This kind of put a damper on Rudy's macho image with his aunt, but in no way did it lessen his marine image of his personal bravado.

Another day, during a small party that was being given at the Stankowski home, Rudy and Charlie, who must surely have already had a few beers each, got into an argument about who was tougher, an army soldier, i.e. Charlie, or a marine, i.e. Rudy.

(Although the author remembers this scene very vividly from his childhood, his Uncle Charlie denied any memory of it when asked about it in his later years.)

"They're fighting, they're fighting," screamed Charlie's sister-in-law, Carrie.

"Where?" asked Stella.

"On the front lawn," said Charlie's wife, Martha.

"Call the cops!" yelled Stella.

Sure enough, as Bernie and others stood watching in a circle around the combatants, Charlie and Rudy were going to it—no holds barred. Their shirts were torn, and blood ran from each of their noses.

Suddenly, around the corner of the house came Stella sporting the garden hose.

"*Diaulo, diaulo,*" she was screaming. "If you're going to fight like dogs, you're gonna be treated like dogs!"

She let the two of them have it with an ice-cold blast of hose water until they broke up. It was the usual method of breaking up dogs that were fighting, or mating when they weren't supposed to.

By the time the police arrived, the fight was over, and the two soaking-wet combatants were standing, laughing through their blood with their arms around each other's shoulders.

"Everything's O.K.," said Ted who recognized the officers who responded to the call. "My brother-in-law and nephew were just having a little fun."

As it turned out, Rudy was given a job by Ted on the railroad—on one condition. The condition was that Ted and Stella would retain a portion of his pay each week as sort of a mandatory savings program so that Rudy wouldn't blow it all on wine and women.

At first, Rudy agreed to the condition. But once he realized that the mandatory savings account was simply being kept in the locked bottom drawer of his Uncle Ted's bureau in the bedroom, he decided it was time to reclaim what was properly his.

One day, when she was in her 90's, Stella asked her son Bernie if she could have Rudy arrested.

"Why do you want to have Rudy arrested?" asked Bernie.

"Because he broke into your dad's dresser and stole the money we were keeping for him there."

"No, Ma, you can't have Rudy arrested," said Bernie trying to calm her down before she worked herself into one of her snits.

"*Musa tu!* Why not?"

"Well, first of all, it was Rudy's money in the first place. And, besides, that was more than sixty years ago. You've got to forget about all that stuff. Besides, Rudy's your nephew."

"He's a dickens, a stinker, and he needs to be arrested!"

That's the way Rudy's Aunt Stella was. Once she had latched onto an idea, it was very hard to get her to release her pit bull bite!

"You know," continued 90-year-old Stella, "The police came one day looking for Rudy."

"Why was that?" asked Bernie.

"He was wearing his Marine uniform after he had been discharged, and that was against the law," remembered Stella.

"What happened?"

"They told him he had to wear civilian clothes, and that he couldn't keep going around trying to pick up girls by pretending he was still in the Marines."

April 19, 1945
Cudahy Wisconsin

Ted was continuing to be recognized as an up-and-comer in the Cudahy community. He not only belonged to the Italian-American Club, and a bowling team, but he was also a member of the Cudahy Kiwanis Club, for which he frequently volunteered to prepare wonderful Italian meals. The following letter was sent to Stella Barcio on Ladish Drop Forge Co. stationary following one of those dinners:

> "Dear Mrs. Barcio,
>
> "In appreciation of the services you rendered the Cudahy Kiwanis Club at our All Sports Banquet, April 19, 1945, we would like to have you accept the attached bill.
>
> "The spaghetti you prepared was very delicious, and a large amount of credit must be given you for the success of the banquet."
>
> "Very truly yours,
"LADISH DROP FORGE CO.
" 'Bud'
"George C. Bitters, Jr.
"Personnel Director"

June, 1945
Cudahy, Wisconsin

Even when school was not in session in Cudahy, Bernie had a penchant for getting into trouble. Thus his father was not really too surprised when he was brought home by a friendly policeman who reported that Bernie had been caught with a friend setting grass fires down by Lake Michigan.

Then there was the day when the family visited Mr. And Mrs. A. Miceli, a family that kept a pig in a pen in their back yard.

"THE PIG IS LOOSE! THE PIG IS LOOSE!"

Sure enough, little Bernie had wandered outside to check out the pig. Trouble just seemed to hang over his head like a black cloud. Whatever he did usually turned out to be the wrong thing.

Sometimes, his mischief was definitely minor. Whenever the ice truck stopped in front of his house to make a delivery, he would sneak around its backside and try to find small chips of ice that he could run off with and suck on.

When he was really bored, and the weather was hot enough, he would look in the gutter for small lumps of loose tar that he could peal up and chew on— sort of like free chewing gum.

Finally, Stella told her son Joe to take his brother over to the playground behind Kosciuszko Elementary School down the street. Since Cudahy was a Polish neighborhood, the school had been named after one of the most honored persons in Polish history, Tadeusz Kosciuszko. On the playground a special booth called "Toyland" had been set up by the city. As the author's brother, Joe, recalls, Toyland was more like an elongated hut, painted a dark green, and it housed all kinds of used toys. It was managed by a kindly, rather rotund older man whose job it was to spend his time repairing toys and, library-like, loaning them to children for a specified period of time. Joe also remembers that there were always parents and children lined up in front of the hut either lending or returning a wide assortment of toys. Because of the war, no metal was available for the creation of new toys, so these toys could be "checked out" by children who needed something different to play with. Stella hoped that Bernie might be able to check out a toy or two that would help keep him out of trouble.

After the novelty of the Toyland lending service wore off, Stella sent Bernie back over to the playground to sign up to play baseball with a summer boys' team that was being formed.

Bernie hurried on over to the field by himself and stood in awe at all the equipment that was being passed out. They were actually passing out gloves, bats and balls for the boys to play with!

WAM!

Suddenly, Bernie lay stretched out on the ground.

"What happened?" asked one of the coaches.

"I was just swinging my bat around, and I guess I hit that kid in the head," answered one of the other boys.

"Are you O.K.?" asked the coach as he knelt down next to Bernie.

Bernie opened his eyes and immediately grabbed at his head where a huge bump was forming.

"I g-g-gotta g-g-go ho-home," stammered Bernie as he got to his feet and started to walk back home.

"Shouldn't someone go with him?" asked another of the coaches.

"Nah, he'll be O.K.," said the first coach. "He seems to know where he's going."

Bernie's head hurt like crazy, but what "hurt" even worse was the pain he knew he would experience when he got home. The usual treatment employed by his mother for head bumps was to run a very wide butcher knife under cold water and then press the flat of the blade firmly against the bump to force it to go down. Bernie didn't know what was worse, the pain caused by the pressure of the cold blade on the bump or the fear that the knife would slip and cut his face off.

Of course, the author wasn't constantly in trouble. If he were given a specific task to perform with careful guidelines, he could usually pull it off fairly well.

Once his mom began to realize this, she started to send him on little errands.

"Here's a dime, Bernard. Run down to Adamczyk's on the corner and buy a loaf of Wonder Bread."

Now that was a mission that Bernie could get into. He loved the colorful windows of the grocery store on which were displayed the large red and white dots that were the trademarks of Wonder Bread.

In June of 2004, the author paid a return visit to Adamczyk's Grocery and was amazed to talk with the owner, Eddie Adamczyk, now 84 years old.

"Do you know Charles Nudi?" asked Bernie after waiting for the owner to finish several candy transactions with local youth who had crowded before the small counter.

"Yes, I do," replied Eddie.

"He's my uncle. I used to live next door to him," said Bernie.

"And I know who you are, too," said Eddie.

"You do?"

"You're a Barcio, aren't you?"

The man was absolutely incredible!

Eddie then explained some of the changes that had been made in the store since 1948 when Bernie had moved to Nebraska with his family. He proudly pointed to black and white photos hung on the store walls that showed how the store used to look when Bernie had been one of the children crowded before the counter to purchase candy and bubble gum.

On Sunday afternoons, before his Mom would sit down with him and his brother to listen to an episode of "The Shadow" on the radio, she would sometimes give Bernie a nickel and send him to Adamczyk's to get some bubble gum that they could chew while they listened.

The radio turned out to be a great way to keep Bernie out of trouble. He would lie down on his belly before it and wait for his brother Joe to tune in to one of the many shows they both enjoyed. Besides such favorites as "The Lone Ranger," "Fibber Maggie and Molly," and "Henry Aldridge," there were also Italian-American shows that amused both Stella and her two boys. Whenever the boys would hear the familiar call, "Rosa, Rosa!" on the radio, they would call their mom to come and listen to "Life with Luigi." On this show, a character named Pasquale was always trying to set Luigi Basco up with his daughter Rosa.

July 4, 1945
Cudahy, Wisconsin

Now that the war was winding down, things were beginning to return to normal in Cudahy. It had been decided that there should be a great 4th of July celebration in Sheridan Park. Instead of being sponsored by the City of Cudahy, however, the event would be a cooperative effort of twenty-three separate community organizations:

Cudahy American Legion Post
V.F.W. Cudahy post 2895
Jr. Chamber of Commerce
Cudahy Kiwanis Club (of which Ted was a member)
Loyal order of Moose, No. 1251 (of which Ted was a member)
Auxiliary of the Moose Lodge
Fraternal Order of Eagles, 2416
Ladies Aux. V.F.W. 2895
Knights of Columbus (of which Ted would become a member after he moved to Nebraska)
American Polish Assn.
American Polish Group
American-Italian Civic League (of which Ted was a member)
First Hungarian Society
G.U.G. Society
U.S. Burns Temple 38
U.S. Burns Temple 178
Cudahy Ev. Lutheran Group
St. John's Lutheran Group
St. Paul's Lutheran Group
St. Joseph's Holy Name Society
Holy Family Holy Name Society (The church which Ted attended with his family)
L.C.O.F. St. Rita's Court.

Ted Barcio served as Music Chairman, one of eight Committee Chairman responsible for coordinating the event.

The Program for the day was as follows:

10:00 a.m.—All children meet at their respective schools, then Parade to corner of Kirkwood and Layton Aves.
10:15 a.m.—Grand Parade down Layton Ave. to Sheridan Park.
11:00 a.m.—Flag Raising ceremonies, conducted by Commander C.H. Meiers. Invocation by Rev. Wm. Bronner. Speaker of the Day, George Haberman, President of the Wisconsin Federation of Labor.
11:30 a.m.—Distribution of Refreshments
12:00 noon—Lunch Hour
1:00 p.m.—Games
2:30 p.m.—Doll, Coaster and Bicycle Parade
3:30 p.m.—Games
4:30 p.m.—Supper Hour
6:30 p.m.—Home Talent Show: 1) Roberta Gunnis Dancing Class, 2) St. Frederick's Home Talent Show, 3) Accordian Class of Peter Maniscalco, 4) Lake School's Junior Majorettes, 5) Rhythm Junction.
8:00 p.m.—Band Concert
9:15 p.m.—Fireworks

7:00 p.m., August 14, 1945
Cudahy, Wisconsin

"Ma, come see. Everyone's going crazy outside," cried six-year old (going on seven) Bernie. He had gone outside with the pretense of sitting on the steps outside the kitchen door, as he frequently did. His real intention, however, was to sneak next door at the first opportunity, and press his nose against the back screen door of his Aunt Martha's house. She was nice. She was always kind to him, although her father, Ignots Stankowski (*JaJa*), was scary and would draw the side of his hand across his throat while making a raspberry sound through the teeth on one side of his mouth whenever he saw Bernard looking over the fence at him—a friendly throat-cutting threat intended to frighten his little neighbor.

Bernie was fascinated by the fact that his Aunt Martha fixed *JaJa* a soft-boiled egg every morning that she served him in a little eggcup. The author would sometimes watch as the old gentleman gently cracked the exposed part of the eggshell, remove it, and begin to eat the egg. Bernie had never seen anything like that before.

The throat-slitting threat of *JaJa*, of course, did not deter Bernie's curiosity—resulting in his watching over the fence the day that the Cudahy cop dragged his Uncle Charlie's dog into its back yard and shot it in the head with his pistol for being allowed to run lose in the streets.

Stella absolutely forbade Bernard (as she insisted on calling him, although most other people called him Bernie) from going next door to his aunt's house. On those occasions when he did and was caught, she might send him down into the basement and order him to kneel in the dark coal bin with his nose pressed against the wall. Then, one day, a new approach was used. She placed a newspaper on the floor of the kitchen and then told her disobedient son to go out into the driveway and bring in a bowl full of the smallest stones he could find.

The first time he was given this assignment, Bernie thought it was fun. A game. He was very proud to present his mother with a bowl filled to the brim with very small stones, some of which were actually tiny fossils. Of course, after she took the bowl and spread the stones out on the newspaper and commanded her son to roll up his pant legs and kneel with bare knees on the stones, the fun quickly went out of the game.

On this day, however, Bernard never made it next door. As soon as he got outside, he heard the horns. He heard the shouts. Gunshots could be heard. A car drove up Hammond Ave. that had four men riding on each running board, hanging on with their left hands while waving whiskey, wine and beer bottles in their right hands.

"Ma, come and see. Look outside."

As Stella came out the kitchen door wiping her hands on her apron, Ted came driving up into the driveway, hat off, hair blowing wild and his shirt collar open.

"Stell," he shouted. "It's over. The war is over. Come on. Get the kids. You've got to see this!"

So Bernard and Joe were loaded into the back seat of the car, and, with windows down to appreciate fully the wild celebrations going on around them, Ted backed out of the driveway and headed up the hill to Packard Ave.

No sooner had he turned north onto Packard, than men began jumping up on the running boards and offering everyone inside a drink. By the time Ted had driven two blocks on Packard, he had two more men standing on his back bumper and two women sitting precariously on his front fenders. Like everyone else, Ted was leaning on his horn and calling out greetings to those who lined the sidewalks.

Five days after the second atomic bomb had been dropped on Nagasaki, the Japanese had accepted the final terms of surrender. This was V. J. Day!

7:00 p.m., August 14, 1945
Indianapolis

"Come on, Pearl, jump in," called her friend from work, Opal. "It's not cold!"

And so Pearl Hacker, who formerly went by the name Pearl Cox (and destined to slip in and out of the name Hacker through a series of divorces and remarriages), got into the spirit of V.J. Day and jumped down into one of the pools on the sides of Monument Circle in the center of Indianapolis. In the pool with her and Opal were more than a hundred others in various stages of sobriety. It was wonderful. The relief and exuberance and anticipation were almost better than sex, as many of the soaked bathers observed.

Pearl Hacker had several identity crises throughout her life. Seldom was she actually who she said she was, at least as regarded her surname. Although her daughter, Lillian, aggressively denied any Kentucky roots, Pearl was, in fact, born in Kentucky. It says so clearly on her "Affidavit of Birth." Pearl's dad was Henry Madden and her mom's maiden name was Nancy Cox. While "Cox" is Welsh, Lillian's grandfather Henry's last name, Madden, is definitely Irish—a heritage Lillian proudly claimed. Pearl, unfortunately, was the product of a marriage that ended almost immediately after she was born.

Pearl's mom next married a man named Henry Heitzman. With this husband she would have five more children: Hester, Herman, Edward, Norman and Mary Jane.

Following her divorce from Henry Madden, Nancy had turned Pearl over to her parents to be raised. Later, when she tried to bring Pearl back into her Heitzman family, her parents refused, insisting that they could do a much better job of raising their granddaughter.

And so, Pearl Madden was raised—and spoiled rotten, according to her daughter, Lillian—by Mr. and Mrs. Cox. Although Pearl was never formally adopted by her grandparents, she chose to tell everyone that her name was Pearl Cox. The name Madden, however, was destined to reappear on her death certificate on September 28, 1985. Death certificates always list the name of the father and the mother's maiden name.

When the war ended, Pearl's fourteen-year old daughter, Lillian, wasn't with her. At that moment she was staying, as she usually was farmed out to do, with her Grandma Nellie Hacker (her father's mother) in a five-room double on Warman Street in Indianapolis. Before that, Lillian had lived with so many different relatives and attended so many different elementary schools in Indianapolis that she felt, at times, like the little matchstick girl walking the streets alone and cold on her way to and from strange places.

Pearl did spend some time with her daughter, but this was usually only in three or four day segments.

"Ridgin," Pearl would say, using her nickname for Lillian, "here's a quarter. Put some clothes in a shopping bag and take the bus to your Grandma's house."

"Where are you going?" Lillian would ask.

"That's none of your business. I have to go out of town with friends. I'll be calling to check on you so you better be good and do what you're told!"

On one such trip, when she was only twelve, Lillian missed her stop and found herself on the street in downtown Indianapolis with no more money for bus fare and no idea about what to do next. So she did what any twelve-year girl in her situation would do. She held tightly to her grocery bag of clothes and cried.

"Hacker!" snapped Lillian's Grandpa Heitzman (her mother's sort-of stepfather renowned for an animated miniature circus that he spent years constructing and later donated to the Children's Hospital in Indianapolis).

Lillian looked up at her Step-grandpa who was accompanied by one of his daughters.

"What are you standing there crying about?" asked Mr. Heitzman's daughter harshly.

"I missed my stop and the driver said I had to get off here at the Circle, and now I don't have any way to get to Grandma Nelli's house because I don't have another quarter," sobbed little Lillian.

"Here," said Mr. Heitzman reaching into his trouser pocket. "Here's another quarter."

He tossed the coin toward Lillian which she was not able to catch, of course, because a slightly mis-aligned eye caused her to have poor depth perception.

"Next time," snapped Heitzman's daughter, "pay attention and don't miss your stop."

Then, to her father, the daughter said, "Come on dad, let's go. We've wasted enough time on the kid."

When Eugene Hacker returned from Europe after the war (he had been sent there after serving in the Aleutian Islands for the first part of the war and only arrived in Europe in time to savor the aroma of thousands of corpses filling the ditches on both sides of the train on which he was riding and witness the mountains of dead enemy troops whose corpses were being stacked for burning in the town squares through which his unit passed) he had not changed much. He was still the carefree man who had resisted promotion to Private First Class because he did not want the responsibility.

Eugene's Enlisted Record and Report of Separation show that he was given an Honorable Discharge on December 23, 1945. His specialty was Heavy Machine Gunner 605, and he had been awarded an Asiatic-Pacific Theater Ribbon, an EAME Theater Ribbon, a Good Conduct Ribbon, an American Theater Ribbon, a Bronze Star Medal and a World War II Victory Medal.

Despite having earned a Good Conduct Ribbon, Eugene still enjoyed getting into bar fights along side his brother Robert, the father of Lillian's cousin, Jack Hacker, and former good buddy of John Dillinger. And, after a few Sunday afternoon beers, Eugene still looked forward to starting arguments with other drivers at red lights and getting out of his car to settle them in the middle of the street, occasions which, as already mentioned, were dreaded by his daughter Lillian.

Pearl finally decided she had had enough of Eugene Hacker, and they were divorced, only to be remarried again in a year or two.

Following their next divorce, Eugene remarried although Pearl did not, preferring to spend a little time each week with her daughter Lillian—although it always turned out to be very little time. Lillian believes she spent most of her early years en route to the house of one relative or another when her mother decided she had something more important to do or someplace she had to go.

Before long, however, Pearl and Eugene were back together again. This time Eugene decided to make a serious effort to support his little family. He opened a bar. But as usually happened when a war buddy opened a bar, too many other buddies and veterans in general expected drinks on the house, and Eugene was soon out of business.

Once again he and Pearl got divorced.

By this time, Lillian had gotten married and was living with her air force husband, John Batten, in Wichita, Kansas. Her mother came to visit her in Wichita and surprised her daughter by taking the occasion to marry the man who had traveled with her from Indianapolis. This marriage, however, was doomed to last only four months, after which Pearl decided to legitimize her life and her daughter by reassuming the surname of Lillian's father, Hacker.

In her old age, Pearl lived the myth of having led a perfect family life with her daughter as she was growing up and easily slipped into her grandmother role with Lillian's children.

As with many of the stories in this book, however, not everyone remembers Pearl Hacker the same way. From the perspective of the author's brother Joe and his wife, Liz, and their four children, Grandma Hacker was always very kind and extremely generous to the kids at Christmas time. Liz, Joey, Bernie and Mary always looked forward to Christmas and nice gifts in Indianapolis. In fact, as far as Joe and Liz are concerned even to this day, Grandma Hacker was really the only gentle and kind "grandmother" their children experienced. When they called her "Grandma Hacker," they meant it.

After divorcing Pearl for the last time, Eugene had decided to settle in Las Vegas where he supported himself by playing black jack each day until he won enough to pay for that day's room and board. After he tired of this, he got himself an ice cream truck and supported himself selling ice cream novelties to the children of Las Vegas. Once again, Eugene remarried.

September, 1945
Cudahy, Wisconsin

"Get to sleep up there," yelled Stella at her two boys whom she had just sent upstairs to go to bed.

"Do you think it will scare her?" asked Bernie.

"We'll find out when she comes up later on," answered Joe.

The two boys had spent some time building a dummy out of their clothes. The whispering that had gotten them yelled at was the discussion they were having about how to set it up in a chair near the door so that their mom would see it as she entered the darkened room and maybe have a fun scare.

Before their little plan could be put into operation, however, two cars drove up into the driveway. The boys pressed their noses against the front windows of their second floor bedroom to see if they could see what was going on.

Before long, they heard guitar and mandolin music and a high-pitched tenor voice singing a lively rendition of "*O Marie*." It was Joe Crapito and his mandolin-playing friend, Luey Marterano, who had his own Italian music show on a local radio station. Tagging along was another friend who played the accordion. As frequently happened, the trio had decided to bring the party to Ted and Stella's house for a while before inviting them to join in the fun and traveling to several other houses as the night wore on.

In a minute, both boys were seated at the top of the stairs listening to the fun.

"Tell the boys to get dressed, Stell," said Ted after awhile.

"Where are we going?"

"They want to drop in on my cousin Emil and his wife Josie, and they want us to go along," replied Ted.

According to the author's Aunt Angeline, Emil Riccio was not really a blood-related cousin of Ted, but rather was the son of a foster child, named Benedetto Riccio, whom Ted's Grandmother had raised in Italy along with another foster son, named Luigi.

It should be noted, however, that Rosella Riccio, the widow of Emil's son, Bennie, did tell the author that her husband insisted that, despite what Aunt Angeline told the author, his father was a blood relation of the Barci family.

The party would continue through the night until daybreak. The amazing thing, however, about the photos that were taken at 5:00 a.m. at one of these parties is that the musicians still look very neat in their ties and vests, and very alert.

Sometimes, when these impromptu, middle-of-the-night parties became rowdy enough to merit a neighbor's complaint to the Cudahy police, the cops who answered the call were generally invited in, treated to some wine and Italian food, and usually joined in the fun.

Life was good for Ted. He was fast becoming a well-respected member of the Cudahy community. He and his father had friends in all the right places, and they knew how to nurture those friendships with generous hospitality.

October, 1945
South Chicago, Illinois

Bernie never really looked forward to his visits with his mom to South Chicago. Too many negative associations.

It was there, when he would be left with his Aunt Lucy while his folks went off to some function or to visit other friends, that he would be teased into crying.

"Your Mamma's never coming back," teased Aunt Lucy.

Bernie's eyes would immediately tear up.

"She doesn't like you, and she's leaving you here with us forever," Aunt Maggie would chime in.

O.K., they had their wish. Bernie was reduced to a total crybaby.

It was in South Chicago that his Uncle Charlie had accidentally burst one of the few balloons Bernie had ever been given as a child. His Uncle was just fooling around. He was a happy-go-lucky, fun loving kind of a guy. Nonetheless, Bernie's balloon was burst. More tears.

Of course, once Bernie arrived at his Aunt Lucy's house, he could usually repress all those negative associations and try to find something to distract himself, hopefully with the help of one or more of his cousins.

"Look! There he is. I hoped he would come today," said Gloria. She and her cousin Bernie were looking out the front window of the second floor flat where they had run to see one of the frequent fire trucks go speeding by.

"Come on. Let's go down the front stairs," said Bernie.

"No," said Gloria, "my mom doesn't want us to use those stairs. We have to go down the back."

So the two cousins raced through the flat toward the back stairs.

"Bernard, where are you going?" asked Stella who was seated at the kitchen table with her sister Lucy.

"We're going out in front for a little while. We'll stay on the front steps."

"Bern," said his Aunt Lucy. "Would you please take that bag of trash out to the alley for me?"

"Sure, Aunt Lucy," said Bernie as he got the bag from under the sink and rejoined his cousin who was waiting for him on the back porch.

Outside, his cousin again waited while Bernie hurried under the grape arbor toward the alley to put the trash in the can that stood behind the garage.

The grape arbor was a hallowed avenue that not only supported grape vines planted by Tony Nudi, but it was also the setting for scores of historical family happenings. It was under this arbor one day that Leonard had gotten into a heated argument with his father-in-law with whom he was drinking wine. His sister-in-law, Stella, happened to be in the garden behind the grape arbor listening in. When her brother-in-law crossed the line—to her mind—and began to be particularly disrespectful to her tipsy father, she flew at him from behind and began to beat on him, knowing that, with his small frame and sense of manly decency, he would not dare to hit her back.

The garage itself was also a mysterious wonderment to all the children. Lucy's husband, Leonard, kept a coop for racing pigeons on the second floor—another gambling venture to which he was addicted. This in addition to the fighting cocks that his brother-in-law Angelo kept for him on his tomato farm near Lansing.

Charlie, Rudy, Gusty and Leonard had spent many nights surreptitiously collecting paving bricks from nearby streets that were being repaved by the city of Chicago. Once they had enough, Leonard said he would build a garage for his father-in-law—no matter that his father-in-law had insisted that he did not need—or want—a garage since he did not drive and never intended to own a car. Nonetheless the brick gathering continued.

Rudy would recall years later that when Leonard began to lay the bricks, they all began to slide and collapse. Paving bricks, it turns out, are covered with a smooth glaze on all sides to keep out water. Mortar does not stick to them very well at all. Once this was discovered, Leonard had to resort to setting only one or two layers of brick a day.

When the garage was finished, Tony Nudi absolutely forbid anyone to park a car in it, and its only use turned out to be as a pigeon coop for Leonard's racing pigeons.

When Bernie had made his way back from the alley, Gloria was swinging on the passageway gate. She quickly jumped down, and they entered the narrow path to freedom.

This was the passageway dreaded by Bernard's brother, Joe.

As a small boy, Joe's mother had insisted on dressing him in a white shirt and white jacket with matching white pants. He was then expected to make his way carefully through the narrow passage without brushing against either side of the soot-coated buildings. Of course, he never made it safely through and inevitably got yelled at once he was upstairs.

Joe's personal memory of one such incident is as follows: "It was a white sailor suit. I never did understand why Ma always wanted us to be dressed so neatly when we were fated to get dirty as soon as we arrived in South Chicago. And as soon as we got dirty, we would catch hell from Ma."

Lucky for the children, this was one of those very rare times when Tony Nudi had a tenant for his storefront. The tenant ran a small store that sold groceries and sundries.

What had brought the children down from their window perch was the arrival of a candy delivery man. The cousins sat on the stoop next to the entrance and waited. As soon as they saw the candy man coming out, they adopted their best "we're good little children—could we please have a candy bar" look.

And it worked. Each was given a Mars Bar by the friendly deliveryman.

Their pleasure, however, would be fleeting. There was no way to eat a Mars Bar on a hot day in South Chicago without getting a messy face, sticky fingers and—horror or horrors—chocolate covered clothing. They would both "get it" when they got back upstairs.

October 15, 1945
Cudahy, Wisconsin

Joe Barcio's daughter Yolanda had entered into a bad marriage with Jerry Dzibinski. The two had met as they worked together at the Line Material Company in South Milwaukee. Although he had asked for and obtained her hand in marriage, Jerry later decided that he was gay and could not, in all honesty, stay in the relationship. When he broke this news to his father-in-law, Joe Barcio responded in macho Italian fashion. Joe was short, 5 feet, six inches tall, but mighty with muscles honed by years of work on the railroad and building homes. He simply picked Jerry up, carried him out the front door and threw him from the porch onto the lawn with words of encouragement not to return.

The following announcement would later appear in the Milwaukee Journal:

> "NOT responsible for any debts contracted by my wife, Yolanda, on or after Oct. 15, 1945. Jerome E. Dzibinski, 3655 E. Holmes Ave."

When Jerome E. Dzibinski showed up later at another party attended by Joe Barcio, Joe went right up to him and punched him square in the face and told him to "get the hell out!"

After she left her job at the Line Material Company, Yolanda always dressed most fashionably as was in keeping with the jobs she next held downtown Milwaukee as a salesperson. Yolanda later married a pleasant Polish pharmacist, Louis Kowolski, in whose drugstore she had found a job.

To the author, his Aunt Yolanda represented elegance. At Christmas time the wrappings on the gifts that she gave were always professionally done, complete with the most beautiful ribbons. On the end table in her living room was always an elegant box of expensive candy. Aunt Yolanda was definitely a very refined lady.

Throughout her life Yolanda has maintained her elegance, and in 2003 was featured in a color photo that ran in the Milwaukee Journal along with an article about the apartment complex in which she lived.

When the author visited his Aunt Yolanda in June of 2004, she gave him a tour of some of the recently remodeled common areas in her complex. As they walked through the halls, Yolanda greeted all she met by name, formally introduced them to her nephew and made personal inquiries into their affairs. They all seemed to appreciate the flair and respect she added to their lives.

May 11, 1946
St. Francis, Wisconsin

Joe and Vrigitta Barcio were marrying off their daughter, Ida. It would be another gala Barcio event, complete with home cooked Italian food, live music, wine, dancing and merriment. Among the guests would be Tony Nudi, who, by this time, had once again changed his last name back to its original spelling.

Tony was not all that fond of Ida's fiancé, but he was Joe Barcio's friend and he would not refuse his invitation to help him celebrate the marriage of his daughter.

After the war was over, Tony's son, Gusty, and Fred Mosacchio had come to St. Francis to look for work since he was having no luck finding any in South Chicago.

"But why are you hanging around with that guy?" asked Tony when Gusty had told him he was going to Wisconsin with Fred Mosacchio to look for work.

"He did his time, Pa," said Gusty, "and he's my friend."

"He stole our horse when he was a kid," countered Tony, still harboring that injustice from years past.

"Yeah, I know. And he spent time in jail. Can't you forget about all that?" said Gusty. "That's all in the past. He's just trying to make a new life for himself."

Years earlier, while attending a dance in South Chicago with some of his buddies, Fred had supposedly shot and killed a policeman. Those days, all young men who considered themselves worth their salt on the streets of South Chicago carried handguns. At one point in the evening, Fred was showing his friends how he could twirl his pistol on his finger and flip it into firing position, like gunmen do in Wild West movies. Suddenly, in mid-twirl, a cop walked up to Fred and said, "Hey!"

Fred jumped, and his gun went off, hitting the cop in the stomach. The wound proved fatal.

The shooting was ruled an accidental homicide, but Fred still had to do some serious time.

"That's not the way we remember it," said Ralph Mallo and Angeline Santostefano in June of 2004 when the author shared this version of the story with them during a visit.

"That's what Uncle Charlie and Rudy Strano told me last summer," countered the author.

"Well," said Ralph, "I always heard that Fred was out driving with some friends of his. They stopped at a store and, without Fred knowing it, his friends went in to rob the owner, whom they shot in the process."

"His friends," continued Aunt Angeline, "ran out the back door when they heard the cops coming. When the cops got there, they found Fred sitting in the car and arrested him."

"As an accomplice," added Ralph.

When the author shared this alternate version of the story with his cousin Rudy Strano in July, 2004, Rudy suggested that this version of the story had been created—as frequently happens in families—to help clean up Fred's image.

At any rate, Fred Mosacchio and Gusty Nudi had traveled to Wisconsin where they were hired as section hands by Raffaele Bruno who was now the foreman of the St. Francis Section of the Chicago and Northwestern Railroad.

Before too long, Fred had been introduced to Ida Barcio, and this was their wedding day. Fred was 14 years older than Ida—a fact that caused much tongue wagging, along with the fact that he also suffered from asthma and would discreetly use an inhaler that he would store on the top shelf of a guest closet whenever he visited his in-laws.

November 30, 1946
St. Francis, Wisconsin

Eugene Barcio had been discharged from his service with the Flying SeaBees/CB's (Construction Battalions) in the Pacific and had returned home to marry the love of his life, Mary Dovi, who lived in nearby Cudahy. Among their wedding party were Eugene's sister, Esther, and her fiancé, Chet Michalski.

Although lumber was still being rationed, Eugene began to support himself by doing what he had learned to do in the service: build houses.

During a visit with Uncle Gene during the summer of 2005, he took the author around St. Francis to show him the first house he built at 1922 E. Eden in St. Francis.

"Were you involved in the fighting on the Pacific islands?" the author asked during a later visit in 2008 after he and Aunt Mary had moved to Winston-Salem, North Carolina to be near their son David.

"We had a Marine unit assigned to us," he explained. "They would guard the perimeter while we either built or took down the barracks on each island. There was a lot of shooting, but most of it was handled by the Marines."

Although Uncle Gene always seemed to be happy-go-lucky during the years following his discharge, he definitely had endured stressful situations, resulting, as reported by the author's brother Joe, in his losing control one day and firing his service revolver in his house. Joe said that Aunt Mary called our dad to hurry over and calm Uncle Gene down and take his revolver away.

May 18, 1947
Cudahy, Wisconsin

It was Bernie's First Communion Day, and a party was being given at his home by his parents.

Bernie had lucked out. Just a few years earlier, when his older brother Joe had made his first communion at Holy Family Church, he had had to memorize all of the special prayers in Polish. It was a Polish parish, and it prided itself on maintaining its national image, right down to the prayers and even the traditional Polish outfits for its altar boys on special occasions.

By 1947, however, things were changing a little, and all Bernie had to do was learn his prayers in English.

In traditional Italian fashion, the celebration was a major one. Stella's father, Tony Nudi, was invited to come from South Chicago, and Ted's parents were also invited to be present, as were Ted's youngest sister, Yolanda. His sister and brother-in-law, Angeline and Henry Santostefano, were also in attendance with their children Jeanie, Francy (as Franny was sometimes called) and Junior (who, as an adult, goes by the name "Hank").

"Wait, Ted. He doesn't have his candle. He should be holding his candle in the picture," said Bernie's mom.

"Where's your candle?" asked his dad.

"It's up on the porch in its little box," replied Bernie.

"Well, run and get it. Hurry," said Bernie's mom.

As Bernie was hurrying back to the porch so he wouldn't keep all his relatives waiting too long to pose with him for the photo, his dad called after him:

"Short memory, long legs!"

Bernie had to stand still, not only for solo shots and a group photo with all of the guests, but also for individual photos taken with his cousins, his grandfathers Nonno and Papa, his grandparents Nanna and Papa, his parents and his brother, and with his *Zia* and *Zio* Santostefano—both of whom he addressed as *Tsitsi*.

June 15, 1947
Carollville, Wisconsins

It was Sunday, and Ted had decided to load the family into his car and drive to Carrollville for a family visit.

On this occasion, Bernie's cousin Junior had the yard swing all covered with sheets as sort of a fort. Things were going well, so long as no one put his leg too far back under the swinging seat and found it pinched against the attached floor rails.

"What you *kits* doing in there," called Aunt Angeline from the back door of the house, using her special pronunciation of the word "kids."

"Nothing, Ma," yelled Junior. "We're just playing."

"Come in now, and wash your hands. It's-a time to eat!"

Truth be told, the kids were not "just playing." The little neighbor girl was with them all and Junior had improvised a quick game of "show and don't tell" that was just getting ready to start.

At any rate, Aunt Angeline, perhaps inspired by that special "second sense" that all good mothers seem to have, had quickly put an end to that little game.

June 29, 1947
Jefferson Park, Illinois

It was Sunday, and Ted Barcio was visiting his parents in St. Francis. He needed to share some important news.

In an attempt to advance his career, Ted had bid on an Assistant Roadmaster's position on the Chicago and North Western Railroad at Jefferson Park, Illinois. It was on a subdivision that ran north from Chicago into the southern portion of Wisconsin. This would require him to be gone during the week, but he was still able to come back to Cudahy on weekends to make the rounds and help his friends and relatives complete their weekly payrolls and other reports for the railroad. Ted had helped most of them get their positions even though several were illiterate, and others had just not had much formal education.

July 4, 1947
Cudahy, Wisconsin

Ted Barcio was once again serving as the Music Chairman of the annual Fourth of July celebration in Sheridan Park, now being sponsored by the Cudahy Sane Fourth Commission.

Sheridan Park was a great place for such events. In addition to playground equipment and open field areas, it featured a large shallow pond in which children could sail commercial and homemade toy sailboats.

The 1947 Program pretty much featured the same events that had been scheduled in 1945. The big difference came at the end of the day when the 6:30 p.m. Band Concert was presented by the Veterans of Foreign Wars Band.

Then, prior to the fireworks display, those in attendance were treated to an elaborate VARIETY SHOW that began at 7:30 p.m.

1) Star Spangled Banner—Miss Cel Cadon and assemblage.
2) Janis Mae All Star Variety Revue—songs, dancing and acrobatics.
3) Cracow Polish Dancers in native Polish costumes, Melvin F. Przybyl, Director.
4) Musical Quartette, under direction of Larry Tonar.
5) Sensational roller skating acts and acrobatics.
6) Additional numbers by local groups announced separately.

September 5, 1947
Cudahy, Wisconsin

"I'm sorry, Mrs. Barcio. I know you would like Bernard to be an altar boy like his older brother, but we just don't think he's mature enough yet."

"What do you mean, Sister? Hasn't he learned his Latin prayers well enough?"

"It's not that, Mrs. Barcio. Bernard just doesn't pay attention to the Mass."

"What is he doing?"

"He's just looking around all the time. He stares at the ceiling, at the side panel decorations, at the statues. He's never ready to do what Father expects him to do."

So Bernie lost his chance to be an altar boy when he was in the fifth grade. Bernard was fascinated by the architecture, by the lights, by the candles, by the art. It was all so different and so impressive. It needed staring at. It needed absorbing. His interest in art and architecture would become something that he would nourish as avocations as he grew up.

He was, however, destined to make up for his shortcomings as an altar boy. Years later, while attending Holy Cross Seminary in La Crosse, Wisconsin, he would first be appointed as Sacristan of the crypt chapel and later as Head Sacristan of the main chapel at the seminary.

But that was still a long way off. In the meantime, Bernie had a lot more mischief to get into.

It was laundry day, and, since he wasn't being allowed to go outside, Bernie decided to watch his mom do the laundry. There were two large sinks in the basement. The clothes would be put to soak in one and the other held a washboard on which stubborn stains were removed with a bar of Fels Naptha soap. The clothes were then put into a washing machine where they would be agitated until his mom decided to run them through the ringer and put them into the laundry basket to be hung up outside.

"Can I put the clothes through the ringer?" asked Bernie who had been watching that device with fascination.

"No! Don't touch anything. You'll hurt yourself!" replied his mom.

His mom started another piece of wet clothing through the ringer and turned to do some more scrubbing. That was when Bernie decided to see what the clothes felt like as they started to be pulled into the wringer.

"OWWW, OWWW, MY HAND, MY HAND!" screamed Bernie whose hand had gotten caught and was being pulled through the ringer.

BAM! Stella hit the release leaver at the end of the roller attachment, and the rollers separated and stopped turning.

"*Diauolo maledetto scataruzo!* Didn't I tell you not to touch anything?" screamed his mom. "Let me see your hand!"

Stella actually pronounced the word "*scataruzo*" as though it were spelled "*shcataruzo.*"

"It hurts! It hurts!" screamed Bernie.

"Move your fingers!" commanded his mom.

"They hurt!" screamed Bernie, now beginning to get worried that he might also be about to get punished.

"Let me see!" said his mom as she roughly examined his hand for torn skin and squeezed each finger to see if she could feel any broken bones.

"Ouch, that hurts!" continued Bernie.

"You're awright. Now go upstairs and sit at the table until your father gets home!"

The road to the seminary was definitely going to be a long one!

September 17, 1947
Cudahy, Wisconsin

Ever since his dad had brought the new 1941 Plymouth home, Joe had been impressed with it. Later, when he 68 years old, he could still remember exactly what the car looked like—inside and out—and he could still recall the new-car smell.

Today, on his twelfth birthday, he would get his very first driving lesson from his dad.

"Here, slide over close to me and put your hand on the gearshift."

Joe did as he was told and grabbed the knob of the gearshift with his hand.

"Okay now, this is how you put it into 1st gear."

Joe gave it a try. It took a while to get the hang of it, but he finally managed to push the gearshift into the correct position.

"Now, you do this to move to 2nd gear."

Moving into second gear was a lot easier, and Joe began to feel very grown up for a twelve-year old.

"Finally, you move it here to put it in third."

Once Joe had the hang of it, his dad started up the car and let Joe shift the gears as he pulled out onto the street for a little ride.

And there was even more yet to come. After Joe was comfortable shifting the gears, he was allowed to hold the wheel and steer the Plymouth along an infrequently traveled road.

He was so proud! A moment he would remember forever.

September 21, 1947
Cudahy, Wisconsin

It was a Sunday morning, and, as usual, Ted had a local church service playing on the upright radio as he shaved.

"Ma, can we go visit *Tsitsi* today?" asked Bernie, eager for something exciting.

Bernie's Aunt Angeline was really the only Milwaukee area relative who had children close to the ages of him and his brother, which made it fun when they got to visit with them at their house on South 5th Ave. in Carrollville. In addition to rolling down a grassy hill behind their neighbor's house, the kids could spend hours swinging on a special double swing, sometimes called a lawn swing or a yard swing, with a moveable floor that *Tsitsi* had built using steel pipes and steel suspension rods. They also would play card games using buttons from *Tsitsi*'s sewing box as "money."

"Go ask your dad," said his mom.

"Dad, can we go visit *Tsitsi* today?"

"*Non-ne*," came the terse reply in what Bernie guessed was Italian.

When Bernie got the old "*Non-ne*" reply, he knew it was no use asking any more.

Sometimes, however, his dad would give the "We'll see" reply. This was a preferred answer because it meant there was a slight possibility. Going to *Tsitsi*'s house for a visit or a party always made the day perfect.

And this turned out to be a "perfect" Sunday afternoon spent in Carrollville. Except for one little problem. Bernie's brother Joe and his cousin Jeannie had gotten into his dad's car that was parked at the top of the driveway which sloped down toward the back of the property. Joe was showing his cousin how he had learned to shift the car's gears. But as soon as he put his foot on the clutch to take the car out of gear, the car began rolling down the hill.

"Ted, your car is rolling down the driveway," called someone from the backyard.

"Who's in it?" called Ted.

"I think it's Joey and Jeannie," came the answer.

Before anyone could get to the car, it had coasted all the way down the hill and came to rest against an out building toward the rear of the property. Big trouble for Brother Joe this time!

"Joe," said Ted in a mean voice, "never play around in a car. You could have killed your cousin. *Capisce*?"

Joe *capisce*-d big time and resolved to stay out of trouble. After all, he was the older brother and needed to set a good example.

In retrospect, Joe recalls that the real reason he so much enjoyed visiting in Carrollville was that it gave him and his brother a change of life pattern. In contrast to his own mother, Aunt Angeline was always kind, warm, open-minded, and she always made them feel welcome. He and his brother may have had to pay for it when they returned to Cudahy, but for a short time they were actually free to have some fun. For that little while they were not subjected to being sworn at, hit or living in constant fear of doing something wrong. Their cousins were close to their own ages, and with them they could play in a manner they were not allowed to enjoy back on Hammond Ave.

October 16, 1947
St. Francis, Wisconsin

After her engagement to Chet Michalski was broken off, Esther met George Duga in a bar owned by his folks on Layton Ave. In fact, George had been born in his folks' apartment on the second floor of the bar. The bar was along side the freight line tracks and near the depot of the Chicago and North Western Railroad for which Esther's dad, Giuseppe Barcio, worked as a trackbed maintenance foreman. Ester and George soon fell in love and were married on this date.

March 31, 1948
Cudahy, Wisconsin

Whenever Ted drove his family to St. Francis to visit his parents, they passed by the St. Francis Seminary. It was a fascinating place surrounded by an impressive black iron fence. In fact, the whole concept of becoming a priest was so fascinating that when Fr. Louis Clarke, a member of the Discalced Carmelite Fathers, visited Joe's class at school to talk about vocations, Joe became seriously interested.

On March 31, 1948, Joe received the following letter:

> "My dear Joe,
>
> "Just these few lines to ask you if you are of the same opinion about going to our Preparatory College in the fall. Did you talk the matter over with your dear parents and have they approved? Let me know as soon as you can.
>
> "I trust that you are enjoying your Easter holidays. May God bless you a lot and may our Blessed Mother and Saint Joseph keep you from all dangers. I am as always,
>
> "Fondly yours,
> "Fr. Louis Clarke, O.C.D."

April, 1948
Cudahy, Wisconsin

The following letter was received by Ted and Stella Barcio concerning their son's interest in attending the seminary preparatory college:

> "My dear Parents,
>
> "I had an opportunity to give a talk on the sacred priesthood and the Carmelite Order in the school which your own son attends. It seems that your son has a feeling that he would like to be a priest and a religious. He would love to go to our Minor Seminary at Holy Hill next September. Are you also willing?
>
> "Now very often it happens that parents become very imprudent when their sons return from school after having heard such a talk and tell their parents that they want to go to a minor seminary in the fall to begin their studies for the sacred priesthood. Often parents discourage them by telling them that they are too young to choose their vocation. They tell them to finish high school and then make their decision. The reason that a boy tells you that he wants to go to a seminary is simply that he is repeating the words of the Vocational Director who has given the talk. A boy who desires to become a priest must be placed in the proper environment and he must be permitted to associate with other boys who have the same ideal that he is entertaining.

"Now, dear parents, your own son has this desire in his heart. He wants to be a priest and a religious. The only sensible thing for you to do is to allow him to go to our Minor Seminary in September. There is nothing wrong in him doing that since we are the ones who are willing to accept him. In this way, at close range, he can study his vocation and do that while he is in high school at our seminary. If you are willing to give him that chance I ask you to use the enclosed envelope to let me know. I shall call on you later when we can discuss the matter at length.

"Dear Parents may God bless you a lot and give you the courage to consent to so important a matter. Other parents have given their consent. In later years you will be the parents of a Catholic priest. What an honor. May our Blessed Mother and Saint Joseph keep you from all dangers. I beg to remain as always,

"Devotedly yours in Mary,
"Fr. Louis Clarke, O.C.D."

Unfortunately for the Catholic Church, but fortunately for the family that Joe went on to have later in life, Joe's father soon accepted a new Roadmaster's position in Norfolk, Nebraska, and Joe's parents were very reluctant to leave him behind attending school in Wisconsin. They finally convinced him that if he were still interested later on, they would think about letting him look into another seminary, maybe one closer to where they would be living.

August, 1948
Cudahy, Wisconsin
An opening for a Roadmaster's position in Norfolk, Nebraska, was posted. Ted hurried home to discuss bidding on the position with his wife. His wife's reply was a practiced, submissive one.
"We go where your bread and butter is."
"I've already told Ma and Pa, and when we go to Angeline's house this weekend, I'll tell everyone else that we're moving," said Ted.
As his brother Joe remembers it, Ted's announcement had not gone over well with their grandfather.
"Why the hell do you want to move way out there?" was his immediate reaction.
By now, however, things had calmed down a bit.
Bernie couldn't believe his ears. They were going to visit his cousins in Carrollville! Even though *Tsitsi*'s house was located near a glue factory that had been built on the shore of Lake Michigan, the smell could usually be ignored. It was a little harder to ignore the fact that hundreds of horses were being killed and processed to make the glue.
When Emil Riccio worked at the glue factory, he told horrendous stories about the rats that infested the building, feeding on whatever they could find, as remembered by Charlie Nudi.

Oh well, if the wind were blowing the right way, there could still be more fun rolling down the neighbor's grassy hill. More fun on the yard swing. And best of all, Bernie had just gotten two new toy guns that shot plastic sticker darts equipped with suction cups on their tips.

As luck would have it, even Bernie's cousin, Bennie Riccio, was in Carrollville when he got there.

Bennie, whose given name was Benedetto (after his grandfather), was one of two sons of Emil Riccio whom Ted Barcio referred to as his cousin.

Bernie and Bennie immediately began to target practice with the toy guns. When the novelty wore off of the usual targets, Bennie suggested that they cross the road and hide down in the ditch. Then, when a car came by, they could try and hit it with their sticker darts.

The first few cars went by too quickly, and neither boy could get a dart to hit even the side of the car as it went by. Finally, Bernie determined that he was going to get a direct hit. As the next car came up the road, Bernie boldly climbed to the side of the road and took aim at the front windshield.

WHACK!

It was a direct hit on the driver's side. And it stuck! Bernie was thrilled.

SCREEECH!

The driver suddenly slammed on his breaks, jumped out of the car and came charging at Bernie who just stood there like a log, taken completely off guard by the driver's aggressiveness.

"I'm gonna kill you, you little son of a bitch," said the driver as he grabbed Bernie by the throat with both hands.

"Arggh," gasped Bernie. He couldn't breathe. This guy really was going to kill him, and his cousin Bennie had taken off to save his own hide.

Just when Bernie thought his little life was coming to an end, however, the man released his grip and threw him to the ground. The man then saw where Bernie had dropped his plastic gun. He picked it up and set it down on the hard surface of the road and smashed it with his heel.

"God damn kids," grumbled the man, "I should smash your head is what I should do."

He then got back in his car and drove away.

Bernie slowly got his breath back and began to look around to determine his situation. Had he been seen by anyone at the house? If he had, he would probably be in even more trouble. Had Bennie gone and told on him?

Luckily, the coast seemed to be clear, and Bernie gathered up his unused sticker darts and casually crossed the road back to his Uncle's house. Bennie hadn't told on him, so all he was out was one gun and a sore neck. He could say he lost the gun, and he knew his neck would feel better again after a while.

The next week, the family put their Cudahy house up for sale and began to pack their belongings into big, round cardboard barrels so they could be shipped by rail to Norfolk. The family would also travel to Nebraska by train since Ted had sold his 1941 black Plymouth.

Ted's sister, Esther, took over the task of helping friends and relatives complete their weekly payrolls and other reports for the railroad.

As they left their home, Bernie looked back to see their dog, Poochie, standing in the driveway of their home.

"What about Poochie? Can't we take him with us?" he asked his dad.

"*Non-ne!*"

"But what will happen to him?" pressed Bernie.

"Oh, he'll be all right here. Don't worry about him."

Years later, Bernie would learn from his Uncle Charlie that Poochie had been taken by him to his Brother Angelo's farm near Lansing, Illinois, where he was accidentally run over by a car.

October, 1948
St. Francis, Wisconsin

In October of 1948, Joe was living with his wife and daughter, Yolanda, at 3545 S. Iowa Ave. in St. Francis. Joe owned a black coup with running boards and large chrome bumpers. He kept his car in a detached garage off to one side of his house.

Joe was also an avid gardener who germinated his own seedlings in hotboxes he built in his garden from small wooden frames and used house windows.

He and his other Italian friends also made their own wine, buying grapes from the Brady Warehouse on N. Broadway Street downtown Milwaukee. His recipe called for a ratio of 14 boxes of dark purple Bouchet grapes mixed with 4 boxes of light Muscatel grapes. Joe was always very generous with his wine, a generosity that easily won the friendship of many local politicians and members of the police force.

Joe Barcio, on several occasions told his grandson, the author, that he had met and was friends with the flamboyant wrestler Gorgeous George. Joe prided himself on his own toughness and enjoyed watching wrestling on T.V., something that Gorgeous George pioneered on November 11, 1947.

Joe and Vrigita hosted many family parties in their various homes, the basements of which could always be set up as party rooms. Sons Theodore and Eugene even built an elaborate portable bar that was kept in the basement for such occasions. Guests always included family, extended family, friends, acquaintances and friendly city officials.

Entertainment was provided by Italians who played guitar, mandolin, accordion and even, on occasion, bagpipe. And, of course, when the time came for the traditional Tarantella to be played, Vrigita would get her tambourine down from the shelf in the front hall closet, and, shaking it regally over her head with her right hand, would place her left hand on her hip and lead the dancing.

Although Joe was only 5 foot 6 inches tall, everyone respected him for his muscularity and powerful Italian temper. When, during one of his anniversary parties, someone asked him how he managed to get along with his wife through all the years, he proudly shared their secret.

"Even though we get mad at each other during the day, we always crawl into the same bed together at night. That's-a the secret!"

Filomena, Tony, Stella, Ted
Stella & Ted Engagement, April 30, 1934

Stella, Filomena, Lucy, Tony Nudi & Leonard
Leo at Chicago World's Fair in August, 1934

Stella and Ted's
South Chicago Wedding Cake
September 2, 1934

Ted and Stella on their porch at 3626 E. Hammond Ave, next door to the Stankowski residence in Cudahy.

1941: Ted Barcio, 34 years old
Hunting pheasants in
Wollworth County, Wisconsin

Author's 3 ½ year old brother Joe in
his white sailor suit, May 30, 1939

3673 E. Holmes Ave., Cudahy, Wisconsin in the 2nd floor flat of which Bernard F. Barcio was born on October 10, 1938

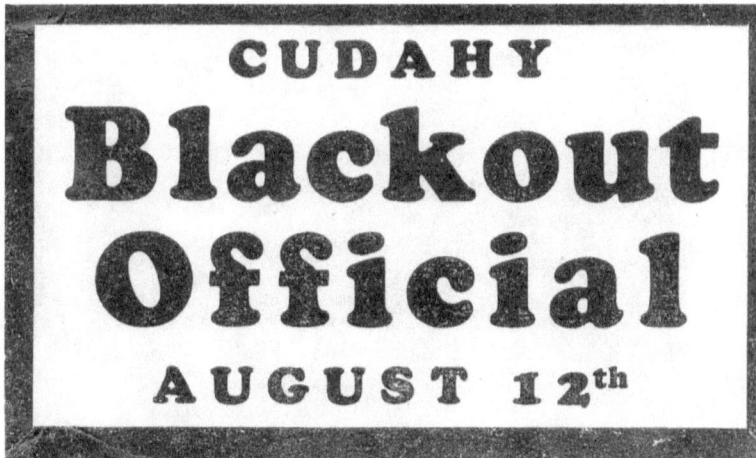

Arm band worn by Ted Barcio In Cudahy, WI, during WWII

Leonard Leo, Tony Nudi, Roco and Joe Crapito
Midnight, Feb. 29, 1942, South Chicago

Tony Nudi in front of his house at 9506 Commercial Ave. in South Chicago

Tony Nudi weaving a willow basket at 3626 Hammond Ave. in Cudahy. With him are his niece Florence Miresso and his goat.

Author's 1st Communion
with grandparents
Giuseppe and Vrigitta Barcio
May 18, 1947

The author's (L, 3rd row up) 1st Communion Class,
Holy Family Church, Cudahy, May 18, 1947

Angeline, Stella, Henry, and Ted
Bernie, Frannie, Junior (Hank) & Joe
Carrollville, May 11, 1947

First house built by Eugene Barcio after his discharge from the Service. 1922 E. Eden, St. Francis, WI

Giuseppe Barcio's house at 3777 S. Ahmedi Ave., St. Francis, In which the author's Brother Joe was born Sept. 17, 1935

Vrigita, Eugene, Giuseppe
1946

Ted (L) and his sisters Esther & Yolanda (R) celebrate the basement bar he helped build for his dad's 60th birthday, March 5, 1946

Mandolin player (L), Sam Dovi on Accordion Ted Barcio on guitar (R)

Ted Barcio harvesting peaches from his tree in Cudahy

Gusty Nudi

Charles Nudi with bi-pod machine gun

Wedding of Martha & Charles Nudi
Holy Family Church, Cudahy
July 4, 1942

Ted (standing) & Charlie with their 1941 Plymouth

Author (L) with his mom and brother Joe in their Polish altar boy vestments Cudahy, April 1946

Ted Barcio badge

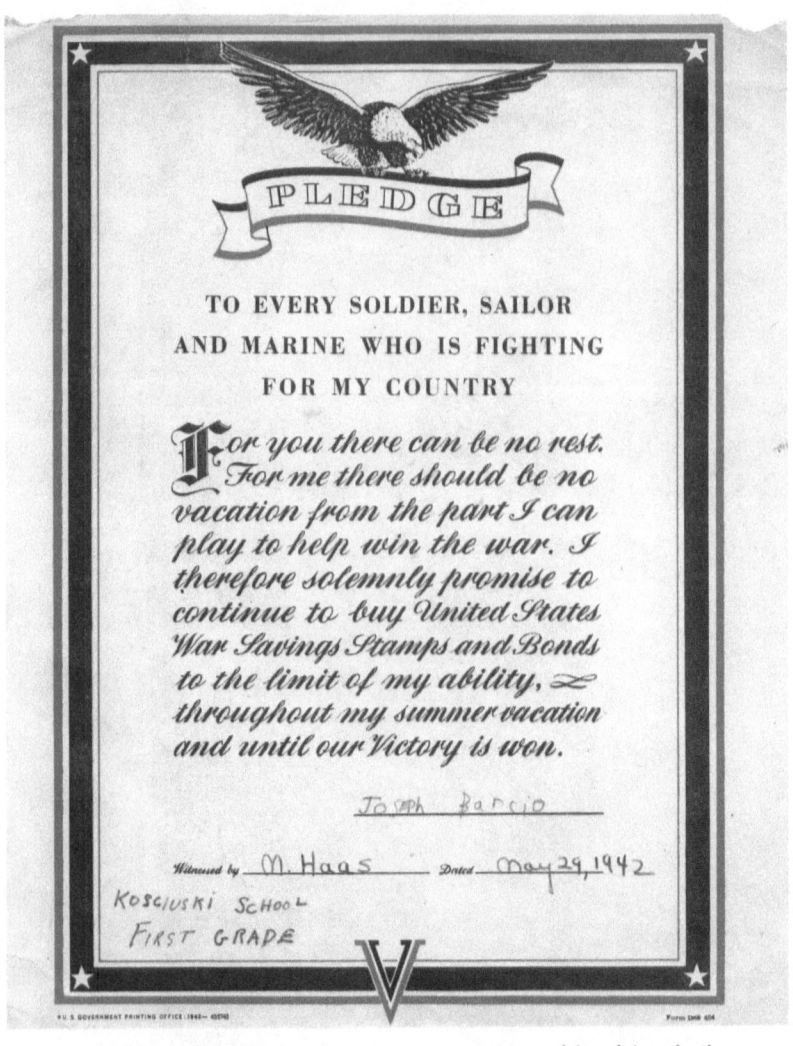

Notice that the Air Force is not mentioned in this pledge signed by the author's Brother Joe in 1942. Initially, part of the United States Army, the USAF was not formed as a separate branch of the military until September 18, 1947 under the National Security Act of 1947.

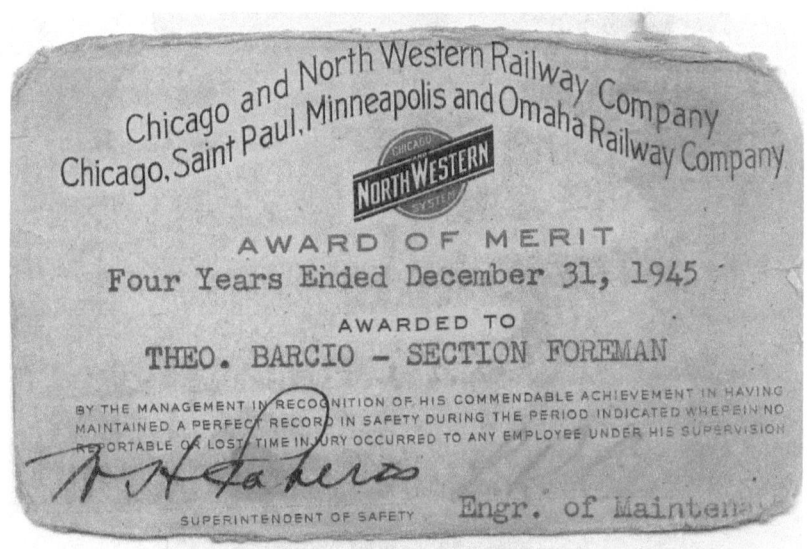

Wedding of Ida and Fred Mosacchio
May 11, 1946

Sally and Joe Mingari
daughter Elizabeth
ca. 1938, Milwaukee

Mrs. Novak, Bernard Grzeca and his mom
3648 E. Hammond Ave., Cudahy

Martha Nudi (R) with
sister-in-law Florence (M)
and sister Regina (L)
3646 Hammond Ave.

Rudy Strano in his
Marine uniform
Cudahy

GRAMA FELOMENA NUDI

Lillian (Hacker) Barcio's Great Grandmother Cox, ca. 1930

Lillian's Grandmother Nelli Hacker
Thanksgiving, 1972, Indianapolis

Lillian Hacker, ca. 1940, Indianapolis

Gene and Pearl Hacker
Indianapolis, 1940's

Gene Hacker and Lillian, 1940's

PART III

November 1948 –May 1955

Livin' Out West in Norfolk, Nebraska

November, 1948
Norfolk, Nebraska
There were a lot of adjustments that had to be made when the family moved into their house at 705 S. Second Street in Norfolk. Although this was the largest town in northeast Nebraska, it was still very small compared to Milwaukee. Most houses were still on party line phone systems, often requiring two or three homes to share one line. If a person needed to make a call, he would have to pick up the phone and be sure no one else was using it before the operator could be contacted. Unfortunately, the Barcio phone line was shared by Mr. Hass, who ran Hass Plumbing and Heating out of the back of his home at 700 S. First Street. Mr. Hass was on the phone a lot, and used the most foul language that Stella Barcio had ever been subjected to (and she had not only heard a lot over the years, but had even used a lot herself, albeit in Italian). If Stella asked him nicely if she could please have the line to make a call, he would let loose a string of invectives that would curl a sailor's hair. Since not even Ted's intervention could do anything to resolve the growing tension over the shared phone line, one of the first luxuries the Barcios would invest in was a private line.

1948 would also turn out to be the year of the Great Blizzard. Just about all of the Albion Line, a cattle line that was part of Ted's Subdivision 2 that ran from Omaha to Long Pine in north central Nebraska, was about to be buried under eight to ten feet of snow.

Although Ted Barcio was the new guy in town, he had dealt with bad weather before in his career. As he listened to the weather forecasts and considered the terrain on the Albion Line, he got an idea that he thought just might save a lot of grief for his crews.

Ted went to talk to his division engineer, A.A. Colvin.

"Mr. Colvin," started Ted, "I think we're in for a very nasty storm that could shut down the whole Albion line unless we take some steps to prevent that."

"What do you have in mind?" asked Mr. Colvin.

"Well, I would like to suggest that I be given a train with a plow, plus a crew, so we could start running back and forth on the line. If we keep the plow moving all through the storm, I think we could keep the line open as the storm moves through, and trains could operate."

"It's actually not my call, Ted. You'll have to get an O.K. from V.A., the Division Superintendent," replied Mr. Colvin.

When Ted explained his idea to the Division Superintendent, V. A. Erickson, Erickson didn't see the wisdom of the suggestion.

"Ted, you're new out here. We've found that the best way to handle these storms is to just let them blow through and then clear the line. Otherwise, we end up just going back over work that's already been done."

So Ted had no choice but just to sit back and wait for the storm to blow itself out, leaving the Albion Line buried under eight to ten feet of snow. It was suddenly impossible for cattle ranchers to have critical feed delivered by rail. It would now be impossible for the same ranchers to ship their cattle as required to satisfy their supply contracts. Getting the Albion line plowed as quickly as possible was a critical matter of financial necessity for the State of Nebraska. While Ted had not been given the tools to prevent this from happening, he was now expected to fix the problem.

Thus it was that Ted Barcio was given a Baptism of Snow as he was forced to spend two weeks away from home supervising plowing operations. Because the winds blowing across the open Nebraska plains created mountains of snow ten to fifteen feet deep in some areas, standard snow plows attached to the front ends of engines proved useless. A Special rotary plow had to be ordered in from Chicago. This unit had a giant propeller blade mounted on its front end so it could cut a path through deep drifts.

On November 21, Ted and his crew were working just east of Oakdale on the Albion line. Two days later, on November 23, they had only progressed to a point a little east of Lindsay, having cleared only twenty-five miles of right-of-way after three days work. And the worst part of it was that almost as soon as the plows cleared a section of track, the wind would blow drifts back over it.

Although Ted would have preferred to work around the clock, union regulations required that the train's crew members be given time off for rest each night in the camp car that was pulled behind the snow plow. Ted also realized he would have to give both the engineer and the fireman their mandated hours of rest, but he was not willing to loose valuable hours allowing the steam engine to be shut down at night and then powered up fresh in the morning. If he and his crew were to be ready to resume plowing at dawn, the engine would have to be kept running all night. Since Ted was the Roadmaster, and union regulations did not apply to him, he simply volunteered to stay up all night to watch the gauges to keep the boiler working, and make sure that the pressure did not get too low nor too high. When dawn came, and the train crew returned to their posts, rested, Ted simply resumed his usual job of directing the efforts to clear the line.

"Here comes the helicopter, Ted," said the engineer who was standing on top of one of the ten-foot walls of snow bordering the track.

"What side is it going to land on," asked Ted so he would know where to go to greet Val Peterson, the Governor of Nebraska, who was flying in to see just how serious the problem was.

As Governor Peterson listened, Ted explained how the wind simply blew the snow back in behind them at the end of each day's work. They were making as much progress as possible and were working as many hours as they could.

"Is there any way that the work could go a little faster?" asked the Governor.

"Well, Sir," explained Ted, "if we try to go too fast, the engine derails, and then we lose a half a day getting it back on tracks. But you can be sure we won't give up."

All the while Ted was out with the snow plows, his wife Stella was left in Norfolk trying to get their new home set up and being sure their children got to school each day. She would leave her radio on during the day and listen to the news reports about how the snow removal was progressing on the Chicago and Northwestern Railroad.

Unbeknownst to Stella, families of some of the other men working the plow with Ted occasionally made arrangements to meet them at railroad crossings along the way and provide them with changes of dry clothing. Ted, unfortunately, had to make do with whatever he had brought with him in his small leather satchel.

When Ted finally returned home to Norfolk two weeks later, his trademark head of black hair had turned completely white. This had truly been his Baptism by Snow, and he had come through it with flying colors. Governor Peterson would later send him a certificate proclaiming Theodore J. Barcio to be an Admiral in the Navy of the Great State of Nebraska.

March, 1949
Norfolk, Nebraska

Even though the family did not own a car, Ted insisted that they all attend the Wednesday night Lenten services at Sacred Heart Church, located at 200 South 3rd Street. So, the family would get dressed and begin their six-block walk, Joe and Bernie in front, followed by their mom and dad. As usual, if Ted was feeling playful and was not involved in a mini-argument with his wife, he would kick a small stone ahead of his two boys to start a little game. Whoever was closest to the stone would give it a little kick, making sure it stayed on the sidewalk and did not go off onto the lawn.

Ted felt strongly about his religion and made sure that his family attended Mass together on Sundays and went to all of the Holy Week Services. And in the 40's, Holy Week Services included a three-hour marathon on Good Friday that began at noon and lasted until 3:00 p.m. Rosaries, litanies and Stations of the Cross filled the time. When the three hours were up, everyone in attendance felt as though they had personally shared the agony of the crucifixion.

The one nice thing about Good Friday was that it was followed by Holy Saturday. At noon on Holy Saturday, one could once again enjoy all those things that he had given up for lent—usually movies and CANDY!

Although Ted would never get as socially involved in the community as he had been in Cudahy, he did decide to become a member of the Knights of Columbus. The Barcio family house would have to be visited by a Knight who would inspect for improper magazines, art or objects and be sure that the family had the right number of crucifixes hung on bedroom walls and at least one picture of Pope Pius XII displayed in a prominent location.

Being Italian, the Barcio family easily passed inspection.

Ted would have liked to become a high ranking Knight—one that got to wear the fancy uniform and sword at special church events—but that required a hefty contribution to the K. of C. that Ted was not in a position to make.

September, 1949
Norfolk, Nebraska

"Ou-ch," said Bernard under his breath. Once again he was in church, and once again he was in trouble. The Nuns at Sacred Heart Elementary School tolerated no student talking when they were all marched over once a week for a school day Mass.

"They're so sneaky," confided Bernie to the boy next to him once he was sure the Nun was gone.

"What did she do to you?" asked the boy.

"She snuck up behind me and pulled the little hairs at the back of my head."

"I hate it when that happens to me," confided Bernie's friend.

Both the good Nuns and the priests of Sacred Heart Parish were skilled disciplinarians, meting out sudden and unexpected pain.

Nuns were deadly with their wooden rulers. A skilled Nun could deliver a cracking rap on a boy's knuckles before he even knew she was near him. They also loved to have boys kneel at the front of the room with their noses to the blackboard for mild offenses. More serious problems would land a boy in the dark basement of the convent, sitting and staring at the ping-pong tables used by the Nuns for recreation while pondering his errant ways.

The pastor, Monsignor Burns, never actually hit anybody, as far as Bernard knew, but he could put the fear of the Lord into any student just by looking at him—with his one eye! Monsignor Burns, word had it, had lost an eye as a boxer and was still as tough as nails. When he called on someone during the catechism class he conducted weekly, he expected a correct answer. Unprepared students risked being caught with their catechisms open in their laps rather than becoming the victim of his wrath by giving an incorrect answer.

"Finally, it's lunch time," thought Bernie as Sister dismissed the class.

"And don't be late," warned Sister. "Everyone should be back in the playground at least ten minutes early!"

Bernie was never quite sure what all the other students did at lunchtime, but he set out for home. He would have an hour of freedom. This gave him enough time to do some exploring, checking out stuff in the street gutters, stuff in the trees, rocks, weeds, flowers, bugs. He wasn't really in all that big of a hurry to get home because he knew lunch would not be ready and waiting.

"Take the basket and pick the clothes that are dry," ordered his mother as soon as Bernie walked into the back yard. If it wasn't "pick the clothes," it would be something else, some job that was just waiting until he got home for lunch.

"But, Ma, I gotta eat lunch, or I'll be late for school," complained Bernie when he was given yet another job that had to be done.

"Then peel some potatoes when you get done, and I'll come in and fix them as soon as I finish."

Scrambled eggs and potatoes weren't really all that bad of a combination—and one that Bernie still has a taste for now and then in his seventies—but it did get a little boring day after day.

"O.K., I gotta go now," said Bernie as he jumped up from the table.

"Wait, carry the basket of laundry up from the basement before you go," said his mom.

"But, Ma, I'll be late!"

"Go fast!"

Now Bernie was in tears—again. He would have to run most of the six blocks back to school, and he would still probably be late and spend another hour after school in the convent basement.

"Quit crying," ordered his mom as Bernie hurried out the front door. "Smile! You want people to think you're silly?"

December 25, 1949
Norfolk, Nebraska

"Can we sit down toward the front?" encouraged Bernie as he entered church with his family.

"Shhh!" said his mom as she automatically brought the back of her hand sharply against Bernard's lips.

As it turned out, however, there were seats down toward the front that the family was able to take. Bernie was fascinated by the crèche that was set up on the side altar. The manger scene was surrounded by tall small-needle evergreens decorated with ochre-shaped blue bulbs. The blue bulbs lent an eeriness to the scene that was totally absorbing.

Bernie's time spent admiring the decorations and architecture of the interior of the church, however, would soon be cut short. Before too long, he would once again be trained to be an altar boy, and this time he would be "broken" so that he could serve properly.

January, 1950
Norfolk, Nebraska

There would never be another blizzard like the Blizzard of Forty-eight while the Barcio's lived in Norfolk, but there would be at least one more time when Ted Barcio would be called upon to display his bravery and ruggedness on the railroad.

It was the middle of January. It was icy cold and the wind blowing the snow around reduced visibility to next to nothing.

At midmorning, the passenger train from Omaha had pulled onto a siding built out in the country, halfway between Stanton and Norfolk, where it usually waited for a regularly scheduled freight train to pass going east before the brakeman would go out and throw the switch for the train to pull back out onto the main line.

Unfortunately, the freight train had not been given clearance to make its run that day because of the poor visibility and icy tracks.

The dispatcher received the news on the railroad telegraph and came downstairs to discuss the situation with the Roadmaster, Ted Barcio.

"Ted, the mid-morning freight will not be making its run, and we don't have any way to notify the passenger train to come on in," said the dispatcher.

"Where is the train now?" asked Ted.

"It's six miles out on the side track. It won't come in until it sees the freight go by out of fear of running into it on the main line."

"Well," said Ted, "we can't just let all those people sit out there in this storm. They'll freeze to death if the engine runs out of fuel."

"What do you think we should do?" asked the dispatcher.

"I think someone will just have to go out there and tell them it's O.K. to come on in," said Ted.

"Ted, I wouldn't want to send anyone out in this weather. The winds are gusting to 100 miles an hour."

"Well, then," said Ted, "I guess I'll go."

The dispatcher returned to his desk upstairs and in a little while, as Ted got ready to set out, Assistant Division Engineer Harold Braden came down the stairs.

"Wait up, Ted," said Harold. "You shouldn't go out in that alone. I'm going with you."

So the two men began their six-mile walk that would become a legend in Norfolk, Nebraska, railroad lore. They donned boots, scarves, heavy hats, gloves, sweaters and heavy coats and started down the tracks toward the siding.

The going was slow, and it was hard to keep their footing on the icy ties with the wind trying its best to blow them off the track bed.

When they came to a trestle bridge, a serious decision had to be made. The wind was blowing the snow so hard that they had little more than a few feet visibility and could not see to the far side of the bridge.

"I think we should go down and cross on the ice to the other side," yelled Harold. "We don't want to be caught in the middle of the bridge if the train has decided to come in."

"I don't think so," countered Ted. "If we fall through the ice, neither of us will make it to the train and we'll all freeze. I think we should cross the bridge carefully. We'll be able to feel the vibration if the engine comes onto the bridge. If it does, we can swing down from a girder and hang on while the train passes."

Ted's wisdom won out, and the two heroes slowly made their way across the trestle.

Several hours later, when the train pulled into the station at Norfolk with Ted and the Harold Braden riding proudly in the engine with the engineer and fireman, word of their brave venture was phoned into the local Norfolk radio station. As Stella listened to the radio that she kept on during the day, she suddenly heard a report about how the Roadmaster, Ted Barcio, and the Assistant Division Engineer, Harold Braden, had "performed an act of heroism."

Later that year, the railroad would install a phone box at the siding so that it would be easier to communicate with the trains that routinely waited there.

When Ted finally walked the eight blocks home through the wind that still blew blinding gusts through the streets of Norfolk, he was presented with yet another challenge. Stella had received a phone call from Sacred Heart School. All of the elementary students were being kept at the school until they could be accompanied home by a parent or adult. Joe, along with the rest of the high school students, had been allowed to walk home on his own.

Ted would have to get bundled up again and walk six more blocks each way through the blinding gusts to bring his son Bernard home from school.

It would take a while for Ted to save up enough to buy another car so in the meantime the whole family did a lot of walking. The boys would be sent to the store, first on foot, and later with bicycles that were bought for them. On Sundays, the family would don their Sunday best and walk two by two to Sacred Heart Church, sometimes playing "kick the rock" along the way.

That summer, Ted celebrated his survival and the move of his family out west by taking them on a bus tour of the Black Hills in South Dakota.

September, 1950
Norfolk, Nebraska

It was during his time in seventh grade that Bernie's initials, B.B., were cruelly turned into the nickname Big Butt by some of his classmates. It was now up to Bernie to prove that he was not one to be fooled with. At first, his best defense was his mastery of vulgar language. When bugged, he would release a stream of imprecations that would have curled the Nuns' ears if they had heard them. In fact, they sometimes did hear them and sentenced him to an extra hour or so in the basement of the convent, thereby causing him to get home late from school and catch hell from his mom.

Soon, however, the time came to do more than talk. Bernie was challenged to a fistfight to be held after school in the parking lot of the grain elevator located across from the school. His opponent was a precocious stud who, as a freshman, could produce seductive line drawings of naked women—a talent that did much to increase his playground popularity.

The fated day came, and Bernie felt fairly confident. He had become a pretty good scrapper and could usually "down" any opponent by rushing in, and while curling his right foot behind the legs of his opponent, push him off balance. Since Bernie had not been given the nickname Big Butt without reason, he could usually overpower his opponents by simply sitting on them and jamming his knees into the insides of their biceps, causing incredible pain and generally resulting in quick surrender.

As the two boys squared off, Bernie saw that his opponent had adopted a boxer's pose. His opponent had been receiving boxing lessons from his dad.

Now Bernie's grandfather, Papa (Joe Barcio who lived in Milwaukee and who was personal friends with the professional wrestler, Gorgeous George), had sent two pairs of boxing gloves to Nebraska. He hoped his grandsons would grow up tough. Bernie and Joe donned the gloves once or twice and had photos taken. The personalities of the two brothers, however, did not allow them to box unemotionally, and before long they sort of mutually decided to "hang up the gloves." So Bernie never really developed any boxing skills. It should come as no surprise that written inside Bernie's boxing gloves (which are preserved in a display case along with a few other toys and the catcher's mitt that he and his brother used in Nebraska) is the name, "Mr. Pleasant."

No matter, Bernie would stick to his usual program. Before his opponent could land a blow, he found himself on his back on the ground with Bernie applying knee pressure to his biceps.

The crowd that had gathered began to yell for Bernie to "clean his plow," and "punch his lights out." This however, was not Bernie's style. He really did not want to hurt any of his opponents; he just wanted them to acknowledge defeat.

"Give up?" asked Bernie.

"No way, Dago!" replied his opponent.

This prompted Bernie to start a slow rocking motion with his knees on the boy's biceps.

"O.K., O.K.," cried the boy. "Get off me, fatso!"

As far as Bernie was concerned, he had won, and he got up. Before he knew what happened, however, his opponent broke all rules of a fair parking-lot fight and, as soon as he got to his feet, he slugged Bernie in the eye.

Now, one might think that Bernie would have been demoralized by the blow, but he wasn't. His opponent knew enough not to stick around and quickly left accompanied by his small group of followers who were patting him on the back and congratulating him. Bernie's black eye became his badge of toughness. He, indeed, was one tough guy, and had the shiner to prove it.

Of course, even tough guys have their moments of panic, but these should not permanently ruin their reputations. Thus his reputation wasn't too seriously damaged by what happened when he had been left home alone one evening.

"You do your homework, now. No listening to the radio until you're done. Understand?" said Bernie's mom.

"O.K. What time will Joe be back?" asked Bernie who was about to be given some rare, unsupervised time.

The only problem was that it was dark out, and being home alone at night really wasn't his favorite thing. In fact the only thing worse was being sent downstairs to get something from behind the furnace after it got dark outside.

This assignment always resulted in serious jitters. The trip down the steps would be slow and careful, and the pace would slow even more once Bernie was in the poorly lit basement. It took conscious determination, in fact, to keep moving one foot ahead of the other and proceed into the black hole behind the furnace. Anything could be back there. Spiders, mice, a bat, or even a criminal who could have sneaked in through the back door that was never kept locked.

"Your brother will be home in a little while. If any emergencies come up, just run next door to Mrs. Sathre's house, and she'll help you."

That was it. Bernie was alone.

"I think I'll just sit here at the kitchen table and do my homework," Bernie thought to himself. "That way I won't have to think about what's going on in the rest of the house."

Bernie had just finished his work and was about to turn on the radio to listen to The Lone Ranger when he saw something run across the kitchen floor. A mouse!

Before he knew what he was doing, he had jumped up, ran out the back door and was half way to Mrs. Sathre's house.

"A mmm, a mmm, mmouse," stuttered Bernie when Mrs. Sathre answered the door. "I was sitting in the ki- ki- kitchen and a big mmm, mm, mmouse ran across the floor."

"Come on in, Bernard," said Mrs. Sathre who was always extra nice since she had no children of her own. "Would you like a cookie and a glass of milk?"

"Tha- tha- thank you."

Mrs. Sathre let him stay for five or ten minutes and then assured him that he would be perfectly safe if he returned home. Besides, he would surely not want to get into trouble by not being home when his brother got back.

Bernie carefully retraced his steps back home through the dark, confident that the kindly Mrs. Sathre would not deliberately damage his tough guy reputation.

The Sathre's would later give Ted and Stella a very fine set of dining room furniture that would eventually be passed down to Bernie's son, Phillip.

When Bernie's parents finally decided it was time for him to have an after school job, he began delivering papers once a week on his bike, fighting off loose dogs that harassed him as he delivered to some of the more rural yards on his route.

With this job, as with every job Bernie would have all through high school and college, he never once saw any of the money he earned. Somehow, his dad would arrange for all the monies to go to him. They were simply added to the family general fund.

In those days, kids had no claim to any money they earned. Whatever it was, it was automatically owed to their parents who picked up all their expenses. This even applied to five-dollar bills that might be tucked into shirt pockets by grandparents during occasional visits. As soon as everyone was back in the car, the boys would be asked if they had been given any money and were expected to hand it over. Nickels, dimes and quarters, however, were fair game and could be kept. Not silver dollars, however. Too valuable.

October, 1950
Norfolk, Nebraska
"Ma, do I have to take the trash out? I've got a bad headache again," complained Bernie after returning from the movies with his brother.

"If you're going to get a headache every time you go to the movies, maybe you shouldn't go," replied his mom.

But, of course, that solution would not work. The only two ways that Ted and Stella had of guaranteeing a little time for themselves, or a least a little time when they wouldn't have to worry about what Bernie would be getting into, was either to give Bernie 50 cents and send him to go get his hair cut, or give Joe money to take his brother to see a Saturday afternoon at the Rialto Theater, usually a western featuring Roy Rogers, Gene Autry, or Hopalong Cassidy in his trademark 10-gallon hat or, Bernie's all time favorite, Randolph Scott.

When Bernie continued to complain about headaches, his mom first took him to an eye doctor whose suggestion was that Bernie not focus so intently on the screen when watching a movie.

"Every so often, you should take your eyes off the screen and look around the theater," said the eye doctor.

"But I'll miss part of the movie," thought Bernie.

"You don't have to look away a long time. Just long enough to give your eyes a chance to focus on something else."

So there it was. It was bad enough that whenever Bernie stepped out of the Rialto with his brother, he had no idea where he was (he always became so totally absorbed in the movie that he was completely disoriented when the hit the street—no telling where he would have ended up had Joe not been with him). Now he had to miss part of the movie as well.

When the headaches continued even after the new look-away policy had been in effect for a few Saturdays, Bernie's mom took him to a eye, ears, nose and throat specialist.

"Your son is suffering from severe sinus headaches, Mrs. Barcio," was the prognosis.

"What can be done," asked Bernie's mom.

"I would like to drain his sinuses at our next appointment, and then see if we need to do it once or twice more after that."

Bernie had no idea what his mom was getting him into, but he had no choice but to allow himself be subjected to whatever so he could finally get rid of his headaches.

"Now, I want you to sit very still," said the doctor when Bernie's first appointment came around.

Bernie watched as the doctor produced a long pointed stainless steel punch.

This was not going to be enjoyable.

"There is a very thin membrane in the back of your nose that I need to pierce. You need to hold your head very still while I'm doing this. Do you understand?" asked the doctor.

Bernie shook his head in agreement, closed his eyes and let his head be tilted firmly back against the headrest. At first the doctor applied a gentle pressure once the stainless steel punch had been inserted into one of Bernie's nostrils. The membrane did not yield. He shoved harder, pushing Bernie's head even more firmly back against the headrest. Still no success. The doctor then produced a small mallet.

"I'm just going to give this a couple of taps," said the doctor.

Bernie couldn't believe it. The doctor was going to drive the stainless steel punch right up into his brain!

THUMP! THUMP!

Success. A small hole had been punched through the membrane.

"O.K.," said the doctor, "we're half done. Now we just need to do the other side."

Absolutely incredible! It was like some sort of medieval torture.

"Maybe I could just learn to live with my headaches," Bernie thought to himself.

Then, just when Bernie thought the doctor had done his worst, the doctor began pushing a small rubber tube through each of the openings created at the back of Bernie's nostrils.

"What we're going to do now," explained the doctor, "is flush out your sinuses. I'm going to run warm salt water through these tubes."

Bernie's eyes were bugged out. He gave no sign of either agreeing or disagreeing with the procedure.

"Now," cautioned the doctor, "it's very important that you keep saying K-K-K-K all the while the water is flowing trough your sinuses. If you don't, all the phlegm is going to go right down your throat."

"K-K-K-K-K-K-K-K-K-K-K-K-K-K-K-K-K-K-K-K-K-K-K-K-K-K-K-K-K-K-K-K-K-K-K-K-K-K-K-K-K," clicked Bernie as the warm, salty, water flushed through his head.

This procedure was repeated during at least three more appointments before Bernie finally announced that he did not think he needed to go to that doctor any more. Either the procedure had worked, or Bernie had decided to cure himself. For whatever reason, his headaches had stopped.

December 1950
Norfolk, Nebraska

Ted had gone through some hard winters in Wisconsin before he moved to Nebraska. The experiences he had with the snow in Nebraska, however, finally moved him to express some of his feelings in a poem.

The Night Before Christmas
'Twas the night before Christmas,
And all thru the yard

Not an engine was moving
The ice was so hard.
The switch lamps and signals
Were lighted with care
In hopes that St. Nicholas
Soon would be there.
But all of a sudden
The wind started to blow
And right along with it
Brought drifts and much snow.
Then came a knock
On old Tom Jones' door,
But he only turned over
And started to snore.
The knock grew stronger
And the fist hit harder.
It seemed strong enough
To knock ice off a retarder.
Tom sprang from his bed
To see what was the matter,
Why all of this pounding,
And all of this clatter.
He opened the door,
And the foreman was there.
"Get out and start shoveling!"
He gave Tom a scare.
So out went old Tom
With shovel and pick
When all of a sudden,
He heard a loud tick.
The snowplow was coming
On track number four.
Tom ran to his shack
And slammed shut the door.
The engine flew past
As fast as a thistle
While the engineer
Gave a blast on its whistle.
For the engineer this night
Was old Santa Claus.
On by went the engine
Without even a pause.
So fast was it going,
So fast and so fair,
That this time, for Tom,
St. Nick would not be there!

January, 1951
Norfolk, Nebraska

Snow and ice offered a whole new world of wonders that could be enjoyed on the walks to and from school. Bernie found it hard to pass by any frozen puddle without stepping on it to break the ice. And there's also some sort of unwritten kid-law that says no virgin tract of snow should be allowed to remain without footprints. This particular morning, however, things were rather more treacherous than usual, and it was slow going.

As Bernie walked to school, he was watching a girl carefully making her way on the icy sidewalk about a half block ahead of him. He thought how funny she looked trying to be so careful not to fall. When the girl got to the corner, she stepped off the curb and fell flat on her butt.

"Ha! Ha!" laughed Bernie out loud. He couldn't help himself. It really was funny to see her go down so fast, books scattering into the street.

Bernie was not old enough yet to consider running up and helping her. Besides, he figured she was so embarrassed she probably just wanted to be let alone.

Bernie was still having a good chuckle about the sight when he got to the same curb.

FLOP! Before he knew what had happened, he lay on the same spot recently occupied by the unfortunate girl. His books and papers were now scattered in the street.

He quickly looked around. Luckily, no one had seen him.

Seventh grade for Bernie also meant, among other things, Boy Scouts. The troop that met in the basement of Sacred Heart Church was small, and their activities were limited. Bernie attempted to learn to tie a variety of knots, as pictured in his Boy Scout manual. Although he participated in only one overnight campout, the smell of canvass in an Army Surplus Store still evokes strong memories of that experience. The troop leader spent a couple of meetings showing films of atomic bombs exploding on western deserts, hoping, it can only be assumed, to turn his boys into tough men ready for the challenges of 20th century warfare.

Bernie and his brother Joe were both enlisted into the Sacred Heart Drum and Bugle Corps. Joe, being older, was the group's drum major, and Bernie was a bugle player. And, oh, how he loved to blow his bugle. He never really quite got the hang of it despite tutoring sessions with the good Nuns. He did, however, like to blast out his versions of cavalry charges while riding his bike to school for practice.

One evening, after a particularly disappointing practice at school, Bernie was riding his bike back home down 2nd street, head down, deep in thought.

CRASH!

Bernie's head hit metal as his groin smashed into the center of the handlebars. He had ridden his bike smack dab into the rear of a parked car.

At about the same place on 2nd Street, a year later, as he was walking home in the dark after a Saturday spent working at Economy Food Market, Bernie was first introduced to the joys of accidental voyeurism. While he usually walked with head hung down, the light in a house he was passing caught his eye. The front door was open and standing in full view in the middle of the room was a teenaged girl in the process of stepping out of her skirt. Although he did not stop to savor the view, the image has stuck with the author over the years.

This chance glance did much to awaken a latent curiosity in Bernie. So it was not too surprising that shortly thereafter, while browsing through some magazines in a deserted isle of a drug store, Bernie decided to remove a particularly interesting small color photo of a young lady wearing only a sunflower on her lap. After secretly placing the folded treasure in his pants pocket, he returned the magazine to the shelf and went about his business. Unfortunately for him, he completely forgot about the picture in his pocket until laundry day when his Mom summoned "Bernard" (as she persisted in addressing him throughout her life) into the kitchen.

"What's this?" she asked as she displayed the unfolded girlie picture before him on the kitchen table.

Bernard's heart skipped a beat as he stared at the forgotten treasure unfolded before him.

"I don't know? Where did it come from?" he asked sheepishly.

"From your pants' pocket. Where did you get it?"

"I must have found it and picked it up."

Once his Mom felt sure no more incriminating admissions could be browbeaten from the accused, she allowed him to leave, doing who knows what with the forgotten treasure.

Summer, 1951
Norfolk, Nebraska

To Bernie Barcio, summer in Norfolk meant freedom. Of course, he would be given some jobs to do by his mother, but would avoid others by hiding under the trumpet vine bush whose drooped branches provided a natural cave at the corner of his house.

If Bernie came across a huge empty cardboard box early in the summer, he would drag it home, and it would become the center of his make-believe solitary games for days.

If he had the good fortune of seeing a movie about knights of old, he would spend hours at the garage tool bench trying to fashion a knight's helmet from scraps of tin and making wooden swords.

On days when he just needed to "get away," he would head down the dirt road that led to a swamp a few blocks from his house at 705 S. 2nd Street. There, amid the marvels of half submerged junk, he could look for frogs. It was a school friend of his that showed him how to push the hollow stem of a large dandelion down the throat of a frog and inflate its little stomach so it would not be able to submerge when returned to the water.

Other days were spent climbing up behind a billboard located on 1st street. After reaching the top, Bernie could let his imagination run wild as he stood concealed by the trees growing behind the billboard and watched the traffic passing unaware of his spying eyes. The only thing more fun than this was climbing the tree next to his garage at home and making his way to the top of his garage roof from where the whole neighborhood could be surveyed.

There was also an empty lot on 1st Street on which new chicken coops were displayed for sale. These could be crawled into for hours of concealed enjoyment.

One day, as Bernie was looking for new distractions that might be located along 1st Street, he happened to enter a small slaughterhouse. He entered so meekly that the workers there ignored him. At first, he was fascinated by the smells, and by the few head of cattle that were standing in the narrow pens. He watched casually as a worker came in to lead one of these cows into a narrow stanchion at the far end of the room. Then, before Bernie realized what was going to happen, the worker grabbed a 22 caliber rifle, held the muzzle flat against the cow's skull and shot it right between the eyes. As the cow slumped to the floor, Bernie decided it was time to go play somewhere else.

On the corner of the road that led from 1st street back to the swamp was a lot on which farm equipment was left on display. It didn't take Bernie long to discover that he could climb up into the seats of these pieces of equipment and actually operate the pneumatic controls to make various parts of the equipment move.

Of course, any boy who moved out west to Nebraska was totally absorbed with the lore of cowboys and Indians. Bernie and his brother Joe had a fine collection of cap guns, including one particularly impressive double-barreled pirate's pistol. When there was money to buy caps, the back yard rang out with "gunfire" and was filled with the stench of gunpowder. When more thrilling gunfights were called for, and no one was home, Bernie would get into his dad's gun closet and get a single-shot 16-gauge shotgun that had a place where caps could be loaded behind the hammer. Then, with this real honest-to-goodness gun held to his shoulder, he could creep through the backyard bushes blasting imaginary enemies that his mind's eye saw passing through the alley.

Once, when a neighbor told his dad that his youngest son had been seen playing with a real shotgun in the backyard, his dad covered for him by insisting that his son had probably just been playing with his toy guns. Later, his dad told Bernie what the neighbor had reported and said, in a way that let his son know he had better not be playing with the real shotguns, that he had told the neighbor he felt sure his son was only playing with toy guns.

When August arrived, the Barcio household in Norfolk became vacation central. Norfolk was just far enough away that relatives and friends from both Milwaukee and Chicago took advantage of Ted's hospitality and Stella's good cooking to write or call and say they were coming to visit for a week or so.

To be honest about it, it is a serious understatement to refer simply to Stella's "good cooking." Stella Barcio was a phenomenal cook. She spent hundreds of hours gathering unique recipes and perfecting them for use during special occasions. Her recipes for traditional Italian breads were closely guarded secrets. Before leaving Nebraska, Stella would even achieve professional status with her cake baking and decorating.

September, 1951
Norfolk, Nebraska

Bernie was now entering the eighth grade. He had made a new friend who lived just up the way on 2nd Street. It gave Bernie something to look forward to in the morning knowing that he could stop at his friend's house and wait for him so they could walk to school together.

Bernie's friend lived in a second floor flat, and every morning, as Bernie climbed the back stairs to meet his friend, he could smell pancakes. It amazed him that his friend's mom got up early and made pancakes for her family every morning. Bernie was just told to fix himself a bowl of cereal, which he had to hurry and eat so he could do a couple jobs for his mom before he left for school at the last minute.

There was also a small store located on 2nd Street on the way to school. It carried a wide selection of penny candies that Bernie used to love to load up on if he happened to have a nickel, dime or quarter that he had managed to "find" at home before leaving for school.

"Bernard," called his mother one day after school.

"Here I am," replied Bernie, deciding to take his chances on what might be expected of him.

"Your pet chicken is getting too big," said Bernie's mom.

At Easter time in Norfolk, one of the stores annually filled its display window with baby chicks dyed different pastel colors. Bernie had begged and finally managed to get one as a pet. He fed it everyday, watched it as it exercised in the yard and penned it up every night.

By September, however, Bernie's pet chicken had lost its color. It was now just a grain-gobbling white chicken that his mom viewed as dinner.

"What should I do?" asked Bernie innocently.

"You'll have to cut its head off so I can clean it and cook it," said his mom coldly.

"But that's my pet chicken," objected Bernie.

"It's food for the table. You knew that when we bought it for you," insisted his mom.

So, Bernie had to be a man about it. He went out into the garage and got the small hatchet from the tool bench. His chicken sensed that something was amiss and did not allow itself to be caught easily. In the end, however, Bernie held his chicken in one arm and the axe in the other as he approached a small chopping block that was set up in the back yard.

"Well, I guess it's got to be done," said Bernie as he laid his chicken's neck on the block and neatly severed its little head with the ax.

The stench of chicken feathers being boiled in a pot of hot water is something no one should have to smell—especially not someone who had raised that chicken as his personal pet for the past five months.

"It's the only way to loosen the feathers so they can be plucked," explained his mom when he asked why his headless chicken had been put into the boiling water.

The transition from boyhood to manhood was not going to be an easy one.

October, 1951
South Chicago, Illinois

While his eighth-grade classmates were in school back in Norfolk, Bernie was hunched over the window ledge in the front room of his Aunt Lucy's flat at 9506 Commercial. His mom was no respecter of schedules when it came to her own feelings and desires. If she got it into her head to travel back home to Chicago, she would simply ask her husband for a railroad pass, pack up Bernie and head out, no matter if school was in session or not.

This she justified because a good Nun had once mentioned to her when she lived in Cudahy that travel was educational for children and school schedules should not prevent parents from providing such opportunities for their children. Of course, the good Nun may have been saying this in the hopes that she would take Bernie the Troublemaker out of her class for a week or two. Bernie was definitely not one who could be left behind when Stella got the bug to visit South Chicago, no matter how old he was.

Of course, just because he was in South Chicago with his mother was no reason to assume that he would stay out of trouble. Bernie's partner in crime in South Chicago turned out to be his cousin Anthony, one of Aunt Maggie's kids that was about his same age. Bernie and Anthony would stage knock-em-down, drag-em-out wrestling matches.

During the daylight hours, when teenage activity tended to be more on the up and up, Bernie and Anthony could sometimes walk under the railroad viaduct into the nearby business district. It was dark, dirty and scary under the viaduct—actually a railroad bridge under which Commercial Ave. made a considerable dip before rising to its original level on the other side—but being allowed to make the trip was sort of a coming-of-age milestone. It was under this viaduct that Florence Miresso, one of Aunt Maggie's older daughters, had been attacked by a mugger as she returned home from work late one evening. Florence had been given the English version of her Grandmother Filomena's name. Florence, however, was tough, having grown up with her half-brother Rudy and her brothers Dickie, Andrew and Anthony. Jimmie was also her brother, but he was too small to pose any challenges. At any rate, no sooner had the mugger tried to steal her purse than she laid into him and pretty much beat the tar out of him before allowing him to escape with his life.

Once Bernie and Anthony re-emerged into daylight, they could make their way up the street to Gayteys, an ice-cream parlor that specialized in eye-popping banana splits and sundaes in addition to high-priced candy. Of course, the two cousins could never actually go in and buy anything. No money. On their way back, the boys would pass by one of the first White Castle's in America. It was located just on the other side of the railroad viaduct from their grandpa's house. Even though the big black and white sign advertised hamburgers for 5 cents, Bernie had never, in all the years that he went back and forth to South Chicago, actually got to purchase one. After all, as his mother reminded him constantly, food was eaten at home and not in restaurants.

As of 2003, Gayteys and the little White Castle were still in business although the neighborhood had become predominantly Spanish-speaking rather than Italian. Bernie's cousin Gloria Leo had once worked at Gaytey's before running away from home after turning 16 in 1955. When she returned to South Chicago years later, the owners of Gaytey's remembered and welcomed her. By 2010 the Gaytey family had moved their store to 3306 Ridge Rd. in Lansing, Illinois.

The most excitement Bernie ever had with Anthony, however, was one night when they joined a group of Anthony's friends in the front of the house for some street fun. There wasn't a lot of traffic that night, but the boys devised a tremendously clever practical joke to play on the next car that would venture down Commercial Ave.

Half of the boys lined up across the street in front of St. Patrick's Church, and the other half lined up just off the curb in front of Tony Nudi's house. When they spotted a car coming down the street, all the boys assumed the pose of a group stretching a rope across the road. As soon as the driver saw the group and assumed they really did have a rope stretched across the road, he slammed on his breaks. Of course, it took only a second for the driver to figure out he had been duped. After a few appropriate curses and negative observations about the genealogy of the boys, the driver would drive on through. But the game came to an abrupt end when a particularly aggravated driver slammed on his breaks, opened his car door and took off after the boys.

Talk about adrenalin! All Bernie could do was try to keep up with Anthony as the boys headed down narrow passageways, over fences and through the alley behind Tony Nudi's house searching for safe hiding places.

Luckily, all the boys escaped unhurt, and, after they were sure the coast was clear, they slowly regrouped in front of St. Patrick's. That's when Anthony's older brother, Andrew, decided to stage a little friendly street fight with a buddy of his. As the other boys watched, the fight began to escalate and there was some question about how friendly it was turning out to be.

RIP!

"You tore my good shirt!" shouted Andrew at his friend.

In a flash, Andrew retaliated ripping all the buttons off the front of his opponent's shirt.

When Bernie, Anthony and Andrew returned to Aunt Maggie's kitchen in the back of the first floor flat, Andrew's good shirt was in shreds.

"We were just playing around, Ma," explained Andrew.

"Look at your good shirt! Do you think money grows on trees? What's wrong with you, anyway?"

"Nothing's wrong with me, Ma. We were just having fun."

Luckily, Bernie had managed to get through the evening with no bruises or torn clothing. He would be able to pass casually through Aunt Lucy's kitchen with little or no hassle from his mom, who perpetually occupied one of the kitchen table chairs outside her dad's bedroom. This provided a commanding view of all comings and goings.

This kitchen was the hub of family activity at Aunt Lucy's. It was at the kitchen table that Tony Nudi would have his morning *piscia lite* that he would dunk into a glass of red wine. In the fall, he would produce his little bottle of Fernet. This was a bitter, miracle-working concoction sold in Italian liquor stores in Chicago that specialized in imported liquors and wines. Tony believed that Fernet was a powerful aid to digestion and that drinking a shot of Fernet each day during the fall would help keep him healthy and regular during the winter.

Believe it or not, Fernet is still available in liquor stores that cater to Italian-Americans.

The dining room in which the player piano was kept was only illuminated and actually used on such very special occasions as a birthday or going away party for Nonno.

The front room was used only as a vantage point to look out the windows. Or it was a place to which kids were sent as sort of a time-out area. And, of course, at Christmas time, one was allowed to go in and look at the Christmas tree. It was here in the front room that Uncle Leonard kept his mandolin leaning in a corner. If he were lucky, Bernie could sometimes manage to pluck the strings for about one minute before his Aunt Lucy would tell him not to touch it.

The front room was also where Aunt Lucy went to nurse her baby daughter, Mary. Bernie did try to go in one day to watch, but was immediately summoned back into the kitchen by his ever-vigilant mother.

Along one side of the kitchen was a huge cupboard that had once stood behind the bar in Tony Nudo's tavern on 93rd Street—the bar he had had to sell to finance his defense after shooting his son-in-law in the back.

One day, when the author was visiting his mom who, in 2002, lived in the Indianapolis Nursing Home, she insisted that the author return to South Chicago and ask to be given the cupboard that had once been in her father's bar. It took some doing to convince her that this would be impossible since the house had been sold years earlier.

It was here in the kitchen that Johnnie Sulek, who happened to be visiting with his wife Carmella (another of Aunt Maggie's older daughters), explained how he argued with the cop that had just given him a speeding ticket. Johnnie was a house builder and drove one of those low-key trucks that were really sedans with their back ends sculpted out so material could be hauled. When not in use, the back could be covered with a snap-on canvass.

"When you're driving in traffic," Johnnie explained with his trademark twinkle in his eyes, "you don't pay attention to the speedometer. You keep up with the flow. If you don't, you find yourself in a lot of trouble."

"Did he buy your explanation," asked Ted Barcio who happened to be visiting that day with Stella and Bernie.

"No. He told me I could go before the judge and contest it, but, hell, Ted, that just means I would lose a whole day's work."

"So you just pay the fine," said Rudy who had been leaning against the refrigerator outside Nono's room as he listened. Rudy was working as a railroad detective at that time, and Stella insisted that he remove his gun and holster and leave them on top of the refrigerator while he was in Lucy's kitchen.

When Johnnie Sulek had first married Carmella Miresso, they intended to drive out west on their honeymoon. But the day after they left they were back in Lucy's kitchen explaining how they had come across a major traffic accident involving both injuries and death. Carmella became so frightened by what she saw that she insisted that they cancel their honeymoon plans and return to South Chicago.

Sometimes, if Bernie were very lucky, Stella would visit her brother Angelo on his farm during one of her Chicago visits. Now that was a fun place to go. Uncle Angelo's son, Raymond, had a BB gun that the boys could shoot. Raymond and Bernie's cousin, Evy, would also show him how to twist an ear of dry corn in his hand so the kernels would fall on the ground for the chickens.

Years later Bernie would learn that the "chickens" were actually fighting roosters that his Uncle Angelo raised for his Uncle Leonard who used to enter them in cockfights.

Uncle Angelo primarily raised Tomatoes on his farm, and when harvest time came, all the children would get to help pick them. Of course, Bernie had to be taught the proper way to do that.

"Pick the stem off the tomato before you put it in the basket," said his cousin Evy.

"Why do we have to do that? That takes too long!" complained Bernie.

"If you leave the stems on," chimed in his cousin Raymond, "They poke holes in the other tomatoes and then they will be rejected by the cannery."

So, once again, nothing was ever totally fun. Too many rules.

There were also rules on the farm that the adults just sort of made up on their own, as it seemed to Bernie. When all the kids were dirty and needed to be bathed, the boys were told to go down into the basement and get undressed. They then had to sit in metal tubs while Bernie's mom and Aunt Helen and Aunt Lucy scrubbed them down. The girls, of course, got to sit on the steps and watch.

So when it came time for the girls to get scrubbed down, the boys all figured it was their turn to sit on the steps and watch.

"You boys get upstairs," called Aunt Helen.

"But the girls got to watch us," complained Raymond.

After Raymond grew up and got married, he and his wife Mary Ellen had five children: Paulie, Chuck, Eddie, Diana and Jean.

Evy always was a beautiful girl. After winning a beauty pageant during a 4-H Fair in her late teens, she married a young man whose last name was Klibofski, with whom she had two sons, Butch and Rick. When that marriage failed, Evy married Cliff Roland, an entrepreneur who tried his hand at everything from racecar driving to hauling sand in barges across Lake Michigan. After Butch and Rick bought and operated Ryan's Bar (which was purchased from Gusty Nudi's second wife, Nettie) in Portage, Indiana, Cliff would manage his multiple business affairs, which now included house demolition and a dry landfill, from a small back office in the bar.

"Never mind!" yelled the author's mom. "Get upstairs right now before you all get it!"

It was unfair how grownups just got to make up arbitrary rules as they went along. Totally unfair!

During the train trip back to Norfolk, Bernie and his mom would snack on the usual tomato and mayonnaise sandwiches, and an occasional piece of fruit. Between-meal hunger pangs could be controlled with a *piscia lite*.

"Mom, I'm going to get a drink of water," announced Bernie about half way through his *piscia lite*.

"Be careful, and come right back," commanded his mom.

When Bernie got to the water fountain located in the wall outside the restroom at the end of the car, he was surprised to notice that this was the last car of the train and that the door to the back platform was open. Since the train was going fairly slowly, he got his paper cup of water and casually made his way out onto the platform. It was fun looking down and watching the ties go by. When Bernie finished his water, he looked at his cup and decided to see what would happen if he tossed it out.

Wow! That was fun. The cup bounced around and finally disappeared into the distance.

Then he tried tossing a paper cup full of water off the back platform. That was even more fun.

"Whatcha doing?" asked a small voice next to him.

"Oh, nothing," said Bernie. "Just throwing water cups off the platform."

"Can I try one?"

"I don't care," said Bernie.

And so, completely unnoticed for at least twenty minutes, the two boys managed to throw almost the entire supply of paper cups off the back platform until they were finally reigned in by the Conductor who had come to see what they were up to.

When the Conductor learned that Bernie was the son of the Roadmaster, he decided to let the matter drop.

Once again Bernie's neck had been saved.

Christmas, 1951
Norfolk, Nebraska

Christmas in the Barcio household came with a lot of mixed emotions. The author dearly wanted to buy into the whole myth of warm family gatherings, decorations, stockings hung by the fireplace with care, gifts and bliss. More often than not, however, the myth was blown away by harsh reality. This holiday came with the most family stress.

Such a simple thing as decorating the Christmas tree would be turned into a tearful ordeal. Everything had to be so complex. Not only would the tree be decorated, but there would be a whole cotton-covered layout created beneath it that demanded the author's help, and, more often than not, generated hostile retribution when any mistake was made or something got broken. Drinking glasses needed to be brought in and gently laid down on the floor. Into these, Christmas lights would be placed. Covered with cotton, the effect was indeed beautiful. Some lights were left sticking up to illuminate small snow-covered cardboard buildings. The center piece of the display was always an over-scale wooden church, complete with detailed interior. This gold-trimmed white and green stucture had been built by Bernie's dad, his Uncles Charlie and Leonard. This, too, was lit with a Christmas tree light.

Although Uncle Charlie really wanted to have this church when things were being moved out of the house in Sparta in July, 1993, Bernie had already told his brother Joe that he should take it since he was the older son. To the author's dismay, he later learned that when his brother moved from Oshkosh, Wisconsin, to Houston, Texas, in September 1998, there was no room for the little church, and it had to be left behind.

Then came the manger set. The figurines in this set were, of course, made to break. They needed to be handled with the greatest of care or else.

Many of these original figurines have luckily survived into the 21st century and are now in the care of the author's daughter, Cyndi.

If either of the boys hoped for toys at Christmas, they were wasting their time. Christmas was a time to buy items of clothing that were needed. They would simply be presented as gifts.

Although there was not a fireplace in any of the Barcio households until 1957 when they moved into their house at 307 N. Water Street in Sparta, Wisconsin, stockings were always hung on Christmas Eve. Somewhere. During the night, while the boys slept, their mother would dutifully stuff the stockings with…oranges and apples. These precious fruit items would, of course, have to be "turned in" as soon as the excitement of finding them in the stockings had worn off.

Christmas, 1951, however, was special. This was the year the boys would be given a genuine Lionel train set. Heaven. An honest to goodness toy, at first controlled by the author's older brother, Joe, until Bernie could learn to deal with it without destroying it.

This train set would eventually end up on a 4′ by 8′ layout board set up in the cleaned out coal bin of the basement. The boys set to work creating a whole city and countryside on the board and on the half wall of the basement into which a concrete coal chute had originally been built.

The gift proved to be a much-needed distraction for Bernie, and one that would help keep him out of after school trouble. The family soon discovered that their trouble-prone son was actually quite talented, both at drawing and at model building.

"I'm going to draw pictures of the store at the end of the alley after school," Bernie announced to his mom one day.

"What for?" she asked.

"I'm going to build a model of it for the train board."

"Here, take a quarter and buy a loaf of bread while you're there."

Bernie's mom always liked to get some personal good out of anything for which she had to give permission.

He would, of course, have to beg money for balsa wood and paints, but Bernie soon began to build models of a number of buildings in Norfolk. After the model of the small grocery store at the end of the alley was completed, he made drawings of a Sunoco filing station, a train station, a number of small railroad shanties and the grain elevator in whose parking lot he had gotten his shiner. Soon, he discovered that he could also build models from plans printed in model railroading magazines. On pages 16-19 of the May, 1954, issue of **Model Railroader**, he found the design for a model of the Madison, Wisconsin, elevated Crossing Shanty which he built, complete with interior controls and a pot-bellied stove.

All of these buildings can still be seen on the model railroad layout that was unpacked by the author in 2003 (after having been packed away in a trunk and several boxes when the family moved back to Wisconsin in 1955) and set up first, in the basement of 6026 Indianola, and later moved to the author's new house next door. In 2013, the author built a special room in his storage and woodworking barn to display what by then had become a two-level layout.

March 5, 1952
South Milwaukee, Wisconsin

Giuseppe (Joe) Barcio had just celebrated his 64th birthday when he finished building his last house. It was located at 627 E. Elm Ave. in South Milwaukee, Wisconsin.

Joe also continued driving his older model car in his advanced years. He made the **Milwaukee Journal** one day when he accidentally hooked his rear bumper onto the front bumper of a car that was parked behind him as he prepared to leave a parallel parking place. Before he noticed it, he had towed the car a considerable distance down the street.

While most people retired from the railroad when they reached the age of 65, Joe had continued to work until March of 1956, when, at age 70, he suffered a stroke that left his right arm paralyzed. He then had no choice but to retire, just two months short of having spent 46 years working on the railroad.

Since he could no longer drive, Joe decided to build two rooms onto the back of his new house that could be used as an apartment for his daughter Yolanda and her second husband, Louis Kowalski. Since Louis owned his own pharmacy, he could also provide the prescriptions that were now needed for Joe and Vrigita to maintain their health.

Just because he had to retire from the railroad, however, did not mean that Joe Barcio just sat back and relaxed. He continued working around the house, gardening and trying to regain the use of his right arm. His son Eugene remembers his father exercising his paralyzed right arm by trying to lift a 5-gallon pail out to the side.

"Every time I went there," Eugene recalls, "he would show me how well he was doing with his arm and brag to me with his laugh. It also made me happy."

April, 1952
Norfolk, Nebraska
"Bernard, come in here and give your mother a hand!"

It was near the end of Lent, and Bernie's mom had agreed to make a wide selection of decorated Easter Eggs for a special party. Of course, when Bernie's mom agreed to undertake a craft project, it meant that Bernie would also be involved.

"Here, poke a small hole in each of these eggs, and then carefully blow the insides into this bowl."

Now, that was kind of fun. Hopefully, Bernie wouldn't get into too much trouble if he broke a couple of eggshells in the process.

Once the eggshells were hollow, they needed to be run under cold water and cleaned out. They then needed to be dipped into different cups of dye to color them as needed.

The reader should not think that Stella simply colored the eggshells or drew simple designs on them. No. Decorating Easter Eggs was an art form for Stella.

"Now, take the scissors and cut little circles in the bottoms of these cupcake baking liners."

If the goal was to create an Indian Easter Egg, a brown colored eggshell would then by glued into the hole in the cupcake liner. Then Bernie would neatly draw a face on the front of the egg, and his mom would attach an Indian feather headpiece made from different colored strips of construction paper and wrap an Indian necklace around the base of the egg.

Other eggs were destined to become little Aunt Jemimas, daisies, rabbits, chickens, Nuns, clowns, sailors, pilgrims, spring-bonneted girls, old ladies with hair in a bun, freckled farm girls with pigtails, etc. The possibilities were limited only by Stella's imagination. In fact, even Bernie was allowed to suggest a new egg-character now and then.

When they were done, all the little Easter-Egg people would be lined up on the floor or on the table and photographed for posterity.

June 2, 1952
The Platt River, Nebraska
Ted had finally saved up enough to buy another car for his family. He had taken the train back to Cudahy so he could purchase it from a used car dealer that he trusted. He then drove his maroon 1949 four-door Ford back to Norfolk. Once school was out, he began to take the family on short outings, including a trip across the Platt River on a ferry on June 2, 1952.

Later it would be with this car that both Joe and Bernie would learn to drive and with which Bernie would learn to squeal the back tires by pulling into a driveway near the pool hall on Norfolk's main street, and, while the car was still rolling backwards as he backed out, popping the car into first gear and laying rubber to impress those inside.

Later that summer, Bernie was taken to the Economy Food Market by his brother Joe who already worked there as a cashier. At first, although not legally old enough to be working, Bernie was taken on as a stock boy. This wasn't too bad since he quickly learned that he could keep an open container of cookies stashed in the back room from which he could snack every time he went back and forth for another box of cans to shelf.

In those days, grocery stores not only kept a covered barrel of sauerkraut in the back room from which bulk orders were filled, but they also sold bulk cookies that were kept in open containers at the front of the store near the cash register. Bernie would love to watch a particular older man, a perpetual drunk it seemed, come into the store and stand directly over the cookies with a drip of snot dangling from the tip of his nose. Bernie never really wanted to sample any of those cookies.

Having a car available now meant that the family could enjoy Sunday drives together. Now, if the reader has ever spent any time at all in Nebraska, s/he will quickly realize that there aren't a lot of wondrous landmarks to visit. Nebraska has gently rolling planes. And dirt roads. And Black Angus cows. And more gently rolling planes.

In reality, most Sunday drives were mere excuses for Ted to drive out to one spot or another on his railroad division and check either on a job that was about to be undertaken or work that was supposed to have been finished. Along the way, however, depending on the season of the year, great fun could be had "harvesting."

"There. In that grass next to the road. Do you see 'em, Bernie?" asked his dad.

"I think so. There are a bunch of them, aren't there?"

"Be sure to break them off close to the ground. Don't pull up the roots," instructed his mother.

So Bernie was dispatched to pick some precious asparagus that his dad had an uncanny eye for spotting either along side the road or near the track bed. If Ted had happened to spot a particularly good patch of asparagus near the track during the week, he would make a point of returning on a Sunday drive to harvest it.

In the fall, the family would leave home equipped with large cooking pots and old sheets.

Because the winds blowing across the open Nebraska plains could remove most of the valuable topsoil in a few short years, landowners usually planted windbreaks along their property lines. The trees planted for these windbreaks had to be fast growing and sturdy. The usual choice was the Mulberry.

"O.K., Bernie, now be careful," instructed his mother after Bernie had made his way up into one of the more fruitful Mulberry trees that the family had spotted on a Sunday harvesting drive.

Bernie's dad and his brother Joe had already spread out the white sheet on the ground under the tree, and had moved back so as not to be bombarded.

"Shake the tree, but hang on!" instructed Bernie's dad.

Bernie shook the tree with all his might, and the harvest was plentiful. Of course, in the process, hundreds of ripe berries struck his face, arms and hands as they fell from above. When he would get down, he would look like a kid with a bad case of the measles.

October 31, 1952
Norfolk, Nebraska

Only in Norfolk do folks celebrate Hallowesta. It's a unique way for a community to socialize on an evening generally marked by youthful mischief.

"Why do they want to put you in jail?" asked Stella, embarrassed at the thought that her husband was being made a fool of.

"It's just something they do for fun, Stell. It's a fundraiser. I just have to stay in the little cell they put up in the middle of the street until enough of my friends stop by to pay my bail."

"And what if nobody pays your bail. Then you just look like an Old Fool!"

"Then I pay my own bail."

Ted was in the spirit of the occasion, but Stella still had a little catching up to do.

Being an upperclassman, Joe had been excused from school early that morning to help paint one of the storefront windows on Norfolk Ave., the town's main business street. Groups of high school students could compete for a chance to paint seasonal scenes on the inside of the windows to be enjoyed by the evening partiers. The windows would then be judged, and prizes would be awarded.

Bernie was feeling left out as usual. He would get to go downtown with his mom and brother in the evening, but that wasn't nearly as much fun as being let out of school for the day to paint a window.

March 1953
South Milwaukee, Wisconsin

Giuseppe Barcio's dream was finally realized. With the help of his son Eugene, he finished building a new house on a lot he had purchased at 627 Elm Ave. in South Milwaukee, and he was now ready to move in.

Of course, this house, like his others, included a dedicated room in the basement equipped with two tiers of 50 gallon oak wine barrels, three in each row.

In another part of the basement was the very heavy wine press with which he had been squeezing grapes since the late 1920's.

After his death on June 3, 1965, the wine press remained, unused, in the basement until the death of his wife Vrigita on October 7, 1971. After that, Eugene gave the press to Giuseppe's grandson, Hank (Junior) Santostephano, who, in turn, later passed it on to Eugene's son, Jim Barcio who, by then, was living in Westchester, PA. During a visit by the author to his cousin Jim in July, 2005, Jim learned that the author was now making his own wine.

"If you'd like to have Pappa's wine press," offered Jim, "I'll bring it to you in Indianapolis the next time I drive my truck back to Wisconsin."

Jim was good to his word, and during the summer of 2011 he delivered Giuseppe's wine press to his cousin. Because the author makes wine only with grapes he grows himself or are given to him gratis, he makes, at most, only 5 gallons a year, squeezing the grapes with a small antique apple press. But even though he does not deal with hundreds of pounds of grapes that would require the use of his grandfather's wine press, the author is still proud to have this wonderful piece of family history in his possession.

April 8, 1953
Norfolk, Nebraska

Bernie was a freshman, and an embarrassment to his brother who, although he was only three years older, had already graduated from Sacred Heart H.S. and was attending classes at Norfolk Junior College, the one-building campus of which was adjacent to the Sacred Heart Church-School complex.

In an attempt to channel his energies into more legitimate activities, Bernie was given the part of "Spike" in a one-act play entitled "A Dress Rehearsal." Fellow actors included one of Bernie's partners in crime, Tony Olson, and a clean-cut young athlete that would later become his idol, John Lawler. While his stage debut proved more successful than his kindergarten participation in "Snow White and the Seven Dwarfs," it did not keep him totally out of trouble.

It was in the basement of the one building that housed Norfolk Junior College that Bernie had been de-pants-ed by a group of older boys looking for a little after school fun. There he was, minding his own business walking home after school, having already been detained for one reason or another in the basement of the convent again, when he was grabbed by two of the boys who appeared to be simply waiting for any likely victim. He was dragged, kicking and screaming, through the double entry doors and down the steps into the deserted basement hallway. While two of the group held his hands, another undid his belt. His pants were then pulled down around his ankles amid laughs, sneers and guffaws. Once this was done, the group ran back up the steps and out the doors, leaving Bernie crying, embarrassed and mad as hell. Now he would be later than ever, and it would be really hard to come up with a believable cover story for his mom.

Bernie was to be introduced to the world of tobacco during his freshman initiation. Not wanting to lose his macho image, he begged for permission from his parents to be allowed to participate. He assured them it would be perfectly safe and that he wouldn't be out too late. As it turned out, however, he got home a lot later than he was supposed to.

Freshmen being initiated met in the grain elevator parking lot and were blindfolded. They were then pushed down onto the back seat floors of a couple of cars and driven out of town. Once the convoy had driven around aimlessly on country roads to disorient any freshman who might have been trying to keep track of where they were going, it came to a stop on a dark, deserted country road. After the initiates were unloaded and had their blindfolds removed, they were each given a slug of chewing tobacco and told to chew until it was completely soggy in their mouths. Then they were instructed to swallow the juice. When this was done, each freshman was made to lie over the fender of one of the cars while the seniors took their belts off and whipped their butts.

The seniors then got back in their cars and drove off, leaving the disoriented, sick-to-their stomach freshmen to figure out where they were and find their way back to town.

Bernie never really had the taste for chewing tobacco after that, but he and a friend did spend several afternoons puffing Lucky Strikes in the park near the dam in downtown Norfolk after school on nice days.

Bernie wanted desperately to fit in now that he was attending high school classes in the four rooms on the third floor of Sacred Heart School. His choice of friends, however, often did little to ensure this general acceptance. One day when Bernie explained some of his experiments with caps to his smoking buddy, Tony Olson, Tony showed him how the tips of wooden matches could be chipped off and hit with a hammer to make them explode. Soon the two boys began to experiment with different ways to use this newly discovered explosive material. To this day, Bernie is not sure whether it was he or Tony Olson that got the idea of nuts and bolts. If a nut was only partially screwed down on top of a quarter-inch bolt, a small space would be left that could be filled with match tips. Then, after a second bolt was gently screwed into the same nut, the set up could be tossed up into the air. When it hit the ground, there would be an explosion and the two bolts would go flying apart.

Since an invention this good could not be kept totally secret, the mischievous duo decided to fix up a nice little nut & bolt bomb and take it to school one day.

Bernie was carefully holding the little bomb on his lap and explaining it to a boy seated next to him when he froze.

"Bernard! What do you have on your lap?"

It was Sister. He was nailed.

"Bring that up here, please!" commanded the stern Nun.

Bernie gave a quick look over at his co-inventor who looked as horrified as he did. He and Tony both knew the consequences if Sister mishandled the device, and it exploded in the classroom.

In sheer dread, Bernie carefully got up and walked to the front of the room.

"Please be very careful with this, Sister," said Bernie as he handed it over.

Sisters, however, are trained never to be impressed with contraband confiscated in the classroom. Without even looking at the device, she took it and placed it in her top left hand drawer. It didn't go off.

Bernie's mind raced during the rest of that period. He imagined the bolt bomb exploding in the drawer. He imagined himself being harangued by the pastor, Monsignor Burns. He imagined the beating he would get at home if his folks found out what he had made. As usual, his dad would send him down into the dark basement to get the "whip" from the ledge next to the furnace.

It would be fifty years before Bernie would come to realize that the "whip" his dad had specially crafted to be used on him was actually modeled after an old Roman *flagellum* or cat of nine tails. There can be no doubt that Ted Barcio was, in fact, modeling his little whip, not on drawings he had seen of ancient Roman soldiers, but on one that had once been used on him as a child by a stern disciplinarian in Italy.

Since there was no way that Bernie was going to allow this sequence of events, he quickly figured out that his only salvation lay in retrieving the bolt bomb as soon as Sister was safely out of the room. Which he did. Sisters never locked their desks. They preferred to count on the Honor System to protect confiscated contraband.

If Bernie could only have been more like John Lawler, life would have been much better for him. John was a neat kid. He was friendly, humble and strong as an ox. Word had it that John's father had him lifting weights every morning in their basement before school. John would make a name for himself that year in a grand showdown with the school janitor, a slim veteran who had had it with boys urinating on the hot water radiators in the second floor boys' bathroom. One day, while John happened to be using that bathroom, the janitor came in and smelled fresh urine. Seeing only John in the room, he grabbed him and threw him up against the wall. Bad move for the janitor. The story that circulated afterwards was that John pretty much cleaned the janitor's plow. The wondrous thing about the incident was that John never got in any trouble. It paid to be a football star at Sacred Heart High School, and John Lawler was a football star.

When Bernie finally decided he wanted to be more like John Lawler, he tried out for a spot on the six-man football team that most small Nebraska high schools tried to field. He got to dress for one game and was amazed at how much pain he endured just running out onto the field in his gear. His football career, however, was cut short by a hernia. He would miss the rest of the season after spending time in the hospital and recovering from his surgery at home.

More discomforting than the hernia surgery, however, was the fact that, as he lay in his hospital bed awakening from the anesthesia, he discovered that something awful had happened to a very personal part of his anatomy. There was a very large and very uncomfortable bandage between his legs. Without giving him any say in the matter whatsoever, his parents had decided it was high time for Bernard to be circumcised—OUCH! Add loss of dignity to loss of foreskin, and it was almost more than he could bear.

Bernie had looked forward to football as a last chance to redeem what little self-pride remained after his earlier disastrous tryout for the middle school basketball team. Bernie felt he could have done well in basketball. He was a good runner, had unbounded energy and was fairly well coordinated. What he hadn't counted on, however, was having to change into basketball shorts in the locker room.

"Hey, check out Barcio!" shouted someone from across the locker room.

"Hey, check out the guy in long johns!" shouted another.

It was winter, and neither of Stella Barcio's boys was allowed to leave the house without long underwear that completely covered their bodies from neck to wrists to ankles. All the other boys, of course, wore much more stylish briefs.

After Bernie fully recovered from his surgeries, his parents decided it was time for him to go back to work at the Economy Food Market where he had started, although not legally old enough, as a stock boy while still in the eighth grade.

Later, during his sophomore year, Bernie would be promoted to the meat department where his small frame—compared to the other full grown men who worked behind the meat counter—made him a perfect candidate to climb into the display case and wash it out at the end of each week. He was also shown how to cut up chickens quickly, without taking too many slices out of his own hands.

As his skills grew, Bernie was finally promoted to hamburger grinder by the manager of the meat department, Virg. Bernie would cut meat scraps into small chunks and push them through the grinder. There was a wooden plunger that he was supposed to use to push the meat down, but he would frequently just nudge it down with his hands until the grinder caught it and began to pull it through.

One Saturday morning, it happened that Virg was telling a dirty joke to another butcher in a low voice while no customers were before the meat counter. Bernie was busy making hamburger. When it got to the good part of the joke, Bernie looked over at Virg so as not to miss any important hand movements or facial expressions. As he did this, he used the thumb of his right hand to push the meat down into the grinder.

"AAAAHHHH!"

Bernie's scream filled the small store and brought his brother Joe running from the cash register.

What had happened was that the very tip of Bernie's right thumb had been caught by the grinder. By the grace of God and the watchful eye of a guardian angel that has had to work overtime protecting him throughout his life, the grinder did not catch the end of the bone. If it had, his entire hand and arm would have been quickly pulled into the grinder and gone home in someone's order of hamburger.

Bernie was quickly ushered into the back room where his thumb and hand were wrapped, and he was encouraged to quit screaming so he wouldn't scare all of the customers out of the store. He was then loaded into the back of the store's delivery van and driven to the hospital.

May, 1953
Norfolk, Nebraska

Summer was approaching and the summer visits by relatives were off to an early start. Bernie's mom would start getting nervous as she worried about having the house ready. This usually meant trouble for Bernie unless he had a well-developed survival plan in place.

"Bernard!" called his mom.

The sound sent a chill up Bernie's spine, and he knew he would have to act fast.

"Bernard, get in here," came the maternal command.

Bernie, however, was already well concealed in his favorite hiding place, a hollow he had discovered under the trumpet vine at the corner of his house. It was close enough that he could "materialize" if his mother flipped out completely, but far enough away that he could pretend afterwards that he had not heard her calling him.

The first visitor this season was Stella's cousin Jean from Pennsylvania.

Two summer guests whose arrival was always most welcome were Ted's cousins, Frank Bufano and his wife, Rose. Frank was the son of Ted's mother's only sister, and he was sort of a factotum. If anything needed fixing, from plumbing to wiring, Frank considered it his duty as a grateful guest to fix it.

It was the author's privilege in 2013 to visit Helen Vanacora, the last living child of Frank and Rose Bufano. Helen, 91 years old and living graciously as a widow in Friendship Village Retirement Home in Schaumburg, Illinois, insisted that lunch be her treat!

The month of June saw Ted's parents, Nanna and Papa, arrive from Wisconsin.

No sooner had they left when Bernie's godfather, Mike Bruno, arrived with his family.

Mike Bruno's father was not the Raffaele Bruno that Bernie's grandfather had known in Cosenza and with whom he worked on the railroad. Mike Bruno's father was the Raffaele Bruno who had emigrated from Sicily to Milwaukee where he worked as a cigar maker. Mike's father, however, had also become close friends with Joe Barcio, which was why Mike had been asked to become Bernie's godfather.

The Bruno's stayed for a few days as they prepared to continue on their way to visit the Badlands and Mt. Rushmore.

"Want a ride on my bike," Bernie asked one of his godfather's little boys nicknamed Mickey.

"Sure," replied Mickey.

"Here, hop up on the center bar, and I'll peddle us down the driveway," said Bernie.

No sooner had they set off when Mickey's foot got caught in the bike's chain.

"OOWWWW," screamed Mickey.

Both Mickey's dad and Bernie's dad reached the driveway at the same time to see Bernie desperately trying to untangle the boy's foot from the chain.

POW!

Bernie caught a good one from his dad.

"Why can't you be more careful? Now go in the house!" commanded Bernie's dad.

Naturally, when Bernie's godfather asked if he could take Bernie with them on their trip to the Badlands and Mt. Rushmore, permission was denied. In his parents' minds, Bernie was a mischievous troublemaker and could not be trusted.

On July 5, Stella's cousin, Anna Artona, arrived from New Jersey for a two week visit.

"My cousins, Stella and Ted, showed me a wonderful time. I will never forget it!" wrote Anna in the Barcio family guest book at the end of her visit.

No sooner had Anna left when Bunny and Mario Nardi arrived. They had chosen Norfolk for their honeymoon destination. Bunny was beautiful, and Mario drove a spectacular red convertible coupe.

Could life get any better?

Bunny and Mario were accompanied by Mario's mother, Mrs. Louie Nardi.

Now, you'll have to admit that not many young men take their mothers with them on their honeymoon!

Later that month, Joe and Anne Parato arrived with their son Joie.

Before July ended, Bernie's godfather was back, having finished his visit to the west. He and his family stayed a few days before continuing on their way back home.

"Look at this, Ted," said Mike as he handed Ted a photo. "We passed through a town that was called Bruno."

And sure enough, there in the photo stood Bernie's godfather under a roadside sign with the name "Bruno" printed on it!

Stella's dad, Tony Nudi, had already stayed with her in Norfolk during the months of February, March and April earlier in the year. When August arrived, he returned.

Stella's sister Maggie also arrived in August for a three-week stay. With her were her youngest children Jimmy, Rosie and Mary Ann.

"Mom" asked Bernie, "Can Jimmy and I get up early tomorrow morning and go see if we can get a job at the circus?"

"Is it safe?" asked Jimmy's mom, Aunt Maggie.

"I think so," said Stella. "The circus is setting up just across the tracks from where Ted works. They should be all right."

Although Bernie also showed Jimmy some of his other favorite hideouts along First Street, all Jimmy would remember later in life—when he supported himself as a full-time gambler in the Gary, Indiana, area—was his visit to the circus with his cousin Bernie.

During the same month, Stella's neice, Florence Pickarski (one of Maggie's older daughters) arrived for a visit with her two children, Carol Ann and Sam.

Carol Ann is now Mrs. Joe Porto of Shererville, Indiana. In 2004 Sam lived in California. When the author saw Sam at the funeral of his mother Florence on Halloween, 2008, he was working for an oil company on the North Slope in Alaska.

Before passing away, Florence's husband Eddy owned a bar in South Chicago and was an avid fan of Indianapolis 500 racing.

Maggie's other older daughter, Carmella, also arrived in August along with her husband Johnnie and their daughters.

Carmella and Johnnie went on to have three children, Carla, Marilyn and John Mario.

This pretty much brought the Barcio Inn schedule to a close for the summer.

The final visitor for the year would not arrive until November 25. He was Raymond Matteo who traveled to Norfolk from San Diego, California, to visit Ted and Stella. It would be to return him a visit that Ted would travel with his family and his mom and dad by train to California in August of 1954.

September, 1953
Norfolk, Nebraska

It was a warm Sunday afternoon and Ted and Stella were at it again. Ted usually tried to avoid these Sunday encounters by spending the morning after church at the office figuring out his weekly expense reports and getting a head start on the next week's job orders.

He usually spent his weekdays going over his line. Nights were spent in small, old-fashioned hotels built near the depots in towns along the way. The rooms in these hotels were equipped with fire escape equipment common in those days: rope ladders attached to the windowsill and rolled up neatly on the floor.

So, weekends were really the only time Ted had free to get caught up on his paperwork. Eventually, however, he did have to come home.

"Ted, today's Sunday! Did you have to go to the office?" pressed Stella.

"Yes-ah," replied Ted.

He had been nailed before he could escape to the front porch and catch a nap with the newspaper folded over his face.

"Nobody else goes to the office on Sunday. Just the Old Fool!" said Stella as she began to push her husband's button.

"I have to submit my expense reports, Stell."

"Can't you do them on Saturday when you go in to the office? And why do you even go in on Saturday? I bet people think you don't even know that there's supposed to be a five-day workweek now. Nobody else goes in on Saturday except the Old Fool! "

"*MANNAGIA CIUCIA VECCHIA!*" yelled Ted at the top of his voice.

Sometimes Ted would vary this imprecation by changing "*vecchia*" to "*mia*" without diminishing its affect.

"Shhhh," hissed Stella. "The windows are open. Do you want the neighbors to hear?"

"God damn it all to hell! Let the neighbors hear. This is my house."

And so it went for at least another half hour. It was Stella's way of getting the attention she lacked during the week while her husband was on the road taking care of his railroad subdivision.

"Come on, boys," said Ted after things had quieted down. "Let's go for a ride."

There were only about three places that the family could go for a ride without drawing unwanted attention. Ted could, of course, drive to the depot and get something from his office. That was always good for about a half hour.

"Let's take a drive through the State Hospital grounds," suggested Stella.

These grounds housed a hospital for the insane. Stella got a special kick out of seeing residents performing their perpetual, absolutely predictable routines such as shaking rugs from the porch of one of the buildings.

"Slow down, Ted, there she is. Let's stop and watch."

"*Non-ne*, we're not going to stop," insisted Ted.

"Well then, drive slow. Nobody's gonna complain. We're just taking a little drive."

The third possible destination was Ta-Ha-Zouka Park located on the far west side of Norfolk. The park had a small zoo featuring a couple of raccoons, a deer, a skunk and a few caged wild birds. Nothing much, just an excuse to get away from home for a while. The park was also where the good Nuns planned their annual spring Field Day for Sacred Heart grade school and high school students.

When they got to the park, and it looked like another argument was about to start up, Bernie decided to excuse himself.

"I'm going to walk over and look at the animals, O.K.?"

Receiving no response, Bernie opened the back door and slowly made his way over to the exhibit area. When he got back, things had quieted down, and his mom had her door open to let in some cool air. Her right foot was hanging off the front seat and resting on the ground. Her window was also down and she was resting her right elbow on the window ledge with the fingers of her right hand wrapped around the top of the door frame.

"Well," said Bernie when he got back to the car, "are we about ready to go home? I've got a little more homework to finish up."

"Why didn't you finish it when you got home from school on Friday?" asked his mom. "Now you can't even relax."

When his mom raised her foot back into the car, Bernie decided to help things along by closing her car door for her—accidentally smashing the tips of her fingers between the door and the car frame.

"AAAHHHHH! *DIAUOLO MALEDETTO*! MY FINGERS! MY FINGERS! *DIAULO! DIAULO!*"

Bernie's dad jumped out of his side of the car and flew around to reopen his mom's door while Bernie just stood there in shock.

Luckily, there was enough rubber insulation on the inside of the door that no permanent damage had been done to his mom's fingers.

Nonetheless, as soon as everyone was in the car, Bernie's Dad sped off to the hospital emergency room. When he got there, however, Bernie's mom refused to go in.

"Why don't we go in and just have it looked at?" asked Ted. "They could x-ray your fingers to be sure nothing's broken."

"*Musa tu!*" snipped Stella, stomping her foot on the floor. "Let's just go home."

The whole incident, however, left Bernie crying in the back seat, his mom crying in the front seat, Joe sitting quietly and nothing to look forward to but a perfectly horrible evening at home.

October, 1953
Indianapolis

Before Lillian's cousin, Jack Hacker, joined the Navy to serve in the Korean War, he had worked at an Indianapolis drugstore. The pharmacist was one of those rare individuals who took a sincere interest in the boys that worked for him and assured them all that if any one of them wanted to study to become a pharmacist after graduating high school, he would pay for their education. When Jack returned from his tour of duty in Korea, the pharmacist renewed his offer.

"Well, Jack," asked the pharmacist, "have you decided what you want to do with yourself now that you are out of the service? My offer still stands in case you want to study pharmacy."

"I appreciate your offer," replied Jack, "but I think I want to become a policeman instead."

This was a natural decision for Jack since he had served as an MP while in the service.

In fact, the only wound Jack ever received while in the Navy was while he was making a raid on an illegal black market ring being operated by a member of the American Navy. As Jack and other MP's were busting into the operation one night, Jack was shot in the shoulder by an American he was sent to arrest.

Before going into the service, Jack, like so many other young men at that time, had gotten married. As soon as he had returned to the States, he had called his wife from Seattle using a phone in a huge room equipped with scores of phones on which service men could make toll-free calls home.

"Hello?" said Jack when his wife's phone in Indianapolis was finally answered. "Is my wife there?"

"Who's this?" asked a man's voice.

"This is her husband."

"Wake up, Honey," Jack heard the man's voice say away from the phone. "It's your husband."

Needless to say, Jack's first marriage was not destined to last.

When he did return to Indianapolis, the first thing he did was beat the shit out of his wife's boyfriend. He then filed for divorce and applied to the Indianapolis Police Academy.

December, 1953
Lincoln, Nebraska

Before Jack had been released from service, however, he was given one more MP assignment. He and a fellow MP were sent to Lincoln, Nebraska, to escort back to San Diego a sailor who had gone AWOL.

Whenever MP's were escorting prisoners by train, they would always be assigned a private sleeping room in one of the Pullman cars toward the end of the train. Jack and his fellow MP took turns sitting with the prisoner as the other would go out to use the restroom, eat meals or take a break in the club car.

One evening when they were almost to California, Jack's fellow MP came back from the club car to announce that he had met two "hot chicks" who were very interested in spending the rest of the evening with a couple of MP's.

"What do we do with the prisoner?" asked Jack.

"I've thought of that," said Jack's buddy.

Jack's buddy then took out his handcuffs and proceeded to cuff the right arm of the prisoner to a secure bar in the sleeping room. He then produced a bottle of whiskey that he handed the prisoner.

"Now," he announced, "you sit here, drink your whiskey, and be a good boy. If you escape, we'll hunt you down and kill ya. Understand?"

The prisoner agreed to the conditions and eagerly accepted the whiskey.

When Jack and his fellow MP returned to their sleeping room the next morning, they found their prisoner slumped on the floor with his right arm still securely handcuffed above his head. He was out like a light.

"Can I have your names?" asked the prisoner as the three were leaving the train depot in San Diego.

"Why? You want to try to get us in trouble?" asked Jack.

"No," said the prisoner. "The next time I go AWOL, I intend to request that you two be sent to take me back."

January, 1954
Norfolk, Nebraska

Before the Barcio's would move back to Wisconsin, they were destined to survive several more severe winters during which their neighbor Mr. Eicher, a retired farmer, would have to show Stella how to get groceries home from the market after a deep snow by loading them onto a sled and pulling them along the un-shoveled sidewalks.

Mr. Eicher was fascinating in many ways to Bernie. He still sharpened his knives on a large whetstone that he spun with a foot pedal while sitting out beside a small shed at the back of his property. Bernie would amble on over whenever he saw his neighbor using the whetstone, sit on ground and watch. Mr. Eicher also had a wealth of country humor he loved to share.

"Bernie, what is it that a poor man throws away but a rich man wraps up and puts into his pocket?"

After some thought, Bernie gave up.

"Snot," said Mr. Eicher. "A poor man blocks one side of his nose with his finger and blows his snot out of the other side onto the ground. A rich man blows his snot into his handkerchief, wraps it up, and puts it into his pocket."

Bernie would get a lot of mileage out of that one breaking the ice with his students during his secondary school teaching career.

"Bernie," asked Mr. Eicher, "do you know what smart pills are?"

Once again, Bernie was at a loss having never heard of smart pills. He did, however, think it would be a good idea to listen carefully to the answer. Never know when a person might need something like that.

"A farmer was out hunting with his son one day," began Mr. Eicker. "As they walked along, the boy looked down and saw something small, round and black lying in the snow. 'See that?' asked the boy's father. 'Yes,' answered his son. 'Know what it is?' 'No,' said the son. 'It's a smart pill.' 'Really?' asked the son. 'Sure,' said his father. 'Pick one up the next time you see one, and see if I'm right.' The two walked along, and after a while the son spotted something small, round and black lying in the snow. He picked it up and ate it. Later he found more and ate those too. Finally, after he had eaten five or six, the boy turned to his father and said, 'Those are rabbit droppings!' 'See,' said the boy's father, 'you're getting smart!' "

This story, too, would also be an icebreaker during his secondary school teaching career.

Mr. Eicher's living room had the comfortable aroma of pipe tobacco. And it contained—wonder of wonders—a stereopticon along with a full set of double-image sepia tone photos. Had he been allowed, Bernie would have liked to spend a lot more time staring into that wondrous device. Visits, however, were always way too short.

Mr. Eicher also spent a lot of time, especially after Mrs. Eicher passed away, talking with Bernie's mom on the small patch of lawn that separated their houses. One day, as they talked and Stella Barcio habitually twisted her loose fitting diamond ring around on her finger, she suddenly made a gesture that sent her ring flying off into the grass.

Even though she and Mr. Eicher spent hours combing the grass in search of the ring, it was never found. Ted eventually bought his wife another diamond ring, a much more expensive one. This she kept until her death in February of 2003. This ring was later converted into a pendant necklace by the author who presented it to his daughter Cyndi as a present on her thirty-sixth birthday in 2004.

The Barcio family would also endure floods, both those that repeatedly washed away the track beds from under the rails on Ted's subdivision, and those that threatened to break the dam that had been built in the center of Norfolk on the north fork of the Elkhorn River that ran through town.

Nebraska is also notorious for its spring tornadoes. It was after one such tornado struck close to Norfolk that the author first heard tales of pieces of straw being blown through the centers of phone poles and people being pelted with kernels of corn that began to sprout under their skin before they could have them surgically removed.

The spring of 1954 once again found Bernie on stage. This time the one act play was entitled "A Cup of Tea." He received the following newspaper review for his portrayal of Mr. Wimpole:

"Bernard Barcio, made up with touches of age, gave an excellent portrayal, in his short stage appearance, of an antique dealer who 'knew his business.' "

March, 1954
Norfolk, Nebraska

"Is that the shirt you're wearing," asked Stella after Ted was all dressed and ready to go.

"Yes-ah!" replied Ted, irritated because he knew where this was going.

"Well, change it. You've got nice clothes. Why do you want people to think you just got off the boat?"

It was Lent, and the family had been invited to watch Bishop Fulton on television by Joe Barone and his wife who lived at 1406 S. 2nd Street. Joe was about the only friend that the Barcio's knew in Norfolk that owned a television. It was a beautiful black and white set. While Monsignor Burns generally discouraged movie going and other forms of entertainment during Lent, he encouraged parishioners who could get to a television set to watch the once-a-week program hosted by Bishop Fulton.

So, not only was this a social visit to the Barone's, it was also a pseudo-religious event. Everyone would have to look his best.

When it wasn't Lent, the family generally participated in social events that were sponsored in the Norfolk railroad depot by the Chicago & Northwestern for their employees. These events would generally feature a square dance and a pitch-in meal.

These were fun. The square dance caller would put on a record, give some basic instructions to everyone and then start the fun rolling. Everyone got fairly good at it. Stella and Ted actually appeared to enjoy themselves on the dance floor, as did Joe and Bernie.

"Allemande left with the old left hand, a right to your partner and a right and left grand!"

Round and round they would go. Usually there were only adults at these events so Bernie was quite surprised one evening when a young girl showed up on the floor. When it came his turn to give her a spin, he was absolutely amazed at how bony her ribs were.

"Is that what all girls feel like?" he wondered to himself.

Joe became interested in learning how to be a caller and soon talked his dad into arranging for him to get lessons from the main square dance caller. Before long, Joe was up on stage calling square dances all on his own as Bernie tried vainly to avoid encountering additional handfuls of bony ribs.

"That's all there is, there ain't no more. So take that girl right off the floor!" said Joe as the set ended, and everyone made their way over to the refreshment table.

Walter Howell was perhaps Ted's favorite foreman on the railroad. Walter Howell was also Bernie's favorite friend of the family because he looked exactly like Randolph Scott, Bernie's favorite western movie star. Walter lived on the second floor of the Fremont Railroad Station with his wife Pearl. They were the first married couple that Bernie ever encountered who slept in separate twin beds.

The Howells helped the Barcios expand their social calendar by inviting them over for dinner occasionally, or inviting them to drive to the State Fair in Lincoln with them and look at the latest Chevy Bel Air models or by stopping over at the house for a game of Canasta. Walter Howell was also street wise, advising Ted not to carry his wallet in his back pocket.

"Pickpockets will come up behind you and slit your pocket with a razor," he said.

Walt also explained how he usually just put five dollars in his front pocket when he went to the Fair.

"When that's gone," he explained, "I'm done spending for the day."

When, however, the Howells invited Ted and his family to join them at their church one Sunday evening, Stella thought they had crossed the line.

"Ted, we're not supposed to attend a non-Catholic church. Do we have to go?" asked Stella.

"It won't hurt anything, Stell. Walt said that their minister asked each family to bring a new family to church, and we're the only ones that he and Pearl are friendly with."

So the whole Barcio family—*horribile dictu*—attended a non-Catholic church service in Fremont with the Howells. Only once, however.

August, 1954
The Grand Canyon National Park, Arizona

Joe (Papa) and Vrigitta (Nanna) Barcio had always dreamed of traveling to California, and they had finally talked their son, Ted, into making the train trip with them along with his family. Ted agreed because he really did want to pay a return visit to Raymond Matteo who had travelled from San Diego to visit him nine months earlier in Norfolk.

When they had gotten off the train for a layover in order to visit the Grand Canyon, they intended to spend the night at a hotel near the train station.

"Ted, we don't need to take all the luggage to the hotel, do we?" asked Stella.

"No, we could leave some here in a locker and just take what we need," agreed Ted.

Bernie watched as his dad loaded the unneeded suitcases into a locker. A couple of them were fairly large. While one went in easily, the other got stuck on the right side of the locker door and wouldn't go in.

"I think it will be O.K.," said Ted. "The locker door will still close. Bernie, you stay here while I get some change."

As Bernie stood looking at the locker, he thought he might be able to fix things. If his dad couldn't get the suitcase to fit in the locker, he bet he could. So he gave it a good shove, and in it went. He closed the locker door just before his dad returned with coins and put them in the slot.

When they were checked into the hotel, there was something about her room that Nanna didn't like, and she had asked Ted to talk to the hotel clerk about it before they left for their Canyon tour. Hopefully, by the time they got back, the problem would be solved.

"Ma, they moved you and Pa to a new room," reported Ted when they got back.

"*Diauolo maledetto*," said Nanna. "I left my stuff all over the bed when we left."

"That's O.K., Ma," said Ted trying to calm her down so she wouldn't pull one of her trademark fainting spells. "They packed everything up and put it in your new room."

"I don't like anyone to touch my stuff," snapped Nanna. "They had no business touching my clothes! I left my underwear and everything on the bed."

It took a little while, but Ted finally calmed his mother down so they could all settle in for the night.

The next day, they barely got back to the train station in time to board the next train for California.

"Stella, you go out on the platform with Ma and Pa. I'll get our suitcases from the locker," said Ted. "Come on, boys, you can give me a hand."

When Ted opened the locker, however, he saw immediately that it would be no easy matter to pull the two big suitcases out. They were stuck firmly behind the too-small door opening.

"How did that suitcase get shoved in there," asked Bernie's dad.

"I'm afraid I did that," confessed Bernie. "I saw you having trouble getting it in, so I thought I would help."

"There you go, sticking your nose in again where it doesn't belong," said Joe.

It took some doing, but Bernie's dad was finally able to wrestle the suitcases from the locker just in time for them to board the train.

November 12, 1954
Omaha, Nebraska

"Can I make some chocolate chip cookies?" asked Bernie one sleepy Sunday afternoon in November when the weather was unusually warm.

"Do you know how?" asked his dad, who had let the newspaper he had been reading fold down over his face, was trying to enjoy a little snooze on the front porch.

"I think I can figure it out. The recipe is on the bag of chips."

Normally, Bernie's mom would be doing the baking in the house, but she had been away for the past week attending the Schulte School of Cake Decorating in Omaha, Nebraska. Stella had already established a solid reputation as a wonderful cook and very competent baker of pastries and cakes, many shaped like roses, books and dolls. When she would receive her Schulte School of Cake Decorating Diploma on November 12, she would know all the secrets of professional cake decorating and would be able to provide absolutely amazing creations for friends and relatives.

Chocolate chip cookies, of course, might just have to be delegated to someone else. Bernie was ready to accept the challenge.

November 25, 1954
Norfolk, Nebraska

"The boys and I are going hunting, Stell," announced Ted.

"Be careful. You know I'm scared to death of guns," said Stella.

Ted still loved to hunt, and now that Bernie and Joe were older, he relished the thought of sharing his love for the sport with them.

"What will we be hunting for?" asked Bernie, eager for the kill.

"Oh, we can hunt pheasants, rabbits or squirrels," said his dad, "depending on what we see."

Since Ted spent his weekdays traveling over sections of his railroad subdivision by motorcar, he usually knew where most of the wildlife could be easily located. When they got to a place in the country near the railroad right of way, he parked the car and passed out the guns and the shells. Bernie got to use a small single shot .410-guage shotgun. Joe got to use a single shot .16-gauge shotgun while his dad would use a double-barrel .12-gauge shotgun.

Now, anyone who has ever hunted pheasants knows that they are among the more tricky of the game birds. If they sense that someone is coming, they will remain hidden until the last minute and then go flying off almost from under the feet of the hunter.

"There he goes!" said Ted.

The three had been walking side by side through a recently harvested cornfield when the pheasant took off. Bernie was in the middle and immediately took aim with his little .410 shotgun. As the pheasant began to veer to the right, Bernie followed it, his eye glued to the sight on the gun.

BLAM!

"Did I get him?"

"No," said Joe, greatly irritated. "But you almost shot me. Watch where you're aiming."

Well, that put a damper on an otherwise fun afternoon.

"Let's go back to the right of way," said Ted. "Bernie, you can walk up on the tracks and Joe and I will walk down in the ditches on each side of the track bed. If we flush out any rabbits, they'll run across the track, and you can shoot them."

"And I guess there will be less chance that I'll shoot Joe, too," thought Bernie to himself.

So the hunting party moved over to the railroad tracks and started its slow trek in silence. Sure enough, as his dad had predicted, before too long a rabbit came bouncing across the tracks. Bernie was on it.

BLAM!

This time his aim was good, and the rabbit tumbled to a stop in the middle of the rails.

"What do I do now?" asked Bernie after he had retrieved his catch.

"Bring him here, and we'll tie him to your belt with a string," said his dad.

So off the three went again, Bernie still walking the ties while his dad and his brother rustled through the weeds in the ditches. Suddenly Bernie realized that the rabbit hanging from his belt was wiggling and trying desperately to get lose.

"Hey," shouted Bernie, "He's still alive!"

Sure enough, the rabbit had apparently only been stunned.

"Now what do I do?"

"You'll have to kill him."

"Should I shoot him again?"

"No, don't shoot him," said Joe. "Up close you'll blow him to pieces."

"I got it!" said Bernie, "I'll take my hunting knife and cut his head off. Will that work?"

"Go ahead and give it a try," said Bernie's dad.

So Bernie unhooked the rabbit from his belt, keeping a tight grip on its two back legs. He then tried to get it to lie still on the ground as he attempted to saw through its neck. No luck. His hunting knife wouldn't even break through the skin.

"Bern," said his dad, "hold the rabbit by its back legs, and hit his head on the rail."

"O.K. This could get brutal," thought Bernie to himself.

WHACK! WHACK! WHACK!

The rabbit finally quit moving and hung limp. Bernie re-hooked his catch to his belt and the hunt continued.

The down side of hunting was that whoever shot something had to clean it. Bernie didn't look forward to that smelly job, but it would be a lot easier than cleaning the occasional squirrel that he was lucky enough to shoot.

And, of course, if they came home with a catch, the family would have to eat it. Stella fixed all wild game in a red tomato sauce (*a la cacciatore*) designed to cancel out the "wild" flavor.

January, 1955
Norfolk, Nebraska

Bernie had gotten off to a rough start in high school and, much to his folk's consternation and the embarrassment of his brother, his grades were rotten during his freshman and sophomore years. Bernie finally managed to get with the program, however, during his junior year.

Having had some success on stage, Bernie had been accepted into the Boys Glee Club at Sacred Heart High School. On January 14 and 15, 1955, he was given permission to travel with the Glee Club, under the supervision of Sr. Mary Catherine Cecile, to compete in the tenth annual Albion Choral Clinic held in the Albion School auditorium in Albion, Nebraska. This meant that, for the first time in his life, Bernie was being sent out of town without being under direct parental supervision. He even got to spend the night in one of the homes that provided sleeping rooms for the participants in the Clinic. And, for the first time, he was responsible for buying his own food. After much careful thought, he had a hot-beef sandwich, topped off with an apple that he bought at a store. This was fun. And to add ecstasy to the whole experience, some of the girls on the trip bought some silver hair spray and provided warm acceptance to a variety of boys by spraying their sideburns with a touch of elegant silver.

On the bus ride back to Norfolk, some of the girls began to encourage Bernie to sing an Italian song for them.

"Come on, Bernie. We love Italian songs. Let us hear one."

As usual, Bernie rose to the occasion and let them have a good and loud rendition of "*Santa Lucia*," a song he frequently belted out to blow off steam after school if he found himself alone when he walked through his never-locked house door. His voice made the bus resonate with an Italian melody, and the girls loved it.

This was living! Bernie was definitely beginning to feel better about his life.

His improved scholastic aptitude could also have been the influence of his Latin teacher, Sr. Mary Angelique. Sr. Angelique was a very young nun, the contours of whose ample breasts beneath her habit were a constant fascination to Bernie. He needed desperately to impress her. In the process, he got with the program and was soon impressing all of the Nuns on the third floor of the building on which the four rooms of the high school were located.

Of course, it could also have been that Monsignor Burns finally made him and most other high school boys shape up one day in catechism class with a well-planned tirade.

"Rick," said Monsignor Burns, focusing his one good eye on a tough looking senior farm boy who was also a football player. "How many persons are there in the Trinity?"

"Three," said Rick, slouching a little in his seat.

"STAND UP when I call on you, young man," said Monsignor Burns in his most authoritative voice.

This was the same voice he used in church when he railed against the vulgar movie, "The Moon Is Blue," that was being shown in the Rialto theater located just a half block away from Sacred Heart Church. Any parishioner going to see that movie was committing a sin, scandalizing their children and contributing to the degradation of community morals.

"Yes, Monsignor," said Rick as he slowly rose to his feet. Once Rick was standing, it was obvious that both of his hands were wrapped in bandages.

"What did you do to your hands?" demanded Monsignor Burns.

"I hurt them playing football," lied Rick.

"DON'T LIE TO ME," shouted Monsignor at the top of his voice. "YOU GOT DRUNK AND BEAT UP A TREE, DIDN'T YOU? GO DOWNSTAIRS AND WAIT FOR ME."

Rick hesitated, wondering whether or not it was time that someone stood up to old One-Eye.

"NOW!" yelled Monsignor.

Rick gathered up his stuff and shuffled out, trying his best to appear non-intimidated.

Every student in the room made a mental note never to lie to Monsignor Burns.

The reason for Bernard's finally getting with the program could also have been the assistant pastor at Sacred Heart Church, Fr. Martin. He, too, conducted religion classes at the high school. He had two good eyes and a deadly aim with erasers. Any boy caught not paying attention would be nailed on the side of the head. If Father happened to be holding a piece of chalk in his hand instead of an eraser, he could hurl a piece of chalk so that it would hit the front edge of the offender's desk and be converted into shrapnel, insuring the immediate attention of the victim. Fr. Martin was also the Driver's Education teacher. Any one who wanted to get his or her license had better not cross him.

April 19, 1955
Norfolk, Nebraska
Glee Club opened up whole new worlds to Bernie. While it was definitely weird, he sort of enjoyed having Sister Cecile push on his diaphragm as she tried to show him the proper way to breathe in order to get the most projection. Yes, there was definitely something very special going on here!

Sister was helping the Boys Glee Club prepare renditions of "You'll Never Walk Alone" by Hammerstein and Rogers (*sic*) and "The Song of the Anvil" by Kountz to be performed during the Sacred Heart High School Spring Concert.

Sr. Mary Michella, the principal, was proud that Bernard was finally living up to his Italian potential. Since the Roman Catholic Church was based in Italy, she was convinced that all Italians had innate intelligence and talent.

April 30, 1955
Norfolk, Nebraska
"Here, Bernard," said Stella who had been looking through the newspaper. "Cut this out and put it in the scrapbook."

Bernie took a minute to read the article:

"Ted Barcio, Chicago and Northwestern Roadmaster, left this weekend for Sparta, Wisconsin, where he has been transferred. Mrs. Barcio and son, Bernard, Sacred Heart High School student, will join him there when school closes. The Barcios came here about eight years ago from Cudahy, Wisconsin. Mrs. Robert Pierce entertained Mr. Barcio's co-workers and supervisors at a farewell party before he left. Guests presented Mr. Barcio a gift. The Norfolkian's other son, Joseph, student at Creighton University, was here for the weekend."

Into the old scrapbook it went. Who knew when anyone would look at it again!

May 18, 1955
Norfolk, Nebraska
"Bernard," said Stella, "get the scissors."
"Another clipping for the old scrapbook," thought Bernie.

Oh, well, at least he wasn't getting into trouble again. Yet.

"Mrs. Rosa Dugan entertained at a luncheon at her home Thursday to honor Mrs. Theodore Barcio who will leave for Wisconsin later this month. Mrs. Margaret Agnes held high bridge score and high canasta went to Mrs. N. J. Rich. Bouquets of spring flowers were used throughout the home. A table centerpiece consisted of a large bouquet of assorted carnations Mrs. Dugan received, made up by a group of Norfolk friends, on Mother's Day."

By the end of his third year at Sacred Heart High School, Bernie was honored as the junior with the highest scholastic average, 92.8. Informally, he was called the junior class valedictorian. Luckily, in view of the rather rough start Bernie had at Sacred Heart, only that year's work was considered in making the award.

As sort of a bonus, Bernie was eventually allowed to attend his Junior Prom, if he could get a date. Of course, he would not be able to use the family car because his dad had driven it back to Wisconsin where he had recently bid on and received the position of Roadmaster of the Winona, Minnesota—Madison, Wisconsin subdivision. He had had to report to his office in the Chicago and Northwestern depot in Sparta, Wisconsin, before the end of the school year.

On May 18, 1955, Ted wrote the following letter from Sparta, where he was already working, to Stella who had stayed behind in Norfolk until the school year came to an end while trying to sell the house.

"Dear Stella,
"Just another note to remind you that if you come out to Sparta, the best way to come out would be to take the train to Omaha 8 o'clock at night. You get in Chicago at 7 a.m. You leave Chicago for Sparta about 10 a.m. Then you get here at 3:10 p.m. the same day you leave Chicago. Otherwise if you go by way of Sioux City to Mankato, you get in Mankato about 5 p.m. Then you will have to wait about 5 hours to get on train No. 518 which gets here 2:30 p.m.

"So your best bet would be to go by the way of Chicago by taking the bus from Norfolk on Friday night for Omaha. Don't forget to pay the house near the end of this month unless you can settle things before that time. You will safe (*sic*) little money by paying it all up on the loan. After you sell it, we will safe (*sic*) most of the interest on the balance we owe, and I think the balance is around $2,700 with interest and all. So by selling for $8,500.00 we still will be O.K.

"So far nothing as far as a nice house for rent. Have couple lined up but I don't know if you will like them.

"You don't suppose Walt [Howell] would like to drive out here with you to look at the country. Then I could talk to him as I could use him here for a foreman right now, if he could take a week vacation to come out and look at it without saying anything to anyone. Talk to him and see what he says.

"I will close now. If anything you need, drop a line. Love to the boys and you.

"Ted"

Finding a date for the junior prom was no easy matter for Bernie. When he found out he would not have a car to use, he questioned his decision to attend the prom and put off asking anyone to go with him. Finally, at almost the last minute, Nick Rich, a friend of his dad's who was a salesman on the railroad, heard of Bernie's predicament and offered to let him use his brand new Pontiac on prom night. At first, Bernie's mom said it was out of the question. Finally, however, after checking with her husband by phone, she was convinced that it would probably be all right.

Now Bernie had to find a date. Always adventurous, he simply walked down to the soda parlor where kids usually hung out after school. He walked in, looked over the possibilities and approached a pimple-faced senior girl who was sitting on the end seat of a booth full of her girl friends.

"Would you like to go to the junior prom with me?" asked Bernie.

The girl was not very popular and, lucky for Bernie, had not yet been asked.

"Can I think about it?" she asked.

"Sure," said Bernie. "I can come back in a half hour."

When he came back, the pimple-faced senior girl who was not very popular agreed that she would go to the junior prom with him.

As he left the soda fountain much relieved, Bernie was confronted by a couple of his date's girl friends who chewed him out for his last minute invitation and his apparent lack of consideration.

"You certainly aren't giving her a lot of time to get ready," one of them scolded. "Don't you know a girl needs time to get a dress and stuff?"

"The nerve of them," thought Bernie as he slowly walked back home. "Don't they know that I'm the valedictorian of the junior class and that my dad's the Roadmaster on the Chicago & Northwestern Railroad? My date should be honored that she gets to go with me."

Digging out on the Albion Line Nebraska, 1948

Walt Howell, wife Pearl, Stella, Joe and Bernard Barcio

Engineer with Rotary Snow Plow, Albion Line, 1948

C&NW RR Foreman, Walt Howell and his wife Pearl, Fremont, NB

Chicago & Northwestern RR Social Club, Depot, Norfolk, NB
Top Row (L to R): Author, Ted (5th), Joe Barone (6th), Walt Howell (10th)
Women Top Row (L to R): Stella Barcio, Pearl Howell (4th)

Author with Mr. Eicker, Norfolk, NB

Author's Godfather, Mike Bruno

Author taken to swim in Fremont, NB

Stella setting up Crèche, Cudahy, WI, early 40's

Crèche with Ted's handmade church

Christmas Crèche display, Norfolk, NB, 1950

Handmade church in Sparta, WI, 1970

Author as a Norfolk, NB cowboy, 1949

Author with bike he shared with his brother

Stella and Ted play Monopoly with family

Nebraska track bed washed out by flood waters

Brother Joe enjoys a midnight snack with Aunt Yolanda, Nanna Barcio and his mom

Stella Barcio hanging laundry in the Backyard, 705 S. 2nd St., Norfolk, NB

Rose and Frank Bufano during a summer visit to Norfolk. Bench & table built by Ted

Middle row: Author and Brother Joe (6th & 7th) from Left), Sacred Heart Drum and Bugle Corps

House built by Giuseppi Barcio at 627 Elm. Ave., South Milwaukee, WI, as it appeared in July, 2005

The 1920's Wine Press used by Giuseppi Barcio until his death in 1965.

Stella Barcio (3rd from R) with Omaha, NB, cake decorating class, November, 1954

Florence Miresso
South Chicago, ca. 1947

Florence (Miresso) Piekarski with author
Schererville, IL, 2005

Author (L), Brother Joe (R)
Sacred Heart Drum & Bugle Corps
Norfolk, May 30, 1952

Cake baked and decorated by Stella Barcio, Norfolk

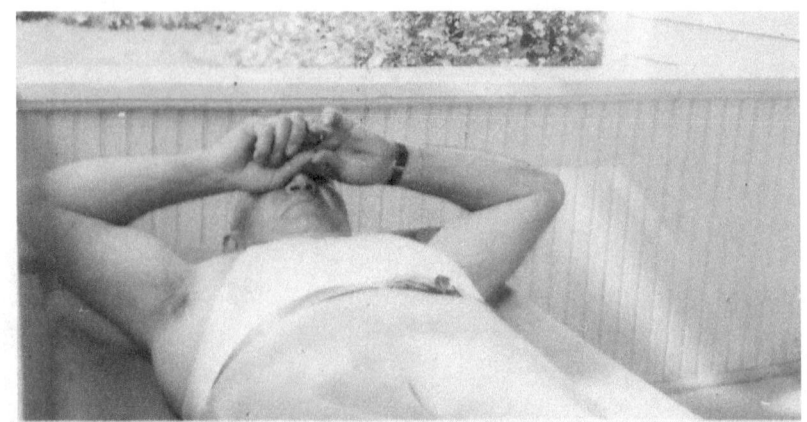

Ted Barcio relaxing on a cot on the front porch, Norfolk

Author visiting a raccoon and a bear, Ta-Ha-Zooka Park, Norfolk, 1955

Brother Joe, Jimmy (son of Eugene) and the author
Basement Lionel railroad layout in Norfolk

Giuseppe Barcio and his coup
3777 S. Ahmeda Ave., St. Francis Heights

Traditional "Bed Doll," Norfolk   Easter Eggs decorated by Stella Barcio

Author (L) and Brother Joe at Knotts Berry Farm, Buena Park, CA, 1954

Brother Joe (L) and the author with grandparents, Giuseppe and Vrigita Barcio, Knotts Berry Farm

Joe Barcio, Norfolk Jr. College
ROTC uniform, 705 S. 2nd St.
Norfolk, NB, October 10, 1954

Lillian (L) and John Batten present
their first daughter Marsha to
Lillian's Grandma Nelli Hacker
Indianapolis, January, 1952

PART IV

October 1955– September 1959

Adventures in the Coulee Region

October, 1955
Indianapolis
Before too long, Lillian's Cousin Jack Hacker was promoted to Detective with the Indianapolis Police Force and began to accumulate stories that would fascinate friends and family for years to come.

One of Jack's more colorful arrests involved a safecracker we'll call "Larry."

"Jack, did you see Larry's car today?" asked a fellow detective.

"Yeah, I saw him driving around."

"Was he riding high or low?"

"His car was riding high so I figured he didn't have anything in his trunk."

All the detectives knew Larry and his habits. They also knew that if they saw his car weighted down, he probably had a safe that he had just stolen in the trunk. That's when they would pull him over and bust him.

One night, while Jack was on duty, a call came in to the station complaining of loud banging and hammering noises in a downtown alley. When Jack and a fellow officer arrived on the scene, there was Larry banging away on a huge safe trying to break the lock.

"Hold it, Larry!" commanded Jack. "Where did you get the safe?"

"I found it here in the alley and thought I would check it out."

Unfortunately for Larry, who really wasn't all that bright, the safe had been too large to fit in the trunk of his car so he had simply tied a chain to it and dragged it all the way into the alley from the building where it had been stolen. All Jack and his buddy had to do after taking Larry into custody was to follow the scraped trail that the safe had left on the streets to discover the building.

December, 1955
South Chicago, Illinois
As has already been observed, the annual trips to South Chicago usually ended up not being very pleasant. South Chicago seemed dirty. There was soot all over the sidewalks. The ground was actually coal black. And, inevitably, Stella would get into an argument with someone or other when she visited her sisters, Lucy and Maggie. They just weren't living their lives right. They let their husbands get away with murder. If they would just listen to Stella, she would show them how to whip them into shape. And they were raising their kids wrong. And they weren't taking care of their father properly. They should

not let him drink so much. And they should be paying him rent for living in his house. Then, later, in the car, Ted and Stella would end up arguing.

The atmosphere in South Chicago was tense. This, of course, would cause Bernie to stick his foot in his mouth more than once by saying the wrong thing.

It was on one such trip that Ted told Stella they were going to drive over and visit his sister Ida and her husband Fred who lived with their two daughters Judy and Barbara in the South Chicago area. Fred had just refinished his basement with paneling and wanted to show off his handiwork.

As the two families were kidding around in the kitchen later, Bernie was listening to the fun banter and just sort of got caught up into it.

Bernie's dad said something, his Aunt Ida answered, and then Stella put in her two cents worth. It was then that his Uncle Fred entered the kitchen and threw in a random comment.

"No comments from the Nigger Gallery!" fired off Bernie, who thought it would be quite funny. After all, he had heard his mom use that phrase a thousand times, and it seemed perfect for the occasion.

The room went cold, and Uncle Fred looked first at Bernie and then at Ted.

Ted, sensing that things could get ugly fast, decided to diffuse the situation.

"Fred, he didn't mean anything by that. It's just an expression! He's just a kid."

Luckily, Uncle Fred decided to overlook the insult, smiled and got back into the spirit of the occasion.

Bernie would eventually learn just how lucky he was that his dad had intervened. He always knew that Uncle Fred was a little different than the other relatives. He was older than his wife, Ida, and, at family gatherings, he would occasionally go over to a closet and use an inhaler that he would temporarily store there to relieve his asthma problems.

Years later, Bernie learned that his Uncle Fred had done hard time for accidentally shooting and killing a policeman—at least according to one version of the story. His Uncle Fred was definitely not a man to whom one should ever say, "No comments from the Nigger Gallery."

February, 1956
Sparta, Wisconsin

Several years earlier, in 1952, Tony Nudi had sailed on the ocean Liner Constantinople from New York City to Naples, Italy. He had finally made it back to Italy to visit what relatives he could find. After travelling to Cervicati where he was born near San Marco Argentano in Calabria, he continued on to the nearby community of Marinello where his family had later moved and where some of his relatives were living. While there, he was so amazed at their still-primitive living style that he decided to help build them an outhouse so they wouldn't have to use their animal barns to do their business. On this trip he also became taken with the young daughter of Fiori Petrassi who was named Rosina. He promised that he would arrange to bring little Rosina to America when he got back.

Good to his word, Rosina arrived in South Chicago and was soon picked up by Stella and Ted to live with them in Sparta for a while. Bernie was along on the trip and rode in the back seat with Rosina on the way back to Sparta.

Because she was, no doubt, more than a little scared, Rosina tried to find a little comfort by holding hands with her cousin Bernie as they drove through the darkness.

After a couple months, Stella—noticing perhaps that Rosina and Bernie were beginning to take quite an interest in each other—decided that it would not work for Rosina to continue living in Sparta and quickly arranged for her to be sent back to South Chicago.

April, 1956
Sparta, Wisconsin

The area along the Mississippi River and inland was basically unaffected by the last glacier that moved down across the United States. The result is a lot of interesting sandstone formations and very scenic hills with gently eroded gullies, called "coulees." Ted Barcio was enamored with the scenery the very first time he went over his new subdivision, and was very pleased that his office would be located in Sparta, right in the middle of some of the best coulee region scenery.

It would be a while, however, before Bernie would learn to appreciate these natural wonders.

"Bernard, get in here."

Bernard was being called into the house from the front porch where, as a senior in high school, he was trying to strike up a conversation with a seductively dressed young lady seated in a lawn chair on the porch. Although she was interesting, Bernie was finding it hard not to notice her atrociously rotten front teeth.

In the house, Stella was deep in whispered conversation with her sister Maggie who had been driven to Wisconsin by a girlfriend (currently seated on the front porch) of her son Dickie. Maggie was on her way to visit her son in a Wisconsin state prison where he was serving time for burglary.

"Here, Stella," said Maggie in a hushed tone. "You keep this watch. Dickie gave it to me, and it is very valuable."

"Why don't you keep it?" Stella asked.

"Because I just know that when he gets out of jail, he'll try to take it back and sell it; or he'll gamble it away."

"How expensive is it?"

"Dickie said it was worth a couple thousand dollars. It's platinum and those are all real diamonds."

Bernard remembered his cousin Dickie from the times he had run into him on the street in front of his grandfather's home in South Chicago. Seven years older than the author, Dickie was flashy. He dressed to kill. He wore several very large diamond rings and held his younger cousins in awe with tales of fast money earned by hiring on to paint dangerously high smoke stacks at the steel mills and the potential of even faster money that could be earned gambling.

Dickie's final gambles, however, did not pay off. He became fascinated by the art of safe cracking and quickly gained the reputation of being one of the best in the nation. While he seemed to be able to get into safes quickly, he did not, however, have very good luck staying out of jail.

It was two o'clock in the morning many years later when Dickie's half brother, Rudy Strano, got the call from the prison chaplain at Terminal Island, California. Dickie had died of a heart attack.

In prison, Dickie, still maintaining a happy-go-lucky front, followed his second vocation, cooking. He compiled a prison cookbook featuring, among other recipes, how to fix spaghetti for 500. Dickie's prison cookbook passed into the hands of his sister Florence who, in marked contrast, supported herself cooking for five priests in a Roman Catholic rectory in Whiting, Indiana.

It is believed that Dickie's tools of his ill-begotten trade had been squirreled away by his half brother, Rudy, who accepted the responsibility of signing for his body and making sure it was given a proper burial. Since Maggie did not want to be buried next to her always-happy but financially-irresponsible husband, Tony Miresso, she insisted that Dickie be buried in the spot originally intended for her in Lot 434, Section Q, in St. Mary's Cemetery in Chicago.

May, 1956
South Chicago, Illinois

Gloria Leo was doing her best to try and live a normal life despite her somewhat dysfunctional family. It bothered her that whenever her little sister, Mary, would return home from the store with a Popsicle or other treat, her Aunt Maggie, whose kitchen door she had to pass, would take it away from her before she could even begin to climb the stairs back up to their 2nd floor flat. Gloria had even taken it upon herself to call the cops on her aunt on occasion, but nothing seemed to help.

By the time she was 16, Gloria was a beautiful young girl, and she wanted to be able to dress nice and fit in with the other girls in her class.

After saving her money, she was finally able to purchase a very stylish pair of jeans, a beautiful top and a few pieces of costume jewelry. She had enough left over to buy some nail polish that she carefully applied before returning home to show off her new look to her mother.

Aunt Lucy was very pleased with the way her daughter looked.

"Gloria, go show your father how nice you look."

Big mistake.

"Dad, how do you like my new clothes?" asked Gloria innocently enough.

Leonard Leo took a long look at his blossoming teenaged daughter. He had, no doubt, already had a few beers. He suddenly lost it.

"*Puttana*! You look just like a little *puttana*!"

Her father grabbed her by the arm and dragged her into his bedroom.

Pointing to a statue of the Blessed Virgin that he kept on his dresser, he yelled, "Do you see our Blessed Mother? She doesn't dress like that. You should be more like her! Get in the bathroom and take those clothes off right now and give them to me!"

"But, Pa..."

"*Vai, vai!*" yelled her father.

After Gloria had taken off the new things she had just bought and gave them to her father, she watched from the back porch window as he took her new clothing out to the alley and burned it all in a garbage can. When he emerged from under the grape arbor on his way back to the house, Leonard looked up and saw his tearful daughter watching him.

"*Veni ca!*" commanded her father. "Come down here right now."

When Gloria met her father at the back door, he once again grabbed her by the arm and pulled her down to the sink in the basement. He immediately began to scrub the nail polish from her fingers.

"The Blessed Virgin doesn't wear this stuff on her hands, and you shouldn't either."

When Gloria explained to her mother that she really could not live like that much longer, her mom tried to smooth things over.

"That's your father, honey. You've got to respect him."

"Ma, I want to leave this house. I can't take this any longer."

May, 1956
Sparta, Wisconsin

The following year, as a new-kid senior at Sparta High School, Bernie intended to get a little earlier start on asking a girl to the senior prom.

Although he was new to the school, and, once again had gotten off to kind of a rough start, he had gained much in self-confidence. He had tried to talk his dad into buying him a car so he could drive to La Crosse and attend Aquinas Catholic High School there. After all, he had spent his entire school career in Catholic schools. Handing Bernie the keys to a car, however, seemed to be entirely out of the question. Especially since a perfectly good public high school was only three blocks away from their rented home at 310 Pine Street.

Enrolling in Sparta High School was something a new student did while standing at the counter in the main office. The school secretary presented the selection of classes and the student signed up for such required courses as English, American Problems, P.E. and chose such electives as Bookkeeping and, if he said he was going to college, Physics.

Unfortunately, Bernie had not studied much math at Sacred Heart High School in Norfolk. During his junior year, the Algebra class was full and Bernie had been counseled into taking Latin with his voluptuous nun.

The result was an F in Physics on Bernie's first Sparta High School report card.

"Bernard," said Mr. Mangino the Physics teacher, "I would like to talk with you."

"Yes, Sir," replied Bernard who had been stopped on the sidewalk as he left school.

"You're having a lot of trouble with Physics, aren't you?" asked Mr. Mangino.

"Yes, I never had much math in my old school."

"You never studied Algebra?"

"No, I was put in Latin instead."

"Well, I looked at your records. You're no dummy, and you should be able to do a lot better in Physics. In fact, I would like to see you getting A's from now on."

This expression of confidence in his ability provided the little push that Bernie needed. He began to ask his neighbor, Ronnie Johnson (who was some kind of a math genius) to help him learn and maybe even partially understand the various equations he needed to know.

Ronnie lived with his family at 312 Pine Street, right next door to the Barcios.

And this seemed to work. Although Bernie had never studied Algebra, or even chemistry for that matter, he managed to learn enough math and memorize enough equations that by mid-year he had earned his A in Physics.

His friendship with Ronnie grew to the point where they would often throw darts together at a board set up in Bernie's basement. One day, while Ronnie was feeling adventuresome, he stood waving his hand up and down in front of the target in an attempt to distract Bernie during his turn. As it turned out, Bernie was an excellent dart thrower and he nailed Ronnie right in the center of his open palm in mid wave.

For all the help he was as a study partner, Ronnie Johnson also had a delinquent streak in him.

"Hey, Bernie," suggested Ronnie as they stood by their lockers before reporting to their 7th period study hall, "let's cut study hall."

"I don't want to leave school and get in trouble," said Bernie.

"We don't have to leave the building."

"What will we do?"

"We'll just walk around. Nobody will catch us. Come on. Let's do it," encouraged Ronnie.

So Bernie was talked into his first—and last—class cutting adventure. The two boys waited at their lockers until the halls cleared, and then they just sort of began ambling about. They didn't cause any trouble. They just relished not being confined to study hall for the period.

"Let's go check out the gym lockers," said Ronnie.

"Isn't there a P.E. class this period?" asked Bernie.

"Nah, the gym is empty."

It felt weird walking around the empty boys' locker room and checking out the shower rooms and sitting in the empty gym, but they had to pass the time some way.

"There," said Ronnie at the end of the period, "now you can say that you cut class at least once during your senior year."

Soon it was prom time. This time around, Bernie asked a petite freshman girl named Clarabeth Fanning who was flattered to accept his invitation. And he asked her early enough so she could have ample time to prepare. Bernie really wasn't a slow learner!

Clarabeth turned out to be too cute by half in her red prom dress with white chiffon shawl.

Even though a senior, Bernie was still kept on a very short leash by his parents, and he would have to drop his date back off at her house no later than 11:00 p.m., no matter that other couples planned to drive to Grand Dad's Bluff in La Crosse afterwards to watch the sunrise the following morning.

One of those unfettered couples turned out to be Larry Vieregge, the baker's son, and his date. They would be married shortly afterwards.

When, in 1986, Bernie attended his class's 30th reunion in Sparta, after having just been honored as Indiana Teacher of the Year, he was surprised to see that Larry and his high school sweetheart were still married, contrary to all expectations for high school romances.

May 27, 1956
Sparta, Wisconsin

Sparta High School was holding its Baccalaureate exercises in the school gymnasium. Bernie didn't realize it at the time, but it turned out to be very prophetic that the Invocation, Baccalaureate Address and Benediction were all delivered by Rev. Floyd J. Dwyer, the Spiritual Director of Holy Cross Seminary in La Crosse, Wisconsin.

June 1, 1956
Sparta, Wisconsin

Bernie was graduating and, in true family custom, all members of the extended family were invited to Sparta for the party.

Bernie's Uncle Charlie and Aunt Martha drove up from Cudahy, along with Bernie's cousin, Bennie Riccio with whom he had had his little roadside brush with death several years earlier. Bernie's Uncle George and Aunt Esther came from Milwaukee with Bernie's cousins Eileen and Henry. His grandparents, Nanna and Papa (Joe and Vrigitta Barcio) also came from Milwaukee. From Chicago came Bernie's other grandfather, Tony Nudi (Nonno), and his Aunt Lucy with her youngest daughter, Mary.

A week or so later found Bernie visiting his relatives again, this time in Milwaukee. It really did seem to be a close knit extended family! Bernie was surprised, however, at how some of those that he always thought were close friends of his dad reacted when he returned to visit them now that he was a Roadmaster.

"*Mow viene il* Big-a-Shot!" observed the aging mother of Mario Nardi when she saw Ted entering her house.

Maybe it was meant as a complement, but it almost smacked too much of jealousy to be something good.

As they were driving back to Sparta, it was pretty much life as usual in the car. Visits to Milwaukee always led to reprisals, regrets, hundreds of "should of's" and "shouldn't have's." The "*Mow viene il* Big-a-Shot" comment was worked all the way into the ground by Stella who focused entirely on its negative connotations.

Finally, Bernie thought he would break the usual monotony and get in one more plug for what he wanted to do that summer.

"But I really want to work on a farm this summer. It's just outside of town. I have to do something besides sit around all summer."

"Why a farm?" asked his mom. "It's a lot of hard work."

"So, I'm strong, and it's something I've always wanted to do."

"You're just a kid," said his mom.

"What do you think, Dad?" asked Bernie.

"We'll see," said his dad, not really wanting to get into it just then.

Bernie knew that when he got the old "We'll see" reply, that pretty much closed the conversation for the moment, but it didn't entirely rule out the possibility.

His dad reached over and turned the car radio on. "Good Night, Irene" happened to be the song playing. They drove along in silence for a while, and then Ted started to sing along with the song. He was definitely feeling mischievous as he knew that when he did this, it would get Stella's goat—Irene being the name of his first sweetheart in Carrollville.

Stella let loose her usual string of colloquial Italian curses.

The song ended. Soon, however, Ted started to sing along with another favorite of his.

"There's a weed in my gar-den!"

This particular lyric was obviously aimed at stirring up some private controversy with his wife, and, whenever he felt particularly adventuresome, he would let her have a chorus or two before she flew off the handle.

The next day, as was usual following any visit to the Milwaukee relatives, Stella was in the kitchen harping on several things to which she had objected during the visit.

"Stell, that's my family."

"Well, if you were more of a man,..."

"God damn it, *state citta*!" yelled Ted, beginning to lose his patience with his wife's prodding.

Stella then slipped into an Italian tirade that pushed the wrong buttons on her husband.

SLAP!

Ted let his wife have a good one across her face.

O.K. So Ted Barcio could occasionally be pushed to the breaking point. He practiced tremendous self-control most of his life, but he was fighting some powerful genes, and, eventually, such inborn traits can be forced to the surface. Ted's cousin on his mother's side, Frank Verta, (son of Vrigita's oldest brother, John Verta) a very tall, very handsome Italian who never once ever addressed Bernie directly all the times that he ever visited them in

Nebraska, was a man rumored to have routinely beat his poor wife, Mini—severe times leaving obvious bruises and black eyes. Bernie always remarked to himself how downtrodden Mini Verta appeared, but, at his young age, he never imagined the hell the poor woman was going through. This he would learn much later from his mother when she was in her 90's and going over aspects of her life that would have probably been better left unmentioned.

"*Diaulo,*" screamed Stella. "*Musa tu!*"

She was not easily cowered by anyone and had begun to hit back.

"O.K., THAT'S ENOUGH," yelled Bernie who had heard all he wanted to from his bedroom. He had walked to the kitchen door and, for the first time in his life, without even thinking about what he was about to do, Bernie had yelled at his parents. They were acting like animals, and he had had it!

"GO TO YOUR ROOM," shouted his dad after a brief moment of shock upon seeing his son in the doorway and hearing him yell at them.

"JUST QUIT IT," yelled Bernie, before he complied.

And, amazingly, it worked. The argument stopped, and the kitchen noises returned to normal. If Bernie had needed to prove that he was man enough to spend the summer working on a dairy farm, he had just done it.

Auggie Terpstra made a good impression when he visited Bernie and his mom a few days later at their rented home. He managed to put all fears to rest as he explained that Bernie would be staying in their extra room in the farm house, would receive all his meals and would be able to come home on weekends. Also, the pay would be $300 for the summer. This was an impressive amount of money, although, as was the family custom, Bernie would never lay his hands on a cent of it.

While Bernie was staying out on the farm getting his first taste of country living, life went on as usual at his parents' house in Sparta. On June 17, Bernie's godfather, Mike Bruno, stopped in for a visit with his family. On June 25, Mr. and Mrs. Mallo paid a visit, followed by a visit by Pete and Joe Crapitto from Cudahy.

Out on the farm, it turned out that Bernie was seemingly made for the life. He thrived on getting up before dawn to help with the milking, although it took him a week or so before he could manage hoisting the 50 lb milk cans into the cooler on his own. And those cow teats! They were a lot more coarse than he imagined they would be. His job was to wash them off with warm water and a paper towel so that Auggie could come along and hang the milking machine from a strap fastened around the cow's middle. When the milking unit was full, it would be poured into the large milk can that would then be covered with its lid and put into the cooler until it was picked up by the dairy truck.

The dairy truck was sometimes driven by a young boy not much older than Bernie. One day, after the boy had driven up and parked his truck next to the dairy cooler, he had stepped out of the truck and walked into the barn to speak to Auggie. Suddenly, a loud crash was heard outside. Bernie went out to see what had happened. When he returned, he calmly reported that the boy's truck had rolled back down the hill and crashed into a fence post. Auggie and the boy were both amazed at how nonchalantly Bernie shared the information. Farm life was definitely having a calming affect on Bernie.

That summer, in fact, was almost the best thing that ever happened to him. Not only did he learn the names of all twenty cows in the herd, he learned their eating habits, how they needed to be let into one field or another to insure they could eat enough to produce the next day's milk, how they needed to have worms squeezed out of holes in their sides and how messy it was when the vet arrived to provide artificial insemination to a cow in heat. He had never seen a rubber glove that went all the way up to the shoulder before.

Then there was haying. This required Bernie to balance himself on a wagon being towed behind the tractor and hay bailer as bales of hay popped out of a chute onto the wagon. These then needed to be carried to the back of the wagon and stacked. When the wagon was full, it sported eight or nine rows of crisscrossed bales of hay. Unbeknownst to Bernie, his thigh muscles were quickly rivaling those of muscle builders he used to stare at in the window of a magazine shop in Norfolk, Nebraska.

Then Bernie was taught how to drive the truck alongside the cornhusker so its load could be emptied on the roll. He would then take this load back to the barn, unload it and be back in place in time for the next load to be poured into the truck.

"Stretch your foot out and stand on the edge of the feeder," said Auggie as he showed Bernie how to pour a 50 lb bag of pig feed into the top of a feeder while standing with his other leg on the back of the wagon hooked to a tractor.

In fact, this is exactly what Bernie was doing when his brother, Joe, drove into the farmyard one day to get him. Bernie was expected at home, and Joe really didn't have much time for, or interest in, farm life. He was not impressed by Bernie's explanation that he would have to wait until he finished feeding the pigs and put the tractor back in the barn before he could leave.

"Have you been accepted into a college?" asked Joe as they drove back into town.

"No," said Bernie. "I'm not sure I want to go to college."

"Of course you have to go to college," demanded his brother.

"I think I would rather become a farmer," said Bernie.

"That's stupid. I'll talk to Dad and make sure that we get you enrolled somewhere."

Believe it or not, that pretty much settled it. Bernie would have to go to college. His mind raced. He knew that in nearby La Crosse there was a branch of the University of Wisconsin that specialized in Physical Education and Athletic Training; but it was commonly referred to as "The Jock College," and he really had no interest in learning to be a coach.

"So, where do you think you'll go to college?" asked his Uncle Gene who was visiting that evening.

"I think I would like to go to the seminary in La Crosse," said Bernie, dumbfounding everyone.

"Have you talked to Father about that?" asked his brother, who, at one time, had entertained thoughts of attending St. Francis Seminary in Milwaukee.

"No, not yet," replied Bernie.

"Joe, why don't you take him over to the rectory while we fix dinner," suggested Bernie's mom.

It was absolutely amazing. When he had awakened that morning, Bernie would have been perfectly happy working on a farm for the rest of his life. As he went to bed that night, he was signed up to enter Holy Cross Seminary in La Crosse, Wisconsin, at the end of the summer.

The power and influence of an older brother in Italian households can sometimes be very awesome.

In 2013, the author would learn that when his brother Joe had graduated from Sacred Heart H.S. in Norfolk a year ahead of his peers, he, too, had not wanted to go to college. But that changed when his dad simply drove Joe over to Norfolk Jr. College, located on the same block with Sacred Heart H.S., and suggested that he enroll. The time Joe spent studying at the junior college later gave him a leg up on his application to attend Creighton University in Omaha.

July, 1956
Sparta, Wisconsin

The word was out. Bernie was going into the seminary. Auggie was certainly impressed, although he still thought it perfectly proper to have Bernie spend hours hoeing endless rows of string beans or walking through pasture after pasture chopping down weeds that the cows weren't supposed to eat.

And Ron Johnson, Bernie's physics study partner, was also impressed. He was so impressed, in fact, that he wanted to take Bernie out for a night on the town one evening during the week.

"Auggie, I'm going to go out for a while with a friend after dinner tonight. I won't stay out too late."

"Did you open the gate so the cows can get into the fresh pasture?" asked Auggie.

"No, not yet. But I'll do it on our way out."

As soon as Bernie got into Ron's car, Ron slid a girlie magazine across the seat to him.

"Aren't you interested in girls now that you're going into the seminary?" teased Ron.

Bernie got so wrapped up in defending his choice not to leaf through the magazine that he completely forgot to open the gate to the pasture.

"That's funny," said Auggie the next morning as he poured half empty milking pails into the big can. "Bernie," he asked, "are you sure you let the cows into the pasture last night?"

This was it. He had forgotten to do what he had promised. As a future seminarian he certainly could not lie about it.

"Auggie, I'm sorry. I guess I just forgot."

"Well, we aren't going to get much milk today," Auggie calmly observed.

Auggie, however, was not one to harbor grudges. He just let it go. Of course, when it came time for someone to climb down into the bottom of the silo to shovel out the stenchy, rotten silage before a new batch was poured in, it was Bernie that was given the job.

One day, because Auggie did not want anyone to think he was a workaholic, he decided that he would take his son and Bernie fishing. Of course, the morning chores would still have to be done and they would have to come home early enough for the afternoon milking.

Nevertheless, Auggie did not want Bernie to end the summer thinking that farming was all work and no play.

September, 1956
La Crosse, Wisconsin

Bernie had reported to Holy Cross Seminary on Mormon Coulee Road and was assigned a roommate. Seminary life turned out to be something for which he was even more suited than farming. He thrived on the companionship, the scheduled life style, the mandated study, recreation and sleep time. He thrived on the structure.

Bernie was put in Latin classes that met twice a day, and was fascinated to find himself, once more, in the wonderful world of biology. He loved learning about nature. In fact, when he had first studied biology in high school, Bernie was a master specimen collector. If Sister wanted students to collect bees, Bernie would show up the next day with a jar filled to the rim. Of course, at the college level, the challenges were a little greater. When he and classmates had to perform vivisections on a family of baby rabbits that the instructor, Father Oswald Schulte, had found on the grounds, he was a little taken aback. But true to his new vocation, he obediently did as he was instructed.

Of course, there were those tense, character building moments when all seminarians who were late to any event in the day had to report themselves to the Rector, Monsignor John Paul, as they filed in for chapel services each afternoon. But even this process proved to be character building. The Rector did not believe in demeaning the seminarians. He simply accepted their admissions and nodded them into the chapel. Of course, if the same seminarian developed a pattern of being late for the same activity, he would no doubt have a private session with the Rector.

Getting report cards was especially stressful. Each seminarian had to wait his turn outside the Rector's office. When his turn came, he would enter and stand erect before the Rector's desk. Monsignor Paul would milk the moment by scrutinizing the report card, sucking air in through his teeth and adjusting his position in his chair. Then, when he felt that he had made the seminarian sweat enough, he would have positive compliments for good grades, and offer encouragements to raise any grades that were on the low side.

Bernie's classmates included a wide variety of students, different ages and even different nationalities. One fellow seminarian, Francis X. Nguyen-Son-Mein, was from Viet Nam where he was committed to return after being ordained.

Albert Brusda fascinated Bernie. This was a seminarian who was at least 30 years old. He had been in the military and was full of stories that completely grossed Bernie out.

"You know, Bernie," said Al one evening as all the seminarians were taking their mandated walk around the building, "I used to work in a hospital emergency room."

"Wow," said Bernie, "I'll bet you got to see a lot of interesting things."

"We had this guy come in one night who complained that his butt was hurting," continued Al.

"What was the matter with it?" asked Bernie.

"He had a light bulb up his butt," said Al, "and when we took it out, all he could say was, 'I wonder how that got there!' "

Al was also the seminarian that first explained to Bernie that some priests and nuns actually broke their vows and slept with each other.

Absolutely unheard of! Bernie was truly scandalized.

Of course, Al also had some rather funny stories that he shared during their evening walks.

"A priest and a Nun were traveling together," began Al one evening, "when their car broke down, and they had to take lodging at the only motel available. Unfortunately, there was only one room left, and they would have to share it. There were, however, two separate beds in the room. They decided simply to sleep in their clothes so that no suspicion would be aroused. After a couple hours, however, the Nun commented that she was chilly. She wondered if Father would be so kind as to bring her one of the extra blankets that she had noticed were on the shelf in the closet. 'I have a better idea,' said Father. 'What's that?' asked the Nun. 'Well,' said Father, 'why don't we just make believe we're married for one night?' 'Oh,' said the Nun, somewhat shocked, 'do you think that would be O.K.?' 'Sure,' said Father, 'It's only for one night.' 'O.K. then,' said the Nun. 'Are you ready?' asked Father. 'I think so,' said the Nun. 'O.K. then,' said Father, "Get your own damn blanket!' "

As they returned to the main building, Al looked up at the carving in the entablature over the entrance to the gymnasium.

"See that carving?" asked Al.

"It is better to aim high and miss than to aim low and hit," read Bernie.

"That would make a good birth control motto, don't you think?" asked Al.

Albert Brusda was definitely a one-of-a-kind seminarian.

The first year went well.

May, 1957
South Chicago, Illinois

Gloria had gotten through her senior year fairly well and, with the help of her mother, was ready to attend the prom in a nice, respectable dress. All seemed to be going well as she awaited the arrival of her date. Nonno was sitting at the kitchen table as usual, as was her mother. Finally, they heard someone making his way up the back stairwell.

"Please, God," thought Gloria, "don't let Aunt Maggie see him and do something embarrassing!"

"Mom, this is my date for the prom," said Gloria when a young man entered the kitchen.

"Hi," said Gloria's mom as Nonno looked up from his glass of wine and eyed the young man.

"*Come si chiama questo? Qualè il suo cognome?*" asked Nonno of his daughter.

"My father wants to know what your last name is," said Lucy.

"Shemanski," replied Gloria's date.

Nonno smashed the table with the palm of his hand, spilling his wine as he suddenly rose to his feet.

"Polack! I'm not going to have any Polacks in my house. Get the hell out of here!"

"But, Pa," interrupted Lucy.

"*State citta!*" ordered Tony Nudi as he grabbed Gloria's date by the arm, pushed him back onto the porch and shoved him down the steps.

At first the boy was at a loss as to what to do, but when he had a minute to regain his composure, he got to his feet on the landing below.

"Come on, Gloria, let's go. I'll wait for you down here."

Before her date knew what was happening, Nonno reappeared at the top of the steps, this time armed with a variety of pots and pans that he began to hurl at the boy.

It was definitely getting harder and harder for Gloria to continue living in such a hostile environment.

August, 1957
South Chicago, Illinois

The account of the following true incident(used here with permission) is told by Mary Leo in an unpublished manuscript entitled **STREET NOISE**, *a novel—originally with names changed—about her life at 9506 Commercial Ave. in South Chicago. To make the story easier for family members to follow, this author has substituted the real names in brackets for the fictional ones diplomatically used by Mary.*

We ran across the flat, [Gloria] staying ahead of me. I followed her to the kitchen doorway, still laughing. When we got there, [Gloria] stopped abruptly. I ran into her back, pushing her into the kitchen.

"Don't you girls have no respect for the people that are still sleeping? Your Uncle [Ted] is still asleep," Aunt [Stella] declared.

Ma, Aunt [Maggie], Nonno and Aunt [Stella] were all sitting around the table eating breakfast. Nonno's radio program echoed in the background. Nonno still wore the blue stocking cap from the night before. I could never figure it out; Ma could never get him to wear a hat when he went outside, even when it was below zero, but at night, in bed, he wore a knit cap. His head got cold at the strangest times.

"We're sorry," [Gloria] said to Aunt [Stella], who glared at her. [Gloria] tried to be serious, but I could hear the laughter in her voice and so could Aunt [Stella].

"You think it's funny?"

"No, [Stell]. [Gloria] ain't laughing at you," Ma said in [Gloria's] defense.

"There's no respect in this house. Lucia, you have to teach your girls respect. My boys know respect. They know how to act to their elders."

Aunt [Stella] and Uncle [Ted] had two sons. The youngest [Bernard] was in the seminary and the other [Joe], at twenty-two was working on [an advanced degree]. Aunt Martha would always compare her sons to [Gloria] and me whenever she wanted to make a point. We should have hated both of them because of Aunt [Stella], but they were the nicest cousins we had, despite having Aunt [Stella] for a mother.

"My girls are good girls, [Stell]," Ma answered, then tried to change the subject. "If we're gonna make ravioli for tonight, we should get started, don't ya tink?"

There was silence in the kitchen even though the radio was blaring. Nonno had turned up the volume. I hurried over to the bathroom. I wanted to be quick and get back to all the food. [Gloria] headed over to the kitchen sink to wash her face and brush her teeth. I'd do that later.

The kitchen really looked pretty good, if you ignored the worn out patches in the linoleum. Daddy, a week ago last Thursday, painted the top half of the kitchen lemon-yellow enamel. Yesterday, Ma hung the new white curtains, with the bright orange ruffles, that she bought on sale at Woolworth's. They hung on all three windows and the back door. She gave the plaster plaque of The Last Supper that hung above the silver radiator a new coat of gold paint. She even took apart the six-foot-high stand-up fan in the corner and cleaned off last summer's grit. She wanted everything to look "spic n' span" for the party.

The table was covered with food. I could see de-skinned boiled wieners, anise cookies, tiny cream puffs, homemade bread and jellies, assorted Stella Doro cookies, and fresh ricotta cheese piled high in a white bowl. And pies, lemon cream pies, with mounds of white meringues waited for someone to cut into them. There was even a bowl of scrambled eggs with cow brains for Aunt [Stella]—her favorite food. Next to Aunt [Maggie], which I'm sure was her contribution, stood a jumbo jar of pickled pig's feet and pickled snouts. [Gloria] loved the snouts the best; they gave me the willies. The snouts still had tiny black hairs poking out through a clear gel. How could anybody eat jellied hair? Yuck!

Aside from the snouts, feet and brains, I couldn't wait to sit down for breakfast.

Once inside the bathroom, with the door closed behind me, I took short little breaths to get used to the outhouse smell. I pulled the brass chain on the bare bulb so I could see where I stepped, which was very important in our bathroom. The burst of light revealed the cause of the disgusting outhouse smell; Nonno's pee-soaked newspapers on the floor around the toilet bowl. I hated it, just as I hated his toilet habits. [Gloria] said that in her new house she would have white tiled bathroom floors that were always spotless, and each bathroom would have its own white porcelain sink. Nonno would never be allowed to use any of her many white bathrooms. She planned on three.

Being careful where I stepped, trying only to step on the tiny dry parts of the now yellow paper, I started to pull down my pants when I felt the wet seep through my sock. It was as if someone came in and poured water on the floor and the newspapers were there to sop it up. Water would have been fine, but, unfortunately, it wasn't water. It was pee. Nonno never seemed to pee in the toilet, always on the floor. Kind of like he aimed for the floor and occasionally a drop or two would actually make their way into the toilet bowl. And forget about sitting on the seat. Ma taught me how to squat over it whenever I saw drops, which was almost always. I hated squatting. I usually wiped the seat off with some toilet paper so I could sit. It was almost as bad as the diseased toilet seats of the world. I could hardly wait until [Gloria] and Louie built their house.

Just as I was about to perch myself over the toilet bowl, I heard a chair fall and Aunt [Stella] scream, "Respect, *puttana*, show some respect."

I quickly pulled up my pants and ran out of the bathroom just in time to see Aunt [Stella] rip [Gloria's] pajamas off her back, all the while yelling at [Gloria] for not saying good morning to Nonno.

"You show respect to Nonno. Say good morning to your grandfather! *Puttana! Puttana!*"

Aunt [Stella] went wild. She grabbed [Gloria's] long hair and pulled as hard as she could. Ma Grabbed Aunt [Stella's] arm, trying to get her off of [Gloria], but Aunt [Stella] was too strong. Nonno turned his chair around to watch. He was smiling and calmly taking sips of his coffee, like he was watching a movie. [Gloria] started swearing at Aunt [Stella].

"Take your hands off me, you bitch!" [Gloria] yelled.

Aunt [Maggie] jumped up and started pounding on [Gloria's] back for calling Aunt [Stella] a bitch. I didn't know what to do, so I started yelling for all of them to stop. Of course, no one listened.

Fights like this were nothing new to me. They happened almost every time Aunt [Stella] came to visit, but usually they were between Ma, Aunt [Maggie] and other relatives. This time the fighting and pounding concerned my sister. I was scared and mad.

"Get off of her, you bitch," I yelled.

I hoped that maybe they would get mad at me for swearing and leave [Gloria] alone. I kept one foot in the bathroom, thinking that if they came after me, I would lock myself in and [Gloria] could run away and it would be over. But no one paid any attention to me or my swearing.

[Gloria] kept fighting, letting out a wild punch or two while [Maggie] and [Stella] kept ripping at her clothes and pulling her hair. Ma yelled for [Gloria] to let go and run, but [Gloria] stood her ground. Then the back door opened and Daddy came in with Uncle [Ted]. Uncle [Ted] hadn't been sleeping after all. He had been out with Daddy.

Immediately, the two men tried to stop it. Unfortunately, Daddy got there first. Daddy was too small to take on [Ma's two sisters]. Aunt [Maggie] turned, and using all of her three hundred pounds, she slammed Daddy against the lemon-yellow wall with her elbow, calling him a "*Merda*." Something white shot out of his mouth when his face hit the wall, and blood splattered on our new white curtains with the orange ruffles. He stood there for a moment, stunned.

Uncle [Ted] stepped in and pulled Aunt [Stella] off of [Gloria]. Ma and [Gloria] stood up. [Gloria's] mouth and nose were bleeding. Her hair, soaked with sweat, stuck to her face. I was shaking, rolling back and forth, my arms wrapped around myself for support. Blood oozed from Daddy's mouth, and there, lying next to my foot, was his bloody front tooth. My stomach did a flip and I felt sick, but I managed to keep myself together. I didn't want to be another of Aunt [Stella's] victims.

[Gloria] ran back to our bedroom. I ran after her. This time we weren't laughing. I could hear Ma in the kitchen trying to get everyone to calm down, and all the while Nonno's Italian radio station played one annoying Italian song after another.

Summer, 1957
Trempealeau, Wisconsin
Bernie would spend his first summer after starting at the Seminary working, not on a farm, but alongside his Brother Joe for the Chicago and Northwestern Railroad. Of course, Bernie would not see one red cent of the money he would earn this summer or any of the subsequent summers that he worked while going to college and living at home in the summers. Both he and his brother Joe had been hired on as painters with a Bridge and Building crew whose job it was to scrape and paint a huge trestle bridge, Bridge # 618, located in the countryside near Bangor, Wisconsin.

"Wake up, Bernie," called Joe at 4:30 a.m.

"Boy, I'm still tired," groaned Bernie from his bed on the second floor back porch of the home their dad had bought at 307 N. Water Street in Sparta from Ronnie Johnson's dad. Bernie had mentioned to his dad that Ronnie had told him that his father wanted to sell it.

"Come on! Our ride's gonna be here, and we have to make our lunches."

That's how each morning began that summer. Both boys would then crowd into the back seat of the car that took them to the railroad station at Bangor.

On the way, they would stop at a sheep farm near West Salem where they picked up Spence, a sheep farmer. Spence chewed tobacco nonstop, and whenever he would say something that couldn't quite be understood by his coworkers, they would say, "Spit, Spence!"

At the station, after the foreman got the Lineup (train schedule) for the day, everyone would help hoist a six-man motorcar onto the tracks and climb on.

It should be pointed out that in more recent years those who work on the railroad usually refer to obtaining a "Form D," instead of using the older term, Lineup.

Most of the crew smoked, and Bernie and Joe had to learn to tolerate both the second hand smoke and the smell of gasoline along with the motorcar exhaust. When they arrived at Bridge #618, the crew would help hoist the motorcar onto the set-off at the side of the track and locate their brushes and paint buckets. No matter how hot it was, each painter was required to wear steel-toed work boots, long pants, long sleeved shirts, a hat and gloves. Some men, such as Spence, preferred to wear coveralls. The trade off for Spence was that he could keep cool by wearing no underwear.

By the end of their first day on the job, both Bernie's and Joe's clothes were covered with black paint. And it would only get worse as the weeks wore on. Their work clothes would get washed once a week, but the paint never came out. They just got stiffer and stiffer.

At first, Bernie was allowed to scrape and paint sections of the bridge that were on ground level. Eventually, however, he had to climb the long ladder that had been strapped to the end beam of the bridge and work on top, some forty feet above ground level. Up there, the two main beams on each side of the bridge were at least two feet wide. Bernie's first day up there, he got around by sliding on his butt. After a few days, his courage increased, and he was finally able to stand upright on the two-foot wide beams as he walked from one place to another to paint.

To get from one side of the bridge to the other, however, one had to cross beams that were only four inches wide. More butt scooting for Bernie—but not for long. A few days later saw him standing perfectly straight—"Keep your eyes on the beam and don't look down at the ground"—while walking across the bridge on the four-inch wide beams.

Whenever anyone would need more paint or would accidentally drop his brush, he would call for the ground foreman named Gus and lower a rope. Gus was a German immigrant whose work ethic insisted that all members of the crew be kept on task as much as possible. Gus would attach whatever was needed to the rope and send it back up to them. If rain happened to be blowing against one side of the bridge, Gus would simply have the crew work on the other side.

September, 1957
La Crosse, Wisconsin

Bernie's sophomore year at Holy Cross Seminary found him enrolled in Chemistry class, something he had successfully avoided during his high school years. Once again, the instructor was Farther Oswald Schulte, and Bernie did just fine.

On Saturday afternoons this fall, the college seminarians had decided to form touch football teams. Because he had beefed up working on a farm and maintained his condition by working on the railroad over the summer, Bernie was invited to be a blocker on one of the teams.

Unfortunately, the man—and he was an older student—Bernie was supposed to block had a square face, a rock-hard jaw and was, as the cliché goes, built like a brick outhouse.

WHAM!

Bernie didn't stand a chance. After the play was over, Square Face came over and offered him his hand.

"Sorry about that, just doing my job," he said with a smile that offered total friendship and no hostility.

Square Face really was a decent fellow. Like Al Brusda he came with military experience, but he was much more shy and remote.

The big surprise this year came while Bernie was attending one of the monthly films that were shown in the gymnasium to the entire student body—high school, college (freshmen and sophomores) and philosophy (juniors and seniors) seminarians. The high school students sat in the first rows, and the college students and philosophers sat in the rear.

"Look what's going on up there," whispered Bernie to the seminarian next to him.

"What are they doing?"

"It looks like the one high school boy is running his fingers through the hair on the back of the other boy's head," observed Bernie.

"Queer!" observed the other seminarian.

"Very!" agreed Bernie.

"Those two will definitely have to be weeded out of the priesthood," thought Bernie to himself.

This would also be the year of the Great Fire.

"Everybody up!" came the cry after Lights Out and the Grand Silence had started.

All the doors swung open and seminarians began sticking their heads out into the hall to see what was happening.

"There's a fire burning on the banks of the river near the seminary, and they want us all to help put it out."

So everyone quickly got dressed and ran down the stairwells to be issued shovels and rakes before heading for the riverbank.

This wasn't the only time the seminarians would be called on for a little manual labor. When there were particularly heavy winter snow falls, seminarians would be mobilized to shovel out the great circular drive that surrounded the seminary so trucks could deliver food and supplies.

October, 1957
South Chicago, Illinois

Rosina Petrassi was moved into the front bedroom of the 2nd floor flat in which Aunt Lucy lived. Because Lucy was perpetually short of money (whenever she did have a few extra dollars, she quickly spent them playing bingo which was her passion), she quickly became a little jealous when she saw that her father was being very generous with Rosina. She would have to take care of this by mentioning it to her sister Stella the next time she visited.

Stella would straighten Rosina out by yelling at her and telling her not to take advantage of their father's generosity.

Later, when Lucy complained to her father that Rosina was dating someone of whom she did not approve, Tony Nudi decided that he had had it with all the negative criticism of his little niece.

"*Lucia, state citta*! That's-a my *nipota*. If I want to give her money, that's-a my business. And if she wants to go out with a nice boy, that's-a her business."

"Pa," said Lucy as she began to set a plate of pasta down before her father, "so long as she's living with me, I'm going to make it my business!"

Before Lucy knew what was happening, her father grabbed her arm and sunk his teeth deep into the flesh, drawing blood."

"AHHHH! *MANAGIA!*" screamed Lucy.

"*Adesso, state citta*. Rosina is my business, and you just-a keep-a you nose out! *Capisce?*" said Tony as Lucy's blood dripped from his lips.

Lucy's daughter, Gloria Leo, would recall in later years that her mother bore the imprint of her grandfather's bite for the rest of her life.

After the author got reacquainted with his Cousin Rosina 50 years later, he learned that Nonno had not always been so supportive of her.

"Bear-nee" confided Rosina in her soft distinctive voice, "one time Nonno found out I was dating a boy he didn't like. He put a gun to the side of my head and said that if he ever saw me with that boy again, he would kill me!"

Rosina eventually did marry a young man named Steve Kwintera, with whom she had two sons, John and Tony. After this marriage ended in divorce, she married Dave Almendarez with whom she had two daughters, Irene and Gloria (named after the cousin with whom she lived for a while in South Chicago), and a son named David.

Thanksgiving Day, 1957
Sparta, Wisconsin

Ted still enjoyed hunting after the family moved back to Wisconsin, but now, since both Bernie and Joe were usually involved with schoolwork during their vacations, he mostly hunted alone. For deer. Ted's weapons of choice were a WWI vintage M30 rifle and his .12-gauge shotgun that fired special shells equipped with balls rather than buckshot. If he was going to do something with his boys, it would have to be something less involved than buying deer hunting licenses for all three of them, equipping them with the required safety outfits and providing them with powerful deer rifles.

"How would you boys like to bowl a few games at Sparta Bowl?"

"Sure," said Bernie.

"Sounds like fun," said Joe.

"Stell, the boys and I are going to go bowling for a little while," announced Ted, testing the water.

"*Musa tu!*" came the quick reply. "Didn't you have enough of bowling when we lived in Cudahy."

"It will just be for a little while, Ma," said Bernie, quickly trying to diffuse a potentially ugly encounter.

"Your father was bowling while I was giving birth to your brother. Couldn't stay home with his wife. Had to be with his friends at the bowling alley!"

"*Ce la luna mezzo mare*," intoned Ted, also trying to keep the holiday from erupting into a squabble.

"O.K. Go. Go. Leave the Old Dope at home," said Stella, changing tactics.

"Why don't you come along, Ma?" suggested Joe.

"Go bowling with your father. I'll stay home and cook. The Old Dope knows her place."

Holidays at home were always so much fun!

January, 1958
La Crosse, Wisconsin

"Want to come skating with me?" Bernie asked his roommate for the year at the seminary.

"Nah, I'm going to the gym and play some basketball."

Every Saturday afternoon, all seminarians were expected to take a break from the books and get in some healthy exercise. Since Holy Cross Seminary had been built on the banks of the back waters of the Mississippi, Bernie had recently asked his folks to buy him a pair of ice skates that he was determined to learn how to use—even if he had to go skating by himself.

"This is awesome," said Bernie aloud as he skated over backwater ice that had frozen absolutely clear.

He could see everything at the bottom of the backwater on which he was skating. Of course, he had to be careful that he didn't hit a thin patch, but there were usually warning creaks and crackles as one of those areas was being approached.

Bernie wasn't totally opposed to playing basketball in the gym on a winter afternoon. It's just that he was so intense when he played that the other guys always seemed to get upset with him.

"I thought I was supposed to guard you," said Bernie when a classmate yelled at him.

"Yah, but you don't have to be right in my face. Give me some room to breathe at least."

It was better down at the river. It was quiet and sunny. And the ice was crystal clear.

Although all of the maintenance at Holy Cross Seminary was performed by an Order of Brothers who lived on the premises, the kitchen was staffed with ladies from the La Crosse community. Meals were served family style, with high school seminarians serving as servers for the college seminarians. During Lent, no talking was allowed during meals and different Philosophy Students (3rd and 4th year college seminarians) would read religious texts to the diners from a podium. The reader would get to eat afterwards.

"What are those things in the spaghetti?" asked Bernie at dinner one evening in January when talking was allowed at dinner.

"They're maggots," replied world-wise Al Brusda.

"Yuck!" said another seminarian who had also noticed them.

"They won't hurt you," said Al. "They're just protein. And besides, they've been cooked so any germs on them have been destroyed. We ate a lot worse than that when we were in the Service."

So that was that. There was no sending the spaghetti bowl back to the kitchen. Bernie would just have to ignore what was in the bowl and eat his dinner.

There was, however, one time when Bernie dared to go to the kitchen door and make a special request of the lady cooks.

"I've got a sore throat," Bernie said, barely able to speak.

"You sure do," said the lady who had come to the door.

"Could you fix me a glass of warm milk with honey in it?"

"Warm milk with honey?" questioned the lady.

"Yes," rasped Bernie, "my mom used to fix that for us at home when we got a sore throat."

"Do we have any honey?" yelled the lady into the kitchen.

"I think so. What do you need it for?" asked another of the cooks.

"One of the students wants us to put it in warm milk for him for his sore throat!"

Bernie really hadn't wanted the whole kitchen staff to be in on his request, but, hey, if that's what it took to get a little down-home comfort, he was willing to put up with the embarrassment. There was an infirmary in the seminary, but it was sort of understood that it was only for "baby" high school seminarians. Bernie knew of no college seminarian who even knew where the infirmary was located in the building.

Summer, 1958
Trempealeau, Wisconsin

This summer Ted only had to find work for one of his boys on the Chicago and Northwestern Railroad. His son Joe had decided to spend the summer in school.

Bernie was once again employed on a Bridge and Building Crew, this time as a Carpenter's Helper. Their job would be to replace a wooden bridge in the swampland near Trempealeau.

This summer, the crew lived in a camp car that was located near the work site to save valuable travel time at the beginning and end of each day. They still needed to get a Lineup each morning so they would know what time to expect train traffic and ride the motorcar to the worksite, but the travel time was considerably lessened.

"Don't touch that tie," ordered the foreman when they had set the motorcar off on its landing.

"Why not?" asked Bernie.

"Because there will probably be a water moccasin or a rattlesnake under it," replied the foreman. "They crawl under there at night because it's warm."

The foreman then got a steel bar and carefully turned the tie over. No snake. But they were around. The swamp was full of interesting creatures, both large—giant swamp birds that could poop 8-foot long and 6-inch wide streams of excrement down the center of the track bed as they flew over—and small, such as the ever-present pesky mosquitoes.

One of the first things the crew had to do was to unload and spread a load of gravel on the side of the track bed in preparation for the bridge work. Once the gravel had been dumped from a railroad car, the crew was sent down on the embankment with long handled shovels to begin spreading and leveling the gravel.

"Slow down, Barcio!" came the quick command from an older worker.

"What's wrong?" asked Bernie.

"Don't work so fast!"

"Why not? I've got a lot of energy," boasted Bernie.

"Because you'll make us look bad," chimed in another older worker.

"Save your energy, and learn to pace yourself. It's gonna be a long day," added a third older worker.

Bernie was slowly learning the work ethic needed to survive among men who endured the hard work year round to support their families.

There were a lot of things to be learned from these men who made their living working with their hands and their backs.

"Don't lay your bar down on the ground like that," said Big Ben.

"What should I do with it?" asked Bernie.

"Pick it up and push the pointed end into the gravel so it stands up," said Big Ben.

"What's the difference?"

"If you leave it flat on the ground, it will get too hot in the sunshine, and you won't be able to handle it," said Big Ben, speaking from years of experience.

Big Ben would soon become the foreman of this Bridge and Building Crew.

When the Pile Driver finally arrived, and the huge piles were dumped off the flat cars down the embankment on the side of the track, the crew was ready to begin building the bridge.

"Tomorrow, the Superintendent is going to come out and look over the job," announced the foreman. "I want everyone to be busy while he's here. So think about what you are going to be doing, and as soon as we see them coming, everybody start doing it."

"What should I be doing?" asked Bernie.

"You take the extension cord and start rolling it up, nice and slow. Make the job last until they're gone."

The next day, work went as usual until the call was heard.

"Here come the Big Shots With the Little Hats," called out Big Ben.

And he was right. The Superintendent and his assistants were all dressed in suits and ties and wore dress hats with very narrow brims—the style at the time.

"O.K., everybody," said the foreman in a low voice, "look busy."

As instructed, Bernie got busy rolling up the extension cord at the suggested pace.

Once that ordeal was over, work could proceed in a normal fashion on the bridge. Pilings were pulled up onto the track bed by the crane and loaded into the pile driver. The pile driver would then move into position and lower the pile into the water to seat it solidly before the hammering would start.

"O.K., Bernie, take this bar and this chalk," said the foreman. "Climb down on that timber next to the pile that's being driven in. Keep making marks on the pile, and let me know when it's moving less than an inch each time it's hit by the pile driver."

"Does that mean it's almost done?" asked Bernie.

"Yup. And be careful," said the foreman.

So Bernie spent his day standing down on the timbers with his bar and his chalk. As one pile was finished, he would move forward to the next one while the one behind him was cut off to its proper length.

When they cut the top off a piling, they would wrap a chain around it that was attached to a crane. Then a worker would step down on a timber and chain saw the top of the piling off. When the top was cut loose, it would swing free on the chain and be set up on the bank by the crane operator.

"LOOK OUT!" shouted the foreman, but it was too late.

The top of the pile that had just been cut off behind him was swinging free on its chain. It swung forward and smashed into Bernie's butt as he stood marking the pile.

SPLASH!

Before he knew what had happened, Bernie had been knocked off of the bridge and into the water, bar and all. He quickly bobbed to the surface and swam over to the shore.

"Where's your bar?" asked the foreman.

"I guess it sank to the bottom," said Bernie, whose dignity had been hurt more than his body.

"O.K., you go sit down over there and dry out for a while," said the foreman.

Another young college boy on the crew volunteered to dive down to the bottom of the river and retrieve the bar.

Later that summer, when the camp cook took his two-week vacation, the foreman was more than anxious to make Bernie the replacement cook and keep him out of harm's way.

After days spent getting up early and fixing bacon, eggs and toast for the crew and then laying out sandwich makings so they could prepare their own sandwiches, Bernie would then do kitchen clean up. Later, he would walk into town and shop for the makings for dinner and spend his day preparing that night's meal. After the dinner clean up was completed, Bernie would change into nice clothes and head off "to see the Boss." This was his euphemism for walking over to St. Bartholomew Catholic Church for some evening prayer time. After all, he was a seminarian. The crew, of course, all assumed that he was secretly paying a visit to some sweet young thing on the side.

One evening, as Bernie was on his way to church, he was attracted by piano playing and singing. He was amazed to see a father playing the piano in his home surrounded by his wife and children, all singing together.

"How neat!" Bernie thought. "It must be nice to be married and have a family to be happy with."

Of course, this little thought had to be suppressed if Bernie was going to be true to his new vocation.

September, 1958
La Crosse, Wisconsin

It had taken some doing, but Bernie had finally gotten his mom to locate a seamstress in Sparta that could custom sew the two cassocks he would need to wear for the next two years as a philosophy student at Holy Cross Seminary.

Once he had his cassocks and his biretta, he was ready to fit in with all the others.

By now, Bernie was becoming quite adept at reading both Latin and Greek. Since a portion of each day was set aside for reading the Bible in chapel, Bernie first read the New Testament through in Latin and then in Greek, which, to his mind, was much more clear and to the point.

This was also the year when Bernie was assigned to serve as Sacristan of the Crypt Chapel. He was responsible for making sure all the altars were ready for the many Masses that were celebrated simultaneously down there each morning and that at least one seminarian was scheduled to serve as an altar boy for each priest celebrating Mass.

Although classes were held on Saturday mornings, seminarians were always given free time on Saturday afternoons for recreation.

"Hey, Bernie, how would you like to run in the one-mile race we're going to have this afternoon?" asked the upper classman who had been put in charge of organizing some formal athletic events that day.

"Sure, I guess so. I've been trying to run the mile every week on my own, so I should be able to handle a race."

As it turned out there were only three other competitors entered.

BANG!

The starter pistol went off, and all four competitors set off with a pace that would be able to be maintained for most of the race. Bernie stayed together with the pack the first three times around the quarter mile track.

"O.K., guys. Pour it on!" came a shout of encouragement from the onlookers.

"Go for it!"

"Burn up the track!"

"Go, Bernie. You can do it," shouted Bernie's roommate.

Bernie kicked it up a notch and stuck with the pack. About half way around the final lap, two other competitors burst into the lead, leaving Bernie and one other runner a little behind. Bernie was a few paces behind his nearest competitor and resolved not to drop back any further even though his side was killing him and his legs were going numb. With pure determination, he managed to maintain his position through the end of the race.

Bernie was, however, about to learn a lesson that might come in handy later on during his life.

"You know," said the runner who had come in 3rd just a few yards ahead of Bernie, "I was really hurting out there."

"Yeah, me too," said Bernie.

"In fact," admitted the 3rd place finisher, "I had pretty much made up my mind that if you caught up with me, I was going to drop out!"

"Oh, man," thought Bernie to himself. "All I would have had to do to beat him is just give one more little burst of speed. I could have done that."

But who knew?

On his Sunday afternoons this year, while other, more adventurous seminarians, managed to sneak into town to go to the movies or partake in otherwise illicit entertainment, Bernie volunteered to walk over to a nearby orphanage and take one of the children for a walk or otherwise entertain his charge for an hour or so.

On days when he wasn't scheduled to report to the orphanage, he loved to spend his free time searching for agates in a nearby quarry. By the end of his seminary years, he had amassed a beautiful collection of fine stones.

This collection was eventually added to a bowl of agates that belonged to Bernie's wife, Lillian. The bowl still remains on display in the author's living room.

June, 1959
Sparta, Wisconsin

This time Bernie's dad was not able to get him hired on a Bridge and Building Crew for the summer. The Chicago and Northwestern Railroad had no openings for temporary summer help. His dad did, however, know the engineer who was in charge of the Sparta Sanitation Department. He was looking to hire someone to cut the weeds along the banks of Beaver Creek that flowed right through the center of Sparta's business district and surrounding neighborhoods.

"Here," said the sanitation engineer, "let me show you how to hold the sickle."

It was one of those big sickles like Father Time carries. Bernie would have to learn how to wield it while balancing himself on the slippery banks of the creek.

"Now," continued the sanitation engineer, "your blade will get dull quickly, so you'll have to stop every so often and sharpen it with this whetstone."

Unfortunately for Bernie, Sparta did not have a gasoline powered weed cutter for him to use. No matter, after a few days on the job, he had quickly gotten the hang of it. The biggest challenge was not to get caught cutting down little trees that residents either had planted on the creek banks behind their houses or had spotted growing there and wanted to preserve.

One day while working along Beaver Creek, Bernie rushed home during his lunch hour rather than eating his sandwich while sitting on a rock as he usually did. He had just been stung on his right temple by a bee.

"Joe," said Bernie's mom, "take your brother over to Dr. Brown's office right away."

"Do you think a person can die by being stung in the temple?" asked Bernie.

"We'll see what the doctor says. Get in the car!" said Joe.

When they got to the doctor's office and explained to the nurse what had just happened, she showed Bernie and Joe into a waiting room.

"Hi, boys," said Dr. Brown when he entered. "What seems to be the problem?"

"My brother got stung in the temple by a bee," explained Joe.

"Hmmm. Let's have a look."

After a quick glance at Bernie's right temple, Dr. Brown sat down at his desk and pulled a medical book down off the shelf.

"Now," he said, "let's see what this says about bee stings."

"Great! A novice," thought Bernie. "He's got to look it up."

"Can a bee sting to the temple be fatal?" asked Bernie.

"Naw, I don't think so," said the doctor. "You're not allergic to bee stings, are you?"

"I don't think so."

"Then you should be O.K."

After swabbing the area with some alcohol and being sure that the stinger was not still imbedded, Dr. Brown gave Bernie a little tube of antiseptic medicine and told him to apply it to the area every so often.

Bernie was going to live!

In a couple of weeks, Bernie finished mowing both banks of Beaver Creek that ran through Sparta and was again about to be unemployed.

At first, Joe had been hired to work at the Sparta lumberyard that summer, and later was hired on as a section hand by the foreman of the Milwaukee Road that also ran through Sparta.

Luckily, Bernie noticed that the State Highway Department was hiring men to paint a bridge on Highway 16 just west of Sparta. With his railroad experience, he was quickly hired on.

On this job, there was a sandblasting crew that worked ahead of the painters. This was a specially subcontracted crew that came out of Milwaukee for the job. These guys were a pretty tough bunch who kept mostly to themselves and didn't interact much with the paint crew. Occasionally one or two of them would get into fights at a bar just west of Sparta, and the job foreman would have to bail them out in the morning. The police had little choice but to cooperate since the City of Sparta desperately wanted to have its bridge painted by the end of summer.

The paint crew would first put on a coat of Red Lead, a rust-resistant undercoating, on the entire bridge and then follow this up with a coat of silver finish paint.

The first day on the job, Bernie had no trouble climbing down onto the girders under the bridge and dropping down onto a scaffold suspended under the girders. After he and his coworker completed that section of the bridge, they needed to swing up and climb back onto the girders so the scaffolding could be moved.

"What's the matter, Bernie? Can't you do it?" asked the foreman who was watching.

"Nope. I just can't get the hang of it," answered Bernie.

"Go back down, and show him how to do it," said the foreman to Bernie's coworker who had already swung himself up.

So the coworker went back down on the scaffolding and explained how Bernie should swing himself up. He even tried to give Bernie a push to help him up. Bernie, however, just didn't have his stomach muscles in shape yet.

"O.K.," said the foreman, "you'll have to slide down a rope and climb back up from the abutment."

How embarrassing! All the other workers stopped what they were doing to watch the new guy shinny down the rope to the ground. Bernie resolved not to be embarrassed again, and by the next day he had figured out how to swing his legs up on the beam above him and pull himself back up off the scaffold.

Just when he had grown accustomed to working under the bridge, he and his coworker were taken up on top. A special ladder had been made that had two large hooks attached to its top end.

"Now, you see, we hang the ladder over the top of the rail, and you just climb over and go down the rungs until you can paint the section that's down there," said the foreman.

One person on this team would paint portions that could be reached while kneeling on the surface of the bridge while his partner would take his turn hanging off the side of the bridge on the ladder.

As usual, Bernie's work clothes were soon stiff with paint. When he noticed that his partner's clothes always looked fresh after each weekend, he asked him what his secret was.

"My dad soaks my clothes in a tub of diesel fuel overnight and all the paint comes out of them. Then we just wash them and they get pretty clean."

Unfortunately, Bernie had no access to diesel fuel so his work clothes just kept getting stiffer and stiffer as the summer wore on.

This was also the summer that Bernie would learn how little secret deals could be arranged with job foremen. Another painter decided that he needed to make some extra money. Bernie had no idea such deals could be made, and was surprised one Saturday when he visited the bridge to see a man out there working on his own.

"How come you're working today?" asked Bernie.

"I asked the foreman if I could work overtime to earn some extra money," replied the other painter.

"I didn't know we could do that," said Bernie.

"You can't," replied the other worker. "This is a special deal that he worked out for me."

August, 1959
Chicago Heights, Illinois

Angeline and Henry Santostefano's son, Junior, had turned 21, and, like almost all of his sisters, he was ready to get married. His sisters Rose and Jeanie had also gotten married when they were 21. Only his younger sister, Francis, would break the pattern and get married younger.

Bernie and Junior ("Hank" as he calls himself later in life) were just about the same age. They had both been born in 1938. Junior had asked if Bernie could come to Chicago Heights a few days early so that he could help paint the apartment they had rented. Of course, Bernie's folks agreed, always ready to help out a relative.

Since Bernie also had a reputation of being a fairly good artist, Junior's dad, whom Bernie called *Tsitsi*, also had a little project for him. *Tsitsi* (Uncle Henry) was earning the extra money it took to afford to live in Chicago Heights by running a lawn care service. He had a truck that he used, and he needed Bernie to hand letter his truck doors for him: SANTOSTEFANO'S LAWN SERVICE. Under this he was to put his uncle's phone number.

The actual day of the wedding turned out to be very warm. Of course, everyone had to get dressed early in the morning to be sure that all the tuxedos, shirts and shoes fit. By midday, the shirts of all the boys were soaking wet with perspiration.

"Take your shirt to Aunt Yolanda, Bern," said Junior.

"What will she do with it?"

"She's ironing everyone's shirts so they look fresh during the ceremony."

And sure enough, there was Aunt Yolanda, herself sweating as she dutifully stood at the ironing board pressing the boys' shirts as they brought them to her.

When Bernie was younger and living in Norfolk, Aunt Yolanda came to visit for a few days. One evening, after a large meal, she felt that she needed to work off some of the calories so she challenged Bernie to a foot race the length of his driveway. She beat him!

As Bernie watched his aunt sweating over the ironing board, he thought, "I bet I could beat her in a race today if she wanted to take me on!" After all, Bernie had beefed up quite a bit over the course of his various summer jobs. Aunt Yolanda, however, was in no mood to race. It was way too hot!

September 5, 1959
Sparta, Wisconsin

"Joe, wake up! They're here," said Bernie.

It was 2:00 a.m. Saturday morning and, as his Uncle Charlie had said in a private phone call the day before, people were beginning to arrive having driven up to Sparta to celebrate the 25th Wedding Anniversary of Ted and Stella.

Ted and Stella had been married on Sunday, September 2, in 1934, but in 1959, September 2 fell on a Wednesday so the surprise party was scheduled for the following Saturday.

"O.K." said Joe, "What should we do?"

"Let's get the shot guns from the cabinet and go down like someone was breaking into the house," suggested Bernie.

As Bernie and Joe reached the bottom of the stairs and entered the living room with shotguns poised, their Uncle Charlie and Aunt Martha were just entering the front door of the house.

"What's going on down here," shouted Bernie, shotgun raised.

After a moment of shock and a look of disbelief on Charlie's face, everyone broke into laughter as the rest of the guests filed in.

Before too long, Louie Marternaro had his mandolin out of its case and Joe Crapito's son, Joe, had his accordion strapped to his shoulders.

Stella's sisters Maggie and Lucy entered, followed by Lucy's younger daughter Mary. Ted's mom and dad entered along with his brother Gene and his wife Mary and their son, Dave. Gusty and his wife, Rose, came in followed by Rudy and his wife Helen. Ted's sister Angeline came in with her husband Henry. They were followed by Ted's other sister Esther and her two children, Henry and Eileen (who continually stuck her tongue out whenever the 8 mm. camera recording the event was pointed in her direction). Stella's father, Tony Nudi, made his way into the living room followed by Ted's sister Yolanda with her pharmacist husband, Louis.

Food and drink came out of nowhere, and the party began.

Soon, as the initial fun of surprising Ted and Stella in the house wore off, Charlie and a few others spilled out into the back yard.

"Hey," came the shout from the second floor window of a neighbor's house, "People sleeping up here!"

"People talking down here," replied Charlie refusing to be intimidated.

It had been years since one of these middle-of-the-night road parties had been organized, but the group definitely had not lost its knack. No one was tired even though they had just spent hours driving to Sparta from Chicago and Milwaukee.

Mid morning, Ted and Stella stepped into their bedroom and got dressed up in their best outfits for the occasion. After gifts and cards were presented, Stella brought out her wedding gown along with the bow tie that Ted wore on their wedding day. She also still had the little pillow that had been used by their ring bearer, Rudy Aloia.

The endurance of the group proved to be absolutely incredible. Meals were served, wine flowed, music filled the morning and afternoon air, and the party didn't begin to break up until late the following afternoon.

It was truly an incredible event that showed the strong family bonds that Ted and Stella still maintained with their families at the time. Eventually, this would change for a variety of reasons, but for the moment it definitely was an astounding experience not to be easily forgotten.

September 15, 1959
La Crosse, Wisconsin

Bernie was now a senior at Holy Cross Seminary. He had been promoted to Head Sacristan of the main chapel. He felt for sure that the Bishop of the La Crosse Diocese, Bishop John P. Treacy, had his eye on him for special opportunities.

Bernie's grades continued to be good, despite the fact that he was now enrolled in a very demanding schedule of classes. In addition to his Education Class that he found fascinating (he was beginning to think that maybe he would enjoy teaching), he took two classes of Ethics each day, and two classes of Metaphysics in which the instructor lectured completely in Latin. Notes and tests in this class were also taken in Latin.

Bernie's voice continued to be improved in his weekly class on Gregorian Chant, and, on occasion, he could make the main chapel resound with his voice when he was chosen to serve as Cantor.

Bernie's History class, however, was different. The seminarians affectionately, albeit secretly, labeled the instructor "Father Tsetse" because, like a tsetse fly, he could put them all asleep in a minute.

"Here are the class textbooks," Father Tsetse had announced on the first day of class.

"They are the texts that are used by the United States Army in their classes and they are what we will be using. I intend to read the chapters to you aloud each day in class. I will appreciate it if you do not interrupt me with unnecessary questions. You may read along, take notes, or simply listen."

Well, that went over for about a month or so. Finally a couple of the philosophy students in the back row could stand it no more.

BLAM! BLAM!

The room filled with the stench of exploding cherry bombs, and Father Tsetse jumped at least two feet out of his seat.

That sort of ended class for the day.

The culprits were properly reprimanded by Monsignor John Paul, but they were not expelled. Too much time, energy and expense had been put into their education.

On Sunday afternoons during his senior year at the seminary, Bernie began to join a small group of friends who enjoyed hiking up the various coulees that overlooked the campus. On one particular Sunday afternoon, Bernie stopped along the way and bought a small watermelon that he thought they could share when they all got to the top. It sounded like a good idea until Bernie realized that he would have to carry it the whole way by himself.

Bernie's big disappointment came in the spring. This was the time that the Bishop annually announced the seminarian that he had specially chosen to be sent to study Theology in Rome. Bernie had thought his chances of being selected were pretty good. His grades were good. He was the Head Sacristan, and he was Italian.

"I've got some sad news," announced Bernie in the car the next Sunday when his folks came to visit.

"What's up?" asked his dad.

"I'm going to drop out of the seminary," said Bernie with a tear in his eye.

"Why?" asked his mother.

"I just don't think I want to go on to Theology."

"What would you like to do instead?" asked his dad.

"I think I would like to go to the University of Michigan and study to become a Latin teacher."

And that pretty much settled it. Bernie had talked it over with his Spiritual Advisor beforehand, and they had both agreed that this would be the best thing for him to do. Besides, Bernie really thought that he was more cut out to be a family man than a priest.

October, 1959
Prairie du Chien, Wisconsin

Joe Barcio had accepted a teaching position at Prairie du Chien High School on the western border of Wisconsin. He taught several classes, including Freshman English. In addition to his teaching, Joe became interested in learning about the Historical Swift Hospital in Prairie du Chien. It was one of the U.S. Army Hospitals operating in Wisconsin during the Civil War, and it became famous for the discoveries its doctors were making while working on soldiers with head wounds that exposed their brains. These doctors pioneered research into how different portions of the brain control different body movements and functions.

Joe also became interested in a young girl who lived with her family on a nearby farm, but that relationship was doomed to fail because of his mother's serious objections—primarily because the young lady was not of Italian descent, which she had decided was a *sine quo non* for the wife of her first born.

Jack Hacker, I.P.D. Motorcycle Drill Team, 1960

Lillian Hacker, Shortridge H.S. graduate
Indianapolis, June 6, 1949

Grave marker installed by Rudy Strano
for his half-brother in
St. Mary's Cemetery in Chicago

49 Ford in which the author learned to drive in 1954 in Norfolk

Author's high school in Sparta, WI, now used as administration offices

South Water St., Sparta, WI, late 1950's

Handmade plywood Christmas decoration used in Sparta, 1956

The Barcio rental home, 310 Pine St., Sparta, 1956

Author with his 1956 Senior Prom date, Freshman Clarabeth Fanning, Sparta, WI

Stella Barcio, Rosina Petrassi, Bernie Barcio

(R—L): Dave and Rosina (Petrassi) Almendarez,
Rosina's son John Kwintera and wife Tammy, Portage, IN, 2013

Author's SmartCar, Auggie Terpstra's farm outside of Sparta, WI, 2011

Author with Mrs. Terpstra at the Morrow Home in Sparta, 2011

Author with Auggie Terprstra's son who now owns the farm, 2011

College Freshman Class, Holy Cross Seminary 1956

Front Row: James Lesczynski (center), later Pastor of St. Patrick's Church in Mauston, WI, Albert Brusda (3rd from R), Francis Nguyen-Son Mein (far R). **Middle Row:** Author (far R)

Holy Cross Seminary, La Crosse, WI, 1958

Holy Cross Seminary Gym entrance, La Crosse, WI, 2011

Author as a Seminarian, with Rose Miresso and Brother Joe

Author with cousins Gloria and Mary Leo, 2007

Joe Barcio, C & NW RR Motor Car
Trempealeau, WI, 1957

Author (R) painting WIS 16
bridge Sparta, WI, 1959

C & NW Trempealeau Bridge paint crew, 1957
Spence (L), Joe Barcio (2nd from L), Big Ben (3rd from R)

Joe Barcio Teaching Freshman English
Prairie du Chien H.S., WI, 1959-1960

Ted Barcio (L) and his brother Eugene during the happy 1950's

307 N. Water St., Sparta, WI, 1975   307 N. Water St., Sparta, WI, 2011

307 N. Water St., Sparta, WI, 1988

Antonio Nudi (L) returns to Italy on board the Constantinople, 1952

PART V

September 1960 – June 1964

Searching for Meaning in Michigan

September, 1960
Ann Arbor, Michigan

Despite the fact that Bernie had been an excellent student at Holy Cross Seminary and had studied four years of college level Latin as well as one year of Classical Greek, the Classics Department of the University of Michigan would not admit him into their Masters Degree program until he had proven himself for one semester.

"I think it's just a way to get extra money out of students," observed Bernie.

And it did seem so. Students who had already spent considerable tuition money getting their undergraduate degrees at U. of M. were readily accepted into the program. Those coming from out of state would have to pay the piper.

But Bernie cooperated and resolved to get straight A's in all the courses they asked him to take during his trial semester. And he did. Since he was on a very tight budget and received no financial aid during his trial semester, he learned to live on Tang mixed with cool faucet water and instant coffee mixed with lukewarm faucet water. A loaf of sliced bread could be made to last a week and used to make sandwiches with cheese slices that could be kept "refrigerated" by being left on the cool window sill.

The next semester he applied for and obtained a Fanny Burr Butler Fellowship that would pay for his courses and textbooks as well as provide a $100 a month living allowance during the next four semesters he would be on campus.

Bernie devoted himself totally to his class work. His only social life during his first year would be attending Mass at the campus Newman Center.

Now when someone spends this much time narrowly focused and keeping to themselves, they tend to become a little self-absorbed.

It was during this time that Bernie began to record his deepest thoughts and observations.

> "An educated, alert man will never really be caught off guard or really surprised by anything because he will have learned to recognize the signs which precede every event. If he cannot predict it exactly, he at least knows that he should be expecting something at this point."

"Rumors are like flatteries. We always enjoy hearing them, and although they're usually not true, we tend to believe them."

"At a certain point in their development, youngsters relax their ideals when they discover that others aren't really perfect after all."

"An income tax form is a Declaration of Dependents."

"A state hospital is for mental patience."

"Crazy people are locked up because the people who think themselves sane happen to outnumber them."

"School: a place where disinterested people go to be taught what interested people learn on their own."

"Casual relationship: She tells you she feels fine.
Intimate relationship: You tell her she feels fine."

"It is really quite amusing to see man darting everywhere, propelling himself on little four-wheeled platforms and paying silent homage to the muffled explosions of gasoline."

"It is really a let down to find yourself in an environment where all your carefully acquired prestige traits count for nothing."

"I don't enjoy technical talks:
If the topic concerns something I'm not familiar with, I feel left out.
If it concerns something I learned in the past, I feel guilty for having
	forgotten so much of the material.
If it concerns something I have just brushed up on, I feel I could be
	up front giving the talk in a much more interesting manner."

"It is healthy to be dissatisfied. This means we will try to improve. But when we get discouraged, this only leads to despair."

"Considering that I spent more than 23 years preparing for it, I think the day could have gone a little better than it did."

At Holy Cross Seminary, Bernie had majored in Philosophy, and, on occasion, believed he could come up with some fairly deep philosophical concepts.

> "Philosophy seems to be a frontier discipline which invades previously unexplained fields of knowledge. As these fields are explored, and respective disciplines arise, philosophy moves on."

"Life must be an art. The basic rules can be learned in a comparatively short time, but putting them into practice is where the art comes in."

"Perhaps it would be good not to tell others how to live. One could describe to them how most of the people in a given community live and then warn them that although the majority will tolerate certain deviations from the general pattern, they will revolt against an individual who refuses to conform in certain modes of action which the majority consider essential—thus the majority have designated officers to handle these extreme non-conformists. It pays, therefore, to observe others and carefully note in which modes of action it is both wise and prudent to deviate from the standard procedures. It view of this, it might be well for councilors to make it clear that they are only 'describing,' and that it is necessary for the individual to 'prescribe' for himself—that's where the art of living comes in."

"Memory is limited to spontaneous recall; thus, to say that we try to remember is a contradiction. We can't exert control over a spontaneous process. All we can do is allow the memory time for the spontaneous recollection. If the memory cannot spontaneously recall something, this thing is forgotten and we cannot remember what is forgotten. Thus it is a contradiction to say we are trying to remember what we have forgotten because to say something is forgotten is to say it is beyond the control of memory. When something is forgotten, we can place it in our minds in two ways: 1) by renewing the original experience, or 2) by simply waiting around for the fact to be spontaneously recalled."

"It seems that one of our most basic drives is to bring to completion that which we start to do. It is in this completion that we find most satisfaction. Thus the more we organize and plan our daily lives and stick to our plan, the more pleasure we derive from having completed what we set out to do. We can satisfy this drive by doing such simple things as planning to walk down a certain side of the street and then doing it. Since some of our plans may be rather large scale ones, we may be deprived of this sense of completion for quite a while— hence, to tide us over, we do such things as smoke a cigarette which is a very deliberate and skilled activity that we can easily execute and by doing so reconfirm our confidence in ourselves."

Before long, Bernie tired of recording his deep thoughts in prose and decided to phrase his observations in poetic form.

"Not to know a specific fact is pardonable.
Not to know where to look it up is ignorance.
Not to look it up when you need to know is laziness."

"Tavern Week is here to stay;
It's overshadowed Mother's Day.
Mother's Day has sprung a leak;
It's Waterloo was Tavern Week."

"I wish I were a non-me
for just a day or two.
I would enjoy meeting me
as though I were a you.
Knowing what I do
about myself right now,
I think I'd be absorbing
to meet if I were thou.
But then perhaps I'm selfish
and egotistic, too.
If I were altruistic,
I would enjoy you."

"Why are you and why are they
And why are others here?
Why couldn't I be here alone
And not have others near.
This may at first seem rather harsh
To question object fact,
And yet another is to blame
For me my brain to rack.
He asked me not too long ago,
Just why are others here,
But at the time, my thought was slow
I couldn't think for fear.
Yet since that day, I've pondered deep
And tried to solve the quiz,
But all I do is look at him
And simply say, 'He is.'
'Others are,' I conjured up
And finished out the line,
'Non nobis est rogare cur.'
I let it rest a time.
But now it's moved me once again

To give it further thought.
I see how much depends, in fact,
Upon the answer sought.
And still, I fear, I'm at a loss,
And once more must demure.
"Allii sunt," is all I'll say,
Non nobis est rogare cur."

As things got rougher in his course work, and Bernie's mood began to change, his darker thoughts also found their way into his prose and poetry.

"High school differs from grade school in that there is no recess.
College differs from high school in that there is no let up.
Grad school differs from college in that there is no way out!"

"You aggravate me:
When you're up, I'm down;
When I'm up,
You're not around."

*"Ego sum tristiculus,
Tristis sum, tristis sum.
Ego sum tristificus,
Tristis sum, tristis sum.
Ego sum tristitia,
Tristis sum, tristis sum.
Tristiculus, tristificus, tristitia—
Tristis, tristis sum."*

"When things are far from going well,
The best key word is C.C.L.
Whenever I get in a mess,
I tell myself I couldn't care less."

"Veiny, hairy, stiff and dry,
the day will come when he will die."

"My landlord has a guinea pig
Up on his T.V. set,
And when I go to pay my rent,
The guinea pig I pet.
Although it has such stiff straight hair
And such a beady eye,
It is his daughter's pet, you see,
It's her *deliciae*.
Too bad it had to die."

"Roses are redolent
Violets too,
But they'll never smell
As much as you do."

"Double dead is really dead,
And Latin, I repeat,
Did die at first among the herd
And then among elite."

"Sweet attempts to revive Latin,
strange as this may seem,
but all he does is prop the corpse
and make its outside gleam."

"It's gotten so I hate to study.
The whole damn day has gotten rutty.
No longer do I schedulize,
All I do is daydreamize."

When Bernie realized, way after the fact, that his landlady had fallen down on the ice while taking the trash out after dinner one evening, hit her head, and froze to death before she was discovered by anyone, he finally decided he had to become a little more involved in the real world. Thus he joined the choir at the Newman Center to lend a little variety to his life and maybe raise his spirits. As it turned out, however, he still had a ways to go.

"After practice Wednesday night
When we've all sung a tune,
The host will serve some Sherry wine,
And then we all commune.

As for myself, I look intent
And try to enter in
Just hoping there's some gain in store
As they begin to spin.

Culture is the topic now
And soon we're in Detroit,
And then administration comes
And now our local plight.

I always think I learn a lot—
I'm not quite sure just what—
Perhaps I really profit most
From watching others strut."

Finally, Bernie realized that he was spending way, way too much time by himself and decided to get a part time job across the street at the Omega Café run by a Greek man and his wife. His wife was as cute as a bug, but it turned out to be a real turn-off for Bernie when he came across her absolutely putrid, stinky socks on a shelf in the back room one day.

The job paid no money, but the Greek owner provided all of Bernie's meals free of charge in exchange for his working in the kitchen three hours each evening washing dishes, peeling potatoes and making pizzas.

"Hey, Bernie," said the Greek owner one day, "you should stop in and meet my brother some time."

"Where is he?" asked Bernie.

"He runs the Alpha Café on the other side of campus," said the Greek owner.

So, one day, when Bernie happened to be on the other side of campus, he stopped in at the Alpha Café.

"Hi, I'm Bernie, and your brother said I should stop in and meet you."

"Oh, yes, Hi. Come on into the back room so we can talk," said the Greek owner's brother.

The back room of this café turned out to be as messy and disorganized as the back room where Bernie worked. Being naturally interested in Greece since he was a Classics major, Bernie was having a nice talk with the Greek owner's brother until…

"Bernie, come back here. I want to show you something," said the Greek owner's brother.

"What do you have back there?" asked Bernie innocently.

The Greek owner's brother opened a door to reveal a lavishly decorated small room with a bed.

"Bernie, if you ever have a girl, and you need some place to come, this room will always be available for you. No charge!" said the Greek owner's brother.

Bernie was totally disgusted, but remained polite.

"Well, that's certainly interesting. I guess I'll keep it in mind. Nice meeting you, but I do have to go now," said Bernie as he graciously made his exit.

Having spent four years in a seminary, Bernie was in no way ready to start taking girls into the backroom of the Alpha Café. In fact, the most progress he had made with girls up to that point was briefly holding hands with a short, chubby, very aggressive girl who had taken the initiative during a Newman Club outing.

Bernie went to school full time in Ann Arbor. After the regular school year was over, he enrolled in summer school so that he could complete his Master's Degree in Classical Studies (major in Latin, minor in Greek) and also obtain his license to teach both Latin and English at the secondary school level. Helping him to do this was his appointment as an American Council of Learned Societies Scholar.

When he graduated in 1962 along with thousands of other students in the Ann Arbor stadium, his mom and dad were present as was his Uncle Gene and Aunt Mary. From Chicago had come Bernie's grandfather, Tony Nudi, along with his Aunt Lucy, her daughter Mary, and one of his Aunt Maggie's children, Rosie. Unfortunately, Bernie had neglected to make reservations for his guests early enough at local hotels and they had to be put up in rooms that people rented in their homes during graduation week.

December, 1961
Sparta, Wisconsin
"Who was that, Ted?" asked Stella after her husband hung up the phone.
"That was Gene."
"What? Does he want you to send him something?"
Stella had picked up just enough of the conversation to have her curiosity piqued.
"Yes-ah. I told him I would send him $300."
"There you go again. All front and no back! Why do you have to send him $300?" demanded Stella.
"He has a chance to be appointed Postmaster and he needs to pay some special dues to get the position."
"What does he think? We have more money than we know what to do with?"
"*Lassa sta,* Stell. He's my brother, and if he wants me to help him out, I'm just glad I can."

Bernie had been listening from the living room as his parents had carried on their discussion with his dad standing in the hall where the wall phone hung and his mom sitting at the kitchen table, one of her favorite spots. He was glad that the discussion hadn't escalated into another out of control argument about his dad's family.

Bernie was especially glad they wouldn't be going to blows over his Uncle Gene whom he really liked. Despite his mom's objections, he had selected his Uncle Gene to be his confirmation godfather and had added the name Eugene to his own list of monikers.

During WWII, Eugene Barcio had served for four years in the Pacific as a member of the colorfully patched Flying C-Bees. It was in this service that he learned the carpenter trade. When he was discharged, he logically tried to find work as a carpenter in the St. Francis area. Since lumber was hard to get at that time, however, he applied at the post office and became a mail carrier, a position he would hold for the next ten years.

Following in his older brother's footsteps, Eugene also became very active in Cudahy social and service clubs and politics. Printing up special matchbook cover ads, he ran for a position on the Cudahy School Board and won. It was a position he would hold for six years until he would be promoted to Postmaster. Post office regulations did not allow Postmasters to hold another public office at the same time.

In 1956 Eugene was promoted to Assistant Postmaster in Oak Creek, Wisconsin.

He now had an opportunity, with this help from his brother, to apply for a Postmaster position. Unfortunately, by the time he received the money from his brother, the position was already filled. When he tried to send the money back, his brother told him to just keep it and use it for whatever.

Everyone should have such a brother!

Before too long, however, another opportunity arose, this time at the South Milwaukee post office. Eugene applied for the position, received it, and was able to spend the next ten years as Postmaster.

Carpentry, however, remained in Eugene's blood, and he always secretly longed to get back into the trade.

"Mary," explained Eugene one evening, "I think we can do a lot better if I get a crew together and go into house building. What do you think?"

"Well, if that's what you want to do. Do we have enough money saved up in case things go bad?" asked Mary.

"We're O.K."

So, Eugene found four men who were willing to work for him part time and went into the house building business.

Before he would finally retire, he would have approximately 30 homes to his credit.

Bernie could not have zeroed in on a more admirable role model. It would be a shame that in just a few years, his mom would be instrumental in creating such a rift between herself and Ted's family that not only Ted, but also Bernie and Joe, would be kept from any interaction with all of their dad's relatives, including Bernie's Uncle Gene.

It is interesting to note that Uncle Gene's older son, David, following in his father's footsteps, would retire, in 2013, from his position as Postmaster in Winston-Salem, N.C.

September, 1962
Bay City, Michigan

Bernie had interviewed for several Latin teaching positions, including one at an exclusive all-girls boarding school on the east coast. Not having been considered for that position, he began to apply for openings in Michigan. After visiting two different schools, he finally decided on Central High School in Bay City.

After living on a $100 a month allowance provided by his Fanny Burr Butler Fellowship to cover room and board while in graduate school, Bernie was awestruck by the $4,977 per annum salary that was being offered for the teaching position.

His brother Joe had traveled to Bay City with him the month before to help him find a place to live and to check out the school and the community. Together they decided on a sleeping room for Bernie that was being let by a high school councilor.

November 1, 1962
Indianapolis

Claude Eugene Hacker lay dying (he would pass away on November 14) in the Veterans' Hospital in Indianapolis with his daughter and his sister by his side.

"Gene, you're a drunk! You're killing yourself with liquor, and you don't know enough to stop. You never were any good, and now you're going to die a drunk."

Lillian never forgave her Aunt Charlotte for those harsh words to her father on his deathbed. For all his faults and shortcomings, he was still her father, and she loved him.

By now, however, Lillian's marriage was itself on rough ground. She had given up her opportunities for post-secondary education to get married and support her first husband, John Marshal Batten, as he obtained his undergraduate degree.

Once her first husband had graduated from college, he decided to join the Air Force.

For nine years, while Lillian was busy having three children and raising them in air base housing, John Batten served as a triple-rated navigator on a B52. He was eventually assigned to Special Weapons and worked with a unit of the Strategic Air Command (SAC). Lillian did her best to raise her three girls, Marsha, Sheryl and Karen, while trying to fill the air base social roles expected of her.

Then, one day, John suddenly announced that he was resigning his commission with the Air Force. He wanted to move his family back to Lafayette, Indiana, so he could earn an M.A. in Airport Management.

So, once again, Lillian assumed the responsibility of supporting her family and sending her husband to school. This time, she worked as the secretary to the President of Berger Steel in Lafayette.

Tragically, before her first husband had even earned his M.A. and qualified for a better paying job, he filed for divorce.

Following this notification, Lillian packed up her three children and left their home in Lafayette to move back to Indianapolis where she had grown up. Having decided to get at least one benefit out of her ungrateful husband before their divorce became final, she took advantage of his GI Bill benefits to purchase a split-level home, located at 5802 Allendale on the west side of Indianapolis.

She had carefully chosen the location because it was right across the street from IPS School 96, an elementary school to which all three of her girls could safely walk.

November 10, 1962
Indianapolis

"This is a beautiful sapphire ring, Miss. Are you sure you want to pawn it?"

"Yes," answered Lillian. "I need money to make my phone deposit at our new house."

"Do you have anything else you want to pawn?" the man behind the counter asked Lillian.

"No," stammered Lillian.

"Do you happen to have a gun you would like to pawn?" asked the clerk.

"If I had a gun," said Lillian, trying hard to keep her composure, "I wouldn't be here."

This last admission proved to be too much for Lillian, and she broke down in tears. The clerk turned out to be a real gentleman. He helped Lillian to a chair at the back of the shop and gave her a cup of coffee. He stayed with her until she could regain her composure sufficiently to finish her transaction and return home.

Later, Lillian was able to redeem her sapphire ring from the pawnshop and pass it on to her daughter Sheryl, who, in turn, gave it to her daughter, Annie.

Lillian walked to her car. It was a nice car. Maybe too nice. She thought she could make a few extra bucks if she traded down and got something less expensive. Perhaps a small Ford.

November 20, 1962
Indianapolis

"This is about as cheap a car as you'll be able to buy," explained the used car salesman.

Lillian had waited until her next payday so she would have extra money for the license and transfer fees.

"Does it run?" she asked.

"Of course it runs. How else would you get it off the lot," came the bravado reply.

Turned out that the car did run. Lillian drove the car off the lot and all the way back to Lafayette before pulling into a filling station. It was then that she discovered just how well the car ran. When she turned the key to the off position, the car continued running and could not be coaxed to stop even by the filing station attendant.

Lillian was still trying to deal with the death of father six days earlier, and this was the last straw. Lillian got back in her traded-down car, backed up—right into the gas pump, nearly knocking it over—and drove directly back to the used car lot in Indianapolis. She created such a scene yelling at the salesman that he eventually went back into his office, got the keys and returned her original car with no charge for the whole ill-fated transaction.

Two days later, Lillian successfully traded down to a small Ford Falcon that proved to be much more economical for her on her limited budget.

December, 1962
Las Vegas, Nevada

The sadness of her whole situation, however, suddenly became too much for Lillian to deal with. She loaded the three girls into her small Ford Falcon and headed west. She had decided on the spur of the moment to start a new life for herself and the girls in California. On the way, she wanted to stop in Las Vegas and drop off a $300 death benefit check that had come to her following the death of her father. She felt that the check rightfully belonged to her father's widow.

"Why, thank you, honey." said the widowed Mrs. Hacker. "I was wondering what was going to become of me now that Eugene was dead."

Lillian had already met her father's final wife in Indianapolis when she had sent her the money to visit her dying husband at the Veterans' Hospital. The woman had very few resources of her own.

Her apartment was very poorly furnished. She was obviously living just barely above the poverty level. It was too depressing by half.

In fact, it was so depressing that it made Lillian reconsider her decision to travel to California. Looking around the dingy apartment of her dad's widow, she recalled the phrase, "No matter where you go, there you are."

Lillian knew then that she really couldn't run away from her troubles. They were inside her, and she would just have to come to grips with them. Where she lived with her girls would make absolutely no difference at all.

"Well, I won't take up any more of your time. The girls and I will be going now. I just wanted you to have the check. I'm glad we got to see each other again," said Lillian as she rose to leave the small apartment.

"OK, girls," Lillian said once they were back outside, "get into the back seat, and be good."

"Where are we going now?" asked the middle child, Sheryl.

"I want to go back home and see Daddy," said the oldest, Marsha.

"Just sit back, and be good and we'll see where we're going."

Lillian drove her Ford back to the highway, but turned east instead of west. She had decided to return to their house on Allendale in Indianapolis.

January 1963
Bay City, Michigan

It was Bernie's first year of teaching at his first job at Central H. S. in Bay City, Michigan. He had two Latin classes that were perfect for him, an English 2A class and a General English 2 class—his class from hell. He needed a teaching minor to get his license at the University of Michigan, but it had not been part of his dream to be confronted with 30+ nincompoops whose only goal in life seemed to be to cause chaos and push him to his breaking point. In fact, by the beginning of November, Bernie had pretty much made up his mind that he would resign from his teaching position at the end of the first semester. There had to be something better that he could do where his talents and efforts would be appreciated.

Not only were the students impossible, but the teacher that came into the room after he dismissed his English classes made him pick up all the paper from the floor before she let him leave. She was the stereotypical spinster English teacher who lived at home taking care of her sickly mother. Her dedication and personal sacrifice raised her to a level of sainthood with the school administration and seemed to give her license to browbeat and lord it over any of the other teachers she chose, especially Bernie.

But Bernie didn't resign his teaching position.

"By God," he had said to himself after a particularly rough day at school, "I have a right to support myself by being a teacher, and those little twerps aren't going to stop me from doing it."

Following the Tenure Meeting that was held for him in Room 212 at 3:00 p.m. on January 22, 1963, this report was filed by his sponsor, Charles Rorrer:

> "Mr. Barcio apparently has no problems with his English 2A and Latin 1 classes. The only problem of consequence in other areas which he feels he has is designing workable teaching techniques for his English 2 group. Also with this group he has had, and is attempting to correct, the run of discipline problems which normally confront a first year teacher.
>
> "Throughout the interview, Mr. Barcio demonstrated a generally conscientious attitude toward his work. He conducted himself with reserve and congeniality; his personal appearance, as usual, was exceptionally neat.
>
> "Miss Harris [the Language Department Chairperson] indicated that she knew of no problem in relation to Mr. Barcio's work. In both her and the sponsor's estimation, he is doing a most satisfactory job. Since he has required very little help in adjusting to his work thus far, it would appear that he progresses easily on his own initiative."

Bernie did not own a television set although the high school councilor (in whose house he rented a sleeping room) did have one. In fact, he was invited to watch for a while the night that President Kennedy came on T.V. to explain his showdown with Russia over the deployment of Atomic Missiles in Cuba.

This councilor rented four rooms on the second floor of her house. Bernie had one, a young high school math teacher (who kept very much to himself) rented the second, a nurse rented the third, and the fourth was rented by a hefty middle-aged woman who was a field agent for the Michigan State Teachers Association. None of the renters interacted with each other at all. Even though the math teacher owned a car and drove to Central High School each day, he never once offered to give Bernie a ride.

The councilor's mother was a creature of wonder, as was the councilor's black cat.

The black cat would amuse himself for hours batting a cellophane candy wrapper around on the floor. Bernie tried to make friends with this feline monster, but all he ever ended getting out of the relationship were multiple scratch wounds on the backs of both of his hands. The cat had a full set of claws and did not hesitate to use them.

The councilor's mother sat in her rocking chair in front of the T.V. each evening. On those occasions when Bernie happened to be passing through the downstairs hall on his way back from dinner, he sometimes witnessed her special ritual for getting out of her rocking chair. She lacked leg and arm strength to rise in a normal fashion, so she would set the rocker in motion, rocking faster and faster, until she had enough momentum to pop out of the seat and onto her feet. It was a wonder to witness.

January, 1963
Indianapolis

Lillian would have to work full time to support the girls, make the house payments, buy gas to get back and forth to work and take care of Maxwell, their cocker spaniel. So she decided that she would hire a housekeeper who could be there when the girls got home from school and make sure they were all right, got along with each other and did their homework before she got home from work herself.

The first housekeeper she hired lasted only a few days. Lillian let her go the first time the children found themselves locked out of the house because she was inside entertaining her boyfriend.

The next housekeeper didn't last much longer. She turned out to have a serious drinking problem.

Lillian finally found Mabel, a kindly older woman who loved the girls and, despite suffering from crippling arthritis, proved to be absolutely reliable. Not only would she welcome the girls home from school with special snacks, but she provided an occasional welcome break for Lillian by having dinner prepared and ready for them all when she got home from work.

Again, as the ironies of life would have it, before long Sheryl was accepted into an accelerated elementary school program and would not be walking across the street to school each day. Lillian volunteered to drive the morning carpool that took Sheryl and several other girls to their special school. After school, Sheryl and her friends would carpool home with another mother.

Then, after Lillian accepted a job as Headmaster's secretary at Park School on its original Cold Spring Road campus nestled smack dab in the middle of the campus of Marion College, her youngest daughter, Karen, was allowed to attend school there as a lower school student. At the end of the school day, Karen was taken home by Park School station wagon transportation.

Only Marsha ended up walking across the street to school each day from her home in Allendale. The advantage was that she got home first and got first shot at the after school treats.

February, 1963
Indianapolis

"When will you be back to pick us up?" Asked Marsha as Lillian dropped her three children off at the home of her ex-mother-in-law.

"I'll be back this afternoon after you've had a chance to visit with your father."

"Is he here? I don't see his car," said Sheryl.

"He'll probably be here in a little while. I think he's driving down from Chicago."

When Lillian returned that afternoon, her ex-husband had indeed arrived. In fact, his big new Buick was neatly parked in the turnaround in front of the house.

"That bastard," thought Lillian to herself. "He thinks he's so Goddamn smart driving his big new Buick while it's all I can do is drive this dinky little Ford."

Without really making a conscious decision to do so, Lillian floored the gas pedal and ploughed the front end of her Ford into the side of the shiny new Buick.

There was a tremendous crash. The hood of the Ford Falcon flew up as its whole front end was jammed back against the radiator. The Buick was hardly scratched.

March 29, 1963
Bay City, Michigan

By now, Bernie had long since decided that, once again, he needed something to provide a touch of sanity in his life. He couldn't just spend every night in his room preparing for the next day's frustrations. So when another teacher had suggested that he join a local theater group called The Bay City Players, Bernie was in.

He had acting experience both in high school (as a senior in Sparta, WI, he had a singing roll in The Pirates of Penzance) and at Holy Cross Seminary where he appeared as a knight in T. S. Elliot's "Murder in the Cathedral" so he had had no trouble landing the part of "Stewart" in "A Majority of One" that was staged for two weekends in December of 1962.

By March, Bernie had a leading role in the spring production, "The Miracle Worker." Bernie played the role of James Keller, Helen Keller's older brother. What amazed Bernie the most was seeing that an elementary school teacher, Ruth Snedeker, was managing to hold the starring role of Annie Sullivan, and a school principal, Ned Baumgardner, was playing the role of Captain Keller. Bernie felt that, as a fellow educator, he was really beginning to fit in. The play was staged on March 29—30 and April 4, 5 and 6.

Bernie still managed to get all his schoolwork done, often while waiting backstage during practices, but it no longer occupied the main focus of his entire life.

June, 1963
Milwaukee, Wisconsin

"O.K., Pa. I'll be over to pick you up in a little while."

Eugene Barcio was about to take his 77-year-old father to his first major league ball game. Although Joe always followed the Milwaukee Braves and frequently used baseball as a conversation starter with his grandsons, he had never actually attended a game.

After attending that game with his son, Joe's interest in the Milwaukee Braves became so intense that he was even interviewed one day by a local Milwaukee radio station so they could share his enthusiasm with other listeners.

September, 1963
Bay City, Michigan

In September of 1963 Bernie was no longer living in a rented room. Once he realized that his landlady viewed him as her "handyman in residence" and began to have him fix windows, clean the basement and trim trees, Bernie decided it was time to move on.

His salary was now $5,132 per year, and he felt he could finally afford to live in a small one-room apartment built into what had once been a garage attached to the back of the home of Charles and Martha Caurse at 1711 22nd Street. This gave him some freedom to come and go without having to pass through someone's living room.

"Help! Someone help me, please!"

Bernie awoke from his nap on the couch in his new apartment. He could have sworn that he heard someone calling for help. He listened carefully.

"Please, someone help me!"

The call was so feint that it could barely be heard. Bernie moved over to the closet that was once a hallway that led into his landlord's house to see if the sound was coming from there. It wasn't.

"Help me, please!"

Bernie opened his door to see if the sound was coming from outside.

"HELP, PLEASE!"

Now the sound was louder and was coming from the house next door. He rushed over to the back door which was open and looked in.

"Thank God, please call an ambulance for me. I've fallen down the steps!" said the neighbor lady as she lay on the basement floor at the foot of the stairs.

Bernie to the rescue. It kind of made up for the time he had not been alert enough to save the life of his landlady in Ann Arbor when she had fallen on the ice outside her home. And froze to death.

Bernie's move into his own apartment, however, did not enable him to shed his "handyman in residence" identity. Before too long his new landlady was inviting him over for Sunday dinner only to ask him to perform "one or two" little jobs for her before he left. He ended up painting her living room walls and ceiling.

Since his new landlady was also getting discouraged by the fact that her granddaughter, Gwen Sabinas, still was not engaged even though she had been dating the same boy for several years, she soon invited both Bernie and her granddaughter to a local beer parlor on a Friday night to see if she couldn't get the two together. She followed up with a couple of Sunday afternoon dinner invitations designed to make her granddaughter's hesitant boyfriend jealous.

The menu of choice was usually succulent fried chicken and twice-baked potatoes—an offering that no single young man could possibly turn down.

Bernie, however, did not take the bait, and Gwen ended up marrying her reluctant fiancé in 1966. She and her husband had five children whom Gwen cared for as a stay-at-home mom while also running a daycare service in her house.

School was also getting better. Bernie was honing his acting skills on stage and using those skills to play the tough guy in his tenth grade English classes. He still had a ways to go, but he could certainly command their attention when he wanted it. And he made them pick up their own trash before they were dismissed each day.

Confirmation of Bernie's marked improvement came over the radio one day.

> "WTAC big 600 is proud to honor Mr. Bernard Barcio today. Mr. Barcio, your pupils have nominated you teacher of the day. You will be receiving a plant as a gift from Boehringer's Greenhouse and WTAC! Congratulations, Mr. Barcio!"

Only his second year in the classroom and already he was being honored as Teacher of the Day. What would be next, Teacher of the Year? Bernie would just have to wait and see.

His singing talents had also been recognized and he was routinely hired to perform solos at Saturday weddings at the neighborhood Catholic Church. He received the following note from St. Stanislaus parishioners, Rita and Ed Bala, telling him how much his contribution was appreciated.

> "May we take this opportunity and commend you on the fine manner you conduct the congregational singing at 8:30 Mass Sundays. One must admit that the children plus a few of us adults are improving weekly thanks to your directing and singing. We'd like to encourage you to keep it up as we do appreciate it."

Bernie's singing ability soon caught the attention of the bishop of the Bay City diocese who invited him to serve as a cantor during a church dedication service in a nearby town. Since it would take a while to drive to the dedication, Bernie decided not to stop for lunch on the way even though he had not had a chance to eat breakfast after he had led the singing during the 8:30 a.m. Sunday Mass.

"You certainly have a wonderful voice," said the bishop after the ceremony.

"Thank you, Your Excellency," said Bernie.

"You must be an ex-seminarian," observed the bishop.

Nailed! You can take the boy out of the seminary, but you can't take the seminary out of the boy!

After that encounter, Bernie walked over to the refreshment tent and decided he needed a drink.

"I'll have a Manhattan," requested Bernie.

There were also snacks available, but he thought that, at the moment, he needed his Manhattan more than he needed food.

Big mistake.

Bernie was about to learn one of the most important lessons of his life: Never drink on an empty stomach.

"*Gira la testa,*" as they say in Italy. Bernie would have to find a place to sit it out until he was finally able to drive back to Bay City.

The 1963-1964 Bay City Players' season would see Bernie on stage in "The Death of a Salesman," "The King and I," and "Write Me A Murder" in which he played the role of the Honorable David Rodingham.

His Latin classes were going great, and the approaches he had adopted building on his training under the renowned Dr. Waldo Sweet at the University of Michigan had him giving Latin workshops to other Latin teachers in the area.

He had so mastered the art of controlling his tenth grade general English classes that he had even been asked to teach summer school the summer before.

And, as an additional bonus, Bernie had been introduced to the challenges and joys of having both men and women share the same dressing room at the Bay City Players.

November 16, 1963
Saginaw, Michigan

It had been two years since the Cursillo movement had made its way to the eastern part of the United States and this was the third year that the special 3-day weekender course on Catholicism was being offered in Saginaw. Since Bernie was fairly active at St. Stanislaus Catholic Church in Bay City, he had been talked into attending.

Cursillos have a definite Spanish flavor to them since they originated in the American Southwest. In fact, for the first couple of years after they were created, they were conducted totally in Spanish.

"Welcome, men, to your first Cursillo," said the priest that would be conducting the total immersion upbeat retreat-like (but not really) experience. "This church basement is going to be our home for the next three days. We'll learn together down here, share our meals together, pray together, and have fun together. We've brought in cots so that we can even sleep down here."

And they did. The group consisted of 48 men, most of them older than Bernie. They were divided up into 4-man study/discussion groups, and after every lecture or presentation by the priest leader, the men would gather around their discussion tables and "personalize" and "internalize" what they had just learned. Each discussion session would end with an impromptu prayer that the men took turns leading.

Every so often, work would cease, and they would be taught an up-beat Spanish song such as *"De Colores,"* or they would sing well-known church hymns or even just fun sing-a-long type songs.

Then it would be back to work. After some presentations, the discussion groups would be given poster boards and markers and asked to illustrate what had just been presented. Before long, the walls were covered with their creative achievements.

By the end of the third day, the group had bonded wonderfully. Although it had involved a lot of prayers, the Cursillo did not have the gloomy all-work-and-no-play atmosphere frequently associated with religious retreats. A Cursillo was actually fun.

And the best was yet to come.

As the novice Cursillistas finished their work on the third day and began to get ready for their final dinner together, Father announced that there was going to be a special Graduation Party after dinner.

"Hey, this could be fun," thought Bernie to himself, completely unaware of the intense emotional experience he was about to have.

As everyone was finishing their final course, the basement of the church was suddenly filled with the joyous sounds of a group of guitar-playing, Spanish singers who were coming down the stairway into the basement followed by a large parade of previous Cursillo graduates.

"Everybody up," called out Father. "Line up around the outside walls and prepare to be greeted by your fellow Cursillistas."

The verses of *"De Colores"* that were now so familiar to all of them filled the room accompanied by the most pleasing guitarists that could have been assembled. Bernie was immediately transported back to his childhood when middle of the night musicians used to pop in to visit his folks when they had all lived in Cudahy.

They say that music and aromas are the most powerful memory evokers there are!

As the musicians and Cursillistas filed into the basement, they began to go around to each of the novice Cursillistas and gave each a big, warm welcoming hug and offer each sincere congratulations and personal encouragement.

A totally enveloping and emotionally taxing experience.

Tears literally streamed down Bernie's cheeks as he accepted and returned each warm hug. And there were women Cursillistas too. They smiled at Bernie's tears and said they completely understood.

"We cried, too, when we finished our first Cursillo. Those are tears of joy and peace you're shedding. Don't be embarrassed. God loves you, and we love you!"

All this social warmth was almost too intense for Bernie after years of living alone and concentrating on his studies and work in lonely rented rooms. For one of the first times in his life he felt as though he was truly loved and appreciated.

To this day, a strain of *"De Colores"* overheard even at the distance is guaranteed to make the author's eyes swell with tears of remembrance.

A month later, all the novice Cursillistas got together at St. Stan's after church for a follow-up meeting. It was good to see everyone again, but the glow of the experience was beginning to wear off. When it was announced that monthly meetings were planned for the group in the future, Bernie saw red flags popping up everywhere. He had a natural aversion to being "sucked into" entanglements and was beginning to think that this would probably be the first and last follow up meeting that he would attend.

"Hey, Bernie," said one of the older men in the group as they were breaking up, "how would you like to come over to the house for coffee before you go home?"

"I don't know," said Bernie eager not to get more involved, "I've got a lot of school work that I need to get done today."

"Come on," insisted his fellow Cursillista. "Just for a little while. I want you to meet my daughter."

So that was it. The man had ulterior motives.

"Run away! Run Away!" said the little voice in the back of Bernie's head, but he didn't want to be rude.

When they got to his host's house, Bernie was introduced to the Mrs. and offered a cup of coffee and a snack. In a little while, the "daughter" ambled in, looking like she really didn't want this introduction to take place any more than Bernie did.

"Hi, I'm Bernie."

"Hi, I know. I met you at the Cursillo," said the daughter.

So she had been one of the ladies in line that gave Bernie a hug while he was emotionally vulnerable.

"RUN AWAY! RUN AWAY!" now screamed the voice at the back of Bernie's head.

"Nice to see you again. And thanks for the coffee," said Bernie as he hastened his departure.

Bernie knew for sure that that would definitely be the first and last follow up Cursillo meeting that he would attend, *De Colores* or no *De Colores*.

November 22, 1963
Bay City, Michigan

"Teachers, pardon the interruption, but we have just received word that President Kennedy has been shot. We will come back on the announcements as soon as we have more information."

Shocking as the P.A. announcement had been, Bernie welcomed the interruption to his English 2 class from hell. Anything that made this group of kids shut their little mouths for a couple minutes was worth it.

"O.K., let's continue with the story. Tom, you read aloud for a while."

Surprisingly, Tom cooperated. He even read fairly well and took correction pleasantly when told how to correctly re-pronounce a word.

"Teachers, please excuse this additional interruption, but we have decided that we are simply going to play the radio news reports over the loudspeaker. We feel this is something everyone has the right to hear."

That did it. Class was over for the day. Not only Bernie's class, but every class in Central H.S. was absolutely quiet as teachers and students listened intently as the events in Dallas were detailed by national news broadcasters.

After about a half hour, the principal broke in once more, this time very somberly.

"Folks, we are going to dismiss school at this time. Please leave in an orderly fashion and return to your homes where you can listen to the news and be with your families. School is dismissed."

The next few days were kind of a blur. Like everyone else, Bernie sat and listened to the radio reports. Since he had a Wollensack reel-to-reel tape recorder at home that he used to make drill tapes for his Latin classes, he taped the funeral procession as the President was being laid to rest on November 25.

Bernie still has that tape although he no longer has a reel-to-reel tape player. After school resumed, he asked his English students to write short essays sharing their reactions to the assassination of President Kennedy, and he recorded several of the more interesting ones on the same tape. Who knows, someday it might get converted to a cassette tape format if anyone were ever interested in it for its historical value.

In 2013, the author did have the reel to reel tape converted to a CD, but either the original tape had deteriorated or the technician did a bad job because the sound is barely understandable.

In July of 2004 the author, accompanied by his daughter Cyndi, was able to visit the former Dallas public school book depository and look out of the sixth floor window at the road below made familiar by repeated T.V. coverage and the notorious grassy knoll.

Because of the terrible tragedy, The Bay City Players cancelled the first two play dates of "Death of a Salesman" which was scheduled to be presented on two weekends, beginning November 22-23. Bernie did, however, get to portray his role of Stanley the waiter when the play was staged as planned on the following weekend, November 28-30.

March, 1964
Ann Arbor, Michigan

Bernie's self confidence had grown considerably over the past year and a half. He felt it was now time to share his Alma Mater with his Bay City Latin Students. He had thus organized a trip involving 120 Bay City Latin students to travel on three busses to the University of Michigan in Ann Arbor for discussions of classical studies. The group had boarded their buses in Bay City at 8:00 a.m.

It was a beautiful Saturday, and the students were now all seated quietly as they listened to a talk by Prof. Frank Copley in Angell Hall. Soon they would visit the language laboratory where its use would be explained by Dr. Waldo Sweet.

Accompanied by Miss Frances Schultz, Central High School's other Latin teacher, and Miss Irma Anschutz, the Latin teacher at St. James school who had taught at Central before her retirement, Bernie would later lead the students on a tour of the Kelsey Classical Museum.

The day would be brought to a perfect close by dividing the students up among the three teacher chaperones who would take them on brief walking tours of the University campus before they re-boarded their buses at 4:30 p.m.

June, 1964
Bay City, Michigan

Bernie was, once again, offered a contract to teach summer school in the mornings at Central High School. Since anything would be better than being reduced to having to return to Sparta to look for summer work, Bernie accepted. To add to his income, he decided to try to earn a little extra money during the afternoons by posting the following notice on the office bulletin board:

> "Attention Teachers:
> "Anyone who would like painting (indoor or out), minor home maintenance or general yard work done at a reasonable rate ($1.50 per hour) during this coming summer, please leave a note in my mailbox sometime this week, indicating the type of work you would like done and any specific date preferences you might have.
> "I will be available from 1:00 p.m. till 5:30 p.m., Monday through Friday, June 1 to July 24."

As Bernie learned later, Central High School teachers had a history of being creative in their efforts to earn extra money. During the depression, Bernie was told, the teacher who taught high school shop supplemented his family income by parking his camper truck in the school parking lot during the day. Any male teacher who was interested, and had $5.00 to spare, could pay a visit to the camper and spend time with the shop teacher's wife.

This was the summer of the World's Fair in New York City. The current shop teacher at Central High School owned a 27-foot cabin cruiser, and he had asked around for a crew to join him as he sailed his boat through the Great Lakes and the Erie Canal to visit the World's Fair. The shop teacher was married and well-respected by the faculty. In fact, he was even rather famous at school because he kept a pet monkey at home.

"You should visit his home sometime," suggested another English teacher to Bernie.

"Does he keep his monkey in a cage?" asked Bernie.

"No, he lets it run free. You know, monkeys can't be house broken," added the English teacher.

"Oh, man, I bet his place really stinks," observed Bernie.

"Hey, Bernie," continued the other English teacher, "could you let me have $5 until payday? I'm running a little short."

Bernie liked the English teacher. He was one of the few members of the faculty that wore a Lone Ranger mask to school on Halloween to show his students he had a human side. And, as it turned out, Bernie did happen to have $5 in his wallet and he gladly loaned it to his fellow English teacher. Of course, it never would be paid back.

The first teacher to join the crew for the trip to the World's Fair was the physics teacher. He was a tall, well-built divorcee who had weathered the charges of making improper advances to a female student in the science lab storage closet.

"She was definitely looking for something," confided the physics teacher to Bernie one day after he had asked him about the charges.

"What do you mean?" asked Bernie.

"She used to sit in the front row in my class. She wore black underpants and always made sure her legs were far enough apart for me to get an eyeful."

It was the physics teacher that talked Bernie into signing onto the crew for the trip to New York.

The third teacher to sign on was a young, very slightly built, single, Jewish math teacher.

Each crewmember would have to chip in $300 for the privilege of making the trip.

At the end of Summer School, all four loaded their gear into the shop teacher's car and headed north to where the cabin cruiser was berthed.

After all their gear had been stored on board, each member of the crew was shown the basic operations of the boat, and, as they headed out into Lake Huron, each was given a chance to familiarize themselves with the controls. Everyone was supposed to take turns.

Everything went fine for the first few days as the cabin cruiser was guided past Detroit and into Lake Erie.

"Be sure to watch the charts carefully," said the captain to the physics teacher who was serving as navigator for the trip. "We don't want to get off course."

The wind was blowing hard, and since Lake Erie is relatively shallow, that meant the waves were high. After hours of slow going, the physics teacher navigator finally had a suggestion.

"There are lights off to the left. I think we should head into shore and find out exactly where we are. It's probably a town in Ohio."

As it turned out, the lights on shore were not in Ohio but in Canada. They had been blown completely off course. After refueling, they headed back out onto the lake determined to make landfall in Ohio before dark.

The next day the group headed out once more. By this time, Bernie had pretty much adopted the back seat of the boat as his favorite spot. Even though he had to breathe in the exhaust fumes of the inboard motor, he could usually get himself situated so that he wouldn't get too sick from the bouncing of the waves. About mid-day, the engine conked out.

"Here, take the helm, while I go down and see if I can get it going," said the shop teacher to the physics teacher.

"Try it now," called the shop teacher.

"It's no good. It won't kick over," said the physics teacher.

"Figures," said the Jewish math teacher. "I just knew this trip was going to be a disaster."

Bernie said nothing. He was just glad that the boat was resting quietly in the water and that there were no gas fumes to breathe in at the moment.

"O.K.," said the shop teacher, "I hate to do it, but we'll just have to put in an S.O.S. to the Coast Guard."

And that's what he did. And did again. And again. No one was sure if the distress calls were even being received, so all they could do was just sit and wait. And keep trying.

"Look," said Bernie, pointing across the water just as it was beginning to get dark. "Here comes a boat. Maybe it's the Coast Guard!"

Sure enough, their message had gotten through. Before too long, a line had been thrown to them and they were being towed to shore at Lorain, Ohio.

This would be as close as the four adventurers would get to the New York World's Fair. Major repairs were called for on the engine that completely exhausted the budget established for the trip. All they could do now was sit tight and wait for the engine to be fixed before starting back home.

"Hey, Bernie, how about going on an excursion to Kelly's Island?" asked the Jewish math teacher.

"Sure, I'm game," said Bernie and off they headed for Sandusky where excursion boats could be boarded.

Kelley's Island had several wineries that offered free samples to visitors. After Bernie and the Jewish math teacher had sampled a number of different varieties, the Jewish math teacher was ready for more adventure.

"Come on, Bernie," he suggested, "we've got plenty of time before the boat leaves. Let's go for a walk around the island."

"I don't know," said Bernie. "It's getting dark. Why don't we just hang around here until it's time to leave?"

"Come on, don't be a schmutz," said the Jewish math teacher. "We'll be back in plenty of time."

There were no lights on any of the island roads, and before either of them realized it, they were further away from the dock area than they should have been.

HOOONK! HOOONK!

"Oh great," said Bernie, "That's the boat horn. They're getting ready to board!"

So off the two adventurers ran, trying their best to remember exactly what turns they had taken to get where they were.

Bernie made sure that the next side trip he took with the Jewish math teacher to Put-in-Bay would be totally in the daylight. They visited the memorials to naval battles that had been fought there, looked at the displays, but stayed close by the dock.

Finally, however, the novelty of life in Lorain began to wear off.

"O.K., everyone," announced the physics teacher, "I've got a pint of plum brandy for us all to share."

"Great idea," said the Jewish math teacher as he passed out some paper cups.

The physics teacher poured shares all around and the conversation began to be loose. Before too long, the physics teacher began to reveal some of his basic anti-Semitic feelings. At first, the Jewish math teacher fended the remarks off in good spirits. But that just made the physics teacher dig deeper into his supply of insults.

"Alright," yelled the captain finally. "This is my ship, and I say it's time for everyone to shut up and go to sleep." Which is exactly what everyone did.

The next day things were pretty quiet until dusk. It was then that another cabin cruiser came coasting into port asking everyone for help. It had broken down on the lake and Jake, a man in his sixties, had taken the dingy to row for help. In the meantime, they had fixed their engine and had set out to find Jake. Since they had been unable to locate him, they decided to come into Lorain and get help.

Bernie's captain took Bernie and the rest of his crew with him on one of the boats that made up the impromptu rescue flotilla.

"JAKE!"

The cry was sent out over the now dark waters, and all would wait quietly for a reply.

"JAKE!"

Silence.

"JAKE!"

No reply.

This went on for hours. Finally, at about 11:00 p.m., the Coast Guard lead boat called off the search. When they all got back to Lorain, word was received that Jake had been found. He had rowed his dingy to shore and was sitting in a shore-side cabin drinking hot chocolate when a Coast Guard vehicle pulled into its driveway as part of his usual routine of checking shore-side cabins for those "lost" on the lake.

Finally, the engine of the 27-foot cabin cruiser was repaired.

"We're all going to have to chip in a little more money to get us back home," announced the captain. "I've put an extra $500 into the repairs, and I'm strapped."

"I've got $40 that I can chip in," said Bernie.

The others all dug down and chipped in also.

The trip back was smooth and uneventful. The shop teacher and the physics teacher stayed at the controls almost the whole way. The Jewish math teacher pretty much disappeared into the hold.

Bernie planted himself at the back end of the boat and thought about his upcoming year abroad in Italy with Tufts University.

The headline had read, "Central Teacher Gets Sabbatical."

"Bernard Barcio, English and Latin teacher at Central High School, will take a year's leave of absence to study classics at Tufts University, Naples, Italy. Recipient of a tuition scholarship from Tufts, Barcio will leave in September, returning to Bay City in May 1965. Announcement of Barcio's scholarship grant was made today by Central Principal Theodore B. Southerland. He explained 'no particular degree is involved,' but pointed out Barcio 'will receive much enrichment and background from his studies.' Southerland explained Barcio will also participate in a series of tours to different classical sites, 'which will complement class work.'"

Giuseppe and Vrigita Barcio help harvest peaches from the trees in Ted's yard on Hammond Ave., Cudahy, WI, 1961

Authors' U of M Graduation lunch
Ann Arbor, Michigan, May 1962
(L to R) Antonio Nudi, Author,
Lucy Leo, Stella Barcio

Bernard Barcio (R) in the roll of The Hon. David Rodingham

Cursillistas attending the Cursillo at Sacred Heart Parish, Saginaw, Michigan, November 16, 1963. Author is in the top row, 3rd from R.

PART VI

September 1964 – December 1965

Back to the Old Country

September 21, 1964
New York City, New York

"Good-bye, Betty Jean. I'll write you every day and let you know how the trip is going," called Bernie to his Bay City girl friend. They had met when they appeared in "The Death of a Salesman" together. Betty Jean Pietryga had played the role of "the woman," Willy Loman's floozy girlfriend. She was a Polish beauty with jet-black long hair. Dyed.

Betty Jean was quickly disenchanted with Bernie's lack of sexual maturity. As early as their second or third date, she started in on her negative observations.

"You hold hands like a little kid holding hands with his mother!"

"What should I do different?" asked Bernie, eager to please.

"Well, the guy should grab the girl's hand and not vice-versa," criticized Betty Jean.

Later she would have something to say about the pathetic way he kissed.

"It's just lack of experience," explained Bernie. "I'll probably get better."

Later on, Betty Jean began to show definite signs of irritation because of Bernie's apparent unwillingness to go much past 1st base. She just didn't seem to understand that he had spent the last six years either in a seminary or devoting all his time to his graduate studies. Finally, she decided to try something different.

"Bernie, how would you like to spend Sunday driving up to visit some friends of mine who own a cabin by a small lake?"

"O.K.," said Bernie, completely unaware of what he was getting himself into.

When they arrived at the cabin and Bernie was introduced to the young couple that lived there, he and Betty Jean took their seats on one of the two couches that were in the small living room. As Bernie settled back expecting to spend the afternoon in pleasant social intercourse, the host couple suddenly began to engage in some very serious making out right before them. Betty Jean had obviously thought that Bernie needed a little demonstration of sexual rather than social intercourse.

Bernie, however, simply got up quietly and left the cabin.

"Where did you go?" asked Betty Jean when he returned about an hour later.

"For a walk," replied Bernie.

"That was kind of rude to my friends, wasn't it?"

"Well, I really didn't want to sit and watch them going at it. I'm ready to leave. Are you?"

Nevertheless, Betty Jean had hoped that Bernie would not go through with his application to attend Tufts University's Classical Year Abroad Program. Perhaps she thought that if she could keep him around a little longer, she might get him to go to 2nd or 3rd base, or maybe even score a home run. Bernie, however, felt that his decision to study abroad for a year was an essential part of his career plans to become an outstanding teacher of secondary school Latin.

Bernie had tried to ease their parting by selling her the 1962 four-door Ford for $300 that he had bought for $1,000 just a few months earlier. Betty Jean had gotten tired of going on walking dates, and Bernie had gotten tired of spending money to rent a car every weekend.

Since Bernie had not driven very much over the past several years that he had been in the seminary and attending graduate school, he was a little rusty. Something that produced more than one embarrassing moment for him.

"Bernie, we're sitting behind a parked car," interrupted Betty Jean.

Bernie had pulled up to a corner to wait for the light to turn green. He was in the lane of traffic closest to the curb. When the light turned green, the lane on his left began to move. Rather than be impatient, he just continued his conversation with Betty Jean as he calmly waited for the car ahead of him to go.

O.K. Just another one of life's little embarrassments!

To further appease Betty Jean for his leaving, Bernie said that if she really wanted to, he wouldn't mind if she managed to come to Italy and visit him half way through the year.

As frequently happens, however, absence does not make the heart grow fonder. Good to his word, Bernie did write everyday while on board the Christopher Columbus. He carefully described everything that was going on at sea, the weather they were having, his trouble with seasickness, the birds, the fish, the meals, and the hot, cramped sleeping quarters located somewhere well below the water line. But these letters just didn't cut it with Betty Jean. She had apparently been hoping for passionate love letters and descriptions of Bernie's personal turmoil now that he had made the mistake of leaving her.

Once Betty Jean made it clear in her first letter to him that she did not intend to serve as the keeper of his historical travel records, Bernie decided it was time to switch to an occasional postcard.

Betty Jean did not travel to Italy to meet Bernie half way through the year. In fact, on his return to Bay City the following summer to teach summer school, Betty Jean had lost all interest in Bernie. She obviously had found someone new, someone who knew how to run all of the bases. So before moving to Indianapolis in August of 1965, Bernie focused on his teaching and painting the farmhouse of his first landlady's brother in exchange for the use of his truck. Bernie had been hired as the Head of the Latin Department at Park School in Indianapolis, and he needed to borrow a truck to drive his belongings down and find a new room to rent. He also agreed to paint a rental house owned by his landlady's older daughter and son-in-law, Mr. and Mrs. Sabinas. At first, he intended to charge them for the job, but when their 18 year old daughter, Marilyn (a girl who had never missed a day of school throughout her high school career), passed away suddenly from liver failure while he was working on the house, he told them he would not charge them for the job.

Later, after Bernie and Lillian founded Pompeiiana, Inc., Mr. and Mrs. Sabinas would become adult members for more than 20 years to thank him for his generosity in their time of grief.

September 26, 1964
Cristoforo Colombo Ocean Liner
Atlantic Ocean
The author sent the following postcard to his parents in Sparta, Wisconsin:

> "Dear Mom and Dad,
> "Boat travel isn't really too bad, but it did take me a few days to get used to it. It is very luxurious. We can swim, dance, play ping pong, drink champagne, stuff ourselves, and have a good time in general—all free. Tomorrow, after 6 days, we arrive in Naples about 1 p.m.
> "Love, Bernie"

October, 1964
Indianapolis
Lillian's cousin, Jack Hacker, was doing well in his career with the Indianapolis Police Department. It was something Jack had determined to do well, especially in view of his father's rather inglorious history of going AWOL from the military followed by numerous run-ins with the law, jail time and prison escapes, all leading to his sad death in a bar-room brawl.

Jack would become a member of the Police Motorcycle Squad, work car theft details and eventually be promoted to the Vice Squad.

While working car thefts, Jack quickly became familiar with a professional thief we'll call "Bill."

Bill could break into a car, hot wire it and be on his way faster than any other professional working the streets of Indianapolis. He was, of course, well known to all those officers working the car theft detail, and whenever a report came in, Bill would be one of the first to be investigated.

He even had the bravado to highjack a flatbed trailer loaded with two pre-built garages. Bill, police would later discover, sold one, and the other he simply put on his own property, daring police to prove that it was one of the stolen garages.

As Jack would recall over lunch with Bernie in April of 2004, Bill was arrested repeatedly. But, to the great chagrin of the arresting officers, before they could even finish their paper work, they would look out the window and see Bill walking out of the station, free as the breeze. Even though the arrests were good and clear and convincing evidence had been collected, nothing seemed to stick.

After a couple years of total frustration, Jack would learn that Bill's one phone call that he was allowed after being arrested was never to his lawyer, but rather to the local FBI office. Shortly after making that call, Bill was always released.

Bill, you see, was an informant that the FBI desperately wanted to keep on the streets. Of course he was a car thief, but that only made him more credible with those whose activities he reported to his contacts at the FBI.

"Guess what, Jack?" asked a fellow detective one evening.

"What's up?" asked Jack.

"Just got a call that Bill has finally stolen his last car. Want to go out and see?"

So Jack and his fellow detective drove over to a railroad crossing where Bill had crashed a brand new Lincoln he had just stolen into the side of a freight train.

"Man, he must have really been traveling!" said Jack when he saw the condition of the Lincoln.

"Guy never had a chance," said the other detective. "Wonder why he didn't slow down?"

"Probably was in such a hurry to get away that he never saw the crossing signs," said Jack.

The next day, Jack got a call from a buddy of his in the department.

"Jack," said his buddy, "did you work the Lincoln wreck last night?"

"Yeah. Old Bill never had a chance," said Jack.

"How are you handling it?"

"We're writing it up as an accident. Why?" asked Jack.

"Did anyone check the breaks on the Lincoln?"

"No, I don't think so," said Jack.

"Check the breaks," said Jack's buddy who then hung up.

Sure enough, when Jack got the call back from impound, all the break lines on the Lincoln had been cut so that they would give out when any serious pressure was applied.

Later, Jack got another call from his buddy.

"Well, Jack, what did you learn about the brakes on that Lincoln?"

"You were right. The lines had all been cut," said Jack.

"So how are you going to handle it now?"

Jack thought for a minute and remembered how slippery Bill had been over the past several years, and how many arresting officers his contacts with the FBI had frustrated.

"I think we're just going to handle it as an accident, just like we decided in the first place," said Jack before hanging up.

Bill had got what he had coming, and there was no point in making life any more difficult for anyone else at this point.

November 1964
Naples, Italy

Bernie's year with Tufts University was off to a great start. All the boys in the program lived separately with roommates in the *Pensione Le Fontane al Mare*, right on the *Via Partenope* that runs along the shore in Naples. When the students were not travelling on special study tours to Rome, Florence, Capua, Pompeii or Sicily, the *Pensione* provided three meals a day, although the students were allowed to bring their own bottles of wine to the table in the evening to save paying extra for house wine. If the students wanted to eat out, they could request a "meal refund" to use elsewhere.

Although the girls in the program were housed in a separate hotel, all the students were close enough to walk to classes held at the Villa Pignatelli located in a park-like setting facing the Bay of Naples.

When the author was in the program, he was told that this magnificent neo-classical villa had once been the residence of Pope Innocent XII, Antonio Pignatelli.

It wasn't until doing further research for this second edition of **That's Not the Way I Remember It** that the author learned they had been misinformed. Pope Innocent XII had died in 1700, while the Villa Pignatelli was not constructed until 1826 by a wealthy Neapolitan businessman named Ferdinand Acton. After changing hands several times, the Villa was finally donated to the State of Italy by the widow of its last owner, Diego Aragona Pignatelli Cortez.

On entering the Villa for class each morning, the author had to pass a security guard who always simply replied "*Giorno*" when greeted with a cheery "*Buon Giorno!*"

The author picked up another colorful expression from a "*Capo*" directing traffic at a busy intersection. This man would yell "*Vai! Vai!*" encouraging cars to move along more quickly.

Tufts did offer a class in spoken Italian, but the teacher was not very good. It turned out he was more interested in publishing a textbook in English that he hired the author to proof for him.

Returning to the Pensione after classes, the author and his roommate, James (Giacomo) Romano, would bypass spending a "*dieci*" to take the "*ascensore*" to their 7th floor room, preferring to take the marble steps two at a time as they raced to their landing.

It was on this landing that the author learned another Italian phrase, this from a lady who had taken a tumble and hit her head on a marble step. As she sat on the floor bleeding, she kept yelling, *"Ai, Ai! La mia testa! Ai, Ai! La mia testa!"*

Since the author had brought his mandolin with him, which he had taught himself to play while in graduate school in Ann Arbor, he liked to relax standing out on their small balcony and singing the Neapolitan favorite, "*Santa Luccia*."

In the evening, he and his roommate would stand on the balcony and watch the *Puttane* argue with Johns who tried to negotiate the best deals before inviting one into their cars.

New Year's Eve
Naples, 1964

Italians have a special New Year's custom: they throw things away that they do not want in their homes at the beginning of the New Year. In Naples they love to throw these things out their windows down onto the street at the stroke of midnight, delighting in seeing them smash to pieces below.

Anticipating this bombardment, all traffic on the *Via Partenope* stopped shortly before midnight. As the author and his roommate stood on their balcony waiting for the barrage of unwanted items to begin, they suddenly spotted a car about three blocks away. The driver waited until it was exactly Midnight and then made a daredevil high-speed drive down the middle of the *Via Partenope* daring folks on the balconies to try and hit him.

January, 1965
Agnone, Provincia di Campbasso, Italy

"Scusi, Signor. Puo dirmi come si puo trovare la casa di Cesare Comperchioli?" said Bernie Barcio after he had made his way from the train station into the streets of Agnone.

He had promised his mother that, while he was in Italy, he would try to find his maternal grandmother's relatives. Since he had already been to Calabria to look up his dad's relatives, he felt he should not put off his trip to Agnone any longer lest his mom feel he was slighting her side of the family.

"Si," replied the helpful stranger. *"Va diretto al angolo e poi gira a destra."*

"Sure," thought Bernie to himself. "Go straight. Turn right. Then I guess I just ask someone else for the exact house."

Which is exactly what he had to do. And, before too long, he found the house along with a whole clan of Comperchioli relatives who welcomed him, fed him, posed for pictures and gave him names and addresses to take back to America.

Cesare, son of Marchucci Comperchioli, was 74 years old and the obvious head of the family. He introduced Bernie to his son and daughter-in-law, Guido and Lucia, along with their small son, Renso. This group proudly posed in front of the house in which Bernie's grandmother, Filomena, had been born.

At the house of Giuseppe Comperchioli, Bernie was introduced to three other Italian-Americans. Clara and Rosmunda Ferrara and Angeline Caroselli lived in Detroit and had traveled to Italy to visit Giuseppe and his family.

Since Bernie had only planned a daytrip to Agnone, he soon had to thank his hosts and deliver a complete round of double-cheek kisses before making his way back to the *stazione*.

If the author were to return to Agnone in 2014, he would find that it is now in the Region of Molise, which was separated from Abruzzi in 1963. He would also find that Agnone is no longer in the Provincia di Campobasso, but in the Provincia di Isernia, which was separated from Campobasso in 1970.

February, 1965
Sansevero, Foggia, Italy

"Giacomo," Bernie had hesitatingly said one afternoon as he and his roommate, James Romano (of Sicilian descent), rested in their room in the *Pensione Le Fontane al Mare*, "how would you like to travel to Foggia with me? You could come along as I try to find my uncle's relatives, and then, on our way back, we could stop and visit a beautiful Italian palace at Caserta. The train goes right by it on the way back to Naples, and I've heard it's fantastic!"

Bernie and Jim didn't know it then, but the "beautiful Italian palace" they would visit would later be featured in several scenes in the **Star Wars: The Attack of the Clones** movie destined to be in theaters at the beginning of the next millennium

Giacomo agreed, and the two of them set out by train across the mountains to the Adriatic side of Italy. If *Napoli* was sunny and mild in the winter, the Apennines were a totally different story. The skies were overcast, and the scenery could not really be enjoyed because of the chilliness of the train cars.

By the time Bernie and his roommate reached Sansevero, it was late, and only with luck were they able to find a room in a nearby *albergo*.

"*Si puo mangiare?*" asked Bernie's roommate after the desk clerk had given them their room key.

The cook had gone home, and the kitchen was closed, but the desk clerk took pity on the uncomfortable duo and invited them into the back room where he found a little food and a couple *bicchieri di vino* which they enjoyed while huddled around a plain wooden table.

"*C'e una stufa?*" asked Bernie, anticipating a cold night in a drafty room.

It cost extra, but the desk clerk was able to provide a portable heater.

In the morning, a breakfast of hard rolls, butter, and *café latte* (not the drink now popular in America, but a whole cup of boiled milk into which a small amount of espresso was poured) was served to the two travelers before they began their random search for the house of Filomena Disantis, aged mother of Bernie's South Chicago uncle, Tony Miresso.

One nice thing about small towns in Italy is that most people do know most other people and, if asked politely, they are usually more than willing to help.

Before too long, Bernie and Jim were being led into a three-story building, the home of Filomena.

Now this was a living situation that the author had never seen before nor encountered since. Most unusual by American standards, to say the least!

The ground floor of the building consisted of cattle stalls. The logic being that not only was it easy to get the cattle in and out on the ground level, but the heat of their bodies (and, unfortunately, the stench of their manure) would rise and heat the upper floors.

The next floor up (the *primo piano* by Italian reckoning) housed chickens with all their familiar noises and smells.

Filomena lived on the top floor, the *secondo piano*. The view was great, but, oh my, the ambience!

Not only did Bernie and his roommate meet his uncle's mother, Filomena, but they also dined with Socorso and Domenico Malizia, Francesca and Alessandro Renna along with Santina Manna.

Bernie noted names and addresses and posed with all the relatives so he would have photos to share with his uncle on his return to The States.

Making their way back to the train station, both he and his roommate felt they had done a good thing. As fate would have it, this would be the last contact his uncle would have with his mother before she passed away and before he would die a few years later in the passageway on the north side of his father-in-law's house in South Chicago.

April, 1965
San Marco alla Mattina, Cosenza, Italy

"Now, Benardo, we are going to stay up a little later tonight because a special person wants to meet you."

This was Bernie's second trip to San Marco alla Mattina to visit his dad's relatives and his own distant cousins. Bernie had traveled to San Marco alla Mattina at Christmas after his dad had sent a letter of introduction advising his relatives of his visit. He had simply taken a train from Naples to Cosenza. When he got off the train, he booked a room at a hotel and began to ask around town for anyone named "Barci."

Bernie was first directed to a bookbinder's shop where he was introduced to a slender young man named Mario Manna who said he was familiar with the Barci families that lived at San Marco alla Mattina. Since it was already late that evening, he said he would pick Bernie up at the *albergo* the next morning. But first, of course, he wanted to show Bernie some very nice black and white photos of nudes (modestly airbrushed) that he had in the back of his shop.

"Un momento," said Bernie when the knock came on his hotel room door the next morning.

"Siete pronto?" asked Bernie's ride.

"Devo farmi la barba et poi saro pronto," replied Bernie who had done his best to learn enough standard Italian to make it through this visit to his relatives.

Before leaving Cosenza for San Marco, Bernie was taken to a small record shop (*Casa di Disci*) that was owned by a cousin of his named Bernardo Barci. Bernardo was the son of Luigi Barci who worked for the railroad at San Marco. On December 26, 1964, Bernie had posed for a photo with Bernardo Barci, his wife Rosetta and their infant son, Luigi, named after his grandfather.

When they got to the town of San Marco, and before driving out into the country to the small village known as La Mattina, Bernie was taken to meet another cousin of his, Francesco. Francesco was a barber and was the son of Bernie's dad's aunt, Violanda Barci.

On the drive out to La Mattina, they were using a small dirt road. Suddenly, apparently in the middle of nowhere, the road was blocked by a railroad gate that had been lowered.

"Who lowered the gate?" asked Bernie as no elevated crossing shanty or gatekeeper's shack or house could be seen nearby.

"The railroad hires the nearest farmer to lower and raise the gate on the road when the train is scheduled to pass. These guys like to come out early and leave the gate down for a half hour or so until the train comes by," explained Mario.

"So what do we do? Just wait?" asked Bernie.

"No. We take a leak," answered Mario who led Bernie over to the side of the road.

It was a quiet and very weird moment he shared with Mario, but it was one that would be imprinted on the old memory.

For that Christmas visit Bernie's Letter of Introduction had been sent by his dad to Domenico Barci, the elder of the Barci clan living in La Mattina. Domenico did have two older brothers, but the eldest, Vincenzo, had emigrated to Pennsylvania, and the other, Giovanni, had never married. Domenico was married to Elvira with whom he had six children: Natalina, Giuseppe, Adele, Marcella, Guido, Nilo.

The first thing Domenico did was arrange to introduce Bernie to the *Padrone* that owned the land on which most of his relatives lived. The *Padrone, Cavalière* Michele Valentoni (the son of the Longare Valentoni who had been the *Padrone* when Giuseppe Barci live in La Mattina) lived in the family *Palazzo* that dated back to the 12th century A.D. On his way up to the second floor where the *Padrone* had his residence, Bernie passed through the *Chiesa di Santa Maria Della Matina* (spelled with only one "t" on its pamphlet) in which his dad had once served as an altar boy before moving to America. The church was located on the ground floor of the *Palazzo*.

On the second floor (the *primo piano*), Bernie was amazed to see that the *Palazzo* was decorated with wooden floors—a covering far more elite and expensive than marble which is a rather common flooring in Italy.

"Va bene," said the *Padrone* once the initial introductions had been made and coffee had been served. *"Che lavoro fa il vostro padre?"*

"Mio padre lavora per la ferrovia. E un capo, un soprintendente."

Bernie's dad really wasn't a superintendent on the railroad, but he had no idea what the Italian word for Roadmaster would be. *Soprintendente* would give the general idea.

"So," said the *Padrone* as he continued his interview with Bernie in Italian, "did your father pay for your visit to Italy?"

The *Padrone* was obviously trying to find out how successful little Tirigi Barci had become after moving to America.

"No, ho pagato Io," replied Bernie. "I worked for two years to save up money, and then I was given a scholarship by Tufts University to come to Italy to study."

"Ma, qual e questo problema dei negri in America?" the *Padrone* suddenly asked rather candidly.

Bernie found it interesting that the Civil Rights Movement in America would be of interest to a wealthy landowner in Southern Italy, but he would give it his best shot.

"Multi credono che i negri sono sporci e pigri," answered Bernie.

"E non vogliono le sue figle andare in spossa ai negri," added the Padrone.

"Si, lèi ha ragione," confirmed Bernie.

On that first visit, Bernie had made a list of more than 100 relatives that were living in the area, and he had determined to pay key family members one more visit before returning to America.

"Chi e questo che voglia incontrarmi e dove habita?" asked Bernie in his best formal Italian about the expected late night visitor. Bernie had managed to pick up a few Calabrese words and phrases by listening to his mom and dad over the years, but these were strictly part of his "recognition only" vocabulary. The few phrases he could repeat from his childhood (such as *"State citto," "Ma tu sei pazzo," "Calabrése e capo tosto"* and *"Diavolo maledetto scataruzo"*) were not really meant for polite conversation.

"This is a very special person named Domenico Penna. He is coming all the way from Mongrassano."

The rap on the door was barely audible, but Bernie's host, Vincenzo Aloise (who was married to Fidarma Barci, daughter of Bernie's dad's uncle, Raffaelli Barci), was on his feet in a second to let his visitor in.

"Buona sera," said Bernie rising to his feet to greet the special guest.

"Buona sera, Bernardo. Io sono Domenico Penna," replied the guest extending a strong hand covered in coarse skin.

After the usual formalities of welcoming their special guest to their home, most of the family disappeared into another room while Bernie and Vincenzo sat at a small wooden table with Domenico.

"Bernardo, I have some very valuable books that I would like to sell in America. I am hoping that you will be able to help me find a buyer."

At this point, Domenico began to place on the table several volumes that had been carefully wrapped in a variety of cloth coverings. Bernie was amazed to see that the volumes were very old sheepskin covered books that had been handwritten by monks. Several were beautifully illuminated texts, the first letters of main paragraphs decorated with colorful and elaborate pictures. Because of his training in classical literature at the University of Michigan, Bernie recognized these books as very rare and expensive volumes and began to understand why Domenico's visit was shrouded in secrecy.

"I have a small gift I would like to give you to thank you in advance for your help," said Domenico as he unwrapped a small sheepskin covered volume of the **Letters of Cicero** that had been printed in the late 1700's. The original first 20 pages of the printed book had been replaced by twenty pages of handwritten copy, which Domenico assured Bernie made the small book especially valuable.

"Grazie, Signor Domenico," replied Bernie. "I'll see what I can do when I get back to America."

Bernie suspected that Domenico's books may have been stolen and that Domenico could well be a black market agent trying to move them. After discussing Domenico's offer with his dad on his return to America, Bernie wrote a letter to Domenico expressing his regrets that he would not be able to help him find a buyer.

"The thing about people like that," had advised his dad, "is that it is better never to get involved with them in the first place rather than try to break it off with them later on."

To this day, the sheepskin-covered volume that Domenico Penna presented Bernie remains a part of the author's small collection of antique books.

That night, as Bernie slept alone in the double bed that occupied the center of the main room in Vincenzo's house, he was sleeping on his back, weighted down by several heavy blankets. The house had no heat, and the mattress rested on legs designed to hold it at least three feet above the cold floor. Perhaps it was the visit of Domenico. Or maybe it was just the weight of the blankets or the fact that Bernie was lying on his back (something that can sometimes produce the same effect). Whatever the cause, Bernie was heard to let out a deep throated frightening moan in the middle of the night that woke both him and the rest of the household.

"So, Bernardo," asked Vincenzo in the morning, "did you have a bad dream last night?"

"I think that happens when I sleep on my back," replied Bernie not wanting to give any indication that he may have been uncomfortable sleeping in their home.

Vincenzo then escorted Bernie out to the cow barn and showed him where he could go to the bathroom in the straw. Vincenzo had neither indoor facilities nor an outhouse on his rented farm.

May, 1965
Naples, Italy

The Tufts University's Classical Year Abroad Program was over, and it was time for Bernie to check out of the *Pensione Le Fontane al Mare* and begin his trip back to America.

"Goodbye, Fink!"

Bernie was stunned. Why was Denise calling him a fink? He thought they had had some good times together. He had struck up an acquaintance with her early in the school year only because he had heard that one of the girls on the trip was sick. So, being a gentleman, he thought he would take the girl a little bouquet of flowers to cheer her up. One thing led to another, and soon they were going to movies together, having dinner together and taking walks through the park along the bay.

"Why is that woman kneeling in front of that guy on the park bench?" Denise had asked innocently during one of their evening *passeggiate*.

"Never mind," said Bernie as he tried not to notice.

A little further along the path another woman was sitting bolt upright on some guy's lap. As he and Denise passed, they sat very still eyeing the two

Americani, and waiting for them to get a respectable distance away before they continued what they had been up to.

Judging by the drab way these two women were dressed, they were either very cheap dates or park prostitutes. The regular street prostitutes, of which there was an open abundance in Naples, dressed more stereotypically in short skirts and bright colors. In fact, one of the first things the boys in the program were taught when they reached Naples was how to say *"Non me scuciate!"* It was a vernacular invective strong enough to thwart any uninvited advances.

As Bernie and Denise became more comfortable with each other, she finally showed him a very special way she had of kissing.

WOW! Bernie had never even heard of, much less experienced, anything like this before.

First, Denise moistened her own lips with her tongue and then asked Bernie to do the same with his. When their lips came together, she began sliding her wet lips over his, back and forth, back and forth, back and forth. It was a spine-tingling, toe curling experience. One that Bernie would come to look forward to in the months ahead.

They spent weekends on romantic Capri together. They traveled through Greece together—always *una camera* to save money, but *due letti* to keep things on the up and up. Denise was a proper Jewish girl, and Bernie, a devout Roman Catholic—regardless of the sly looks they got from an occasional wispy-eyed bellboy. Their entire relationship never really got much past those slippery kisses.

But, hey, those were enough to keep anyone interested.

At the end of the school year, Denise had been sent money by her father to purchase a VW that she was going to drive through Northern Europe for the rest of the summer before returning home.

She had asked Bernie to chip in and join the others who had agreed to travel with her. Bernie couldn't. He was so broke that he had even had to cash in his return trip boat ticket to get some extra money. He had to turn Denise down. Special kisses and all.

Maybe that's why she was calling him a fink.

As Denise drove off with her new travelling companions, all Bernie could do was sing a little chorus of "Go Away, Little Girl" to himself, a song that was popular that year.

Spending the year studying and traveling throughout Italy, Sicily and Greece had filled Bernie with a burning desire to stay in Italy if at all possible. He had visited the American School in Naples hoping to be hired on as a secondary school teacher. Unfortunately, he was told, all their teachers are hired stateside.

Nella, the daughter of Ernesto Barci who lived in San Marco alla Mattina had made at least two trips to visit her aunt in Naples while Bernie was there. Her real motive, Bernie suspected, was to interest him in marrying her. Granted she was very cute, but she was a little older than Bernie and, to his mind, very aggressive and strong-armed. When she went walking with him on the streets of Naples, she was very much in control. A real turn off.

Then there was the Italian lady Bernie had met on Capri who owned a wool weaving shop. She was very open about wanting to marry an American so she could spend her winters in America and her summers catering to the tourist trade on Capri.

Somehow, Bernie didn't think that his life had been saved when he accidentally fell backwards off a piece of column at Olympia in Greece so he could marry either of these young women.

Of course, there was the stunning beauty who sang in the nightclub on the first floor while living in the *Pensione* with all the Tufts male students. But she was definitely way beyond Bernie's reach. Besides, her plans for the future did not involve being married to a secondary school teacher in America. She was saving up to become a lawyer and get rich in international trade.

So Bernie resigned himself to returning home. Besides, his brother Joe had delayed his wedding plans at the insistence of his parents so Bernie could be home for the wedding. And his grandfather, Joe Barcio, was nervously awaiting the safe return of his grandson from his visit with the relatives he had left behind all those years ago.

To come up with extra money, Bernie had decided to cash in his return boat trip ticket and travel by train to England where he could board an Icelandic Airways flight to New York for half the price of his boat fare. Since he would end up being in England for a few days, he would also be able to look up the relatives of Charles Caurse, his Bay City landlord, who lived in Wales. When his landlady had given him the address and asked him to do this for her quasi-senile husband (who insisted on calling all dogs "puppy" regardless of their size or age), Bernie hadn't thought he would be able to accommodate her since the Tufts program did not have an excursion to England in its curriculum. Now that he could make the side trip, it turned out to be fun. There's nothing like knocking on a door in a foreign country and announcing to a strange family that you are an acquaintance of a relative of theirs who had asked you to stop in and say, "Hi!"

Stories connected with Bernie's trip from Naples to London, as exciting as they are, will have to wait a couple of pages to be told.

June 3, 1965
South Milwaukee, Wisconsin
Bernie had returned safely from Italy and had been taken to visit his grandfather, Giuseppe Barcio. It was as though this was all his Pappa had been hanging on for. Not long after the visit during which Bernie had tried to tell his grandfather as much as possible about the relatives he had met, Giuseppe died from a heart attack. It was definitely the end of an era.

Bernie's brother Joe had already taken his seat in the back in his dad's car following the burial of his grandfather when his mom started in on him from the front seat.

"You'll have to cancel your wedding, Joe!"

"No, by God, I don't, Ma!" shouted Joe back at her from the back seat.

Like the grandfather whose namesake he was, Bernie's brother Joe also was renowned for his Italian temper. In fact, he had even dared to match his temper with his grandfather's one Sunday after he had taken his fiancée, Liz Mingari, over to their house in South Milwaukee to meet them. While they were visiting, an argument broke out between his grandfather, his grandmother and several others who happened to be in the house. Joe was humiliated.

So, after he took Liz back home, he simply returned to South Milwaukee and proceeded to give his grandfather holy hell for embarrassing him in front of his fiancée.

"If you all want to yell and argue, you can just do it when we're not here!" screamed Joe into his grandfather's face.

Giuseppe Barcio, the man who had come from Italy to start a new life, had raised six children, had shot and killed an assailant who left a bullet in the back of his neck, had been a foreman on the railroad, had built numerous houses despite his illiteracy, and was trying desperately to recover from a stroke, just stood and looked at his grandson, his namesake, the firstborn son of his firstborn son. He said nothing. He did nothing. He just stood there. His lame right hand hanging uselessly at his side.

While, in his later years, Joe felt proud to have taken his stand against his grandfather, he was probably very lucky to have survived the day. Those who knew his grandfather would not have been surprised if Giuseppe Barcio had taken that opportunity to defend his honor one last time, stroke or no stroke.

If Joe had survived standing up to his grandfather, he certainly wasn't going to be cowered by his mother.

"Damn it, Ma. First you don't like any of the girls I date because they're too fat, or they live on a farm or they're not Italian. Then you don't like an Italian girl I date because she's Sicilian. And now you want me to cancel my wedding. No, by God, I won't do it."

Bernie was still standing outside the back car door waiting to get in, although he was in no hurry to be in the middle of the argument that sounded like it was going to be a doozy.

"Ted," screamed Stella when she saw her husband open his car door and get in, "talk some sense into your son's head!"

"What's the matter now, Son?" asked Ted as he sat down behind the wheel.

"Ma wants me to cancel my wedding, and by God, I'm not gonna do it."

"Well, you can just go to hell then," screamed Stella at her son. "And take your Sicilian with you!"

Suddenly, it was all just too much for Ted. While he, too, was renowned for his Italian temper, and would normally not have backed away from the fray, this would not be his day for a stand. Ted slammed his head against the steering wheel, covered his eyes and started bawling, openly and unashamedly.

The shock was too much even for Joe and his mom. They both shut up immediately while Bernie stood outside the back door of the car not really knowing what to do.

Finally, Ted got out of the car, removed his handkerchief from his pocket, wiped his eyes and blew his nose.

"I'm sorry, boys," he said in a subdued voice. "I'm sorry. I just buried my father, and I really don't want to argue just now."

As Joe recalls the event, his fiancée, Liz, was also standing off to the side of the car during the whole exchange.

The trip back to the airport was quiet. Very quiet.

Bernie flew back to Michigan where he would teach his last session of summer school at Bay City High School.

The first opportunity Bernie had, he took a bus back to Ann Arbor (having sold his car to Betty Jean before leaving for Italy) to consult with the Classics Department there and see if they knew of any new Latin teaching positions for which he could apply.

They had two. A school in Hawaii needed a full-time Latin teacher and had contacted the University of Michigan in the hopes that they could refer one of their graduates.

Hawaii sounded exotic, and Bernie did consider the position—for about 15 minutes. He decided it was too far away from his family.

The second opening was for someone to head the Latin Department at a private school in Indianapolis called Park School. The position paid an incredible $7,800 per year. Bernie couldn't believe his good luck.

He contacted the school immediately and made plans to meet the headmaster, Bill McCluskey, and visit the campus as soon as possible.

June 19, 1965
Milwaukee, Wisconsin

"Go, Bernard. Sing a song for your brother," instructed Bernie's mom.

"But I don't have any words with me," said Bernie.

"You know the words. Go. Go," insisted his mother.

Good to his promise, Joe did not cancel or delay his marriage plans. Bernie had flown back from Michigan, and the Milwaukee Barcio's attended in full force, albeit dressed in black since they were still in mourning for the recent death of Joe's grandfather.

Liz's dad, Joe Mingari, played the role of proud father and passed out aperitifs to those who came through the reception line. Liz's Mom had passed away when Liz was a teenager. A live band played, and Bernie was finally coaxed into giving an unrehearsed rendition of *"Santa Lucia."*

December 31, 1965
Times Square, New York City, New York

Although Bernie had traveled back to Sparta to spend Christmas with his family, he had already bought his plane tickets for his trip to New York City.

"Why are you going to New York?" his mom had asked.

"One of the boys that was studying in Naples with us invited everyone to New York for a reunion. We're all going to go to Times Square on New Year's Eve."

When Bernie got to the host's house in an upscale neighborhood to the north of New York City, he found that very few students had accepted the invitation.

The boy was there who had traveled with Bernie by rail from Naples to London. This was a student who had managed to enjoy very little of his year with Tuft's in Italy. It was his personal philosophy that life was simply a waiting room for death. When a middle-aged American divorcee, who was also living at their *Pensione*, had suggested that he should at least get out and watch the fishermen haul in their catches along the bay one morning, he agreed to give it a try. The experience left him nonplussed.

Bernie and his dour companion had both decided to cash in their return boat tickets to fly from London to New York on Icelandic Airways. On the way, they would first make a stopover in Milan to see La Scala and later in Paris to see the Louvre and the Eiffel Tower.

After their stopover in Milan, they had re-boarded the train and were settling back to enjoy the scenery to which they would soon be treated as they passed through the Swiss Alps. When the train reached the Swiss border, however, it was boarded by Inspectors who came through the cars checking everyone's passports. Bernie had his ready and easily passed inspection. His friend, however, was having a problem.

"This is not your passport," said the Inspector.

Bernie's friend took it back and looked at it carefully.

"Oh, man, the hotel clerk in Milan gave me the wrong passport. What do I do now?" he asked.

"Well, you will have to get off the train and retrieve your passport before you can enter Switzerland," said the Inspector.

Rather than get permanently separated, especially since he needed his friend's knowledge of French to tour Paris successfully, Bernie decided that he, too, would leave the train and wait in the depot until his friend returned from Milan.

Dawn, a girl with permanently tanned skin and an elongated face that sported a scar over one eyebrow, attended the New York reunion with another girl with whom Bernie had never become well acquainted during the program.

Denise, however, chose not to attend with her slippery kisses.

So much for that friendship!

On New Year's Eve, they all boarded a train and headed for Times Square. The Square was packed, and it was cold. For a while they just walked around and watched people shivering as they carried drinks from one bar to another.

"Hey, the party's up here," came a slightly inebriated voice from a window overlooking the Square.

"Let's go up," suggested Dawn.

"Might be fun," agreed the reunion host. But then, this boy's idea of fun in Italy had been to scoop his own turds out of the toilet in his 7th floor *Pensione* room and drop them on the gas tank that had been installed at the curb below.

Once in the building, they made it up to what they thought was the correct floor, only to find that almost every room had its door open and was filled with partiers hanging out its window. They finally decided just to pick a room, any room, and make their way over to a window to watch the ball drop.

At midnight, Bernie got a little peck on his left cheek from Dawn.

Happy New Year!

The crowd in the Square began to disperse almost immediately. When the Tuft's group made their way back down to street level, they thought they would hang around just a little longer to enhance their memories of the occasion.

The New York City Mounted Police, however, had other ideas. It was now quarter past midnight, and they wanted Times Square cleared.

"Look out!" shouted the group's poop-dropping host. "That horse almost kicked you."

Sure enough, the Mounted Police were positioning their mounts in the middle of each small gathering of partiers and then giving their horses signals to make them spin in circles while kicking their back legs out.

That would have to be the group's final memory of Times Square on New Year's Eve, 1965.

Cristoforo Colombo Ocean Liner service New York to Naples, Italy

The author on the grounds of the Villa Pignatelli, Naples, Italy, 1964

On-site archaeologist explains Etruscan burials to *"Il Grupo"*, Etruria, Italy, spring 1965. Author (front row L), roommate Giacomo Romano (4th from L)

Author performing "Santa Lucia" on his mandolin. Naples, Italy, October 1964

Author (R) and his dour travelling companion, Naples, Italy, Spring 1965

Apartment (top of stairs) where Tirigi Barci was born in La Mattina, Italy, Aug. 6, 1907

(L to R) Guido, son Renso, wife Lucia, Cesare Comperchioli in front of house in which Filomena was born July 8, 1890 Agnone, Italy, January 1965

(L to R) Mario Manna, The Author & Bernardo Barci
Casa di Disci, Cosenza, Italy, Dec., 1964

Postcard from Cosenza, Reggio di Calabria, Italy, 1965

Author's cousin Nella,
daughter of Ernesto Barci
La Mattina, Italy

PART VII

March 1966 – April 1972

National Limelight and

Adventures in a River House on Ferguson

March 15, 1965
Indianapolis
"Is everything ready?" asked the headmaster, Bill McClusky.

"I think so," said Bernie. "We broke the bow last night during a test fire, but the lumber yard worked all night to rebuild it. They put it together with Elmer's Glue."

"Do you think it will work?" asked Bill.

"Well, it's very stiff, so one of the engineers here has suggested that we wrap it with wet towels to limber up the wood," replied Bernie.

It was Bernie's first year as Head of the Latin Department at Park School and there he was smack dab in the middle of the national limelight.

"You're not planning to fire the rock that your students brought in last week, are you?" asked Bill.

The week before, in response to a contest to find the best 100 lb. projectile to be fired on national television, Geoff Reynolds had brought in a rock that weighed exactly 100 lbs. On its face he had neatly painted the words, "FLYING BALLS MEAN DYING GAULS."

"No," said Bernie. "We rejected that entry and are using a different rock. It weighs a few pounds more but it should be O.K."

"What does this one have written on it?"

"This one just says GAUL BLASTER."

This had all started, as Bernie later wrote in a book entitled **Catapult Design, Construction and Competition,** at a routine meeting of the Academic Development Committee of Park School held in December, 1965.

"I want you all," said headmaster Bill McCluskey, "to review continuously the content and method of your instruction. We want our students to be challenged. Don't be afraid to try unusual methods of stimulating the interest and involvement of the students."

Since this advice matched perfectly with Bernie's teaching philosophy of encouraging all of his Latin students and of never putting down their ideas in class, he soon found himself helping the students of his Latin II class to build a full size Roman catapult. Their goal was to hurl a 100 lb. rock 100 yards.

Since Park School had recently hired Ed Cervone to serve as a public relations coordinator for their efforts to move the school to a new campus, Ed thought the project was novel enough to gain the attention of the national media.

"The N.B.C. camera crew is here, Bernie, and they want to ask you a couple questions," said Ed as he came up to the catapult.

Not only was the camera crew on campus, but there was also a motorcycle messenger standing by who would rush the film to the airport so it could be broadcast from New York City by the Huntley-Brinkley NBC news team. Bernie had already been interviewed several times as the show picked up on the early stages of the project and did short reports during the preceding weeks to hype the firing of the Mars I catapult.

"Bernie, the phone's for you," called Bernie's Orchard housemate, Bill Hopper.

It was a reporter from the **New York Times**.

Other evening calls came from **Sports Illustrated, Indianapolis Star** reporters, and various network newsrooms.

Bernie had quickly and competently adjusted to his national celebrity and handled all calls with decorum and efficiency. If his heart was pounding with excitement, his calm voice and collected demeanor gave no indication.

If this was destined to be his "15 minutes of fame," he was going to handle it with aplomb and enjoy every second of it.

Three p.m. on the Ides was scheduled as the "Ides of March Castoff." At that time the entire school body paraded to the athletic field where the Mars I had been set up. Parents and alumni were present. The drum and bugle corps from nearby Marian College provided military background marches. Present to cover the firing for the Huntley-Brinkley NBC news team was reporter Pat Trese.

The crowd hushed as Bernard Barcio, the Latin Master of Park School, addressed his students:

> "On a day when the key word is Gemini and the conversation treats of projectiles, missiles and countdowns, let's remind ourselves briefly of the first Gemini, the sons of Mars—Romulus and Remus. Imagine, if you dare, the full scale of the accomplishments of a nation which made studied and extensive use of projectiles, missiles and countdowns to gain almost complete control of the then known world. A nation synonymous perhaps with no man's name as much as with Gaius Julius Caesar's.
>
> "Caesar was indeed a Roman, a man with the creative intuition to conceive a challenge, the imagination to formulate the approach, the courage to bring it to completion, as well as the rashness to ignore the threats to 'Beware the Ides of March.'
>
> "Park School's second year Latin class has not only met the challenge of reading Caesar, but has gone so far as to try to emulate him. Though on a small scale, they are discovering the incredible

complexities in which the Romans were involved. They are experiencing the factors of cooperation, foresight and determination which necessarily had to be employed before success, to the degree that the Romans enjoyed, could have been realized.

"From the Mars I Catapult Project we have learned that the ancient [world] was equally as challenging as the modern, equally as dangerous, and unpredictable enough to tax man's rationality to its fullest.

"As our nation and our space program today, Caesar and his policies were also subject to cutting criticism. Just as NASA has its defenders so too did Caesar. In tribute to Caesar, I would like to read to you today the defense which Cicero offered on Caesar's behalf."

Bernie then read a text in Latin to the assembled crowd, very few of whom would understand a word. But, hey, he had the eyes of the nation on him, and he was going to take advantage of the opportunity to promote his subject. When the Latin selection was finished, Bernie was ready to continue preparing the crowd for the launching.

"The Mars I is ready for launching. Before beginning our countdown, I exhort you in the traditional manner of a general before battle. *'O passi graviora, dabit deus his quoque finem.'* "

This address was also in Latin. Bernie had borrowed the words of encouragement that Aeneas had given to his men when they landed in Lybia after being shipwrecked off its shores. The closing line of the oration proved to be the most ominous, as future years would reveal.

"Forsan et haec olim meminisse iuvabit."
Perhaps it will help to remember these things some day.

And what a day it turned out to be! The chemistry teacher, Mr. Daniels, (a man who himself tipped the scales at nearly 300 lbs.) had volunteered to help hoist the 103 lb. rock, politely christened Gaul Blaster, into the firing tray. During a brisk tattoo of drums, the order was given to fire.
CRRRAACKK!
Under extreme pressure, the bow cracked and Gaul Blaster tumbled to the ground, setting the first modern catapult record of 3 feet with a 103 lb. rock.

The bow that was used on that first catapult was still on display during the year 2000 in a what was now called the Park-Tudor Lower School hallway.

When, however, the author requested permission to display the original bow during a party held on March 12, 2011, to commemorate the 45th Anniversary of the Inception of Modern Catapulting, he was told that it could no longer be located.

The rock christened Gaul Blaster, now with most of its red paint and lettering worn off, currently rests under a flowering crab apple tree in front of the author's new home.

May 29, 1966
Park School, Indianapolis
Two weeks had passed since Bernie's Latin class had made national news with its Mars I catapult. Bernie had been invited to address a gathering of Park School parents, students and supporters.

> "It is a great honor to address such an audience this evening. A teacher is always flattered when he finally addresses a group that is actually listening to what he has to say.
>
> "It is a fitting way to approach the end of a month that has been both tense and marked by anticipation. A month which dotted the U.S.A. with U.F.O.'s, roused college students with L.S.D. and put Park School on the map with P.C.B.'s.
>
> "P.C.B.'s are among the latest of Nature's creative forces to be released—to date they remain unharnessed, captivating and unpredictable in their combined force. No other energy can change the conceptual to the tangible so quickly.
>
> "Briefly, P.C.B.'s are **P**ark's **C**atapult **B**uilders. They are a group of students taking second year Latin who have had their minds sparked by the past to such a degree that they surged forward to a unique accomplishment.
>
> "They are a group of boys who moved so quickly that I did not have ample opportunity to advise not to be so daring, to be more cautious, to avoid approaching the limits of their inexperience and capabilities, not to rile up the student body, to avoid jamming the roads of Park with horses, drummers and a parade, to avoid taking a risk while the whole nation—long accustomed to viewing the spectacular in their T.V. rooms—critically looked on.
>
> "In short, Mars I was created before we at Park knew what force a Gaul Blaster really contained.
>
> "Mars I is a full scale Roman catapult inspired by a study of Caesar's Gallic Wars. It was recklessly suggested in class [by David Leve], it was built before plans could be drawn up. It stands 5 feet high, is 8 feet long, and, if the energies of its 5000-pound pull bow can be properly controlled, will hurl a 100 pound rock at least 100 yards.
>
> "Mars I is brutally handsome. If I may, I would like to show you, at this time, just a few slides of a very momentous Ides of March."

August, 1966
Stratford, Ontario

Fresh from his year abroad with Tufts University, Bernie firmly believed in the educational advantages of travel for students. He therefore wasted no time in planning Park School's first Stratford Shakespearean Festival Trip. The school agreed to provide a transportation van to be driven by Bernie. The group would leave Indianapolis on Monday, August 1, at 7:00 a.m., and return by 8:00 p.m. on Thursday, August 4. On Tuesday and Wednesday they would attend three different plays at the Shakespearean Festival Theater in Stratford.

Most of the students were housed in sleeping rooms made available through the Festival Agency with local families.

Two boys, however, obtained parental permission to camp out at the Stratford Camp Grounds. Since one of these boys was the son of Madame Sebastian, a teacher of French at Park School, Bernie's natural reluctance to leave them unsupervised was allayed.

He was not really surprised to learn afterwards that the boys had cavorted through the night instead of sleeping soundly in their tent as they had promised.

September, 1966
Indianapolis

"What a great house," proclaimed Bill Hopper, the Park School art teacher. Bernie and Bill had just moved into the old farmhouse on the Lilly Orchard located on the northwest corner of 71st and College Ave. Their job would be to keep an eye on the property as Park School's plans for construction moved along. There were three bedrooms on the second floor, two small and one large that faced east.

"Wanna flip a coin to see who gets the big bedroom?" asked Bill.

Bernie won the coin toss, and Bill chose the small bedroom on the south side of the house.

Not only did Bernie and Bill have the run of the house and the orchard, but they also had the key to Foster Hall, a stately, all-stone Tudor construction that housed a huge working pipe organ.

The orchard also featured two ponds, on the larger of which lived an ornery goose that they affectionately named George.

Bill Hopper set up a painting studio in what had once been the dining room of the old farmhouse, and both he and Bernie took turns cooking fairly decent meals each evening.

Life was good on the orchard.

It would not be until years later that Bernie would come to appreciate the full historical value of the house in which he and Bill Hopper were now living. In May, 2003, when the author was editing, for a **Special Early History Edition of the Village Sampler**, historical articles that his wife Lillian had published earlier (based both on her own research in 1998 and on an interview conducted by Shirley Vogler Meister in 1993), he came across the following historical account of life in the Lilly Orchard farmhouse.

"Mary Martha Washington was born Jan. 29, 1914, in a house which once stood on the location of the Lower School building of Park-Tudor school, 7456 N. College Ave. at a time when the location was known as the J. K. Lilly Farm. Her parents were Wanetta (an Indian name) and William Anderson. Wanetta's physician when Mary Martha was born was Dr. Mason Light, whose father [no doubt, Dr. Robert C. Light who once owned a small house on the southwest corner of College and Westfield Blvd. and was a co-leaser of White City Park when it was built in 1907] 'owned the property where The Vogue now stands.'

"Her maternal grandparents, William and Mary Engelken, were the farm's caretakers. Her grandfather and 'hired help' planted the first apple orchard on the farm. Mary recalled how J. K. Lilly often brought guests to the Engelken home for a traditional chicken dinner served by Martha's grandmother.

"When the Andersons and Engelkens lived together in the house on the J. K. Lilly farm, they attended St. Mary's Church which the German Catholic community had built between 1910 and 1912 at 317 N. New Jersey St. They had to start out from the Lilly farm by horse and buggy which they left at a livery stable once located approximately where Ossip's Optometry now is located on Broad Ripple Ave. and board the Interurban for the ride to church."

What would happen later to the farmhouse would be a terrible travesty considering its long and colorful background.

October 1, 1966
Guelph, Ontario

"No, Mr. Barcio, the Governor cannot provide transportation for you and your students to Canada," reported an aid to the Governor of Indiana.

"We thought maybe the National Guard might be able to fly our catapult to Canada along with our students," countered Bernie.

"No, the Governor says he is only authorized to use the National Guard in times of emergency."

That had settled the matter, and Bernie was only able to accept the invitation to take part in the 11th Field Artillery Regiment's Centennial Celebration in Guelph, Ontario, by renting a van into which the disassembled catapult could be loaded. Accompanied by his students and Park School's public relations manager, Ed Cervone, the group arrived and set up in the middle of a baseball field on which the Centennial Celebrations were to be held.

The organizers had seen the Park School catapult featured on the Huntley-Brinkley show and had invited Mr. Barcio to bring his catapult and his students to Canada. They even provided official-looking Roman costumes borrowed from the Shakespearean Festival Theater in Stratford, Ontario.

"Tres, duo, unus," said Mr. Barcio into a microphone on the field as he gave the countdown to fire the redesigned Mars I.

This time, the bow had been crafted from a solid piece of limber wood. More importantly, the projectile would be an old bowling ball cleverly coated in plaster of Paris to resemble a rock. This time the bow did not break and the projectile was hurled a whopping 20 feet across the infield. Unfortunately, when it hit the ground, its plaster of Paris coating shattered, revealing its bowling ball core.

November, 1966
Park School, Indianapolis

Bernie had worked closely with the headmaster's secretary, Lillian Batten, throughout the whole catapult hullabaloo. They had, understandably become quite friendly.

Bernie happened to be visiting Lew Berkeley and his wife, Anne, at their home on campus one evening when Lew's phone rang.

"What? Are you sure, Lillian? Have you called the police? O.K., get out of there as soon as possible and come over to our house," advised Lew.

"What's the matter, Lew," asked Anne.

"Lillian's working late at the office, and someone took a shot at her from the road," said Lew.

"Is she hurt," asked Bernie.

"No, but it scared her half to death."

When the police arrived, Lew and Bernie went over to the office to look over the scene. The police then came to the house and interviewed Lillian to see if she could think of anyone who might have wanted to shoot her.

She had recently gone through a divorce with the father of her three children, but she doubted that her ex would stoop to such extremes.

The bullet was recovered from a wall in the office, but it was never determined who fired the shot.

In the future when Lillian had to work late, she made it a practice to keep the blinds closed.

December 1, 1966
Park School, Indianapolis

Bernie was scheduled to deliver a short address to the Wednesday Morning Assembly. It would be a full assembly of both Upper and Lower Schools and all faculty and administrators. With the help of the school's P. R. man, Ed Cervone and the Headmaster's secretary, Lillian Batten, he and his students had brought national attention to the school, and he had become somewhat of a local celebrity.

After the usual acknowledgements and thanks, Bernie got right into the main body of his address.

"Today, as you know, is December 1st, the first day of National You'd Better Be Good Month. It is a month which gives each of us an opportunity to renew our interest in the reward that comes from having met a challenge—whether that challenge is to be good for 24 days or simply to listen carefully for 10 minutes.

"Not all of us like the word 'challenge' although it is actually quite harmless. A challenge is simply a task which we know could be done, but which we also know would demand our full concentration and serious effort.

"There was a football game once in which a challenge was turned down. The game was between Bay City and Saginaw, Michigan. During the course of the game, the team from Saginaw was loosing, and its coach began shouting from the sidelines, 'Give Calhoun the ball!' During each play that followed, however, the ball was never given to Calhoun. Whatever player did get the ball was quickly wiped out by the very powerful and aggressive Bay City defense. Calhoun was one of the better Saginaw players, and the coach felt that their only chance was to put the ball into his hands. So once again the coach shouted, 'Give Calhoun the ball!'

"This time, however, when the Saginaw quarterback came out of the huddle, he looked over at his coach who was about to be disappointed yet one more time and yelled, 'Calhoun, he don't want the ball!' (*pause for laughter*) I would like to narrow the challenge of December down to its smallest part, today, December 1st. Today is a challenge. The challenge lies in spending the day as perfectly as you are able to spend it. The challenge is to do the right thing, at the right time, in the right way. The challenge is to do everything the best way you know how—even making a routine trip to your locker. The challenge is not to let yourself down today.

"While each of us has a fairly good idea of what we'll do today— at least the students, if not the teachers—unfortunately, there is no one who can tell us exactly what we must do every second of the time in order to spend a perfect day. Yet, somehow, we'll know. Somehow each of us will have an idea of what each situation calls for and immediately afterwards we'll know whether or not we've done the best we could.

"The way to go about facing up to today successfully is to break it up into its smallest parts and take it one part at a time. Concentrate on 'now' and be concerned with what is coming tomorrow only in so far as you have to prepare for it today.

"Should you decide to accept this challenge, please take the precaution of retaining a sense of humor and a ready smile, for these will help you over the rough spots and make the day enjoyable for others. Perhaps we teachers should remember this more than the students. Exemplifying this is a note a Lower School student once left on her teacher's desk. It read, 'Dear Teacher, if you feel all right, would you please notify your face.'

"The day is here. The challenge is ours. Do we dare to accept it?"

January, 1967
The Lilly Orchard, Indianapolis

"Bernie, you and Bill are going to have a roommate. Do you think that will be O.K.?" asked headmaster Bill McCluskey.

"Why sure, Bill, there's a third large bedroom on the second floor, so there shouldn't be any problem," replied Bernie. Bernie agreed to give up the large bedroom which he had won with a coin toss, and graciously moved into a smaller room on the north side of the second floor.

However, there would be a problem. A big one. His name was Joel Tennis, and once he moved into the orchard farmhouse, along with his Doberman pincer and his pet snakes, things were never the same.

The first thing that went wrong was that Joel's Doberman chased down and killed George the goose. It was truly a sad evening as the three tenants dug a grave near the foundation of the Commons Building that was already under construction on the property.

The next thing that happened was that Joel decided that the dining room of the farmhouse that had once been Bill's painting studio would now be used for arena-style feeding of his snakes. He would release the snakes and then introduce mice. Let the games begin!

When trash day came and went and the trash had not been picked up on the orchard property, Bernie called the collection service.

"Hi, we live on the Lilly Orchard. We had our trash out on the right day, but your crew never picked it up," said Bernie in a calm, business like voice.

"You keep your Doberman indoors, and we'll pick up your trash," was the reply.

So the Doberman was moved onto the front porch of the farmhouse—an area that was quickly turned into a putrid dog run.

"Has anyone seen my coral snake?" asked Joel.

"Your coral snake? Isn't he poisonous?" asked Bill.

"Yes, he is," replied Joel. "If you see it, don't touch it. Let me get it."

Thus began a two-day search for the snake. It could be found nowhere in the house.

"I see your snake," yelled Bernie a few days later. "Joel, come and get your snake."

"Where is it?" asked Joel as he came downstairs from his bedroom.

"It's in here in the bathroom. I checked under the plunger as I usually do when I come in here. Then I happened to look up above the window. There it is, sitting on the top of the curtain rod."

Life was no longer good on the orchard. And would get a lot worse.

Joel decided that it was too much trouble to cook a new meal each night. He also said that the three should alternate whole weeks instead of nights to cook. The idea seemed O.K. until it came to be Joel's turn to cook. He simply prepared a huge pot of cooked beans that he announced would be dinner for the rest of the week.

Then came the magic markers. And the garbage bags.

At first, Bernie had looked into getting permission to move the farmhouse off of the orchard and setting it up on a foundation on a nearby lot. The school even agreed to give the house to the three of them if a lot could be found that they could afford. Unfortunately, no lot could be found, and it was announced that the house would be torn down.

"What the hell is all this?" asked Bernie as he entered the kitchen after school.

"Art!" announced Bill proudly. "Since the house is going to be torn down, Joel and I thought we would decorate the walls with creative graffiti. Check out all the neat quotations!"

It was a mess. And it didn't stop with the kitchen. In a few days all the walls, and ceilings, on the main floor were covered with magic marker sayings, drawings, game boards and crude instructions.

"What the hell is all this?" asked Bernie once more as he came home to see sacks of garbage stapled to the kitchen ceiling.

"Well," said Joel, "Bill and I decided that since they're going to trash this place anyway, we would just help them out."

Bernie decided it was time to move out, and, before too long, managed to purchase an old river house at 6544 Ferguson in Old Broad Ripple. He was able to buy it on contract for $6,000 from a man who had just purchased it a couple months earlier for $3,000.

The art teacher, William H. Hopper, left for NYC the following year to try and make it in the Mecca of the American art scene. He did fairly well, and, in 1975, landed a Solo Exhibition of 20 of his paintings in American Cultural Centers in Japan. When the author tried to locate him in 2013, he discovered that Bill had passed away in 1997. The author is still in possession of a large painting which Bill had given to his wife, Lillian.

The first thing Bernie did to his new house was have a wood burning fireplace built into the north wall of the living room. This was something he had always wanted. He then installed random-width oak flooring—something else he had always wanted.

Bernie then invited Lillian to go up to Zionsville with him to look among the antique shops there for an ornate mantel for the fireplace. Such a piece represented the first step toward elegance for Bernie, even if it would be installed in an old river house. Together, they finally decided on an intricately carved walnut mantel that Bernie was able to buy for $450.00. It was a financial stretch for him, but, hey, priorities are priorities!

June 11, 1967
Meridian Hills, Indiana

Lillian had finished her lessons with Fr. Courtney, and had recently been baptized as a Roman Catholic, thereby opening the door to a church wedding for her and her fiancé, Bernie.

Theirs had been an unusual courtship.

There is no denying that other single faculty members at Park School used their associations with the wealthy Park community to their personal advantage. Bob Eckles, who taught the Middle School Latin program under Bernie's supervision, struck up a relationship with Margo Lacy of Inland Container fame and fortune, and was soon married to this multi-millionaire. Madame Sebastian, the school French teacher, began to date the elder Mr. Block, owner of a chain of Block Department stores, and ended up providing a very comfortable life for herself and her two children with the help of her new husband's fortune.

Bernie, however, had no such aspirations. As the Head of the Department of Latin at Park School, he had been thrust into the national limelight by the fact that his Latin students had built and deployed a full-sized working catapult on national T.V. He had worked closely with Lillian as the headmaster's secretary in coordinating the press releases, and things just sort of blossomed from there.

Lillian, however, seems to have been most impressed by the fact that Bernie was one of the first faculty members who had ever requested a student's file so he could gain a better understanding of a student's past academic history.

Luckily, Lillian's first husband had never bothered to be baptized, an oversight that facilitated the granting of a Pauline Privilege and the subsequent blessing of the church on their marriage.

Bernie was treated to the traditional Park School faculty bachelor's party in the basement of the Athenaeum and presented a coffee table book on Romantic Art.

Since Lillian had been married before, she chose not to wear white, opting instead for a knee-length pink dress. Her three girls, who had mostly interacted with Bernie throughout his courtship of their mother by untying his shoestrings to the point of annoyance, wore cute spring outfits. The wedding party would be one of the smallest that any in attendance would ever witness. Besides her three children, Marsha, Sheryl and Karen, Lillian's Mom, Pearl, was in attendance along with Lillian's Great-Uncle, James Cox, and his wife, Jenny.

James Cox was a fascinating gentleman who, in his younger days, had ridden as a mechanic on Indianapolis 500 racecars. In those days, Indy race cars were double-seated, and the mechanic rode alongside the driver during the race so repairs could be made right on the track.

Bernie's Mom and Dad were in attendance as was his brother Joe and his sister-in-law, Liz.

Following the brief ceremony held on a Sunday—something not usually allowed in the Catholic Church, thereby necessitating the marriage certificate to have been dated the day before—the wedding party drove to a small restaurant on College Ave. called Hollyhock Hill—reservations recommended.

There the usual friendly banter took place accompanied by quasi-surreptitious stealing of food morsels from each other's plates.

Fr. Courtney had played such a central part in facilitating their marriage that Bernie and Lillian were truly saddened years later when they attended the 50th anniversary of his ordination.

"Hi, Father," said Bernie as he approached Fr. Courtney prior to the ceremony, "Do you remember me? I'm Bernie Barcio."

"Hi," replied Fr. Courtney. "No, I don't. They tell me I'm a priest, and they have me all dressed up like this. I guess I'll just have to cooperate and go along with it."

Fr. Courtney had become the victim of Alzheimer's Disease. A sad circumstance for a man who had been known all his life for his quick wit and sharp intellect.

June 18, 1967
Broad Ripple, Indiana

"Hey Bear-nie," called Jake from his side of the fence that divided their two houses.

Jake and his wife were Latvians, and it had taken Jake a while to understand that his neighbor did not teach Latvian but "Latin" at nearby Park School. Jake was also a packrat. His yard was a storage area for all sorts of building materials that he had scavenged from the neighborhood. When his wife got angry with him, she would chase him with a hammer up and down the paths that separated the stacks of materials. Jake was also a busybody who prided himself on not letting anything escape his attention.

"Hey, Bear-nie," Jake confided after Bernie had come near the fence. "Your Pa has quite a temper."

"What do you mean?" asked Bernie.

"Well, the day you and your wife left to go on your honeymoon, he had a big argument with your mother in the front yard."

"Yeah," said Bernie, "they're Italian. They yell a lot."

"Bear-nie," Jake continued, "your Pa knocked her so hard she fell flat on the ground. He wouldn't even help her get up. He just walked to his car and waited for her to get up by herself."

"Yeah," said Bernie, "My Ma wasn't all that happy about my marrying a divorced woman with three kids. She must have still been arguing about it."

Bernie's parents had indeed been arguing about it, ever since he had first called them a month earlier to invite them to the wedding. In his mother's mind, her son Bernard had fallen into the proverbial divorcee-with-three-kids trap that she and her friends had talked about for years as the most awful thing that could ever happen to any woman's son.

To Stella's way of thinking, if her husband was any kind of a man, he would have done something—anything—to prevent the marriage. He hadn't. And she wouldn't let it go. So he knocked her down in the front yard while Jake was watching.

So many years would pass before Bernard was allowed to introduce his wife and family to any of his relatives that people thought he had married a black woman and was therefore being kept in the closet.

September, 1967
Old Broad Ripple, Indianapolis

Before they were married, Lillian had been renting a half of a double in the first house at 6944 North College Avenue on the north side of the White River Bridge. The first thing Bernie and Lillian had to do before they could move themselves and the girls into the house Bernie had bought at 6544 Ferguson in Old Broad Ripple, was to build a two-bedroom addition on the south side of the house. One bedroom would be the master bedroom, and the other would be a special bedroom for Marsha. Karen and Sheryl each could have one of the two original second floor bedrooms.

Although Bernie had few tools besides a hammer, a screwdriver and a small square that had been given to him by Jim Wasson, the maintenance man at Park School to use building his catapult, he jumped right into the project. After watching Bernie and Karen work on the addition, Sam, a neighbor who lived across the street, finally walked over and offered them the use of some of the tools from his garage. Sam was a retired farmer and had a nice selection.

The fates were smiling.

"Can I have a hanging bed?" asked Marsha.

Bernie thought about the idea for a while. He considered himself to be fairly clever and finally decided he knew how he would do it. Since the two-bedroom addition was being built with an open raftered ceiling, Bernie contrived a way to suspend a wooden bed frame he built for Marsha from four nylon ropes attached to the rafters.

Marsha was content. For the moment, at least. Before too long, however, she would become discontented and would start demanding, once again, that she be allowed to live with her father in Chicago.

During an earlier episode when Marsha had insisted that she be allowed to live with her father, her mom had allowed Marsha to listen in on an extension while the question was posed. Marsha's dad did not know she was listening.

"Marsha wants to come and live with you," said Lillian.

"No way, Lillian. It's just not possible," said Marsha's dad.

"She'll want to know why not."

"Tell her that my wife and I now have a new family, and she just wouldn't fit into the picture. Besides, I pay more than enough support money each month for her to have everything she needs living with you."

Marsha was crushed.

January 16, 1968
St. Vincent's Hospital
on Fall Creek Parkway,
Indianapolis

"Hi," said Bernie at the emergency registration desk, "I think my wife is having her baby."

"Did your doctor tell you to come to the hospital?" asked the receptionist.

"Yes," said Lillian, obviously in some pain, "he said he would meet us here."

After the wheels of registration rolled along at their usual slow pace, Bernie and Lillian were finally told which elevator to take to go up to the Maternity Ward.

"Mrs. Barcio, let's have you come in here," said a nurse as she took control of the wheel chair away from Bernie. "You can wait in the waiting room, Mr. Barcio, and we'll come and get you when it's time."

This all was way unexpected by both Bernie and Lillian. This was happening way too early. The doctor had assured them there was plenty of time before the baby would be ready to be born.

"Maybe it's just one of those false labor pain things," thought Bernie to himself as he looked around for a comfortable chair.

Heck he hadn't even thought about buying cigars to give away yet or anything. All they had had time to do was to call Lillian's mom, Pearl Hacker, to come and stay with the girls while they hopped into the car and headed downtown.

All of a sudden, the doors to the maternity ward swung open and a man in a white hospital jacket came rushing into the room.

"Is Mr. Barcio here?" asked the man.

"Yes, I'm Bernie Barcio."

"Please hurry and come with me."

As they walked, the man began pointing to signature lines on forms he had attached to a clipboard that Bernie needed to sign immediately.

"We're going to have to do an emergency C-section to save the baby, and we need you to sign off on all these forms."

As Bernie was hustled into the Maternity Ward, bloodcurdling screams filled the air. Women in various stages of pre-delivery pain were letting the world know just what they were going through. As they drew near to the bed on which Lillian was lying, Bernie noticed she was not one of the women screaming. She just lay there looking very uncomfortable and a little frightened.

"They're going to have to do a C-section," said Bernie.

"I know, they told me," said Lillian.

"O.K., Mr. Barcio, just a few more forms for you to sign, and then we'll have to ask you to leave."

As soon as Bernie finished signing, one nurse began to push Lillian's gurney out of its slot as another took Bernie by the arm and hurriedly escorted him back out of the Maternity Ward.

When the procedure was finished, Bernie was taken to a room where he could see his wife.

Their baby, to be named Cynthia Lee, was too fragile to be seen, however. She would have to be confined to an isolette for a week or so until they could be assured of her survival.

When Bernie finally did get to see his daughter for the first time, he did what all fathers do. He counted fingers and toes.

"What's that taped to her stomach?"

"That's a quarter," said the nurse. "We need to keep pressure on her belly button until the opening heals."

"Will the mark on her lip go away by itself?" asked Lillian.

"It may lighten after a while, but the doctor thinks it's a port wine birthmark. She should be able to have it taken care of when she gets older," said the nurse.

No matter. Both mother and daughter had survived and that's all that was important. Everything else, including the locating of cigars, could be taken care of in due time.

July, 1968
Pompeii, Italy

Faithful to his commitment of providing travel opportunities for his students, Bernie had put together a special summer course that began with class work at Park School, where students were taught the rudiments of archaeology, ancient Roman history, mythology and modern Italian.

Following their successful participation in these classes, Bob Crandall, Doug Kuhn and Bernie's new stepdaughter, Marsha Batten, flew from Indianapolis on Thursday, July 11, on their way to Rome, Italy. Marsha could not believe the opportunity being given to her. Not only was she traveling to Europe, but she was traveling as the only girl in the group with two handsome young boys from Park School. Bernie and Lillian had decided this would be a good experience for Marsha since she seemed to be having more trouble than her two sisters adjusting to her mom's remarriage. In the end, the trip seems to have done little to allay her misgivings, but that is a whole separate story that will be told shortly.

"Sir, they don't have my luggage," said Bob Crandall after everyone else had retrieved theirs.

"Let's go to the lost luggage office," comforted Bernie, hoping that it would show up. "When they find it, we can arrange to have it sent to our hotel."

In Rome, the group stayed at the Hotel Tizanio while enjoying a bus tour of that city's main attractions.

But Bernie had insisted from the beginning that this would not be a whirlwind tour of Europe as was being offered to students by other organizations. This was designed as a study-tour. They would visit only a few chosen locations, and they would get to know them well.

By Saturday night the group was in its quarters at the Hotel Grande Rosario in Pompeii that would be their home for the next five days. Bob Crandall's luggage had not been found. Among the ruins of the ancient city of Pompeii, each student was assigned a large home, a small home and one public building that s/he would study thoroughly. Each site was to be measured, sketched and carefully described.

Setting the pace for his students, Bernie selected the large House of Marcus Loreius Tiburtinus as one of the sites he would study in detail. He would later develop the Persona of Marcus Loreius Tiburtinus and present his life in 1st century Pompeii to hundreds of audiences across the United States and Canada.

As Bernie was walking to his selected site early one morning, he saw a tattered local *ragazzo* ambling toward him through the ruins. As the boy passed, Bernie noticed he was carrying a large basket covered with a cloth.

"Piglia, piglia il ragazzo!" shouted a guard from down the street behind Bernie.

Bernie looked back at the guard and then at the boy who immediately took off down one of the side streets.

"Piglia, piglia," continued to shout the guard as he ran up to Bernie.

"You could have grabbed him," puffed the guard in Italian once he saw that the urchin had escaped.

"Che faceva?" asked Bernie.

"He was stealing artifacts from the ruins. These *ragazzi* come in every day from the back walls and plunder for their parents. If I ever get my hands on that one,..." sputtered the guard before giving Bernie another look of disapproval and returning to his post.

By Thursday, July 18, the students had all successfully completed their assignments and they departed for Naples where they boarded a steamer to the Isle of Capri for the night. Marsha could not believe it. There she was on the Isle of Capri made famous both in movies and in song. It just seemed so unreal. This surely couldn't be happening to her, a young girl whom her father had seemingly rejected when he divorced her mother.

On Friday night the group stayed in Resina, a modern town built directly over the ruins of ancient Herculaneum. After he had taken them on a tour of the excavated portion of the ancient city, called the *scavi,* Bernie offered the group a unique opportunity if they were up to it.

"How would you guys like to spend Sunday climbing to the top of Mt. Vesuvius?" he asked.

Would they! This was going to be great. The boys were all in good shape and Marsha prided herself at being able to keep up with any boy her age.

Very few students, or adults, for that matter, can claim to have ascended on foot to the top of Mt. Vesuvius, but Bernie's little group managed to pull it off. Half-way up they came to a small shop, and Bernie treated every one to an *aranciata* and some bottled water.

When they reached the mouth of the volcano, they joined other tourists who had either ridden up on tour busses or in the cable car. This cable car was, in fact, the descendent of the funicular cable car first built on Mt. Vesuvius in 1880 and made famous by the Neapolitan song, *"Funiculi, Funicula,"* composed and set to music by Peppino Turco and Luigi Denza.

Monday was spent in Naples visiting the *Museo Nazionale* and staying in the same *Pensione Le Fontane al Mare* in which Bernie had been housed when he was a student with Tufts University in Naples.

Wednesday found the group back in Rome on another tour bus. They had only managed to work in about half the important sites in Rome during their initial visit. This time they would spend both morning and afternoon filling in the gaps.

By Friday, July 26, it was all over. Bob Crandall's luggage was lost forever. Marsha never seemed happier than when she was on this tour. For a while she kept in touch with her traveling companions, but when she attended a house party with one of them at which liquor was secretly being served to the students in the basement, Bernie and her mom decided they really weren't cut out for Park School's student social circle. Bernie had called the parents of the student hosting the party, only to be told that Marsha was obviously lying since absolutely no liquor was being served in their house during that party.

Slowly the glow disappeared from Marsha's eyes as she slipped back into her earlier morose ways.

September, 1968
Indianapolis
"Bernie, have a seat," said the Headmaster, Bill McCluskey.

Bernie had a fairly good relationship with Bill, and, up until very recently, felt that he was encouraging and very supportive. But that was before Bernie had married his secretary.

"Bernie, we intend to hire someone, and I wanted to see if you would have a problem with our decision," said Bill.

"Well, Mr. McCluskey, you have a right to hire anyone you want. You really don't have to check with me. Is it a new Latin teacher?" asked Bernie.

"No," said Bill, "It's a new music teacher, in fact. His name is David Collver. Do you know him?" asked Bill.

"No, I don't think so," said Bernie. "Where is he from?"

"He's from Bay City, Michigan, and he says that you once dated his fiancée, Betty Jean."

Now that was a blast from the past. Bernie hadn't given Betty Jean much thought at all since he left Bay City. She, however, had obviously kept track of him and had decided that he had been hired by a pretty good private school. So she had no doubt encouraged David to apply for the opening of which he had become aware.

"No, I don't see any problem there," said Bernie.

"How will you feel about working along side David," asked Bill.

"Well, I would say that David will have his hands full. His fiancée can be a bit of a challenge, so I would only offer him every encouragement in his work here at school."

While Bernie had every intention of not having very much to do with Dave Collver, Dave quickly came to rely on him as his one friend in Indianapolis.

"Hi, Bernie," said David when he called early one Sunday morning. "Hope I didn't wake you up."

"No, Dave. That's O.K. What's up?" asked Bernie.

"Well, I was on my way back to Indianapolis when my car broke down. Can you drive up here to Gas City and give me a ride?"

There was not much else Bernie could do other than help him out.

October, 1968
Palmyra, Wisconsin

"That concludes this morning's announcements. Have a good day," said Joe Barcio whose job it was, as principal of Palmyra High School, to read the morning announcements.

He was just beginning to look over the day's paper work in his office when his secretary came to his door.

"Mr. Barcio, the Superintendent's in the building and would like to see you."

Joe walked out into the hallway and saw the Superintendent standing outside of the school's front doors.

"Good morning. You wanted to see me?" asked Joe.

"See that door-closing lever up there at the top?" asked the Superintendent pointing to the top of one of the main entrance doors. "It's way out of line."

"Boy! You're right. I'll have the…"

"That lever is way out of line," repeated the Superintendent before Joe could even say that he would have the custodian take care of it.

"I'll have it fixed as soon as I find the custodian," said Joe quickly finishing his previous thought.

"You know, Joe, if you're going to be a good principal, you should stay on top of things like that. A really good principal would not let things like this occur."

"Yes, sir, I'll certainly keep a closer eye on the building."

As Joe stood there outside the door of the building next to the Superintendent, he was just beginning to wonder if he was going to lose his job as high school principal all because a door latch was out of line when he suddenly caught a whiff of the Superintendent's breath. Although it was only 9:00 a.m., the man had obviously already been drinking. Quite a bit!

"I'll have that door latch taken care of immediately, and I'll make it a point to inspect the building periodically," promised Joe as the Superintendent turned and walked away toward his office.

Shutting the door, Joe sat at his office desk and worked alone for about a half hour until he had finalized his plans.

"I'm going over to the elementary school for a while," said Joe to his secretary as he quickly made his way out of the building.

Now the principal of the elementary school in Palmyra was an older, more experienced educator whom we'll call "Carl." Carl was wizened in the ways of local Palmyra politics, the board, and—as Joe soon was to learn—the Superintendent. Carl would surely know the best way to deal with the problem.

"Yah. What's your concern, Joe?" said Carl after Joe had shared his observations on what was obviously the Superintendent's drinking problem.

Joe was shocked.

"Carl, this is serious stuff. The man could ruin his career. He could ruin ours!"

But, to Carl, all this was old hat. Not only was he and everyone else in town aware of the problem, but they had even had to make repairs to the high school after the Superintendent drove his car into one of the supporting pillars of the roof near the front door of one of Palmyra's elementary schools. Yes, he was inebriated. No, nothing was done about it.

"Well," said Joe, "What are we going to do about it?"

"Nothing, Joe. Just forget it."

So, while Joe realized that there was nothing to be done, he did take advantage of the experience to re-evaluate what he thought he knew about the School Board, the Superintendent and his own official role as Principal of the high school—which consisted mainly of being wary from that point on.

March 6-7, 1969
Indianapolis

Bill McCluskey, continued to view Bernie as the school's factotum. Since Bernie didn't coach a sport, he was the logical candidate to handle all other student activities that might need coordinating. It became Bernie's job to plan and coordinate a special Spring Institute that would bring the senior class members of Park School and Tudor Hall together for academic interaction. It was hoped that such an event, well planned and carefully executed, could ease tensions that might be building concerning the merging of the two student bodies.

On the two days of the Spring Institute the student participants would be excused from their regular classes and would follow a special schedule at Park School.

The format Bernie had established would have the students meeting together in the library to hear a series of lectures. Following each lecture, students would break out into pre-scheduled discussion groups led by faculty monitors. It was through participation in these discussion groups that the schools hoped to establish a positive, friendly dialogue between the two student bodies.

On Day One of the Institute, students attended a lecture entitled "The Meaning of Culture," by Leslie Frost, daughter of the Poet Laureate, Robert Frost. A second lecture entitled "Too Important to Leave Just to the Scientists" was given by Alfred Chiscom of Purdue University. After a lunch break, the students were shown a film entitled, "The World of Carl Sandburg."

On the second day, Phinias Cambel of Wabash College lectured on the topic, "Toward a Meaning of Afro-American Culture," and Richard Yoakam of Indiana University lectured on, "Communications Science and Culture."

Once again, true to his talents, Bernie pulled it off. The Institute was considered a complete success.

April, 1969
Indianapolis

Bernie and Lillian had been surprised to receive an invitation to attend the wedding of David Collver and Betty Jean in Bay City, Michigan. Of course, they would not go. How awkward would that have been?

Once the Collvers were back in Indianapolis, however, Bernie did try to keep the relationship casual and initially declined offers for social occasions with David and his wife.

Once it became obvious, however, that the Collvers had few, if any, social contacts in Indianapolis or, as far as that went, among the faculty of Park School, Lillian suggested that she and Bernie give a little get together at their home to introduce them to a few of the faculty members and their wives—just to show how "big" they could be about the total awkwardness of the whole situation.

On the night of the get together, all of the other guests had arrived except the Collvers.

"Bernie, I've got a problem," David confided when he finally called to explain why they were late.

"What's up, Dave?" asked Bernie.

"It's Betty Jean," said David.

"What's the problem?" asked Bernie.

"Well, she's got a bug up her pants and is being a real pain. She's climbed up on the top shelf of our hall closet and refuses to come out."

"Dave," said Bernie, "I really feel sorry for you. I know she has a temper, but I don't think there's really anything I can do to help. Everyone's here, Dave. Why don't you just leave her in there and come on over by yourself? Eventually she'll get tired and come down."

David Collver didn't stay at Park School too long. He tried to get into real estate investment by buying a double on north Meridian Street, but he must certainly have sold it before he and his wife moved to Valparaiso, Indiana, not to be heard from again until January 4, 2004.

May, 1969
Indianapolis

It was a rather long and tense faculty meeting—the last one of the 1968-1969 school year, but Lew Berkeley wasn't going to let it end without having some of his major concerns addressed.

"Mr. McCluskey," said Lew (he was always formal during faculty meetings), "there are several issues that deserve the professional consideration of the faculty as a whole before we merge with Tudor Hall. They really shouldn't be left hanging over the summer."

"Well, Mr. Berkeley," said Bill McCluskey, maintaining an air of formality, "we really don't have time today to deal with them, and I don't think we can honestly expect the faculty to make themselves available over the summer."

"Would you object to a group of us getting together over the summer to spell out some of these concerns so they can be addressed next fall?" asked Lew persistently.

"I won't have any problem with that. Just be sure you come to me with your results before you put anything before the faculty. I'm still the Headmaster, and I don't want you circumventing my authority."

When the meeting broke up, Lew Berkeley, Bernie Barcio, John Riggles and Dean Hawver continued sitting around the table.

Bernie felt obliged to help Lew out, a man whom he had come to respect.

"Lew, how would it be if we all met at my house a couple times over the summer and try to come up with some ideas that we could present next fall?" asked Bernie.

"Fine with me," said Lew. "Are you other fellows available to work on this over the summer?" he asked.

The others said they were willing.

"I think we should invite Jim Foxlow to be in on this too," suggested Lew.

Jim Foxlow was respected and revered by the students, alumni, his fellow faculty, the administrators, the Board of Directors and the community. Having Jim join the group would validate its purpose and insure careful thinking.

June, 1969
Indianapolis

Bernie was nominated and agreed to serve as the Chairman Pro-Tem of the group that was soon calling itself the Faculty Committee for Professional Advancement, the F.C.P.A. for short. By the end of the summer, Jim Foxlow, also an uncontested scholar, had typed up Version 5 of the group's purposes.

"The purpose of this committee shall be to represent the faculty in strengthening the Park School program by
- a) identifying, investigating and discussing matters of concern to the entire teaching staff, especially professional growth and conditions of employment;
- b) communicating the results of its deliberations to the Headmaster and the rest of the faculty, together with recommendations for action on such issues as lie with the province of the various faculty committees;
- c) apprising the Board of Directors, or the appropriate committees thereof, through the Headmaster, of current faculty thinking and suggesting to these bodies, also through the Headmaster, reconsideration of existing policies or institution of new ones."

Being the conscientious scholar he was, Jim Foxlow also felt it necessary to attach explanatory footnotes to each of the above.

Note: The proper scope of a) would necessarily have to be determined through discussion and agreement between faculty and Headmaster as issues arose for serious consideration.

Jim was definitely walking on eggshells and he did not want to appear pushy or belligerent. By this time the originator of the movement, Lew Berkeley, had decided to distance himself from the group and go about his coaching and teaching responsibilities.

Note: b) implies that there is desired a certain overlap between this committee and other committees consisting of faculty but having been appointed by the Headmaster. This overlap would allow for the faculty as a whole to bring matters more strongly to the attention of these committees. At the same time it is not intended that the F.C.P.A. would make any attempt to supercede the authority invested in the Headmaster-appointed faculty committees.

Jim Foxlow knew that Bill McCluskey would not tolerate any threats to his authority and was only allowing the existence of this committee to quell the discontent that had been voiced by Lew Berkeley and others at the final faculty meeting of the year before.

Note: c) expresses the desire of the F.C.P.A. to speak representatively for the whole teaching staff and to be assured that its thoughts can be represented to those within whose authority the responsibility of decision rests.

This was a meek attempt to let the Headmaster know that, even though he was the acknowledged authority at Park School, the F.C.P.A. was still claiming final access to the Board of Directors.

As it turned out, this access was always denied, and Bill McCluskey would frustrate almost every effort of the F.C.P.A. to function as a meaningful committee. He had never intended to address any of the problems that had been brought up at the final faculty meeting and had allowed the existence of the F.C.P.A. only because he thought that those serving on it would eventually burn themselves out and disband.

September, 1969
Indianapolis
On September 11, 1969, the F.C.P.A. met in the Park School Library from 3:15 to 5:00 p.m. The original five faculty members that had met over the summer were now joined by Ed Harris, a 6th grade teacher and Marian Smith, a 4th grade teacher. Bill McCluskey was also present and wore a dower expression as the committee that he had hoped would go away began to lay some aggressive proposals on the table.

The committee wanted to address:
a)   the duties of department chairmen

    b)   the role of the Academic Development Committee
    c)   precise details of the school-provided Travelers Insurance coverage
    d)   priorities for the year
    e)   a Master Teacher Plan
    f)   Faculty in-service training.

Bill McCluskey definitely felt that he was "being pushed" by the F.C.P.A., and he didn't like to be pushed.

Following the meeting, Bill casually discussed with Bernie his preferences for dealing with faculty concerns.

"You know, Bernie, in other schools that I've been at, they did not feel the need for all these committees. The faculty has too much to do to spend extra time serving on committees," confided Bill.

"But the faculty has a right to have some input," countered Bernie.

"What I would really prefer, Bernie, is that you serve as sort of an ombudsman, a low-key person who informally serves as a go-between for me and faculty with concerns," said Bill.

"Well, Bill, I'm just trying to do what I think will be best. I agreed to serve as chairman of the F.C.P.A. so the concerns of the faculty could be addressed and worked out," said Bernie. "But if you want, I would be willing to try simply passing concerns on to you."

"That would be great. And, by the way, let's just keep this little arrangement private between me and you, O.K.?"

Well, Bernie innocently fell into that little trap, but quickly saw the light.

The first time he passed along a problem that had been brought to his attention, Bill McClusky privately confronted the faculty who had mentioned it.

"You know, Bernie," said Bill who later called Bernie into his office after school, "I mentioned the problem that you referred to me to Larry, and he said he never had a problem with that. He suggested that you were just trying to push your own agenda."

O.K. Now Bernie knew how it was going to work. His fellow faculty members wanted to dump on him in the hopes their problems could be solved for them, but they did not want to be personally identified by the Headmaster as teachers who were rocking the boat.

September, 1969
Old Broad Ripple, Indiana

Lillian's three girls had gone through a lot of adjustments since their parents had been divorced, but, on the whole, they were doing quite nicely. They seemed to be accepting Bernie's role in their lives.

The only time that Bernie ever had to take charge of a disciplinary situation with Karen was shortly after they had all moved into his house on Ferguson. As he and Lillian stood talking in the kitchen one afternoon, Bernie looked out the back window of the house to see Karen hanging down over the eaves waving at them. Bernie shot up the steps to the second floor window out of which Karen had crawled.

"Karen!" he shouted, "Get in here right now. And be careful. You could fall and kill yourself."

Karen obeyed immediately, responding to the authority in his voice.

"NEVER DO THAT AGAIN," yelled Bernie sternly once she was back in the house.

Sheryl was the quiet one. She seldom got in trouble except when she complained to her mom about things at school. Her mom, however, was pregnant again, and things were getting a little tense. Sheryl wasn't feeling that she was being given ample opportunity to vent her concerns to her mom who now had her own problems on which she needed to focus.

"Karen, can you carry a bag of groceries into the house?" asked Bernie as they all, except Marsha, got back from the store early one evening.

"Sure," said Karen, always eager to cooperate.

Lillian had her hands full with Cindy, and Bernie was carrying the rest of the groceries. Half way to the porch, he noticed that Sheryl wasn't carrying anything.

"Here, Sheryl," said Bernie turning around and handing her a bag. "Carry this bag with the eggs into the house."

"No!" said Sheryl. "I won't"

SMACK!

Bernie had not been allowed to grow up rebellious. So he automatically did what would have happened to him if he had he ever sassed one of his parents. He simply slapped Sheryl in the face.

Sheryl was shocked, but she carried the bag into the house, and then immediately disappeared into her room for the rest of the evening.

It was the only time Bernie ever felt that he needed to interfere with her discipline.

October, 1969
Indianapolis

Having had no success in getting Bernie to let the F.C.P.A. die or maintain a subversive role as an ombudsman, Bill McCluskey decided to frustrate Bernie's efforts by loading him up with extra assignments.

"But, Bill, I'm already serving as the Advisor to the Proctors," said Bernie.

"You know, Bernie," said Bill, "the other faculty members all coach sports, most of them coaching a different sport each season. They feel you're not pulling your weight."

So Bernie was appointed the Advisor to the school yearbook. He was also in charge of Morning Assemblies, an after school Honors Program that brought in outstanding community speakers, as well as teaching all of the classes of Latin and coordinating a catapult competition that continued to draw national attention. McCluskey had also "suggested" that Bernie and his wife Lillian should run the Lilly Orchard apple and cider sales during the late summer, and after school and on weekends during the fall.

November 1, 1969
Broad Ripple, Indianapolis

Bernie and Lillian decided that they would set an 11:00 p.m. curfew for Marsha when she began dating a boy named David, a friend she had made when Lillian and the girls had lived in Allendale on the west side of Indianapolis.

"You're late!" snapped Bernie when Marsha walked in the door at 11:20 p.m.

"Oh, it's just a little late. Besides we were just outside sitting in the car.

"11:00 o'clock means you're in the house at 11:00 o'clock," said Lillian. "We shouldn't have to come outside to look for you."

Marsha kept pushing her curfew limits and kept getting more and more annoyed reactions from Bernie and her mom. Finally, Lillian and Bernie decided that she simply would not be allowed to date David any more if they couldn't honor her curfew.

October 17, 1969
Broad Ripple, Indiana

"Okay," announced Lillian, "I think I'm ready. Can you get that small suitcase?"

"No problem," said Bernie.

"We're going now," said Lillian to the three girls. "Listen to Gramma and take turns watching Cindy."

Lillian and Bernie were on their way back to St. Vincent Hospital on Fall Creek Boulevard in downtown Indianapolis. The delivery of their second baby would not catch them off guard as the birth of Cindy had done. This time the caesarian delivery was pre-planned and the date pre-set. All they had to do was show up, and everything would go according to schedule.

Since they knew it was going to be a boy, Bernie had already bought a whole box of "It's A Boy" cigars that he was looking forward to distributing.

When Lillian had asked him what he wanted to name their son, Bernie chose the name "Phillip."

"Is there someone in your family with that name?" Lillian had asked.

"No. I just like the name. It means 'horse lover.' "

"Do you want to spell it with one 'L' or two?" asked Lillian.

"Two," replied Bernie.

Only later would he come to realize that Phillip is usually only spelled with two 'L's when used as a surname. Oh well, that would only make his son's name more unique!

"Do you have an idea for a middle name?" asked Bernie.

"Eugene," replied Lillian. "That was my dad's name."

"That's okay with me, but my mom is sure going to hit the roof."

"Why?" asked Lillian.

"Because she'll think that we're naming him after my Uncle Eugene.

"What's wrong with that?"

"Well, she's not exactly on speaking terms with him right now."

"Well, you can just tell her that Eugene was my dad's name."

And so Phillip Eugene Barcio was born in a room at St. Vincent Hospital on Fall Creek Boulevard. Years later, after St. Vincent Hospital moved to its new location on the north side of Indianapolis, the original building was converted to an old age home.

"You know, Phil," said Bernie one day when Phil was already a teenager and they were driving by the building in which Phil had been born, "wouldn't it be ironic if you ended up spending your final days living in this old age home in the same room in which you were born?"

Phil was not particularly amused by the thought.

By the year 2000, however, the building in which Phil was born had become part of the Central Indiana Ivy Tech Community College complex.

November 23, 1969
Indianapolis

Bernie was becoming increasingly frustrated but was too conscientious to give up his responsibilities as Chairman of the F.C.P.A. At a meeting of the full faculty, he was proud to announce: "Since its election in September, this year's committee has met weekly."

The F.C.P.A. had come up with four recommendations concerning faculty salary and career development.

December 1, 1969
Broad Ripple, Indianapolis

During her senior year at Broad Ripple High School, Marsha was living a fairly full life. She had a part-time job and occasionally volunteered as a Candy Striper at St. Vincent Hospital on Fall Creek Parkway. She was, however, not taking her forced breakup with David very well.

"Marsha didn't come home from school today," said Lillian when Bernie got home.

"Have you called around to see if any of her friends know where she is?" asked Bernie.

"Nobody knows."

"Well, let's just call the police and report her as a runaway," suggested Bernie.

But, as anyone knows who has ever had a child run away, the police won't even get involved during the first 48 hours. They chalk it up to family problems that tend to work themselves out in a day or two.

When Marsha still had not been heard of after two days, the police finally did agree to get involved.

"We've found your daughter," said the policeman who called Lillian.

"Where was she?"

"She was staying with a friend of hers named David and a bunch of other kids who are all living in a house on Pennsylvania Street."

"Where is she now," asked Lillian.

"She's here in Juvenile Detention. Would you like to come down and pick her up or should we keep her overnight?"

At first, Bernie suggested that it might be a good idea to let Marsha experience a night in detention to make her think twice before putting her family through that turmoil again.

"I don't think so, Bernie," said Lillian. "You hear too many horror stories about what goes on down in Juvenile Detention."

So Marsha was picked up and brought home. At the suggestion of the police, Bernie and Lillian arranged to begin meeting with a counselor at the Catholic Social Services to see if he could help her work through her anger and confusion.

Marsha seemed to take the meetings well and even enjoyed having someone's total attention for an hour a week.

December 18, 1969
Indianapolis

By December, Bernie had been encouraged to expand the list of items concerning which the F.C.P.A. should seek clarification from the Board of Directors through the Headmaster.

The list of concerns now numbered 20:

a) teacher liability
b) disability insurance
c) pension plan
d) sick leave policy
e) workmen's compensation
f) graduate study
g) distinction, if any, between elective and appointive committees
h) definition of grounds of dismissal
i) work load (academic, extracurricular, administrative)
j) terms for continuation of employment
k) compensation for extracurricular activities
l) non-administrative nine- and eleven-month contracts
m) faculty secretarial help
n) percentage of contribution by faculty and school to insurance program
o) school philosophy (goals and objectives)
p) duties and responsibilities of administrative officers and committees
q) professional leave of absence
r) salary schedule including base pay
s) option for biweekly or monthly pay
t) evaluation of teachers (apropos of merit pay and continued employment)

Even though the headmaster was apprised of all the workings of the F.C.P.A., he was definitely feeling threatened. All of these areas had been part of his unquestioned bailiwick (his favorite word), and he didn't welcome suggestions that written guidelines be produced that would limit his freedoms.

Bill McCluskey would continue to block any efforts of the F.C.P.A. to interact directly with the Board of Directors and would continue to make all decisions unilaterally.

January, 1970
Old Broad Ripple, Indiana

About a year earlier, Bernie and Lillian had decided to build a second, two-story addition onto their home on Ferguson. By now Karen had become quite a carpenter, having gained precious experience by helping with the first two-bedroom addition. Since the new campus for Park-Tudor school was being constructed on the Lilly Orchard, Bernie had been able to borrow enough plywood to build his own forms for the foundation concrete. When it came time to begin the carpenter work, Bernie's brother Joe and his wife and children had driven down from Wisconsin to help.

The wall dividing the old master bedroom and Marsha's old room with the swinging bed was removed and the area was turned into a sort of great room, the east side of which served as the new living room and the west side a dining room.

As Mary Blake's aunt, a kindly neighbor who lived across the street, was preparing to move, she offered to sell Bernie and Lillian her complete ornate oak dining room set for $200.00. It fit perfectly into the new dining room area.

The new master bedroom occupied the first floor of the new addition. On the north end of the master bedroom was a large walk-in closet. On the west end was a small nursery.

"Lillian, I think the baby's crying," Bernie said one night, and Lillian forced herself out of bed to try and quiet him down.

After a while, all was quiet, and Lillian came back to bed. But just for a little while.

WAAHHH.

"Shhh," hushed Lillian when she returned to the nursery. "Go to sleep now. Here, I'll wind up your little music box for you. Shhh."

Once again Lillian returned to bed.

WAAHHH.

Now Lillian was getting mad. She flew out of bed and into the nursery.

"WHAT'S THE MATTER WITH YOU? GO TO SLEEP!" yelled Lillian, half in tears.

After a while, Bernie became aware that there were no sounds coming from the nursery, and that Lillian had not returned to bed.

"Oh my God!" he thought to himself. "She's killed him!"

Bernie quickly got out of bed and quietly walked over to the nursery.

There was Lillian leaning on the rail of the crib, half asleep. Sound asleep—and alive—in the crib was baby Phil.

He had finally gotten the message and had managed to save his little life.

January, 1970
Park School, Indianapolis

The committee's suggestions for professional advancement, however, were soon shot down.

"Seminars are a waste of our time," countered one faculty member.

"We're already professionals. We don't need anyone coming in and telling us how we should be teaching. This is why we choose to teach in a private school. To avoid all that bull shit," chimed in another.

"Well, what do you suggest?" asked Bernie, trying to play the role of a calming leader.

"Let's talk salaries. We've got to find out how much the Tudor teachers get and be sure that we get as much," said another teacher.

So Bernie went to see the headmaster. He would simply ask him for a list of the salaries being paid to both faculties.

"Can't do it, Bernie," said Bill. "That's confidential. It always has been and it's going to stay that way after the two schools merge."

"But shouldn't there be some guidelines so that people feel they're being treated fairly?" asked Bernie.

"If your committee wants to make some suggestions, I'll pass them along," promised McCluskey.

So Bernie called another meeting. He thought that most of his fellow committee members were sincerely interested in discussing salaries, but he was surprised when Bill Browning observed that if they were given higher salaries, they would simply have to pay more taxes. Bill indicated that higher salaries weren't really his highest priority.

Nonetheless, Bernie worked hard and, using the pay scales of the Indianapolis Public Schools and the township school systems that were provided to him by the I.S.T.A., he came up with a suggestion for minimum pay scales for both faculties. The headmaster would still be able to offer higher salaries if needed to obtain quality teachers, but these minimums would insure that the Park-Tudor faculty salaries would at least be in line with the public school teacher salaries in the area.

When Bernie presented the minimum scale to the members of the F.C.P.A., everyone seemed to be in agreement that this was what should be asked for from the Board.

"You know, Bernie," said Bill McCluskey, "I've been talking to some of the people on your committee, and they indicate that a minimum salary schedule is not at all what they are interested in. They claim you're doing this on your own. Is that true?"

So, once again, Bernie was the victim of double-dealing and backstabbing. He had been encouraged to lead his fellow faculty and had done his best to try and get something for them that he thought they all wanted, and, as usual, they had simply turned on him when confronted by the headmaster.

February 12, 1970
Indianapolis

A brick wall did not have to fall on Bernie Barcio. He realized exactly what Bill McCluskey was doing. Since all his efforts to work openly and honestly for the betterment of the school were being thwarted at every turn, he thought he might give sarcasm a try. Maybe the school administration and faculty could be shamed into making more serious efforts to improve their school.

Bernie composed the following anonymous letter (phrased to appear to have been sent out by board members to the school community) that he would put in all of the school mailboxes over the weekend and then watch the reactions of the faculty and administration on Monday.

"Dear Parents and Friends:
"Our school now stands at the threshold of a new and exciting period of its history.

"When the two schools shall have the use of fully completed buildings and the educational impact can be felt of the fine combined faculties, the school ultimately will be able to offer a program second to none. The future of the school must be viewed with enthusiasm.

"It is to be understood, however, that our school will, next year, maintain its tradition of paying its faculty less than these dedicated men and women are worth to the surrounding community and could be earning in the public school system. It's not because these men and women are worth less than their peers in the public school system, it's just that we value them less. Besides, aren't they being given the chance to work in some pretty plush surroundings?

"The faculty did have an emotional reaction to the discrepancies existing between their salaries and those of public school peers, but we allayed any stirrings by promising them substantial raises soon, by promising them that big money was coming the school's way soon, and by asking them to trust us.

"The faculty, therefore, is content. Luckily, they do not realize that there is no basis for any trust on their part. They need only to consider the status of those faculty members who have been with the school the longest and have trusted the most. These dedicated souls receive up to 2 or 3 thousand dollars less than their public school peers. Luckily, they do not consider that when they confronted the academic committee of the board, the committee (whom they trusted faithfully during the past years while the school was building its new multi-million dollar campus) admitted readily that it had been most negligent in furthering the academic cause of the school. To repeat, the faculty is now content, and there is no fear that they will realize that the time for trust has long since passed, nor will they suggest that it is now time for a solid salary commitment from us if they are ever to better their plight.

"To re-emphasize, the future of the school must be viewed with enthusiasm. Our school will continue to offer its standard education with its modestly paid staff in pleasant surroundings. Since our school pays its faculty conservatively, no additional burdens will be placed on the community by raising tuition or bothering the community for endowment contributions. And, after all, if you're happy, we're happy.

"P.S. Plans are moving ahead well for new construction involving doubling the size of the gym (to include an Olympic size pool) and a Fine Arts Building. Such construction is costly, but, after all, we do realize where the proper priorities lie."

So Bernie drove over to school and stuffed all the mailboxes with his anonymous letter.

"Did you reset the school alarm when you left the building?" asked Lillian after he had returned home.

"Yes, I did," replied Bernie.

"Was anyone else in the building?" asked Lillian.

"No, I don't think so. The alarm was still armed when I punched in my code," said Bernie.

"Your code?" asked Lillian.

"Yes, we each have a different code that we need to punch in when we de-activate or reactive the alarm," said Bernie.

"So, they'll probably be able to figure out exactly who was in the building today, right?" asked Lillian.

"I guess so," said Bernie.

"How long do you think it will take them to figure out that you're the one who put the letter in all the boxes?" asked Lillian.

Of course she was right, and as soon as Bernie realized this, he drove back over to the school, punched in his code once more, removed all of the letters from the mailboxes, reset the alarm and returned home. All of the copies were destroyed except for one that was kept in a special F.C.P.A. file in case Bernie ever wanted to write this book at some point in the future.

March 6, 1970
Indianapolis

To make matters worse for headmaster Bill McCluskey, some of the students were also beginning to challenge his decisions and authority. Bernie Barcio and the F.C.P.A. he felt he could still deal with, but he was not about to tolerate insurrection from the student body.

"But Mr. McCluskey, if the dress code allows white jeans, why should blue jeans not be allowed?" asked one of two students who had asked to meet with him.

"Because blue jeans repulse me and remind me of overalls," answered the Headmaster.

"Mr. McCluskey, we would like to ask you to please read a paragraph in this book entitled **The Reasonable Exercise of Authority**," said one of the students as he placed the book on the Headmaster's desk. The paragraph read:

> "The courts have clearly warned that freedom of speech or expression is essential to the preservation of democracy and that the right can be exercised in ways other than talking or writing. From this generalization, it follows that there should be no restriction on a student's hairstyle or his manner of dressing unless these present a 'clear and present' danger to the student's health and safety."

Mr. McCluskey refused to pick up the book.

"Mr. McCluskey, I can't believe that you are so close-minded that you won't even read it!" said one of the students.

After picking up the book, glancing at it, and tossing it back on his desk, Bill McCluskey repeated his stance about overalls.

"You're obviously angry and cannot talk about this calmly," observed the Headmaster.

"No, Sir, we are not angry. We came in to discuss this calmly," said one of the students.

"You're pushing me, and I want you to stop," said the Headmaster in a commanding voice.

"Well, Sir, could we at least discuss this matter again in the near future?" asked one of the students.

Bill McCluskey replied that they would discuss it when <u>he</u> called them in. Not before.

Bill McCluskey had definitely had it. In his mind he saw Bernie Barcio as the thorn in his side that was ruining a really cushy position that he and his wife Betsy had going for them at Park School. He would have gone to see Bernie that very night to resolve things once and for all if Bernie and Lillian weren't entertaining Lesley Frost, the daughter of Poet Laureate, Robert Frost.

To earn extra money for the yearbook for which he served as advisor, Bernie and his student staff had sponsored a Park School Lecture Series. A $5.00 season ticket entitled ticket holders to attend lectures by John Spencer Churchill, nephew of Sir Winston Churchill, Geoffrey Bocca, Lesley Frost and Dr. Thomas Melady.

Bill would just have to delay his visit a little while.

March 8, 1970
Indianapolis

"Hi, Bernie, this is Betsy. Is Bill there by any chance?" asked Betsy McCluskey.

"No, Betsy, he's not," said Bernie.

"Did he stop in to see you and Lillian last night," asked Betsy.

"No. We were home, but he never came over."

"If you see him this morning, would you please have him call home?" requested Betsy.

Bill had told his wife that he wanted to go discuss some things with Bernie the night before, and then he had never returned home. He had no doubt wanted to get a lot off of his mind and to convince Bernie to quit being a pain.

Although Bernie never learned for sure just what had taken place the evening before, he and Lillian figured that Bill must have stopped off somewhere to have a beer or two and formulate his plans. Or he may have stopped in to see a faculty or board member in whom he felt he could confide. Or he may simply have gone downtown and tied one on—spending the night in a friendly or rented bed somewhere.

Even though he hadn't "had it out" with Bernie that evening, he had definitely made up his mind. Bernie would have to go.

March 14, 1970
Indianapolis

Once again, Bernie was about to be featured on the NBC nightly news. Pat Trese had returned to Indianapolis to bring America up to date on Park School's big catapulting venture that he had covered four years earlier. His coverage of that first tragic-comic event later won him several awards in national news coverage competitions, and he was back to give Bernie and his students a chance to redeem themselves before the nation. This time Latin students from Culver Military Academy had been invited with their teacher, John Roose, to join in the games.

Reporter John Ramsbottom gave this account of the encounter in Park School's newspaper, the **Red and Black** (March 20, 1970, Vol. L, No. 8, pp. 1 & 2):

> "True to the *Ordo Eventuum*, the parade consisting of the armed Latin students of Park, the Culver *Equites*, the opposing *duces* (resplendent in their war garb) and a vociferous group from the far reaches of the empire, moved away from the gym at 3:30. It immediately encountered a blizzard reminiscent of the worst Gallic winters. Upon its arrival at the firing site, the acting troupe of Latin II hurried into a rendition of the Death of Caesar. Lance Hamilton was permitted no more than ten minutes to die, and judging from his continued writhing, he used all the allotted time. Following on the heels of his final expiration, the Culver Rough Riders presented a display of Roman horsemanship with a few close calls. But to give them due credit, standing on the backs of two horses simultaneously cannot be an easy feat to sustain while riding into a twenty mph headwind. Promptly at 4:00 David Noling began reading the Latin challenge to Culver, which was answered by a Culver representative with much tongue rolling and addition of syllables. This exchange was followed by the flipping of a Roman coin, which Park won. Another good omen. At approximately 4:15 Park fired its first shot."

This time Pat Trese got the footage for which he had hoped years before. Park School's new catapult, a trebuchet, hurled its ten-pound projectile a stupendous 228 feet.

April 10, 1970
Indianapolis

"Bernie, this is Lew," said Lew Berkeley who had called him late in the evening.

"Hi, Lew, what's up?" asked Bernie.

"I just got a call from Mr. Howard Sams, one of the Directors on Park School's Board," said Lew, "He said McCluskey is going to fire you tomorrow."

"O.K.," said Bernie, "I can deal with that."

"He also wanted me to tell you that he is willing to put up whatever money you'll need to defend yourself since he respects what you have done for his son and for Park School."

As soon as Bernie got off the phone with Lew, he called an acquaintance he had made at the I.S.T.A., explaining what he had learned and asking for advice.

"O.K., here's what you do," said the I.S.T.A. representative. "You'll have to leave your classroom if you are relieved of your duties, but don't leave the school building. Go down to the teachers' lounge and stay there until the end of the day."

"What would happen if I just left school?" asked Bernie.

"If you leave the building, they can say that you walked off the job and had, in effect, quit. If they can claim that you quit, you won't be entitled to any of the benefits you would have coming if they fired you."

The next day, however, nothing happened. Bernie taught his classes as usual, and he was not summoned into the Headmaster's office. He did, however, realize that it was time for him to begin looking for a new place to teach the following fall.

May 6, 1970
Indianapolis

On May 6, Bernie had mailed a five-page letter of resignation directly to Mr. Kuhn, president of the Board of Directors of Park School, a copy of which had also been sent to Bill McCluskey with the following personal note attached:

> "Bill,
> "After much soul-searching and, in my estimation, an honest effort to give Park and Park-Tudor a very generous benefit of the doubt, I have decided to reject an offer for employment at Park-Tudor School for the school year 1970-1971.

"For the record, my reason for leaving Park is dissatisfaction with seriously unprofessional conditions and orientations of the school and the school community. I have considered the many problems of Park in great detail and have tried to do what I could to improve them or to offer suggestions for their improvement via a most sincere and persistent effort.

"I think the minutes of the F.C.P.A. meetings and the recollections you may have of the many talks you and I have had throughout the year will sufficiently document these problems.

"I should like to point out, however, that the one official response to the many recommendations and requests of the F.C.P.A. (dating back to September '69 with the great insurance inquiry) was a minimum pay scale for next year which both insults the faculty and violates the one area of trust which the 'new' Board invoked so carefully and so warmly promised in the 'new deal,' namely, faculty involvement. To my knowledge, no faculty member sat in on the working sessions which actually produced the minimum pay scale put into effect. This is no 'new deal.'

"I personally learned many things this year and it is upon them that I base my decision to leave."

A week later, Bernie learned of a Latin teaching opening for the 1970-1971 school year in Thornton, Indiana. As he sat in the Superintendent's office at Thornton High School, the Superintendent's phone rang.

"It's for you," said the Superintendent as he handed Bernie the phone.

"Hello, this is Mr. Barcio."

"Mr. Barcio, this is Mr. Kuhn, president of the Park School Board of Directors."

"Yes, Mr. Kuhn, how can I help you?"

"What in the Hell do you think you're doing at school?" yelled Mr. Kuhn into the phone.

"Mr. Kuhn, I'm in a meeting right now, but I definitely want to talk to you. When can we get together?" asked Bernie.

"We can damn well get together tomorrow morning," said Mr. Kuhn, sounding very out-of-breath.

"Tomorrow is Sunday, Mr. Kuhn," countered Bernie.

"You be at my house by 11:00 a.m."

Bernie couldn't figure out whether Mr. Kuhn was on the verge of tears or simply having a hard time breathing. He agreed to meet with him the following morning.

Even though the rest of the faculty at Park School had resisted any efforts at professional development, Bernie had personally invested a lot of his own time into researching and reading up on some of the most recent educational trends. He had become fascinated with books by John Holt in which some of the old tenets of education were being seriously challenged, and he had tried several of Holt's suggestions for "real learning" in the Latin classroom. Mr.

Kuhn had heard of some of these experiments and had decided that Bernie was simply trying to undermine the quality of education at Park School.

It turned out that Mr. Kuhn was suffering from a heart condition that resulted in his shortness of breath. Bernie listened to all that Mr. Kuhn had to say, and, when given an opportunity, calmly explained how he was simply experimenting with some new educational approaches. He wasn't trying to undermine anything, but rather, was trying to improve his own teaching methods in the Latin classroom.

When he left, he loaned Mr. Kuhn three or four of the books he had been reading and encouraged him to at least glance at them to see where Bernie was coming from.

The following week, Bernie was asked to meet with the Headmaster after school.

"Bernie, things are not going well for you here, are they."

"Things are going fine in my classes, Bill," replied Bernie, "It's just that I'm finding it very hard to respect the way I'm being treated by you, the members of the Board, and the faculty members who wanted me to put myself on the line to represent their interests."

"They tell me that you weren't representing their interests but following your own agenda, Bernie."

"If that's what you're hearing, you should talk to Bill Robinson. I think he'll give you a little different story. He's worked with me from the beginning. He won't be afraid to tell you the truth about what has been going on with the F.C.P.A. In fact, he may be one of the few faculty members willing to stand up for what I have tried to do."

"You know, Bernie, if you're that dissatisfied here, why don't you submit your resignation right now," said Bill.

"Well, Bill, I would, but I have a family to support, and I can't just walk away from my income."

The next interview Bernie went to was for a Latin opening at North Central High School.

Bernie's teaching record looked great on paper.

"Why are you wanting to leave Park School," asked the interviewer at Washington Township Schools.

"Well, Sir, I had been asked to represent the faculty as Park School prepared to merge with Tudor Hall, and, frankly, the whole experience left me with a very negative impression of the administration and faculty. I just don't think I could continue working with people I no longer trust."

"You've made quite a name for yourself with your catapults, haven't you?" asked the interviewer.

"Yes, that was a class project that really caught the eye of the national media. I think it has helped to promote the study of Latin."

"Well, we like what you're doing in your classroom and we would like you to teach Latin and English at North Central High School next year. Would you be willing to accept a contract?"

"Yes, I would. I look forward to spending my time teaching instead of trying to represent the concerns of teachers. I've definitely had enough of that for a lifetime," said Bernie as he breathed a sigh of relief to have found nearby employment for the following school year.

May 21, 1970
Park School, Indianapolis

Despite the fact that he had apparently stirred up a hornet's nest, Bernie decided to go ahead with an after school meeting that he had arranged earlier. He had been able to get the author of **How Children Fail**, John Holt, to accept an invitation to visit Park School and meet informally with its faculty.

The flyer in the faculty room advertised "informal conversation" with John Holt in the Lower School Library from 3:00 p.m. to 5:00 p.m.

Showing the chutzpah that had become his trademark, Bernie included a caveat at the bottom of the poster that warned, "You too may be considered unprofessional."

June, 1970
Nitta, Gunma Prefecture, Japan

It's never easy for the middle child. The oldest tries desperately to hold on to the limelight and the youngest usually ends up getting everyone's care and attention. The middle child has to rely on intelligence, wit and cleverness. The good thing is that the middle child usually has a lot of free time to work all this out, since folks tend naturally to give most of their attention to the other two. Sheryl Batten was the middle child. Of her Mom's "first family."

Sheryl was indeed intelligent, a mixed blessing as far as she was concerned. Because she was smart—and talented—she would not be able simply to walk across the street to school from her new house on Allendale in Indianapolis where she lived with her Mom following the divorce. No, Sheryl would be carpooled to a new school where the curriculum would be more challenging for her.

Later, after her mom remarried and started in on her "second family," Sheryl would be enrolled in School 84, another school with a challenging curriculum. She hated it there.

"Why aren't you happy at School 84?" asked her Mom one day after Sheryl had delivered a powerful and eloquent diatribe.

"Nobody likes me!" proclaimed Sheryl. "I have no friends. Everyone there has been going to school together for years, and they all know each other."

"That's not true," countered her mom. "I'll bet a lot of them are new to the school, too. They probably just make friends quicker than you do."

Barely had Sheryl had a chance to adjust to School 84 when she found herself among strangers again, this time at Broad Ripple H.S. Sheryl, however, focused. She excelled in her classes and soon made a name for herself among her teachers.

For a time, Sheryl talked about wanting to become a nurse. But that was before she got to witness her new little brother, Phillip, learning to walk.

Phillip tripped. Frequently. And it took Phillip a little while to learn how to put his hands down before him when he sensed that he was falling. The result was that he routinely fell flat on his face, breaking baby teeth off or shoving them through his lips. After two or three experiences with her baby brother's encounters with the floor, Sheryl decided that she really did not have the stomach to deal with bloodshed.

"Besides," she concluded, "I'm too shy and withdrawn to be a nurse."

This shyness of Sheryl's was about to come to an abrupt end, however, as she rose to the language challenges of her two month (July and August) foreign student exchange and adjusted to life with her host family in Japan.

Because of her step dad's association with Youth for Understanding—and especially because her family had agreed to host Vera, that organization's first exchange "woman" from a communist country (Yugoslavia)—Sheryl had been accepted into Youth for Understanding's Summer Exchange Program with Japan. Sheryl would never be the same. While she increased her intelligence on the program, she lost her shyness and returned a self-confident, aggressive young lady who knew what she wanted in life and was willing to go after it. Of course, there would be a short delay as she married and had two children, but she would eventually get her degree in Social Service from Purdue University and a degree in Law from the I.U. School of Law in Indianapolis where she made Law Review. Sheryl's law career would be refined in the federal court system of the United States.

July 8, 1970
Chicago, Illinois
Leonard Leo, who had spent the final years of his life bedridden with cancer of the jaw, was interred in St. Mary's Cemetery. He died not ever seeing his daughter Gloria again after she had run away from home to get away from the abuse of those who lived around her, including her father who misunderstood her attractiveness and insisted on berating her as a *puttana* for the way she dressed.

After staying with friends in Chicago, Gloria had made a new life for herself in Las Vegas where she eventually became very wealthy working as a waitress in the High Rollers sections of major casinos.

Although Gloria's mother, Lucy, always told everyone that no one knew where Gloria was, Gloria had contacted her mother secretly to let her know that she was fine so she wouldn't worry.

Later, after her father passed away, Gloria invited her mother to come live with her in Las Vegas where she could enjoy her favorite pastime—Bingo.

Gloria now lives in a million dollar house on a hill overlooking Las Vegas. The house, located on a multi-acre estate surrounded by a high security fence and graced with an in-ground pool, had originally been built for the sister of Janet Jackson. Although born in 1939, Gloria has taken very good care of herself, is still very attractive and continued to work in the High Roller section at the new Stardust Casino until it was closed in 2006. The Stardust was supposedly the last of the "mobster run casinos." So far as the author knows, Gloria is the only member of the two extended families who owns a Hummer!

August, 1970
Old Broad Ripple, Indiana

Bernie and Lillian were thrilled to receive a phone call from Bernie's cousin, Kathy. She was the daughter of his Uncle Gusty and Aunt Rose. They were wondering if it would be O.K. for them to drive down from Lynwood, Illinois, and visit over the weekend.

"Why sure, Kathy, we would love to have you and Aunt Rose visit us. We've sort of been cut off from the family, and it would be great to see you again."

No sooner had the visit been arranged than the phone rang again. It was Bernie's mom calling from Sparta, Wisconsin.

"Your dad and I are planning to drive down and see you this weekend. Will you have a place for us to stay?"

"Well, Ma, actually this weekend would not be a good time," said Bernie.

"*Shuda mi!* Why not?" demanded his mom.

"Well, because Kathy and Aunt Rose are driving down to visit us this weekend."

"Just call them back and tell them they can't come," insisted Bernie's mom.

Bernie's Uncle Gusty had divorced his wife, Aunt Rose, a number of years earlier. Although Bernie's mom had always given her sister-in-laws a lot of grief over the years, she wasn't quite sure what to make of the divorce. Her solution was simply to avoid Aunt Rose whenever possible.

"I'm not going to do that, Ma," said Bernie. "I've already told them they could come."

"*Shuda tu!*" cursed Bernie's mom. "You call her right now."

"Who was that?" asked Bernie's wife, Lillian.

"That was my mom. She said they wanted to come down this weekend, but I told them they couldn't because Kathy and Aunt Rose were coming."

"Can't they just all come at the same time?" asked Lillian.

"That wouldn't be a good idea. My mom doesn't always get along well with her sister-in-laws. I just don't think it would work."

"So are you going to call Kathy and tell her they can't come?" asked Lillian.

"No, I'm not!" insisted Bernie. "My folks can just come down on another weekend."

It wasn't five minutes later when the phone rang again. This time it was Bernie's dad on the phone.

"Bernie," he said in a calm voice that Bernie had come to recognize as one that should not be resisted, "call your cousin Kathy, and tell her that they can't come to your house this weekend because we're going to be there."

Bernie was silent. He was used to sometimes-irrational demands from his mom, but he had always respected all requests made by his dad. He knew he would have to do as he was asked.

"O.K. They'll probably be upset with me, but if you want me to do it, I guess I'll do it," said Bernie.

Years later Bernie would learn from Kathy that she had been one of the few people in the family to have successfully stood her ground against her Aunt Stella—a feat almost unrivaled.

"When did that happen?" asked Bernie.

"Oh, a number of years ago. Your mom had just finished being totally nasty to my mom, and I just wasn't going to stand for it," said Kathy.

"What did you do?"

"Well, when I had a chance to get Aunt Stella alone, I simply told her that I did not appreciate the way she treated my mother, and that I didn't want that to happen again," said Kathy, in her soft, calm voice.

"Wow! Did you have to duck?" asked Bernie.

"No, Bernie. In fact, her whole attitude changed immediately. She said she was sorry, and she even kissed my hands."

Absolutely incredible!

It was no wonder that Bernie's mom was not willing to spend the night under the same roof with Kathy and Aunt Rose.

After her divorce from Bernie's Uncle Gusty, Aunt Rose had remarried briefly, but as soon as her new husband insisted that he be given total control of her finances, she immediately filed for divorce.

After spending nearly ten years in the company of another lady friend, Uncle Gusty later became interested in a lady named Netti who owned a bar near Portage, Indiana, and they were eventually married.

In the 1980's, however, Netti would become so seriously enthralled by the visions of the Blessed Virgin that Mary Ann Van Hoof claimed to have seen beginning in 1950 near Necedah, Wisconsin, that she insisted that they sell the bar and move as close as they could to the Way of Peace Shrine that had been built commemorating the visions.

Netti agreed to sell her bar, now called Ryan's, to Butch and Rick, the two sons of Gusty's brother Angelo's daughter, Evy Roland.

Even though Mary Ann Van Hoof broke with the Roman Catholic Bishop of her dioceses in 1975 and became affiliated with a radical schismatic movement, Gusty and Netti continued to live in their remodeled trailer home in the countryside near Necedah. After breaking with the Bishop of her diocese, Mary Ann Van Hoof began to warn her followers of a movement by the Devil to place the world entirely under one leader so he could better control it. After 9/11, Mary and her followers began to claim that the whole disaster had been coordinated by agencies of the United States Federal Government to allow President Bush (whom the group believes is operating as an agent of the Devil) to make his initial moves at world conquest.

September, 1970
Marian College, Indianapolis

"This is our request: To increase our chest! This is our request: To increase our chest!" Marsha was parading down the hall with several other girls who had come out of their dorm rooms to join the impromptu parade. The girls had their arms raised before their chests, with fingers tightly grasped together as they pulled their arms outward to flex their pectoral muscles.

At Bernie's suggestion (in keeping with his appreciation of the values of a Catholic education), Marsha had been enrolled in Marian College and was living in a dorm just off of Cold Spring Road. Marsha had been through some hard times with her mom and Bernie, and they were taking her enrollment as a positive step toward a brighter future.

During her first weekend home visit, Marsha went on and on about how awful her roommate was and how badly she would like to have a room of her own.

"What does she do that's so bad?" asked her mom.

"She's a pig. Her stuff is slopped all over the room, and she leaves the sink a mess," complained Marsha.

"Have you asked her to clean her stuff up?" asked Bernie.

"All she does is ignore me. I finally began cleaning the sink myself because I didn't want to wash up in her filth."

"Did she get the message?" asked Bernie.

"No, she just began taking it for granted that I would do the cleaning. But I showed her!"

"What did you do?" asked her mom.

"Now I just clean my own half of the sink!"

September, 1970
Old Broad Ripple, Indiana

Vera had arrived. While the Youth for Understanding staff had told Bernie and Lillian they would be hosting an exchange student from Yugoslavia, they hadn't told them the student would be an exchange "woman."

Vera was 19 years old, and she would be staying in the new room that had been built for Marsha at the back of the new two-floor addition. Since Marsha was now living at college, the arrangement would work just fine. Vera had already finished the equivalent of her high school education in Yugoslavia, and she was not pleased to learn that she would be attending Broad Ripple High School as a senior. Somehow or other she thought she was coming to America to attend college in California.

Things just didn't get off to the greatest start with Vera.

On the drive to Indianapolis from her orientation city, Lillian mentioned to Vera that Mr. Barcio, her host, was Italian.

"I hate Italians!" proclaimed Vera.

"I don't go to church," announced Vera on Sunday morning. "We are atheists, and we don't believe in God!"

"Well, why don't you come with us anyway? Consider it a cultural experience, not a religious one," said Bernie trying to smooth over the objection.

"No!" said Vera, and that settled it.

"Your bread is like mush," said Vera as she squished a whole slice of bread into a ball at dinner.

"That's what American bread is like," said Lillian, shocked at Vera's rudeness.

"My mother always went out and bought a fresh loaf of hard crust bread for our family every day. We would never eat anything like this in our country," countered Vera.

Somehow or another, Vera soon managed to contact others from Yugoslavia that were already living in Indianapolis.

"I will be going with my friends for dinner tonight," announced Vera one evening.

"What friends?" asked Bernie.

"Friends from my country who live here. We will be out late. May I have a key to get in, please?"

"That won't be necessary," said Bernie. "We'll wait up for you and let you in."

Later that evening, Bernie and Lillian were startled when the front door of their living room was rudely pushed out of its frame, lock and all.

"What are you doing?" called Bernie as he jumped up from his chair in the living room.

"The door was stuck," explained a hefty Yugoslavian man who had shouldered in the door.

"It wasn't stuck. It was locked. I would have opened it if you had just knocked," explained Bernie.

Vera was definitely not interested in the American experience. Her mission here was to convert as many people as possible to the merits of Communism. She argued at school, she argued at home and she argued with Lew Berkeley and Bill Robinson when they were invited over to meet her.

Because Vera continued to complain and refused to adjust to her placement with Bernie and Lillian, Bernie had no choice but to contact the Youth for Understanding office and request that she be resituated as she was completely disrupting his home and family.

When she left, Vera thought she had won and was going to be sent to California, where she claimed to have a rich uncle who was waiting for her. Unfortunately for those plans, however, she was simply relocated in Michigan where she spent the remainder of the school year before being returned to her native country.

October, 1970
Old Broad Ripple, Indiana

Although she was supposed to be spending her time at Marion College studying, Marsha had met a young musician named Lonnie from the west side of town. When she came home one weekend to share this news, she surprised everyone by announcing that she was in love and wanted to drop out of college.

"Why do you want to do that?" asked Lillian.

"It's just not what I want to be doing right now."

"If you would just spend more time at Marion and less time studying in Lonnie's bedroom at his house, you might find that college can be fun," said Bernie.

"I'm going to drop out of college, and Lonnie and I are going to get married."

"I don't think so," said Lillian.

"Why not?" insisted Marsha. "If I can't live with my dad, at least let me start living my own life."

"For starts, you're only 17 years old," said Bernie, "and you have no idea of what you're getting into."

"Nah doy! I'll be 18 in two months."

"That's still too young," said Lillian.

Marsha decided to drop her little bomb that she thought would guarantee her getting her way.

"We've already slept together."

Silence. Lillian stared at Marsha and Bernie stared at Lillian.

"Are you pregnant?" asked Lillian.

"No-o," said Marsha, "I'm not stu-pid!"

Lillian arranged for the two families to get together to discuss the situation. Lonnie's parents were invited to Old Broad Ripple.

"We think they're too young too," agreed Lonnie's mother after Lillian and Bernie had shared their thoughts.

"Well, then we'll just elope," stated Marsha.

"I don't think so," said Bernie. "You each need to have your parents' permission to get a license, and it doesn't look like Lonnie's folks are any more willing than we are."

Lonnie seemed to take the decision fairly well. In fact, Bernie thought that he even looked a little relieved. Marsha was pissed and was, no doubt, already plotting her next move.

January, 1971
Old Broad Ripple, Indiana

The holidays were over and Marsha was still on semester break. Because she and Lonnie had not been able to convince their parents to sign for them so they could get married, she had not had a very good first semester at Marian College. She was now more depressed than ever.

"Where are you?" demanded her mom when Marsha finally called home about 1:00 a.m.

"I don't know. I'm somewhere! I've decided I'm just going to get in my car and keep driving until I run out of gas!"

"Marsha, don't be dumb. Just come on home!"

Too late. Marsha had hung up.

"Well, we can try calling the police and telling them what kind of car she's driving," suggested Bernie.

That idea, however, was destined to be pointless.

"How old is your daughter?" asked the police dispatcher.

"She just turned 18," said Lillian.

"Well, Ma'am, then there's nothing we can do. Once they turn 18, we can't pick them up for running away."

So that was it. Marsha was turning their lives into a nightmare, and there was nothing they could do about it.

A few days later, however, Marsha called and said she was coming home to pick up her things.

"Well, I think it's time for a little tough love," suggested Bernie.

"What do you mean," asked Lillian.

"Instead of letting her announce that she's running away, we should just ask her to leave. Hell, we can't just continue to let her turn our lives upside down every time she feels like it. Let her see what it feels like to be completely alone, and maybe she'll shape up."

Marsha drove up accompanied by a black girl friend. Bernie went outside to meet them.

"I think you'd better have your friend wait for you outside," commanded Bernie. "Your mom and I want to talk with you."

As soon as Marsha got in the house, her mom led her into the master bedroom, and Bernie closed the door behind them.

SMACK!

Lillian gave Marsha a well-aimed slap.

"Why in the Hell are you doing this, Marsha?"

WHACK!

Bernie landed a slap on one of Masha's legs before she had a chance to scramble onto the bed and perch up on the headboard with her back to the wall.

"You're not going to keep making our life a living hell," yelled Bernie. "You're 18, and there's nothing we can do to keep you from running away. If you don't want to be here, you can just pack up your stuff and get the hell out!"

Marsha stared at them with wide-open eyes. Her adrenalin was pumping and she was obviously scared, but she wasn't going to shed any tears. When the coast was clear, she scampered off the bed and up the steps to a new bedroom that had been built for her when a second addition had been added to the house on Ferguson, *sans* hanging bed.

"Say goodbye to your sister," said Bernie to Sheryl and Karen who stood stunned in the living room watching events unfold.

Once Marsha and her friend had her stuff loaded into the car, Bernie went outside for a parting remark.

"And if you ever do come back to visit your mom, you'd better make damn sure I'm not here!" threatened Bernie.

January 5, 1971
Sparta, Wisconsin

Tony Nudi often spent a month or more at a time living with his daughter Stella and his son-in-law, Ted, in Sparta. Stella took good care of him and Ted was always most pleasant with him. They could converse in Italian and share stories about the old days. Also, Ted always listened respectfully to his father-in-law's views on life and other philosophical observations.

Both Ted and Stella were obviously concerned when Tony became seriously ill. Dr. Brown, the family doctor in Sparta, was called to the house. He examined Tony and wrote out prescriptions that he thought would help.

Tony Nudi, however, got worse instead of better. When he passed away, Stella was not happy with Dr. Brown's efforts and openly shared her feelings.

"You should have done more!" she complained to the doctor after he had come to the house to sign the death certificate.

"Mrs. Barcio, we did all that we could for your father," replied the doctor.

"Nope! There was something else you could have done!" insisted Stella.

"Mrs. Barcio, what else would you have liked us to do for him? He was very sick, and he just wasn't responding to the medications."

"Nope! You're wrong!" insisted Stella. "There was something that could have been done to save him."

"Mrs. Barcio, your father was 94 years old," said Dr. Brown in desperation.

Dr. Brown made it a point to be as courteous as possible with his patients, especially when they were going through times of stress, but Stella Barcio was pushing his limits. Finally, he could take it no more. He had to end the discussion even if it meant he needed to be a little rude.

"Mrs. Barcio, how long did you want him to live? He couldn't live forever, you know!" said Dr. Brown sternly. "I'm sorry for your loss, but, if you will excuse me, I do have to go now. An ambulance will be here in a little while to move your father to the mortuary."

This wasn't quite the angry, serious, truthful conversation into which Stella may have hoped to prod Dr. Brown, but it was as far as he was going to allow her to go.

All she could do to revenge herself on him was to repeat his heartless—in her mind—statement to her son Bernard years later to show how awful Dr. Brown had treated her:

"Mrs. Barcio, your father was 94 years old. How long did you want him to live?"

February, 1971
Wishard Hospital, Indianapolis

"Your mom is here to see you," said the policeman as he led Lillian into the emergency room cubicle where Marsha lay on a gurney.

The police had called Lillian after Marsha had been rushed to the hospital to be treated for a drug overdose. She had unsuccessfully tried to kill herself.

"I don't have a mother," grumbled Marsha. "She's dead!"

"Hey, young lady," said the policeman, "don't talk to your mother that way!"

That brief encounter turned out to be one of the few times Marsha would ever see her mother again—none of which were pleasant.

After she recovered, Marsha decided to bond with her dad's relatives, the Battens, who lived in Indianapolis. They would be her new extended family.

After a brief marriage to Lonnie doomed to end in a divorce, she eventually met a nice Catholic boy named James Louzon whom she married.

Before Lillian passed away in 2004, she confided to Bernie that she had visited Marsha again in the hospital after hearing that she had given birth to a boy, who was named James after his father. Once again, however, Marsha had insisted that she had no mother and demanded that Lillian leave the room.

At first Marsha attended beauty school and worked as a beautician for a while. She then went to nursing school and became a nurse. As a high school student, Marsha had enjoyed working as a Candy Striper at St. Vincent Hospital when it was still in its downtown location. Perhaps with the encouragement of her husband, she finally decided to become a professional nurse. She found employment at St. Francis Hospital and at Kennedy Living Center in Martinsville, Indiana.

The last that Bernie and Lillian heard, via the Robinsons with whom Marsha has kept in occasional contact over the years (knowing that what she told them would reach her mother), Marsha and her husband had four children and one grandchild.

When Cyndi was about 34 years old, she said she would like to meet her half-sister Marsha and was told how to get in touch with her.

"We're going to have lunch at Appleby's on Broad Ripple Avenue," announced Cyndi. "Marsha insisted that no one come with me."

Lillian and Bernie had no problem with that and hoped she would have a pleasant experience.

"It was awful," announced Cyndi when she returned home. "The black lady who drove when Marsha left home was with her. All she did was put everyone down. It wasn't a very pleasant meeting."

Marsha's sister Karen, however, did persist in getting back in touch with her. Karen remains the only one of Marsha's siblings with whom she stays in contact—even bringing her daughter Tracy with her in 2013 to visit Karen at the Governor's Mansion after Karen's husband, Mike Pence, was elected Governor of Indiana.

March 15, 1971
Indianapolis

Bernie was now teaching Latin and English at North Central High School in Indianapolis, and he had been challenged by his old Park School Latin students for a return catapult match on the Ides of March. His students would be competing with a double-towered trebuchet called Pacator.

By now catapults had definitely become a newsworthy national event, and, once again, Pat Trese and his NBC news team were on hand to cover the contest.

This contest was described by reporter Steve Wolf in the North Central High School newspaper, the **Northern Lights** (March 31, 1971, Vol. XV, No. 12, p. 1):

> "The Ides arrived. Dressed in Roman costumes, the [Park-Tudor] 8th period [Latin] class paraded across the field. The [North Central] Latin Club was bussed to the scene of the battle to lend moral support, but hundreds of other North Centralites turned out to cheer the team.
>
> "From the start, however, it looked like there wouldn't be much to cheer about. [Pacator's] first shot went backwards, and the crowd gasped as [David] Dortch [—a Spanish student who had been allowed to compete in the contest with a catapult of his own design—] followed it with a 337′ smash of his own. Park-Tudor's Latin class catapult followed with a modest 47′, and North Central again shot— and again flubbed; straight up, straight down. The first volleys set the pace for the remaining rounds and Dortch's lead was never challenged.
>
> "Pacator, however, provided an ironic twist to the battle. After four mediocre shots in the actual contest, it let loose with a 337′ exhibition blast that tied Dortch's newly-set record. Sighed senior Ruthann Tornes, 'I just wish the regular contest could have been as good as the exhibition.' "

June, 1971
Versailles, Indiana

"If it's raining, we must be camping," thought Bernie to himself as he fruitlessly tried to pile sand around the outer edges of their blue tent with its two-room bedroom unit inside. He had carefully situated a campground dining table inside the zip-on kitchen wing of the tent so they could be dry while they ate. All he had to do now was keep the water from getting inside.

Bernie and Lillian had bought their tent, a French tent no less, from a retired army sergeant in Indianapolis. The sergeant and his wife had bought it in Europe and were more than willing to share many happy memories of its use in campgrounds throughout France and Italy. Camping was really the only way Bernie and Lillian could afford to vacation with their family that had quickly grown to five children. The tent had a common area with no floor, an add-on (by means of a giant zipper) kitchen area with see-through plastic windows and a specially suspended two-room sleeping unit that came with built in canvass floors.

Suddenly, there was a flash of lightening and Bernie felt an electric tingle spark up his legs as he stood ankle deep in the water outside.

"This could get dangerous," he thought to himself.

Then came the screams from inside the tent.

"My potty! My potty!"

Bernie abandoned his sand project and quickly stuck his head through the opening of the door. His work with the sand had apparently all been in vain. The floor was covered with a good four inches of water, in which, slowly floating back toward the kitchen unit, was Cindy's potty.

No sooner had he rescued the potty and placed it high and dry on the camp table than Cindy's voice again filled the rain-soaked tent.

"My Boy! My Boy!"

Her little rubber squeak-doll boy, her nighttime companion, was floating away toward the door.

This was almost getting to be too much. Camping was fun and something they all looked forward to each summer. But, really! Cooking steaks over an open fire only to have them curl up and make rain-water pockets definitely took the edge off of the whole fun experience.

And he wasn't quite sure how many more late nights he wanted to spend sitting in small town Laundromats waiting for their sleeping bags and sacks full of clothes to dry.

July, 1971
Mammoth Cave, Kentucky

"Will you folks be tent camping?" asked the ranger at the entrance to the Mammoth Cave campgrounds.

"Yes," replied Bernie. We hope you have some nice grassy sites."

"We do," said the ranger. "Staying long?"

"Just overnight," replied Bernie.

"Ask him about the copperheads," said Lillian from the passenger seat. Phillip was in a car seat between them. Karen and Cindy were in the back seat.

"My wife thinks you have copperheads here," said Bernie smiling condescendingly.

"She's right," said the ranger.

"But they usually don't crawl around the campground at night, do they," stated Bernie hoping for official ranger confirmation.

"I'm afraid they do, folks. Enjoy your stay."

Lillian had heard more than she had really wanted to. Once they got to their assigned campsite and got the gear unloaded off the roof and off the top of the trunk of the big white Oldsmobile, Bernie went to work setting up the tent while Lillian and Karen took care of fixing something for them to eat.

Once they had eaten and cleaned up and made the usual trips to the campground outhouses, the family settled into their separate sleeping quarters and prepared to zipper up for the night. That's when Lillian produced the masking tape. She had decided that the only way to insure that no copperheads would invade the bedroom units was to secure all the zippers with masking tape, making any further excursions to the outhouses impossible, of course.

The family survived the night with no copperhead visits and Cindy spent the next morning being carried through Mammoth Cave on the shoulders of her father—this after having assured everyone that she would have absolutely no problem making the hike through the cave on her own two feet.

The next night found the Barcio family setting up their tent in a new state park. A light mist of rain was in the air.

"We've really got to look into getting a camper trailer," Bernie confided to Lillian later that evening after the sky had cleared and they were relaxing around a small campfire. "That way we would at least be up off the ground."

Before the Camping Trip of the Summer of 1971 ended, Bernie had taken an interesting branch he had found, stripped the bark off it and carved it into a walking stick. After it dried, he invited Karen to paint scenes on the walking stick that highlighted the summer's adventures which included getting rained on, visiting Mammoth Cave with its snakes, stick figures of all family members present, horseback riding, wreath making, omnipresent raccoons, swimming, deer spotting, bicycling, flower and fern collecting, and loading the roof and trunk of the big white Oldsmobile with camping gear. This walking stick was still used for hiking by the author, along with several others he had made after returning to tent camping following his final retirement from teaching in 2005. In 2012, however, he finally presented the decorated walking stick to Karen since it contained her own early art work.

March, 1972
Indianapolis

Bernie and Lillian had been looking at homes on the north side of Indianapolis for several months before they finally saw one at 6026 Indianola that caught Bernie's eye. It had extra lots and a certain character that appealed to Bernie.

At first, Lillian was repulsed by the property because it was surrounded by a six-foot high wire fence that had been installed by one of its original reclusive owners.

"We'll have to see if it has a fireplace," reminded Lillian.

When they were finally able to tour the house, Lillian and Bernie arrived with a yardstick to measure the fireplace. They had to be sure that their prized ornate carved walnut mantel—the first thing they had bought together before they were even married—would fit. It would.

Not only did the house turn out to have character, and more than enough room for the four children who would be moving in with them, but it also had a colorful history.

The first year that the address, 6026 Indianola Ave., appeared in an Indianapolis directory was 1932 when it was listed as the residence of Charles and Blanche Layman. Charles Layman owned a good deal of stock in Barbasol, a product that had been invented by his friend, Frank B. Shields. The Barbasol Company had begun producing its products on the second floor of a building located at 1324 N. Meridian St. in Indianapolis. According to a neighbor, Wayburn Sheeks, who lived at 6001 Indianola during the 1950's and 1960's, Charles and Blanche traveled the country extensively promoting the sale of Barbasol products.

In 1936, Frank B. Shields sponsored the Barbasol Special #12 in the Indianapolis 500 race. It was decorated to look like a tube of shaving cream and finished in 12th place.

A 1935 aerial photo of Broad Ripple High School that Lillian would come across years later while publishing the Broad Ripple **Village Sampler Newspaper** would show that the house was one of the few then existing in the addition. While looking through the second floor of the two-car garage that came with the house, Bernie came across an old wooden sign proclaiming,

> NO HUNTING, FISHING
> OR TRAPPING IN THIS
> ADDITION.

Blanch Layman, who lived alone in the house as a recluse after her husband passed away, finally sold it to Lloyd and Anah Scholl on September 14, 1962. After the Scholls were divorced, Anah had put the house on the market just in time for Bernie and Lillian to make their bid for the property.

Several years later, a letter was delivered to the house from a fur storage company. The letter said that a Russian sable fur coat was still being kept in storage and requested that Mrs. Layman claim it. All Bernie and Lillian could do was let the storage company know that Mrs. Layman was deceased and they had no idea how to contact any of her heirs.

April 22, 1972
Culver, Indiana

The NBC Chronolog news team had returned to Indianapolis to cover the annual Latin catapult contest in 1971, but in 1972 it was totally amazed at the line up of catapults that filled the horizon of the catapult field at Culver Military Academy. What had started as the project of a single Latin II class at Park School had now turned into a National Catapult Contest. Catapults were being fielded not only in Culver, Indiana, but also in Wilmington, Ohio and Mauston, Wisconsin among other locations.

As far as catapult records were concerned, Bernie would lose the battle, but win the war. Pacator, the catapult built by his North Central High School Latin students, would not win the contest on the Culver field, but Bernie's goal of using the catapult project to promote interest in the study of Latin was a total winner. Never again would so many authentic reproductions of Roman catapults ever be assembled on one field for friendly competition.

The winner of the First National Catapult Contest turned out to be the same Spanish student, David Dortch, representing Park-Tudor School in Indianapolis. Bernie had permitted David to submit an entry in an earlier contest held on the grounds of Park-Tudor school, and David had continued his interest on his own after Bernie had began teaching at North Central.

David Dortch was soon invited to appear as a guest challenger on ABC's "To Tell the Truth."

Lillian Batten at her desk
at Park School on the
Cold Springs Road Campus
1966

Park School Campus on Cold Spring Rd., Indianapolis, 1968

Photographed by John Krauss

The farm house on the Lilly Orchard in which the author lived while the new Park School campus was being planned

The Mars I catapult Ides of March, 1966

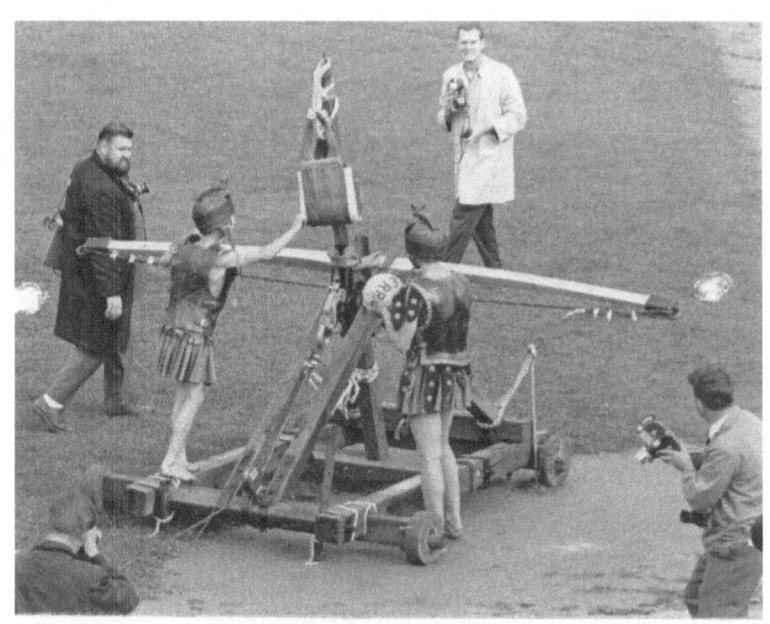

The Mars I catapult in Gwelph, Ontario
October 1, 1966

Claudia Somes (R) and other N.C.H.S. Latin
students prepare their catapult Pacator
at Culver Military Academy, April 22, 1972

(L to R) Lillian, Sheryl, Marsha & Karen Batten, 1967

Author and his bride, Lillian, June 11, 1967

The author's home, 6544 Ferguson, Broad Ripple, with both additions complete, 1971.

The author's home, 6026 Indianola, Broad Ripple, March, 1972, before the high fence was removed.

Mountains seen from Gloria Leo's estate
Las Vegas, 2006

(L to R) Cyndi (author's daughter), Gloria Leo, Anna-Marie (Gloria's daughter), Mary Leo (Gloria's sister), Dionna (Gloria's daughter), Las Vegas estate, 2012

PART VIII

May 1972 – July 1993

Life on Indianola
Before Moving Stella Barcio to Indianapolis

May 1, 1972
Broad Ripple, Indiana

"Lillian, here's what you have to do," said Bernie to his wife from the phone in the faculty room at North Central High School. "Go to the Washington Township Small Claims Court, it's just off Keystone on 54th Street, and file an Eviction Order."

"Are you sure we want to evict the family?" asked Lillian.

"We have to, Lillian. They knew that we needed to move in on May 1, and they've had plenty of time to find a new place to rent."

"What if we just found a place to rent for a while?" asked Lillian.

"Why should we pay money to rent an apartment for our family when we bought a perfectly good house to move into. Besides, if we bend on this, there's no telling how many months they would drag it out," insisted Bernie.

Two days later, Lillian and Bernie's house that they had bought at 6026 Indianola in Broad Ripple was empty. The tenants who had been renting from the seller had quickly complied with the court order once they saw that Bernie and Lillian meant business.

Lillian and Bernie had managed to sell their previous home in Old Broad Ripple for more than four times what Bernie had paid for it because the area was being developed by small business owners.

"I think I would like to have my bedroom in the basement," said Sheryl.

"I've got dibs on the large bedroom on the 2nd floor," said Karen.

Phillip and Cindy each got one of the two smaller bedrooms on the east end of the second floor.

No arrangements had to be made for Marsha since she had separated herself from the family.

Tullia, Bernie's cat that he had had since 1966, moved in with the family and soon claimed her own favorite areas. Tullia was a beautiful calico cat that Bernie had gotten as a kitten from the French teacher, Madame Sebastian at Park School. Bernie always claimed that Tullia was French. Bernie had, of course, named Tullia after the daughter of Marcus Tullius Cicero. In their old house on Ferguson, Tullia had pretty much had the rule of the roost. If she felt feisty during the night, she would go tearing through the house into the den and climb right up the burlap wallpaper to the ceiling. Or, if she were properly spooked, she would simply shoot right up the curtains to the top of a window.

During one phase of the remodeling that Bernie and Lillian had done to the house on Ferguson, there were open beams in the ceiling above their bed. Tullia loved to make her way up on the beams early in the evening. Then, in the middle of the night, after they were both asleep, she would jump down right onto their pillows and scare the living daylight out of both of them. Sometimes, she would decide to go through the house meowing for lost kittens. She had given birth to several litters over the years and every so often she just sort of forgot that they were all grown up and gone. In fact, she gave birth to one of those litters right in Karen's hair as the family was camping one summer. Since Tullia was pregnant, Bernie had decided to take her along, and Tullia had simply curled up in Karen's sleeping bag when the urge to give birth suddenly struck her.

"AAHHH!" screamed Karen when she felt something warm and slippery against her forehead.

"What's wrong?" called Lillian.

"It's Tullia. Oh, no! She's having her kittens in my hair!"

Once Karen was extricated from the mess, everyone just decided to let Tullia finish her work right where she was.

"What about my hair?" asked Karen.

"It'll wash out," said Bernie flippantly.

"Nah-Doi!" said Karen twisting the knuckle of her index finger into her cheek as she always did when someone said something that she considered to be totally stupid.

Although Tullia mellowed a little in her new house on Indianola, she could still take a spook every now and then and go tearing through the house.

"OH MY GOD! GET HER OFF! GET HER OFF!" shrieked Lillian's mom, Grandma Hacker.

Grandma Hacker was not a cat lover. She tolerated the fact that Bernie and Lillian had pets, but she usually gave the pets a very wide berth whenever she came over.

Grandma Hacker had just settled herself down in a dining room chair for a visit when, all of sudden, from out of nowhere, came Tullia. Something had spooked her, and she tore straight through the dining room and right up Grandma Hacker's legs, lap and chest, coming to rest squarely on her shoulders and looking around the room all bug eyed.

In fact, it was hard to tell whose eyes were bigger at that moment, Tullia's or Grandma Hacker's.

If pressed into service, Grandma Hacker could be coerced into coming over and feeding the cats while the family was on vacation, but, on those occasions, she let the cats know exactly who was boss.

During one such occasion, Karen's black and white cat, Charlotte, had managed to slip outdoors when Grandma Hacker was going in. Charlotte had decided to cross the street just as a car came barreling along.

SCREECH! THUMP!

Grandma Hacker hurried back outside to see what was going on, only to see that Charlotte had just been struck by the car and was lying motionless in the middle of the road.

"Charlotte, you get yourself in that house right now!" yelled Grandma Hacker.

There was so much authority in her voice that Charlotte immediately jumped up and came running back into the house despite the fact that skin on the inside of her back leg was torn completely open.

May 15, 1972
Indianapolis

Despite his spot in the national limelight and the tremendous publicity Bernie was attracting to his students and to the study of Latin, he quickly found that Mr. Cloncs, the principal of North Central High School, was not all that enamored with what Bernie had to offer.

"Bernie, we find that we really don't have a need for you in our classrooms here at North Central next year," said Mr. Cloncs after school one day.

"Am I being fired?" asked Bernie, having been in a similar situation earlier at Park School.

"No, you're not being fired," said Mr. Cloncs.

O.K., Bernie knew they really had nothing on him that would justify their trying to fire him. So it must be political. Perhaps his notoriety, obtained through a program that he had brought with him and promoted all on his own, was somehow a threat to the administration and other faculty at the school.

"So what are my options?" asked Bernie.

"Well, you could resign," stated Mr. Cloncs.

"I don't think I want to resign, Mr. Cloncs. I have a family to support," said Bernie.

"Well, Bernie, if you want to stay at North Central next year, all we can offer you is study halls and lunch room duty. I don't think you would enjoy that very much would you?"

"No, I don't think so," said Bernie.

"Or, you can accept a transfer to Eastwood Junior High School," suggested Mr. Cloncs, glad to have some alternative to having Bernie under his feet the following year.

"Do they need a Latin teacher at Eastwood?" asked Bernie.

"No, they don't offer Latin there. You would be teaching five classes of eighth grade English. One preparation, plus study hall and lunch room duty."

August 26, 1972
Sparta, Wisconsin

The long awaited day had finally come when Ted could retire from the railroad. Bernie and Lillian and his brother Joe and his wife, Liz, came home to attend their dad's retirement dinner that was held at the Friendship Inn in La

Crosse. Seated next to Bernie's dad at the main table was the Superintendent of the Bridge and Building Crews who had retired a couple of years earlier.

"Bernie, do you remember this gentleman?" asked Ted.

"Yes, I do. I believe you came to visit our job site when we were building a bridge one summer."

"Yes, I believe I did," said the retired superintendent.

"Our foreman was so nervous that day that he assigned everyone a job that we were supposed to do as soon as he saw you and your assistants coming. I was supposed to coil a long extension cord. He wanted us all to look busy."

"STUPID," thought Bernie to himself as soon as he had said it. "Now he's going to think that he was being made a fool of. When am I going to learn to keep my big mouth shut?"

Bernie immediately decided it would be best if he just avoided saying anything more for the rest of the meal. He would focus on eating his dinner without making too big of a mess.

Since it had long been Ted's dream to revisit his boyhood home of San Marco alla Mattina in southern Italy, Ted immediately went to work applying for passports for his wife and himself.

Although Stella seemed to have no problem coming up with the documentation she needed to be issued a passport, Ted was having some real problems. He would have to write many letters in order to obtain a copy of his baptismal certificate from Italy, records of his father's processing on Ellis Island, and get statements from the grade school he attended in St. Francis in Milwaukee. It was a horrendous effort that produced a veritable mass of documentation—all of which Bernie happened to discover in a small drawer of an end table that had been moved to Indianapolis and placed in his mother's apartment.

"Stell, we're going to have to delay our trip to Italy a little while," explained Ted one day.

"Why? You got your passport didn't you?"

"Yes. There's no problem with our passports. But there's a little job I have to do before we can go."

"Don't they know you're retired? Why do you still have a job you have to do?"

As it turned out, the owner of a Sparta factory needed a railroad spur installed so he could ship and receive directly. He had asked Ted about the possibility of having a spur built before Ted had retired, and Ted had assured him it could be done. Now, however, since Ted's division was being shut down, the work crew was no longer available.

"I'm going to build the man's spur, and then we can go," said Ted.

"*Ma, tu sei pazzo*! How are going to build the spur. You're supposed to be retired!" pressed Stella.

"I've got some men lined up who promised to help. It's just a short spur."

So, Ted ordered the materials that would be needed for the job; but when everything was ready, he suddenly found out that the men who had initially agreed to help with the project were no longer available. He would have to build the spur himself.

Now, building a railroad spur, no matter how short, is no easy matter. Each tie weighs more than 200 lbs. (and they are laid in at 10 inch intervals). The lengths of rail generally require a team of 6 to 8 men to lift into place. Ted would have to drag them into place all by himself. Then all the spikes would have to be individually driven and the gravel tamped under each tie so the trackbed would be level and stable.

Bernie and Joe knew nothing of their father's commitment. He contacted neither of them to ask if they could take some time off to help him with the project. He had promised the man a spur, and, by golly, the man would get it if Ted had to build it himself.

Which he did.

In the process, Ted ruptured himself and would eventually need an operation to repair the damage.

All of which pretty much put the kibosh on any travel plans to Italy.

September 1972
Indianapolis

Bernie accepted his assignment to Eastwood, determined to make the best of a bad situation. Teaching five classes of eighth grade English would provide a wonderful opportunity for him to sell his students—and their parents—on the merits of studying Latin. He was determined to start a Freshman Latin class at Eastwood as soon as possible.

Of course, he was also determined to continue his sponsorship of the National Catapult Contest.

It is interesting to note that, although Gene Cloncs no longer wanted Bernie working in his high school, he continued to call Bernie whenever he took a cow to be slaughtered at a Fisher's slaughterhouse. Gene would use some of the meat himself and offer a quarter to Bernie. Not wanting their previous troubles to interfere with an opportunity to provide quality meat for his family, Bernie usually complied and filled a large freezer that he and Lillian had at home.

October 1, 1972
Bloomington, Indiana

Lillian's daughter Sheryl and her boyfriend Jeff Donnella had been straight-A students together at Broad Ripple High School during their senior year. Both had promising futures. Sheryl had even been recognized as a National Merit Scholar during her senior year.

Although Sheryl was quickly accepted as a freshman at I.U. in Bloomington, Jeff decided he wasn't quite ready to start college. He wasn't sure just what he wanted to do. For the moment, he just wanted to be wherever Sheryl was until he had it all figured out.

November 1972
Chatard High School, Indianapolis
"I'm not going to do it," whispered Karen to her biology lab partner.

"But you'll get in trouble!"

"I don't care. He's too cute, and I won't chloroform him and cut him open," insisted Karen.

"What will you do with him?" asked Karen's lab partner.

"I'm going to put him in my purse," whispered Karen, "and let him loose in the field at lunch time."

"Well, if you're going to let yours loose, I'm letting mine loose too. We'll just both get in trouble."

So Karen and her lab partner went through the motions of keeping busy during the class period and at the end of class gently concealed their live frogs.

Their biology teacher was disappointed, but both girls were such good students that he decided to let the matter ride without getting them into serious trouble.

Ever since that incident, frogs have become a symbol close to Karen's heart. She has much frog realia among her prized personal possessions and has even painted pictures of frogs to give to her family.

March 1, 1973
Indianapolis
Wayne Walls (who went by the name Pete), the principal of Eastwood Junior High School, was a retired naval officer. He had been given the task by Washington Township to "deal with" this Barcio character, hopefully getting him to leave the school system.

"SEE ME" said the note that Bernie found in his school mailbox at lunchtime. It was from the principal and it was meant to be intimidating. It would be the first of a long series of "SEE ME'S" that Bernie would find in his box as Mr. Walls engaged in "walk by" classroom observations of Bernie and his teaching methods for which he would write Bernie up on afterwards and discuss during a "SEE ME" session.

"I noticed your shoes weren't shiny when I walked by your classroom yesterday, Bernie," said Mr. Walls. "Do you think that sets a good example for your students?"

"I can certainly try to shine them before I come to school each day," replied Bernie.

Next time it would be, "Bernie, I noticed that you touched your mustache a couple times while you were talking to your students. That shows you're nervous. Are you nervous about your teaching here, Bernie?"

Sometimes the principal would criticize the cleanliness of the Bernie's classroom, the neatness of the books stored on his shelves, the arrangement of items on his teacher's desk, the way he wrote on the blackboard, or the way he erased the blackboard.

One day, as Bernie was walking by the main office on his way to prepare for his next class, Pete Walls spotted him and beckoned him to come into his office and close the door behind him.

"Bernie," said the principal looking at a folder that lay open before him, "you know, your folder is thicker than any other teacher's at Eastwood."

If this comment was meant to intimidate Bernie, it wasn't going to work.

"Well, Mr. Walls, I guess that's because I do more than most people do. When a person does a lot, a person takes a lot of risks, and he's bound to make a few mistakes along the way."

"Bernie," said Pete Walls, pausing to let the drama of the moment build a little, "what do you think my role here is as principal?"

"I think," answered Bernie without the slightest hesitation, "that the role of the principal, and all administrators, is to facilitate the work that we teachers do in the classroom. Teaching is the most important thing that goes on in a school."

Pete Walls just sat there with a stilted ex-military grin on his face, not sure whether he should charge Bernie with insubordination or congratulate him for a fairly good insight into the educational process. Bernie saw that this meeting could get sticky and easily turn into a lengthy confrontation. He suddenly took a step forward, leaned over the desk, and extended his right hand to shake hands with the principal.

Caught off guard by this gesture, Pete Walls automatically extended his right hand and returned Bernie's firm handshake

"Mr. Walls, thank you for taking the time to talk with me," said Bernie as he firmly grasped the principal's hand, looking him straight in the eye. "Now, if you'll excuse me, I have a class to teach."

Flashing his most friendly smile, Bernie turned and walked out of the principal's office, leaving Pete Walls to wonder what had just happened, and what, if anything, he should do about it.

Bernie was not only given lunchroom duty, but he was also given restroom duty. And once the weather became cold, he was assigned outside supervision during the lunch period to keep track of those students who chose to step outside for a few minutes after finishing their lunches.

No matter, as Bernie had decided years ago in Bay City, Michigan, he had a right to support himself by teaching if he chose, and, by God, no one was going to run him out of his chosen profession.

One day, as he was teaching one of his eighth grade English classes, a student came to his door and told him to report to the office immediately.

Had he overlooked a "SEE ME" note? He didn't think so. He told his class to be extra good while he was gone, and hurried to the office.

"Mr. Barcio," said the school secretary, "you have a phone call. It's from the Pentagon in Washington, D.C."

Absolutely incredible!

The Pentagon had seen the national coverage of the catapult contest, and they were intrigued. As it happened, the Viet Cong were using catapults to knock down helicopters as they flew over the jungles of Viet Nam, and the

Pentagon thought it was time they learned how these machines worked. The Viet Cong, of course, were not concerned with authenticity. They were simply making giant sling shots out of surgical rubber cord and hurling logs up into the air to foul the propellers of the American helicopters as they flew over.

"Mr. Barcio, we want the army to learn all about the catapults your students are constructing. To this end we have instructed officers at Ft. Benjamin Harrison in Indianapolis to provide you with whatever personnel, equipment or machinery you may need as you do your work. We want the soldiers assigned to that base to work along side you and your students."

Bernie couldn't believe his ears. When he returned to his classroom and shared the news with his students, they were thrilled.

Mr. Walls, however, was totally frustrated. All his efforts to thwart Bernie and his projects had apparently been to no avail. When he shared his frustrations with administrators from other Washington Township schools, Bob Lattimer, as Bernie would learn years later, tried to offer him some good advice.

"Instead of fighting him, why don't you just call the news media and pose for pictures with him in front of your school?" suggested Bob.

April, 1973
Mauston, Wisconsin

"Knock, knock," said the Assistant Principal as he stood in Joe's office door. "Joe, I have a police officer in my office who has asked to question a student. What should we do?"

Now this was a question for which Joe had been carefully prepared by his course in School Law that he had taken at Marquette University in Milwaukee. Since the course had been taught by a professor who had once worked as school attorney for the Omaha, Nebraska, Board of Education, Joe respected the information that was being passed along. Joe was especially impressed since he himself had done graduate work in Omaha while attending Creighton University.

"If a policeman or juvenile officer shows up at school with a warrant for a student's arrest," advised the professor, "the best thing to do is to take the officer directly to the student's classroom, open the door, point the student out, and step back."

That was very clear cut advice that any future administrator enrolled in the course could easily remember.

"If, however," continued the professor, "a policeman or juvenile officer shows up at school and asks to question a student, there are certain legal procedures that must be followed."

This was going to be the professor's instruction that would serve Joe's purposes on this particular day.

"First, call the parents and tell them an officer is at your school to question their child. If the parents say it's okay, then the principal or the assistant principal must sit in while the student is being questioned," instructed the professor. "The school administrator is thus acting *in loco parentis*."

Joe had obviously been instructed by a professor who knew his school law.

"But there is an interesting twist to this law," continued the professor. "If the parents refuse to have their child questioned by the officer, it is the school administrator's legal responsibility to inform the officer that the student's parents have refused to give their permission and that the officer is to leave the school building."

Joe felt confident he could handle this situation easily while preserving everyone's rights.

"Okay," said Joe, "call the parents right away to keep them informed."

A few minutes later, the assistant principal returned to Joe's office.

"The parents said they do not want their child questioned unless they can be present. And they simply can not come over to the school at this time," said the assistant principal. "Now what do we do?"

Once, again Joe was well prepared.

"No problem," said Joe with confidence. "Just inform the officer that the student's parents have refused to give their permission so he may not question the student."

The assistant principal returned to his office and passed the message on to the officer who quietly left the building.

As principal, Joe liked to leave his office door open whenever possible to advertise his approachability and to keep an ear open to what was going on in the outer office.

About an hour later, as he sat quietly working at his desk, all hell suddenly broke out in the outer office.

"Mr. Barcio," shouted the local Juvenile Officer from behind the reception desk, "when I send an officer to this school to question a student, he will be questioned! And if that doesn't work, Mr. Barcio, then I will have a warrant issued for your arrest!"

Having vented, the Juvenile Officer stormed out of the building.

When Joe shared the incident with his superintendent, he was advised to check in with the school attorney in Mauston. This man, who handled school matters only as a sideline to his regular work, seemed to know as much about school law as the juvenile officer.

"What's the problem, Joe?" asked the attorney. "If the police want to question a student, there should be no problem."

Rather than arguing with someone who was obviously not up on school law, Joe, after discussing the whole encounter with his wife, Liz, that evening, decided to contact his School Law professor for reinforcement of his stance.

A week later, armed with a definitive letter from his professor, Joe met with the Superintendent of Mauston Area Schools and shared the legal bases for his earlier stance.

"Joe's stand was the correct one," explained the Superintendent to all Mauston school administrators when they met later in the week. "No permission from parents means the police do not question their child in school."

When Joe made copies of his professor's letter and sent them to all the members of the school board and other officials who had become involved in the incident, he was shocked by their responses.

Instead of admitting that Joe's stance had been the correct one, as the Superintendent had wisely done, every one of them—yes, every one: the school attorney, the Chief of Police, the Juvenile Officer and the County Judge—became enraged by the copy of the letter that they received.

Nevertheless, the Constitution of the United States and the laws of the State of Wisconsin made a small inroad into the Mauston Area School District because of Joe's courage, and new procedures protecting parent and student rights remain in effect to this day.

Another little incident that sheds light on how the legal authorities in small town America work involves a meeting Joe and his Superintendent had one day with the District Attorney in Mauston.

The District Attorney had been contacted by some folks who were questioning the legality of a private school that had been set up by the folks who had clustered around the Shrine at Necedah, Wisconsin.

"Joe," said the D.A. as he pointed to a variety of texts that he had on his desk before him, "these are some of the textbooks they are using in their school. Are they educationally sound?"

"I believe so," said Joe. "In fact, they are some of the very same ones that we have adopted for use at Mauston High School."

"Well, then," concluded the D.A., "since they appear to be using valid textbooks and they take attendance and display a U.S. flag in their classroom, I guess they meet minimum qualifications for a school in Wisconsin."

Ah, the wondrous simplicity of small town life.

May, 1973
Indianapolis

The catapult season was over, and Bernie found himself in the office of an assistant Superintendent of Washington Township Schools, Gerald DeWitt.

"Bernie, we want you to quit sponsoring the National Catapult Contest."

"Why is that, Mr. DeWitt?" asked Bernie.

"The township does not want the liabilities connected with activities that are scheduled to take place off its campuses."

"There is a tremendous national interest in this project," stated Bernie, unwilling to commit to such an agreement.

"No matter. If you want to continue working for Washington Township, you and your Latin Club can no longer sponsor the contest. Is that understood?"

Bernie left realizing that he would have to come up with some way to satisfy both the national interest in catapulting and the wishes of Mr. DeWitt.

"I've got it, Lillian," announced Bernie after he had given the matter some thought. "We need to form our own non-profit organization that can sponsor the catapult contest independently of Washington Township Schools. The organization can provide its own insurance and assume the liabilities. What do you think?"

"Sounds like a good idea," said Lillian. "Who do we know that could help start such an organization?"

"The father of one of my North Central catapult team members is a lawyer. His name is Kappes. I'll call him and see if he has any ideas."

"Skip" Kappes, as Bernie would come to know him, knew exactly how to go about setting up a non-profit organization. He told Bernie what had to be done, how to form a board of directors, draw up articles of incorporation, and spell out goals. Skip volunteered to complete all the legal work *pro bono*.

Bernie next made an appointment to meet with Allen Clowes, whom he had met while working at Park School. He knew that Mr. Clowes had experience with non-profit organizations, was well respected in the community and was very affluent. Mr. Clowes agreed to serve as the Vice-President of Bernie's non-profit organization which would be called Pompeiiana, Inc., and would serve as a "National Center for the Promotion of Latin at the Secondary School Level."

Mr. Carl Dortch, father of Park School's Spanish winner of the First National Catapult Contest, and Chairman of the Indianapolis Chamber of Commerce, also agreed to serve on the Board.

On Pompeiiana's Advisory Board would appear such notable names at Mrs. Pulliam, owner of the Indianapolis Star and News (whose son had studied Latin under Bernie at Park School) and Mrs. Howard Sams, owner of Sams Publishing Co. and the Park 100 complexes in Indianapolis, whose son had also studied Latin at Park School and who was a close friend of David Dortch.

In record time, Pompeiiana, Inc. was offered official recognition by both the IRS and the State of Indiana. Bernie was in business, and the catapult contest would continue.

True to his interest in students, however, Bernie immediately formed a committee of high school students who met at his house in the evenings over reconstituted frozen orange juice and popcorn to create a *Consilium Catapultarum* which would coordinate future national contests.

June, 1973
Indianapolis

A youth for Christ International publication called **Campus Life** had run a feature article entitled "A Mighty Heave in Indianapolis" in the spring of 1972. They had returned to the catapult field this year to cover the event one more time. The article in their spring 1973 issue was titled simply "...CATAPULTS."

"Can you believe the coverage the contest is getting, Lillian?" asked Bernie.

Lillian worked right alongside Bernie as they annually sent out news releases prior to each catapult contest in an effort to generate publicity that was so vital to keeping public interest in Latin alive. The coverage in **Campus**

Life, however, was spontaneous, unsolicited coverage. The kind that is most rewarding!

"And check out this article in **Outdoor Indiana**," said Bernie. "The photos are all black and white, but the title is in Latin and the article is great!"

The title of the article in the spring 1973 issue of **Outdoor Indiana** was entitled "CATAPULTA MAXIMA."

One would think that positive media coverage of their students' extra curricular activities would be prized by high school administrators.

Au contraire, mon ami! The coverage only seemed to generate suspicion and perhaps jealousy. Barcio was not working under their thumbs. He was not generating slush funds that could be tapped for the private purposes of the top school administrators. Just what was he doing?

Barcio was doing his best to promote public interest in the study of Latin at the high school level.

August 4, 1973
New Castle, Indiana

After one year at I.U., Sheryl dropped out of college to marry Jeff Donnella. Since Jeff's mom, who had died of cancer, had spent her final years living in New Castle near members of her family, and since one of Jeff's most beloved relatives was his "Grandma on the hill" in New Castle, the couple chose to get married in a Catholic Church in New Castle. Jeff was brought up as a Catholic and Sheryl had converted, as had her mom, her sister Karen and her Grandma Hacker, Lillian's mother. Sheryl's sister, Marsha, true to her stance on individualism, was not interested in becoming a Catholic. Besides, she had recently "been saved" when she attended a service at a Baptist church with a friend.

Following their wedding, Sheryl and Jeff moved into a second floor apartment in New Castle and Jeff got a job in a refrigerator manufacturing plant.

It's not a long drive to New Castle, and it was one that Bernie and Lillian had made several times already, often with Grandma Hacker who loved to eat at a Lobster Bar that served whole lobsters to guests who sat at very tiny tables. The owners had wasted little on fancy decorations, but it was one of the few places that one could get whole lobsters served at reasonable prices.

"This is a nice apartment," observed Lillian when she and Bernie visited Sheryl and Jeff in Newcastle.

"It's small, but it meets our needs," observed Sheryl.

"Can I get you guys anything to drink?" asked Jeff.

"Sure, I'll have a Dr. Pepper," said Bernie, knowing that that was Jeff's favorite drink, and that he was most likely to have some on hand.

Jeff went into the kitchen to fix the drinks for everyone and get the glasses out of the wall cabinet.

CRASH!

"What happened?" asked Bernie who went running in to see Jeff standing a little dumbfounded as the wall cabinet lay collapsed on top of the kitchen counter.

September, 1973
Broad Ripple, Indiana
"Mom, Phil is calling me names again!" cried Cindy.
"Well, she's such a dork," countered Phil. "Get a life!"
"O.K.! That's enough," said Lillian sternly.
She had had about all the bickering she could take for one day.
"I want you both to sit down at the dining room table and just get it all out of your systems," said Lillian.
"What do you mean?" asked Cindy, not exactly sure what she was getting herself into.
Maybe if she acted fast, she could just escape to her room and the whole thing would blow over.
"I mean I want both of you to sit there and look each other in the eye while you call each other every name you can possible think of. Just get 'em all out of your systems once and for all. Then maybe you'll be able to get along better, and we can have some peace and quiet around here," instructed Lillian.
Lillian had used this and other methods in the past in dealing with Marsha, Sheryl and Karen, with varying results. Sometimes she had the girls sit down with paper and pencil and spell out all their grievances before they would be released to go about their business. She had even sat Sheryl and Marsha down at this same table when the family lived on Ferguson and had them do the same name-calling exercise that Phil and Cindy had just been ordered to perform. The jury is still out on how effective either of these methods actually is.
"Goofus!"
"Dork!"
"Ninny!"
"Klutz!
"Skinny!"
"Ugly!"
"Idiot!"
"Dumbbell!"
Before long, however, when one sibling is sitting just a few feet away from another, looking him or her right in the eye, it gets harder and harder to keep a straight face. Soon both Phil and Cindy had broken up with laughter and could no longer continue.
"O.K.," said Lillian. "Is it all out of your systems now?"
"Ye-hes," laughed Cindy.
"I, heh-heh, think so," choked Phil, unable to keep a straight face.
So, for the moment, at least, the tactic seemed to have worked. The tension had been diffused and the next time either was tempted to bad mouth the other, a teasing smile would make the remarks a lot less caustic.

January 30, 1974
Newcastle, Indiana
"How soon can you get home from school?" asked Lillian.
"I think I can get away right after my last class," said Bernie. "What's up?"
"Sheryl had her baby this afternoon. Karen and I are driving to the hospital in Muncie, and you should try to get there as soon as you can."
When everyone was together at the hospital, Bernie, Lillian and Karen made their way to the Maternity Ward where they met Jeff.
"How's she doing?" asked Bernie.
"She's worn out, but I think she's fine," said Jeff.
"How's the baby?" asked Lillian. "Have you chosen a name yet?"
"She's tiny, but seems healthy. Sheryl wants to name her Ann," said Jeff.
After they were allowed in to see Sheryl, Lillian gave her daughter a little hug and congratulated her on her new daughter.
"How are you doing, Sheryl?" asked Bernie.
"Well, I'll tell you one thing," said Sheryl, "I'm never doing that again!"
But, of course, she did. On August 27, 1975, Sheryl gave birth to a bouncing baby boy she and Jeff named Erik.

March, 1974
Broad Ripple, Indiana
"*Magister*," asked Mary Hyde, one of the eighteen students on the *Consilium Catapultarum* during one of their monthly planning meetings, "did we ever hear from the **Guinness Book of World Records**? Are they going to include our catapult records?"
Bernie finished placing a large bowl of popcorn on the table along with a pitcher of freshly blended frozen orange juice before answering. "I just got a letter back from them the other day, Mary," replied Bernie, whose formal classroom name was *Magister* (teacher) Barcio.
"What did they say?" asked Karen Cecere, a close friend of Bernie's stepdaughter, Karen, who happened to be serving on the *Consilium* during the 1973-1974 school year.
"Well, first of all, people in England use the word "catapult" to refer to a sling shot. When they finally realized that we were talking about full-sized replicas of Roman *ballistae* and mediaeval trebuchets, they said they did not want to endorse the project by accepting our records."
"Why not?" asked Cindy Romer.
"Because they think the contest is potentially too dangerous. I guess they don't want people all over the world killing themselves trying to beat our distances."
As fate would have it, however, even though the **Guinness Book of World Records** would not carry the official distances of the National Catapult Contest, the media coverage generated would spawn an interest in catapulting that would continue to grow over the years, resulting, eventually, in enthusiasts in England building piano-hurling trebuchets, re-creationists in

California building frozen-turkey hurling *ballistae*, and eccentrics in Arizona building automobile-hurling Roman catapults.

One never does know how an idea will grow once it is thrown out to the masses!

October 10, 1974
Broad Ripple, Indiana

"O.K.," said Bernie whose birthday was being celebrated around the dining room table, "let's get down to some serious present opening!"

"Here," said Karen, "open this one first."

"Sure," said Bernie, eager to see what surprise Karen had in store for him.

Karen looked over at her mom who smiled at her. They had worked together on having the gift custom made.

"Oh, wow!" exclaimed Bernie as he carefully unwrapped Karen's gift from its tissue paper.

He couldn't believe his eyes. It was a custom carved pipe, the bowl of which had been shaped to resemble the Mars I catapult.

"Where did you ever find something like this?" asked Bernie.

"I had to have it specially carved," beamed Karen.

Bernie had first taken up smoking a pipe to fit in with the prep school teacher image at Park School. At every faculty social event, pipe smokers would show off how dexterous they were in lighting a match with one hand while it was still attached to the matchbook, how cleverly they could ream out the bowl of their pipes before refilling them with redolent tobaccos (the aromas of which were oohed and aahed over by other faculty), how handily they could wrap the warm bowls of the lit pipes in the palm of one hand while shaking hands or gesturing with the other, how amazingly, yet casually, they could curl the smoke both from the bowls of their pipes and from their mouths.

It was a habit Bernie would keep up for many years, even after his friend Bill Robinson had finally given it up when he nearly burned his house down by leaving his lit pipe in his jacket pocket when he hung it up in the living room closet.

Even though Bernie would also eventually give up smoking his pipes, he would always keep and treasure this one, perhaps the only genuine catapult pipe in the world.

May, 1975
Indianapolis

"Hey, Lillian," called Bernie as he walked into the house holding a magazine. "Check out this neat coverage of the catapults."

"Did you know they were going to run it?" asked Lillian.

"I had done a phone interview with someone from the magazine but had no idea they would do such a great job with the story."

Because it was a magazine about teenagers for teenagers, **Seventeen** had run an article in its May, 1975, issue on the rising fad of catapulting that seemed to be taking the country by siege. The color photos included with the article were totally awesome!

May, 1976
St. Meinrad's Seminary, St. Meinrad, Indiana

"I've got some bad news, everyone," said Clem Morman, the pilot of the small one-engine plane. "We're almost out of fuel, and we're going to have to put down real soon. Somewhere."

Bernie had hired Clem, who taught with him at Eastwood Jr. H.S., so that he could fly down to St. Meinrad Seminary and give a talk, wearing his Roman soldier costume, to those attending the spring meeting of the Indiana Classical Conference. Accompanying him was Claudia Somes, a senior Latin student and catapult builder from North Central High School, also in costume. After his talk there, the pair needed to be flown back up to Fort Wayne, Indiana, to judge the regional catapult contest that was being sponsored by Wayne High School Latin teacher, Nancy Mack.

"Can't we just land on a road down there?" asked Bernie.

"That's against Federal Aviation rules," said the pilot. "I would lose my license."

They would have actually had plenty of fuel if they hadn't gotten lost. Lewis Lyons, a counselor from Eastwood Jr. High School, had also come along to serve as navigator, but all he ended up doing was getting them lost somewhere over Kentucky. This they finally discovered by dropping down and buzzing a water tower with a town's name emblazoned on its side.

"There's an open field," said Clem. "I'm going to try and put it down there. Every one watch for power lines and fences!"

"If our wheels hit a wire," chimed in Lewis, "the plane will flip over, and we won't have a chance."

As they began their descent, Bernie felt Claudia's finger nails biting deep into his bare arm. She was hanging on for dear life.

"There's a farmer plowing in the next field, let's try and get his attention," said Bernie after the plane had coasted to a bumpy stop.

Bernie, Claudia and the counselor got out of the plane and began waving and calling to the farmer. He seemed to notice them a couple of times but just as quickly turned away and focused on his work.

"Oh, man, do I feel stupid," said the pilot.

"What's wrong?" asked Bernie.

"This thing has an auxiliary fuel tank and it's full. All I would have had to do is flip a switch."

"Great," said Bernie, "so let's get back in and head for the airport. We're still O.K. on time."

"I don't think so," said Clem.

"Why not?" asked Bernie.

"The field is too bumpy to risk trying to take off with all of us on board. I think I can get it in the air, but I'll have to go alone."

"So what do we do?" asked Bernie.

"I guess you'll have to try and bum a ride from that farmer if you can get his attention."

So Bernie and Claudia, each dressed in their Roman military costumes, began walking toward the fence along with the counselor. Before long, the tractor made its way around the field, and the farmer was back.

"Didn't you see us waving at you?" asked Bernie.

"Yup, I did," said the Farmer. "But I couldn't believe my eyes, so I just went about my business. I figured that when I looked again nothing would be there. You know, like one of those hallucinations."

In the end, they all climbed on board the farmer's tractor and rode over to his farmhouse where he got his truck and drove them to St. Meinrad's. Clem Mormon had called the seminary from the airport and told them to announce that the I.C.C. speaker was going to be a little late, but that he would be there.

The flight to Fort Wayne was a smooth one. Lillian was awaiting Bernie and Claudia at the airport and they quickly drove to Wayne High School for the remainder of the day's activities.

It was the last time Bernie was ever interested in flying in a small one-engine plane.

Claudia Somes grew up to become a pediatrician and currently practices in Carmel, Indiana. It is not known whether or not she avoids riding in small planes.

May 18, 1976
New York, New York

The **New York Times** (p.31) ran a syndicated article on the National Catapult Contest which was picked up by major newspapers across the country.

June 7, 1976
Indianapolis

"How about this, Lillian," boasted Bernie. "I've finally made it into **Sports Illustrated!**"

After publishing a brief article on catapulting in their April 6, 1970, issue, **Sports Illustrated** (pp. 64 & 66) had sent writer Bruce Newman to Indianapolis to cover the 1976 National Catapult Contest thoroughly in an article entitled, "First Among Those Who Cast Stones."

August, 1976
Indianapolis

Bernie and Lillian could usually tell when Karen returned from a date with her current boyfriend, Steve Whittaker. As they would stand talking on the front porch, Karen would lean back against the door jam on which the doorbell was mounted. After a few times Bernie knew enough not to open the door and embarrass them. Tonight, however, there had been no telltale doorbell ring. Karen had simply come right into the house, slammed the front door shut and gone directly to her room.

Suddenly all Hell broke lose outside in the driveway.

"Either you get a squad car over here immediately, or I'm gonna go out there and handle it myself," said Bernie sternly into the phone. He was so angry his hands were shaking.

In their usual cold, aloof manner, the 911 operator just went right on with her questions.

"What seems to be the problem, Sir?"

"Our daughter's boyfriend has completely freaked out and he's lying down yelling and screaming in our driveway," said Bernie trying his best to keep as calm as he could. "I want him out of there. Now!"

"Did he hurt your daughter, Sir," asked the operator.

"No," replied Bernie. "She's in the house. I think she broke up with him, and he just flipped out!"

THUMP-A-THUMP-A-THUMP-A-THUMP.

"I'm gonna hang up now," said Bernie. "I think there's a police helicopter over our driveway."

Sure enough, when Bernie got outside, the spotlight from the helicopter was shining directly on Steve who remained curled up on the pavement, crying and gasping.

Almost simultaneously, a police car arrived, and two officers got out and began to talk to Steve. After a while they had him calmed down enough that he was ready to quit crying and get to his feet. One of the officers then came over to talk to Bernie.

"We can take him with us if you like, Sir, but if we do, we'll have to put him under arrest," said the officer.

"What else can be done?" asked Bernie.

"Well, Sir, I would suggest that you volunteer to drive the boy home yourself," said the officer.

"And that would keep him from having to be arrested?"

"His parents would probably really appreciate that if you're willing to do it, Sir."

So Bernie agreed to drive Steve home. Karen remained in the house with her mom throughout the whole ordeal, and it was decided that Steve's Chevy Blazer would just be left parked at the curb until his folks could come and get it the next day."

"I really love her, Mr. Barcio," sobbed Steve as he was being driven home.

"Well, she's a terrific girl, Steve, but I just don't think she wants to be with you right now," observed Bernie.

"I'll do anything, anything, for her," proclaimed Steve.

"Well, Steve, I would advise just giving her some time. She's definitely worth waiting for. If you win her over, you'll have quite a woman," said Bernie.

"O.K.," said Steve.

The two rode in silence the rest of the way to Steve's house.

"Thanks for not having me arrested, Mr. Barcio," said Steve as he got out of the car.

September, 1976
West Lafayette, Indiana

"You know, Sheryl," Jeff had observed one day as he looked around their small apartment in New Castle a year earlier, "we were both two of the most intelligent people in our senior class at Broad Ripple. I think we can do better than this!"

So Jeff and Sheryl had both quit their jobs in Newcastle and moved to Indianapolis while Jeff applied for admission to Purdue University. In the meantime, Sheryl worked in the evenings in the main office of Bank One, downtown Indianapolis, and Jeff worked as a courier for an office in the City County Building.

When they were ready, they moved their growing family into married student housing in West Lafayette, where Jeff worked on a degree in chemical engineering.

Not to be outdone, as soon as they were able and could arrange the proper student loans, Sheryl enrolled and began working on her own undergraduate degree in Social Services.

After they both graduated, they moved back to Indianapolis where Jeff got a job as a chemist with Eli Lilly, and Sheryl enrolled in the I.U. School of Law where she would quickly make Law Review.

They definitely were able to do a lot better and were proving it to themselves and their families.

November, 1976
Mauston, Wisconsin

"Joe," began the school psychologist who had been instructed to obtain parental permission to test students suspected of having learning disabilities by their high school teachers, "I have identified sixteen of your high school students that, according to the new State of Wisconsin guidelines, should be with a teacher specially licensed to work with Learning Disabled students."

Joe discussed the psychologist's findings with the Superintendent, and they agreed that the School Board would have to comply with the new state guidelines and hire a special teacher for the Learning Disabled in addition to the teacher already on staff who worked specifically with the more seriously mentally retarded students. That teacher not only taught her charges reading and math but also trained them in personal hygiene.

"Can you have the Request to Hire ready for the next board meeting?" asked the Superintendent.

At the next board meeting, Joe began by reviewing the new state requirements for dealing with the learning disabled. He then described the special needs of Learning Disabled students as contrasted with the more seriously mentally retarded and explained why a specially trained teacher would have to be hired.

The matter really was fairly cut and dried, and the decision should have been a no-brainer. But Joe had been working with Wisconsin rural school board members for some years by now, and really wasn't all that surprised at their reaction.

"Hell, no!" said the board President after the group had discussed the proposal. "We already have a special education teacher on the payroll, and we're not about to hire another one. Let's move on to the next agenda item."

When the meeting finally adjourned at 11:30 p.m., and the members of the school board had all left, Joe remained seated at the table along with his Assistant Principal, the Superintendent, the Assistant Superintendent and three other Mauston area principals.

After another hour of discussion trying to figure out how they could keep the School Board from being in violation of the new state law, the superintendent got up suddenly from his chair.

"Stay here!" he instructed and turned to leave the room.

When the Superintendent returned, he tossed the high school transcript of the board President—who had been a student at Mauston High School some 25 years earlier—onto the table.

"Gentlemen, in view of the unusually low grades our board President earned in high school, I would like to suggest that we are dealing with a man who is both ignorant and incompetent."

None of those at the table argued the point.

The Superintendent's new plan of attack was to invite a supervisor from the State Department of Public Instruction (DPI) to drive the 70 miles from Madison and attend the next school board meeting scheduled, as always, to begin at 8:00 p.m.—a time agreed upon to allow those board members who farmed to finish their evening chores first.

To accommodate the DPI supervisor, the Superintendent assured him that he would be given the first spot on the agenda.

"Gentlemen," announced the School Board President when the meeting was called to order, "I suggest that there are several other items on the agenda that we need to handle first before we turn the floor over to our visitor from the DPI."

It would be a good hour and a half before the board finally agreed to listen to their guest.

"All right," announced the President haughtily. "Now what's this business with the State Department?"

The DPI supervisor, no doubt well acquainted with resentful rural politics, had sat patiently throughout the evening. He would now have his moment.

The supervisor calmly rose to his feet, gave his name and DPI title, and proceeded to review the current Wisconsin State School Law on teaching Learning Disabled students. When he was done, he was ready to drive some final nails into Mauston Area School Board's coffin.

"Gentlemen, the Mauston Area School District currently receives about 39% of is annual budget from state department funds. These funds will be immediately withheld if you do not agree to hire a special teacher to meet the needs of your Learning Disabled students," said the DPI supervisor before sitting down to await the board's decision.

"Well, uh, Mr. President," one of the board members finally said, "I, uh, would move (*he cleared his throat*) that the board, um, direct Mr. Barcio to, uh, hire a teacher for the, uh, Learning Disabled."

Silence.

"Uh, yes," said another board member finally. "I second that motion."

Silence.

"Is there any discussion?" asked the President in a somewhat more subdued tone than his original haughty introduction.

Silence.

"All in favor say 'Aye.'"

And the president's request was followed by a humble chorus of nine "Aye's."

"Opposed?"

Silence.

"Motion carried."

His job done, his point well taken, the DPI representative quietly stood up and calmly left the room to drive 70 miles back to Madison.

Joe posted the job opening the very next morning with both public and private state universities, and, before too long, was able to interview a mature and experienced 4th grade teacher who had taken her master's degree in the field of Learning Disabilities.

When the candidate's credentials were presented to the School Board at their next meeting, no one questioned them, and she was hired on Joe's recommendation.

So, Mauston Area High School now had an excellent teacher for its students with learning disabilities, and Mauston Area Schools got to retain their state funding.

Another job well done!

April 21, 1977
Indianapolis

Eleven years after Latin teacher Bernie Barcio had first challenged his students to help build an authentic Roman catapult capable of hurling a 100 lb. Rock 100 yards (a distance required in order to set the ancient machines up outside of enemy bow and arrow range), the dream was finally realized.

"One, two, three, fire!"

A crewmember on Mary Hood's Zephyrus catapult team pulled a rope that safely stretched some 100 feet away from the giant six-story-high machine. A release hook opened, and the one-ton counterweight began to accelerate toward the ground. The 100 lb projectile was cradled snugly at the end of a 30-foot long sling.

As the sling flew through its awesome arc, an eerie "swoosh" was heard—perhaps the "awful sound" of a catapult that had once been described by the Roman engineer, Vitruvius.

The large stone released at the carefully planned 45-degree angle and climbed steadily in an awe-inspiring parabola.

Silence.

Then, way down field, dirt flew straight upwards and a slight vibration could be felt beneath the spectators' feet.

The 100 lb. missile had been hurled 565 feet 6 inches down field. A modern day catapulting record had been set that stands to this day, and Bernie's long-held dream had just been fulfilled.

Bernie looked around the field. The spectators stood awe struck. It was almost a religious experience, and no one wanted to be the first to break the mood; however, no TV news crews, local or national, were present to document the achievement.

NBC had responded to news releases by saying that they felt they had really given their audience about all the catapult coverage in which they might be interested.

All the local TV stations had originally committed to covering the event. Unfortunately, the moment was overshadowed by a very unusual local news story that had developed just blocks away from the catapult field.

As it turned out, Marjorie Jackson, a millionaire Safeway Grocery Store heiress, had recently withdrawn all of her cash from several bank accounts and had squirreled it away in her home, including in several large indoor trashcans. This she had been instructed to do by the voices in her head.

Since Marjorie set a place nightly for Jesus at her dinner table, she felt perfectly safe.

A few weeks earlier, however, thieves had broken into her home during a routine "hit" on the neighborhood. They hadn't expected such a trashcan treasure, and had left taking only a small portion of the fortune.

The woman did not report the crime to the police since she did not want to alert anyone to her monetary and religious peculiarities.

The thieves had paid a return visit to the woman's house the night before, murdering her and taking the rest of the trashcan bonanza with them.

The story broke just as Bernie's catapult dream was about to be fulfilled, and all local news teams had been reassigned.

The thieves were later caught after they went on a spending spree in downtown Indianapolis bars. Ironically, in their hurry to escape the house, they had missed millions more also hidden there.

Another such serendipitous event was destined to deprive Bernie of a different "moment in the sun" in 1986.

As Bernie would walk down the hall to a TV studio about to be interviewed for having been selected as Indiana Teacher of the Year on January 28, 1986, he would glance at a bank of T.V. monitors to see the explosion of the Space Shuttle Challenger being broadcast live on all networks. His interview was, of course, put on hold.

June, 1977
Broad Ripple, Indiana

It was a pleasant day as Lillian sat behind the wheel of the family's big white Oldsmobile [*parked in front of 6544 Ferguson in the photo included above*] waiting to turn off of Kessler Boulevard onto Indianola Ave. With her were Cindy and Phil and a bag full of treats that they had purchased at the Hostess Bakery Day Old shop on the west side of Indianapolis.

CRASH!

Everyone in the car was jolted forward and the bag of treats fell to the floor as another car smashed into the back of the Oldsmobile.

After checking to see that the children weren't hurt, Lillian got out of her car and hurried back to talk to the driver of the other car.

"Didn't you see me stopped here with my turn signal on?" asked Lillian.

"Honey, I didn't see anything," replied a little old lady driver as blood flowed from her lip where it had banged into her steering wheel."

Not wanting to jeopardize the safety of her children, Lillian quickly exchanged insurance information with the little old lady and, as soon as traffic allowed, turned the corner and drove up the street to her own driveway at 6026 Indianola.

"Bernie, the back end of our car is smashed in," announced Lillian as she hurried into the house and into the bathroom.

After Bernie made sure no one was hurt, he helped bring the Hostess treats into the house and went out to survey the damage.

"Did the police come and file a report?" asked Bernie after Lillian came out to join him.

"No," said Lillian, "I didn't want to wait in the middle of the street for the police, so we just exchanged information, and I came on home."

"Well," protested Bernie, "we're going to have to have a police report for our insurance. Let me go in and call and have someone come to our house to write up the accident."

"Won't I get in trouble for leaving the scene of an accident?" asked Lillian.

"I don't think so. You exchanged information. I'll just explain that you didn't want to endanger the children by leaving the car in the middle of the street until the police came. It'll be alright," assured Bernie.

And it was. The officer who arrived understood completely and took down Lillian's statement about what had happened and provided an accident report that could be used to file with the insurance company.

Luckily, the Oldsmobile was a heavy enough car that only the bumper was damaged.

July, 1977
Broad Ripple, Indiana

"Where's Phillip?" asked Bernie.

"He's outside playing with David," answered Cindy.

In one way, having a large, two-lot wide yard that served as the neighborhood summer playground did have its drawbacks. Since Lillian now worked as a typesetter at the Northside Topics, Bernie needed to serve as the playground supervisor for all neighborhood kids as well as Phillip and Cindy's school playmates. Or, at least, Phillip's. Cindy didn't have many friends who came over to play. She generally just ended up playing with Phillip's friends or neighborhood kids who showed up, such as David and his little sister, Tiffany, who lived across the alley.

BAM! BAM! BAM!

"What's going on?" asked Bernie who rushed outside to check on the noise.

"David wants to see how hard he can ram my Big Wheel into the garage door," said Phillip.

"David, quit that," ordered Bernie. "You'll break Phillip's Big Wheel. Why don't you guys go play in the sand area?"

Bernie had had a ton of sand delivered and dumped onto the southwest corner of their property. He then brought home as many scrap catapult timbers as he could from the catapult field and built a rather elaborate raised platform with ladders, a slide and a balance beam. Not only did all the kids enjoy playing on this new equipment, but even Phillip's dog, Olive—half schnauzer, half dachshund—could be set on one end of the balance beam. Olive would then run the length of the beam, jump up onto the raised platform and scoot head first down the slide.

As ordered, David stopped crashing into the garage door. But it would be just a few more days before he would devise some other test that would finally do the Big Wheel in.

David was just a rough neck. And Cindy had a little girl crush on him.

August, 1977
St. Augustine, Florida

"Be careful of the undertow on this beach. It's pretty strong here," cautioned a swimmer as he passed Lillian and Bernie on his way out of the surf.

Bernie had been invited to give a twenty-minute persona presentation as Fabius the Tribune at a General Assembly during the National Junior Classical League Convention that was held in Florida that year.

"Did you notice that the whole place gave you a standing ovation?" asked Lillian when Bernie had rejoined his family after having changed out of his costume.

"I didn't really notice that, but they sure were enthusiastic in their applause."

"How can you do that?" asked Lillian.

"Do what?" asked Bernie.

"One minute you're standing there being cheered by a couple thousand people in an auditorium, and the next you walk calmly out to your car as though nothing happened."

"All in a day's work, Ma'am!" quipped Bernie who, however, had thoroughly enjoyed his reception by the students.

But now that was over, and it was time to focus on the vacation time they had planned into their Florida trip. Bernie and Lillian had taken Phillip and Cindy to visit some of the historical sites in St. Augustine during the morning, with a promise that they would spend this time on the beach in the afternoon.

While Phil and Cindy played in the sand, Bernie and Lillian decided to borrow the two small floats they had rented for the children and test the water. They had both heard the caution about the undertow, but figured that it must be something that threatened those swimmers who ventured out fairly far from shore.

Bernie began swimming around with Cindy's float while Lillian was just resting on Phil's float and letting her feet dangle in the warm water off shore.

After a while, Bernie decided to go check on the children for a minute, and when he returned to the water, he looked around for Lillian. She wasn't where he had last seen her. He looked way out and, sure enough, he could just barely spot her head calmly bobbing above the waves. She was slowly being carried out to sea by the undertow.

"Come on!" called Bernie to another young man who was swimming nearby. "I think my wife is caught in the undertow. Let's go out and get her."

Bernie dropped Cindy's float in the water and the two of them swam as fast as they could out to the small bobbing head. When they got within voice range, Bernie called out.

"Lillian! You're caught in the undertow. Raise your legs up and start swimming back to shore as fast as you can. We're coming out to get you."

Once Lillian understood what she was supposed to do to escape from the undertow, she raised her feet behind her and began kicking her way back to shore. Bernie and his helper reached her about the same time. Since the other man was a stronger swimmer, he told Lillian to let go of her float and hang onto his shoulders while he swam back to shore with her. Bernie grabbed the abandoned float and followed behind to make sure they both made it O.K.

"My floatie! My floatie!" shouted Cindy as Lillian and her helper made it back to shore.

Sure enough, the float that Bernie had dropped in his hurry to swim out to Lillian was by now bobbing about in the waves far from shore. Of course, nothing would do except for Bernie to swim back out and retrieve it.

"Didn't you know what was happening?" asked Bernie once he and Lillian were safely back on the beach and they had thanked the other swimmer for his help.

"I was just resting on Phil's float and really didn't know I was being pulled that far out until it was too late. Then I really didn't know what to do until you came out to get me."

"Well, now you owe me your life," chided Bernie.

"Well, that was your chance to be free," kidded Lillian. "Now you're stuck with me."

When they got back to Indianapolis they shared the story with Grandma Hacker.

"Well, you damn well better have saved my baby," said Grandma Hacker in her inimitable pseudo-harsh manner. "If you hadn't, you would have had me to deal with when you got home!"

February, 1978
Mauston, Wisconsin

At the beginning of the school year, Joe had gotten ambitious and asked the Mauston High School guidance counselor to identify a dozen or so students who wanted to study British Literature. Joe had enjoyed teaching such a class before going into administration, and he thought he would enjoy teaching it again, this time as a sideline to his administrative duties.

Sometimes, however, his role as Principal conflicted with his teaching role.

"Mr. Barcio," said one of the students in the class who had come to the principal's office one day, "you're supposed to be in class with us."

Sometimes when this happened, Joe could drop what he was doing and return to the classroom with the student, but at other times, he had to excuse himself.

"Oh my gosh," Joe would have to say, "I can't be with you today. Just continue with the assignment until tomorrow."

One of the students in Joe's British Literature class had been the older son of the high school art teacher to whom the fictitious name of "John" is hereby assigned. He was a fine young man of whom his father was proud to have attending school where he himself was teaching.

In view of Joe's friendship both with John and his son, it is understandable that he was quite concerned late one Sunday afternoon when he received a disturbing phone call.

"Joe," began John, "I didn't know who to call, so I guess you're it."

"What's up, John?"

"Joe, I've got a real problem. I guess I'm sort of in distress here."

"Is there something you would like for me to do?"

"No, not really," said John. "Joe, I've been sitting here at home just sort of looking at my rifle."

Joe quickly realized what must be going through John's head. The man was obviously considering suicide.

"John, what do you say I drive over and we just talk a while?"

"No, I don't want you coming over to my house."

"Okay, I understand," said Joe. "Is there someone else I can call for you?"

"I wouldn't mind if you asked the speech teacher to stop over for a while," said John.

"Great, I'll call her right now. You just sit tight, okay? Don't do anything foolish. I'm sure she'll be there in a few minutes."

As soon as Joe hung up, he called the Mauston police department and asked them if they would accept a gun and hang onto it, no questions asked. They said they would.

Then Joe called the speech teacher.

"Thank God you're home," said Joe when the teacher answered her phone.

He explained the whole situation, and she readily agreed to drive right over to John's house.

"Just make every effort to get him calmed down, and, most importantly, take his gun away if you can."

After that, all Joe could do was sit at home and wait—anxiously.

"Joe," said the speech teacher when she called about two hours later, "I was able to convince John to let me drive him to the hospital, and I dropped his gun off at the police station—no questions asked."

John eventually wound up in a hospital in Madison for about six weeks. Basically, he had suffered what lay persons call a "nervous breakdown." Since he had accumulated a healthy supply of unused sick days, John was able to recover with no loss of pay while a substitute was hired to teach his art classes for him.

It was a great day when John returned to Mauston High School. He and Joe had some fine discussions, and Joe was convinced that John's life had taken a turn for the better. He was a skilled teacher and a definite asset to Mauston High School.

At the end of the school year, Joe was proud to present John's son with his diploma.

Shortly afterwards, John's son joined the Army.

March, 1978
Indianapolis

After eight years at Eastwood Jr. High School, Bernie had pulled it off. He had introduced Latin. He had continued to coordinate the National Catapult Contest under the aegis of Pompeiiana, Inc. And he had used his achievements to apply successfully to teach the most outstanding junior high Latin program in the Indianapolis area at Fulton Jr. H.S.

Over the years Bernie had come to expect almost anything in his teaching, and he had pretty much steeled himself to rise to any number of occasions.

He had even been kicked in the ass by one of his less talented students as he walked back to his car after supervising a late-night event at Eastwood. Unfortunately for his assailant, the parking lot was dark and deserted.

"You little shit," said Bernie as he turned and grabbed the chubby little boy by his two arms.

The boy, shocked to see a teacher fight back, stared at Bernie with wide-open eyes.

"We're not in school out here," said Bernie, "and it's just you and me. You attacked me, and I have a right to defend myself!"

Bernie spun the boy around and threw him on the hood of his car.

"You just made a big mistake, and you're lucky I'm not going to beat the shit out of you."

The boy quickly realized just how lucky he was, and, without saying a word, meekly slipped off the hood and disappeared into the night.

Junior high teaching was a lot more physical in those days, and teachers frequently had to protect themselves and do whatever it took to maintain their control over their classes. As a teacher Bernie later met at Fulton Jr. H.S. would confide to him one day, teachers seldom had to do this more than once. Word would get out, and students would come to respect them.

"I had this one boy in class that simply got up and called me an asshole."

"What did you do?" asked Bernie.

"I took him out in the hall and let him have it good."

"What did he do?" asked Bernie.

"He said he was going to tell his dad, and that his dad would make sure I would be fired."

"What did you say?"

"Hey, I told him that I was looking for a job when I found this one, and that I really didn't care what his dad had to say about it."

"Did anything ever come of it?"

"No. But no one else has ever given me a problem in any of my classes," boasted the teacher.

Of course, no teacher ever intends to get physical with a student. It is, after all, a no-no that is drilled into every teacher's head in education courses, by school principals and by union representatives. But there are times when natural defense mechanisms simply take over.

"PUT HIM DOWN," screamed Bernie as he glanced back into his classroom from his assigned hall duty.

A renowned troublemaker had been deliberately put in his class at Eastwood after having been taken out of the classes of several other English teachers.

"HE JUST HAD AN OPERATION, PUT HIM DOWN!" repeated Bernie as he rushed back into the room.

The troublemaker refused to comply and began to shake the boy whom he held in a tight bear hug.

SMACK!

Bernie hit the side of the troublemaker's arm with the back of his hand, and the troublemaker set the boy down. And that seemed to settle the issue. Apparently no permanent harm had been done to the boy who had been the troublemaker's victim.

The next day, as Bernie was preparing to leave his room during his one assigned prep period, he looked up to see an office assistant point a very irate mother into his room and then quickly disappear.

As Bernie watched in disbelief, the mother walked past him and stopped in front of his desk. Then, without saying a word, using both her arms, she knocked everything from his desk onto the floor. She then put both her hands under the front of the large teacher's desk and hurled it over, causing all the drawers to scatter their contents.

"I'm sorry, Maam," said Bernie in disbelief. "Is there a problem?"

"The problem is that my son came home with a black and blue mark on his arm that was caused when you hit him."

"That's because he had a bear hug on a boy who had just had an operation, and he wouldn't release him when I ordered him to," countered Bernie.

"If you ever touch my son again," shouted he mother, "I haul your ass to court."

Bernie surveyed the mess after the mother had left and decided it was something his principal, Mr. Walls, needed to see.

Mr. Walls, who continued to be Bernie's antagonist at Eastwood, said that the mother had stopped into his office afterwards and shouted what she had done and why.

"Did you hit her son?" asked Mr. Walls.

Bernie explained that he had and why.

"Well," said Mr. Walls, "Get your room straightened up. I hope your realize that I don't think her son can be in your class anymore."

To Bernie's mind he should never have been put there in the first place.

Neither Bernie nor the school system ever pressed charges against the mother, and the mother did not seem to cause any future trouble to her son's other teachers or the school. She probably knew very well that she had a troubled boy and that she was lucky he was allowed to attend a public school anywhere.

July, 1978
Central Station, Indianapolis

"Stand back here by us, Phil and Cin.," said Bernie. "You don't want to get sucked onto the tracks when the engine comes by."

"Look how many cars long it is," said Lillian.

"Our car will probably be way toward the back," said Bernie who not only had ridden trains constantly during his younger years, but had also worked for the railroad during his summers at Holy Cross Seminary.

"Will we all get our own seats?" asked Cindy.

"We'll see," said Bernie, repeating a phrase that had once been used on him by his own father.

Bernie and Lillian had decided to share the experience of a cross-country train trip with their children while such a thing was still available. Both had their own train-riding memories. Now it was their children's turn.

Always on a limited budget, Bernie could not afford Pullman tickets for his family. They had to ride coach. Day and night.

At first, it wasn't bad. It was all so new for the children. They enjoyed the walks back to the restroom, the trips to the Dining Car and an occasional random tour through all the cars of the train.

After a few days aboard, however, Bernie and Lillian began to realize that not much had really changed from what they remembered negatively about train travel.

There was no escaping "Smelly!" This was a late middle-aged woman who sat directly behind them and was awash with very obnoxious perfume or toilet water or some other foul-smelling mixture.

"What's that?" asked Phil as he awoke with a start in the middle of the night. "I think I hear Darth Vader!"

Sure enough! The snores coming from across the isle could easily have been taken from the soundtrack of **Star Wars**.

"Bernie, wake up," said Lillian in the middle of another night. "Why are we stopped?"

Bernie got up and looked out the window. Blackness! He walked back to the end of the car to see if a window was open between the two cars. It was. The train appeared to have stopped in the middle of nowhere on a sidetrack.

"They're probably waiting for another train to go by on the main line," said Bernie when he got back.

Another night while everyone on board was sound asleep, the train suddenly shrieked to a grinding halt. The lights came on and conductors came hurrying through the car.

It turned out that an elderly lady had suddenly become completely disoriented and had pulled the emergency brake cord. She was turned over to local authorities at the next town.

Another elderly person, a man this time, would have to be put off the train on a subsequent night after he came through the car hitting all the windows shouting, "Air, we've got to have some air in here. I can't breathe!"

Of course, there was also the occasional drunk who simply peed in the corner of the car in the middle of the night if he couldn't make it all the way to the restroom on time.

And there were the all the kooks and oddballs that have always—and probably always will—ride public transportation.

"I never brush my teeth," announced a young man in his 30's as Bernie stood at a sink in the men's restroom taking care of his morning hygiene.

"Why not?"

"I had them all pulled out."

"Why did you do that?"

"I just got tired of all the cavities and the pain and the dentist bills. So I simply told my dentist to pull them all out and fix me up a pair of false teeth. It's the best thing I ever did for myself."

"O.K.," thought Bernie to himself, "that's another kook for the books!"

On the return trip from California, four passenger cars at the head of the train, between the Dining Car and the rest of the passenger cars, were filled with Boy Scouts either going to or returning from a Jamboree. These scouts had no concept of what seats were for. They and their stuff were spread out everywhere—under the seats, in the aisles and spilling out of the overhead racks. Making one's way to the Dining Car was like walking through a minefield of human bodies, luggage and trash.

"Well," said Bernie after they had finally returned to Indianapolis, "at least we'll have a lot of memories to talk about when we get old. You know, sometimes it's the negative things that prove to be the most memorable."

"You may be right," said Lillian.

Years later, after retiring from his teaching and administrative positions, Bernie mused about the possibility of riding the Canadian railroad across Canada. As of January, 2014, he still has not figured out the logistics of travelling to Toronto to ride the Canadian Railroad round trip, via Pullman, to Vancouver.

He did, however, ride roundtrip (via Pullman) on Amtrak's Empire Builder from Chicago to Portland, Oregon, during January of 2007. In May, 2010, he next travelled coach on Amtrak roundtrip to Charlottesville, Virginia, to rent a car and visit Shenandoah National Park. Finally, in June of 2010, he rode coach on Amtrak roundtrip to Salt Lake City, Utah, to rent a car and visit both Grand Teton and Yellowstone National Parks.

August, 1978
Oklahoma City, Oklahoma

"Come on, Lillian," encouraged Bernie, "there won't be anyone at the pool that we'll know."

Lillian was wearing a very small bikini that was skimpy on her when she was 20 pounds lighter. Now she was ashamed to be seen in public wearing it.

"It's the only suit I have," said Lillian. "Do you think it looks bad?"

"Hey, it looks fine to me," said Bernie who was anxious to get in a little swimming before the pool closed that evening.

They had put in a long day driving from Indianapolis, and they were both tired.

When they had returned home after their train trip to California, Karen had handed her parents one of the wedding invitations that she and her fiancé, Steve Whittaker, had been preparing in their absence. Lillian and Bernie were now on their way to southern Texas where Karen and Steve had decided to be married on a bluff overlooking the Rio Grande River.

No sooner had Bernie and Lillian settled into the water at the pool when someone called out to them.

"Hey, is that you Mr. and Mrs. Barcio?"

It was Steve Whittaker's parents. They had decided to stop at same motel and were also enjoying a late evening swim. Needless to say, Lillian pretty much stayed in the water until it was time to get out and return to their room.

When they all got to the pre-arranged rendezvous point in Texas and met with Karen and Steve to have breakfast together, Karen reported that there had been so much rain in Big Bend National Park the previous few days that the rangers weren't letting anyone enter. The wedding would have to take place in a small chapel in town.

While Bernie and Lillian and the Whittakers packed up and started their return trip to Indianapolis, Karen and Steve remained behind in Texas to wait for the high waters to recede and enjoy a camping honeymoon in the park.

September, 1978
Broad Ripple, Indianapolis

"We do have furniture," explained Bernie sheepishly to the reception guests who were seated on rented chairs that had been set up in the dining room and living room for Karen and Steve's Indianapolis wedding reception. "We just put it all in storage for the occasion."

There were more chairs and tables set up on the large lawn on the south side of the house on Indianola. Karen had always talked about having a lawn wedding in the yard when she was married, but she had decided to settle for a lawn reception instead.

November, 1978
Mauston, Wisconsin

"Mr. Barcio," said the school secretary who had come to Joe's office door, "there's an Army Chaplain who would like to see you."

When the Chaplain entered Joe's office he said that he had come to see "John," the art teacher whose son Joe had taught in his British Literature class the year before.

"John is teaching class at the moment," said Joe after checking the schedule. "Is this important?"

"Yes," said the Chaplain. "Extremely important!"

On his way to John's classroom, Joe stepped into the teachers' lounge and asked a free teacher to cover John's class for a minute while the two of them returned to Joe's office.

"John, this is an Army Chaplain who has asked to see you," said Joe after they were in the office and the door was closed.

"Sir," said the Chaplain, "your son is dead. His throat has been cut, and we don't know who did it!"

At this news, John simply collapsed into the chair that was behind him, and he broke down and cried and cried and cried.

Joe sat behind his desk, his mouth open. He could say nothing. He, too, was in shock.

The Chaplain sat down next to John and gave him time to adjust to the news. Finally, as chaplains do, he helped John calm down.

"Joe," said John as soon as he had composed himself a little, "my younger son is in my art class this period. Could you please have him come to your office?"

"I'll go down and get him myself," said Joe.

The walk back to the office was personally dreadful for Joe. Since he found it difficult to say anything to the boy, the two walked in silence.

When they reached the office, Joe and the boy walked in. As Joe closed the door behind them, John told his younger son the news about his older brother. And the crying started all over again.

(*As Joe shared this story years later, he couldn't help but start crying all over again!*)

After Joe made arrangements to have John's classes covered so he and his son could go home, he sat back down with the Army Chaplain.

"That was a rather harsh way to tell a parent about his son's death," said Joe.

"I have found," said the Chaplain who was, in fact, one of a small group of Chaplains who had volunteered to handle such assignments, "that the best thing to do is tell the facts—frankly and quickly—and then let the family take it all in."

A week later, Joe attended the funeral services for John's son and was pleased to note that the U.S. Army had two extremely courteous soldiers in attendance.

October 10, 1978
Broad Ripple, Indiana

It was Bernie's birthday and Karen and Steve had come over to join the family for the celebration.

"Bernie," called Lillian from the kitchen, "would you see what's wrong with Tiger? She's been kind of moping around today."

Tiger was Cindy's cat. She had gotten her after her first cat, Sappho, had gone to the Great Litter Box in the Sky.

"Where is she?" asked Bernie.

"You'll have to look around for her," said Lillian.

Bernie finally found Tiger behind a couch in the living room. From the way she was lying, with her mouth slightly open and one of her canine teeth pressed against the floor, Bernie knew that Tiger was no longer with them. He hated to ruin the occasion by telling Cindy that Tiger was dead, so he got a small box and gently set the cat in it.

As he walked through the kitchen, he whispered to Lillian.

"Tiger's dead, but we're just going to tell Cindy that she's not feeling well and that we're putting her in the breezeway until after dinner when we'll check to see how she's doing."

Bernie also confided the situation to Karen and Steve.

"Has anyone seen Tiger?" asked Cindy when she came down from her bedroom for dinner.

"Yes," said Steve, "I've looked at her. She's not feeling well, so I think we should just leave her rest."

Since Steve was in med school, he felt that his reassurances would lessen Cindy's concerns about her cat.

"Where is she?" asked Phil.

"She's resting in a box in the breezeway," said Bernie to Phil quietly.

The family went on with dinner. After the traditional off-key rendition of Happy Birthday, Bernie blew out his 40 candles and began to serve the cake. Unnoticed by anyone, Phil decided to slip out in back and check on his sister's cat.

Suddenly, he was back standing wide-eyed in the doorway between the kitchen and the dining room.

"Well, Cin, it looks like you've got a dead cat. I keep picking her up, and she keeps falling back down."

"Oh, she's fine," replied Cindy. "I've seen her do that lots of times."

Like so many of the family pets over the years, Tiger was laid to rest wrapped in a little towel and tucked into a shoebox. Her unmarked grave is somewhere on the property at 6026 Indianola.

Cindy's next cat was all black except for his four white paws. She named him Boots.

Cyndi would let Boots out every morning and call him back inside in the evening to spend the night in her bedroom. It wasn't until 2013 that Scott Patten, who lives across the street, shared a little secret about Cyndi's cat with the author. Having just lost his most recent pet, Scott walked over to show the author a photo of his deceased cat. He then showed the author a picture of cat his family loved years earlier.

"We called it Bootsy," said Scott.

Every morning "Boots" would simply cross the street to his house where his dad would let "Bootsy" in, feed him, and let him spend the day before putting him back outside in the evening.

February 8, 1979
Indianapolis

The death of Lillian's Grandma, Nelli Hacker, at age 97 was sad. In a lot of ways, Lillian's Grandma Hacker had been her mother-away-from-home. As an only child, Lillian had grown up with her Aunt Dood (Helen Kemp), Uncle John and their children, although she always felt a little like Cinderella. In a moment's notice she might be told to throw her stuff back into her shopping bag and go home with her mother or go to stay with someone else for a while.

Nelli Hacker was, no doubt, one of the most colorful of Lillian's relatives. Nelli was remarkable for a huge goiter that hung beneath her chin. It didn't seem to bother her during most of her life, so she simply ignored it. After a while, those who loved her also became oblivious to its presence.

Nelli's parents were Charles Henry Bunnell and Nancy Jane Ozmunt, the aunt of John Dillinger, Jr.'s stepmother, Lizzie Fields Dillinger. As fate would have it, after Nelli married Winfred Ellsworth Hacker, she and her husband lived on a farm right next to the one on which her cousin Lizzi lived with her stepson who was destined to become a notorious bank robber. At least one of Nelli's sons, Robert Hacker (the father of Lillian's cousin, Jack Hacker), misspent a good portion of his youth hanging around with John Dillinger, Jr., and with some of his other "bad crowd" friends. But that story has already been told earlier in this book.

It is interesting to point out that when the author visited the Dillinger family graves located in Crown Hill Cemetery in Indianapolis during August, 2004, it was obvious that the grave of John Dillinger, Jr., had become an object of cult activities.

Visitors chip off corners and edges of his gravestone as souvenirs and leave coins for good luck. Someone has even added an additional small carving bearing the following message: "Our hearts still ache with sadness, and secret tears still flow, what it meant to lose you, no one can ever know."

Visitors also chip mementoes from the headstones of Dillinger's father and mother, buried next to him. The headstone of John Dillinger's stepmother, Lizzi, however, remains intact, perhaps because no one realizes her connection with the notorious bankrobber.

By the time Nelli was 93 years old, her goiter had grown to the extent that it was beginning to press on her windpipe and interfere with her breathing. For the first time in her life, she was forced to enter a hospital. Prior to that, her health had been just fine despite the fact that she began each and every day with a generous helping of bacon or sausage with eggs.

In the hospital, Nelli seriously resisted any attempts of the nurses to give her injections that had been prescribed by her doctor.

"If I can't take it by mouth, I don't need it!" insisted Nelli.

When Nelli was offered sleeping pills following her goiter-removal operation, the 93-year-old once again refused on the grounds that she had heard they were habit forming.

In her advanced age, Nelli lived with her daughter Helen (Dood) and her son-in-law, John Kemp, at 2609 E. Hanna Ave. The house had been built by John and his brother. Nelli had her own living quarters in the house which were simply closed up after her death. Although Lillian's Aunt Dood later suffered from MS, she continued to live alone in her house following the death of her husband on March 15, 2002. As of 2004, all of her Grandma's belongings were still right where she left them.

The entire house was eventually cleaned out and sold in 2007 after Aunt Dood had passed away on March 13, having spent the last year of her life in a nearby nursing home.

May, 1979
Broad Ripple, Indiana

"Karen," asked Bernie, "What's all this stuff on the floor of the garage?"

"The engine on my VW wasn't working right, and Steve thinks he can fix it," explained Karen.

"But it's all in a million pieces," observed Bernie.

"Well, he said he needed to take it apart to figure out what was wrong. He'll put it all back together in a while," said Karen.

Karen didn't realize it at the time, but she had just lost her VW.

Either Steve couldn't figure out what the problem was, or he just never got around to giving the project the attention it deserved.

When Bernie couldn't stand the clutter any more, he put the all pieces in a big box and asked Karen to have Steve take them away.

That was the end of Karen's first car.

Another year would also see the end of Karen's first marriage.

Unfortunately, Steve turned out to be very disappointed with his ongoing schooling to be a doctor—something his grandfather had insisted on and had even offered to pay for. His dissatisfaction led to one thing and another, and within a little more than a year Karen came home to announce that she and Steve were getting a divorce.

"What does Steve want to do if he doesn't want to be a doctor," asked Bernie.

"You know, Bern, I really don't know. And I don't care," said Karen.

"Will he finish med school?" asked Karen's mom.

"He probably will. His grandfather is paying for it."

"Well," said Bernie, "He'll probably find something he enjoys doing."

"I think he wants to be a professional mountain climber," said Karen.

May, 1979
Mauston, Wisconsin

It had been a traumatic year for "John," the art teacher at Mauston High School, a year that had led him to a hard decision.

"Joe," John had confided after asking to meet with him in his office, "I've decided to resign my position here in Mauston and move to Florida with my youngest son. We've had some hard times lately, and I'm sure you understand."

Joe certainly did understand and wished John all the best. He then set to work posting the 1979-1980 school year opening for an art teacher with colleges and universities. He also consulted the teacher listings at the Capitol in Madison.

Although one of the applicants turned out to be a graduate of Mauston High School whom Joe had known to be a fine young man when he was a student there, the young man did not, in the end, come through as the most qualified among those who applied for the position.

"I've looked through all the applicants," announced Joe when he met with the Superintendent to share his final choice, "and I believe this young lady outshines all the others."

"What about the young man who is a graduate of Mauston High School?" asked the Superintendent.

"Well, he's a fine young man and seems to be a competent applicant, but the young lady was the best of the lot," said Joe.

"Did you know that his family is well known in Mauston and owns a retail store in town?" asked the Superintendent.

"Yes," said Joe. "But I think we do have to make our selection based on qualifications rather than on ties to the community, don't you?"

"I agree. Just thought I would ask."

So, as usual, Joe gathered all the references for the young lady and made copies for the board members. The normal procedure was for the administration to handle the interviews and present their recommendations to the board for final approval. Without meeting the applicants, the board normally accepted the administration's recommendations.

"Joe," said the Superintendent one morning before the board meeting, "the board President has asked us to have our young lady candidate attend the board meeting so the School Board itself could interview her before approving our recommendation."

Although this was very unusual, Joe contacted his chosen applicant and she was present when the School Board met.

When the board reached the agenda item that concerned hiring a replacement art teacher, they asked the young lady several questions about her qualifications. When they were finished, a member of the board made a motion.

"I would like to move that we instruct the Principal to hire the young man to fill the position who is a graduate of Mauston High School."

All those in favor said, "Aye," and the motion carried.

"Mr. President," said another board member, "I believe it would be appropriate if the administration had a check for $100 sent to this young lady to help pay for her time and expense in attending the meeting tonight."

Both Joe and the Superintendent were shocked!

The young lady, with head and chin held high, simply got up and walked out of the boardroom.

Contrary to the usual protocol, both Joe and the Superintendent also got up and left the boardroom to offer their apologies to their preferred candidate. They tried to explain that things like this are not supposed to happen.

"I'll have the check sent to you at your home address," said Joe as the young lady left the building to return to her car.

"You know," replied the young lady, "it doesn't matter to me whether you do or not."

This definitely was a courageous young lady who, unfortunately, had just had a harsh introduction to small town politics in Wisconsin.

Joe likes to think that her courage landed her a good job teaching art elsewhere.

April, 1980
Broad Ripple, Indiana

"Hey, Barcio, come here!" The raspy voice belonged to the notorious Rick, the holy terror of Christ the King school whose antics were routinely overlooked by the good nuns because a relative of his had been generous to Chatard High School.

Phil was collecting for his **Indianapolis News** route that he delivered after school.

"Yeah, Barcio, come here!" chimed in Pat, a Rick wannabe who basked in the protection enjoyed by his partner in crime.

"Whadda you want?" asked Phil, knowing full well that what they wanted was to start trouble.

Both Rick and Pat carried sticks in their right hands.

"You know what we want. Give us your money," said Rick.

"I don't have any money yet," replied Phil.

"Show us your pockets, then," said Pat.

Phil proved his point by turning his pockets inside out, revealing only a few scrap candy wrappers and a special red Eraser Mate pen. Rick gabbed the pen.

WHACK!

"You're a loser, Barcio," said Pat as he struck Phil from behind with his stick.

Rick and Pat turned and walked away, no doubt in search of other prey, while Phil gathered up his stuff and made his way home.

That night Phil explained to his dad that he didn't want to do his paper route any more.

"Why not?" said his dad. "You've only had the route for two weeks. I used to deliver papers after school when we lived in Norfolk, Nebraska. It's good for you."

"I'm not so sure it is," said Phil's mom.

"Why not?" asked his dad once more.

"Because some bullies tried to steal his collection money from him today and they hit him with a stick."

"What bullies?"

At first, Phil was reluctant to reveal the names of his attackers knowing that if they got in trouble, he would probably have to pay for it after school another day. Finally, however, he broke down and named Rick and Pat.

"It won't do any good to report Rick," said Phil's mom.

"Why not?" asked his dad a third time.

"Because his family is some kind of big wig family at Christ the King. I think they gave money to the high school. Others have tried to report him, and nothing comes of it. Neither the priest at the church nor the nuns at the school want to rock the money boat."

"Who's this Pat kid?" asked his dad.

"I don't think his parents know what he's doing with Rick," suggested Lillian.

"Well, they're by God going to find out," proclaimed Phil's dad.

After dinner that evening, Phil was made to accompany his dad as they went calling.

Their first stop was at Rick's house. After explaining what had happened to Rick's mother, she instructed her son to go get the red Eraser Mate pen that he had taken from Phil. He handed it over and, at the instruction of his mother, reluctantly shook hands with Phil.

At Pat's house, his parents asked their son to join them in the living room as all three listened to Phil tell what Rick and Pat had done. Pat displayed his much-practiced innocent pan-face that he used whenever he was charged with something he wanted to deny. His folks just looked blankly at both Phil and his Dad, neither denying the charges nor apologizing for their son.

"I just want you to know," said Phil's Dad, looking Pat straight in the eye, "that we are Italian, and we stick up for each other. If you attack our son, you are attacking our family. If it happens again, you will have me to deal with."

Pat and his parents just sat there, showing no emotion or reaction. They had obviously been in similar situations before and had learned that the best way to diffuse the anger of those who came to complain of their son was to stay calm and say absolutely nothing.

"Come on, Phil, let's go. I think they have the message," said Phil's Dad as he rose to leave.

Phil was allowed to resign from his paper route.

That summer, however, Phil would have a new bike stolen out from under him in the street behind Broad Ripple High School by a gang of blacks, one of whom had a gun tucked into his waistband, as Phil reported. But, after all, he did get to bring the junky bike home that the gang left behind after one of them rode off with his new one. The junky one was turned over to the police who were called to investigate the theft.

Phil also was involved in Little League Baseball at the Haverford Field that summer. As fate would have it, Pat was a pitcher on an opposing team. Whenever Phil would be at bat, Pat would fire at least one bean ball his way, just to let Phil know he still had his number.

Phil would get a season's relief from Pat's bean balls after breaking his finger while playing football with Joe Weisinger and Richie Orban. The cast for the one broken finger turned out to be humongous, extending most of the way up his arm. Phil would spend the rest of the season cheering his teammates on from the bench.

May, 1980
Indianapolis

Bernie had decided to become a little more active in the Indiana Classical Conference (I.C.C.). He had enjoyed attending their annual meetings over the years, and especially enjoyed renewing his acquaintance with Prof. John Helms at the meetings. He and John had attended graduate school together in Ann Arbor, Michigan, and they had spent many Saturday afternoons conversing in the library stacks at the University.

Bernie had been slated to run for Secretary-Treasurer of the I.C.C. and he had won. Only afterwards was he told that the position would be a life-long one.

"I don't think so," thought Bernie to himself. "Everyone needs to have an opportunity to serve."

Bernie did keep the position of Secretary-Treasurer for the next 12 years before he finally decided it was time to pass the torch to a new candidate.

June, 1980
Broad Ripple, Indiana

School was out, and the summer fun was beginning. Joe and Liz had driven to Indianapolis for a visit, and the kids were all out in the big yard having fun.

"Hey, Cindy," called David Perkins from the ally, "what are you guys doing?"

Normally, Cindy was pretty much ga-ga over David who, with his too-cute-by-half little sister, Tiffany, lived directly behind her at 6025 Haverford. Today, however, her cousins were visiting from Wisconsin, and she had no time for him.

"Cindy, I'm talkin' to you!" insisted David.

"Do you hear something?" Cindy asked her cousin Joey.

"Cin, come over to the fence, I want to ask you something," insisted David.

"Gee, I wonder why I don't hear anything?" asked Cindy in a loud voice intended to irritate David.

David, however, had had it, company or no company. He bent over and picked up a nice size stone and pitched it at Cindy as hard as he could, hitting Cyndi near her right temple.

"AHHHH!" screamed Cindy as she grabbed her head and ran into the house, followed closely by her cousin Liz.

"What happened?" demanded Cindy's Aunt Liz?

"Cindy got hit in the head with a rock by a boy in the alley!"

"What boy?" demanded Bernie who had hurried into the kitchen.

"David," sobbed Cindy.

That was it! Bernie had about had it with David Perkins. Not only did he break Phil's toys, but now he had hit Cindy in the head with a rock. Bernie flew out the back door, followed by Cindy and her cousins who wanted to see what was going to happen.

Bernie put the toe of his right foot into the wire of the ally fence, and quickly climbed over. In a flash, he was through the gate into David's yard and pounding on the side door of the Perkins residence. Whoever answered was going to get a full taste of Bernie's Italian temper.

It would be quite a while before either David or Tiffany would be welcome in the Barcio play area.

July 18, 1980
Malibu, California

Brenda Waddle, who taught at Castle H.S. in Newburgh, Indiana, was enjoying an all-expense paid visit to the J. Paul Getty Museum in Malibu, California.

Ever since Pompeiiana, Inc., had been officially founded on July 19, 1974, the author, serving as its Executive Director and President of the Board of Directors, needed to give constant attention to fund raising—the bane of any not-for-profit organization. Although Pompeiiana did receive occasional grants from both the Clowes Fund and the Lilly Foundation, it needed to come up with additional ways to supplement the income it received from membership dues and subscription fees teachers paid to purchase monthly issues of the Pompeiiana NEWSLETTER for use in their Latin classrooms.

One venture the author tried was to have Indianapolis area Latin students sell Pizza Coupon booklets.

Another way funds were raised was through the sponsorship of Chariathons, in which participants would either obtain pledges or pay entry fees to pull each other in home-made two-wheel chariots around a parking lot deck over the Canal in Broad Ripple, around the obelisk in the Indiana World War Memorial Plaza, around the racing oval at Raceway Park in nearby Clermont, around the city block containing the Study of General Lew Wallace, the author of Ben Hur, in Crawfordsville, and finally at the Indianapolis Motor Speedway—initially around the entire 2 ½ mile course, and then around the 1000 ft. long pit wall at the speedway.

The author came up with a "Bottles for Latin" fund raising contest during the 1979-1980 school year.

Latin teachers were encouraged to raise funds for Pompeiiana by having their students collect and redeem recyclable bottles. The teacher whose students raised the most money by the end of the school year would win an all-expense paid trip to visit the J. Paul Getty Museum in Malibu, California.

This museum is of special interest to Latin teachers because it is a re-creation of the ancient Roman Villa of the Papiri discovered, but never fully excavated, near Herculaneum in Italy.

The winner of the Bottles for Latin contest was Brenda Waddle.

July 21, 1980
Milwaukee, Wisconsin

On this date, Michael Bruno, the son of Raffaele Bruno and Godfather of Bernard Barcio passed away.

As Bernie looked into his family's histories and talked with his uncles and aunts, he was amazed to learn just how many different Bruno families had become intertwined with their stories.

Bernie's godfather was the son of Raffaele Bruno who had moved to Milwaukee from Sicily. He supported himself as a cigar maker and had even sent his two sons, Michael and Angelo, back to Italy to study when they were young. The father of Bernie's godfather had eventually moved to New York, leaving his sons to remain friends with the Barcio family in Milwaukee.

Because Michael Bruno had become close friends with Ted Barcio over the years, he had visited him in Nebraska while on vacation with his wife and sons. One of Mike Bruno's sons was named Ralph, no doubt named after his grandfather, Raphaele.

Then there was the Bruno family that Giuseppe Barcio had known when he lived in Cosenza, Italy. It was that Raffaele Bruno that worked with Giuseppe on the Chicago and North Western Railroad in the Milwaukee area.

Of course, there was also this Raffaele's cousin, Dominic Bruno, in South Chicago. Dominic's wife was a cousin of Filomena Nudi who had asked him to help her husband, Tony, find a safe refuge after he had shot his son-in-law, Frank Strano. He helped by taking Tony to Milwaukee and introducing him first to his cousin Raffaele who later introduced him to Giuseppe.

Although some of these Brunos were not related to each other, yet all were intertwined with the lives of the Barcios and the Nudis.

As Bernie would learn years later from his Uncle Gene who had worked as Postmaster for the U.S. Post Office, there was even another Raffaele Bruno who was a mail carrier in the Chicago area. This Bruno, however, was known only by name, as far as Bernie was told.

August, 1980
Leiber State Park, Indiana

"Come on, Dad," said Cindy, "you promised you would take Phil and me for a walk."

"In a little while," replied Bernie.

"Says it, does it!" said Cindy applying the phrase guaranteed to get results.

Heavens knows, it had been used on both her and her brother enough over the years to get them to keep their word.

Later that evening, after the campfire was ready, the usual makings for S'mores were assembled on the campground dining table. Cindy loved to make the treat, but she seldom chose to eat it.

"Who wants a S'more?" asked Cindy.

"Makes it, eats it," said Bernie.

Finally, it was time for campfire entertainment.

"Come on, Gary. Do your duck walk!"

Camping was always so much more fun when the Robinsons and the Linards joined Bernie and Lillian and their children. And this was one of those fun outings.

"O.K. Is everyone ready? Here goes," said Gary Linard who proceeded to squat down, raise his elbows from his sides and waddle around the campfire quacking.

The laughter generated was spontaneous and sincere.

"You just quack us up, Gary," said Gary's sister Sharon.

Gary's dad, George Linard, was still holding out in his tent. George taught physics at Park School and had been invited to have his family join the Barcios and the Robinsons at Leiber for the weekend. George, however, suffered from an emotional malady that would sometimes turn him into a recluse. He had confined himself to his tent until he could work through it.

As the night grew darker, and the circle tightened around the campfire it was time for stories. Of course, there were the usual Chicken Heart tales that Steve Robinson loved to tell. Both Bernie and Bill Robinson, however, prided themselves on being able to spin original stories on the spur of the moment to entertain the children. Many of these stories would incorporate the names of Cindy and Phillip and other little ones gathered around the campfire.

"Why don't we let Mr. Barcio go first," said Bill Robinson after everyone had been properly frightened by the dramatic conclusion of the latest rendition of the Chicken Heart story.

"Once upon a time," began Bernie, "there were two little children named Phillip and Cindy who went camping with their parents in the woods. After dinner one night, Phillip asked if he and his sister could take a little walk before bedtime. 'O.K.,' said Phillip's daddy, 'but don't leave the path. You don't want to be caught by the Yucca Lurkers.' "

Back in the Park School library there were large plastic Yucca plants in great pots that had been brought in for decoration. The middle school boys used to love to tease the library proctors by hiding behind the Yucca planters. One day, when the English teacher, Jim Foxlow, happened to be working in the library, he spotted some of the middle schoolers and called them "Yucca lurkers." This was where Bernie was getting the term.

" 'What are Yucca Lurkers?' asked little Phillip.

" 'Oh, nobody can see them,' said his mommy. 'but you can always know when they're around because you can hear their tiny footsteps.'

" 'O.K. said little Cindy,' eager to start her walk with her brother. 'We'll stay on the path.'

" 'And be sure and stay away from the Itchy Goomey Tree," cautioned their daddy.

"The children's daddy had pointed out the Itchy Goomey Tree to them earlier during the day when they had been scouting around. It was a big old tree that had a large hole in one side.

" 'We'll stay away from the Itchy Goomie Tree,' said Phillip as he and his sister set out."

Now Bernie was basing the name of terrible Itchy Goomey Tree on a line he had read in the poem "Hiawatha" by Longfellow. The line began, "On the shores of Gitche Gumee..."

"The little children walked and walked and were having so much fun that before they knew it, it was pitch black outside, and they were not exactly sure how to find their way back to the campsite.

" 'I think we should go this way,' said little Phillip.

"But as they began going down the path that Phillip had suggested, they began to hear feint pitter pat sounds behind them.

" 'What's that noise?' asked little Cindy, as she and her brother quickly turned around to see.

"They couldn't see anything behind them, so they turned around and continued walking. Pretty soon there it was again. Pitter pat. Pitter pat. Once again, as soon as they turned around, nothing could be seen.

" 'I've got an idea,' said little Phillip. 'Let's walk backwards, and then we'll be able to see what's making that pitter pat noise.'

"And so the two little children began to walk backwards through the woods. All of a sudden, they felt some prickly branches beginning to wrap around them.

" 'Something's got me,' said little Cindy.

" 'Me too," said little Phillip. 'Let's turn around and run!'

"But when the two little children turned around and ran, they ran right into a giant hollow of a big tree. The poor little children didn't know it, but the Yucca Lurkers had tricked them into walking backwards right into the branches and the mouth of the dreaded Itchy Goomie Tree!

"Later that night, their parents decided to get their flashlight and go looking for their children. After a long time, they finally reached the spot where the children's daddy had shown them the Itchy Goomie Tree. When he shined his flashlight into the big hole in the tree, there on the ground lay the bones of two little children."

After a sufficient pause to allow the horror of the situation to sink in to the campers, Bernie attached a moral to his story.

"And that's why little children should always listen to their parents."

"And never walk backwards in the woods," added Phil.

"And keep away from Itchy Goomey Trees," said Cindy.

Once again, Bernie had risen to the occasion and was now ready to share the honors with Bill Robinson.

"O.K., Bill," said Bernie, "It's your turn."

"Come on, Mr. Robinson," said Gary Linard. "Make it be a scary one!"

"Well, I don't know if I can make it be scary," said Bill, "but I'll tell a story about a boy who wanted to have his own peach tree."

Once again every one grew very quiet so they could be sure to hear every one of Bill Robinson's words. He was naturally soft spoken, and here in the dark, with the crackling of the fire and the rustling of the leaves in the trees, they would have to listen very closely.

"Once upon a time," began Bill Robinson, "there was a little boy named Steve who lived on a peach orchard with his parents. Every year Steve would watch as his father carefully pruned the peach trees in the hopes of producing a peach that would win first place at the county fair. When his father would come across a tree that looked sickly or was misshapen, he would take his hatchet and cut it right down.

"One day, as little Steve was walking with his father through the orchard, he spotted a very small and scrawny looking peach tree that the wind had bent almost down to the ground. Little Steve felt sorry for the ugly peach tree and went over to try and straighten it out.

" 'Don't bother with that ugly tree, son,' said Steve's father, 'I'm going to cut it down.'

" 'Oh, Dad, please don't cut it down. It just needs a little help. If I can get it straightened out, I'll bet it will be just fine.'

" 'Come on, now, Son,' said his father, 'it's just an ugly peach tree, and we shouldn't waste our time with it.'

" 'But, Dad, you have so many other peach trees in our orchard. Can't I just have this one and see if I can help it grow strong?'

"Finally, little Steve's dad agreed not to cut the ugly peach tree down. Every day after that, little Steve would go out into the orchard and care for his ugly peach tree. He tied strings to it to help it grow straight. He carried buckets of water to pour on its roots. He picked off any little bugs that he saw crawling on it. But despite all the care he gave his peach tree, it remained ugly.

"When spring came, and all the peach trees were full of beautiful blossoms, little Steve's ugly peach tree had only one blossom. But Steve still wasn't going to lose hope in his tree. He built a windbreaker around his little deformed tree so nothing would happen to its one precious blossom. And every day he continued to water the tree's roots and to offer it encouraging words.

" 'Come on, little peach tree. I know you can do it. You may only have one blossom, but I'll bet you can grow a really nice peach if you just try.'

"Before long, the bees had visited little Steve's ugly peach tree and had fertilized its blossom. A tiny fuzzy peach could be seen growing in the sunlight.

" 'How's your little peach tree doing?' asked Steve's father one day.

" 'It's doing great. It just has one peach, but it is one of the prettiest peaches I've ever seen.'

" 'I guess I'll have to stop by some time and have a look at it.'

"And sure enough, when Steve's father finally got around to visiting the ugly peach tree, he was amazed to see the most beautiful, luscious, rosy cheeked peach in the whole orchard.

" 'Why, Son,' said Steve's father, 'I believe your little tree has grown the best peach in our whole orchard. Would you like to submit your peach as an entry in the county fair this year?'

"And sure enough, when the judging was all finished at the fair, the peach that had grown on little Steve's ugly peach tree was awarded the first place ribbon."

After allowing a few moments for the ending of his story to sink in, Bill Robinson decided that he, too, would add a sort of moral to his story.

"So, I guess the moral is that even something small and ugly can still do something very good if it just gets a little encouragement."

"Tell us another one," said Gary Linard who was still not ready to turn in for the night lest his dad not be ready for company in their tent.

"Well, I think it's Mr. Barcio's turn again."

"No, that's alright, Bill. My stories are way too scary for this late at night. You go ahead and tell another."

Bill sat for a moment and played with a stick in the campfire before starting. Finally he was ready.

"Once upon a time there was an elephant named Herman who dreamed of seeing the ocean."

This story, once Bill had finished spinning it, made such an impression on Phil Barcio that Bill finally did a little pen and ink drawing that showed Herman the elephant sitting in an old bathtub as he floated down a river on his way to see the ocean. When it was finished, he gave it to the Barcios.

As of 2014, the drawing still hangs in the author's guest room!

September, 1980
Godfather's Pizzeria, Indianapolis
"Come on, Phil. You can do it!" encouraged Steve Hurst.

"One more piece will make it 14!" said another of Phil's friends, Richie Orban.

"Oh, man, guys," moaned Phil, "this is more pizza than I've ever eaten at once in my whole life."

Steve, Richie and Phil had been joined by Chris Sheek and Joe Weisinger at a pizzeria on 56th and Keystone. The boys all knew each other from Christ the King grade school, and many of them had played either Haverford Little League baseball or Tabernacle soccer with each other.

"O.K., guys, here goes!" said Phil as he took a giant bite out of his 14th square of Chicago style pizza.

"Well, that was the last piece," proclaimed Joe, whom his friends affectionately called Weewee. "What do we do now?"

Chris Sheek had been looking out the window at a pet store that was located right across the street.

"Let's go over to the Reef and look at their pets," suggested Chris.

"Wait," said Phil. "Let's see how much money we have left between us. Maybe if we all pitch in, we can buy something."

When the boys all got to the pet store, they began to look around at the kittens, the fish, the puppies, the hamsters and the birds, checking the prices. By the time they would have to pay for a cage and supplies, all they would be able to afford was one hamster.

"What are going to do with one hamster?" asked Steve.

"Well, we could all share it," suggested Chris.

"Yeah, right. So like who would get to keep it first?" challenged Richie.

"I think Phil should get it first," said Joe. "He won the pizza-eating contest."

"I came in second," said Chris, "So I should get it next."

When the boys had it all worked out, they laid their combined funds on the counter and made their purchase. They all decided to name their jointly-owned pet "Hempster the Hamster."

"Where did the hamster come from that's on the front porch?" asked Cindy when she saw the cage that had been secured in the sunroom with the sliding glass patio doors closed so the cats wouldn't bother it.

"That's Phil's pet hamster," said Cindy's mom. "He's keeping it here for a few days before Chris Sheek takes it to his house."

Cindy's sister Sheryl had once had a pet hamster when the family lived in its house on Ferguson. It managed to get out of its cage one morning as everyone was getting ready for school. Karen's ever-vigilant cat, Charlotte, had pounced on it almost immediately and took off running through the house with the hamster hanging from her mouth.

"MY HAMSTER! THE CAT'S GOT MY HAMSTER!" screamed Sheryl.

Bernie quickly managed to make Charlotte release her catch, and the hamster was returned to its cage where it was doomed to die in just a short while from internal injuries.

"Be careful," warned Cindy's dad. "Close the sliding glass door when you go in there so a cat doesn't get in."

Cindy entered the sunroom and carefully closed the sliding glass patio door behind her. Hempster eyed her warily for a second before taking another turn on his exercise wheel. Cindy then decided to take Hempster out of his cage and hold him for a minute. As she started to lift him out, the cage door fell down on the hamster's head. Cindy put Hempster back in the cage for a minute while she secured the cage door so it wouldn't fall again. She then picked Hempster back up and slid his rear end into her shirt pocket. As she looked down at him looking up at her from her shirt pocked, she saw that one of his little eyeballs was hanging out. It had been poked out by the cage door when it had fallen.

Cindy felt terrible. It was a vision that would stick with her for years to come.

To make matters worse, Hempster got lose one day after it was Chris Sheek's turn to keep it, and since one of its eyes had been poked out, he got eaten because he didn't see Chris' cat sneaking up on him.

Years later, Phil could wax philosophical about the whole experience.

"If you want to share possession of a pet with four other 10-year old boys, pick a pet with a reputation for toughness. Maybe something with armor, like a turtle. Although I recall that I once had one of these, too, briefly—Myrtle the Turtle—and it didn't fare much better than old Hempster. In Cindy's defense, the cage door was already damaged. We guys should have gotten a better cage."

When Cyndi (as she later spelled her name) was reminded of the story later in life, she was a bit taken aback.

"I have been trying to get over that for years now, but someone keeps bringing it up. Now, if you'll excuse me, I'll be scheduling an appointment with my therapist."

December, 1980
Broad Ripple, Indiana

Christmas vacation had finally come. Whole days with absolutely nothing that had to be done.

"Who wants to play Risk?" asked Bernie.

"I do," said Phil.

"How about you, Cindy?" asked Bernie.

"No. I'm too tired. I don't want to play," said Cindy.

When Bernie and Lillian had first begun to play board games with Phillip and Cindy so they could spend some family time together, the rule had been that the loser would have to put the game away. That, however, proved to be counterproductive. Since either Phil or Cindy inevitably lost the first several times, they soon refused to play lest they be strapped into the embarrassment of having to put the game away.

"O.K.," Bernie announced one evening as he brought out a board game. "New rule. Winner puts the game away!"

All right! That simple rule change managed to put new life back into family game night.

When Phil came back upstairs from retrieving the Risk game from the shelf behind the furnace, Bernie noticed he had forgotten the game board which, for some reason, had been placed separately on the shelf.

"Where's the game board, Phil?"

"Oh, man, I must have forgotten it on the shelf."

As Phil took off through the kitchen on his way back downstairs, Bernie called after him:

"Short memory, long legs!"

So the Risk game was set up and major warfare was initiated. Since everyone was on vacation, the game could be left set up and be continued for days. Of course, precautions had to be taken so the cats wouldn't jump up on the game board and mess everything up.

This proved to be so much fun, that it soon became sort of a family winter vacation tradition. When it wasn't Risk, it was Monopoly or some other potentially long-lasting board game.

Of course, once Pacman would be introduced into the house, the days for board games would be over. Then it would be hours—literally hours—of competition as Phil and his dad sat crouched in the corner of the living room facing the T.V.

Phil would turn out to be the unbeatable all-time champion of Pacman as well as of all future video games that became the rage, each in its turn.

February, 1981
Christ the King School, Broad Ripple, Indiana

Cindy was also destined for her share of pain before leaving Christ the King School.

"Hey, Barcio," chided Ann Kouchkowski and Jill Bradford, "Bet you can't push us off."

The girls stood on one of the concrete parking lot wheel stops that were placed along the side of the playground.

Cindy had a birthmark on her face that her classmates liked to remind her of daily, so she was always happy to be the recipient of any sort of friendly attention. She put her books down and went over to the girls. It took her a few tries, but she finally managed to push them off their perches.

"O.K., it's your turn, Barcio," said Amy Gould. "Climb up there and see if we can push you off."

Cindy had always been small for her age having been born prematurely and spending the first few weeks of her life in an isolette.

No sooner had she stood on the concrete stopper than Amy Gould had run up behind her and shoved her to the ground violently.

"OU-CH!" cried Cindy as she lay on the pavement.

"What's the matter?" asked Ann and Jill.

"I think I hurt my shoulder," moaned Cindy.

Since it was school policy to chalk up all playground injuries to unavoidable accidents, the nuns at Christ the King always refused to investigate any charges of cruelty or unnecessary roughness.

Cindy's shoulder had been fractured by her fall, and there was nothing her parents could do but take her to the hospital and foot the bills.

On the playground at Christ the King School kids learned early on that they could literally get away with murder.

February, 1981
Mauston, Wisconsin

"Joe," said the President of the School Board, a former social studies teacher who had once been fired by another school district in Wisconsin, "why aren't you recommending the dismissal of the band teacher?"

"Because his current record of performance does not really warrant such severe action," replied Joe.

The School Board was out to get the band teacher because, over the 25 years that the man had been working at Mauston High School, he had frequently refused to comply with School Board requests that his students perform marches at football games and take part in community parades. Although the band teacher was himself an excellent musician and parents and students generally felt he was great, he did have a sometimes-abrasive personality and he wasn't thoroughly convinced that public performances by his band were all that important.

"Joe," countered the School Board President, "either you fire this teacher, or this board will fire you!"

Even though the School Board was meeting in a closed executive session, everyone in the room—both board members and administrators—were stunned.

"Please consider," explained Joe, "that this teacher is attempting to be a caring spouse for his wife who has Multiple Sclerosis. If he were to be fired, the action could be highly disastrous to his whole family."

The President was unmoved, and his warning stood.

It was after midnight when Joe returned home and woke his wife, Liz, to tell her of his situation.

The next day, after preparing copies of every report the band teacher had received during his tenure at Mauston High School, Joe called the teacher to his office to inform him that his contract would not be renewed for the following year.

"By God," screamed the band teacher who had immediately become extremely livid and angry, "if anyone is going to lose his job, it's going to be you and not me!"

Things went down hill from there. The band teacher demanded, and got, an open meeting with the School Board at which community members could speak on his behalf.

When Joe arrived at school on the night of the meeting, he discovered that so many people turned up that the meeting had to be moved into the school library. Not only was the full board present along with all of the other school administrators, but there was also a large group of parents and an even larger group of students—all present to defend the teacher!

Instead of defending its request, the board sat back and assigned Joe the role of "prosecuting attorney" while its members pretended to be present as impartial judges.

For 45 minutes, as local newspaper reporters took notes and parents and students listened, Joe reviewed every supervisory report made on the teacher, starting with principals who had been at the school long before his own tenure there. Then he moved on to his own reports in which he had had to remind the teacher of the board's expectations of the band program. He finished by saying that he would recommend to the board that the teacher's contract not be renewed.

For the next two hours or so, the board listened to pleas from parents who really wanted the teacher to stay on, many of whom directed their comments directly at Joe. Then students were also given an opportunity to speak, and many of them chose to attack Joe angrily.

"You know, Mr. Barcio, there was only one perfect man in this world, and they hung him from a cross!"

"Oh, my God," said Joe to himself after the student had angrily taken her seat.

At that point, the board announced that it would retire to another room briefly for a brief executive session, after which they would announce their decision.

"The Board has decided," said the President when the group returned to the library, "to accept Mr. Barcio's recommendation and not renew the band teacher's contract."

Joe suspected that only the board members would sleep well that night.

"Joe," said the board President at a subsequent meeting, "when you fill this band position, I want you to conduct a nation-wide search and get the best band teacher there is in this country to come here."

Startled, Joe replied, "I don't think you will be able to get the best band teacher in the country to come to Mauston."

"Well, why not, Joe," said the board president as he angrily banged his fist on the table.

"Because you don't pay the best salary in the country to hire the best teacher in the country."

Silence.

"You will get," continued Joe, "the best teacher who is willing to work for the current salary you pay."

Silence.

"Well, you better try to get the very best teacher you can!" said the board present.

Then, addressing the other members of the board, he said, "Next item on the agenda."

The band teacher, of course, appealed the board's decision to the Wisconsin State Department of Education, and the following year a special arbitration hearing was held in the Mauston Court House.

This time, the members of the school board were not required to be in attendance to defend their decision.

During this hearing, Joe learned a hard lesson about school administration. The school board needed him to be the "fall guy," and, as far as it was concerned, he was on his own. The Superintendent of Mauston Area Schools was in attendance along with the school system's attorney, but they would only sit and chat quietly with each other during what was to turn into a two-day ordeal. To Joe, it seemed that the only person in the room who was actually on his side was his wife, Liz, whom he had asked to be present.

As representatives from the State Department of Education listened, the attorney for the Wisconsin Education Association, which was defending the band teacher, began a long, calculated attack designed to wear Joe down, hopefully break his resolve, and, if at all possible, make him look foolish. The man would not even let up enough to allow Joe an occasional rest room break.

At one point during the final day of his "toying" with Joe on the witness stand, Liz overheard the attorney remark to a colleague, "You know, I could jerk this guy around for two more days if I wanted to."

By the time the attorney had decided that he had had all the fun he wanted, Joe was exhausted.

In the end, however, the board's decision not to renew the band teacher's contract was reversed, and it had to pay a substantial sum of money to the reinstated band teacher who had temporarily found work in the insurance field in another city.

The emotional anguish of that open board meeting and the two-day hearing at the court house remains with Joe to this day—even though it has been helpful to record his experience for the very first time for inclusion in this book.

May, 1981
Fulton Jr. H.S., Indianapolis
"Are you sure you won't reconsider and stay on here at Fulton?" asked Fern, the retiring head of the Language Department.

"Well, Fern, if they were willing to create a separate Foreign Language Department here, I would probably stay on to serve as its head," said Bernie.

"I don't think they're going to do that."

"Well then," said Bernie, "I think I'm going to accept the Latin position at Carmel High School. It's a four-year Latin program and one of the best in the state."

So, Bernie was moving on again. The great thing was that where he was living in Broad Ripple enabled him to change school districts at will and never have to move his family.

"Well, Lill, they decided not to accept my offer and make me department head of a foreign language department at Fulton."

"So, are you going to accept the Carmel job?"

"I think so. Donna Wright is definitely leaving, and it's a great program."

"Even though it means another cut in pay?"

"Well, I guess that's kind of the way it is. As we've said over the years, money isn't everything. No point in staying somewhere that doesn't appreciate your talents when there are so many other job opportunities available close at hand."

"Well, you could just swallow your pride and stick it out."

"Oh, sure, and turn into a scarab," countered Bernie.

"A scarab?"

"Do you know that the scarab is one of the oldest insects on the planet? It's remained basically unchanged for centuries."

"So?"

"Do you know what the secret of its survival is?"

"No. What?"

"Somewhere along the line, scarabs figured out that the secret to survival in life was to learn to eat shit. So they just made that their main diet. I don't think I want to stick around and be a scarab. Think I'll move on even if it means a couple thousand dollar cut in pay."

The problem—although it really wasn't a problem since both Lillian and Bernie agreed on the principles behind all his moves— was that every time Bernie had switched jobs in Indianapolis, he had had to take a cut in pay. When he had left Park School to go to North Central High School, Washington Township told him they could not give him full credit for his five years experience at Park School. Park was a private school, and they only gave full credit for public school teaching experience. That resulted in a $5,000 a year cut in pay. When Bernie finally left Eastwood Jr. H.S. after his eight years in Limbo there, he again took a couple thousand dollar cut in pay to move into the Wayne Township school system. And now, here he was again, accepting another pay cut.

But no matter. He had his dignity. And, besides, the Carmel job was much more prestigious. And, unbeknownst to either Lillian or him at the time, the switch would eventually result in his being honored as Indiana Teacher of the Year!

July, 1981
St. Maur's Seminary, Indianapolis

Bernie's dream of putting together a Latin Weekender Conference that would totally immerse Latin teachers into the culture of the Ancient Romans had come true. He had written proposals, obtained funding from the Lilly Foundation and the Indiana Committee for the Humanities, and arranged to use the secluded facilities of St. Maur's Seminary in Indianapolis for the gathering. Twelve teachers from Indiana, Kentucky, Ohio and Pennsylvania gathered for what the **Indianapolis Star** ("Pompeiiana helps 'dead' language survive," Aug.2, 1981, Sec. 5, P. 8) called a weekend-long toga party.

The Latin Weekender included movies, games and workshops in which the teachers learned ancient techniques for making jewelry, mosaics and clothing. The climax was a Saturday night Roman feast. The participants dined while reclining on *triclinia* (similar to low couches) and leaning on their elbows. Dinner included authentic ancient appetizers for *gustatio*, Cornish game hens for a main course (*primae mensae*) and such specialties as *placenta casei Athenaea*—Athenian cheesecake—for dessert (*secundae mensae*).

The event proved so successful that Bernie was able to sponsor several larger Latin Weekenders to which Latin teachers were even invited to bring their students.

Bernie was definitely doing his share to help revive interest in high school Latin, not only in Indiana but throughout the United States.

October 1, 1981
Broad Ripple, Indiana

Phil was now in the sixth grade at Christ the King School. It would turn out to be the Year from Hell for him and most of the others in his class. Sr. Mary Theresa had been brought in to teach the sixth grade class that year. Sr. Mary Theresa had just spent two years recovering from a nervous breakdown.

Phil's Dad knew something was seriously wrong at Christ the King School when Phil would come home and report that he had received a zero on homework that his Dad knew he had carefully worked on the night before.

"Why did you get a zero?" his dad asked.

"Because I didn't get it on her desk on time," said Phil

"How much time did you have to get it there?"

"Sr.'s crazy," said Phil. "She sits down at her desk and says, 'OK, you all have five seconds to lay your homework on my desk. If it's not here in five seconds, you get a zero.' "

"Does anyone make it on time?"

"Only those who already have it out of their folders and are sitting in the front rows," said Phil.

Since Phil's Dad was a licensed teacher in the public school system of Indiana, he knew that these were not valid classroom practices. He thought he would address the problem diplomatically by making an appointment to talk with the pastor of Christ the King parish, Fr. Kenny Sweeney.

"I'm sorry," Mr. Barcio, said Fr. Sweeney after he had listened to the complaint, "but the good Sisters have complete and sole authority over how they run their school. I make it a practice of not interfering."

"But what they're doing is not educationally sound and may even be illegal," said Phil's Dad.

"Don't forget," said the pastor, "that Christ the King is a parochial school and is not bound by the same rules as the public schools. If you are not happy with Christ the King School, you do have the right to place your son in the public school system."

Thus, the pastor planted the seed, and although Phil's Dad was a firm believer in Catholic education, he realized that Phil might, in fact, have better luck in IPS School 59 the following year.

Phil was encouraged to try and make the best of the year without getting into too much trouble. He did his best, but when Sr. Mary Theresa gave him a C on a paper that both he and his parents knew deserved an A, he lost his little Italian temper. When Sister wasn't looking, Phil, who was sitting near an open window, began tossing books from a shelf out onto the playground below.

Suddenly, in the doorway of the classroom stood the person who had hired Sr. Mary Theresa, Sr. Mary Luke, the principal. Or, as Phil's parents preferred to think of her, "Sr. Mary Lukewarm." With her was the school janitor holding the books that he had gathered from the playground.

Phil was nailed, and it strengthened the family's decision to have him switch to IPS School 59 the following year. It was just a little further down the street, and he would still have to walk right past Christ the King, but he would have a new set of friends to walk with. So far as anyone knows, Phil had no further problems with Rick, Pat, Sr. Mary Theresa or Sr. Mary Lukewarm.

At School 59 Phil excelled in academics and music. He impressed the neighbors by walking to school each day wearing a neat pair of slacks, a sport shirt and a tie. It was an unofficial dress code that had been adopted by academic achievers at School 59. No longer did Bernie need to stand at the foot of the steps each morning and call out, "Up, Up, Up!" to get Phil out of bed. He actually looked forward to going to school each day.

October 29, 1981
Broad Ripple, Indiana

"Where's Cindy?" asked Lillian when she walked into the front room and saw Cindy's guest, Mary Jane, sitting by herself.

Cindy didn't socialize all that much with her friends from school so her mom was always pleased when Cindy reached out. Lillian had done her share by serving as a Troop Leader for Cindy's Girl Scout troop. She would even volunteer to help coach Cindy's Little League softball team, The Gators.

"I'm not sure," said Mary Jane.

Lillian looked around the main floor of the house with no luck and finally went upstairs to Cindy's bedroom.

"What are you doing up here?" asked Lillian.

"I'm tired," said Cindy. "I wanted to come up and go to bed."

"Cindy, you invited Mary Jane over. You can't just leave her downstairs all by herself."

But that was it. Cindy was done entertaining. The only thing Bernie and Lillian could do was offer their apologies to Mary Jane and drive her home.

Later that month, Cindy decided to try hosting a sleepover, something her mom encouraged in the hopes that it would help boost Cindy's self-confidence and enhance her social acceptance.

"What's that," asked Cindy as one of her guests produced a game for the girls to play.

"It's a Ouija Board."

"Those things are scary," said Cindy, not sure of what she was getting herself into.

At any rate, all the guests retired into Cindy's room and closed the door. The squeals and cries and hoots that followed totally intrigued Phil who was listening from his bedroom down the hall. Finally, the girls had had all they could take—Ouija Boards really are spooky. The board was put back in its box, and things quieted down.

Phil continued listening to see if he could figure out what was going on behind his sister's closed bedroom door. Finally he heard whispering.

"I can't sleep with that thing in here," he heard his sister say.

"Are you afraid of it?"

"Yes, I am. I'm going to take it downstairs."

That's all Phil had to hear. He quickly hurried down the steps and found a convenient hiding place.

This was going to be fun.

Before long, he heard his sister making her way slowly down the steps in the dark.

"UAHH!" shouted Phil as soon as Cindy turned the corner into the dark dining room.

"AHHHH!" screamed Cindy as the Ouija game box flew from her hands and spilled its contents all over the dining room floor.

"Gotcha!" yelled Phil with glee.

"You big jerk! You can just help me pick all that up now."

As far as Phil was concerned, it was totally worth it. Another great memory for posterity!

November, 1983
St. Thomas Aquinas Church, Indianapolis

"You have a beautiful voice," said Mike Pence who had gone up to the front of church after Mass to congratulate the attractive young lady who sang and played guitar during the service.

"Thank you," said Karen, "glad you enjoyed the music."

"Oh, I did. Especially the songs that you sang! Would you like to go somewhere for coffee?" asked Mike.

Following her divorce from Steve Whittaker, Karen had busied herself with a variety of activities such as scuba diving, skydiving, earning her pilot's license and singing with the guitar group at St. Thomas Aquinas Catholic Church.

A native of Columbus, Indiana, Mike Pence was attending the I.U. School of Law in downtown Indianapolis. He had a small apartment downtown, but had decided to attend mass that evening at St. Thomas—a decision that made all the difference in their futures.

April, 1984
Carmel, Indiana

"Congratulations, Mr. Barcio, you have been selected as the Teacher of the Year for Carmel-Clay Schools!"

So, 22 years after having been briefly honored as the Teacher of the Day by Central High School in Bay City, Michigan, Bernie Barcio had just been honored once again. Of course, the *bonus* of the recognition came with a tremendous *onus*. Bernie would now have to enter into statewide competition to see if he could be chosen as the Indiana Teacher of the Year. He would have to work with the staff in the central office to create a great scrapbook documenting and highlighting all of his achievements and noteworthy undertakings over the years. He would also have to begin collecting letters of recommendation from as many significant and respected individuals as he could think of. But, hey, Bernie was always up to a challenge.

May, 1984
Chatard High School, Indianapolis

"Let's hurry, Lill. We want to get there a little early to get some good seats," encouraged Bernie.

"Almost ready. Is the front door locked?" asked Lillian.

"Yup, we're all set."

Bernie and Lillian were on their way over to Chatard High School to see their daughter Cindy perform in the spring musical production, **Godspell**. Although Cindy had a beautiful voice, the choir teacher, Tammy Anderson, rarely gave her a chance to star or solo. At any rate, Cindy, following in the footsteps of her older sister, Karen, who had also stared in Chatard High School musical productions as a student, was great in the role she had been given.

When Karen attended Chatard, she had dazzled her audience when she appeared in the annual talent show wearing a body-hugging outfit and long black stockings. Perched daintily on a high stool, Karen sang a tune from **Cabaret** that left the audience google-eyed.

July, 1984
The ShenandoahValley, West Virginia

"I'm going over to the payphone and check our messages, Lill," said Bernie who was camping with Lillian, Cindy and Phillip on their way back from giving a talk in Richmond, Virginia.

"When you get back, I want to find a Laundromat and dry some things out," said Lillian.

Camping would never change. Living in the elements was always a challenge.

"Well," said Lillian after Bernie returned. "Were there any messages?"

"Just one from some guy who said he wants to talk to me when we get back in town. Who the hell is Mike Pence?" asked Bernie.

"Oh," said Lillian, "that might be the boy that Karen has been seeing."

When they got back to town, Mike Pence called again and arranged to come over to the house to talk to Bernie. Sure enough, he was the boy that Karen had been seeing for nine months. The two had fallen in love, and Mike wanted formally to request permission to ask her to marry him.

Bernie was flattered. Although he had never been given the opportunity to adopt any of Lillian's three girls, he felt especially close to Karen, maybe because she had been the youngest and had enjoyed more opportunities than her two sisters to bond with him. Karen had even chosen to work closely with Bernie as they were building the two additions onto their house on Ferguson. She wanted to learn how to do everything that he knew how to do.

"Well, Mike, you can certainly have our permission to ask her. I've got to tell you. She's a great girl, very talented. There is one thing, though," cautioned Bernie.

"What's that?"

"You'll have to be ready to make yourself available for her debriefing every night."

"Is that right?" asked Mike.

"She usually comes home bursting with things to say and report, and she just won't stop until she has had a chance to tell somebody everything on her mind," said Bernie.

"Oh," said Mike, "I think I can handle that."

And that was that. Karen would accept his proposal, and the two were ready to begin their lives together.

August, 1984
Indianapolis

After Lillian was hired as an assistant to the Director of Publications at Butler University, she enrolled in an evening class on Feature Writing, one of her long-time interests. The class was being taught by Adjunct Instructor, Pegg Kennedy. Before long, Pegg assigned Lillian several articles to be written and submitted with an eye on their being published in **Indianapolis Magazine**.

Her first article accepted for publication was "PUB-LIC RELATIONS," and told the stories of three budding Indianapolis restauranteurs, Jack Bayt (Courtyard restaurant), Rick Rising-Moore (Union Jack's) and Ken Meiring (Common Market). The article appeared on pp. 21-23 of the August, 1984, issue.

The September **Indianapolis Magazine** contained Lillian's article entitled "Living Aloft" (p. 13) about Scott Keller's restoration of the Harness Factory Loft.

On page 20 of the December, 1984, **Indianapolis Magazine**, Lillian featured "The Peanut King," Richard Green, who owned the largest nut processing business in Indiana.

The Publications Department of Butler was proud to have a published writer as a member of its staff.

Saturday, August 18, 1984
Madison, Wisconsin

It was Ted and Stella's 50th Wedding Anniversary party, and most of the guests had already found their seats in the Parlor Room of the Inn on the Park, 22 South Carroll Street in Madison.

"Bern," said Bernie's dad who was all decked out in a white tux jacket, fancy white shirt, black pants, baby blue bowtie and cummerbund, "Mom wants these corsages passed out to the ladies on this list. Can you take care of it?"

"Sure. No problem. Are we sure there are enough for everyone?"

"There should be. We even bought a few extra."

"O.K.," said Bernie, "we'll get them passed out. Are you and Ma ready? It's almost one o'clock."

Even though Bernie, Lillian, Joe and Liz had made every effort to plan everything as carefully as possible on a meager budget, Stella wanted there to be something special that she could bring to the party. Thus the two large boxes of corsages that had been specially made by a local florist.

Of course, things being the way they are, there weren't enough corsages to go around, and as Bernie began to pass them out, he quickly realized that key guests were about to be slighted.

"Lillian," he quickly confided to his wife, "I don't have a corsage for Aunt Martha. Would you mind if we gave her yours?"

Before it was over, Joe's wife, Liz, and Cindy also had to give up their corsages in order not to slight other important guests who had decided to attend at the last minute not having RSVP-ed.

This, of course, also led to an imminent shortage of finger-food that had been ordered for the party.

Finally, Stella was ready to make her grand entrance. As she and Ted began walking down the hallway from the private room Bernie had reserved for them, Mario Nardi's mother, arriving late, suddenly appeared in the hall.

"Ah, *Commare Stella*!" called out Mrs. Nardi happy to be among the first to see the guests of honor.

"Oh-ah. *Shuda mi! Musa tu!*" said Stella upset that someone was about to ruin their grand entry. "Go inside! Go inside," she hissed indicating with a harsh gesture of her hand where she wanted Mrs. Nardi to go.

"Oh, *si. Capisco. Mi dispiace, mi dispiace! Compare Tirigi, come sta?*"

"*Bene grazie, Commare*. We'll see you inside, O.K.?"

Another little bit of unanticipated awkwardness.

But, no matter. Bernie had located a local Italian D.J., Russ Loniello, who not only played Italian tapes but also sang traditional Italian songs to specially prepared sound tracks. Bernie had done his best to try to locate live musicians who might be able to play the accordion, guitar and mandolin while belting out traditional Italian folksongs as had once resonated in their home on Hammond Ave. in Cudahy during all those middle of the night traveling parties. Unfortunately, there just didn't seem to be any live Italian folk song performers available.

On his mom's suggestion, Bernie had contacted Henry Mastronardi, the accordion player who had played at their wedding 50 years earlier. Henry, however, was living in a nursing home in Illinois and no longer able to travel. All Henry could do was make a cassette recording—he was still able to play the accordion very professionally—in honor of their 50th. This he mailed to Bernie complete with appropriate dedicatory remarks included on the tape.

"And now," said Russ Loniello, "one of our guests of honor would like to say a few words. Please welcome Ted Barcio!"

Ted accepted the microphone from the D.J. and looked out over those assembled. It took him just a minute to gain his composure and begin his welcoming remarks and thank you's.

Finally, Ted took a deep breath and said, "Hello!"

Everyone broke out in friendly laughter.

"There," said the D.J., "that wasn't so hard."

"Oh, goodness. I want to thank everyone. My neighbors, my friends. My cousins. My neighbor next door. When Joe was born, my neighbor was next door. He's here. And his brother, which is Joe's [?] grandfather, isn't here, but his grandmother is here. That makes us happy. I see my cousins from Chicago. There's the Paraino's, the Sciani's, all my friends. And there's the Nardi's, and Riccio, Benny Riccio, my cousin's son. And our friends from Sparta. And there are my friends from the railroad. Oh, I hope I don't leave any of you out. And my sisters-in-law. Thank you for coming."

"What about your brothers-in-law?" called out Charlie Nudi, wanting to have a little fun.

"Of course, there's Angelo and Charlie. And Gusty. Welcome! Welcome all! Thank you for coming."

The full comments that Ted delivered during the party were recorded on a cassette tape by the D.J. When the author listened to the entire tape with his Uncle Charlie in August 2004, they were both moved by the nostalgia of hearing Ted's signature voice again after so many years and of hearing the touching references to who were in attendance.

Among all those being recognized by Ted at his 50th Wedding Anniversary Party, no Barcio other than the families of his two sons could be spotted in the hall. Neither Ted's brother nor any of his sisters were present.

In their defense, however, it must be stated that, no doubt, none of Ted's immediate family had been sent an invitation. Bernie had designed the unique invitations that featured a photo of their wedding party, and he had had an ample supply printed. His mother had insisted, however, that she and his dad be allowed to address and mail them. Ted had obviously chosen to avoid any additional conflicts between his wife and his family by simply not including them in the celebration.

Stella's family, however, was present in force. In fact, apart from an occasional funeral, this would be the last time that all surviving members of the Nudi family would be together until a special birthday party would be planned for Stella's 90th Birthday at the Indianapolis Retirement Home held on April 22, 2000.

April 26, 1985
St. Maur's Seminary, Indianapolis

Bernie had felt that the Latin Weekenders he had sponsored for Latin teachers throughout the United States had been a little unappreciated by the majority of the high school and university classics teachers in Indiana, so he devised a plan.

"Nancy, if you run for 1st Vice President of the I.C.C., you'll be able to host the spring meeting and provide whatever format you like," suggested Bernie.

"What do you have in mind?" asked Nancy Mack, an Indiana Latin teacher who had built catapults with Bernie for the past several years.

"What I'm suggesting is that we structure the spring meeting as a total immersion Latin Weekender Conference," said Bernie. "John Helms from

Valpo will be the President. He and I are friends from our University of Michigan days, and he'll go along with the idea."

"Won't the cost be prohibitive?" asked Nancy.

"I believe I can get a matching grant from the Indiana Committee for the Humanities that will make it affordable," said Bernie.

And it worked. The financing fell into place, and Bernie, Nancy and John pulled off their coup. A good portion of Indiana's leading secondary and post-secondary classical teachers were successfully introduced to the magnificence of the Latin Weekender Conferences that had already been so well received by others.

Out of these conferences, grew the development of several *Personae* presentations by Latin teachers Nancy Mack, who portrayed a professional Roman mourner, Donna Wright who portrayed Julia, the daughter of Augustus Caesar, Diane Werblo who portrayed a Pompeiian clothier, Bill Gilmartin who portrayed the Emperor Caligula, and Tod Wright who portrayed a Roman school teacher.

Bill Gilmartin became so deeply engrossed in his portrayal of the insane Emperor Caligula, however, that he actually frightened himself and decided to retire the character at the end of the Weekender Conferences.

Nancy Mack, Donna Wright, and Diane Werblo all decided to join Bernie in offering their *Personae* presentations to audiences across the nation. Bernie's *Personae* included Marcus Loreius Tiburtinus (a citizen of Pompeii), Fabius Loreius Tiburtinus (a Roman military Tribune) and his own version of Fr. Guido Sarducci as a renegade Italian priest trying to convince high school students to consider becoming Latin teachers. They were all soon joined by Dr. Paula Saffire, a professor of Classical Greek at Butler University, who portrayed the Greek poetess, Sappho, and an Illinois Latin teacher, Lois Dion, who portrayed a Roman marriage coordinator.

June 8, 1985
Speedway, Indiana

Bernie and Lillian had been formally introduced to Mike's parents at a downtown Indianapolis restaurant, and all plans had gone smoothly for their wedding. They had chosen a Catholic Church in Speedway and had planned the wedding reception at a nearby motel.

"I've got a little surprise for Karen," confided Bernie to Lillian as he was about to escort Karen down the aisle.

"I hope you're not going to embarrass her," said Lillian.

"No, I wouldn't do that," assured Bernie.

"What are you going to do?"

"After the ceremony, while they're taking pictures, I'm going to stuff cotton into my cheeks and pose with her wearing my Godfather fedora. It'll be just like the movie."

This, of course, started a family tradition. Later, Bernie's neice, Liz, insisted that Bernie also do a Godfather photo with her on her wedding days (first with Ted Biggs in 1996, and then with Chris Miller in 2005). Sheryl's daughter, Annie, also posed with Bernie for her Godfather photo. When Bernie's son, Phil, married Audrey on the beach in Bahai Honda State Park in the Florida Keys, Audrey also insisted that she have an opportunity to have a Godfather photo taken with Bernie. This time, though, the "Godfather" would be wearing white Bermuda shorts in addition to his usual dark shirt, light tie, black jacket and black fedora.

At the reception, Mike and Karen invited Phil to play keyboard at which he was becoming quite proficient.

Unfortunately for Mike, the motel also had an indoor swimming pool next to the reception room. Toward the end of the evening, Mike's brothers muscled him away from his new bride and dragged him into the poolroom to start another long-standing family tradition.

Despite his appeals and the fact that he was wearing a rented Tuxedo that was about to be ruined, his brothers heaved him, fully dressed, into the pool. As Mike was climbing out, his dad walked up to the side of the pool. Mike held up an arm so his dad could help him get out. But as soon as Mike had made it back up on the pool wall, his dad simply pushed him back in again.

This event made such an impression on the male members of the Barcio family in attendance that they all secretly planned similar escapades for future weddings.

When Phil got married to his first wife, Kim, their reception was held at the Marott Hotel on Meridian Street, downtown Indianapolis. Since the Marott did not have an indoor pool, his cousins decided to douse him with water in one of the small rooms surrounding the main lobby. Unfortunately, just as they all let loose their cascade of water, Phil bent down and most of the water hit his cousin Joey who happened to be standing behind him.

Joey would also get doused at his wedding, and his brother Bernie would later get barraged with water balloons at his. Since Phil's second wedding, to Audrey Liphard in 2003, took place on the beach in Bahia Honda on the Florida Keys, there was no escaping his being tossed into the ocean by the men in his wedding party.

August, 1985
Sparta, Wisconsin

Bernie and his son Phil had driven up to Sparta together to visit his folks. On the way they had stopped at Wisconsin Dells, a town that had, in fact, been the Honeymoon destination of Bernie's mom and dad back in 1934. Now it was a very upscale, flashy, over-commercialized resort town.

At a novelty photo shop in Wisconsin Dells Phil posed for a photo that would feature him on the cover of **National Lampoon**. Almost prophetically, Bernie, wearing his Godfather fedora and sporting a slender cigar, posed for a **Newsweek** cover with the caption "Our Man Of The Year" printed in reverse print over his photo. Sideline captions read, "The World Celebrates A man for All Seasons," "Legend Tells His Own Story," and "How the Man Won and Why."

When Bernie's selection as Indiana Teacher of the Year would be announced to the faculty at Carmel High School the following year, Bernie would proudly display the magazine cover on the buffet table set up in the faculty room.

In addition to visiting his folks with his son, Bernie decided to take Phil out to the farm on which he had worked in the summer of 1956 and introduce him to Auggie Terpstra, his old boss.

"Hi," said Bernie when the farmhouse door on which he had rapped was opened. "Is Auggie here?"

"Are you looking for my father?" asked the young man who had answered the door.

"Yes, I'm Bernie Barcio and I worked for him one summer a number of years ago."

"I'm his son. My dad doesn't live here any more," said the young man.

"Are you running the farm now?"

"Yes," said the young man. "My wife and I run it now with my children. If you want to see my dad, you can find him at an auction that's being held just up the road."

So Bernie and Phil drove on up the road to find Auggie.

"Hi, Auggie," said Bernie. "Do you remember me?"

Auggie looked Bernie up and down and looked at Phil for a while without saying anything.

"I worked with you in the summer after I graduated from high school back in 1956," said Bernie.

"Bernie! Of course, now I recognize you," proclaimed Auggie.

Auggie looked pretty much as he had 20 years ago. Hadn't changed a bit.

"So, you're not running the farm anymore?" asked Bernie.

"No," said Auggie. "You knew that we were only renting the farm when you worked for me, didn't you?"

"Yeah, I think so. Is your son renting it now?" asked Bernie.

"No, Bernie," said Auggie. "I was finally able to save up enough money to buy the land from my landlord. When I retired, I gave it to my son and his wife."

Life did indeed go in circles. Bernie was glad that Phil had a chance to meet his old boss. He was good Wisconsin farm stock, and Bernie was proud to have had a chance to work and learn from him all those years ago.

September 28, 1985
St. Vincent Hospice, Indianapolis

"Hap-py Birth-day, dear Gramma, Hap-py Birth-day to you!"

It was Pearl Hacker's 72nd birthday and her daughter, Lillian, was at her bedside along with the author and their two children, Cindy and Phil. It was hard, however, to be very festive, for as hospice nurses are skilled at observing, "it wouldn't be long now."

When Pearl first became sick with what later were confirmed to be definite signs of cancer, she was reluctant to admit her illness and chose to be treated at a chiropractic hospital in Indianapolis rather than be seen by an oncologist. She preferred to believe that her pain was due to a misalignment of her spine. When the pain persisted and spread, however, her daughter Lillian was finally able to convince her to seek more standard medical analysis. An oncologist detected a large cancerous growth behind her heart that was putting the pressure on her spine and causing her back pain.

At first, in August of 1985, while her husband and son were visiting his parents in Sparta, Wisconsin, Lillian invited her mother to move into their spare room so she could look after her. Pearl, however, was not a pleasant patient. All her life she had been strong-willed and independent, and she wasn't going to mellow now, even though bed ridden. Lillian explained her initial decision to her husband by phone, but called a couple days later to say that it just was not going to work and that she was looking into having her mother moved into a room at the St. Vincent Hospice.

By the time the author had returned from Wisconsin, Pearl had come to grips with the finality of her condition and had, in a very business-like manner (as was her wont as an ex-manager of American Fletcher's Bank branch in Broad Ripple), sold her car to her son-in-law for $1.00. And, yes, she insisted on being handed the dollar bill as she lay in bed.

Gramma Hacker needed help in blowing out the candles on her cake, and shortly after slices had been distributed to her guests, she quietly passed to her eternal rewards.

January, 1986
Indianapolis
"And now, it gives me great pleasure," said the State Superintendent of Education, Dean Evans, "to introduce the 1986 Indiana State Teacher of the Year, Bernard Barcio."

At the official Indiana State Department of Education presentation of the award, both the winner and the runner up were given an opportunity to make brief statements to those gathered. As fate would have it, the State Superintendent of Education presenting the award to Bernie was Dr. Dean Evans, the man who had been the Superintendent of Washington Township Schools when Bernie was given no choice but to leave North Central High School. In another twist of fate, the runner up was Richard Dick, an outstanding orchestra leader from North Central High School who was renowned nationwide for his Stradivarius performances with the Henry Mancini Orchestra.

Following his acceptance speech, Bernie casually walked over to the table where Eugene Cloncs sat, the Principal of North Central High School who had asked Bernie to leave his school. Seated with the Principal was the Asst. Superintendent of Washington Township Schools, Gerald DeWitt, who had pressured Bernie into giving up his Latin Club sponsorship of the National Catapult Contest. Bernie shook hands with both men and looked them straight in the eyes as he congratulated them on having sponsored the Runner Up in the contest. Such moments in life as these are rare indeed.

February 4, 1986
State House, Indianapolis

As Ted Barcio had once been honored by the Governor of Nebraska for his heroic work in cleaning the snow from the Albion Line in 1948, Bernie was now being honored by the Governor of Indiana, Robert Orr, for having been selected by the Indiana State Department of Education as the Indiana State Teacher of the Year.

The award was the coveted Sagamore of the Wabash.

And there would be more state honors to come. During the 1986 2nd Session of the 104th Indiana General Assembly, Bernie would be honored with House Concurrent Resolution No. 37.

Having spent most of his professional life in classrooms, Bernie was dumbstruck as he was ushered into the chamber of the House of Representatives in the State House.

"This place is a mad house," thought Bernie.

And it really sort of was. Someone was at the podium addressing the group, most of whose members were busy laughing it up or deep in discussion with each other on the floor. The room never did get absolutely quiet, but enough of a semblance of order was finally obtained after aggressive gavel banging to enable a speaker to announce Bernie's congratulatory Resolution and call him forward to accept it.

Bernie was then escorted to the opposite side of the State House where he entered the very quiet, very sedate Senate Chamber. Plush! Since there are fewer Senators than Representatives, each Senator had his own massive, leather covered reclining chair. Bernie could not believe the difference in the atmosphere and decorum of the two chambers.

When the Concurrent Resolution congratulating Bernie as the 1986 Teacher of the Year was announced, the room was absolutely quiet. Those in attendance were actually listening with interest.

Amazing!

Later, Bernie would be further honored by the Indiana Department of Education by being asked to serve as a member of the Indiana Foreign Language Curriculum Task Force, 1993 through 1995. Travel expenses and meals were provided, as were professional days from teaching responsibilities at Carmel High School.

Once again, life was good.

March, 1986
Winona, Minnesota

"Good morning, Father Barcio," said the caller when Joe answered the phone in his office.

"Good morning, this is Mr. Barcio. How can I help you?"

Since Joe had replaced a priest who had served as Chief Administrator of both the Junior and Senior High Schools for the Winona Diocese, it was hard for callers to get out of habit of addressing him as "Father" Barcio.

In fact, as far back as anyone could recall, there had always been a priest serving as Principal of the two schools. Having a lay administrator was something new.

When Joe had first moved his family from Mauston, Wisconsin, to accept this position, he had a young man serving as Assistant Principal. This young man's duties were mainly to supervise the junior high school while Joe handled the duties of Principal at the high school. If Joe needed to be out of town on occasion, the Assistant Principal was left in charge, and he handled things quite well.

Two years later, however, Joe had some bad news for his assistant.

"I'm afraid," began Joe after the two of them were alone in his office, "that the members of the diocesan school board have decided to cut expenses by eliminating your job."

"Great! Now what do I do?" asked the young man parenthetically.

"You've done a great job here," continued Joe, "and I am more than willing to give you whatever recommendations you will need to find work in a new school next year."

As it turned out, with Joe's help the young man was soon hired to serve as principal of a Catholic elementary school in Minnesota.

To help Joe out with his now double work load, the school board—which, by the way, consisted of five priests and four lay people—contacted an experienced nun who was serving as principal of all the local Catholic elementary schools. She agreed to come in periodically to help with the junior high administrative duties. She did prove very helpful, especially with the two young priests who were assigned—with no formal training in teaching—to teach religion at the junior high and the high school. With the help of the good Nun, these two "stumbled" their way through their first year in their classrooms.

For her help Joe was very thankful. He really did not have time to help two newly ordained priests to become effective classroom teachers.

That same year, the school board made another momentous decision. For the first time ever, they decided to elect a Lay member of the board to serve as Board President. Previously, each of the five priests on the board used to take turns holding that office.

Joe, of course, was anxious to cooperate as best he could with this new Lay Board President. So, when she called him at home on a Saturday evening, he received her call with great interest.

"Joe," began the Board President, "I just picked up my son at St. Mary's College where the eighth graders were supposed to be having a sled and skating party."

"Yes," said Joe interested in what else he would hear.

"Joe, there was no teacher-supervisor at the party, and my son broke his wrist."

"There wasn't?" asked Joe incredulously.

"Joe, I want to know who was responsible for organizing the party and then didn't show up to supervise it."

"I'm sorry about your son's wrist. I'll look into the matter first thing Monday morning," said Joe as he imagined how the poor teacher who had mismanaged the event would no doubt be let go at the end of the school year.

Monday morning, Joe met with the Nun who was helping with the junior high school.

"Sister, we have a serious problem with a staff member in the junior high," began Joe. "I need you to find out which teacher organized a sled and skating party at St. Mary's College on Saturday night and then failed to show up to supervise it.

Sister sat quietly listening to Joe speak.

"The worst part is," continued Joe more gravely, "that the Board President's son was at the party and broke his wrist. Needless to say, Madam Board President is very concerned!"

At this point, the good Sister put her hand to her mouth and said, "Oh, my gosh! You know, Joe, that was me. I organized it and told the eighth graders when and where it would be. Then I got so busy Saturday that I forgot all about it!"

As Joe listened to Sister's explanation he was thinking to himself, "Oh boy. This is probably going to call for an executive session of the Board. Poor Sister is really going to catch holy heck!"

Joe wondered what it would be like when a Nun catches "holy heck."

"Sister," said Joe, "I want you to call the Board President immediately. Explain what happened and then get back to me."

As it turned out, Joe never got a chance to see what kind of "holy heck" befalls a Nun who gets herself in trouble. In fact, not only did Sister never get back to him about the matter. Neither was the matter ever referred to again. Not even at the next Board meeting.

The matter was apparently dropped. No one ever asked Joe about it again, and he never asked anyone else about it either.

The power of Holy Mother Church is awesome, indeed.

May, 1986
Chatard High School, Indianapolis

"Sorry, Cindy, but the lead female role has been assigned to someone else," said choir instructor, Tammy Anderson.

Cindy's voice was better than ever since she had been taking private voice lessons from Sharon Searles at Butler University. Miss Anderson, however, still refused to give Cindy a staring role in that year's musical performance of **The Wizard of Oz**. Cindy suspected that her choir teacher may have been taken aback by the fact that Cindy had been able to be accepted as a voice student of Professor Searles—something Tammy herself had been unable to achieve.

But, no matter. Cindy decided to go ahead and enjoy her role as Mayor of the Munchkins. She got a special kick out of the fact that her brother Phil had been given a chance to play keyboard in the production.

May 18, 1986
Butler University, Indianapolis

"It gives me great pleasure," announced John G. Johnson, the President of Butler, "to present you with an Honorary Doctorate of Humane Letters."

The president then handed Bernie a diploma as a dean draped his new academic hood over his shoulders and arranged the doctoral colors so they would be properly visible from behind.

In the back of Bernie's mind was the awareness that he had once been the recipient of a Fanny Burr Butler Fellowship at the University of Michigan, and he was now being awarded an honorary doctorate by Butler University in Indianapolis.

Ah, the curiosities of fate!

Since Bernie had taught as an adjunct instructor of Classical Greek and Latin at Butler since 1972, the faculty decided to honor him at a special luncheon. Bernie was asked to describe his experience of being selected as Indiana Teacher of the Year.

"I don't want to get all spiritual on you, but I do have to say that being honored in this way, gives a person a feeling of what it must surely be like to be in a "state of grace." The feeling of total well-being is most relaxing. In fact, one begins to feel as though he can do no wrong."

"What has been the reaction of your parents to the honors that you have received?' asked one of the faculty members.

"Of course, they were very impressed. But when I told my dad that I had been given an Honorary Doctorate of Humane Letters by Butler, he just asked me when I was going to earn a real doctorate. But that's the way he is, always encouraging his sons to aim a little higher."

August 1, 1986
Sparta, Wisconsin

It was Bernie's 30th Reunion of his high school senior class, and he had decided, for the first time, to attend.

"You know, Joe, I think I only remember one or two boys from the class. I was only with them for one year," said Bernie.

Joe had been invited by his folks to come to Sparta for the occasion and attend the Reunion Dinner with his brother. Joe was serving as a high school principal at that time and enjoyed chatting with Bernie's former principal, Mr. Gardner.

The only classmate Bernie recognized immediately was Larry Viergge, the baker's son. He was there with his wife, the girl he had married right after graduation. Another boy began to look more familiar the more Bernie talked to him. He had been in Bernie's Physics class and had been specially chosen by Mr. Mangino to learn how to land survey. He was Vernon Zieglar and he had been a very bright student that Mr. Mangino thought might do well as a surveyor. Vernon was now a very rugged farmer, with muscles and meaty handshake to match.

Bernie's neighbor, Physics study partner and dartboard opponent, Ron Johnson, was not in attendance.

So much for close friendships.

Bernie looked around the room for the blond girl who used to wear her hair in a pigtail that showed off the very seductive backsides of her tiny pink ears. There were a lot of women present, but most of them were the wives of other students. Bernie recognized none of them.

The next day Bernie and his brother Joe drove out into the country so Bernie could show his brother the road he used to drive up to climb Sugar Loaf Hill. Sugar Loaf Hill was on private property, and no one was supposed to trespass, but as seniors in high school Bernie and his friends had managed to make it to the top several times. Bernie and Joe didn't trespass this time, but they did park their car in the road at the base of the hill and get out to enjoy the view.

"It's so peaceful here," observed Joe.

"It really is," agreed Bernie. "All you can hear are the sounds of the insects."

Bernie and his brother were creating a memory. A very peaceful moment that they would remember for years.

This special moment, however, turned out to be the calm before the storm. Not too many years later they would both return to Sparta, first to bury their father, and then, much more traumatically, to attempt to pack up their mother's belongings so that she could be moved out of the house that she could no longer manage and down to Indianapolis where Bernie could decide how best to care for her.

August 17, 1986
Sparta, Wisconsin

"Bernard?"

The name, the voice and the tone could pretty well immobilize Bernie, especially when he was answering a late night phone call.

"Hi, Ma. What's up?"

"You have to come home for a couple days," said his mother.

"But I was just there for my reunion. What's going on?"

"Someone's coming from Italy," said his mom. Then, calling to Bernie's dad, she yelled, "TED-a, come here and talk on the phone! Tell your son what's going on. Hurry! It's long distance."

"Hello, son."

"Hi, what's going on?"

Bernie's dad proceeded to tell him that he had received a letter from Italy and that one of the relatives that Bernie had met when he was there in the 1960's was coming to Sparta for a visit. Bernie would have to be there.

The relative turned out to be Giuseppe, the son of Domenico Barci. When Bernie had last seen Giuseppe, he was a small boy with a bad burn on one of his cheeks. He had tripped in his house and fallen face first into a *stufa,* a large bronze platter filled with hot charcoal that was placed in a circular wooden frame in the middle of the floor to heat the main room of the house.

Giuseppe had grown into a handsome young Italian and there was now no evidence of the burn.

At first Bernie wondered how any of the extremely poor relatives he had met in San Marco alla Mattina could possibly afford to travel to America, but that was quickly cleared up.

Giuseppi explained that *Cavalière* Michele Valantoni, the *Padrone* to whom Bernie had been presented during his visit, had died, leaving his wealth and his estates to his son, who subsequently fell in love with and married Giuseppi's sister, Marcella. By a strange twist of fate, the *Padrone*'s son then suddenly passed away, leaving all of his wealth and estates to Marcella who now lived in the Palazzo.

"Adesso, siamo ricci. Viaggio ogni settimana a Roma a fare la spesa," bragged Giuseppe.

And what did he go to buy every week in Rome?

"Vestiti nuovi! Tutti di moda! Siamo ricci!"

As a memento for Bernie, Giuseppe had brought a small ceramic replica of the *Torre Normanna*, the landmark near San Marco about which Bernie's dad had told him as a boy and which Bernie had seen when he visited the city.

The replica had broken on the trip from Italy, but Bernie was able to glue the pieces back together, and, as of 2014, it too remains on display in the author's guest room.

May 17, 1987
Butler University, Indianapolis

"Lillian Rose Barcio," announced the Dean of the Liberal Arts College.

Lillian made her way across the stage of the Hilton U. Brown Theater in which the graduation ceremony was being held.

"Congratulations, Lillian," said Bernie, wearing his doctoral academic hood, as he proudly presented his wife with her college diploma, B.A. with a major in Journalism.

Years earlier, Lillian had interrupted her college education to raise her first family. Then, for many more years, she had worked to help others get their college and post-graduate degrees. And now, at age 55, it was finally her turn. Since she had been employed full time as a Publications Assistant at Butler, she qualified to attend classes tuition-free.

What triggered Lillian's decision to get her college degree was the fact that Butler University had brought in an efficiency expert to see where the University could save money. The expert proceeded to focus primarily on lower echelon positions. After a year of careful scrutiny, his recommendation to save the University money was to dismiss Lillian, one or two other secretaries and some maintenance folks.

In true corporate style, Lillian was given a golden handshake by Sally Walker, Dean of Students.

"As Dean of Students, I have had the pleasure of working with Ms. Lillian Barcio, University Relations Secretary. She has proficient design and publication skills and is a talented and creative person. During the past seven years, she has designed covers for the Butler University <u>Student Handbook</u>, Rush Guide and <u>Guide to Residential Life</u>. She has recommended paper stock and selected pictures.

"She is a delightful person with whom to work. As tension builds up because of publication deadlines, she maintains a pleasant demeanor and sense of humor. Ms. Barcio would be an asset to any work environment."

Lillian, however, had determined to work only for herself in the future. She would work at home both as a typesetter and typist as well as help the author run Pompeiiana, Inc. out of their basement offices.

When spring came, Lillian signed up for 24 tuition-free hours that would enable her to receive her undergraduate degree by the end of the term. Her major was journalism.

Once Lillian was presented her diploma by Bernie, she was ready to begin following her long time dream of publishing a small, neighborhood newspaper.

"Is that a Rolls Royce Limo?" asked Phil as the family moved toward the parking lot.

"Neat, isn't it?" asked Bernie who had hired it for Lillian's special day.

The Limo was an older model Rolls Royce, but it was pure white and very elegant. Lillian had definitely earned this and more.

June, 1987
Broad Ripple, Indiana

Following her graduation, Lillian and Bernie took steps to form a Sub-S Corporation that would be called BLB Enterprises. Working under its aegis, Lillian began to fulfill her aspirations.

Before long, she was laying in the final corrections on the boards for Vol. I, No. 1 of the **Broad Ripple Village Sampler Newspaper**. It would be ready for distribution during the first week of June. She had personally visited all of the merchants in Broad Ripple as soon as she had graduated and had sold them on her idea. She helped the merchants design their ads, she created them on her computer (on which she had installed Ventura Publishing and taught herself how to use it), she came up with all her own story ideas, wrote and edited the stories, took her own photos, and laid in original art and clip art.

She was a one-woman dynamo riding high on the exhilaration that comes from fulfilling one's long-held aspirations.

To supplement the income of BLB Enterprises, Lillian continued typesetting for other publishers as well as typing manuscripts and personal resumes.

Lillian was tirelessly dedicated to making her dream come true—even if it meant having to spend 14 hours a day working at her keyboard and light table in the basement offices.

September 1, 1987
La Crosse, Wisconsin

"Not bad for an old Dago," confided Ted Barcio to his son, Bernie, who was seated in a chair in his hospital room. "I started out as a water boy and ended up as a Roadmaster. I'll bet Johnny Cash could make a good song about my years on the railroad."

"I'll bet he could," said Bernie. "Or maybe someday Joe or I will write a book about all your stories. All those snow and flood stories. They would make an interesting book."

After letting that thought ride for a moment, Bernie asked if it would be O.K. for him to use the restroom in his dad's room.

"Sure. I think so," said his dad.

When Bernie was done, he bent over to flush the toilet and got the surprise of his life.

SPLASH!

"Oh, Man!" said Bernie as water dripped from his face.

"What happened?" asked his dad from his bed.

"I guess I hit the douche lever instead of the flush handle. I'll clean it up."

What an awkward time to do something so stupid! Bernie guessed it must be in his genes or something.

Ted had recently suffered chest pains, and his doctor was about to perform an aortic valve replacement operation. Bernie and Lillian had driven up from Indianapolis and had stopped in at Sparta to drive Bernie's mom to La Crosse. Bernie's Uncle Charlie and Aunt Martha were also on hand to lend moral support.

At first, everything went well, until the time came for Ted to be taken to the operating room. This was apparently more trying than Stella had imagined it would be. She suddenly became a different woman.

"Ma, the lady in the waiting room said that if we want to spend the night here in La Crosse instead of driving back to Sparta, there are homes nearby in which people rent out sleeping rooms very reasonably. How would it be if we looked into that?" asked Bernie.

"Why can't we drive back to Sparta so I can sleep in my own bed?"

"We could, but it would just be a lot more convenient if we stayed in La Crosse. That way, if something happened that we needed to hurry back to the hospital, we would be right here."

"*Musa tu*! What's going to happen?"

"Well, you never know," said Bernie.

At that point Stella decided that Lillian was somehow responsible for her not going to be able to sleep in her own bed that night, and she immediately started standing as far away from her as she could. Nothing Lillian could do to try and talk to her mother-in-law would work. Stella would simply move further down the hall and keep to herself.

After Bernie finally got everyone to agree to at least drive over and look at one of the homes with sleeping rooms, the idea was immediately rejected.

"It's too dark in there. They have too many rugs on the floor. I could trip and fall. Why can't we just drive back to Sparta? It just takes five minutes," observed Stella, still trying to get her way.

"Because it's silly. We should stay here so we can be close to the hospital. Just in case," said Bernie.

"Is there a motel handy, Bernie?" asked his Uncle Charlie. "Maybe your mother would be more comfortable there."

So, they all got back in their cars and drove over to the nearest motel where Bernie was able to get three rooms for the night.

"Bernard. You pay for Charlie's room. Understand?"

"Why sure, Ma. I'll pay for all of them."

In the morning, Bernie, Lillian, Uncle Charlie and Aunt Martha were all refreshed and ready to face the day. Stella, however, looked bedraggled.

"Didn't you sleep well, Stell?" asked Charlie.

"Hell, No! A person can't sleep in a strange bed," replied Stella, ready to make everyone pay because she had not been taken back to Sparta the night before.

"What did you do all night?" asked Bernie.

"I sat in a chair. What do you care about your mother? Your wife wouldn't let you even drive your mother home so she could at least rest in her own bed."

O.K. No point in beating that dead horse any more.

Ted, on the other hand, had a wonderful night. The operation had been a total success, and in a few days he would be released to return home, almost as good as new.

December, 1987
Butler University, Indianapolis

Cindy Barcio had recently finished four successful years at Chatard High School. She was a good student, and had quickly become known for her outstanding voice. She had been a member of Chatard's elite Show Choir, and had sung key roles in school productions of Godspell and The Wizard of Oz.

Since both Cindy's mom and dad worked at Butler University—her mom had worked in the publications office and her dad was still an Adjunct Instructor of Latin—she was offered a full ride scholarship to attend classes as a day student. Cindy, however, wanted the full college experience and chose to live on campus.

Her roommate during her first year at Butler was Christine, a girl fanatically interested in Elvis and The Monkees. Cindy naturally tried out for the choirs at Butler. In typical snooty university fashion, she was told that her voice did not qualify her for the best choir, but she could sing with a lower choir. When she took a class on radio broadcasting, she was told she did not have the "voice" to be a radio announcer. When she signed up for a class on horse riding, she was also quickly disillusioned by the fact that she would have to spend more hours grooming her horse than riding it.

Because the classes at Butler offered little that interested Cindy, she and her roommate quickly got into the social scene on campus.

A year and a half later, Cindy was invited to leave Butler since she had not really been attending classes and seemed to have found no class offerings that either welcomed or enticed her.

January, 1988
Sparta, Wisconsin

There is an old Latin saying that goes, *"In vino veritas."* It means "In wine there is truth." Stella Barcio, however, had her own views about getting to the truth. Her motto, if it had been translated into Latin, would have read, *"In ira veritas"*—"In anger there is truth."

As far as Stella was concerned, she really wasn't getting down to brass tacks with anyone unless she made them angry. In anger she saw sincerity. She believed that what people said to her in a fit of anger—especially when accompanied by cuss words— was really the truth about how they felt. Never mind all that polite stuff that was part of normal social interaction.

Stella, therefore, became a master at "pushing people's buttons" whenever she wanted to have a sincere conversation with them. This, of course, could often produce some unwanted and unpredictable results from those she prodded.

Her husband, Ted, had long since become a master of tempering or re-channeling his angry reactions after she had pushed him to his breaking point. While there were occasions when he could not help but deliver a well aimed slap or shove, he was a very muscular man, even in his old age, and he could have inflicted much more physical damage had he not practiced great self control.

It was in January 1988 that Stella so enraged Ted that, in order to keep from seriously harming her, he simply re-channeled his anger by hurling an armchair against the wall of their living room, breaking the chair and knocking a hole in the wall.

Stella recounted this story to the author when she was in her nineties to show what a temper his father had—not realizing that it also showed to what an extent she prodded him when she needed some angry, serious, truthful interaction.

March, 1988
Sparta, Wisconsin

"Ted, what are you doing?" called Stella from the back door of their house.

"I'm trimming some branches," replied Ted from the ladder on which he was working.

Stella stood for a while and watched. She loved to be a casual observer when someone was working so she could make small—or major—suggestions.

"Ted, don't you see those wires up there?" asked Stella.

"Yes-ah! *Lasa ma ide*!" replied Ted trying to focus on what he was doing.

"Ted, those are electric wires!"

"*Mannagia ciuchia mia*! Yes, Stell, I know!" replied Ted.

"You're going to electrocute yourself, Ted. Come down!" ordered Stella.

"Ce la luna mezzo mare,..." sang Ted as he attempted to diffuse the anger he felt rising in him.

Stella, however, would not let go. She was determined to make her husband come down off of the ladder. She walked over to the garden hose, turned it on, pulled the hose over to the bottom of the ladder and directed the spray at Ted.

"MA TU SEI PAZZA!" yelled Ted as he felt the blast of cold water on his back.

"Musa tu! Come down now, Ted!" ordered Stella.

No matter that she might have caused her husband to fall from the ladder, Stella somehow determined that the risk was worth it to get him to comply with her wishes.

In late August, 1987, Ted had suffered a heart attack. In his old age, his body had become less able to deal successfully with the stresses that were built into his lifestyle.

May 5, 1988
Chatard H.S., Indianapolis

"Let's hurry, Lill. We want to get there a little early to get some good seats," encouraged Bernie.

"Almost ready. Is the back door locked?" asked Lillian.

"Just checked it."

"Are all the cats in?"

"Yup. I think we're all set."

Bernie and Lillian were on their way over to Chatard High School to see their son Phillip perform in the spring musical production, **Grease.**

Although Phil had a decent voice, he was more into instrumental music such as piano, keyboard and guitar. He would, in fact, play accompaniment for his sister Cindy on several professional quality recordings they would make in the future. Cindy recorded both cover songs and original songs that were written by her brother.

In September, Phil would move into the dorm at Ball State University to begin his college career.

September, 1988
Anderson University, Anderson, Indiana

Cindy had always admired the singer Sandy Patty. After she learned that Sandy was a graduate of Anderson University, Cindy decided to apply for admission there.

The story at Anderson, however, was similar to that at Butler. Cindy became more involved in the lives and problems of fellow students than she did in her classes—which she somehow failed to attend. After one semester, Cindy returned home to work as a salesclerk at L. S. Ayres in Glendale.

During all of her college experiences and work as a salesclerk, Cindy continued to sing with a group called The Gathering at the 12:30 p.m. Sunday Mass at Christ the King Church. Her voice constantly earned her uncharacteristic applause whenever she sang an after-communion solo. The leader of the group, John Lenahan, did little, however, to promote her singing and continued to abuse her good will be making her the all-time songbook collector after Mass. When Cindy tried to learn to play the guitar so she could enrich her participation in the group, John seemed to put her down constantly.

February, 1989
Muncie, Indiana
"Hey, you two!" said the campus policeman who had spotted Phil and Shelly near the Ball State library. "Did you two happen to see who wrote all those colored chalk messages on the walls of the library and the theater?"

As he drew closer to Phil and Shelly Redman who were sitting next to the library having a cigarette, he noticed that their faces and hands were stained with red, green, blue and yellow chalk.

"Is that your box of chalk on the grass next to you?" asked the cop.

Phil and Shelly were busted, but good! They had just returned from a Nuclear Freeze activist group meeting and had decided to chalk some nuclear freeze messages on the outside walls of the Ball State Library and theater.

Years later, Phil would muse, "What do they call those criminals who foolishly/arrogantly stay at the scene of the crime so they can see people's reaction to their work? Oh, yeah. They call them stupid!"

Phil and Shelly complied with all the orders of the policeman who finally figured out that he had cornered the culprits. They actually did not know how lucky they were. Not many years later, another Ball State student would be shot dead by a campus cop for not complying immediately with his commands.

"Man, I don't believe this is happening to me," thought Phil to himself.

Sure, at Chatard High School Mr. Stevenson used to predict that all the senior boys were nothing but jailbirds. But Phil had never taken him seriously. He certainly had never imagined that he would find himself being booked and locked in a cell in Muncie, Indiana. At 11:00 p.m. Phil was allowed his one phone call.

"Hey, Laura. This is Phil. Can you do me an big favor and come down and bail us out?"

"Hey, man, why were you busted?" asked Laura.

"Shelly and I were just chalking some signs. How much cash do you have on hand?"

"Oh, wow, Phil! I've only got about twenty bucks."

"Can you do anything to help us out?"

After Phil hung up, Laura thought about what she could do. She didn't have the $200 cash that would be needed to bail Phil and Shelly out. So she called another friend of theirs, Giles, who always mysteriously had cash on hand.

"How much cash do you have on you, Laura?" asked Giles.

"I've only got $20."

"Well, I've got some I can part with, but we'll have to get a few more people to help."

As Phil and Shelly sat in the detention cell, they had some time to think.

"It was just a minor misdemeanor. All we were doing was writing peace messages with chalk. Hell, it would have washed right off in the next rain. No need to get all red about it."

Luckily, Phil kept these thoughts to himself as he calmly awaited his rescuer.

At three a.m., Laura, Giles and six other kids, all with punk rock haircuts and leather jackets, approached the front desk of the Muncie jail. As far as any of them knew, this could just as easily have happened to them, and they, too, would certainly appreciate the help.

Had they not been bailed out, Phil and Shelly had been promised morning donuts by the cop on duty—something neither one of them really missed.

September, 1989
Indiana Business College, Indianapolis

Cindy decided it was time to change her life dramatically. She finally realized that John Lenahan could not be counted on, neither as a close friend nor as one who would be willing to help her promote her singing. Also, she couldn't see herself selling Monet jewelry at L. S. Ayres for the rest of her life.

Also, Cindy had some very weird experiences while sharing apartments first with Rhonda (in which apartment she began routinely to "see" the "Black Shadow Man" lurking in and around one of the apartment closets) who enjoyed openly entertaining male guests on the apartment living room floor, and then with Robin whose life-style turned out to be more than Cindy was prepared to deal with.

The first thing Cindy did to re-orient her life was to get an apartment of her own and then change the spelling of her name to "Cyndi."

These small steps became symbolic of her new outlook on life.

Next, Cyndi applied to and was accepted by Indiana Business College where she successfully earned an Associate's Degree in Business Administration. This degree enabled her to find work and make new friends at Major Tool and Machine Co., (MTM) and Data Processing Services (DPS) in Indianapolis.

When she decided to move to Dallas, Texas, to be closer to Dave Tanner with whom she had become friends while at MTM, she was hired first by International Computer Graphics (ICG) and then by Affiliate Computer Services (ACS).

Although Cyndi has made several sound recordings, and has tried out for lead singer positions with bands, she has not seriously pursued a career in music. If invited, however, she gladly graces wedding services with a variety of excellently performed solos.

February 14, 1990
Columbus, Indiana

"Hi Bernie. Mike Pence."

"Hey, Mike, how's it going?" asked Bernie.

Bernie's son-in-law had decided to go ahead and follow his political aspirations even though his own family did their best to discourage him. Forever the teacher, Bernie had strongly encouraged Mike to go for it.

"If you don't give it a try, you'll wonder all the rest of your life whether or not you could have done it," Bernie had encouraged.

So Mike had put together a campaign committee and obtained the endorsement of the State Republican Party to run for congress against the incumbent Democrat, Phil Sharp.

"Say, Bernie, the State Republican Party has asked me to address a special Valentine's Day gathering, and Karen and I would love it if you and Lillian could attend," said Mike.

"Hey, that's great, Mike. I'll check our schedule. If we can make it, I know we would both be honored to be there," said Bernie.

"One thing, Bernie," continued Mike. "Would you and Lillian be coming alone or would Phil be joining you?" asked Mike.

"Why do you ask?"

"Bernie, the committee and I would really prefer it if Phil didn't attend," said Mike.

Bernie just stood there dumbfounded, holding the receiver in his hand and saying nothing.

"You there, Bernie?" asked Mike.

"Yes, I'm here. Why don't you want Phil to be there?" asked Bernie.

"Well, with his long hair and all, he just doesn't fit the image that Karen and I would want to have seated at our table. I'm sure you understand," said Mike.

"Oh, I understand, Mike," said Bernie. "You know, Mike, we're a family. If Phil isn't welcome, then I'm afraid that Lillian and I won't be able to be make it either."

"O.K., Bern. No hard feelings, I hope," said Mike.

Bernie hung up the phone. He had heard that politics could do strange things to a person. He had never imagined that this would be one of them.

As it turned out, Mike Pence would lose his bid for Congress in 1990 even without Phil in attendance. He would lose again in 1992. The way the district was laid out, Phil Sharp was just too powerful of an incumbent to beat at the polls.

Sunday, May 27, 1990
Muncie, Indiana

"I think you'll like this next song," announced Phil from the stage on which he was performing with his college band, FIRE HYDRANT, MAN. "It's called 'Big Ass El Dorado' ."

Guitars and bass twanged, drums and tambourines beat, and a flute blew as Phil belted out the words to the song he had written. He was being accompanied by Chris Barton, Todd Hamilton, Kriss Luickett, Matt Hart and Kevin Martensen.

Before the set was over, Phil invited his sister, Cindy, on stage to sing one of her signature songs that she did so well.

Even though FIRE HYDRANT, MAN hadn't been allowed to set up on stage at The Flying Tomato until 9:00 p.m., the audience held and broke into wild applause at the conclusion of "Big Ass El Dorado."

"Could it be that our kids have a future in the music business?" Bernie tried to yell into Lillian's ear over the blasting decibels.

Although the group would spend April 7th and April 14th at Flat Production Studio in Muncie recording **Thirty-five Songs In Dog Years**, a professional quality recording of their five original songs ("Some War-Torn County," "Big Ass El Dorado," "Telephone Pole," "I Wanna Be A Non-Conformist (Just Like You)." and "Flower Lady"), competition on campus was severe, and the group would eventually disband having earned no state, national or international recognition.

Phil, however, was destined to receive some <u>unwanted</u> international recognition within the next several months.

August, 1990
Indianapolis International Airport
"Got your tickets and passport?" asked Phil's dad.

"Yup, they're right here in my jacked pocket."

"Phil," said Gideon Navarro who had also come to the airport to see his high school friend off, "we're gonna try and fly over and see you while you're in London."

"Hope that works out. I'll take you around and show you the sights," said Phil.

Phil had been accepted into Ball State University's London Center Program at Regents College, and he was more than a little excited to begin his adventure.

"This is going to be a great experience for you, Phil," encouraged his dad.

"I'll try to see if I can visit some of the places you saw when you lived in Italy."

"That's right, your program does have several tours arranged on the continent, doesn't it?" asked his dad.

"I think we go to France, Germany and Italy."

"Well, be careful, and stay out of trouble," cautioned his dad.

"O.K.," said Phil as he gave his final hugs to his mom and dad and Gideon before heading down the Jetway.

Although Phil did his best to stay out of trouble, he wasn't entirely successful. When Gideon and a couple other friends flew over to London to spend time with him, their youthful exuberance got them into a couple of scrapes that his parents wouldn't even hear about until Gideon was deliberately trying to embarrass his friend at Phil's Wedding Rehearsal Dinner in Key West, Florida, some 13 years later.

Also, while Phil was visiting Paris, he had decided to purchase a neat walking stick that came with a concealed sword. When December came, and it was time to fly back to The States, Phil knew there might potentially be a problem taking the walking stick on board, so he made some initial inquiries at the ticket counter.

"I have a walking stick that I'm taking back with me. It has a concealed sword in it, and I'm wondering how I can handle it so that it won't be confiscated," asked Phil.

"That should be no problem, Sir," assured the young lady at the ticket counter. "When you get up to the gate, present it to the attendants and ask them to have the captain take it into the cockpit with him. You can retrieve it from the captain after you land in Indianapolis."

Sounded like a good plan, so Phil calmly approached the attendant at the gate and explained what he had just been told to do.

Before he knew what was happening, Phil was being ushered away by airport security and placed in a small holding zone.

"Why are you trying to board the plane with a weapon," pressed the security guard.

"But, I wasn't," explained Phil. "I was just doing what I had been told to do at the ticket counter."

No matter how many times he went over his story, the security guards still did not believe him. He had a certain "trouble maker" look about him that they just loved to profile.

"I'm going to miss my flight," pleaded Phil.

"This is our supervisor," said the security guard as yet another person entered the small room. "Tell him your story once more."

Phil guessed they were trying to get him to trip himself up, but all he did was keep repeating the truth of the situation. In the end, his walking stick was confiscated, and Phil was released with barely enough time to board his plane.

January 16, 1991
Broad Ripple, Indianapolis

"Hap-py birth-day dear Cin-dy. Hap-py birth-day to you!"

No sooner had Cindy cut her cake and passed out the pieces than all the guests at her birthday party were glued to the television set that had been left on in the living room.

Live from Kuwait, the CNN News Team was bringing America the beginning of the Gulf War.

Somewhere among all the Special Forces assigned to fight in that war was a tall young man named Dave Tanner. Dave and Cindy would later work together at Major Tool Co., in Indianapolis and kindle a relationship that would last for at least 10 years and see them both move to Dallas, Texas.

February, 1991
Carmel, Indiana

During his 41-year career in the secondary school classroom, Bernie had had the privilege of working with only two Fifth Year Latin students.

His first was John Soper, a senior at Park School in 1965 when Bernie was hired as Head of the Latin Department. John was a linguistic genius. He had even created an artificial language, complete with vocabulary and grammar. He was way beyond the usual Latin IV authors such as Virgil, Horace and other lyric poets, so Bernie taught him some of the basic linguistic principals he had studied at the University of Michigan and had John reading such exotic texts as Canon Law, the Latin version of the letter that Christopher Columbus wrote after discovering America (Cuba, actually) and selections from Medieval Latin. After college and university where John mastered several modern European languages, he was hired by a department of the United States Government that specialized in international intelligence gathering. Unfortunately, John was soon to be stabbed to death in Turkey while on a plainclothes mission.

Bernie's next opportunity to work with an extremely talented student came when he met Kathleen Harlow, a Latin student at Carmel High School. As soon as Kathy appeared in his Latin II class, Bernie knew that she was a special student. She could read Latin fluently and was definitely ready to be challenged. Over the next couple of years, Bernie worked with Kathy as an Independent Study student and let her go at her own speed. When Kathy took the Fifth Year National Latin Exams that were offered to her as a senior, she earned all perfect scores. She was honored by the **Indianapolis Star** as a 1991 Indiana Academic All-Star.

As an Academic All-Star, Kathy was invited to nominate the Carmel High School teacher who had most influenced her academic career.

> "Mr. Bernard Barcio, my Latin teacher made it possible for me to take an unusual yet highly rewarding approach to my studies and to go beyond what even I thought I could accomplish. From the time I entered Mr. Barcio's Wonderful World of Latin, my respect for him and his subject grew. Without his enthusiasm and his unique, flexible teaching style, I doubt I would ever have come close to my present love for the Latin language and language studies in general. Mr. Barcio is not merely an adequate or a good teacher, but an outstanding one, for he has given me encouragement, confidence, integrity, and the power to think at a higher level. I would like to address my final statement specifically to him: *Tibi satis gratias agere numquam potero. Namque talibus ex factis gratiae numquam morientur.* (I will never be able to thank you enough, for the benefits of such deeds will never die.)"

Unlike John Soper, Kathleen was able to thrive in her chosen career—a family physician. Bernie would later receive the following e-mail from Kathleen Harlow, who now signs her name Dr. Kathleen Yang.

> "Dear Dr. Barcio,
>
> "Greetings! This is Kathleen Yang (formerly Kathleen Harlow), and I am writing you from my home in Cincinnati. I've found it is a very small world. I am a family physician practicing in Northern Kentucky/Greater Cincinnati. I started my first job out of residency this past August and am still accepting many new patients to build my practice. One of my new patients a few months ago was Kathy Ellifrits, a colleague of yours in the community of Latin teachers. As soon as I found out she taught Latin at Walnut Hills High School in Cincinnati, I asked her if she knew you. She said you were quite a legend in the Latin community.
>
> "I said, 'That's the man! He was my high school Latin teacher and my most memorable teacher during those years.'
>
> "I'm sorry to say that my husband, Dr. Michael Yang (who is a pediatric ophthalmologist) took only one year of high school Latin. But he has many other fine qualities! I have found my years of studying Latin to have reaped me many benefits, from winning at 'Balderdash' to easy mastery of medical lingo. Thanks again for many fun and rewarding years!"

April 25, 1991,
Sparta, Wisconsin

"Can't you hurry and get him out of there?" insisted Stella.

She had been working in the yard for quite a while that morning, and when she finally went back into the house to use the restroom, she discovered her husband, Ted, collapsed on the bathroom floor. She had called 911 immediately, and was now not happy about how slowly the Sparta Policeman seemed to be reacting to the emergency. Unfortunately, although Stella did not yet realize it, Ted was already dead, and there was little for the policeman to do.

"Look, Mrs. Barcio, he's already stiff. There's nothing that can be done to help him."

It was a terrible ordeal for Stella, one that she would recount years later while living in an Indianapolis retirement home.

She and Ted had lived a full and busy life after his retirement from the railroad. They both took evening classes at Sparta High School where they studied oil painting, baking, cooking and woodworking. They also kept a very well tended yard and vegetable garden.

Stella continued to bake voluminously on holidays, mailing out scores of special loaves of Easter Bread and hundreds of Christmas cookies.

Ted refinished used furniture that he picked up at bargain prices, and he produced hundreds of woodcraft items—none of which he was ever allowed to sell or give away.

Over the years, they had slowly filled their house with their craft items and collectibles—to the point that it became necessary for their sons to rent two storage units in town to which rooms of items could be transported.

As the author was settling his parents' estate following the death of his mother in 2003, he carefully distributed his father's wood craft items and paintings to family members. He mailed the contents of two extra-large plastic bags filled with crocheted items to family members, including one small box sent to Lillian's estranged dauther, Marsha.

Stella was now suddenly alone.

April 30, 1991
Sparta, Wisconsin

Bernie couldn't believe it. His dad had been an executive on the Chicago & Northwestern Railroad. He always seemed to have scores of friends. And he came from a large extended family. Yet his was one of the most sparsely attended funerals that Bernie had ever experienced. He just couldn't believe it.

He had personally called at least half of the relatives in Chicago and Milwaukee and had shared the specifics of the funeral arrangements.

After a while, it would, of course, come to make sense. Stella had effectively alienated just about all of Ted's family over the years, and they did not relish traveling across the state of Wisconsin just to expose themselves to further insults. There was, however, one of Ted's sisters, Esther and her husband George Duga, who simply decided that this was her brother. She was not going to let her sister-in-law's tongue or habits prevent her from attending his funeral.

Years later, after Bernie had taken steps to re-establish relations with all of the Barcios, Ted's brother Gene would write: "Bernie, NO ONE LOVED my brother more than I did even though we were not allowed to spend much time together, including at his funeral, which hurt me very, very much."

Months later, Bernie would learn that both his Uncle Angelo and Aunt Helen, although they had taken his call and seemed to be communicating rationally, were both suffering from mild Alzheimer's disease and could not process the information or pass it onto their children so they could attend.

Most of Ted's railroad buddies, as it turned out, had either passed away themselves or were too infirm to attend. Those friends that he had made in town or through his affiliation with St. Patrick's church were also put off by Stella's sharp tongue and unpredictable responses.

Only a few members of the Knights of Columbus, to which Ted belonged despite the objections of Stella, attended.

And what, at that time, seemed like adding insult to injury, Stella insisted that her husband be buried in the Nudi family plot in St. Mary's Cemetery in South Chicago. The final separation from his family in Milwaukee.

Bernie and Joe couldn't believe it! They objected. They looked to their Uncles Gusty and Charlie for some support, but neither of them dared to tangle with their sister in her emotional state. Stella won, and an even smaller funeral party traveled to South Chicago for the interment.

Years later, Stella's brother, Gusty, would tell her by phone that her husband should not have been buried in the Nudi family plot. He didn't belong there. He even told Stella that she should have her sons move the coffin elsewhere. Bernie only wished that his Uncle had lent his support in Sparta when the initial decision was being made. He definitely was not about to move his father's coffin after the fact. Besides, he had already had his mother's name and birth date engraved next to his father's on the grave marker. She would share the burial plot next to his, both of which were located directly behind the burial plots of Stella's mom and dad. In fact, all four share the same granite gravestone, now engraved on both its faces. This stone had been imported from Italy when Tony Nudi had originally purchased it.

June, 1991
Milwaukee, Wisconsin

Bernie and Lillian had paid a return visit to Sparta to see how Stella was faring. Since she frequently refused to answer her phone for days on end, it was really the only way to check on her. Of course, Bernie could always call the Sparta Police Department and have them go over to the house to check on her, but that only works once or twice.

"Yes-ah," said Stella very annoyed to have been forced to answer her door. "Why were you pounding on all my windows?"

"Mrs. Barcio, are you all right?"

"Of course I'm all right!"

"Is something wrong with your phone?" asked the Sparta cop who had agreed to visit her house.

"No. There's nothing wrong with my phone," snapped Stella.

"Then why don't you answer it? Your son has been trying to call you."

"Well, if he wants to call me, he should just keep trying. I don't answer unless someone keeps trying for a long time. Then I know it's important."

Since Stella did not know how to write checks, Bernie went ahead and used this trip to convince his brother Joe to travel to Sparta once a month and write checks for their mother. Joe tried to stick to the agreement, but after finding himself locked out of the house and finding his mother absolutely impossible to deal with during his visits, he quickly abandoned the job.

Check writing was next taken over by a local Sparta woman until Stella became suspicious of her asking too many questions. After that, her brother Gusty would drive over from Necedah and try to manage her affairs for her.

Although both Bernie and Joe knew that their mother could not go on living alone in her house, they also knew that any attempt to get her to sell enough stuff to be able to move into an apartment would be futile. So they pretty much just decided to leave her be and see what happened.

After this particular trip to Sparta, Bernie suddenly made a decision.

"If it's all right with you, Lill, I think I would like to drive through Milwaukee on our way home and visit my dad's relatives."

Something in the back of Bernie's head told him that this was the right thing to do. Too many years had passed since all relations had been broken off with them. Not only had they not attended his 50th Wedding Anniversary in Madison, but only one of his sisters, Esther, had been brave enough to attend his funeral.

Uncle Gene and Aunt Mary were tearfully happy to see Bernie and to finally meet Lillian. After spending time catching up and resolving to maintain a closer relationship in the future, Bernie and Lillian next visited Aunt Yolanda who was also thrilled to re-establish contact with her nephew and have a chance to meet his wife.

"On the way home, we would like to stop in and visit Aunt Angeline," announced Bernie before leaving Yolanda's apartment.

"Oh, Hon, she'll be thrilled to see you," said Yolanda.

"You'll have to tell us how to find where she lives."

"Oh, Honey, I think you'd better call Uncle Gene for that. I know where she lives, but I wouldn't be able to tell you how to get there."

Because of the impromptu visits, everyone got a chance to get a lot of things out into the open, and Bernie felt that he and Lillian had done a good thing by helping to erase a lot of the guilt everyone felt for having severed relations with their brother because of run-ins they had with Stella over the years.

Aunt Angeline was both surprised and relieved to put an end to years of tense separation from her brother's family. After spending some time catching up on all the lost years, Aunt Angeline, true to her Italian background, made a special point of reminding Bernie that he still had filial responsibilities towards his mother.

"She's still your mother. You have to love and respect her, no matter how difficult she is to deal with."

Point well taken!

"Aunt Angeline," said Bernie before he and Lillian got ready to leave, "I think it would be nice if we could arrange a reunion of all the Barcio family. That way Joe and his family and I and my family would be able to see all our cousins and their families."

The seed was planted. Before too long, Rudy and Rose Aloia would arrange for the whole family to get together for a Dutch-treat dinner (cash or check only) at a country club to which they belonged.

After that wonderful event—which gave Bernie a chance to renew his acquaintance with his cousin Franny and finally move past their embarrassing encounter all those years ago—everyone was invited to Jeannie and Ralph Mallo's house to keep the party going.

Bernie couldn't believe it. It was like stepping back 40 years. Jeannie and Ralph had their basement set up as a party room exactly as Nanna and Papa had used their basements for all family events. Even some of the same knickknacks were displayed that Bernie had once seen as a child in his grandfather's house.

The side trip to Milwaukee to re-establish relations with the Barcio relatives turned out to be the absolutely best thing that could have been done. For everyone's sake.

June 5, 1992
St. Louis, Missouri

"This is actually exciting," said Bernie. "All those years we lived near the Mississippi River, I used to see these big steamboats go by and wonder what it would be like to be on one."

For their 25th Wedding Anniversary, Bernie and Lillian had reserved luxury accommodations on the Mississippi Queen, an old-fashioned paddleboat that still traveled between St. Paul, Minnesota and New Orleans. Since the entire trip would have taken more time than they had (and cost twice as much), they had opted to board the paddleboat at the half-way point in Memphis and enjoy the relaxing ride to the mouth of the Mississippi.

Their 25th Wedding Anniversary party in Indianapolis was a little smaller than the one that had been staged for Bernie's folks in Sparta. Cindy invited her brother and Karen and Mike over to her Broad Ripple apartment to help cut the Anniversary cake. But even though the gathering was modest, she did do it up properly. There were silver balloons and a silver Happy Anniversary banner taped to the wall. It really was an enjoyable get-together. And, after all, no big event could have been planned involving extended family and friends since Bernie and Lillian had announced way in advance that they were going to celebrate their anniversary aboard the Mississippi Queen.

Such are the tradeoffs of life.

Neither Bernie nor Lillian knew exactly what to expect on the Mississippi Queen, other than that their room would be large, luxuriously located above deck, have its own balcony and bath, and that the trip would be slow and relaxing. They were, however, both a little shocked as soon as they entered the main salon of the boat.

"Look at that!" said Bernie, staring in disbelief. "It's a sea of white heads! It's Geriatric Central in here!"

"Shhh," hissed Lillian. "There's sure to be some younger passengers somewhere."

If there were, they pretty much stayed in their cabins during the entire cruise. But then, what had Bernie expected? This was, after all, a nostalgic trip down memory lane. Something most young people wouldn't even know about.

During meals on board, Bernie and Lillian managed to get fairly exclusive seating at a two-person table so they could enjoy their "youth" together and not get sucked into Oldfolksville conversations. On the evening of their anniversary, the two lovebirds shared special wine with dinner, followed by a tour around the dance floor—a rare event for Bernie whose legs inevitably turn to lead as soon as he is talked into dancing with anyone.

Afternoons featured old-folk type board games and variety talent shows that Bernie and Lillian boycotted, preferring to spend their afternoons relaxing in their cabin or reading on their private balcony overlooking the muddy Mississippi. They did, however, attend the session at which a Mark Twain impersonator entertained the passengers.

He was good!

"Think I'll go swimming, Lill," said Bernie one afternoon, hoping that maybe some younger folk might be gathered around the ship-board pool.

No such luck. The pool area resembled a beaching area for retired walruses. The pool was miniscule, and the water was cold.

Every so often, the Mississippi Queen would pull into a port to allow passengers to disembark and visit local sites. On one of those stops, Bernie and Lillian got to visit the plantation where the black and white movie **Hush, Hush, Sweet Charlotte** had been filmed. Of course, they would have to watch it on video when they got home.

Another excursion found them photographing a tombstone for a town's special three-legged pet cat. "Tripod" had gone to the Big Litter Box in the Sky on October 15, 1953, and had been buried, complete with elaborate marble headstone, on the lawn of the courthouse. In another southern town, they would photograph the butt end of a civil war canon that had been planted half way down in the center of a main street sidewalk.

Since these excursions almost always turned out to be hot and sweaty events, it was always refreshing to return to the boat and enjoy the cool, complementary, alcoholic drinks that awaited them.

On the final morning, seating in the dining room was up for grabs, and they were forced to mingle. Turned out, many of those on board had traveled all the way from Europe and other parts of the world just to make the historic trip down Mark Twain's River. The one couple from England that they talked with actually was quite interesting.

C'est la vie!

Once they disembarked in New Orleans and located their luggage that was laid out with all the rest on the stone-covered bank of the river, Bernie and Lillian took a cab straight to the airport. They had spent several days in New Orleans to celebrate their fifth wedding anniversary and had done all their local sightseeing at that time.

This time there would be no drive across Lake Pontchartrain, no visits to historical plantations, no late night walks down Bourbon Street to watch the scantily glad girls swinging in and out of bar windows.

Twenty additional years can do a lot to slow a couple down.

May, 1993
Sparta, Wisconsin
"I think it will be the best thing to do, Ma," said Bernie.

This was his fourth or fifth phone call to his mother trying to convince her that she should let herself be moved to Indianapolis so Bernie could better look after her.

"You know how hard it was for me to have a new furnace installed in your house in Sparta last winter. I just live too far away to be able to look after things with you living in Sparta."

"What are we going to do with all my furniture and all my things?"

"We could have a sale in Sparta if you like. Maybe an auction. You like auctions, and you're always saying how people make a lot of money when they auction their stuff off."

"NO! I don't want all the gawkers here looking at everything. All you and Joe want to do is sell everything. You don't appreciate how hard your father and I worked to have what we have."

"I tell you what, Ma. How about if we just pack everything up and move it all down here. Then we can go through it all in our own sweet time and decide what to do with everything."

"Where would I live?"

"We have some nice apartments near our house. It's where Lillian's mother used to live. They have little ponds with ducks and everything."

"I don't know."

"Come on. It will be fun. You'll be able to bake cookies with Cindy and show her stuff you know."

"But I'm more comfortable here. I've got my doctors, and a van takes us to Tomah to get our toenails trimmed. Gusty comes and takes care of my bills. He's smart, and he knows what he's doing."

"Yes, but what if you fall down in the yard again? You said yourself that you were lying out there for a long time before someone helped you."

"Yeah, I finally called to a couple boys who were going down the ally. They helped me up."

"Well, that's dangerous. You shouldn't be living there alone."

"And where will we put all my furniture?"

"We can put it in storage. It will be safe until we get a chance to go through it all."

In the end, Stella finally agreed to have moved to Indianapolis all the stuff in the house—which amounted to a considerable amount of furniture, clothing, handicraft work, photos, memorabilia, sheets and pillowcases, quilts, antiques, tools, and more—as well as all the stuff in a two-car garage that was packed literally to the rafters, including many boxes and barrels that had never been unpacked when the family moved from Norfolk, Nebraska, back in 1955, and all the furniture that Bernie's dad had refinished that occupied two commercial storage units in Sparta.

"Lillian and I will drive up once school is out, and we'll help you to start packing."

"Why do you have to bring her?"

"Because she's my wife! And she's your daughter-in-law. We need her help, so be good about it!"

July 10, 1993
Sparta, Wisconsin

"Is the front door open, Joe?"

"Nope. It's still locked."

"Does she know we're here?"

"She just looked out through the curtain and told me to go to hell. I say we just leave. She can just stay here and rot for all I care."

"I think I know what to do," said Bernie. "Wait here."

Bernie walked around to the back door of the house, which was unlocked, walked into the house and told his mother that he and Joe were there. He then walked over to the front door and let his brother in. Of course, before anything could be packed, the whole discussion concerning the move to Indianapolis had to be reopened, and Stella had to be allowed to vent all her pent up hostilities against her two sons, the "bastard" across the street, etc., etc. Eventually, work did get done, however, and stuff got sorted through and boxed up or stuffed into large plastic trash bags and tied off.

"Why don't you let us take some of dad's old clothes to the Goodwill in Tomah, Ma?"

"There you go. You just want to give everything away. They just sell it. Why should they make the money? Besides, you and Joe should go through it. There are things there you could wear."

Ted's clothes hung from two large pipes that Bernie had suspended from the ceiling in the upstairs kitchen during an earlier visit. They also still took up a lot of room in the master bedroom closet, and on shelves. And in boxes. Bernie intended to get most of his dad's clothes to a Goodwill drop off box in Indianapolis eventually, but, in truth, when the time came for the final move to be made, there was not even room for all of them in the Stewart's Moving Van, in the two large U-Haul trucks or in the small trailer that was hitched behind Bernie's Chevy Blazer. Many had to be surreptitiously and unceremoniously discarded in a huge dumpster that was brought into the garage driveway for the final move.

"I've got a small trailer hooked up to my car, Ma. I'll just take some of these smaller things with me now so we don't have so much to move later on."

Actually, Bernie had been transporting small trailers full of stuff out of Sparta during most of the summer. He had made several trips back and forth. Some of the things Bernie brought back to Indianapolis, and many—especially items personally requested—were delivered to Bernie's Uncle Charlie in Cudahy.

When their time in Sparta was up, and it was becoming evident that there wasn't enough time in the summer for Bernie and Joe to finish packing things by themselves, they tried to get their mom to agree to hiring someone locally to help.

And, believe it or not, Stella finally did hire a young woman to come in and help box up things in the upstairs bedrooms.

"She was a dickens," complained Bernie's mom when Bernie called to see how things were going. "I told her not to come back any more."

"Why? Wasn't she a good worker?"

"All she was doing is asking if she could have this or that for her kids. She said they were poor, and that I had so many things that they could use."

So much for that plan.

July 20, 1993
Sparta, Wisconsin

"So why did you have to call the police?" asked Bernie as his mother told of the latest problems she was having living in the house alone.

"A boy from the County Home next door knocked on my door. When I asked him what he wanted, he said he was thirsty and wondered if he could have a glass of water."

"You didn't let him in did you?"

"I told him to stay in the entryway while I got him a glass of water from the kitchen. But after I gave him the water, and he left, I saw that he had gone through my purse that was on the table under the phone and took $60."

"What are the police going to do?"

"Well, they're going to make him pay it back. The little stinker!"

"Well, don't let those kids in any more. I've got the moving van all lined up so we're going to come up and finish all the packing next month. Try to have everything ready as best you can, O.K.?"

When the police interrogated the boy from the County Home, he insisted that he had only taken $20 which he returned. It was his word against Stella's, and, as far as the police were concerned, the case was closed.

July 30, 1993
Sparta, Wisconsin

When Bernie, Lillian and Joe returned to Sparta for the final move, they really weren't too surprised to see that nothing much had been done in their absence. But they had four days to finish before the Stewart's Moving Van would arrive from Indianapolis, and they felt sure they could do it. To maintain a little sanity and provide a sane refuge for themselves each night, they had booked rooms at the Sparta Inn at the end of Water Street.

The work was very strenuous, and the hours were long with hardly a decent break for meals. Finally, however, everything was boxed, wrapped, sacked or packed except for the kitchen.

The kitchen was Stella's last bastion of defense. She had refused to let anyone touch anything in the kitchen all week. She wanted to handle everything in the kitchen herself. In her own way. By the last day, however, it was obvious that she wasn't going to be able to do it. There would have to be a showdown.

"O.K., Ma," began Bernie when everyone arrived at the house early the next morning to begin the final day's work. "The first thing we're going to do today is pack up the kitchen."

"*Musa tu*! Don't touch my kitchen!"

"Ma, we have to. The truck is coming tomorrow, and we have to be ready."

"Well, you'll just have to come back another time and finish."

That was it. That was the final button. And Stella had just pushed it.

"NO, BY GOD, WE'RE NOT GOING TO COME BACK ANOTHER TIME!" screamed Bernie at the top of his lungs as he moved closer to where his mother sat so she could get the full effect of the anger in his face.

Joe immediately jumped to his feet and threw himself on his knees between his mother and his brother, thinking that Bernie was about to lose total control and get physical.

Bernie would actually never have done that, but he <u>was</u> going to win <u>this</u> argument on *this* day.

"WE'RE GOING TO PACK THE KITCHEN TODAY, AND WE'RE GOING TO LOAD THE TRUCK TOMORROW, AND WE'RE MOVING YOU DOWN TO INDIANAPOLIS. YOU'VE GOT TO GET IT THROUGH YOUR HEAD. WE-HAVE-NO-MORE-TIME! *CAPISCE*?"

To make a long story short, the kitchen got packed. The Stewart's Moving Van arrived and was packed to the roof. A large U-Haul truck got stuffed. The small U-Haul trailer hitched to Bernie's Chevy Blazer was not only packed full, but it also had things tied to its roof. There was still too much stuff left to be loaded.

"We're going to have to get another truck," said Bernie.

The first thing he did was to ask the Stewart's driver if his company could send another moving van from Indianapolis. That turned out to be impossible. He then called the U-Haul dealer in La Crosse to see if it had another large truck that could be rented. They did.

Success! Sort of.

Once the 2nd large U-Haul truck was loaded, Bernie noticed that there was something drastically wrong with it and it would not be able to make the trip to Indianapolis. So he had to drive the loaded truck to La Crosse and watch as the U-Haul crew took the stuff out of the disabled truck and reloaded it into one that would be able to make the trip.

"Who's going to drive the second truck?" asked Joe.

Bernie intended to drive the first U-Haul while Lillian would drive the Chevy Blazer with its small trailer in toe.

"I know," suggested Bernie. "Let's ask the guy from across the street that we hired to help us pack. You know him from when you were a principal in Mauston, don't you?"

"Yes, I do. He was a bit of a trouble maker in school, but he does seem to have settled down."

The guy from across the street was more than willing to make an extra $100 driving the 2nd U-Haul truck to Indianapolis, but when Bernie asked to see his driver's license, he turned out not to have one.

A back up driver was located by simply walking into a Sparta bar and asking if there was someone available to drive a U-Haul Truck to Indianapolis.

"We'll pay you $100 and pay for your bus ticket back to Sparta along with an allowance for meals and motel."

Now, granted this is not the best way to hire someone that you intend to trust your belongings to, but at this point in the game, there weren't that many options.

"What's the worst thing he can do?" asked Bernie. "Drive off with a truck load of stuff? That would just mean we would have less to deal with in Indianapolis."

The new driver, however, in addition to being able to show a valid driver's license, turned out to be absolutely reliable.

Everything ended up getting loaded except for an antique shelf in the basement and Stella's beloved kitchen table that she had had since the beginning of her married life.

"Ma," explained Bernie, "We'll just have to come back and get it later."

"No. Find room. Tie it on top of something."

This was, in the end, the final showdown, and Bernie was learning how to win.

Since Joe was unable to drive down to Indianapolis with the caravan, he returned home. There was no way that Stella could have been gotten into the front seat of the U-Haul truck with Bernie and there wasn't any room for her in the Chevy Blazer either. The solution was to hire a local Sparta cab driver and his wife, with both of whom Stella was friendly and comfortable, to drive Stella to her new apartment in Indianapolis.

Once everyone was loaded up and ready to roll, Stella announced that they should all go for breakfast first at a small restaurant near the tracks where she and Ted occasionally ate.

"What harm can there be in that?" asked Bernie. "Why don't you come along, Joe. We'll all eat, and then we can head out."

What harm, indeed.

"I want no cholesterol eggs," said Stella.

"But, Ma'am, we only have real eggs."

"Sure you have them. They're called Egg Beaters or something."

"No, Ma'am. I'm sorry, but we don't have them."

"Go talk to the cook in the kitchen. He'll know what I want."

"Mom, she knows what you want, but they just don't serve them here," interrupted Bernie.

It wasn't easy, and it wasn't pretty, but the message finally got through.

Stella would have to lose her last argument over her last meal in Sparta.

Both the kitchen table and the antique shelf in the basement were eventually sold by the realtor to a collector to whom she had shown the house prior to its sale.

But the sale of the house at 307 N. Water Street in Sparta is, as they say, a whole "nother" nightmare.

Tullia (R) and her kittens

Ted Barcio Retirement Party
August 26, 1972

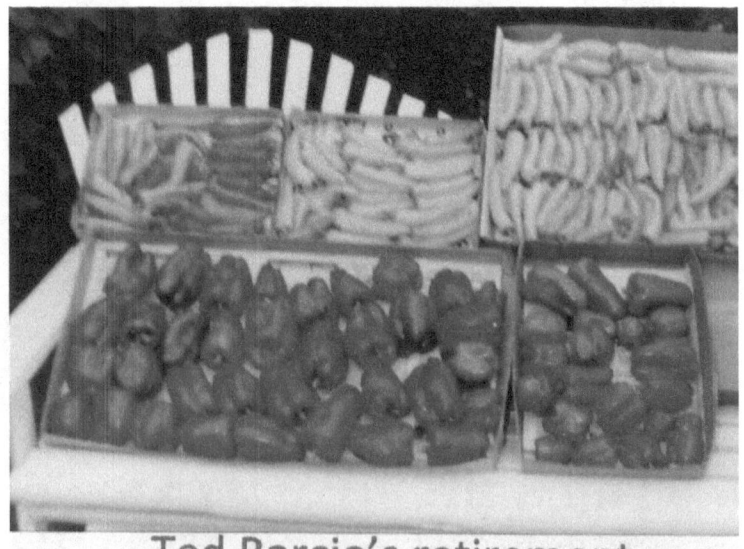

Ted Barcio's retirement garden produce

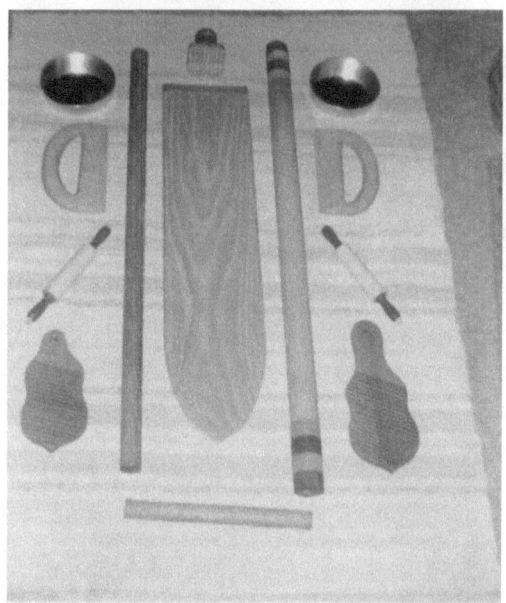

Ted Barcio's retirement woodwork projects

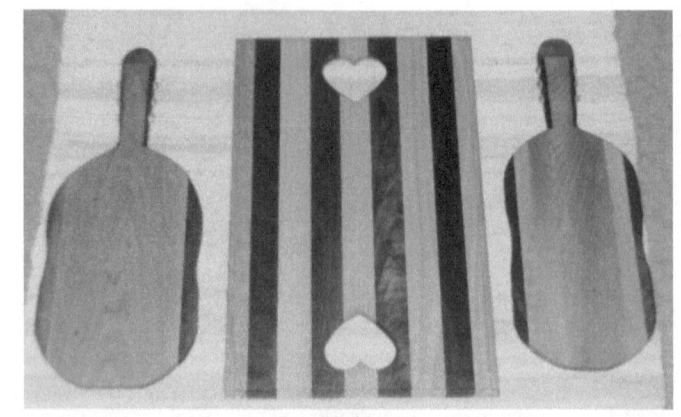

Ted Barcio's retirement oil paintings

Stella Barcio knitting projects

Stella Barcio's Easter Bread and Italian *Piscia Lite*

Stella Barcio Easter Bread varieties displayed on Ted's cutting boards

(L to R) Lillian, Shirley & Jack Hacker, Author
August 4, 1973

Author (3rd from L): Pompeiiana display at Penrod Art Fair, Indpls., Sept. 1974

Author presents travel prize to
Latin teacher Brenda Waddle
May, 1980

Brenda Waddle visits the
Getty Museum, Malibu,
July 18, 1980

Author gives orientation at a Chariathon held at the Indpls. Motor Speedway, 1984

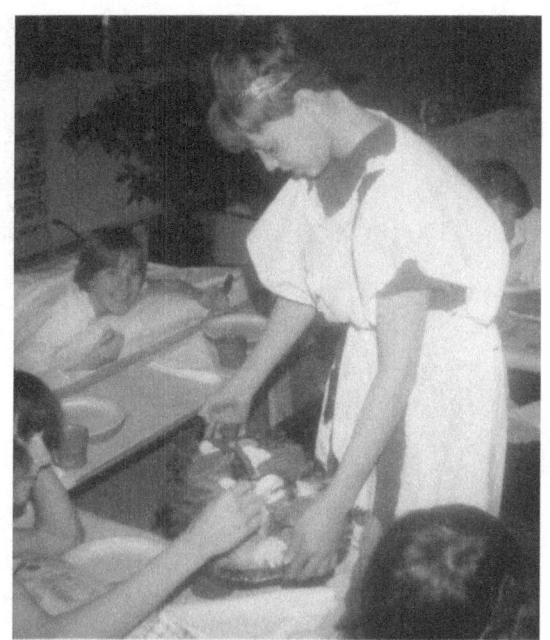

Philip Barcio serves at a Pompeiiana Latin Weekender Conference

The author: Marcus Loreius Tiburtinus

Author: Fabius the Tribune

Author: Fr. Guido Sarducci

Mary Hyde's NCHS Zephyrus sets a catapulting Record, April 21, 1977

Cyndi Barcio hangs stockings from the walnut mantel, December, 1973

Phillip Barcio on his Big Wheel, 1977

Playground the author built from catapult timbers, 1977

Aunt Helen (Dood)
(b. June 17, 1917—d. March 13, 2007)
John Kemp
(b. Sept. 25, 1915—d. March 15, 2002)

Stella and Ted Barcio
50th Wedding Anniversary
Madison, WI, August 18, 1984

Stella Barcio wearing her
1934 marriage negligee,
holding a recreation of her
wedding bouquet, August 18, 1984

Author with step-daughter Karen Pence, June 8, 1985

Author with daughter-in-law Audrey Barcio, May 17, 2003

Author with niece Liz Biggs, 1996

Author with niece Liz Miller, 2005

(L to R) President Johnson, Grace Mullen, Joe Lamberti, Author
Butler Univ. Honorary Dr. of Humane Letters, May 18, 1986

Mother of Lillian Barcio, Pearl Madden Hacker
September 28, 1913—September 28, 1985

Giuseppe Barci & Ted Barcio
Sparta, WI, August 17, 1986

Author (L) & Giuseppe Barci
La Crosse, WI, August, 1986

Author presents his wife Lillian with her Butler Univ. Degree in Journalism, May 17, 1987

(L to R) Phil, Cindy, Lillian, Bernie Barcio, Karen and Mike Pence, May 17, 1987

PART IX

August 1993 –August 2004

Life on Indianola
After Moving Stella Barcio to Indianapolis

August 15, 1993
Indianapolis

"You ready, Lillian?" called Bernie. "It's *Mezz' Augusto*, you know. Can't be late."

"When we pick your mom up, am I going to have to sit in the back seat?"

"Well, she usually likes the front seat, but we can try and see what she does."

Bernie had settled his mom into a nice ground-floor apartment at the Glenbrook Apartments, no more than five minutes away from his home on Indianola. Her most precious belongings and favorite furniture had been moved in, and she even had a spare bedroom in which all her quilts could be stored. There was, of course, a lot more things with which she refused to part that would not fit in her apartment. A commercial storage unit had to be rented for these a couple blocks further south on Keystone.

At first, things seemed to go fairly well. Then Bernie discovered that although his mom had always been a renowned and excellent cook, she was no longer able to prepare her own meals. Thinking back, he realized that for the past few years of his parents' life together, his dad appeared to have been doing most of the cooking. After her husband passed away, Stella had apparently been living on fresh fruit and pre-cooked food such as whole cooked chickens that can be bought at the grocery. So one of the first things that Stella did after she was moved into her apartment was to insist that Bernie come over each evening and cook for her.

This was not going to work at all.

Also, since he realized that his mom needed help keeping her apartment clean, he quickly found an efficient young black woman to clean and help prepare meals.

Before long, however, Stella convinced her helper that her son was trying to take over her life and take control of all her finances. The young black woman agreed to help Stella find legal help so she could maintain her independence.

While it was true that Bernie was managing all his mom's financial affairs, it really could not be any other way since she was unable to write checks or deal with the public effectively. She did, however, quickly discover how to contact the main office of the apartment complex and insist that she had ants and cockroaches in her apartment. They, of course, checked and even treated the apartment. The complaints, however, did not cease.

Bernie was finally forced to admit that his mother really was not in any condition to be living on her own. The apartment complex managers no longer wanted to deal with her endless complaints, and she not only needed help with her cleaning and cooking, but she also needed someone to oversee her medications, which Bernie discovered she was not taking as prescribed.

"You know, Lillian," Bernie finally had said, "I think we need to have my mom evaluated by someone to see whether she should be in an assisted living setup rather than on her own."

"Why don't you call the St. Vincent Geriatric Center to see what they suggest?"

Bernie quickly learned that it indeed was possible to have a geriatric psychiatrist evaluate his mom and make some recommendations. When he suggested the plan to his mother, however, she absolutely refused to have any part of it. She saw the move as another indication that Bernie was trying to deprive her of her rights.

"Isn't there some way to have her evaluated against her will?" asked Bernie as he continued his discussions with the Geriatric Center.

"Only if you can show that she is a potential danger to herself."

"How do I show that?"

"If she gets herself into a problem, you will have to involve the police and have your mom transported to Methodist hospital for evaluation. Once police involvement and hospital evaluation have been documented, then we can hold her here against her will until we have a psychiatrist evaluate her ability to live on her own."

When they drove into Glenbrook Apartments that Sunday morning to take Bernie's mom to *Mezz' Augusto* Mass, they had no idea that this was going to be Intervention Sunday.

"Hi, Ma, you ready to go to church?"

"Is your wife with you?"

"Well, yes. We always go to church together."

Stella tensed up, but made her way to the front door of her apartment hallway. As soon as she stepped outside the door and saw Lillian sitting in the front seat of the car, she flipped. Releasing her walker, she raised both her hands to the sides of her head and proceeded to put a double-*cornuto* curse on Lillian.

"Ma, what are you doing?" said Bernie.

"Musa tu. Diaulo maledetto scataruzo! Cadu mano! Cadu mano!"

And it went on from there. Nothing Bernie could say or do could get his mom to quit her deliriously worded string of Italian curses and imprecations. She was a raging woman totally out of control. Bernie could not believe the contorted expressions on her face.

"This is it," Bernie thought. "She needs help. Now!"

Bernie walked back to the car and told Lillian to drive over to a pay phone and call 911.

When the police arrived and began talking with Stella, she suddenly lapsed into her pleasant little old lady routine. After Bernie finished getting rid of his frustrations by taking a few well-aimed punches at a tree with his bare knuckles, he was finally able to explain to one of the officers what had just taken place. He formally requested that they help in having his mom taken to Methodist Hospital for the prerequisite exam.

"But I just want to go to church. Bernard! Come here. Let's go to church. It's *Mezz Augusto!*" she said in a weak, humble little voice.

"No, Ma. We're not going to do that today. They are going to take you to the hospital in the ambulance and make sure that everything's O.K."

Now, nobody actually believes in Italian *cornuto* curses anymore, do they? While Bernie and Lillian certainly don't want to believe that his mother had any special pull with the Devil, it does seem to be more than coincidence that this event coincided with the beginning of a long series of health problems that Lillian would have to endure, everything from macular degeneration to cancer.

Bernie and Lillian figured that once an evaluation was completed at Methodist, his mom would be held there until alternate living arrangements could be worked out. Instead, about 10:00 o'clock at night the call came that Stella had been released and returned to her apartment.

"But she really isn't able to stay there alone!" insisted Bernie.

"I'm sorry, Sir. We had no legal grounds to continue to detain her here."

The next day, Bernie quickly located a service that provided home nursing care. Arrangements were made for a nurse to meet Bernie at his mom's apartment.

"Hi, Ma," said Bernie as he unlocked the door and let himself in.

"What the hell do you want?"

"I'm your son. I want to help you. *Capisce?*"

"Get the hell out! Who's that you have with you?"

"Ma, this is a nurse who is going to stay with you and help."

"Musa tu! Tu sei Pazzo! Diauolo maledetto!"

As Bernie tried to let the nurse into the apartment, his mom suddenly used her walker to attack the woman and push her back into the hall.

This was all that Bernie needed. He dismissed the nurse and drove home to contact the Geriatric Center. He now had all the legal precedent he needed to have her evaluated against her will.

August 21, 1993
Vancouver, British Columbia

"Here, Mom and Dad, this poster for **Little Rabbit** is for you," said Phil.

"Is this the poster for the film you wrote and directed?" asked his dad.

"Yes," said Phil. "We each had a chance to pitch story lines for film projects, and both of mine were chosen to be produced."

Phil was completing his eight-month term at the Vancouver Film School to which he had been accepted after he decided he wanted to pursue some career related to filmmaking. After he had been accepted, a friend of his from Indianapolis, Ross Simpson, also applied and was accepted into the program.

"Did Ross help with **Little Rabbit**?" asked Phil's mom.

"He served as the Chief Lighting Technician, and then he and I and a couple of other guys did the music for the film," said Phil.

"How much time do we have before the films are screened?" asked Phil's mom.

"I think they'll start in about a half hour so we had better head on over to the theater," suggested Phil.

Phil's other idea that he had pitched for a film the class could make was to do a documentary on a bus driver that Phil had met and come to know and respect as he traveled around Vancouver.

"The guy is incredible," Phil said. "He's a real bundle of energy. He's a musician and he's got more stories than a person has time to listen to."

"What's the name of that film?" asked Phil's dad.

"It's just called **Bus Driver**."

During his months at Vancouver Film School Phil had been introduced to every aspect of film making from story line pitching, script writing, lighting and key grip to directing, camera operations, sound mixing and editing. He and Ross could hardly wait to enter what they had heard could be a very lucrative line of work.

"Did you ever work out that little problem you had over the trash incident?" asked Phil's dad.

"Oh, yeah. That was just a lot of hassle over nothing," said Phil. "I think they just wanted to flex their administrative muscles. Nothing came of it."

Phil had called home about half way through the school term to explain that he had gotten into trouble in the editing room one night. He and others were editing film, and the process was long and tedious. To break the monotony, Phil had rummaged through a trash container in the room and fashioned what he decided was a fairly decent piece of modern trash-art from the things he had found. It was so neat that he left it on display in the room when they finished their work for the evening. The editing instructor, however, did not think it was neat at all and threatened to have Phil expelled for wasting valuable equipment and resources.

"Do you think this is all a big joke?" he had yelled at Phil after he called him in the next day. "Well, it isn't! If you're not going to take your course work seriously, we can just have you out of here," said the instructor.

Phil tried to look repentant and serious even though it was hard not to smile when a Canadian pronounced the word "out" in that funny way all Canadians have of saying it.

After graduation, Phil and Ross returned to Indianapolis where they founded BIG DONUT MOVIES for the express purpose of producing the motion picture creations of the partners. They hoped that **Life On Mars**, a script written by Phil, would be their first feature length production.

Indianapolis, however, turned out to be a very hard market. They quickly learned that the Indianapolis film scene was very in-group-ish and next to impossible to break into.

Eager to make a start somewhere, the partners finally decided that there were more opportunities to find work in the film business in Houston, Texas. So, in mid-winter they loaded their things into a rented truck (once they finally found one that could actually run in cold weather) and headed south.

September 1, 1993
St. Vincent's Stress Center, Indianapolis

It took some doing, but Bernie had managed to get his mom to get into his Chevy Blazer and let herself to be driven to the "hospital" so she could see a doctor.

"Ma, do you remember when you had a nervous breakdown in Nebraska?" asked Bernie daring to open a touchy subject.

"*Musa tu*. I never had a nervous breakdown."

"Don't you remember when you were in the hospital in Omaha for a while, and then when you got back home, dad had a special metal cover made with light bulbs under it so you could lie under it to relax your back."

"What? Do you think your mother's crazy?"

It was a tense ride over, and Bernie kept an eye on his mom to make sure she didn't do anything stupid like grab the wheel and crash them both into oncoming traffic. When they got to the Stress Center, they were met by a pleasant young receptionist who welcomed them into her small office where some paper work could be completed.

"Mrs. Barcio, would you like a glass of orange juice?"

"*Musa tu*!"

"Ma, she just wants to know if you would like something to drink," explained Bernie. "She's just being polite."

"How do I know she won't put something in it to knock me out?"

"Mrs. Barcio, we would never do anything like that. If you don't care for anything, that's perfectly all right."

Finally, all the paper work was done, and two orderlies appeared in the doorway.

"Mrs. Barcio, these two gentlemen are going to help you back to your room where you'll be staying for a few days while the doctor works with you."

Amazingly, Stella cooperated. In fact, it seemed to be harder on Bernie than it was on her as he watched his mom slowly being ushered down the hall and into the facility. Noticing what a hard time he was having, the receptionist tried to offer some comfort.

"Mr. Barcio, it's hard, I know. But you're doing the right thing. You're just trying to help your mom. You've got to remember that."

Bernie hoped she was right.

September 8, 1993
St. Vincent Stress Center, Indianapolis

Dr. Joseph V. Edwards was assigned to Stella's evaluation, whenever he could get her not to lock herself in the bathroom the moment he arrived. He did manage to get enough opportunities for interaction to make some very competent observations and recommendations. Whenever he finished working with his patient each day, Stella went about her business making herself at home in the facility. She even took to raiding the refrigerator during the late evenings so she could be sure she was eating food that was not "drugged."

When Dr. Edwards said he was ready to meet with Bernie and Lillian to present his findings, Bernie invited his niece, Liz Marie, who was practicing nursing in Indianapolis at that time, to join them in the consultation room.

> "Stella suffers from senile dementia of the Alzheimer's type. This is a progressive deterioration of brain function including memory, judgment, personality and others. She is very paranoid.
>
> "She is an irritable, depressed woman focused on physical illness. She has impaired ability to conceptualize or comprehend complex information. She shows mild problems with memory. Her judgment is impaired by her lack of awareness of her deficits, her unwillingness to accept help, and her inability to cooperate with others. She is physically frail and on a number of potentially dangerous medications.
>
> "She needs assisted living (if she will accept the help) with management of her meals and medicines, assistance with hygiene and social activities. She would need to show an appropriate adjustment to a nursing home setting before assisted living could be attempted. Otherwise, she needs permanent nursing home placement."

Since both Bernie and Dr. Edwards were not sure how successful they would be in getting Stella to cooperate with decisions that were being made for her own benefit, Bernie had proceeded with a petition to be appointed as her legal guardian. The hearing was scheduled to take place on October 29, 1993, at 3:00 p.m. in the Marion County Superior Court of Probate Division. Part of Dr. Edward's job was to give his opinion about what effect this hearing would have on Stella.

> "Her physical health would not be endangered but her emotional health would be injured by the court process due to her paranoia and inability to understand the purpose of the proceedings."

Bernie wanted to be able to provide a safe and reliable living situation for his mother, but he did not want to traumatize her in the process. In the end, he decided to cancel the petition and the court appearance and just tell her that her living arrangement had to change, and that he was going to help her through it all. The only leverage he would have would be sheer determination and will power. He would have to hope that this would be enough, and that she would agree to cooperate.

Stella was moved from the St. Vincent Stress Center to a private room in the Americana Health Care Center at 8350 Naab Rd., across from St. Vincent hospital. It was there that Bernie had to face the first of a series of challenges and explain to his mother that she would not be able to return to her apartment, and that he would have to move her things out and put them all into storage until new living arrangements for her could be made.

This was one of the most difficult encounters Bernie would have, but he stuck to his guns, remained calm and persistent despite everything that his mother threw at him verbally and emotionally.

September 15, 1993
Carmel, Indiana

Things were getting a little uncomfortable at Carmel High School, and Bernie needed to focus on this main source of bread and butter for a while. Dr. Dale Graham, a man who sincerely appreciated Bernie's talents, contributions and sense of humor, had retired. He was replaced by Dr. Bill Duke who did not really appreciate the full academic importance of Latin in the curriculum. He immediately began to make noises about cutting back the Latin offerings. Seeing that eventually there might be a suggestion that the Latin teacher be reassigned to teach English or, worse yet, let go, Bernie decided to get active in the Carmel-Clay Education Association (C.C.E.A.). If a school tried to get rid of an association officer, they could easily face an uphill legal battle with the Indiana State Teachers Association.

So, during the 1993-1994 school year, Bernie served as Membership Chairman of the C.C.E.A. The following year (1994-1995) he would get himself elected as President and during the 1995-1996 school year he would serve as the Negotiations Chairman. He was hammering away for both his fellow teachers and his own Latin program.

During this same time period, Bernie decided to enhance his standing among state Latin teachers by running for the position of First Vice-President of the I.C.C., a post he easily won. During the 1996-1997 school year, he would automatically serve as the organization's President. Thus in the course of his career as an Indiana Latin teacher, he managed to hold all of the offices of the I.C.C. except one. That one was the honorary position of 2nd Vice-President which the I.C.C. offered to the teacher selected as the Secondary School Latin Teacher of the Year. Since Bernie had been an officer of the I.C.C. ever since he helped initiate the selection process for an I.C.C. Teacher of the Year, he remained ineligible to be considered for the honor.

October, 1993
Westside Village, Indianapolis

"This is a nice place, Ma. You can have your own private apartment, and as much of your furniture and things as we can fit. And you even have a small kitchenette with a refrigerator and stove."

"*Musa tu!* I want all my crocheted things with me."

"O.K., I can do that. I know right where they are."

"And my quilts."

"O.K. We can probably put them on the shelf in your closet."

Luckily, the staff at Westside Village was able to overlook Stella's negativity during her initial visit and interview. It was a great place. Stella's room was on the second floor, but it was very near the elevator, and the building wasn't so big that she would become disoriented. The nursing staff was exceedingly kind and bent over backwards to do everything for her that she asked.

Stella's visit to the Little Sisters of the Poor assisted living facilities had not gone half as well. The main interviewer and screener, Lucy Khemke, picked up almost immediately on Stella's negative vibes and pretty much decided that they did not want to deal with her in their facility. She didn't really ever come right out and say this, but the fact that Stella's name has remained very low on the "waiting list" and never, ever, seemed to work its way closer to the top quickly confirmed her mindset. In fact, almost a full year after Stella passed away, her name still remained locked in near the bottom of the "waiting list." Bernie decided just to leave her name there and see if he ever would be notified that an opening was available for his mother. Maybe after Lucy Khemke retired.

Bernie had visited other assisted living facilities in and around Indianapolis and was fairly disappointed in all that he saw. The Morristown Health Center was in an older, dark, foreboding building, and residents were housed three to a room.

That would never work.

Roland's Independent Living Club was basically a motel converted into a health care facility. Stella would have had to put on her coat and scarf every time she walked over to the building where meals were served.

In fact, before he discovered Westside Village, the only other facility to which he even gave serious consideration was Bethany Village located on south Shelby Street in Indianapolis. The only drawback there was that they housed residents two to a room with a curtain separating them and their belongings. That may have had to work in an emergency, but it wouldn't have worked for long.

Things went fairly well at Westside Village with only an occasional call from Rodney, a nightshift male nurse who every so often decided he just couldn't take another minute of Stella.

"Bernie?"

"Yes?"

"This is Rodney at Westside Village."

"Hey, Rodney. What's up?"

"Would you please come and get your mother?"

"Why? What's the problem?"

"Please. I just need a break. Just take her for a ride or something for an hour or so. Can you do it?"

So, by cooperating with the staff at Westside Village, Bernie was able to provide very comfortable and almost luxurious accommodations for his mother for a couple of years.

September, 1994
Jacksonville, Florida

Phil and Ross had been right. The film industry could be very lucrative when one was hired on to work with a crew. The pay was often more than $1,000 a week. The trade off, however, was that when the job was done, the money dried up. So when Phil had a chance to be hired on as a Boom Operator for the crew that was producing the T.V. series called The Point Man, he jumped at the chance.

"You'll have to live in Jacksonville, Florida, the entire time, Man," pointed out Ross who had no intention of leaving their apartment in Houston just yet.

"That's O.K.," said Phil. "I don't mind Florida, and besides, the pay is great."

So Phil headed for Jacksonville to join the film crew by which he had been hired. At first, he was put up in a motel with the rest of the crewmembers, but Phil soon realized that he wouldn't be able to take that for too long.

"Why do you want a separate living allowance?" asked the crew director when Phil talked to him about it.

"I have to get away from the rest of those guys at night," explained Phil. "They're into a lot of shit that I don't want to have anything to do with, and they're always riding me to join in."

"Well, it will have to come out of your regular salary," explained the crew director.

"Fine with me," said Phil. "It'll be worth it."

"You'll have to find your own transportation to the set every day. We're not going to make a special trip to pick you up, you know," said the crew director.

"I can handle that," said Phil.

October, 1995
Indianapolis

"Bernie, Dr. Nation wants me to have some special tests," announced Lillian one evening.

"Is this just routine, or does she suspect a problem?" asked Bernie.

"There was something about the report that came back from the samples she sent in after my last office visit," said Lillian.

As it turned out, a pre-cancerous ovarian condition was revealed that would require the removal of Lillian's ovaries.

The good news was that the condition had been discovered early and could be quickly remedied. There was no indication that there would be any further trouble.

November, 1995
Houston, Texas

By this time, Phil was beginning to get very frustrated by his various jobs on movie crews. He was creative and talented enough to be bothered by some of the decisions that were being made by the directors. If he dared voice any opinions, he was quickly reminded that he had been hired on only as a technician, and that he should mind his own business.

Phil had agreed to help his dad make a professional video of one of the Roman *Personae* that his dad performed for school audiences across the country. The video would be entitled **The Life and Training of a Roman Legionnaire**. He would round up the equipment and a helper to do this, but he was beginning to think that maybe he would rather be focusing on script writing than on the production end of filmmaking. As a writer, Phil would have total quality control and not have to put up with several other people telling him how things would have to go.

Phil and Ross would, however, continue their collaboration on the script for **Life on Mars** which they had started earlier.

March, 1996
Houston, Texas

"Hi, Mario, I'm Phil Barcio. I'm the Production Assistant for the commercial we'll be filming today."

"Hi, Phil, Mario Andretti."

"My folks are big fans of you when you race in the Indy 500."

"Thanks. Where can I get something to drink?"

Phil pointed to the catering cart and stepped out of Mario's way and out of his life. Mario, his son Michael and Mike Ditka were all on set, and they were being paid handsomely by Texaco to film the commercial. None of them really enjoyed mingling with the crew.

The commercial would air on national T.V. during the 1996 Indianapolis 500 Race.

Phil was able to get Mario's signature on a copy of the storyboards before the day was over, but he knew enough to stay out of Mike Ditka's way.

May, 1996
Carmel, Indiana

As Negotiations Chairman for the C.C.E.A., Bernie had pushed hard to get an early retirement incentive package included in the contract. Fellow committee member, Dave Bardos, had crunched the numbers and could demonstrate that the school system could actually save money by providing a monthly early retirement benefit to teachers at the top of the pay scale and replacing them in the classroom with teachers earning entry level salaries. At first the school board's negotiation's team resisted the proposal, but suddenly decided to agree to it. Bernie later discovered that while only he and a few other classroom teachers were able to take advantage of the benefit, more importantly the head football coach would be able to take advantage of the offer.

A year later, the school system decided to cancel the program on the grounds that it might be considered illegal. Of course, they continued paying the monthly benefits to those who were initially allowed to take advantage of the package.

"Bernie, we've discovered a small problem," said Asst. Supt., Jim Burrell.

The administration had viewed Bernie as a royal pain during his years of leading the C.C.E.A. and seemed to relish opportunities to turn the screws on him whenever they could. Bernie pushed hard for teacher benefits, was well-liked by the teachers he led and was efficient and well-organized—a threat to any school administration.

"Bernie, we've discovered that you were over-paid on a number of your paychecks," said Jim Burrel, flashing his trademark smile.

Bernie had asked Jim Burrel to calculate just what his retirement benefits would be. Since he had used very few of his sick days over the years, he had almost amassed the maximum unused sick day payment allowable. He was, however, about to be screwed out of a big chunk of that payment.

"How much was I overpaid?" asked Bernie.

"$5,000," said Jim smiling. "We'll just withhold that amount from your lump sum retirement benefits."

"Why wasn't that error discovered a lot earlier?" asked Bernie.

"Well, that's the funny thing, Bernie. If you hadn't taken early retirement this year, we probably would not have reviewed your payroll records and any record of the error would have been lost once the new payroll program was installed."

Bernie neglected to ask if anyone else had been accidentally overpaid and whether they, too, were going to be required to pay the school system back.

So that was it. Bernie would get to take advantage of the early retirement incentive package he had helped negotiate, but the school system was definitely going to screw him in the process. Having, however, previously lost thousands as he moved from Park School to Washington Township in 1970 and then to Wayne Township in 1978 and finally when he accepted his teaching position at Carmel H.S. in 1981, he and Lillian had become inured to these financial disappointments and took them in stride.

C'est la guerre!

January, 1997
Indianapolis

Joe's oldest daughter, Liz Marie, had decided to move to Indianapolis after graduating from the School of Nursing at Marquette University in Milwaukee, Wisconsin. She was attracted by the employment possibilities at St. Vincent Hospital and also looked forward to having her Aunt Lillian and Uncle Bernie near at hand.

Since Liz Marie was diabetic herself, she was trying to specialize in pediatric diabetic education and even worked out a learning game that she was interested in trying to market.

"Uncle Bernie?" asked Liz Marie as she called from Kokomo, Indiana.

"Yes, is this Liz Marie? How's it going?"

"Not well, Uncle Bernie. I had to drive up here to Kokomo, and my car broke down. I was wondering if you could drive up here and tow my car back to Indianapolis?"

Hey, that's what uncles are for. Bernie relished an opportunity to rescue his niece and immediately set off on his mission of mercy.

Liz Marie had also joined The Gathering at Christ the King Church where she was able to play flute and sing with her cousin Cindy at the 12:30 Mass. She and Cindy even got to share some great Christmas caroling memories.

"Hi, Aunt Lillian," said Liz Marie after she had entered her aunt's kitchen.

"Hi, Liz Marie, how are you?" asked Lillian.

"I'm a little shook up, I'm afraid."

"What happened?" asked Bernie who had just entered the kitchen.

"I almost killed myself on the College Avenue Bridge over the White River," exclaimed Liz Marie.

"How did that happen?" asked Lillian.

"I guess I didn't see the ice on the bridge until it was too late. Before I knew it, my car was spinning in a circle right in the middle of the bridge."

"Did you hit the rail?" asked Bernie.

"No, thank God. I was able to stop just in time!"

"Lucky there weren't any cars right behind you," said Lillian.

Liz had, in fact, spun out almost directly in front of the duplex on the north side of the river where Bernie had moved in with Lillian and the girls until the family could occupy his house on Ferguson.

Liz Marie had grown up in Wisconsin and was certainly used to driving on snow and ice. She had just been caught a little off guard.

March, 1997
Broad Ripple, Indianapolis

"It looks like your mother," observed Lillian.

"Well, it's not. It's Pomona," explained Bernie.

"Who's Pomona?" asked Phil.

"She was a Roman goddess of fruit trees," explained Bernie, forever the Classics teacher.

A few months earlier, Phil and his film-school friend, Ross, had helped Bernie cut down the tall basswood tree that stood menacingly on the southeast corner of their property.

"Why do you want to cut it down?" Phil had asked.

"Because it's not real stable. See that chain up there?"

"Yeah."

"I had to put it there to hold the two trunks of the tree together. They used to sway and creak something terrible."

"Won't the chains keep it from falling now?" Ross had asked.

"No, the trunks have gotten a lot taller. If they fall, I'm afraid they'll fall on the Hulvershorn's cars in their driveway. Bad enough that our Itchy Goomey tree fell on the back of their house right after they moved in."

"Did we have to pay for that?" Phil had asked.

"I thought our insurance would pay for it, but it would only pay to remove that portion of the tree that was left lying in our yard. The Hulvershorns' insurance had to pay for the damage to their house and the removal of the tree in their yard. I did give Mr. Hulvershorn $100 to cover his deductible. I figured that was the only fair thing to do."

After the three of them had felled the top part of the tree, they spent the rest of the day cutting the trunk and larger branches into firewood size logs. Ross' young daughter, Kelsey, helped break up and add the twigs to the wood pile being stacked behind the one story 15 foot by 20 foot storage barn that Bernie had built with the help of Phil and Ross back in 1992.

Pompeiiana, Inc., had been paying more than $600 a year to rent commercial storage space for its catapults, supplies and display items that it loaned to teachers, and Bernie and Lillian had decided they could save Pompeiiana some money by providing storage on their own property.

The twigs would come in handy as fire starters.

Once the weather warmed up a little, Bernie went to work on the 4-foot-high basswood trunk that he had deliberately allowed to remain. Using a chainsaw, an ax, a hammer and a chisel, he soon fashioned the trunk into a bird feeder that represented a seated Pomona holding a bowl on her lap into which bird feed could be placed.

Much to the surprise of Bernie and his neighbors, several of whom frequently brought their grandchildren by every so often to admire the feeder, the stump did not die, but re-grew two healthy branches that Bernie later kept trimmed to provide umbrella coverage for Pomona.

June 27, 1997
Lone Mountain Guest Lodge, Colorado

Karen wanted Mike's 40th birthday celebration to be special. So, here the whole family was, up in the mountains of Colorado. Once the kids were settled in, and Karen and Mike had a few moments to themselves, they decided to go out on the balcony and talk while taking in the scenery.

"So, Mike, have you decided whether or not you're going to accept the invitation to run for Congress again."

"I'm giving it some serious thought."

"If we do run again, let's do it differently this time."

"What do you mean?"

"I mean, let's not push it. If things fall into place, we'll know we're meant to do it."

"You up for a little prayer, Kare?"

So, since this would be a major family commitment, the two stood together and asked God for a little guidance, some sign perhaps.

"Karen. Look!"

"Oh, wow! They're beautiful!"

As Karen and Mike stood looking out over the mountains, two red tail hawks came soaring into view.

"What do you think, Karen?"

"That's the most wonderful sign I've ever been given. And look, Mike! They're hardly even moving their wings at all. They're just letting themselves be carried."

"They're just soaring over the tree tops."

"That's how we should run for office this time. No flapping. No pushing it. Just soaring as we let ourselves be carried where God wants us to go."

In August of 2004, Mike was serving his second term in Congress and was now running for a third term.

July 21, 1997
Danville, Indiana

Because of Stella's peculiar eating habits—she avoided all fiber as much as possible, considering it to be trash—she eventually developed diverticulitis and had to have an operation to remove the infected portion of her colon. Following that operation, which left her with an ostomy bag, the staff at Westside Village determined that they were no longer in a position to provide Stella with the kind of care she needed.

Bernie would need, once more, to try and locate a health care facility for his mother.

Lucy Khemke was still in charge of new admissions to The Little Sisters of the Poor facility. No there still was not a room available for Stella. Yes, her name still was on the waiting list and she would notify Bernie if an opening occurred.

Following her operation which had been performed in the Hendricks County Hospital in Danville, Indiana, Stella had recuperated in the Danville Regional Rehab Center located across the street from the hospital. A new assisted living residence had just been built adjacent to the Center called Emerald Gardens, and the director had invited Bernie to consider the facility for his mother. The place was immaculate and all on one floor. It even had a formal dining room where Bernie would be able to enjoy Thanksgiving meals with his mother and Phil and Cyndi.

All moves for older people are, however, upsetting. While Stella adjusted fairly well, she still had her moments.

"Will you be coming here first thing tomorrow morning?" asked Bernie's mom when she called on Saturday evening.

"No, but I will stop in after lunch."

"*Musa tu!* It's Mother's Day. You only have one mother, you know!"

"Yes, Ma, I know."

"That's right. So you'll be here in the morning?"

"No, Ma. I'm going to spend the morning with Lillian and Phil and Cyndi. We're taking her out for breakfast for Mother's Day. I'll be there in the afternoon."

"You can't say mother without putting your lips together, you know."

"I know. I have to hang up now."

"No. Wait!"

"What?"

"What are you going to bring me?"

"I have a nice corsage for you to wear."

"Why don't you bring it tonight?"

"Because I can't"

"No time for your mother, right?"

"Ma, I gotta hang up now. I'll see you tomorrow."

"In the morning, right?"

"No, Ma, after lunch. Bye now!"

When Bernie arrived at Emerald Gardens after lunch the next day, his mother was nowhere to be found. Her room was empty. He walked around to all the common areas of the facility and asked the Charge Nurse if she knew were Stella was.

She hadn't seen Stella since breakfast.

Finally, as Bernie stood in the main dining room wondering whether or not he should just leave, one of the residents caught his eye and pointed to an outdoor seating area.

"Is Stella out there?" Bernie asked.

The resident nodded, giving Bernie a sly little grin.

"Hey, Ma. What are you doing out here?"

"*Musa tu*! What do you want?"

"Happy Mother's day. Here I brought you a nice corsage."

It took a while, but Bernie finally smoothed things over, and the day was saved.

Eventually, Bernie was informed that Stella was no longer a viable candidate for Assisted Living and would require nursing home care from now on.

"But there is no way that she can afford nursing home care. That would be twice as much as we are paying right now, and, frankly, she ran out of money a long time ago. I've been covering for her, but I've only got limited resources," explained Bernie.

"Don't you have other family members who can help?" asked the administrator.

"Not really. My brother lives in Texas, and he really doesn't have any more extra money for her care than I do. Besides, he's kind of on non-speaking terms with her at the moment."

"You're kidding!"

"No, I'm not. But I can't really hold it against him. Our mother pretty much drove him right up the wall. Permanently! It's not really his fault. So it's kind of all up to me at this point."

"If your mother is out of funds, she should be able to qualify for Medicaid," explained the administrator.

So, Stella was transferred into a double-occupancy room in the Danville Regional Rehab Center attached to Emerald Gardens.

Once again, Bernie had to pack up his mother's belongings and put them into temporary storage until new living arrangements could be made.

August, 1997
Broad Ripple, Indianapolis
The inscription on the plaque read:

> To Lillian Barcio
> The Village Sampler
> With gratitude, affection and recognition of
> your efforts to inform, entertain and above all
> chronicle the life of our Community.
> Broad Ripple
> Village Association

Lillian had just published the final issue of **The Village Sampler** in its newspaper format. She was retiring due to failing eyesight. She was now turning the business over to Phil who wanted to try changing the format into that of a magazine featuring four-color slick covers.

For the past several years, many Broad Ripple businesses had been encouraging Lillian to try a magazine format and offer them the chance to run four-color ads. Phil thought he would give it a try.

"Well, I'm not going to pay that much to run an ad in the **Sampler**. That's twice as much as it used to be," complained one of the first businesses that Phil approached to renew its ad in the September, 1997 issue.

"Well," explained Phil, "**The Village Sampler** will have a whole new format. It's going to be a magazine which is what many of the Broad Ripple merchants have been pushing for."

"Not if it's going to cost that much more!" insisted the disgruntled merchant.

"Our rates," continued Phil, "are still a lot less than you would have to pay to advertise in any other Indianapolis publication."

"Well, then, I just wont advertise. Besides, I get most of my business from word of mouth anyway," concluded the merchant, ending the interview.

Phil forged ahead anyway. Each month he managed to come up with three or four businesses that saw the value of running four-color ads on the inside and outside of the back cover. He did, however, have to adjust the B/W ad rates for the inside of the magazine low enough so some of the regular advertisers would stick with the **Sampler**.

Since the magazine format was a lot more expensive, and funds also had to be spent to construct custom designed display racks, the venture needed more serious underwriting by the Barcio family than it had required when the **Sampler** was being published in a newspaper format.

September, 1997
Indianapolis

"Hi, this is Dr. Youngblood's office. Is Lillian there, please?" asked the nurse.

Bernie watched as Lillian listened to the findings on the colonoscopy that she had been given a day or two earlier.

"What is it?" asked Bernie.

Lillian took a minute to process what she had just been told, and did her best to maintain her composure.

"They think they've discovered colon cancer," Lillian finally managed to say.

"What do they want you to do?"

"I'm supposed to make an appointment with a specialist to find out how they are going to approach it," said Lillian.

Once again, Lillian had lucked out. The colon cancer was only in its first stages which allowed the infected section to be removed before any metastasis could take place.

December 10, 1997
Broad Ripple, Indianapolis

"Lillian, I wanna read you a letter that I would like to send to Marsha," announced Bernie.

"Why?" asked Lillian.

"Well, she's obviously a lot more hard-headed than we thought she would be. I thought if I broke the ice, we might be able to get back together with her sometime."

"Are you sure you want to open that can of worms?" asked Lillian.

"Why not? What could it hurt?"

"She's been saying some pretty awful things about you, you know."

"Like what?"

"She told the Robinsons that you mistreated her when she was living at home."

Bernie was dumbfounded. So that was how she had decided to justify her craziness. That was a shame.

"So the Robinsons have had that in the back of their minds all these years when we've visited with them," thought Bernie to himself.

"Well, if that's how she chose to justify her actions, that's her choice," said Bernie. "I still think it would be worth while to send the letter."

After much editing and discussion, a version of the letter that was acceptable to both of them was finally placed in an envelope and mailed.

There was no reply.

The next year Bernie would send an unacknowledged Christmas card.

December 22, 1997
Hendricks County, Indiana

"Hi, I'm Bernie Barcio, and I have an appointment with Jennifer Buddenbaum."

Luckily, Bernie had been able to schedule his appointment at the Hendricks County Office of Family and Children for the first Monday of Christmas vacation. This was not going to be easy, but very few things related to the care of his mother following the death of his father had been easy. In response to his mother's repeated exhortation to "just be a man" whenever he invited outside help in dealing with her, he had done just that. She had, in her own way, toughened her son up to the point that he could now make hard decisions about her care with a minimal of emotional involvement.

"Your mother's financial records do indicate that she qualifies for Welfare aide," said Jennifer after the meeting had started.

"Welfare!"

Now that's a word that comes with a lot of negative connotations. Bernie really did not want to focus on the fact that his mother, a woman of intense personal pride who had managed to live quite well with her husband and raise two college-educated boys, would now be living on Welfare.

Better not to dwell on that. In fact, it was a bit of information that Bernie would manage, with the help of the healthcare professionals who dealt with her, to keep from his mother for the rest of her life. But there was really nothing else he could do. When Bernie and his brother had finally managed to sell the family home in Sparta—after it had been ravaged by kids living at the County Home next door—he had set aside $10,000 of his share of the profits for the future use of his mother. By this time, not only had he used up all of that money (her monthly bills in the various Assisted Living facilities topped $3,500 a month), but he had also spent thousands of additional dollars of his own money to supplement her monthly expenses. By now, however, his personal resources had also been depleted. Welfare was the only answer.

"This means, of course," said Jennifer, "that you will have to locate a nursing home facility that accepts welfare residents."

"Don't they all?" asked Bernie.

"No. Some don't, and others have a quota that limits how many welfare residents can live there at any one time."

"Do you happen to know if the Little Sisters of the Poor accepts welfare residents?" asked Bernie.

"I believe they do."

O.K. Bernie would try one more time and see if Lucy had allowed his mother's name to move any closer to the top of the waiting list.

No such luck. The woman was adamant!

Bernie also tried to get his mother into American Village Retirement Home located closer to Broad Ripple on 54th Street, but when the administrator there called Emerald Gardens for a reference on Stella, she received such a negative report that the administrator had no choice but to turn down her application.

February 18, 1998
Indianapolis Retirement Home, Indianapolis
"There is a God!" said Bernie to himself when he heard that his mother had been accepted onto the nursing care floor of the Indianapolis Retirement Home (IRH), located across the street from Methodist Hospital in Indianapolis.

"Why do I have to move? Why can't I just go back to my room?" asked Bernie's mom.

"Because the doctor says you have to have nursing home care, and Emerald Gardens doesn't provide that."

"Well, I don't want to stay here!"

And that was for sure. Stella had already gotten into at least one confrontation with a male resident because he wouldn't move his walker out of her way so she could hurry into the dining room.

"The bastard hit me! What are we going to do about it?"

"We're going to move somewhere else," replied Bernie.

"But what are we going to do about the bastard. We should call the cops on him."

"No, Ma. We're not going to call the cops. The nurses handled the situation just fine. He's just an old man."

"*Musa tu*! He's a bastard!"

The Indianapolis Retirement Home was a wonderful old facility located at 1731 N. Capitol Avenue. It housed only 40 residents, 20 of whom lived in private Independent and Assisted Living apartments on the first floor, and 20 of whom lived in Assisted Living or nursing care rooms on the second floor. The building had been built in the 1800's and, under the guidance of the wife of the Governor of Indiana, had opened as a home for unwed mothers. The place was a godsend.

To the nurses and staff of IRH Stella became quickly and affectionately known as Miss Stella.

On good days (which is meant to remind the reader that Miss Stella also had her bad days), she would kiss their hands and give her usual benedictions as they left for the day.

"God love and bless you. God be with you. You'll be treasured in Heaven."

"Nigh', night, Miss Stella."

"Nigh', night, honey doll. Take it easy on the road!"

Miss Stella loved to sing at sponsored sing-a-longs. She loved to attend the holiday parties in the Clowes Memorial Garden. She took an active interest in the cooking demonstrations that were held in the basement party room. She gladly attended special events in the beautiful Solarium. She adjusted wonderfully. She dressed nicely and proudly wore the clip-on earrings and necklaces that her son bought for her. When in her room, she listened nicely to her portable radio while snacking on fruit stocked in her small refrigerator by her son—except for the bananas that had to be left out on the dresser top. And, boy! Did she ever like bananas! No one would have ever guessed that she was one of the facility's welfare residents.

As fate would have it, the Indianapolis Retirement Home was destined to close its doors and go out of business—but not until a few months after Stella passed away.

Was somebody up there looking out for her and her son?

And what about the fact that by the year 2003, the Americana Health Care Center—in which Stella had been first placed after being evaluated by Dr. Edwards—had been torn down!

And isn't it just a little unusual that Dr. Edwards himself resigned and went into early retirement shortly after completing his work with Stella?

What was there about this woman, this admittedly spoiled daughter of Tony Nudi, that unusual occurrences followed in her path?

February, 1998
Broad Ripple, Indianapolis

Bernie had sent Marsha a letter in 1997 encouraging her to get back together with her mom, but there was no response. When Cyndi asked if her mom and dad would mind if she arranged to meet Marsha, she was given every encouragement.

"Wanna get together for lunch at Applebee's on Broad Ripple Ave.?" asked Cyndi.

"O.K.," said Marsha. "Just be sure you come alone. There better not be anyone else with you."

Although Cyndi was good to her word and showed up alone, Marsha was accompanied by the same black girlfriend that had been with her the day she moved out back in 1971.

All Cyndi ever told her dad about the encounter at the time was that they had a nice visit, and that she was glad to have had a chance to meet her sister. Cyndi was only about three and a half years old when Marsha had left.

Six years later, during her mother's wake, Cyndi would share with her dad and her cousins that Marsha had spent the entire luncheon putting down Bernie and Lillian and complaining about how she had been mistreated.

That's certainly not the way the author remembers it!

May 10, 1998
Indianapolis Retirement Home, Indianapolis

"Hi, Cyn?" said Bernie when he called Cyndi from the Detroit airport.

"Hal-loh? Where are you guys?" asked Cyndi in her usual cautious manner.

"We're on our way back, but we're going to be late getting home."

Bernie and Lillian had flown to New Hampshire so Bernie could deliver a *persona* performance. They had intended to be home for Mother's Day, but their return flight had been delayed, and they now realized they weren't going to be able to make it.

"So I guess you won't be back so Phil and I can take Mom out for her Mother's Day breakfast."

"No. I'll have to take care of that for you, but I do have to ask you and Phil to do me a favor."

"Ye-es?" said Cyndi beginning to get suspicious.

"We'll all go out to dinner when we get back if you guys will stop in and visit Grandma for me today. Buy her a small bouquet of flowers, and I'll reimburse you."

Luckily, for Bernie, Cyndi and Phillip would be able to cover for him. He did not want another Emerald Gardens episode.

When Cyndi and Phil got to the Indianapolis Retirement Home, they found that a special afternoon social was being sponsored in the Solarium for the occasion, and they agreed to accompany their grandmother to the event and stay a while.

"Honey doll," said Cyndi's grandmother, "would you get your Gramma a nice big plate of those strawberries from the table?"

"Sure," said Cyndi, eager to please.

"Be sure and get good ones. Big and ripe. Not rotten!"

"O.K., Grandma. I'll try and do it right."

When Cyndi returned with a heaping plate of strawberries, it quickly became obvious to Stella that she would not be able to eat them all herself.

"Phillip, eat some strawberries."

Phillip complied not wanting anything to ruin the pleasant afternoon.

"Honey doll, here, eat some strawberries."

"No thank you, Grandma. I've had plenty," said Cyndi.

"These are strawberries! You don't get these every day. Here. Eat!"

"No, really, Grandma. I'm full!"

"*Musa tu. Mangia! Mangia*! They're good for you."

This was it. As a little girl, Cyndi had lived in fear of her grandmother, and had either always tried to avoid her or do what she was ordered so as not to antagonize her. But Cyndi was not a little girl any more. It was time for her to join the ranks of those who had dared to take a stand against the Great Stella and who, hopefully, would live to tell about it.

"Grandma, NO! I don't want any more strawberries!"

"*Diauolo*! You little dickens. Come here and give your grandma a kiss."

"Here, Grandma," interceded Phil, who quickly bent over and kissed his grandma on the cheek. "We have to go now, but we really enjoyed being with you today."

"Would you like us to help you carry your flowers back up to your room?" asked Cyndi, hoping to leave on a positive note.

"No, Honey Doll, that's O.K. Someone will help me."

"O.K. Happy Mother's Day," said Cyndi as she tried to deliver a quick kiss and make her break.

Stella, however, was much more practiced at controlling situations than Cyndi was. As soon as Cyndi bent down, her grandma reached up and, with vice-like hands, gripped her by the arms and proceeded to plant kisses on her that too-closely resembled Mafia kisses of death that Cyndi had seen delivered in **The Godfather**. It was a long time before Cyndi ate another strawberry.

September, 1998
Indianapolis

Phil and Ross were now back in Indianapolis where they had formed their own production company called Big Donut Movies. They would use the corporation to try and market **Life on Mars** and to try and break into the market for filming local commercials.

"Phil!"

"What's up Ross?" asked Phil.

"You know the Modern Times Restaurant on College?"

"Yeah. I've eaten there. It's kind of an interesting place," observed Phil.

"I think I've talked the owner into hiring us to make a few commercials for her," said Ross.

So that was it. Phil and Ross had their first big break and before long they had scripts written, cast members chosen, equipment rented and a film crew assembled.

The four commercials they shot were not only creative, they were clever and effective. They ran on local T.V. stations for as long as the owner could afford to pay for the spots.

December, 1998
Broad Ripple, Indianapolis

"Well, that's it," said Phil as he laid in the final corrections on the boards for the last issue of **The Village Sampler Magazine.**

The masthead read, "**THE VILLAGE SAMPLER**, FREE Take One, Vol. XII, Number 7, December, 1998."

No taps were played. The final issue would be distributed and once all the copies had been taken, Phil and Bernie would make the rounds and gather up the custom-built distribution racks and store them in the attic of the garage until they could be sold at a future garage sale.

Phil had given it more than the old college try. The advertising dollars just weren't there, and the Barcio family simply could not provide any additional underwriting for the venture.

"Should we have said something in the issue pointing out that it would be the final issue?" asked Phil.

"No," said Lillian. "It's better this way. Just let it die. Who knows? It might even be a few months before a lot of people realize it's not being published any more."

It had been her dream, and the whole family had helper her give it her best shot.

What Lillian enjoyed most during her years as an editor was her research for articles on the early history of Broad Ripple. She had also made acquaintance of several descendants of early Broad Ripple settlers and of others who had done extensive historical research on the early days and residents of the community. She drew all these resources together and featured special historical articles in each of the issues.

Even though she had technically retired as editor of the **Sampler**, Lillian had continued to provide historical material that Phil included in the new magazine format.

January, 1999
Houston, Texas

When Joe retired from teaching in May, 1998, he and his wife, Liz, eventually sold their house in Oskhosh, Wisconsin, and, in September of 1998, they moved to Houston. Since Liz was the primary caretaker of her father, Joe Mingari, they also moved him to Houston with them.

At first, they all stayed at the home of their son and daughter-in-law, Joey and Alisha, whose hospitality proved to be exceptionally kind.

Shortly after arriving in Houston, Joe Mingari became quite ill and was hospitalized for about four weeks. During this time, Joe and Liz made almost daily trips to the hospital while, at the same time, looking for a house to buy.

At length, Joe and Liz bought a house at 15835 Roxton Ridge Drive, resettled Joe Mingari into a nearby home that offered assisted living arrangements, and they all became official Houstonites.

Joe recalls that without the emotional support and the generous hospitality of Joey and Alisha, the transition would have been most difficult.

"I wonder if they take part-time workers there?" said Joe to Liz one day as they were driving past Johnson Space Center Houston.

Joe was thinking that it would be nice to stay active even though retired.

"Why don't you stop in and ask some time?" said Liz.

Thus, in January of 1999, after having carefully filled out an application, Joe was called to the Space Center. Several orientation sessions later, he was put to work.

At first, he was assigned inside the Space Center which involved being rotated among twelve (yes, 12) different locations in the course of a day.

"Susan," said Joe who found the constant rotation to be somewhat less than appealing, "I thank you for the chance to work here, but I think I'm going to look around a bit more. The constant rotation is a little more than I'm up to."

"Joe," said Susan, "would you like to try the tram area?"

"Well, okay," said Joe, "I'll try it."

When Joe discovered what his new assignment involved, he was thrilled. Working "the tram area" meant that he would be taking guests on tours of the Johnson Space Center and visiting Building 9 (the astronaut training facility for shuttle and space station deployment), Building 30 South (the mission control rooms for both the shuttle and the space station), Building 30 North (the historic mission control room used to send astronauts to the moon), Building 220 (where the X-38 was being built for the International Space Station) and Building 5 which contained the motion-based shuttle simulator.

This was right up Joe's alley! He would actually be "teaching" guests about the space program. Wow!

Five years later, Joe would be invited to lead the elite "Level 9" tours which are VIP tours of the Johnson Space Center. Limited to twelve guests,

Joe would be provided a van and a driver and would absolutely delight in taking guests once a week to such places as the Neutral Buoyancy Lab (the big pool in which astronauts train underwater) and to the Mission Control Centers for the Shuttle and Space Station (places which were off-limits for General Tours after September 11, 2001). Joe would also lead VIP guests to Building 32 that houses the two vacuum chambers which reproduce conditions of outer space, to Building 9 (the astronaut training facility), and to Teague Auditorium which houses many mementoes of the early space program as well as memorabilia of Lyndon Johnson.

One privilege that Joe especially enjoys as part of his "little retirement job" is the opportunity to walk guests along side a real Saturn 5 Rocket which is displayed lying on its side at Rocket Park. The rocket was actually built for a moon mission but was never used after the missions were canceled by Congress and President Nixon in the 1970's. Here Joe gets to explain how each stage of the rocket worked to get the astronauts first into earth orbit and then how it fired its last rocket engine to propel itself to the moon.

Not a bad way to stay active even though retired!

By 2013, a protective building had been constructed over the Saturn 5 Rocket to protect it from the elements and provide informational displays concerning its history.

July 27, 1999
Houston, Texas

At this time, Joe and Liz were attending St. Bernadette's Catholic Church in Houston. It was there that they had had an opportunity to hear a talk by another parishioner of the same church, Eileen Collins, the first woman to be assigned as a Shuttle Commander.

On July 23-27, 1999, Collins commanded the STS-93 Columbia which highlighted the deployment of the Chandra X-Ray Observatory. Designed to conduct comprehensive studies of the universe, this telescope would enable scientists to study such exotic phenomena as exploding stars, quasars and black holes.

"There it is," exclaimed Joe to Liz as they both stood outside their home on the evening of July 27.

He was pointing up at a long orange streak appearing in the sky overhead. It was the shuttle Columbia commanded by Collins as it made its way toward Florida.

A minute later, it was gone, leaving an intense orange glow from horizon to horizon.

Joe and Liz hurried back into the house and turned on their radio.

Sixteen minutes later they heard the report that the Columbia had successfully landed in Florida.

December, 1999
Houston, Texas

One of the first perks that Joe enjoyed as VIP tour guide was to receive an invitation to attend a Christmas party in the beautifully spacious home of Bo Bobko. Bobko had flown on the shuttle Challenger on its first mission and had made two other shuttle flights into space.

Whenever the shuttle is in orbit, Joe's current parish, St. Paul's Catholic Church, proudly displays the American flag that Bobko took into orbit on the first Challenger mission.

December 23, 1999
Carmel, Indiana

"Hey, Bernie," said Genene Kambs, a German teacher at Carmel H.S. with whom he had carpooled for several years, "what is there about you that you keep getting into the paper?"

"What did I do now?" asked Bernie.

"Haven't you seen the article?"

"No. What paper was it in?"

"In the Thursday **Star**. Page 2 of the B section. Want me to mail you a clipping?"

"That would be great, Genene. Thanks. I'll watch for it."

As it turned out, each day in 1999, Monday-Saturday, a special column called "Flashback" presented a look at the past from the photo archives of **The Indianapolis Star** and **The News**. This time the photo was of Bernie during his early teaching years at Park School.

> "Latin instructor Bernard Barcio (far right) conducted a class at Park School in February 1968 as students sat at a double-butterfly conference table Barcio designed and patented. Barcio taught from 1965 to 1970 at Park School for boys, a private school that began in 1914 and eventually merged with Tudor Hall for Girls (founded 1902). When the school moved to its current campus at 7200 N. College Ave., Barcio drew up plans for the desk that put him in closer proximity to students. He went on to teach at Washington and Wayne Township schools and Carmel Clay schools and was named Indiana State Teacher of the Year while at Carmel. He also received an honorary degree from Butler University and was named a Sagamore of the Wabash. Barcio took early retirement three years ago and now teaches part time at Indiana University-Purdue University Indianapolis and Butler. He still visits schools to portray a Latin-speaking Roman soldier or Pompeian citizen."

April 22, 2000
Indianapolis Retirement Home

"So, who's going to be there?" asked Stella as Bernie explained some of the details of her 90th Birthday Party that was going to be held in the Solarium.

"Everyone. Sonny, Evy, Charlie, Gusty, Rudy," said Bernie.

"Rudy! That little dickens!"

"He's your nephew. Be nice to him."

"How are we going to keep people out who don't belong? You'll have to stand at the door and tell them to leave!"

"No one's going to come in who isn't invited. Don't worry about that!"

"Now, I don't want your wife to be there!" said Stella.

O.K. Here they were going to go again. They had already had this argument several times before.

"Well, she's going to be there. She's my wife."

"No! *Capo tosto!* No! No! *Cadu mano! Cadu mano!*" cursed Stella.

"IF LILLIAN'S NOT THERE, THERE'S NO PARTY!"

Now Bernie was yelling at the top of his voice, completely impervious to the fact that there were other residents and staff members on the floor. But it was too late. She had pushed all his buttons. Again.

"BY GOD, WE'LL JUST CANCEL THE WHOLE DAMN THING!"

"Good! Good!" said Stella, refusing to be intimidated. "I don't want her at my party!"

That was it. Bernie determined to get it through his mom's head once and for all that Lillian was going to be there regardless. He bent over and gently placed his right hand on her face, as one would grab a little kid's face to command her attention.

"AHHH, don't hit me! Don't hit me!" screamed Stella.

"Nobody's hitting you, Ma. Just listen to me. Lillian is my wife, and if there's going to be a party, she's going to be there.

"*Musa tu! Diaulo!* No Lillian!"

"Then no party! *Capisce?*" yelled Bernie who suddenly realized it was probably time for him to take a little walk down the hall to cool off.

When he got into the hall, a couple of the nurses on duty looked at him, but not accusingly. They had all had their own encounters with "Miss Stella," and they knew exactly what he was going through. In fact, she had almost strangled one of them by twisting the cord from which her pen was suspended around the nurse's neck. Stella had not wanted to change her top that was soiled, and the nurse was determined to take it off of her.

"O.K., Ma," said Bernie as he walked back into the room. "I have to go now. I'll bring over a nice corsage for you to wear, and I'll make sure the nurses have you all dressed and ready for your party next Saturday. Remember, everyone will be there. It will be fun."

"Just make sure your wife isn't there!"

"O.K., Ma, whatever you say. It's your party!"

Bernie knew the argument was unwinnable. Lillian would be there. He would just make sure the two of them kept out of each other's way. And who knows? Maybe that's all Stella really wanted.

April 29, 2000
Indianapolis Retirement Home

The Solarium was beautifully arranged with tables shaped in a large U-shape. Serving would be buffet-style with all the food having been fixed beforehand by Bernie and Lillian at home and transported in a huge rolling thermo-box that Bernie had built special for the event. Angel hair spaghetti, Italian sausage, dried hot Italian peppers fried to a crisp in olive oil and generously salted, *frese, ensalata*, garlic bread, gallon upon gallon of Chianti, *pizzelle, cumbitte* (Jordon almonds), and stella's favorite, strawberry torte cake.

"Ray, nice to meet you," said Bernie as the accordionist, Ray Massa, looked up from his sound equipment.

"Hi, you must be Bernie. This is Tony Di Malfi, my Italian tenor."

"Hey, *Piacere!*" said Bernie.

One thing Bernie was bound and determined to do for this party was to have live musicians on hand. It had taken almost a year to locate them, and they had to be brought in from Ohio. But it was worth it. Bernie had dreamed of showing Lillian and his own children the kind of party that he had grown up with. Ray and Toni were going to make that dream come true.

Just about all the guests had arrived, many of them not recognizing other members of the family that they themselves had not seen for years.

"Who's that?" asked Gusty as a short, petite young woman entered the room.

"That's Mary Leo, Uncle Gusty. She came all the way from California."

Bernie thought he would be able to handle seeing his cousin again after all those years, but he couldn't. They were both forced to share a tear-filled hug.

Mary had not seen either her Uncle Charlie or her Uncle Gusty since Bernie had given her away the first time she was married at St. Patrick's Church in South Chicago many years in the past. Since then, she had had two children, now grown, and had remarried. But she was still as cute and petite as always.

"Who's that with Sonny?" asked Uncle Charlie.

"That's Raymond!" said Bernie.

"Oh, my God. I would never have recognized him!" said Charlie.

"Rosie!" cried Bernie as he rushed forward to give a big hug to his cousin Rosie who had come with Rudy Strano despite the fact that she herself was fighting cancer.

Rosie Miresso is a whole wonderful story all by herself. When she was growing up, she appeared to be a little slower than most of the other children in her family. Mary Leo claims that this was because Aunt Maggie had taken some drug while she was pregnant that had a negative effect. Rosie, however, was a bundle of fun and joy. She had become the mother of two boys, and was handling her cancer in such a positive manner that it repeatedly went into remission. In fact, she was even invited to appear on the Oprah show, and would have, if her sisters Carmella and Florence hadn't talked her out of it.

"Everyone's gonna look at you and talk about you. You don't want to do that!"

"But they said they would pick me up in a limo and even pay me to be on the show," insisted Rosie.

"Don't do it! We don't want you to look foolish on national television."

So Rosie didn't do it.

Today, just about every Nudi relative was present for Stella's 90th except for Florence, another of Aunt Maggie's daughters.

Florence had gotten into a bit of a tiff with her half-brother, Rudy, over the control of the house in which their mother, Aunt Maggie, had been living at 510 Pulaski Rd. in Calumet City. The result was that the two of them could no longer stand to be in the same room together. Even if it meant she would have to miss her Aunt Stella's 90th birthday party.

"Rudy should have brought Florence," Stella would complain to Bernie afterwards.

"I don't think so, Ma. They don't get along."

"They're family. They have to get along."

Since Stella had had hundreds of knock-em-down-drag-em-out encounters with almost every member of her family over the years, and still managed to make believe nothing had ever happened when she saw them again, she just didn't understand why Rudy and Florence just couldn't get in the same car together and drive to Indianapolis.

Lillian helped to serve the food and managed to stay out of her mother-in-law's line of vision during the entire event. Wine flowed. Song filled the room.

When it came time to sing the traditional "*C'è la luna mezz'o mare*," Rosie lit up. This was her favorite song, and her voice soon dominated. The musicians surrounded her like moths to a flame, and before long, with everyone watching her through happy, tear-filled eyes, she belted out the x-rated Italian verses to the song that she had heard her father sing so many times when she was growing up.

It was a great family event. Bernie regretted none of the trouble, expense or abuse he had shouldered to make it happen.

October 10, 2000
Jeffersonville, Indiana

"What was that?" asked Lillian as she and Bernie sat relaxing and watching a little TV in their motel room.

"Someone's pounding on the door to the next room," said Bernie who had gone over to the window and peaked out of the curtain.

"Open the Goddam door," yelled one of the men standing outside.

"Go to hell! You're not getting in here," came the scream from inside the next room.

"Then I'm just going to come through the door, old man!"

"You do and I'll blow your fuckin' head off," came the counter threat.

That did it. If there was going to be gunfire, Bernie knew something had to be done immediately. He grabbed the phone and called the motel office.

"We know what's going on, sir," came the reply. "The police are on their way."

CRASH!

The door to the next room was suddenly broken open and the sound of bodies being hurled against the wall reverberated through Lillian and Bernie's room.

Lillian's Cocker Spaniel Rudy, who was also along for the trip, sat quietly on his blanket, apparently impervious to all of the commotion.

"Let's pack our stuff, Lill," said Bernie. "I'm going to get us switched to another room on the other side of the motel before this gets completely out of hand."

As Bernie was on the phone telling the motel manager to find them a new room as far away from the commotion as possible, it suddenly got very quiet next door.

"What do you suppose happened?" asked Lillian.

"A police car is outside," said Bernie who had hurried over to the window and peaked out.

Since the police seemed unsure about where the commotion had been taking place, Bernie pulled open the curtain and, catching their attention, he pointed to the room next to his so they would know where to investigate.

"Okay, everything's packed," said Lillian.

"All right," said Bernie. "The first chance we get, I'll get you and Rudy into the car and then I'll grab our stuff."

Just then there was another loud rap on the door next door, this time with the butt of a police flashlight.

"Open up in there. This is the police," shouted a commanding voice.

"Just a minute, officer," came a meek reply. "I'll be right there."

This was followed by a lot of hoarse whispering and shuffling about that Lillian and Bernie could hear through the door.

CRASH!

The police had heard the whispering too and quickly decided to take the initiative and let themselves in.

"GET DOWN! DOWN ON THE FLOOR! THAT MEANS YOU TOO! PUT YOUR HANDS WHERE I CAN SEE THEM!"

"HE'S GOT A GUN, OFFICER!" yelled one of the occupants of the room.

"THROW THE GUN ON THE BED! NOW!" yelled an officer.

These police commands were accompanied by yells and cusses and loud thumps and screams of pain.

As things began to quiet down, the phone in Bernie's room rang.

"Sir, we have a room for you on the other side of the motel. If you would like to stop by the office and turn in your key, we can give you your new key."

"We'll be there as soon as we can," said Bernie.

THUMP!

This time the thump was up against the outside of the door to his own room, and Bernie rushed to look out of the curtain to see what was happening.

"Can we go now?" asked Lillian.

"Not yet," said Bernie. "A cop has a guy pushed up against our door and he's putting the cuffs on him. As soon as he puts him in his car, we'll go for it."

Still Rudy sat quietly. No barking. No fidgeting. Maybe he figured he really didn't have to do anything unless some threat entered his immediate space.

When all of the police action was finally confined to the interior of the room next door and to the patrol cars that had converged on the scene, Bernie decided it was time.

"Okay. Let's go!" said Bernie.

It wouldn't be easy, but Bernie was going to have to try and get some rest that night because in the morning he was scheduled to deliver a couple of *Persona* Performances at a Kentucky Junior Classical League convention being held the next day across the river in Louisville.

But who could possibly go right to sleep after all that?

October 15, 2000
Broad Ripple, Indianapolis
"Now, who's that supposed to be? A monk?" asked Lillian.

"No. That's Vertumnus, the husband of Pomona," replied Bernie.

"What did he do?" asked Phil.

"Well, he was the Roman god who watched over plants as their blossoms turned to fruit. I figured he would be a good guy to have here in the garden."

Vertumnus stood at least 6 feet tall. He had been carved from the stump of a black walnut tree that Bernie had allowed to remain after the rest of the tree had been felled.

The tree had been a lot smaller when they had moved into the house back in 1972, and a swing had once been hung from one of its branches for Cindy and Phil. A line had also once been run from the trunk of the tree to the far corner of the garage onto which the leash of Phil's dog, Olive, could be hooked so she could run freely back and forth. Lately, however, the tree had grown very tall, and since it overhung the corner of the house in which the master bedroom was located, Lillian lived in fear of being crushed every time there was a nighttime windstorm.

Since this tree was much more dangerous to remove, being thicker, taller and closer to the house than the huge basswood had been, Bernie had hired a one-eyed independent tree cutter to "lay it on the ground." The man was absolutely amazing. He had to be in his late 40's, but even with his handicap, he scooted right up to the highest branches and carefully dropped them one at a time.

Bernie had asked him to leave a 6-foot high stump and to leave the rest of the trunk in as large a piece as possible. He intended to rent a 2-foot long chain saw and slab the wood for some special project.

Although there is an urban myth about the tremendous value of black walnut trees, Bernie had carefully looked into the matter and discovered that saw mills are reluctant to purchase hardwood trunks that have stood on residential lots. Since the main value of such trunks is for veneer production, the saw mill operators are afraid to risk ruining their veneer blades by running into nails that are frequently left imbedded in residential trees. One sawmill had expressed an interest in Bernie's black walnut log, but he would have had to pay to have it loaded onto a truck and delivered to the mill. Then, what he was being offered for the log would barely have been enough to cover his expenses.

So he decided to slab the log and let the slabs dry until he could think of what to make from them.

October 31, 2000
Our Lady of Peace Cemetery, Indianapolis

"How soon can you guys get here tonight?" Cyndi and Phil were asked by their dad who had a special Halloween surprise planned for them.

"They can't get here until after 5:00 p.m.," Bernie explained to Lillian. "I'll have to make special arrangements so we can still get in."

"This is too weird. Why are we doing it?" asked Lillian who really wasn't all that excited about taking the kids to see their recently purchased burial crypt at Our Lady of Peace Cemetery.

"Well, someone should know that we bought it, and, besides, it will be perfect for Halloween," replied Bernie.

When Cyndi arrived, she was still wearing her "Grim Reaper" costume that she had just worn to a Halloween get together.

As she and Phil sat in the back seat, their dad drove the family out to the cemetery entrance. When they got there, it was locked, but special arrangements had been made. In a little while, an attendant drove up, glanced into the car and stared briefly at Cyndi draped in black in the back seat.

"Thank you for letting us in," said Bernie, looking as solemn as possible. "It was important for our children to be here this evening."

The attendant gave no indication that he thought the whole ritual weird in any way. He opened the gate and went back to wherever it was that he had come from.

As they entered the cemetery, there was still enough light to see how to get to the mausoleum, on the north outside wall of which was a marble square with the names Bernard F. and Lillian R. Barcio carved into it. Beneath each name was a date of birth.

As they all took turns posing under the marble nameplate, photos were taken that Cyndi would later post in her cubicle at work in Dallas in an effort to explain some of the perceived oddities of her own personality.

November, 2000
Columbus, Indiana

"It's early yet," said Karen, "But Mike is looking real good."

"How close is he to having the votes he needs?" asked Bernie.

"Shhh," said Karen, "look! They're doing an update."

The room full of Mike Pence for Congress supporters grew absolutely still. Everyone had their eyes and ears focused on the television sets that had been set up in the motel banquet room rented for the occasion.

"That's it, folks," said the announcer. "It looks like Mike Pence has just obtained the lead he needs to move to Washington!"

The room exploded with cheers and whistles as everyone wanted to shake Mike's hand at once.

Karen and Mike's three children, Michael J., Charlotte and Audrey, sat with their grandparents and watched. They knew that something good had just happened, but they had no idea how this was about to change the rest of their lives.

March, 2001
The Sundance Film Festival, Park City, Utah

"Dear Phil & Ross," the postcard read that came in the mail, "We got the **Carlos & Alejandro** stuff you sent us! Sincerely, The Sundance Film Festival."

Although Phil had shifted his focus to fiction writing, Ross was still determined to break into the film business. He had an idea for a silent movie telling of an attempt to bring an exotic animal called a Kuheamundi into the country from South America, and he had enlisted Phil's help to write and produce the film. It must be noted that Phil believes the animal's name is spelled "kudamundi," but the author obtained his spelling by calling a store that dealt in exotic animals.

The opening boards of the silent film read:

"There were three
German peanuts walking
Down the road...

...und von vas assaulted!"

CARLOS & ALEJANDRO

A BIG DONUT MOVIES PRODUCTION"

Ross had financed most of the cost of shooting and editing the movie although he and Phil collaborated on all the technical aspects of the film. After an introductory screening at a local coffee house, Ross was ready to throw his bread out onto the waters and see what would happen.

The acknowledgement postcard (which Phil had had to pre-write and pre-address so it could be dropped in the mail to them when the film arrived) was all that ever came of the venture.

But, hey, how many people can actually say that they've submitted a film to Sundance?

July 10, 2001
Misty Mountain Campground, Charlottesville, Virginia

"Hap-py Birth-day dear Lil-lian (Mom), Hap-py Birth-day to you!"

Bernie and Phil had decorated the camp table with balloons and managed to locate a small cake for the occasion. They were celebrating Lillian's 70th birthday at Misty Mountain Campground near Charlottesville, Virginia.

As Lillian and Bernie had discussed their forthcoming retirement years, one of the ideas that Lillian had shared was that she would like to buy a motorhome and tour the country, visiting the children and seeing the sights.

Over the course of his teaching career, Bernie had seen so many fellow teachers plan carefully for their retirement only to die almost immediately after they had turned in their school keys. He hated the thought of something like that happening to them before they began to realize any of their retirement dreams.

"You know, Lill," Bernie had announced one day, "I've got three East Coast *Persona* performances scheduled for July. Rather than driving out there by car and paying for motel rooms and meals at restaurants, I'll bet we could rent a motorhome for about the same amount in travel expenses."

A few calls to Cruise America confirmed Bernie's supposition.

"Phil, JoMamma and I are planning to drive to the East Coast in a rented 27-foot motorhome for a couple weeks in July, would you be interested in joining us and share the driving?"

Phil had been thrilled to be invited and gladly accepted.

Now he was joining in the on-the-road birthday party for his mom.

The trip had gone well. They had even been able to arrange to visit briefly with Karen in Virginia and Sheryl and her daughter and granddaughters in New Jersey. As they got back to Indiana, however, Lillian said she was not feeling very well.

"Why don't you lie down on the bed in the back?" asked Bernie.

"No," said Lillian, "I'll just sit here at the table. I really don't want to move."

No sooner had Bernie driven the Cruise America motorhome into the driveway at 6026 Indianola on the evening of Sunday, July 15, than Lillian said she would like to be driven to the hospital. Immediately!

Dr. George, the surgeon on duty that evening at St. Vincent's decided that Lillian's gallbladder was ready to burst and would require emergency surgery to be removed.

After Lillian had been wheeled off to be prepped for the operation, Bernie called Phil who was unloading the motorhome and brought him up to date.

"Can you take care of Rudy and the cats until I get home?" asked Bernie.

"Sure, Dad," assured Phil. "The motorhome is unloaded and cleaned up."

"Will you be able to drive over with me to return it in the morning?" asked Bernie.

Phil agreed and, after ending the phone call, Bernie wandered off to get a cup of soup from the vending machine.

"A member of the Barcio family," announced the volunteer in the surgery waiting room.

Bernie was shown into a small sitting room where he was to wait for Dr. George.

"Hi," said a strange doctor who suddenly entered the room and took a seat opposite Bernie.

Bernie didn't recognize him, but sat quietly as the doctor looked over his notes.

"We had to remove a very large mass from her stomach," said the doctor.

"How is she doing?" asked Bernie.

"She's resting comfortably, but she's going to be a good twenty pounds lighter when she's released."

"Well,' said Bernie smiling, "she'll certainly be happy about that."

The doctor looked at Bernie over the tops of his reading glasses. He wasn't smiling.

"Did you do the operation instead of Dr. George?" asked Bernie.

"Dr. George?" asked the doctor with a puzzled look on his face.

"Yes, Dr. George talked to me beforehand and said that he would be removing her gallbladder."

"I didn't remove her gallbladder," said the doctor looking even more puzzled. "Aren't you Mr. Thomas?"

"No," said Bernie, "I'm Bernie Barcio. My wife, Lillian, was having her gallbladder removed."

"I'm sorry," said the doctor. "I thought this was the right room."

The doctor simply got up and left with no further explanation.

"My God," thought Bernie to himself, "I'm glad he didn't come in here and tell me that his patient had died!"

As Bernie sat in the consultation room and pondered the chances of what had just happened, in walked Dr. George, looking happy and encouraging.

"That was the worst gallbladder I've ever had to remove," announced Dr. George. "It was a miracle that it hadn't burst!"

So Lillian had escaped another close call, and Dr. George now had a story that he could share with his colleagues.

September 11, 2001
Indianapolis

"Hey, Phil, do you have your T.V. on?" asked Phil's Dad.

"No. What's going on?"

"Turn it on. All hell is breaking lose on the east coast. They're crashing airplanes into buildings."

Bernie Barcio had been in the bathroom listening to W.I.B.C. on the radio as he brushed his teeth. A brief phone interview was being broadcast with a caller from New York.

"What?" the D.J. had asked.

"It looks like a plane just crashed into the side of the World Trade Center."

"Was it a big plane?"

"It looked like a small plane from here…Oh my God!"

"What? What's going on?" asked the D.J.

"There's another one! Another plane just hit the other tower. A full sized jet!"

Well, that ended the tooth brushing for the morning. Bernie and his wife, Lillian, both glued themselves to the television coverage in the living room, watching first-hand as, later in the morning, both towers imploded and collapsed in a cloud of dust.

During the initial live T.V. coverage, Bernie swore he saw bodies falling from one of the towers, but the networks were very careful to edit out any such further scenes.

Months later, when a film documentary aired that happened to have been being made that day of the life of a rookie fireman in New York City, the sound track would record an ongoing series of thumps on the roof above a twin tower lobby in which the camera crew was set up. The thumps were the sounds being made by the bodies of those who were leaping from the upper story windows.

In Arlington, Virginia, where Karen Pence was teaching in the school attended by her children, she was unaware of what was happening until much later in the morning. Unbeknownst to Karen, her husband, Congressman Mike Pence, had been quickly hustled away to a secure holding area when it was discovered that additional targets for the attacks included the Pentagon and the White House near which Mike had his office.

It would be much later that evening before Karen and her children and Bernie and Lillian and Phil would learn just what had happened to Mike after he went incommunicado following the attacks.

October, 2001
Broad Ripple, Indianapolis

Bernie had just finished what he considered to be one of his all-time masterpieces and had proudly engraved "*B.F.B. faciebat MMI*" on the backside of the headboard. Like Antonio Stradivarius, the famed Italian violin maker who also signed his creations with the Latin word "*faciebat*" instead of the usual "*fecit*" because he "was making" (*faciebat*) them for a long period of time, rather than simply stating that "he made" (*fecit*) them, Bernie had spent months constructing his *magnum opus*.

Bernie's *magnum opus* was an ornately carved solid black walnut four-poster queen-sized bed frame that, using only simple tools, he had handcrafted from the slabbed log of the black walnut tree that had once overhung their master bedroom.

As Lillian would joke to all the neighbors and friends who dropped in to see the wondrous creation, "I used to worry about the black walnut tree falling on us, and now we're sleeping in it!"

Mrs. Hulvershorn, Bernie's neighbor to the south, was so impressed with the bed that, for a while, she would call once or twice a week to request permission to bring guests and members of her family over to admire it.

December 11, 2001
Lynwood, Illinois

Aunt Rose Nudi, Gusty's first wife, had been handicapped since her stroke on January 31, 1990. Now, a little more than eleven years later, she had passed away.

"Mom passed away in my arms," said Kathy to her cousin Bernie who had driven to Chicago with Lillian to attend his aunt's funeral.

As far as Bernie and Lillian were concerned, Kathy was a saint for the care she had given her mother over the past eleven years.

Before Aunt Rose had her stroke, Kathy was working as a secretary for the CIA in Washington D.C. When she heard on January 31, 1990, that her mom had had a stroke, she flew back to Chicago and was at her mom's bedside on February 1. She had simply locked the door to her apartment in Virginia and left. It would be another year before she would return to Virginia, and then only to put her belongings in storage and give up her lease.

Since she already had her security clearance, Kathy was able to get work with the Department of the Army in Chicago where she worked for the next eleven years as she cared for her mom. During the workday, Kathy arranged for a very dear and reliable home care provider to be at the house that Kathy's dad had built himself beginning in 1954.

That first year, Gusty had only enough money to finish the basement of the house. Once that was done, complete with water, sewer, power and heat, he covered over the floor joists with tar paper and moved his family into the basement. He would finish the main floor of the house the following year, although Kathy recalls moving into the main floor during the summer before any of the windows had been installed.

"It was unbearably hot and we were eaten alive by mosquitoes as we all slept in what would end up being the kitchen," recalled Kathy years later.

As Kathy cared for her mom on the main floor of their house, her brother, Rocky, lived in the basement apartment. Since, however, his work as a heavy equipment operator often took him out of town for days at a time, Kathy assumed all responsibility for her mom's care. Rocky helped by taking care of the yard work which was substantial since the house had been built on a rather large lot.

At Aunt Rose's interment service, those gathered smiled as Elvis Presley's "Green, Green Grass of Home" was played as per Aunt Rose's request. Then the priest invited all present to share their favorite Aunt Rose story before he concluded with one of his own.

"Kathy, I still remember that Sunday when your mom absolutely refused to return home with you after church. She certainly was a strong willed woman. You were so patient with her that those of us who were watching from a distance could only marvel how you slowly calmed her down and finally won her over. You definitely have the patience of a saint!"

After her mom was laid to rest, Kathy was finally able to seek employment in Washington D.C. again. This time, however, she stayed with the

Department of the Army and simply requested a transfer from the Chicago office.

Kathy's life goal remained, however, to gain an overseas assignment with an agency of the United States Government.

January 5, 2002
Indianapolis

"Phil," said Ross, "I think we've been ripped off."

Ross had met a film producer in California that was interested in an idea for a movie featuring rap stars and a road trip that he and Phil had come up with. They had worked for a couple of years co-writing the script. They had even made changes that the California producer had suggested be made before he turned it over to his selection panel.

After the panel had nixed the script, Ross had gotten the idea of posting the script on a web site that was frequently consulted by directors and producers seeking ideas for films. Ross had just gotten a call in response to that posting.

"Now what's wrong?" asked Phil.

"I just got a call from a guy out west who saw our script on the website."

"Is he interested in it?" asked Phil.

"He said he likes the idea, but said that there was already a very similar script in production and he thought that we should be aware of that," said Ross.

So there they had it. All the traffic their script had seen going from one office to another in California seemed to have given someone else the opportunity to steal its unique concept and have a similar script created.

It's a vicious business.

Not long afterwards, Phil decided he no longer wanted to be in business with Ross. They disbanded BIG DONUT MOVIES, and Phil began to concentrate on his writing.

January 10, 2002
Houston, Texas

Just when Joe thought it would be a normal day of tours at Space Center Houston, he had the honor of being asked to lead a VIP tour for a group of Russians, one of whom happened to be Igor P. Farkhutdinov, the Governor of the Sakhalin Region.

Definitely not just another normal day in the life of a retired educator!

April, 2002
Houston, Texas

"Excuse me, Mr. Barcio," said Paulo Bauer, the Vice Governor of the State of Santa Catarina, Brazil, "but I'm wondering why the Brazilian flag is not on display with the others?"

Joe had been in the process of explaining the operation of the pool in the Neutral Buoyancy Laboratory to his VIP tour group when he was interrupted.

The group consisted of about five state officials from Brazil along with several Brazilian reporters.

During Joe's explanation, Vice Governor Bauer had been looking at the flags on display in the laboratory, one for each nation taking part in the International Space Station.

Joe couldn't think of a reason why the Brazilian flag had not been included and was just about to say this when he noticed the Building Manager and his assistant entering the building.

"Excuse me," called Joe to the Building Manager, "These are guests from Brazil and they were wondering why the Brazilian flag has not been included in the display."

"Actually," replied the Building Manager, "I've been trying to get a Brazilian flag, but for some reason I've had a very hard time. In fact, I only just recently received a lead on how to obtain one."

Later, when the group had left, Joe was contacted by the Building Manager and asked if he would like to be present when the flag was hung.

"I would love to," said Joe.

Three weeks later, Joe and Liz were present in the Neutral Buoyancy Laboratory at 9:00 a.m., camera in hand, to witness the hanging of the Brazilian flag.

"Smile," Joe said to the workman climbing the ladder, "this picture is going to be sent to Brazil!"

Two weeks later, Joe received a beautiful letter from Vice Governor Bauer on State Department stationary. Because the letter is written in Portuguese, Joe can only assume that it is a thank you letter and has added it to his collection of memorabilia.

April 29, 2002
Houston, Texas

"*Buon Giorno*," said Joe as he tried out his somewhat limited command of the Italian language on his special visitors. "*Buon venuto!*"

"*Buona trovata*," came the traditional reply from one of the members of the group.

At times like this, he wished his brother Bernie were present who was a little more comfortable with the *lingua patriae*.

The group consisted of a large number of Omega watch dealers from Italy under the special leadership of astronaut Tom Stafford. Joe's job was simply to accompany Stafford and his group on the Johnson Space Center Campus.

Joe was more than a little pleased by this unique opportunity. Not only would he have a chance to try out more Italian on his guests, but he would be spending the day with an astronaut who had flown on the Gemini 6 Mission in December, 1965, and the Gemini 9 Mission in June, 1966. Stafford had also flown on the Apollo 10 mission to the moon in May, 1969, and, with his fellow astronaut, he orbited the moon more than 20 times, tested out the Lunar Lander (which they did not land), and took pictures of the moon's surface to prepare for Apollo 11. Tom Stafford had also been the commander of the Apollo-Soyuz Mission in July 1975.

Che bella fortuna for Joe!

Memorial Day, 2002
Dallas, Texas

"You know, Cyn, if you're lookin' to be married, you're livin' in the wrong house," announced Dave one Sunday after he had had more than his usual quota of weekend beers.

Cyndi knew that Dave had a weekend drinking problem, but she thought that he had gotten it under control when he had moved down to Dallas by himself several years earlier. In fact, he had even assured her that he had it under control when he invited her to come to Dallas and move in with him in a little house he had bought.

Cyndi had believed him and had moved to Dallas where she easily found work.

"Cyn, anytime you want to get married, you just say the word and we'll go look at rings," Dave had said to her repeatedly during the years that she was living with him.

They had even built a new home together in Allen, just outside of Dallas. Although they had not yet gotten married, both their names were on the title.

Finally, Cyndi decided it was time.

"O.K., Dave," she announced one Saturday. "Let's get married."

Dave had to think—and drink—about it for a while, but he had finally phrased his answer.

When Dave came home from work a few days later, he was shocked to see that Cyndi had moved out, lock, stock and barrel. She was gone. Her stuff was gone. Her cats were gone.

Cyndi had easily found a very convenient location at the Gaston Apartments. She couldn't believe it when she learned that the neighbors in the apartment directly below hers were named Liz and Joe, just like her Aunt and Uncle in Texas.

Good move, Cyndi!

A year later, Cyndi would move again, this time to a new apartment complex closer to her work.

June 15, 2002
Houston, Texas

When Joe met his VIP tour group, he was somewhat taken aback by the number of security agents who were assigned to accompany the tour.

"Your primary guest is Nguyen Manh Cam, Deputy Prime Minister of Vietnam, and he is not to be given a normal tour," confided one of the Secret Service agents to Joe.

"Why Not?"

"Since Mr. Cam is a Communist, we are not allowing him to visit the Johnson Space Center. Too many security problems."

"He wanted to meet with Governor Rick Perry," added an F.B.I. agent who was also standing nearby, "but the Governor refused to meet with him."

With the tone for the day having thus been set, Joe introduced himself to Mr. Cam and his entourage, which consisted of eight other Vietnamese officials, American Secret Service Agents, members of the F.B.I. and a Houston Police Officer who served as interpreter. The officer had been born in Vietnam but spoke impeccable English.

Three hours later, as the limited access tour was drawing to a close, Joe made so bold as to ask Mr. Cam if he had a business card. Courteous to a fault, Mr. Cam searched his suit jacket pockets but found none. He then had his aide open a brief case, searched there and found none.

"That's okay," said Joe to the interpreter. "Please tell Mr. Cam he doesn't need to bother. It was just a thought."

But, no! The Deputy Prime Minister of Vietnam continued searching through other brief cases his aides carried until he found his business card, which he politely handed to Joe.

When the tour was over, Joe accompanied the group to a caravan of four limousines that awaited them. Joe intended to offer Mr. Cam a final handshake before he entered his limo, but at the last minute a Secret Service Agent, a huge man with crossed arms, put himself directly between Joe and his guest.

Joe moved over to the side a bit and gave his guest a wave instead.

Mr. Cam politely waved back.

"Communist!" said one of the Secret Service Agents in a surly voice as the limousines drove off.

And, of course, he was right. Joe had just spent the day with the second highest political official from Vietnam. Mr. Cam, however, was the most polite Communist Joe had ever met.

And he has the pictures and business card to prove it!

June 22, 2002
Houston, Texas

"Tell us about your selection as an astronaut," said one of the guests whom retired astronaut Joe Edwards had brought to Space Center Houston.

Joe Barcio had been asked to serve a tour guide for the special group. As is usual, he joined the group for their lunch break half-way through the tour and was able to be in on the casual conversations with Edwards.

"Well, you know," began Edwards in reply, "there were many other candidates that I believe were equally qualified."

"Why do you think they chose you?" asked another guest.

"I guess I was just fortunate," said Edwards with the humility that Joe has come to recognize in almost all of the astronauts whom he has been privileged to meet.

July, 2002
Houston, Texas

Joe had already put in a full day at Space Center Houston when he happened to overhear the Director expressing their regrets to a late arriving group.

"I'm very sorry, Mr. Kamigahira, but the last VIP tour has already been conducted for the day. Would your guests be able to come back tomorrow?"

"No, that will not be possible. They are representatives of the Japanese Space Agency and will be flying back to Tokyo in the morning."

"I would be honored to give them a special tour," spoke up Joe. "If that would be permissible."

Joe didn't believe that America's partners in the Space Station should be turned away.

"You wouldn't mind working late?" asked the Director.

"No. I'll just call my wife and let her know that I'll be home a little later than usual."

"Thank you very much, Sir," said Mr. Kamigahira. "My guests will be most appreciative."

So, setting out, Joe made the acquaintance and earned the lasting gratitude of Yuki Kamigahira, the Public Affairs Representative of the Japanese Consulate in Houston, Makiko Hayashida, a Public Relations Representative from Tokyo, and Minoru Yonekura, the Director of Public Relations, also from Tokyo.

True to what Joe had already learned many times in the past, his Japanese guests were extremely courteous and expressed their thanks in profound words.

August 4, 2002
Broad Ripple, Indianapolis

It had been nearly four years since Dr. Youngblood had recommended that Lillian have any serious diagnostic tests. This time, because of some of the symptoms that Lillian was displaying, Dr. Youngblood sent Lillian to have a CT-scan performed at St. Vincent Hospital. Unfortunately, Dr. Youngblood turned out to be about three years too late with her recommendation.

The CT-scan revealed cancerous growths in Lillian's kidney and lesions in her left lung. The biopsy report indicated that it was Stage 4 kidney cancer. This was followed by several weeks of waiting and additional tests while the doctors tried to determine whether they were dealing with lung cancer that had metastasized to the kidney or vice versa. They finally decided that neither was the case, and that Lillian was suffering from two completely separate cancers that had nothing to do with each other.

Lillian's Oncologist, Dr. Schultz, and another kidney specialist at St. Vincent Hospital were up front with Bernie and Lillian from the beginning.

"There is no cure for kidney cancer!" they both stated matter-of-factly.

"We can treat the lesions in the lung with radiation," said Dr. Schultz, "but all we can do is try a few treatments to see if we can get the infected lymph nodes surrounding the kidney to reduce in size."

"What happens then?" asked Bernie.

"If they do shrink, we may be able to remove the infected kidney," said Dr. Schultz.

"Can a person survive very well with one kidney?" asked Lillian.

"Certainly," assured Dr. Schultz.

"Well, when do we start?" asked Lillian, taking a positive attitude from the very beginning.

The first series of treatments involved the use of Interluken 2. Unfortunately, Lillian was not able to tolerate more than one full treatment. Additional treatments had to be cut short, and the size of the lymph nodes were not reduced, although their growth did seem to have been stunted.

After 21 radiation treatments, however, the lesions in Lillian's left lung were successfully treated.

August 20, 2002
Broad Ripple, Indianapolis

"Hey, Dad, what are you working on?" asked Phil as he entered the former offices of **The Village Sampler** and the **Pompeiiana NEWSLETTER**, both of which had been prepped for publishing in the basement of the Barcio home at 6026 Indianola.

"Well, you know how your mom always wanted to put all of the historical articles that she ran in the **Sampler** in a special publication?" asked Bernie.

"Yeah, I know. We even wrote to the Indiana Historical Society to see if we could get a grant to do the publication, but we never got a reply," mourned Phil.

"Well, I've decided to do the publication for her. I'm going to lay out the articles in a 12-page tabloid newspaper format," said Bernie.

"How will you afford to have it printed?" asked Phil.

"It will be published by Pompeiiana, Inc., as a fund raising project. We can have 10,000 copies printed in B/W on newsprint fairly reasonably and then sell them for $1.00 a copy to raise money for Pompeiiana," said Bernie.

"Think it will work?" asked Phil.

"I think so," projected Bernie. "We can sell the copies at special Broad Ripple events and offer them at bulk rates to Broad Ripple business for resale to their customers. It should work."

Thus, in May of 2003, 10,000 copies of the **Special Edition of The Village Sampler Early History of Broad Ripple, Indiana**, were picked up from the printer.

In the end, Pompeiiana, Inc., not only recovered its initial expenses, but was also able to raise money to be applied to its not-for-profit operations. In December of 2003, the remaining copies of the Special Edition were purchased by the Broad Ripple Village Association for distribution at future Broad Ripple Events.

Lillian's hope of someday putting all of the historical articles that she ran in the Sampler in a special publication had been realized.

October 14, 2002
Johnson Space Center, Houston, Texas

"Joe," asked his supervisor, "how would you like to spend the day with Buzz Aldrin?"

Would he! Aldrin was an astronaut who had flown on Apollo 11 to the moon and was the second man to walk on its surface on July 20, 1969.

"Mr. Aldren, welcome home," said Joe when he was introduced since Aldrin had trained at the Johnson Space Center.

"Thank you, Joe," replied Aldrin.

It turned out to be Joe's privilege to serve as tour guide for Aldrin and his guests as they visited the Center, and to have lunch seated next to him.

What Joe cherishes the most from the day, however, is the picture taken of him and Aldrin standing under the five giant rocket engines of the Saturn 5 rocket located on the Johnson Space Center grounds.

January, 2003
Johnson Space Center, Houston, Texas

As Joe was organizing his group to begin a scheduled protocol tour, a young woman with a noticeable French accent came up to speak privately with him.

"Excuse me, Sir," she began. "I am a member of your tour today, and I am hoping that we will be able to visit the Neutral Buoyancy Laboratory."

"No," said Joe, "I'm afraid that the Neutral Buoyancy Lab is not part of our official itinerary today."

"Oh, please," persisted the young lady. "We must visit the lab because I am hoping to see my uncle whom I have not seen for ten years."

"And who is your uncle?" asked Joe.

"My uncle is Claude Nicollier. He is a French astronaut with the European Space Agency, and I was told that he would be training in Neutral Buoyancy Laboratory today. I absolutely must have a chance to see him."

"I'm very sorry," said Joe again, "but if a building has not been put on our official itinerary, I'm not allowed to take a tour group to visit it."

"Here," continued the young woman. "Here is my uncle's phone number at the Lab. Please be so kind as to call him, and I'm sure he will tell you that it is alright to visit."

So Joe pulled out his cell phone and dialed the number. He was more than a little surprised when he found himself speaking directly with astronaut Claude Nicollier.

"Mr. Nicollier," began Joe, "I am a tour guide here at the Space Center, and I have a young lady in my group today who says she is your niece."

"But, of course! I was hoping she would contact me if she visited the Space Center. Joe," continued Nicollier, "give me just a few minutes, and I'll arrange for all of you to have special passes to visit the Lab."

Wow!

As soon as he hung up, Joe contacted his Duty Manager and told her where he was planning to go and why. She gave her immediate approval.

When the tour group arrived at the Neutral Buoyancy Lab, they were ushered right onto the main floor where Claude Nicollier and his niece had a warm, and long overdue, reunion.

Ever since that day, Joe has an open invitation to call upon Nicollier any time if he would like to bring another group "on the floor of the pool."

February 1, 2003
Houston, Texas

Once again, Joe and Liz were standing outside their home hoping to see the reappearance of the orange glow as the shuttle Columbia once again made its way toward its intended Florida landing site. On board was astronaut David Brown whom Joe had been privileged to meet in December 2002, just about four weeks before he launched into space aboard the Shuttle Columbia for the first time. Brown had come up to Joe as he was working with a small group of guests just outside Building 9.

"Hi," Brown had said in a very friendly manner.

"Hi," replied Joe.

"Would it be okay for me to give each of you a mission decal?"

"Sure," said Joe. "Please go right ahead."

Brown handed every one in the group a decal before finally handing one to Joe.

"May I ask your name?" said Joe.

"I'm David Brown," said Brown pointing to his name on the decal he had just handed Joe. "I'm going up on the next mission."

Brown was 40 years old, a bachelor, a doctor of medicine and an astronaut. He was obviously very excited about his forthcoming first mission in space.

This time however, instead of hearing that the Shuttle Columbia had safely landed in Florida, Joe and Liz were horrified to learn that the Columbia, with David Brown on board, had disintegrated as it flew over northern Texas, killing all on board.

February 22, 2003
Indianapolis Retirement Home

When the phone rang this morning, it was 5:30 a.m., and Bernie knew his mom had passed away before he even picked up the receiver.

He had received several phone calls from the Charge Nurse at the Indianapolis Retirement Home over the past month. They all reported that his mom was on the verge of dying. The first couple of times he had hopped into his truck and driven down. He even had the priest from St. Peter and Paul come and administer the Blessing of the Sick.

Then it was decided that Stella Barcio was simply suffering from Potassium poisoning. Her doctor had ordered her daily dose of Lasix to be drastically reduced, but he had not ordered a similar reduction in the number of Potassium pills she was given daily to counter the effect of the Lasix.

So after a few days in the Cardiac Intensive Ward at Methodist Hospital, Stella was sent back to her room.

Still the calls came. One Charge Nurse after another would call every couple of days with the news that Stella's demise was imminent. Bernie had taken to spending a half hour with his mom daily all through the month of February ever since he had first been alerted to her critical condition.

"But I just left her not 20 minutes ago," said Bernie when another call came in.

"Well, Mr. Barcio, I just came on duty and thought I should let you know. The bottoms of her feet are turning yellow and that's usually one of the final signs."

"Thank you for calling," said Bernie. "I'll check back with you later to see how she's doing.

The next day, Stella was about the same. She slept a lot, but would wake up when he came into the room and look at him for a moment. She was no longer speaking, but she would accept an occasional sip of water through a straw when he offered it to her. Bernie stayed for a while, said a rosary for his mom as was his custom throughout this final month, and returned home.

When another call came in about 11:00 p.m., Bernie thanked the Charge Nurse and said he would come down the first thing in the morning to see how Stella was doing.

Now, after the 5:30 a.m. call, there was no sense of panic or urgency. Bernie had pre-arranged and pre-paid her funeral several years earlier, complete to the details of the church service to be held in Chicago and burial next to Bernie's dad in St. Mary's Cemetery. In fact, her name and birth date were already engraved on the headstone.

Earlier in the month, when the first calls had alerted Bernie to his mom's impending death, he had selected a dress and jewelry that he would take to the undertaker. He had even made a commemorative video of her life that he intended to show at the funeral luncheon. All he had to do now was simply follow things through.

He felt no panic. In fact, as he met with the undertaker to finalize the arrangements, he was completely composed. He had already "experienced" her death, complete with privately shed tears, so many times earlier during the month that the actual event seemed to be post climactic.

March, 2003
Broad Ripple, Indianapolis

"Well, we've got one extra box left," said Bernie to Phil who was watching him pack up samples of Grandma Barcio's crochet handiwork to mail to relatives and friends.

"Why don't you send it to Marsha?" suggested Phil.

"Hmmm," said Bernie. "Not a bad idea. I could put the Retirement Home's return address on it so she just wouldn't toss it as soon as she got it."

So the last box of Grandma Barcio memorabilia was mailed to her sort-of granddaughter, Marsha. In it Bernie had placed a typewritten note explaining that Stella Barcio had passed away and that her crochet work was being distributed among family and friends. No signature.

May, 2003
Johnson Space Center, Houston, Texas
"Would you be willing to pose for a few pictures?" Joe asked Nancy Currie who happened to be in the Building 9 Robotics laboratory as Joe was leading a VIP tour of the facility. On this particular day, Joe's wife, Liz, also happened to be in the group.

At first, Currie was hesitant.

"As taxpayers," Joe continued, "they would really treasure a picture of you."

"Okay," said Currie finally.

This was indeed a rare opportunity for Joe and his guests since Nancy Currie had already made four flights into space on various space shuttles.

May 17, 2003
Bahia Honda State Park, The Keys, Florida
Phil and Audrey had fallen in love on the beach at Bahia Honda State Park located along the Florida Keys.

Before this wondrous event, they had known each other for a couple years having worked next door to each other in Broad Ripple. Phil was a waiter at Mezza Luna, an upscale Italian restaurant, and Audrey was a waitress at La Jolla, an always-packed Mexican restaurant. Audrey was also an airline hostess (she resented being referred to as a "Stewardess") for ATA and only waited tables between flight assignments. They had caught each other's eye as they waited on customers seated at the patio tables that each restaurant featured. They talked occasionally, but nothing serious.

Then, suddenly, Audrey was gone. Phil learned that she had moved to Phoenix so she could accept ATA flights originating from that hub. So that was that. Or was it?

One day, as Phil went out on the patio to do some set ups, he looked over and there was Audrey. He couldn't believe it. Now he wished he had her phone number, but didn't really want to come right out and ask for it.

Audrey was also happy to see that Phil was still working at Mezza Luna. So, when Brian Brothers, a friend of Phil's, came in to La Jolla for lunch one afternoon, Audrey wrote her phone number down on a slip of paper and gave it to Brian.

"Tell him that you knew he wanted it, and that you were able to find it out on the sly," said Audrey.

Brian agreed, and after he had finished his lunch, he walked over to see Phil.

"Here, Phil," said Brian bluntly, "Audrey wanted me to give you her number."

Since Audrey could get guest passes for air travel, she and Phil were able to take several flights together, one of which had included a romantic layover in the Florida Keys.

Now they had invited family and friends down to Florida to witness their marriage on the same beach on which they had fallen in love. All the guests stayed in Key West in accommodations that Phil and his fiancée had arranged beforehand. This was definitely the most unique and special wedding any of the guests had ever attended. Phil's sister, Cyndi, sang a special wedding song on the beach; Phil's friend, Brian Brothers, who had recently become an ordained minister in addition to being a lawyer, performed the ceremony, and all of Phil's other male friends and cousins in attendance performed the traditional "dunking" ceremony by carrying Phil out into the surf and giving him the old heave-ho.

When Phil and Audrey returned to Indianapolis, they lived briefly in one half of a double in Woodruff Place, but immediately began serious house hunting. They knew that it was silly to spend money on rent that could be going toward building equity in a home of their own.

Phil was still as dedicated as ever to his writing—when he wasn't working as a Black Belt Karate instructor at Broad Ripple Martial Arts Academy and waiting tables at R Bistro in downtown Indianapolis. These jobs provided the income needed so he and his new wife, Audrey, could maintain the little 1890's Victorian home they eventually bought at 925 Prospect, near Fountain Square.

July 11, 2003
Houston, Texas

Joseph Mingari, Joe's father-in-law whom he and his wife Liz had moved to Houston with them from Oshkosh, Wisconsin, passed away.

Although Joe Barcio celebrated his birthday on the same day as his father-in-law, Joseph Mingari had been born in Sicily on September 17 in 1908. After coming to America, he married a cousin of his, Sarafina (called Sally in English) Galati, and they both went to work to make a life for themselves and their daughter, Elizabeth whom Joe Barcio later married.

Liz recalls that both her mom and dad were hard workers, with her mom working nights at the Square D Company in Milwaukee, and her father frequently working two jobs at the same time. When needed, Joe Mingari would be called in to work on the line at American Motors which manufactured the Nash automobile in Milwaukee, and then, when his shift ended at 3:30 p.m., his wife Sally would meet him outside on the street corner across from their house as he drove by and hand him a sack with dinner which he would eat while working the night shift at the Pfister and Vogel Tanning Company.

During this time, Joe Mingari lived with his family in a flat they rented near Holten and Meinecke in Milwaukee while saving up to purchase a home of their own.

Unfortunately, before their dream could be realized, Sally passed away in 1960, when her daughter Liz was only 19. She had suffered a heart attack while praying the rosary in church.

Joe Mingari went ahead with their plans, however, and eventually was able to purchase a double at 48th and Chambers where he lived with his daughter before she and Joe were married.

Because he wanted his daughter to be familiar with her roots, he traveled with her back to Sicily during one of the summers in the early Sixties. He had even managed to convince his father, who was still living in Sicily, to come to America for a trial visit, but his father quickly returned to Sicily where he preferred to live.

As anyone knows who has ever had to deal with tenants, some are good, and some turn out to be less desirable. This was the case with the first couple to whom Joe Mingari rented the second floor flat of his home. The next tenants, however, were pleasant renters, and the third couple, the Gluchers, actually turned out to be Joe Mingari's life-long friends. After Mr. Glucher passed away, Joe would frequently drive back to Milwaukee from Oshkosh (where he was living to be close to his daughter and son-in-law) to visit Mrs. Glucher. In fact, in his later years, when he was becoming a little forgetful, he would sometimes make the trip more than once during the same day. (Eventually, after Joe Mingari was involved in a serious auto accident while returning from one of these visits, his daughter and son-in-law were forced to take away his driving privileges for his own safety.)

Like many Italian immigrants, Joe Mingari had very definite likes and dislikes as well as clear cut ideas about sports, politics, economics and other immigrants. This author recalls the great pride Joe took in a small fig tree that he grew when it finally bore figs—a little bit of Sicily right there on the side of his house in Milwaukee!

Whenever Joe Mingari met the author, the first topics of conversation were always the Milwaukee Braves and what kind of team did Indianapolis have.

"They're all a bunch of crooks," Joe Mingari would say if asked about investment strategies or politics.

Joe also had little patience for immigrants from other countries who took their time learning English after coming to America.

"You comma dis country, you speaka da English," was his rule of thumb.

At his funeral, Joe's grandson, Bernie Barcio, recalled several bits of wisdom that his grandfather had tried to instill in his grandchildren.

"When-a you drive, you always gotta watch da guy in front of da guy ahead of you!" was the most poignant.

Some people manage to avoid a lot of complications during their lives because they have well-developed bullshit detectors. Joe Mingari was one of these fortunate people, and he tried hard to pass on the ability to his daughter and grandchildren.

August 1, 2003
Broad Ripple, Indianapolis

"Did you mail the builder the house plans we came up with?" asked Lillian.

"Yeah, I did that this afternoon. Kurt said he wouldn't be able to look at them carefully until after the Home Show, but at least he'll have them on his desk," Said Bernie.

For the past several years, Bernie and Lillian had been planning on making a change in their living arrangements as soon as their involvement with Pompeiiana was completed. Since they owned an empty lot and a half just to the south of their home on Indianola, they had sort of dreamed of having a home of their own design built there in which they could live. It would be a lot smaller, and there would be less yard work. Also, the goal was to eliminate stairs as much as possible and have everything on one floor.

Years earlier Bernie had designed a dream home that he had suggested that the Board of Directors of Park School build on that campus for him and Lillian. The idea was nixed, but Bernie had put a lot of effort into those plans, so he simply pulled them out and used them as a basis for the plans they had now drawn up.

While waiting to see one of Lillian's doctors, Bernie had seen an ad in **Indianapolis Monthly** by a custom builder called Kurt Schmadeke.

It was to this builder that he had sent their dream house plans.

September, 2003
Johnson Space Center, Houston, Texas

Joe stood in the viewing area of Space Station Mission Control with his tour group that included several high school students. They were all watching the main floor below as workers ceremoniously hung the mission plaque commemorating the six months that astronaut Ed Lu had recently completed on board the International Space Station.

Present at the ceremony was astronaut Lu himself who had recently returned from Russia where he had landed in a Russian Soyuz.

When the ceremony concluded, Joe was making a few summation remarks to his tour group when—lo and behold—who should enter the viewing area but Ed Lu himself.

"Excuse me, Mr. Lu," said Joe walking over to introduce himself. "I'm Joe Barcio, a tour leader here at the Space Center, and I was wondering if you would say a few words to my tour group."

Lu was very gracious. He spent a few minutes chatting with Joe and the group before excusing himself to attend another meeting.

Talk about being in the right place at the right time!

September 1, 2003
Broad Ripple, Indianapolis

"You know, Lillian," observed Bernie as he entered one of his occasional philosophical moods, "we've made a lot of changes over the years. And, you know, I think every time I switched jobs, we ended up taking a pay cut."

"Yup, we sure did," agreed Lillian.

"But, you know," continued Bernie, "I think I was better off after every move. You can kind of get a sense when what you have to offer is no loner being appreciated, and it's time to move on."

"Oh, I think you did the right thing every time you moved."

"We would probably have a lot more money if I had just stayed put somewhere."

"Well, money isn't everything."

"I guess not. We've also spent a lot on our various projects."

"Like catapults!" observed Lillian.

"Yes, and BLB Enterprises and **The Sampler**."

"Yup, I guess they were all non-profit ventures," agreed Lillian.

"Well, you have to take risks in life."

"That's for sure!"

"I mean, if all we needed was security to be happy, God would probably have made us all be trees."

"Trees?"

"Did you ever think about trees? Like, they grow wherever their seeds are planted. No objections. No say in the matter. They simply put their roots down, mind their own business and hope every one leaves them alone. Trees aren't aggressive; they don't resist whatever anyone tries to do to them. They bend with the wind. Their main goal just seems to be survival."

"So what's your point?"

"My point is we're not trees. We were meant to take chances and to be aggressive in trying new things and avoiding situations that cause grief. I know you've heard me say this before, but if all we wanted to do is eat shit during our lives, we would be better off being scarabs."

"I guess you're right."

"We've taken a lot of chances and made a lot moves," continued Bernie. "And I really don't regret any of them. It means we're alive! It's like I told Pete Walls, the principal at Eastwood, one day when he called me into the office and pointed out that I had one of the thickest teacher files in his cabinet. I told him that was because I probably did more stuff than most other teachers."

September 20, 2003
Broad Ripple, Indianapolis

"I wonder what part of $100,000.00 he didn't understand?" asked Bernie after he and Lillian had met with Kurt Schmadeke.

Kurt had taken the house plans that Bernie had sent him and reworked them a little to come up with a one-floor home to be built on a concrete slab.

Even though Bernie and Lillian had made it as clear as they could that they only had $100,000.00 of equity with which they could work in building the house, Kurt had presented them with a proposal priced at $165,000.00.

"I guess we can begin to look around at some of the other houses on the market and see if there's one we like that we can afford," suggested Bernie.

"I want to stay in this area, though," said Lillian. "Everything is so convenient here."

"And it is a comfortable area to live in!"

October 1, 2003
Broad Ripple, Indianapolis

Audrey Barcio, Phil's bride, was now following her dream. After 9/11, she had become seriously disenchanted with her work as a flight attendant for ATA.

"What would you rather be doing?" Phil had asked her one day.

"I would really like to go back to school and finish getting my degree in Art Therapy," said Audrey.

"Then, why don't you?" encouraged Phil.

So, Audrey had gone back to school.

Audrey's main interest was in abstract art, and before long she was producing canvases that were catching the eyes of some influential art patrons—even though her instructor at the Herron School of Art persisted in offering her nothing but negative criticism.

"Phil," announced Audrey in an excited voice one evening, "I've been invited to display my paintings!"

"Where?"

"In the Upper Room of the Broad Ripple Steak House! They'll be on display for a full month!"

Thus, on Wednesday, October 1st, Audrey's parents and her sister Cheryl drove down from Lafayette to join Audrey, Phil, Bernie and Lillian for the opening reception.

This was Audrey's first big break.

October 4, 2003
Broad Ripple, Indianapolis

For the past several years after Bernie had retired even from his teaching assignments at Butler University and I.U.P.U.I. to devote himself full time to the work of Pompeiiana, Inc., he would often begin his day by telling Lillian that he was "going to work" in the basement.

"You know," Lillian would say, "you are retired, and you don't really have to rush downstairs immediately after breakfast every day."

"Ah, but I do," Bernie would tease. "I'm important, and I have important things to do. Gotta work, work, work!"

That routine was finally about to change.

According to its bylaws, Pompeiiana, Inc., was supposed to hold its annual meeting of the Board of Directors on the fourth Saturday of September. This year, however, a variety of circumstances had prevented the members from being able to get together. So, by mutual agreement, they met around the dining room table at 9:15 a.m. on Saturday, October 4, to hold their final meeting.

After pointing out how a $5,000 grant received from the Allen W. Clowes Charitable Foundation on May 1, 2003, enabled Pompeiiana to operate successfully through the spring and summer, Bernie explained that the current cash on hand and projected income, totaling $627, would be adequate to cover its final projected expenses, which came to exactly $627.

"So, I guess that means Pompeiiana will be closing its operations for good," observed its newest board member, John Broyles.

"We have no other choice," explained Bernie. "We were only able to raise $9,200 of the $500,000 endowment needed to remain in operation after my retirement."

"We really made every effort over the years to raise funds," commented Lillian.

"Teachers did seem to enjoy the **NEWSLETTER**, although, in spite of mass mailings, membership has been falling annually," said Bernie.

"And you feel that we've tried every viable fund raising effort?" asked Gordon Wishard, one of Pompeiiana's longest serving board members.

"Over the years we've done all sorts of things, beginning with a Bottles for Latin program. We even framed that as a contest and were able to send the winner, Brenda Waddle, to visit the Getty Museum in California. Then there was the Pizza Coupon Book that I spent a summer putting together. It was a good idea, but did not generate much money," said Bernie.

"Don't forget the Chariathons," said Lillian.

"Of course. We sponsored the National Chariathon for Latin for a number of years as a fund raising effort. We started out holding it on a parking deck over the canal in Broad Ripple, and then moved it to Obolisk Square downtown. Students would get pledges for the number of laps that they would pull each other around in Roman style chariots. Later, the format changed to an actual race and funds were generated from entry fees. Those races were held at Raceway Park and around the block in Crawfordsville where the Ben Hur Museum is located before we finally sponsored them annually at the Indianapolis Motor Speedway. The kids had a lot of fun, and we had participants coming from a number of surrounding states, but no great amounts of money were ever raised."

"The money did help the general fund, though," observed Lillian.

"Yes, it helped us to keep the cost of the **NEWSLETTER** affordable for students," said Bernie.

"Pompeiiana also produced educational materials to sell like the Roman Emperors Posters that I helped with," observed Donna Wright.

"And bumper strips, buttons, terra cotta plaques, drill tapes, videos, you name it. I think we tried it all!" said Bernie.

"I really don't think there was anything else we could have done," said Lillian.

"I even donated all the proceeds from my *Persona* presentations during the past couple of years, but that basically provided operational funds," said Bernie.

"The foundation support just wasn't there, was it?" asked Gordon.

"No, Gordon, it wasn't. Over the years I personally drafted inquiries and funding proposals to every foundation in the country whose guidelines suggested they might fund an educational venture such as ours. We've gotten a number of small grants earmarked for such specific things as publishing our **Persona-Presenters Speakers Bureau** pamphlet, our Latin Weekender Conferences, *Persona* presentations in the Detroit area and some general help with operating expenses, but nothing major enough to fund the Endowment needed to stay in business," explained Bernie.

"We had a long run," observed Gordon.

"Yes, and I believe we made some real contributions to promoting the study of Latin during the 70's and 80's when it was in danger of being dropped from the nation's secondary schools."

"Don't forget the Textbook Giveaway Program," reminded Lillian.

"Yes, I believe that was one of the most helpful programs that we sponsored. It didn't generate any extra income, but we were able to help teachers recycle thousands of textbooks and teaching materials that were no longer needed in some schools or by some retired teachers, and put them into the hands of those that could use them simply for the cost of postage and handling. I know that there are several schools that are offering Latin today only because they were able to get sets of textbooks through this program," said Bernie.

So that was it. Pompeiiana, Inc., having been initially formed as a framework to continue the sponsorship of the National Catapult Contest, was going out of business. Bernie and Lillian had made it their labor of love over the years, but now they had to step away, and it would not be able to survive their leadership.

October 5, 2003
Broad Ripple, Indianapolis

It would take a while for teachers to realize that Pompeiiana had gone out of business, and Bernie would have to spend a little time each day returning purchase orders and sending notes to teachers explaining that memberships were no longer available. But things were definitely beginning to slow down.

Now, instead of rushing downstairs after breakfast each day, Bernie would have time to take their dog, Rudy, for a casual walk down the alley where they could pause and share doggy treats with such other doggy denizens as Eddie (a feisty little white dog with black spots), Freddie (a very noisy black dog with white spots who took a little extra time to get with the program), Sam (a very old, but sweet tempered, chocolate lab who insists on circling the fence line of his yard to get his treat rather than crossing the lawn) and, Bernie's favorite, Emma (a long-snouted English terrier who spins circles before sticking her nose through the fence to get her treats).

Any dogs new to the neighborhood are addressed as "puppy" until Bernie can learn their names. New dogs that insist on barking at Bernie and Rudy are encouraged to "talk about it" until they can be coaxed over to the fence to get in on the free treats. It usually only takes three or four encounters to win a new dog over so that no barking arguments are started with Rudy, and, instead, they can both calmly enjoy a dog biscuit or two together.

It's a relaxing way to start the day after one is not quite as "important" as he was before.

October 10, 2003
Broad Ripple, Indianapolis
"Hi, Bernard, Happy Birthday," said the female voice on the phone.
"Well, Hi! Thank you," said Bernie.
"Do you know who this is?" asked the female voice.
"No, I'm afraid you have me at a loss," admitted Bernie.

It turned out that the female voice belonged to a Sparta High School classmate who has made it her business to keep in touch with all of those who graduated in the Class of 1956.

Bernie wondered if she could be the blonde who wore her hair in a ponytail. He didn't ask. After all, he would sound pretty silly saying something like, "Are you the girl the back of whose ears I used to fantasize about when we were in study hall together?"

They ended up having a long talk, reminiscing about their senior year and about the City of Sparta. Bernie never did catch her name. But, who knows? If she calls again—although she said her health was bad, and that she was basically homebound—he might even ask her is she was the blonde that used to wear her hair in a ponytail during their senior year.

October 13, 2003
Indianapolis
In addition to teaching Karate, waiting tables and remodelling the 1890's house he and Audrey had recently purchased near Fountain Square, Phil was still pursuing his main passion: writing.

And things were beginning to look up.

"Dear Writer," began the e-mail that Phil received. It was from autonotify@glimmertrain.com.

Phil had submitted one of his short stories to a **Glimmer Train Press** contest, and he was about to read some very encouraging news.

> "We had the pleasure of reading hundreds of wonderful submissions for this competition; thank you SO much for participating. Your entry made it all the way to the Top 25. Great Work! Keep writing!"

And, of course, Phil will. He knows that if he sticks with it long enough, his big break will come. He has already completed scores of short stories, several film scripts and two novels. It will be just a matter of time before one of them sells.

October 20, 2003
Houston, Texas

"I've got a big day today," said Joe as he left for Space Center Houston in the morning.

"What's going on that's special?" asked Liz.

"I've been invited to spend five-and-a-half hours in Mission Control."

"What will you be watching?"

"I get to observe four simulated launches of the space shuttle."

During the course of the day, Joe was privileged to meet four individuals key to the NASA Space Program.

Leroy Cain was the director in the Mission Control Center. It was Cain, in fact, who had been on duty there when the Shuttle Columbia disintegrated over Texas. Joe had the honor of sitting with him as he worked a shuttle simulation.

Joe got to learn a lot about how "Houston" talks with the Space Shuttle by spending an hour with Mark Polansky, the Astronaut on duty at the CAPCOM position as he worked the shuttle simulation.

Another man present was Bill Foster, the Ground Controller in Mission Control Center who had also been on duty during the Columbia disaster. Foster, in fact, has become quite friendly with Joe and frequently takes time from his duties to meet with VIP guests that Joe brings on tour to Building 30 South.

Another person with whom Joe got to spend an hour during the day was Steve Sides, who works at Instrumentation and Communications in Mission Control Center.

It was quite a day!

October 27, 2003
Broad Ripple, Indianapolis

"Lillian, this is Tim Walsh of Walshbilt Homes," said Bernie as Lillian joined Tim and Bernie at the dining room table.

Bernie and Lillian had looked at more than 15 homes that were on the market and found none that they could see themselves moving into. So Bernie had resubmitted his original house plans to a new builder who was specializing in building in the Broad Ripple area. Tim Walsh was also a graduate of Chatard High School and came well-recommended.

"So," asked Lillian, "can you build our house for the $100,000.00 we mentioned?"

"Well, Mrs. Barcio, I can come close, but I'm afraid it will be a little more than that," said Tim.

Tim had come up with some good suggestions to improve the plans Bernie had given him, but, even with Bernie doing most of the interior finish-work, Tim's estimate still came to $138,000.00. So much for that idea.

November 5, 2003
Broad Ripple, Indianapolis

Bernie had been invited to deliver a presentation of his *persona*, Marcus the Citizen of Pompeii, at Springfield High School and at Wittenberg University in Springfield, Ohio. On his way back, he decided to stop in at Tom Raper Homes on the east side of Indiana just out of curiosity.

"Lillian," Bernie announced when he got back home, "I think I've found a way that we can still have a home built on our lot that's within our budget!"

"How's that?"

"We can buy a modular home and have it installed over a crawl space for about $80,000.00."

"Will the city permit one of those homes on our lot?"

"They don't allow manufactured homes, which are really mobile homes, but they do allow modular homes. They have some really great floor plans that almost match exactly what we were trying to build."

As they looked into modular homes a little more, Bernie decided to see if there might be a local distributor that it would be easier to work with. That's when he discovered Bob Young Homes on the east side of Indianapolis.

After just two visits to the show houses on their lot and after talking with Bob Young, Jr., in person and on the phone, Bernie and Lillian had picked out the modular home they wanted.

Bernie had already looked into all the financing issues earlier when they were planning to have a home custom built, so that aspect was already well addressed. The only thing he needed to do before they could proceed would be to be sure that the lot and a half on which they intended to build was properly separated from the rest of the property by the Washington Township Assessor.

Now, one would think that such a simple task would not take very long, especially since the lots had been so designated on the original deeds that Bernie and Lillian had drawn up when they bought the property back in 1972.

This one task, however, would manage to put things on hold for the next couple of months.

November 16, 2003
Broad Ripple, Indianapolis

"Lillian, Pegg Kenedy is here," announced Bernie.

Pegg was a realtor with Tucker that Lillian had met years earlier at Butler. At that time, Pegg was teaching the Feature Writing class in which Lillian was enrolled. The two had hit it off well, and when Bernie and Lillian decided they needed to put their house on the market if they were serious about building on their extra lots, Lillian had insisted that they work with Pegg.

"Do you have an asking price in mind?" asked Pegg.

"Yes," said Bernie. "We would like to list it for $199,900.00."

"That's a little high for what I think it's worth without the extra lots, but if that's your price, we can list it that way."

"We figure that if anyone's really interested, they can always make us an offer."

Pegg thought that the house alone on 80 feet of property could easily bring $165,000 or $170,000. If Bernie and Lillian were selling all of the property, she thought that they could realistically expect to get at least $250,000.

"We actually do need to sell for close to our listing price in order to end up with what we need to pay your realtor commission and the two loans that we'll need to get to build the house," said Bernie.

"Okay," said Pegg. "You're the boss. We'll list it at $199,900.00 and see how it goes."

November 19, 2003
Herron Art Gallery, Indianapolis

"It's a juried exhibit," explained Audrey to Bernie and Lillian who had gone to the Herron Art Gallery to see one of Audrey's paintings that had been selected for special display.

"It's quite an honor to have had one of your paintings selected," complimented Lillian.

"Yeah. I kinda feel sorry for those students who didn't make it."

"Were the entries chosen by instructors here at Herron?" asked Bernie.

"No-o," said Audrey, beaming. "They brought in professors from Bloomington, headed by the curator from the Indianapolis Museum of Art, so they wouldn't know any of the students."

"Well, that makes it even more special that your painting was chosen," said Lillian.

"You know what I really like?" asked Audrey.

"What's that?"

"Well, they have another display upstairs. All the students whose entries weren't selected, get to have their work shown up there. I think that's so neat for them!"

Audrey was coming along nicely with her work; still, showing her teacher instincts, she was concerned for those who had not been so lucky.

December 1, 2003
Indianapolis

"You know, I wonder what people think who see all these rubber bands hooked up to the doors," observed Lillian.

Bernie had come up with an ingenious method of excluding their 20-year old pet cat, Patches, from certain rooms in the house.

Actually, to tell the truth, Patches was originally Cyndi's cat. After Tullia had passed away, Cyndi had come home one day with a new calico replacement that she hoped her dad would take to. Bernie, however, was unwilling to let Tullia be replaced so easily. He distanced himself from the replacement calico by naming it Nemo (after a character in **20,000 Leagues Under the Sea**, by Jules Verne, who chose a name that meant "Nobody" in Latin since he wanted to separate himself from his fellow men). Later, when Cyndi decided to move, Bernie traded her Nemo for Patches, whom he had become somewhat more attached to.

But to get back to the rubber bands and the doors.

Bernie put a small nail in the door jam up near the top of a door, and another nail into the face of the door near the top. Then, one or two large rubber bands were hooked around the nails. The doors could still easily be opened but would gently close immediately afterwards.

"Who knows? Maybe they'll just think we've come up with a clever way to close doors in the house. If we take the rubber bands off, Patches will just get in the bathroom or bedroom and pee."

"What do you suppose is wrong with her," asked Lillian.

"Well, Cyndi thinks that when cats start peeing around like that, the end is near," said Bernie.

"But Patches has been doing it for almost a year now!" said Lillian.

"Tell me about it," said Bernie.

Over the course of the past year, he and Lillian had had to replace the carpet on the front porch, put a cardboard box barrier to keep Patches from going in the corner behind the phonograph and another barrier across one entire end of the living room to keep her from peeing on the hearth.

Now Lillian pointed to the cardboard barrier in front of the hearth and suggested, "We should be sure and take that down if someone comes over."

By December 1st, Patches had begun peeing in the front entry—on both sides of the toy box, under the server in the dining room and in front of the clothes closets in the master bedroom. There's nothing more shocking than stepping in cold pee with bare feet!

Lillian's bedroom dressers had already had to be rearranged a couple of months earlier because Patches had taken to peeing in the corner next to the bedroom register on which she slept most of the day.

By December 3rd, both the bathroom door and the bedroom door had been equipped with rubber-band door closers.

"O.K., I've got it," said Bernie after they were both in bed. "Since she's sleeping on the rug in front of the refrigerator in the kitchen with Rudy, I'll just block the kitty door so she can't get back into the dining room."

Years before, Bernie had installed a louvered half-door between the kitchen and the dining room so they could confine their first dog, Olive, in the kitchen at night. In the center on the bottom of the door, he had cut a small arched passageway so the cats they then had could still go through and go into the basement to use the litter. A similar opening had also been cut into the Dutch door in the kitchen above the entrance to the side door of the house and the basement.

"But her litter is in the dining room," countered Lillian.

This had been the original concession to Patches who insisted on peeing in a corner of the dining room near the china cabinet. Bernie had at first solved the matter by simply putting a litter box in that corner for her. Of course, the litter box had to have a cardboard barricade around it. The barricade was entered via an arched entrance large enough for Patches but small enough to keep Rudy, the family's pet cocker spaniel, out. Gross as it is to realize, Rudy relished cat poop!

"Well," said Bernie, "she has two litter boxes in the basement. She can just go down there and use one of them."

"Two litter boxes?" asked Lillian.

"Yeah, I had to set up another litter box down there because she was deliberately peeing on the opposite end of the room from her basement box. I think she's just being ornery!" complained Bernie.

When all these new arrangements were in place, Patches suddenly started to show signs of instability when she walked or tried to turn. She could still jump up into a kitchen chair and onto the kitchen table on which her hard cat food was kept—although she preferred a buffet of soft people food—along with her bowl of whole milk. Her food had to be up on the table to keep Rudy from stealing it all.

Bernie and Lillian were definitely going the extra mile for Patches. Since she seemed to be living mostly on milk, Bernie even thought they should buy whole milk for her instead of having her drink the low-fat milk that Lillian preferred.

Almost a year ago, when Patches had first stopped eating her hard cat food, she became dehydrated. After a visit to Dr. Williams, the vet, where she received a life-saving shot and was given appetite enhancer drops that would have to be administered twice daily, she was kept alive with scores of jars of baby food.

Then, after she refused to eat any more of that, Bernie had discussed the situation with Karen's daughter, Audrey, about to be given the name Dr. Audrey.

"Audrey, Patches won't eat any of her food. What do you think we should do?"

"Well," replied Audrey giving the problem her most careful consideration, "I think you should pet her. Then she'll want to eat."

And as frequently happens, from the mouths of babes do come the most profound insights.

After applying generous petting, Patches was finally coaxed into eating a small piece of cooked chicken breast. In fact, the more petting she received, the more she ate.

So now, a supply of frozen chicken breasts had to be laid in so a new one could be cooked specially for her every two or three days. Then, when she suddenly lost interest in chicken, additional petting encouraged her to try some calf liver. So then, calf livers had to be pre-cooked and frozen for her so she could have a new piece thawed out for her each day. When she lost interest in liver, more petting encouraged her to begin a diet of Braunschweiger. Soon, she would only eat the Braunschweiger every other day, preferring smoked turkey, ham or Kentucky Fried Chicken—or whatever else Bernie and Lillian were eating—on the off days.

So long as she was eating, however, Bernie and Lillian did all they could to encourage her. She was skin and bones. Heck, they even let her jump up on the dining room table each evening to check out that evening's entrée in case she might be interested in a taste or two.

By the evening of December 5th, however, Patches was obviously complaining about something. She walked around the kitchen in which she was now confined making short complaining noises before plopping down in weird places. She was also having a great deal of trouble going up and down the stairs to her litter in the basement.

"I think it's her claws," observed Bernie after he and Lillian were in bed that night. "You know how long two of them are on each of her back feet. I'll bet her other claws are ingrown, and they hurt when she tries to walk on them. That's probably why she's so unsteady."

"That could be," murmured Lillian who was trying hard to fall asleep, distracted by her own pain and discomfort. Lillian was suffering from Kidney cancer that was slowly spreading to her liver and lungs.

"Think I'll take her in to the vet tomorrow morning and have him look at her feet. I think he's open on Saturday mornings."

As Bernie lay there thinking about Patches and listening to her low, growl-like complaints from the kitchen, he got a new idea. He figured that if her feet hurt her, she was probably having trouble jumping up on the kitchen table to eat and probably would be pained to go down into the basement to use the litter box.

"Where did you go," asked Lillian when Bernie came back to bed.

"Well, I took Patches down into the basement so she could have her food, milk and water on the floor without Rudy stealing it. I also opened a can of salmon for her. She was very interested in that. I put the hot pad on the floor and placed her sleeping mat over it."

"I hope you didn't set it on High," said Lillian. "You don't want her to burn herself."

"No, it's on Medium. Besides the concrete floor is cold, so I don't think it'll overheat. I also took the cardboard barrier from the living room and set it up to keep her in one part of the basement. I left a light on for her, and she's got two litter boxes. What more could she want?" observed Bernie.

About one o'clock in the morning, Bernie went back down to see how Patches was doing. Instead of being sound asleep on her warm mat, as he had hoped, he found her sitting in a far corner near a storage closet.

"Hey, you silly kitty," said Bernie as he gently picked her up and lay her down on her warm sleeping mat. "Now, stay here so you'll be warm."

Patches purred as he pet her and looked up appreciatively with her clear expressive eyes.

About 4 a.m., Bernie went back down to check again. There she was standing in the corner by the closet again.

"O.K.," Bernie said to himself, "she obviously wants to have her sleeping mat in that corner. Maybe it's darker over there or something."

So Bernie moved the heating pad arrangement into the darker corner, laid Patches on her side on it and petted her coat smooth. Once again, she purred appreciatively and looked up into his eyes.

When Bernie awoke again at 6 a.m. to get ready to do some house cleaning because a realtor had arranged to show the house between 1 and 2:30 p.m. that day, he quietly went down the steps to see what Patches was doing. Great! She was curled up on the heating pad in her corner, sleeping soundly. Success at last!

"Are you going to take her to vet this morning?" asked Lillian when she got up.

"Well, she's finally sleeping; so I thought I would just let her be. She seems to be doing fine with her dish of salmon and her milk and water. It even looks like she has been eating some of her hard cat food. There are little chunks scattered on the floor around that bowl," said Bernie.

By the time Bernie had finished mopping the bathroom, the front entry way and the kitchen, it was 10 a.m. He went down once more to check on Patches. To his shock, he found her splayed out flat in one of her two litter boxes. It was as though she had managed to get in and was trying to pee, but she just didn't have the energy. It was too sad.

"Hi," said Bernie when the vet's nurse answered the phone, "Could we get in to see Dr. Williams this morning?"

Cyndi didn't like Dr. Williams. In fact, she preferred to call him "Dr. Kervorkian." When Cyndi had been living at home, it seemed to her that every time she took one of her cats to Dr. Williams, he put it to sleep. Although Dr. Williams is a perfectly fine vet and a wonderful man, she was convinced that this was his only treatment for her sick cats—albeit they had all literally been on their last legs when she took them in.

"Do you want to make an appointment?" asked the nurse cheerily. "Which of your pets will be coming in?"

"It's Patches," said Bernie, beginning to find it hard to speak.

"And what seems to be Patches' problem?" asked the cheery voice.

"I think she's dying," gulped Bernie.

"Oh, I'm sorry," said the nurse, adopting a more somber tone. "Let's not bother with an appointment. Why don't you just bring her in right now, Mr. Barcio."

"I'm taking Patches to the vet now, Lill," said Bernie in a deceptively cheery voice. "I was able to get her in this morning."

"Do you want me to come along and hold her in the car?"

"Naw, I don't think she'll be a problem."

Bernie didn't want to upset Lillian by his fears for Patches. Heavens knows she had enough troubles of her own.

"I'll wrap her up in a towel. She'll just sit quietly on the seat, I'm sure."

When he got into the car with Patches, Bernie didn't have the heart to plop her down into the seat next to him. He held her cuddled in his left arm as he drove. Patches calmly looked out the window, not struggling to get out of the towel as she usually did whenever she was wrapped up to be given a squirt of medicine.

At the vet's office, Bernie checked in at the nurse's window and took Patches over to a large fish tank to see if he could interest her in the tropical fish that swam up to the glass wall to tease her. She looked at them, but showed no interest.

"Yes, it's a Lassa Apsa," said a man sitting in the waiting room holding a small dog on his lap.

"Do you have to trim the hairs off his face so he can see?" asked Bernie, eager for a conversation so he wouldn't have to think about what was about to happen.

"No. They don't require much care. Lassa Apsa's don't shed, you know," observed the man.

"It's so tiny," said Bernie.

"It's only nine weeks old," said the man. "We just got it. We had to put down my wife's last Lassa Apsa a few weeks ago. I didn't want to get another one, but my wife said that she either got a new one, or I could just move out," kidded the man. "What's wrong with your cat?"

"Oh, she's just old," said Bernie, reluctant to discuss Patches lest he lose control of his emotions.

"O.K., Mr. Barcio," said Dr. Williams who came around the corner just then. "Let's bring Patches back into the examining room."

Bernie complied, gently carrying his little bundle.

"Just set her up here on the table."

Bernie set her on the table and unwrapped the towel. Poor Patches looked so pitiful just lying there. She seemed scrawnier than usual, and her fur was all mussed. She just looked at him with those haunting big, clear eyes.

"She's in bad shape," said the vet. "I think the best thing to do is to put her down, don't you?" asked the vet.

Bernie couldn't speak. He just nodded, fighting back his tears as best he could.

"How old is she?" asked the vet.

Bernie thought the answer, "Twenty," but he couldn't speak to save his life. He just shrugged.

"No matter," said the vet.

Then to his assistant he said, "Take her into the other room. We'll give her the shot in there."

"Would you like her interred in the Pet Cemetery?" asked the vet.

Bernie shook his head "NO."

"We'll have her cremated then, Mr. Barcio," said the vet. "Would you like the ashes?"

Again Bernie shook his head "NO," still unable to speak. He just wanted to pay the bill and leave with what little dignity he had left.

The nurse carefully rewrapped Patches and picked her up. Bernie did not have the heart to look at her again. He turned and left the room to return to the waiting room.

Two more people had entered with their pets. Bernie went to the farthest window and tried to disappear as he pulled out his wallet to get a credit card.

"We'll bill you, Mr. Barcio. You won't have to pay now," said the Dr. William's secretary.

Bernie nodded his understanding and returned his wallet to his pocket. As he was turning to leave, the secretary called him back to the window.

"Mr. Barcio, if you could, we do need you to sign this form please. It just shows that you gave Doctor permission to euthanize Patches."

Boy, was she pushing it.

As Bernie turned once again to leave the office, the man to whom he had been talking looked up at him.

"Sorry," the man said as Bernie went out the door, unable to thank the man for his kind sentiment.

December 7, 2003
Indianapolis

"OK. I think I've figured out...," wrote Bernie in an e-mail to his son, Phil.

It was Sunday morning, and he had spent the last 24 hours alternately trying not to think about the whole ordeal and trying to come to grips with it.

"I think I've figured out why a pet's passing is more wrenching than a person's can be. We communicate with people mostly through words. As a person fades and can no longer communicate effectively, we begin to distance ourselves from that person to such an extent that by the time they pass away, we have already insulated ourselves from the loss."

This seemed perfectly logical to Bernie. He had sat daily with his mother as he watched her weaken prior to passing away the February before. Remarkably, he was able to handle all her funeral arrangements and even get through the entire funeral and burial with hardly a tear. In fact, he was perfectly upbeat about the whole experience.

He had had a much harder time dealing with the death of Tullia, his pet cat that had managed to live some 22 or 23 years, and with the loss of Heathcliff, Lillian's pet cat, the year before.

"With pets, the communication is all through the eyes and body language—a communication they can keep going right up until the very last minute as they look up at you that final time, asking, 'Why?' I mean, really, it's almost more than a person can stand."

December 8, 2003
Indianapolis

Lillian had recently had a follow up CT-scan to check the effects of the Interferon shots she had been receiving weekly since her Interluken 2 treatments had been stopped.

"I'm afraid the news isn't good," said Dr. Schultz. "The cancer has spread to your liver and new lesions have appeared on your right lung."

"What does that mean?" asked Bernie.

"It means the Interferon shots have not been effective in keeping the kidney cancer from spreading."

"Do you think we need to give it more time to work?" asked Lillian.

"No, I don't think so. If the Interferon were going to be effective, it would have stopped the cancer from spreading."

"So what do we do now?" asked Lillian hoping for yet another possible treatment.

"The only treatment that's available at this point is Thalidomide."

"How does that work?" asked Bernie.

"Lillian would take two pills a day. What Thalidomide is supposed to do is dry up the blood vessels that nourish the cancer cells. I have to be upfront with both of you, however," said Dr. Schultz, "It only has about a 15% success rate."

"Well," said Lillian, maintaining her positive attitude, "someone has to be in the 15%, don't they?"

"Yes, you're right," said the doctor. "I can write you a prescription and get you started on the pills next week if you like."

"Can't we start right now?" asked Lillian. "If it's going to work, I'd rather start sooner than later."

"There will be some forms you need to sign before you'll be allowed to start the Thalidomide," said the doctor. "This is the drug that caused so many birth defects in the 1960's and the company has to be very sure that those who use it will not get pregnant."

Not only did Lillian have to sign a two page statement guaranteeing that she would not get pregnant (something that was, in fact, physically impossible since she had already had a hysterectomy and had recently had her ovaries removed), but she had to phone the drug company and complete a phone interview during which she gave the same assurances. Before the CVS drugstore pharmacist could fill the prescription, the pharmacist had to see the signed affidavits and check with the drug company to be sure Lillian had completed the phone interview.

"Pat," said Lillian after calling her friend Pat Robinson when she got home, "I've got some bad news."

"Oh, Lillian, what's that," asked Pat taking the bait.

"I'm afraid I can't get pregnant!"

"Bill," said Pat to her husband on the other end of the phone, "Lillian just learned that she's not supposed to get pregnant."

"Were they trying to?" asked Bill, only to kick himself a few minutes later for even thinking that they might be.

Lillian was going to continue putting a positive spin on her situation. She might even have a little fun with it.

December 10, 2003
Broad Ripple, Indianapolis

"I think Joe's really going to like his gift," observed Bernie.

"Is it for both of them?" asked Lillian.

"Yes it is. Both of their lives are so involved with NASA that I think Liz will enjoy it as much as he will."

The Danbury Mint in Norwalk, Connecticut, had just recently come out with a stunning replica of the various key components of Apollo 13: Command Module, Service Module, and the ascent and descent stages of the

Lunar Module. The model was created in 1:50 scale and measured 13 ½ inches in length. Its silver, black and gold foil coloration was very attractive.

Bernie and his brother had grown up in the heart of America's early space program as the country rushed to play catch-up after Sputnik. Although neither they nor their parents owned television sets during those early days, they always managed to be near a T.V. screen for the really big events.

Joe also had a natural interest in astronomy, something that Bernie considered to be well out of the realm of his understanding. Joe talked space to his children as they grew up. He shared his interests in that special way he has that can always fascinate his listener. It was no surprise, therefore, when his oldest son, Joey, came home one day to announce proudly that he was moving to Houston, Texas, where he had found work with a company associated with NASA.

Not only that, but Joey would also fall in love with and marry an actual NASA scientist, Alisha Hector.

After all of Joe's children eventually ended up finding work in the Houston area, Joe and Liz had moved to Houston where Joe, as has been related earlier, eventually became a V.I.P. guide for the historic Apollo Mission Control Center. Wearing a replica of the white vest (complete with the Columbia Mission Patch STS-107) that Flight Director Gene Kranz always wore when he worked in Mission Control, Joe has had the honor of posing for photos with V.I.P. guests from China and the Chinese Consulate. From Beijing, he has met the Chief Trade Representative, Liu Jianhua, the Director of Foreign Investment, Qiu Guangling, and Yusong Chen from the Department of Treaty and Law, and Yang Zhe, the Deputy Director, Refining Division, China Petroleum and Chemical Corporation. From the Chinese Consulate in Houston, Joe has met the Consulate General of the Peoples Republic of China, Chen Jianping, the Vice Consult, Li Jianbin, and the Economic and Commercial Consult, Jianguang Lu.

He has also given VIP tours to personages from such places as Aruba, Chile, Brazil, Argentina, France, Norway, Sweden, Germany, the Ukraine, Muldava, Russia, England, and most recently, Egypt. In fact, by request of a Major General of Egypt, Joe had the honor of standing next to this remarkable personage with his very neat mustache, his precise English and his firm, courteous handshake as his son took their picture.

Joe was in retirement heaven.

He would love his Christmas gift!

December 12, 2003
Broad Ripple, Indianapolis

"Phil, glad you're here," said Bernie after Phil had gotten out of his white VW Jetta.

"What's happening?" asked Phil.

"Well, I was hoping you could give me a hand putting Vertumnus up on his new stump."

"I see you've already got Pomona moved," observed Phil.

"Yeah, she was a lot lighter. I was able to pick her up by myself. This guy weighs a ton though."

In anticipation of the modular home about to be installed on the south 60 feet of their property on Indianola Avenue, Bernie had hired Indy Tree and Landscape Co. to cut down and remove the new Itchy Goomey tree that had grown in the spot of the old one and another huge black walnut tree that would, once again, overhang the master bedroom of their new house. He had marked how much of each stump he wanted the tree cutters to leave.

Since the original Pomona stump would now be in the middle of their new home's proposed driveway, she would have to be moved. Her bust had been cut off and placed on the stump of Itchy Goomey tree #2 by Bernie.

Also, since Bernie was reluctant to abandon Vertumnus in the yard of their old house once it sold, he had had the bust of Vertumnus also cut off by the tree cutters.

"Just leave it sitting on its stump," Bernie had said to Mike whose chain saw had just cut through the black walnut carving. "I'll get it moved myself."

It turned out to be a bit harder than Bernie thought it would be. The bust of Vertumnus was much fresher than Pomona had been. It was also larger. It was also harder and heavier wood.

After Bernie had rolled a heavy-duty railroad wheelbarrow, that had once belonged to his dad, in place, he thought he would simply be able to tip Vertumnus off the stump and into the bucket of the wheelbarrow. Down Vertumnus went, and over tipped the wheelbarrow.

Great! Now Bernie had to wiggle between the grapevines he had planted and the overturned wheelbarrow to get Vertumnus and the wheelbarrow upright.

"It's all leverage," was Bernie's mantra. "Never actually lift anything heavy. Rock it, tilt it, balance it. Let the weight of the object do the work." This was something he had learned working on the railroad.

Before long, Bernie was backing his load across the garden toward the small gate in the ally fence. When it came time to pull the wheelbarrow's pneumatic tire up over a small log that served as a gate threshold, Bernie noticed that the tire was almost flat.

"No problem! I've got a pump," he thought to himself.

Before long the tire was rock hard, and Bernie was on his way down the ally wheeling Vertumnus to his new home.

Once the wheelbarrow was in place at the new walnut base, Bernie fixed up a wooden ramp so he could slide Vertumnus, butt end first, up onto the stump. After wrapping a chain around the bust, he hooked it to an old catapult winch that he had fastened to another nearby tree.

He had gotten the bust cranked high enough on its slide that, with two people working, it could be lifted into place.

This was where Phil's help was needed.

December 14, 2003
Broad Ripple, Indianapolis

"It isn't time so much that heals," thought Bernie as he knelt in church waiting for the distribution of communion to be completed, "it's a memory filtering process. We have to decide what we are going to think about when we remember a lost pet. Some images definitely have to be avoided unless we just want to spend all our time feeling sad. I'll have to figure out how I'm going to remember Patches without feeling sad. I'll have to filter out the unpleasant memories and focus on the fun ones, the pleasant ones. That's the process that heals!"

Bernie and Lillian had not eaten dinner at the dining room table for several days after Patches had been put to sleep because of the memories. Sure, everyone knows that pets aren't supposed to be allowed on the table during meals, but Patches was such a finicky eater, and she had been so skinny the last couple of years since her bout with dehydration that Bernie and Lillian were thrilled to see her show any interest at all in food—even if it meant feeding her tidbits from their own plates as she surveyed the nightly dinner offerings. Patches had become such a part of dinner that it just took a while to be able to eat at the dining room table and not be overwhelmed by her absence.

"So, how are you both dealing with it?" asked Phil a few nights after Patches was gone. "Cyndi said that we should get you another cat right away."

"Definitely not," replied his mom. "We have our hands full with Rudy."

Rudy the cocker spaniel is already 13 years old. Thousands of dollars have been spent for knee surgery on both his back legs, and he has his own way of taking command of the household each evening after dinner. He is definitely a handful!

"Some people," said Bernie, "do use immediate pet replacement as a way to distract themselves from their sorrow, but that's not how we want to deal with it. Patches was a special personality, and it would do her memory an injustice simply to replace her. She deserves her own special niche."

So, when Phil had asked, "How are you both dealing with it?" Bernie had given the answer, "Time. Time helps a person deal with it."

It wasn't until several days later, in church, that Bernie finally figured out that it would, in fact, take more than just time. Their memories of Patches would have to be filtered.

December 15, 2003
Broad Ripple, Indianapolis

Since Lillian was finding it almost impossible to climb the three stairs up into the kitchen after coming in the back door, Bernie had decided to build a handicap ramp on the back porch for her.

He had already built a smaller version for Rudy after he had had both of his back legs operated on and needed to avoid stairs for a while.

Lillian's ramp, however, would be larger and more gradual. He had already completed the small ramp that led down the one step out the back door onto the porch and had built the three gently sloping sections that would enable her to go down from the porch to the brick patio floor that she had laid in two decades earlier with the help of her grandson, Eric Donnella. Bernie had a center rail installed, but before completing the outside rails, he had decided to put up some Christmas decorations at the front of the house.

"Well begun is half done," said Bernie aloud, taking pleasure in another of his oft-repeated mantras.

He had worked for about an hour on the decorations and was returning to the garage when he heard Lillian call to him in a weak voice.

"Bernie, help me. Help!"

Bernie dropped what he was carrying and ran into the breezeway.

"What happened?" he asked when he saw her sitting on the ramp holding her forehead that was covered with blood.

There was also a great quantity of blood on the bricks before her.

Lillian had hit her head on the bricks once before several years earlier when she fell off a small stool while trying to clean some spider webs off the rafters. This time it looked much more serious.

"I was calling you and calling you. Where were you?"

"I was in the front of the house putting up decorations."

"I didn't know where you were and wanted to ask you about this sweet potato. I guess I forgot that the ramp turned."

"How long have you been here?"

"Quite a while. At first I couldn't even get up off the bricks and thought I was going to bleed to death down there. I finally managed to hang onto the fireplace and pull myself up."

It had indeed been quite a while because when Bernie looked carefully at the deep gash above Lillian's eye, the blood was already clotted.

"O.K. Let me be sure everything is turned off on the stove and lock the doors. We'll drive over and get you taken care of right away."

"Let's just drive over to the Med Check on Broad Ripple Avenue," suggested Lillian.

Unfortunately, when they drove into the parking lot behind the facility, they discovered that it had closed and moved to a new location.

"Let's head for the St. Vincent emergency room," said Bernie. "Of course, that means we won't be done there until midnight. We'll call Phil and see if he can come over and let Rudy out."

True to his prediction, it took several hours in the emergency room before Lillian would have her wound cleaned and receive stitches. In addition to the usual signing-in procedure and endless questions, there would have to be a CT-scan taken to be sure she had not suffered a concussion. Luckily, she had not. Before the long evening was over, Phil arrived at the hospital to check on his mom and assure her and his dad that he had taken care of Rudy.

Later that evening after they returned home, Bernie went out in back with a bucket and mop and washed up as much of the blood as possible before it would set permanently into the bricks.

The next day, he quickly finished building the rest of the outside rails on the ramp to prevent future accidents.

He then cut the sweet potato in half that Lillian had been carrying when she fell and put the two halves in glasses to see if they would grow.

One died, but as of August, 2004, the second half was still growing beautifully.

December 31, 2003
Sussex, Wisconsin

"5, 4, 3, 2, 1. Hap-py New Year!"

Bernie's Aunt Esther Duga had decided to accept an invitation to ring in the New Year with friends. Although she was 82 years old, she was still very spry and young in mind and heart. She still enjoyed an occasional glass of wine or even something a little stronger.

"Esther," said a friend at the party, "come over here once. There's someone I want you to meet."

"O.K., give me a minute to get down off this stool," answered Esther.

CRASH!

Before she knew what had happened, Aunt Esther found her face pressed flat on the floor, wrist and shoulder in great pain and blood from her cheek quickly staining the carpet.

"Oh, my God! What happened?"

"I think she caught the heal of her shoe on one of the rungs of the stool as she was getting off!"

"Someone call 9-1-1!"

Recovering from that little accident would take 8 stitches below Aunt Esther's eye, a cast on her wrist, a sling for her arm since there's no way they can set a cracked shoulder bone, and weeks in therapy. Luckily Esther now lived fairly close to her daughter, Eileen Ascher, who would be able to drive her mom to her doctor appointments—as soon as her own wrist healed that she had recently broken when she tripped over a pillow lying on the bedroom floor while she was making the bed.

Happy New Year!

January 4, 2004
Broad Ripple, Indianapolis

"Hi, how can I help you?"

"Hi, is this Dr. Bernard Barcio?"

"Yes, it is."

"Is this Dr. Barcio who is the Roman centurion?"

"Yes. Is this Betty Jean?"

"How did you know? Do you have Caller ID?"

"No, we don't have Caller ID. You've still got that unmistakable twinkle in your voice."

"Thank you."

So there it was. More than 35 years after moving to Valparaiso from Indianapolis, Betty Jean Collver had searched the web and located her old boyfriend from Bay City, Michigan. Turns out that her husband Dave Collver had divorced her several years ago, and almost immediately afterwards was diagnosed with cancer that took his life in a short time.

The couple had moved from Valparaiso, where Betty Jean had finally obtained a college degree and earned a teaching license (although she never did teach afterwards), to the Detroit area. There, Dave had worked for the American Cancer Society and the Michigan Masonic Home as well as keeping his hand in church choir directing. Betty Jean went to work for the Detroit Free Press as a secretary, a job she held for some 25 years.

After asking Bernie some catch up questions to see what his life had been like during the past 35 years, Betty Jean said that she had had two children, Mary Elizabeth and David Christian, and that her daughter was married and would soon be presenting her with her first grandchild.

The strange twists of life never do cease to amaze!

Betty Jean would follow up with an e-mail in a few days, but Bernie decided to let it go unanswered and to keep no record of her e-address. No point in offering any encouragement to someone who no longer had any place in his life.

January 6, 2004
Indianapolis

"Well, how are you doing?" asked Dr. Schultz as he peaked around the door of the examining room. Dr. Schultz always seemed to enter the examining room very cautiously, as though he wasn't sure of what kind of reception to expect.

"Well, we were hoping you could tell us," said Lillian.

"Your blood count is actually higher than it was on your last test."

"That's something positive," stated Lillian. "And I've also lost four pounds of fluid since last week."

"Well, that might be muscle loss instead of fluid loss," said Dr. Schultz, knocking the positive wind out of Lillian's sails.

"You mean the Lasix isn't working? I'm taking 80 milligrams a day plus the booster pill."

"I'm afraid the swelling in your lower body and legs is not fluid that can be reduced through urination," said the doctor solemnly.

"What's it from?" asked Bernie.

"It's coming from the surface of the kidney and is getting into the tissue. It can't be flushed out by circulation."

"Should I keep taking the Lasix then?" asked Lillian.

"Yes, I would. Just in case it can do some good," said the doctor. "And you should continue the Thalidomide for a while longer. It's still too early to determine if it's having a positive effect."

When Lillian left the doctor's office, she was scheduled to have a follow up CT-scan on January 23.

January 7, 2004
Christ the King Church, Indianapolis

"A lot of people want to serve God, but only in an advisory capacity," read the billboard in front of the Broad Ripple Methodist Church. Bernie had seen it on his way to get a half-gallon of fat free milk at the "Moscow" Kroger Store in his neighborhood. (It was called that because of the growing scarcity and lack of variety of items stocked.)

"I guess it does sound like all we do is advise God on what he should do to help us," thought Bernie, "but who else can we look to for help?"

So, for the last several months, Bernie had begun to walk over to Christ the King church on weekday mornings for either the 7:00 a.m. or 8:00 a.m. communion services. Lillian and he were definitely going to need all the help they could get.

Undeterred by the Methodist observation, Bernie decided to begin adding one additional prayer to his usual morning routine. He would begin praying for **S**piritual confidence, **P**hysical stamina and **E**motional Stability, all of which would be needed if he and Lillian were going to get through the coming months.

"Hmm," thought Bernie to himself, "that creates the acronym **SPES**. The Latin word for 'hope.'"

How very appropriate.

January 8, 2004
Broad Ripple, Indianaolis

"Hey, Lill, Mary Leo's book came," announced Bernie.

"What is it called?" asked Lillian.

"**Stickshift**. I'll start reading it to you tonight. We can do a chapter a night after dinner."

So, little Mary Leo, who grew up in Nonno's second floor flat at 9506 Commercial Avenue in South Chicago, little Mary who graduated from high school but never made it to college like the two sons of her successful Aunt Stella, turned out to be the first one in the family to land a professional writing contract!

After Mary's first marriage—at which Bernie had given her away in St. Patrick's church across the street from her house—had gone bad, she had left Las Vegas where her first husband was a card dealer, and where she had worked as a cocktail waitress and keno runner, and headed for sunny California.

Once in the Sunshine State with a brand new husband, Rick (Richter) Watkins, Mary worked first as a bartender in Silicon Valley and then as a production assistant in Hollywood. But she wanted more. She eventually became an IC layout engineer and lived in the San Diego area.

As it turned out, however, Mary's secret passion over the years was to become a writer, having been inspired by her cousin, Rick Leo, who lives in Alaska and who has published two books about his experiences there: **Way Out There** and **The Edge of the Earth**.

While working as an IC layout engineer, Mary joined a local Writers' Club. Aspiring writers got together weekly to share their creative efforts, critique, get critiqued and encourage each other's efforts.

At first, Mary wrote sort of an autobiographical novel—with names changed—detailing some of the horrendous experiences she and her sister Gloria went through while living at 9506 Commercial. When she submitted a draft of this work to a publisher, she was told that there was no longer interest in the Italian-American bit. This was just before "The Sopranos" became one of TV's biggest hits!

A selection from that book was quoted in the **August, 1957** entry in this work.

Now, in January 2004, Mary had a contract with Harlequin Books to provide a new Lighter Side novel every three or four months! She and her husband now live in Pennsylvania, having moved away from San Diego just before devastating forest fires raged through their old neighborhood in the fall of 2003.

Good job Mary! And good move!

"Hi, Mary," said Bernie when he called his cousin to congratulate her. "I love the lead character's name, Lucy Mastronardo. Hmmm, now where have I heard those names before?"

"I know, I know. Just had to work my mom and some familiar names into the story."

"You know that Henry Mastronardi was the accordionist that played at my folk's wedding, don't you?"

"I had heard the name a lot, but I wasn't exactly sure who he was. I changed the name to Mastronardo just because that sounded better."

"Every time I read Lucy's name in the novel, I can't help visualizing your mom. That's neat how you've immortalized her!"

As Bernie and Lillian continued their nightly readings of **Stickshift**, they were pleasantly surprised to come across a character named Joe Strano. Mary's cousin Rudy was obviously still on her mind.

January 11, 2004
Broad Ripple, Indianapolis

"Now, Lillian," said Bernie as they were sitting down to breakfast after 7:30 a.m. Sunday Mass, "I would like to discuss something, and I don't want you to get upset."

Lillian got that look on her face that said, "Oh, God, what is he going to get into now," but she said she wouldn't get upset.

"I think I would like to call someone from Flanner and Buchanan and pre-plan our funerals. You know, having my mom's funeral pre-planned, and pre-paid, was one of the best things we ever did. It just made everything a lot more manageable."

"O.K."

"I've already done a little work on this and have even written my own obituary for the newspaper. Would you like to hear it?"

Lillian looked up at him incredulously.

So, after breakfast, Bernie got the Pre-arranged Funeral file out of the file cabinet on the front porch and proceeded to read his own obituary aloud.

> "Dr. Bernard F. Barcio, L.H.D., _____(insert age attained). Born October 10, 1938. Founder and Director of Pompeiiana, Inc., Adjunct Instructor of Classical Studies at Butler University and I.U.P.U.I., Teacher of secondary school Latin at Carmel H.S., Fulton Jr. H.S., Eastwood Jr. H.S., North Central H.S. and Park School. Survivors: Wife Lillian R. Barcio, Children Cyndi and Phillip Barcio, Brother Joseph A. Barcio, 2 nieces and 2 nephews. Extended family members include the families of Sheryl and Jeff Donnella, Karen and Mike Pence and relatives in Chicago, Milwaukee and Italy. Calling at Broad Ripple Flanner and Buchanan Mortuary _____(insert date/time); Funeral Mass at Christ the King Church ____(insert date/time); Entombment at Our Lady of Peace Cemetery.

"I don't think you need to say 'Wife Lillian R. Barcio,' " said Lillian. "You can just say 'Wife Lillian.' They charge by the line, you know."

"You're probably right. I'll change that. Wasn't that clever how I worked in Sheryl and Karen's families?"

Bernie had been concerned about that. He really couldn't call Sheryl and Karen his stepdaughters since they had never been adopted. And he really didn't want to leave them out completely from his list of survivors. Their children would feel as though their "G-Pa," "Pappa," or "Don Barcio" didn't love them. So he just decided to make them be a part of his "Extended family." Pretty clever move! Marsha's name, of course, would be omitted.

How's that for a great way to start the day—reading your own obituary?

On the following Tuesday, Bernie and Lillian met with Len Yanavich, CPC, Family Service Advisor from the Broad Ripple Flanner and Buchanan Mortuary.

"Is that Polish?" asked Bernie.

"No, it's Lithuanian," replied Len.

"Reminds me of the musician. I think his name was Yankovich."

"Yea, I think they call him Weird Al Yankovich," said Len.

"I wonder if he's Lithuanian, too?" pondered Bernie aloud.

"I really don't know."

Then it was time to get down to business. Len went over some basic information such as, names, social security numbers, birthdates, father's name, mother's name complete with maiden name—all of which are needed to obtain death certificates later on.

"I think I would like to have a bronze colored casket," volunteered Bernie. "But I think Lillian is going to want blue."

"No," said Lillian, "I don't want blue. I want something brown. Maybe bronze would work."

"I would like a casket floral spray made from carnations," said Bernie. "It's an Italian thing. And I believe Lillian would like pink sweetheart roses."

"No, I wouldn't. I wish you would quit speaking for me," countered Lillian.

"What would you like?" asked Len.

"Daisies!"

Lillian's other all-time favorite flower.

"We already own a burial crypt at Our Lady of Peace Cemetery," stated Bernie.

"How did you happen to buy one there?" asked Len.

"When they first opened that cemetery, they were offering some great prices," Bernie said. "Hard to pass up a good deal! We already have our names engraved on the end stone."

"Bernie considers that part of the real estate we own," kidded Lillian.

"It's a two-coffin crypt," added Bernie. "I think we want the coffins put in so we're head to head."

"And which organization would you like to specify for memorial contributions?" asked Len.

Bernie looked at Lillian who just looked back at him. He thought he knew what the answer would be.

"None," said Bernie, "unless you want to say that memorial contributions should be made to the family."

"No," said Len, "we don't do that."

"It's kind of an Italian tradition that all those attending a funeral slip an envelope to the bereaved that contains a small contribution to help offset the cost of the funeral. But that doesn't have to be spelled out anywhere."

As Len was leaving he said that he had to go out of town the following week.

"I won't be able to get back over until a week from now so that you both can sign the final arrangement agreements," said Len.

"Well," joked Lillian, "We'll try to hang in there 'til then!"

When Len returned the following week, Lillian once again reminded Bernie that he really shouldn't always speak for her.

"I would like memorial contributions to be made to the St. Vincent Oncology Foundation, or whatever its exact name is," said Lillian.

Bernie would have to watch himself more carefully in the future.

January 12, 2004
Indianapolis

"Hi, Hon," said Phil, "how did it go?"

"I got it done," replied Audrey, "but I'm bushed! I worked thirteen straight hours up there on the scaffold."

"Ready for some pizza?"

"You bet!"

"It should be here any minute now. I ordered it at least 20 minutes ago," said Phil. "When will everyone get to see it?"

"I guess not until The Vogue reopens."

Steve Ross, the owner of The Vogue, a theater converted into a band-performance bar in Broad Ripple, had seen some of Audrey's paintings and had commissioned her to paint the ceiling above the front bar in The Vogue as part of the redecorating he was doing.

Another great break for the budding artist/teacher!

January 15, 2004
Broad Ripple, Indianapolis
"Who was that who called?" asked Lillian.

"Rudy. He was just calling to see how you were doing," said Bernie.

Rudy, or Frank Strano, as he is formally known, has known a lot of stress and turmoil throughout his life, beginning with the tragic death of his own father five months before he was born. Despite the fact that there were those family members who doubted that he would ever make anything of himself, he has handled himself admirably over the years, beginning with his acceptance into the Marine Corps.

Later, when he was working as a railroad detective in South Chicago, he slept on a cot in Nonno's basement as he tried to jumpstart his life.

After a while, Rudy became affiliated with the labor union and did quite well for himself. Beginning as a membership promoter, he worked his way up to such high offices as Business Manager in the union and he even eventually became a regular card player with major politicians in Washington, D.C.

Over the years, Rudy also came to be respected by key Alderman in the Chicago area, and, building on these connections was able to help numerous members of his family find work and obtain benefits.

Rudy also worked as a building inspector and, using those friendships with contractors, was able to build himself a beautiful home in Munster, Indiana.

Although Rudy never had any children of his own, he has generously shared both his inside knowledge and his money to help his stepchildren set themselves up in variety of business ventures.

"Rudy turned out all right, after all," observed Uncle Charlie one day as he sat next to Bernie at a family reunion that was being held by Bernie's cousin, Evy, at her lakeside home in Ogdon Dunes, Indiana.

"Yes, he has. He learned how to work within the system and used it to his best advantage. He's a very clever guy," said Bernie.

Since Rudy lost his own wife several years ago, he knew what Bernie and Lillian were going through and tried to keep in touch to offer what support he could.

And it was sincerely appreciated.

January 16, 2004
Broad Ripple, Indianapolis
Bernie and Lillian were once again seated at the dining room table, this time to sign papers arranging the Swing Loan that was needed before a construction loan could be granted by Bank One. Just days before, Bernie had

finally been notified that the Washington Township Assessor's Office had completed the necessary adjustments in their computers and had notified all proper offices of the changes in the way the lots were to be designated.

"Now it's getting exciting," said Bernie after the bank officer had left with the completed paper work.

"What's next?" asked Lillian.

"Paul Davenport said that he could have the construction loan papers ready for us to sign by the end of the month. Things finally seem to be falling into place."

January 26, 2004
Dallas, Texas

"So," wrote Cyndi in an e-mail to her dad, "how did Mom's CT-Scan go last Friday? And what do you mean she's not on any cancer meds at the moment?"

Bernie and Lillian had just returned from meeting with Lillian's oncologist, Dr. Schultz, or as Bernie sometimes referred to him in private, Dr. Doom and Gloom. As they both had secretly suspected, the prognosis was not encouraging, but Bernie knew he would still have to answer Cyndi's e-mail.

> "Cyn,
>
> "JoMamma was on a cancer-targeting med (Thalidomide), but her Dr. stopped it about a week-and-a-half ago (would not renew her prescription) because he did not think it was working. The CT-scan confirmed his opinion.
>
> "Today he said he is out of tricks. He has no other treatments to suggest and is afraid that if he were to suggest something else at this point, it would cause her more discomfort than do her good. So she is to continue going in every two weeks to have her blood tested and get transfusions if they are indicated, and she is to continue getting the booster shot every two weeks for a while.
>
> "Her appetite is great, and the Vicadin she takes seems to alleviate her pain sufficiently. He wanted to prescribe something stronger, but he said the side effect is constipation—something she definitely does not want to flirt with. Other than that, he said we should just go on about our business. He wants to see her again in about a month.
>
> "So that's kinda where we are. Wherever that is!"

Bernie never told Lillian that each prescription of Thalidomide was costing him $1,000 out of pocket since its use was not covered by insurance. If it had proved effective, however, he would gladly have gone into debt to continue filling the prescriptions.

January 27, 2004,
Broad Ripple, Indianapolis

"Hi, I'm Bernie Barcio, and I'm supposed to meet Cindy Flatten here at 8:30 this morning."

"I think she's running a little late because of the snow," said Rose, the secretary at Christ the King Church.

Since Lillian didn't feel up to going to church on Sunday and missed being able to receive communion, Bernie had called Eleanor Seaver who coordinates the Lay Ministers at Christ the King to see if he could arrange to take communion home with him for Lillian. Eleanor had put him in touch with Cindy who would be able to give Bernie a pyx (a small host container) and explain the ritual for home communion services.

"Hi, sorry I'm late, but the road from Carmel was brutal today," said Cindy when she arrived. "Let's go into the sacristy, and I'll get you what you need."

After Cindy had given Bernie a pyx and a little white zipper pouch in which to carry it, she explained the prayers that should be used for home distribution of communion.

"Have you ever been in a sacristy before?" asked Cindy.

"Yes, I have," said Bernie suddenly realizing how little anyone at Christ the King actually knew about him. "In fact, I spent four years in a seminary where I served as the Head Sacristan of the main chapel."

Bernie couldn't tell if Cindy was impressed or not.

The next morning, when Bernie walked over to church for the 7:00 a.m. communion service as he had begun doing in the fall, he was able to have an extra host placed in his pyx and begin serving communion to Lillian at home.

So Bernie, the ex-seminarian, was now a Lay Minister with a one-person ministry.

How about that!

January 27, 2004
Germany/Switzerland, Europe

When Bernie taught at Park School back in the 1960's, he had encouraged the school administration to introduce a student Foreign Exchange Program. One of the students that came to Park on the program was Uli Friedrichson. Uli studied Latin with Bernie and kept in contact with him over the years. As an oncologist who now teaches in Germany and practices in Switzerland, Uli has made several return trips to the United States and has nourished his friendship with Bernie and Lillian.

In response to an e-mail from Uli concerning Lillian's health, Bernie wrote the following reply.

> "*Salve,* Uli. *Gut Morgan!* Sorry I haven't kept in closer touch lately, but we've been sort of distracted here of late. After the Interleuken 2 treatments were abandoned, Lillian's oncologist had her on Interferon. When that was not stopping the spread of the cancer to her liver and lungs, he put her on Thalidomide that was supposed to

cut off the blood supply to the cancer cells and impede their growth. No luck.

"Her doctor has now run out of tricks. He told us yesterday that he can no longer treat her. He will remain her doctor and will be available to Rx pain meds as needed. All he could do now, he said, was to put us in touch with a Hospice nurse so that when we decide we can no longer handle things by ourselves here at home, we will have an open door to Hospice care.

"I read the latest CT-scan results/reports this morning, and it sounds like the cancer is rampant throughout her lungs, liver, left breast and abdomen. The report said the cancer has completely obscured the left kidney. She also has cardiomegaly, which I am interpreting to mean an enlargement of the heart.

"Remarkably, Lillian still doesn't feel all that bad. Her appetite is healthy; she can still get in and out of bed by herself, dress herself, and use the restroom, all with the help of her cane.

"Her attitude is great. We are both trying to be upbeat and pleasant. She rests a lot and listens to murder mysteries on tape.

"So, I think we'll just keep going on about our business and sort of take one day at a time."

January 30, 2004
Johnson Space Center, Houston, Texas
"Good Afternoon. I'm Joe Barcio, your tour host for your visit today."

Joe had been asked to provide a VIP tour to approximately 50 ESPN reporters. After sharing lunch with the group, he would show them a display of capsules that have been in space and moon rocks before loading them onto a tram for the ride to the Johnson Space Center. There, wearing his specially re-created mission control jacket, Joe would take them through the historic Mission Control Center, the X-38 building and the Shuttle and Space Station training areas.

Upon returning to the Space Center, he noticed that it was already 3:50 p.m. and that time was running short since the group was scheduled to re-board their bus at 4:00 p.m. He decided to give only a very brief introduction to the special astronaut who had been asked to address the group.

"Ladies and gentlemen, it is my honor to introduce to you astronaut Eugene Cernan, the last human being to walk on the moon!"

The applause was shattering, and it became immediately obvious that the group had no intention of re-boarding its bus at the assigned time.

From the time Cernan began sharing his stories, he had everyone's undivided attention.

" 'My suit has over-inflated,' I said when I tried to re-enter the hatch door after completing a space walk during a Gemini Mission. 'I can't fit back through the hatch.' "

" 'You'd better give it your best shot,' said my fellow astronaut, 'or we'll both die when our oxygen gives out!' "

Cernon proceeded to talk to the group for a good 45 minutes before opening the floor to questions.

"What was it like to orbit the earth?"
"What was it like to leave the earth behind?"
"What was it like to approach the moon?"
"What was it like to orbit the moon?"
"What was it like to land on the moon?"
"What was it like to walk on the moon?"
"What was it like to drive a car on the moon?"
"What was it like to look up and see the earth?"
"What was it like to leave the moon?"
"What was it like to return to earth?"

Before the group was willing to take their leave, Cernan had spent another 40 minutes fielding their questions.

"Joe," said Cernan before dismissing the group, "I should not be the last person to walk on the moon."

He then went on to explain his vision of other astronauts who will someday make the walk, just as he once did.

Joe had already met Buzz Aldrin and was thrilled to have the opportunity to meet a second astronaut who had walked on the moon.

The talk had been a real treat both for Joe and for the ESPN reporters.

February 1, 2004
Houston, Texas

Joe and Liz were attending Mass at their new parish, St. Paul's Catholic Church, when the priest offered a special prayer for the astronauts on the Shuttle Columbia. As each of the Columbia astronaut's names were called, astronaut Michael Massimino, of Italian descent, lit a candle, seven in all.

Joe had had an opportunity to meet Massimino on March 5, 2002, while he was training at the Neutral Buoyancy Lab in preparation for his shuttle flight to repair the Hubble Space Telescope.

Because Massimino is an active member of St. Paul's, Joe and Liz are privileged to see him from time to time.

February 4, 2004
Broad Ripple, Indianapolis

"Who was that on the phone?" asked Lillian.
"That was Bob Young, Jr.," said Bernie. "Guess what!"
"What?"
"He's placed the order for our house. It should be ready to be delivered in five or six weeks!"
"Incredible," said Lillian. "When will they start work on the foundation?"
"Bob says they'll probably be out to start that about February 18th or 19th if the weather cooperates."
"Do the driveway people have to have the rough driveway in by then?"

"No. The rough driveway just needs to be done by the time the house is delivered. And by then Phil and I will have all the trees down that need to be out for the foundation work to begin."

Okay. Now this was really getting exciting!

February 22, 2004
Houston, Texas

Joe's daughter, Liz Marie, and her fiancé, Chris, were attending an Encounter Weekend for Engaged Couples. As one of the exercises during the weekend, individuals were asked to write a letter to a special person who had a positive influence on his/her life.

Liz wrote the following letter to her Aunt Lillian.

"Dear Aunt Lil,

"Chris and I are at our Engaged Encounter this weekend and it's been wonderful. We have grown closer and throughout the activities have had time to reflect on who and what is important to us.

"I realize that YOU have had a very positive impact on my life!

"You have gone through a lot: raising three daughters, coming into our family, providing two more cousins for us, finishing a degree and dealing with a sick mother and mother-in-law. You and Uncle Bernie ran two successful small businesses for many years and, of course, are now dealing with many health issues.

"I remember with fondness sitting at the kitchen table talking to you about events in your life and the perspective you have. You seemed at peace, and I know it influenced me when I was going through events in my life—the divorce, the annulment, and now marriage preparation to a Wonderful Man! You learn from those events, and love is better and certainly more appreciated with family, friends and those special people in your life.

"You helped me recognize that I need to make my own decisions—especially when I had to buy my own car—not my parents' idea of what I should get. Boy, was that an eye opener! I want to thank you for that!

"As your health has changed, I never saw you complain; instead you learned to adapt and find resources to use, such as books on tape.

"All this is very inspiring! You are an amazing strong woman whose calm demeanor can and should be emulated.

"Please know that I love you very much—my favorite aunt!
"All my love,
"Liz"

February 23, 2004
Broad Ripple, Indianapolis

"Hi," said Bernie when he called Dr. Schultz's office. "Lillian was scheduled to have a blood test this morning and then meet with Dr. Schultz this afternoon, but she's not able to stand up today. I'm afraid we'll have to cancel."

"Okay, Mr. Barcio. I'll tell the Doctor."

"Uh, the last time we were there," continued Bernie, "Dr Schultz said he was going to put us in touch with a Hospice Nurse. I think we need to do that at this time."

"I think you're probably right," said the receptionist. "I'll have Nurse Karen call you as soon as she is free."

When Nurse Karen called, she said that everything had been put into motion and that Bernie would be contacted immediately by an RN from the St. Vincent Hospice program. Before the morning was out, an RN named Beth was at Lillian's bedside making a quick evaluation and explaining the program. Although Lillian could not stand, she was very much in control of her senses and not really in all that much pain (4 on a scale of 1 to 10). Lillian signed her own enrollment papers as Bernie listened and watched.

Early the same afternoon, a truck pulled into the driveway and the At Home Health Equipment Company delivered an adjustable hospital bed with an automatically inflating air mattress, a wheel chair, a portable potty, a long-term oxygen unit and a small emergency oxygen unit along with an adjustable bedside table—all provided courtesy of Medicare's participation in the hospice program.

The next day an RN named Tracey arrived during the morning to draw blood. She also brought a more powerful pain medication that would last for 12 hours. Tracey called later in the day to report that Lillian's potassium level was a little low, but nothing to worry about. Also Lillian's blood reading of 8.7 did not warrant having to transport her to the hospital to have a transfusion.

With Bernie's help, Lillian was able to slip from the side of the bed into the wheel chair so she could eat a small breakfast at the dining room table and look out the picture window at the work that was progressing on the foundation for the modular home that she and Bernie had chosen. After breakfast, Bernie gave Lillian a sponge bath, helped her into one of the three new nightgowns that Cyndi had bought for her the previous weekend and then helped her return to bed.

On Wednesday, Bernie finally met Nicki Sherer, the RN that was being permanently assigned to Lillian's care. Lillian was still feeling fairly well, was kidding around and sleeping several hours at a time.

February 26, 2004
Broad Ripple, Indianapolis

"Hi," said the social worker as Bernie opened the front door, "I'm John Nuland."

John was shown to a bedside chair in the master bedroom where the hospital bed had been set up next to Bernie and Lillian's custom crafted black walnut queen-sized bed.

"Is there any way that you think you have let Bernie down?" asked John as he tried to get Lillian to share what he obviously was figuring would be among her final thoughts.

"Not really," said Lillian, keeping her trademark cool composure.

John probed and questioned, but was unable to shake Lillian's calm demeanor. She was definitely a strong and confident lady!

"Bernie, do you want to know what is probably going to happen next?" asked John.

"Yes, I would like to know, but I would rather we talked privately."

So Bernie and John retired to the front room where John suddenly began to paint a very gloomy picture.

"Bernie, Lillian is very near the end. Did you realize that?"

"No, not really. We thought she was doing fairly well. She had a good blood test, and she feels that if her back can stop hurting, she should be able to be up and around again."

"Bernie, I don't think so. I don't think Lillian's back pain is due to sprained muscles. It's most likely due to the progression of the disease. I believe she could pass within a week or so. Do you want to know what to expect?"

"Yes, I think I should know, but I don't think we have to tell Lillian."

"Okay, Bernie, I'm going to call Nicki and have her share the details with you tomorrow when she stops by."

This was definitely going to take a little while to sink in. Neither Bernie nor Lillian imagined that things were moving as fast as John was suggesting.

When Nicki returned on Friday, however, she was very definite.

"Do you really think she only has a week left?" asked Bernie as he and Nicki sat outside on the patio to talk.

"Maybe even less time than that, Bernie. In fact, I would be surprised if she lasted through the weekend. Her body is just shutting down. It's the way that her cancers are working."

When Nicki went into the house to look after Lillian, Bernie called his stepdaughter Karen's cell phone number to tell her Nicki's projection. Then he remembered that Cyndi had said she was preparing to buy a ticket to return to Indianapolis on March 19 to help some more with the packing.

"Cyndi," asked Bernie when he called her at work, "have you bought your plane ticket for the 19th yet?"

"No. Why?" asked Cyndi.

"Well, don't. You may need to come home sooner than that."

"Why? What's going on?"

"Well, the nurse just said that JoMamma may only have about a week left. But, you know, I would just hold off on buying any tickets just yet. That's what they told me about Gramma Barcio at the beginning of February last year, and she lived for 22 more days. I just didn't want you to commit to any ticket purchases until we see what's happening. Okay?"

Cyndi agreed. After a phone call like that, however, her day at the office was almost entirely ruined. She found it hard to maintain her composure and focus on what she needed to be doing. And her co-workers turned out to be somewhat less than supportive.

February 28, 2004
Broad Ripple, Indianapolis

"How are you at making phone calls?" asked Bernie as he and Phil were talking over the predictions that Nicki had made the day before.

"I think I can do okay," said Phil.

"That's great," said Bernie. "I can't. I think I forget to breathe and then I get all choked up. If you could make the phone calls when the time comes, I would really appreciate that."

"I've got it covered," assured Phil.

Lillian had had a pretty good day on Saturday. She drank a vanilla Glucerna (a drink made especially for diabetics) for lunch and dinner, and then, at bedtime, she said she wanted Bernie to fix her a bowl of apples and cinnamon oatmeal. When Bernie offered to feed it to her as she lay slightly raised in bed, she insisted on holding the bowl and feeding herself, even though small quantities occasionally missed her mouth and needed to be cleaned up with a Kleenex. Rudy waited expectantly at the side of the bed to lick the bowl, but Lillian wouldn't give it up until she had scooped up every possible drop of milk and cereal.

Bernie took this as an encouraging sign and looked forward to a restful night.

February 29, 2004
Broad Ripple, Indianapolis

Unfortunately, Lillian was to have a terrible night. She called to Bernie about every 45 minutes to help her get comfortable. Sometimes, she felt that she needed to use the bedpan, but then was not able to do anything. Then she would call that she needed to get up, but when Bernie tried to raise the bed, she would grimace with pain. Soon Bernie figured out that it did not pay to go back to bed after he had helped to readjust her position. He began to sit in the chair at the side of her bed and try to rest a little as she would think about the new position for about five or six minutes and then quietly comment that it wasn't quite right yet. A pillow needed moving. She needed to be scooted up higher. She needed to be rolled over a little—no...that was too much. Sometimes she asked Bernie just to wait while she tried to think about how to tell him what she wanted him to do.

Finally, about 5 a.m. Bernie decided it was time to call the Hospice Hotline and talk to the nurse on call, who turned out to be Carol.

"Lillian is in a lot of pain, and she's not scheduled to take her next pain pill until 6 a.m.," explained Bernie after he brought Carol up to date.

"Ouch," said Carol suddenly.

"What happened?" asked Bernie.

"My 5-year-old daughter just rolled over and poked me in the eye. My husband's gone, and she decided she wanted to sleep with me. What kind of pain medicine are you giving Lillian?"

After Bernie explained that they had been given two different strengths of Oxycodone, a form of synthetic morpheme, Carol was ready to make some suggestions.

"Give her the 20 milligram pill now and also give her two or three of the 5 milligram pills," instructed Carol.

Bernie did as he was instructed, but a half hour later, Lillian was complaining loudly that she was hurting and was begging Bernie to help her.

"Did Nicki leave you any of the anti-anxiety medicine?" asked Carol when Bernie had her paged a second time.

"Yes, I believe it's in the refrigerator," said Bernie.

"Put about a third of a dropper of the liquid under her tongue. That will help her to calm down and maybe get to sleep. I'll try and get there by 8:30 a.m. If I'm not there by 8:45, have me paged again."

When Bernie had Carol paged at 8:50, she told him to go ahead and go to church and she would definitely be there by 10:15 or 10:30.

Since Bernie did not want to leave Lillian alone, Audrey volunteered to stay at the house while he and Phil attended the 9:00 a.m. Mass.

"I forgot to tell Audrey not to call 9-1-1 if something happens while we're at church," whispered Bernie to Phil half-way through Mass. "I'm going to go out and use the car phone to tell her to be sure to call the Hospice Hotline if she needs help."

When Bernie and Phil got home, Audrey and Phil noticed that Lillian had spit up a small quantity of blood and that her left hand was hanging limply off the side of the bed.

"Can you please page Carol and tell her to get here as soon as possible?" said Bernie to the nurse who answered the Hospice Hotline. "We have a crisis here!"

Bernie, Phil and Audrey tried to make Lillian a little more comfortable as they waited for Carol's call.

"Where are you?" asked Bernie when Carol answered her page.

"I'm at a pharmacy on 86th Street getting a couple things I'll need to care for Lillian. I should be there in about 15 minutes," said Carol.

When Carol arrived, she placed patches behind Lillian's ears that would help to dry the saliva in her throat so she wouldn't make the "death rattle" and gave her a stronger dose of pain medicine.

"She's very close," announced Carol to the stunned trio, and then she walked into the sunshine beaming through the picture window in the dining room.

Audrey sat on the edge of the large queen-sized bed that was next to the hospital bed and held Lillian's right hand, squeezing gently as Lillian squeezed back.

Bernie sat in the chair on Lillian's left and held her other hand while Phil embraced his Mom's head and comforted her.

When Bernie noticed Lillian looking directly at him, he waved at her with his left arm. Lillian released Audrey's hand and raised her right arm to return a bad imitation of a drunken sailor salute.

"I think we should say a little prayer," suggested Phil.

Bernie nodded in agreement but found he could not talk as he looked sadly into Lillian's now half closed eyes.

"Dear Lord, please look down on our Mom," began Phil, with his right hand placed on his mom's head, "She deserves the best."

And then, just as Lillian was about to breathe her last, Phil, with all the composure of a veteran chaplain, said, "Please receive Mom's soul into heaven and look after her and reward her for all the good she has done in her life."

At that moment, all movement ceased in Lillian's chest, and Carol came back into the bedroom to announce that Lillian had passed.

It was 11:20 a.m.

The sun shone brightly into the dining room window as all four stood silently near the bed for a few minutes.

Lillian Rose, beloved wife, mother, grandmother and great-grandmother, had passed away in a beautiful way on a beautiful day as those who loved her held her hands and her head and prayed her soul into heaven. *Requiescat in pace!*

March 1, 2004
Germany

Although Bernie had asked Phil to handle the more difficult phone calls notifying immediate family members and close friends of Lillian's passing, he was able to send e-mail notifications to several others whom he knew were following Lillian's illness. The following reply was received from Uli Friedrichson in Germany:

> "Dear Mr. Barcio,
> "I really regret the passing away of your wife. I hope she had not to suffer a lot. My prayers are with you and all of your family. If everything turns out right, I'll be over in Indy sometime this year. I'll contact you as soon as I know when—maybe we could meet and go for a drink or dinner. Many regards."

March 4, 2004
Christ the King Church, Indianapolis

Friends and family came together for the 10:00 a.m. Mass for Lillian at Christ the King. Bernie made a careful effort to involve family members in the service by having his grandchildren—Michael, Charlotte and Audrey—bring up the gifts, Sheryl and Karen do the readings from the Old and New Testament and Mike deliver the eulogy. Cyndi had helped Bernie pick out the musical selections to be sung by the Resurrection Choir, but the goal was to avoid putting Cyndi and Phil through any more emotional stress than they had already experienced during the past week.

When the time came for the eulogy, Mike took his place at the lectern.

"I'm Mike Pence, husband of Lillian's third daughter, Karen, and I am humbled to speak for Lillian's family today. I regret that this eulogy has fallen to a politician. It seems Lillian Rose Barcio's life has been punctuated by family associations with bank robbers [*an allusion to her dad having hung out with John Dillinger as a teenager*] and politicians. [*laughter*]

"Lillian loved to laugh. Her keychain read CERTIFIED CRAZY PERSON.
[*more laughter*]

"From her youth in Indianapolis as an only child, she was able to count on her grandmother, her Aunt Dood and her Cousin Jack—an only child as well—who lived down the street.

"Jack told me, 'when any boys gave her trouble, I'd have to beat them up or get beat up for her.' Thanks, Jack.

"Jack and friends like Delores [Lillian's classmate from their days at Shortridge High School] and Pat [Robinson] brought Lillian Rose through many trying times.

"Then came a relationship that left her with three beautiful little girls aged 6, 4 and 2: Marsha, Sheryl and Karen. As a working single mother, she still made sure of every detail of their lives. Her little girls were Girl Scouts and had dancing lessons.

"While working at Park School as the Headmaster's secretary, Lillian met a dashing young Latin teacher and forged lifelong friendships with Anne Berkeley, Bill and Pat Robinson and Marilyn Linard.

"One of the first movies that Lillian and her dashing young Latin teacher, Bernie, saw together was Dr. Zhivago—the review of which would become a theme for their life together: 'Turbulent were the times and fiery was the love story.'

"Lillian and Bernie were married in June of 1967, and from the turbulent times came romance, a home and her second family consisting of Cyndi and Phillip.

"As the years rolled by, the fiery love story only became stronger. Daughters and son would marry, eight grandchildren and 3 great-grandchildren would be born.

"While her family was the center of Lillian's life, her indomitable spirit would lead her back to school, obtaining a college degree in her 50's. She would also found and publish the **Village Sampler Newspaper** which, for more than a decade, was required reading for every citizen of her beloved Broad Ripple.

"As I close and I think of Lillian and her beloved Bernie, I can't help but think back once more to the 1965 movie, Dr. Zhivago. While Lillian would agree that she was no Julie Christie and that Bernie was no Omar Sahriff, there is definitely something of an epic notion in her brave life and her love for Bernie and her whole family.

"As I stood yesterday in the master bedroom of their home, the room where she left us Sunday morning, I saw the framed words of Laura's Theme from their movie, done in calligraphy by her daughter Cyndi, on the wall. In my heart, I read the words almost as a note that Lillian had left behind for Bernie and for all of us who will miss her so much.

" '*Somewhere, my love, there will be songs to sing although the snow covers the hope of spring. Someday we'll meet again, my love. Someday, whenever the spring breaks through. Somewhere a hill blossoms in green and gold, and there are dreams—all that your heart can hold.*' "

When Mike finished, Lillian's nephew, Bernie Barcio, approached the lectern to deliver a second eulogy.

"When my brother and sisters and I gathered around recently to recount the wonderful memories of Aunt Lil, it occurred to us that each memory had the same underlying image: Not only was she a wonderful wife, mother, grandmother, godmother, aunt and friend, but she was also a friendly, humorous peacemaker who had the ability not to let negative things in life rile her up but, instead, to deal with them and move on. She would have soft, one-on-one conversations about the here-and-now with simple topics. As my brother recounts, 'Now, do you like to be called Joe or Joey?'—start with the basics. She appreciated the simple things in life.

"For me, Auntie Lil is my Godmother and only Aunt, but I had a separate, rather special distinction to her in that I was 'not much of a hugger.' Apparently, she had very high standards, so this must speak very well of Uncle Bernie. Nonetheless, I'd still get a smile and a little chuckle. It's the simple moments that perhaps we don't appreciate enough that perhaps can have the biggest impact. Let me share a couple examples.

"When I was much younger, I was sitting in Uncle Bernie's car waiting for Auntie Lil to come out with some groceries. When she crossed in front of the car with a bag of groceries in each arm, my Uncle says with his pipe in his mouth and his hands on the wheel, 'Let's have a little fun with Auntie Lil.' He then blared the horn just as she was close to the car to get the full shocking effect. She practically fell over while clutching the two bags of groceries as she tried to prevent the contents from crashing to the ground.

"At that point, I thought I should start working on *his* eulogy, but then a strange thing happened. She smiled and started laughing. I was amazed at his success in this matter, so I dutifully took note of the details of the event so I could use it in the future. I was about 8 at the time, so for the next 15 years or so I attempted the same joke in a variety of manners with parents, friends, girlfriends (I should say ex-girlfriends) and never did I achieve anything that could be described as successful. After a thorough review, I finally realized what I was missing. It had little to do with the joke itself or its delivery, but rather with the person on whom it was played. Only a remarkable person such as Auntie Lil could appreciate the spontaneity and have the sense of humor to laugh at herself and have the supporting, nurturing demeanor to say, 'Oh, you are so clever!' With Zen-like efficiency she seemed to appreciate the simplicity, beauty and humor of the moment.

"Several months ago I was asked a question during an official Enron investigation about how people in the same company can have completely different accounts of what happened. In response, I retold a story about Auntie Lil and Uncle Bernie. Uncle Bernie was recounting some personal story to us about something or other he had done, and Auntie Lil waited patiently until finally, unable to endure any more of his Homeresque exaggerations, she piped up and said, 'Why is it that whenever you tell this story, you make it out like you are some super-genius and I'm some helpless idiot?'

"Uncle Bernie said, 'That is because I am telling the story. When I'm telling the story, I'm the hero. When you tell the story, you can be the hero.' At which point she just smiled and rolled her eyes and then patiently let him finish the story, not bothering to take him up on his offer—she didn't need to. She probably never knew that her impact and legacy is now recorded in the Enron investigation as the 'Lillian Effect.'

"Even during times of challenge and strife, Auntie Lil's Zen-like qualities shined through. From patiently appeasing our Grandma's eccentricities to taking her own ailments in stride, Aunt Lil rose above her more-than-justified opportunity for anger and, instead, exuberated an amazing sense of patience, acceptance and peace. In short, as my mom describes her, 'She's a saint!'

"And so, now when I think about 'not being a hugger,' I think of what was so surprising to her and perhaps what she was telling me. How can you go through life studying and working so much and overlook something as simple as a hug. I am not sure if she is a Zen Master, but it sure seems like it. I am sure that when I join her at the Pearly Gates—she with her claddagh ring and 'Kiss me, I'm Irish' button—despite shedding all my corporeal limitations, she will say, 'Still not much of a hugger, eh?' Then she'll smile the same supportive smile and chuckle. Perhaps I can spend the rest of eternity learning that which she seemed to know naturally—the wonderful beauty of the simple.

"We love you, Auntie Lil.

"Let me end with an Irish Blessing by Grace E. Easley that seems appropriate. I'll spare you my Irish accent.

" 'May you live a full life—
Full of gladness and fun,
With a pocket full of gold
As your least fortune.

" 'May the dreams you hold dearest
Be those which come true,
The kindness you spread
Keep returning to you.

" 'May the friendships you make
Be those which endure,
And all of your gray clouds
Be small ones for sure.

" 'And trusting in Him
To Whom we all pray,
May a song fill your heart
Every step of the way.' "

March 6, 2004
Selinsgrove, Pennsylvania

"Bernie," wrote Mary Leo in an e-mail when she returned home, "it was quite a moving and highly spiritual experience. I think everyone came away from it feeling Lill's presence. She would have loved how caring Joe and his family were to you, Cyndi, Phil, her two daughters and to us.

"It was an extremely rough time for everyone, but through love and understanding and some healthy laughter, we all seemed to bond together for a common cause. It was almost magical. It's comforting to know that we can depend on each other when times are truly difficult. Thank you for keeping Rick and me close to your side."

Bernie was glad to hear from his cousin and was looking forward to obtaining a copy of her second Harlequin Flipside novel, **For Better or Cursed**, which was being released later in the month. He had heard that he would be included as a character (a "cousin Bernie from Indiana who played the mandolin) in the book.

Mary Leo's writing career would, of course, continue to move forward. In March of 2005 she would have a third Harlequin Flipside novel, **A Pinch of Cool**, published, and she was already under contract to have an Anthology, HQ Signature novel, **Coffee House Dating**, published in March of 2006.

Bernie indeed felt privileged to have Mary close by his side.

In 2007, Mary had her book **CABIN FEVER** published by Harlequin, while her husband, Rick Watkins, published **THE BIG BURN** in 2006, and an Athena Force novel called **STACKED DECK** in 2007.

March 8, 2004
Broad Ripple, Indianapolis

Things were finally settling down a little at 6026 Indianola. Those who had traveled across the country to be together for the sad event had all returned home, and it now fell to Bernie to sort through the names of those who had given flowers, had masses said, made donations to the Oncology division of the St. Vincent Foundation, had provided wonderful food dishes both for the house and for the family room at Flanner and Buchanan Mortuary during the viewing.

As Bernie sat writing the Thank You notes at Lillian's desk that he had now adopted as his own, it was rewarding to realize just how many people had come together in support of the family.

Cards of condolence would, of course, continue to arrive for days afterwards. And just when Bernie would think that he had finally "gotten it together," he would open another card and suddenly find it hard to read through blurry eyes.

Of all the cards that would come, however, one would remain in his mind as being especially touching. It was sent by Linda and Bob Soel, a man who had once been Phil's Little League coach. The Soel's usually sat in the chapel on Sunday mornings in seats immediately in front of Bernie and Lillian. After church, they would visit and recall old times as they returned to their cars.

> "We are so sorry to hear of your loss. We always enjoyed our little chats outside of church. Lillian always appeared to be a fragile little angel waiting for her eternal reward in heaven. We pray God gives you the grace and courage to accept it."

March 10, 2004
Washington, D.C.

Lillian's son-in-law, Congressman Mike Pence, asked and was given permission to address the House of Representatives for 1 minute and to revise and extend his remarks.

> "Mr. Speaker, I rise to remember the life of the devoted wife, courageous mother, publisher and journalist Lillian Rose Barcio.
>
> "Lillian Barcio died February 29, 2004, in Indianapolis where she was born in July of 1931. She is survived by her loving husband of 37 years, Bernard; her daughters, Marsha Louzon, Sheryl Donnella, Karen Pence, Cyndi Barcio, and her son, Phillip Barcio. In addition, she is survived by eight grandchildren and two great-great grandchildren.
>
> "Through many hardships, Lillian Barcio kept her faith in Christ and her humor and optimism about life. The Bible says that charm is deceptive and beauty is fleeting but the woman who fears the Lord is to be praised.
>
> "Lillian Barcio, my mother-in-law, was such a woman whose life would merit remembrance in this Congress even if she had not raised the most wonderful woman I have ever known. May God rest the soul of Lillian Barcio and bring rest and comfort to her loving husband Bernie and all those who mourn her passing."

March 12, 2004
Broad Ripple, Indianapolis

"Whenever you're gone," Lillian used to say to Bernie, "Rudy just lies on the rug at the top of the stairs looking at the side door waiting for you to come home."

And it was true. Sometimes Bernie would come into the house through the door on the back porch, and, because Rudy had lost most of his hearing, he wouldn't hear him come in. There he would be, lying down, staring at the side door waiting. Finally, he would feel the vibration of Bernie's footsteps and jump up to see him.

A few days ago, Lillian's high school friend, Delores, had asked if Rudy seemed to miss Lillian.

"No, he hasn't yet," Bernie had said. "He is a lot more feisty lately, however. After dinner, he wants to play more than he has in a long time."

But after Bernie had put Rudy to bed in the kitchen last night, he noticed something unusual when he re-entered the kitchen to put the cordless phone back in its holder before going to bed himself. Instead of being sound asleep on his blankey in front of the sink, where he usually slept, Bernie noticed that Rudy was sleeping on the rug at the top of the steps, facing the side door.

That was different.

Then, this morning, Bernie noticed it again. After Rudy finished his breakfast, instead of lying down between the table and the window—his usual daytime sack-out location—Rudy was lying on his tummy on the rug at the edge of the landing, staring at the side door.

Rudy must have finally realized that he hadn't seen Lillian around for a few days, and he was obviously waiting for her to come back home.

He was, after all, her dog.

March 22, 2004
Broad Ripple, Indianapolis

"Here comes the house!" announced Phil as he hurried in to tell his dad that the truck delivering the first half of the new modular home Bernie and Lillian had selected was coming down the street. It was such an anticipated event that even one of Lillian's best friends, Ann Berkeley, had come over to watch the delivery.

The lead trucks arrived first, blocking off traffic as the seventeen-foot wide section slowly made its way up Indianola from Kessler Blvd.

When the trailer pulled up in the front of the 60-foot lot on which the home was to be located, everyone just sort of stood and looked at it in amazement for awhile.

"That opening cut in the retaining wall isn't going to be wide enough," announced one of the workers who was studying how the section could be backed onto the property before being rolled over onto the foundation.

So, two or three other workers got busy knocking out additional slabs of limestone and stacking them over to one side so Bernie and Phil would be able to rebuild the wall afterwards.

After the initial amazement of seeing the first half of his new home wore off, Bernie began to look carefully at the unit.

"That's the wrong half," Bernie said calmly to the delivery crew.

"No," countered the head man, "It's the right one. They loaded it at the factory. See, that's the end that faces the street."

"No," countered Bernie. "That's the end that faces the back. That's supposed to be the south half of the house and it's loaded backwards on the trailer. I'll go in and get the floor plan and show you."

It took quite a bit of convincing, but Bernie finally made everyone realize that the wrong half had been delivered first in addition to having been loaded backwards on the trailer.

Meanwhile, the driver who had driven the unit down from the factory was busy unhooking his tractor from the trailer. His job was just to deliver the unit. He was out of there. Someone else would have to figure out what to do next.

"Well, I guess we'll have to hook up one our tractors to the trailer and take it back to the lot for the night," said one of the men from Bob Young Homes who was there with his crew to install the unit.

"What happens then?" asked Bernie.

"We'll have to jack it up and pull the trailer out from under it, and then load the other half on."

"Make sure the right end is facing the street," cautioned Bernie.

"We will," said the man, "but we won't be able to bring it back today. We'll have to try again tomorrow."

So, after weeks of waiting, everyone would have to wait a little longer.

March 24, 2004
Broad Ripple, Indianapolis

"Yesterday they delivered the correct half first," wrote Bernie in an e-mail to his neice, Liz Marie, "and, yes, it was turned correctly on the trailer this time. But then they found that the trailer did not sink down deep enough into the mud as they had hoped it would. They even let the air out of the tires. So they left it sitting there all night, hoping that it would sink deeper by this morning."

Bernie got up from his keyboard and walked over to a basement window to look over at the workmen.

"I believe," he continued, "they're outside right now probably trying to decide what to do next. The house is beautiful—if they ever get it placed on the foundation correctly."

March 25, 2004
Broad Ripple, Indianapolis

"Look at that," thought Bernie to himself as he noticed the small Star Magnolia tree that Lillian had bought for him and which they had planted next to the swing area. "I guess it decided to welcome the new house with a full array of beautiful blossoms."

Both halves of the modular home had now been delivered and successfully rolled into place onto the foundation. Workers had "raised" the roof peaks of each half and they were now busy "marrying" the two halves of the house together, plugging in wires, putting up siding, laying down the final capping layer of roof shingles.

It was beautiful. Just as Bernie and Lillian had planned and imagined. Or, almost.

"You know, Bob," said Bernie to Bob Young, Jr., with whom Bernie and Lillian had worked while ordering the house, and who had come out to see how things were going, "Those shingles aren't the brown color we ordered. They look gray to me."

"Oh," said Bob, Jr., "that's what they call 'brown' at the factory."

Bernie really wasn't in a mood to argue, but he knew that Bob, Jr. was wrong. Later, when he found a wrapping paper from a pack of the shingles, clearly printed on the package were the words, "Gray Shingles."

Bob, Jr., however, had been most cooperative working with Bernie and Lillian over the past several months as they struggled to straighten out the plot descriptions with the Washington Township Assessor—something that had delayed the project by several months—that Bernie really did not want to make an issue. Lillian had wanted brown, but Bernie was so glad to see the house finally coming together that he figured he could live with gray shingles.

The weather was beautiful—in the 70's, after being in the 60's all week.

This was also the second weekend for the Big Garage Sale. Bernie and Phil had started the sale the weekend before, but there was so much stuff that still needed to be gotten rid of that they decided to let it run for one more weekend. This time Bernie specifically advertised some of the larger items that most folks wouldn't expect to find at a garage sale.

The beautiful oak dining room set that he and Lillian had bought very reasonably from a friendly neighbor when they lived on Ferguson proved to be way too big for the new house.

"If we move all the pieces in there," explained Bernie to his son Phil, "there won't be room for anything else in the kitchen or the living room."

The dining room set was advertised separately in the paper and was quickly sold for $1,400 to a postal carrier and his dad who intended to strip the set down and refinish it in a lighter shade.

"I'd love to see it when you're done," Bernie had said to the father.

"We'll give you a call," assured the man.

As of August, 2004, however, Bernie had yet to hear from either the postal carrier or his father, and he had, by this time, misplaced their phone number.

So much for that. Probably better to remember it as it was in those hundreds of special occasion photos that had been taken of the family gathered around it over the years.

As fate would have it, in July of 2006, a bad hail storm damaged almost every roof in the Broad Ripple area. When Bernie hired contractors to replace the roofs on both his house and barn, he made sure that the new shingles were brown.

March 27, 2004
Broad Ripple, Indianapolis

Bernie and Phil had gone to MCL for dinner, and over dessert Phil had shared some of his serious concerns about what he considered to be the lack of proper care given to his mother by her doctor and some of the nurses.

Bernie had listened to his son's concerns and tried to allay his fears. He was, however, reluctant to get into too serious of a conversation lest he begin to choke up and completely break down in public. There were a lot of things he needed—and wanted—to share with Phil, but he would need to choose a more comfortable venue for the exchange.

Later that evening, he decided to compose an e-mail to Phil.

"I sat with Rudy as he finished eating his pig's ear, and am now taking a moment before I put him to bed to share a little.

"I've given more thought to what you said over dinner about wishing we had done more to force JoMamma's caregivers to show more aggressive concern over her treatment. That bothered me quite a bit also, and I frequently shared my feeling with JoMamma until I finally figured out why she wanted me to butt out.

"She was the one who was trying desperately to adjust to living with a terminal illness. She was the one who was doing all the suffering (she frequently confided to me in desperation how tired she was of hurting). All she was really asking of the rest of us was that we do everything in our power to help maintain a calm and hassle-free environment in which she could attempt to deal—with as much dignity as possible—with her personal challenges.

"Thus she did not want me—or you either, as you have shared—getting into any hassles with her doctor or her nurses. Nor did she want anyone in her family getting into any hassles with each other in her presence—as she made a strong point of mentioning that day when we were walking and discussing politics with Karen near your double.

"Our job—and the best thing we could do for her in her mind—was to maintain a dignified and hassle-free environment for her. She wanted to handle the rest on her own in her own way.

"And I think we did that for her by not engaging her doctors and nurses and creating tension and conflict.

"Because this is really all she was asking of us, I believe that neither you nor I need feel any guilt for not having grappled with her healthcare providers. This would only have made her situation all the more intolerable for her.

"She (and I) both knew that there was really nothing that could be done for Stage 4 kidney cancer. She (and I) knew that the best that could be hoped for from all the treatments was perhaps a delaying of the progress of the disease so that she could enjoy a slightly longer life than would have been otherwise possible. She did not want the extra moments that she was buying by putting herself through the discomfort of the treatments to be clouded by the hassles of her own family members. She only wanted us to be peaceful and help her enjoy whatever extra time she was earning.

"And, this I firmly believe, we did by honoring her requests not to engage, challenge or beat the shit out of her doctor or her nurses—even though we may have dearly wanted to.

"In the end, with the help of you and Audrey and the Hospice nurse, I sincerely believe we made it possible for her to pass away in a beautiful way—on a beautiful day. Exactly the way she would have wanted it.

"We can only be thankful that we had the spiritual confidence, physical stamina and emotional stability to be able to honor what she really wanted us to be doing right up until the end.

"So even though we both dearly wanted to speak up and give someone 'what for,' I believe we did the right thing by biting our tongues and keeping our peace and thereby making it possible for her to keep hers as she dealt with the really serious aspects of the whole ordeal.

"And perhaps you did a better job of biting your tongue than I did.

"I definitely went against her wishes when I insisted that we go to the IU Med Center and get a second opinion. She considered this confrontational and resisted it all the way—although afterwards she did admit that she felt better knowing that Dr. Schultz really was, in fact, offering the only on-label treatments that were available. And being a person with Stage 4 kidney cancer, we learned that she really did not qualify for any of the alternative or experimental approaches that are being tried at various centers across the country. She really did not like the stress that this whole second-opinion business created and, I think, resented the fact that I was introducing this stress into what little time she had to try and enjoy what was left of her life.

"About two weeks before she passed away, when Annie and Sheryl were scheduled to visit, she had a front tooth fall out. This happened a day or so before Annie was scheduled to arrive. She was embarrassed as all get out by the fact that she would have to face Annie with a tooth missing. She called Dr. Vaughn to see if she could get in right away and have the tooth reinserted.

" 'No,' the receptionist said. 'Dr. Vaughn won't be able to see you until the middle of next week.'

"JoMamma was crushed and in tears, but refused to press the matter.

"I had had it. I told JoMamma I was making a run to the bank and the post office and got in my truck and drove directly to Dr. Vaughn's office where I insisted on seeing the doctor personally.

"Dr. Vaughn invited me into her office, and I explained that JoMamma was home crying because she would have to face her granddaughter with a front tooth missing. I asked Dr. Vaughn to make an exception and see her that very afternoon to fix her tooth.

"She said, 'Okay.'

"Then I said that I wanted her to have her nurse call JoMamma back—giving absolutely no indication that I had intervened in the matter—and casually tell her that an appointment had suddenly come open for her.

"The doctor agreed and had her nurse call. When I got home from my trip 'to the bank and the post office,' JoMamma was thrilled to tell me that Dr. Vaughn's nurse had called and that she would be able to get her in right away after all.

"She was happy. I was happy. And Dr. Vaughn and her staff kept the secret.

"In this way, I was able to intervene without upsetting the 'peace' with which JoMamma was trying desperately to surround herself.

"So any help you offered by not upsetting this 'peace' should be considered a blessing and should not be anything over which you should be feeling guilty.

"Hope this helps. Now I'll go back upstairs and put Rudy to bed.
"Thanks again for all your help today and for being willing to share your concerns and feelings.

"*Vostro* (not quite entirely over it either) *Padre*"

March 29, 2004,
Fountain Square, Indianapolis

It had now been a month since we had all sat together with Lillian as she peacefully passed away. Phil continued to reflect on all of the things that happened, the final deathbed moments, the arrangements, the phone calls, the funeral. Today would be the day that he would sit down at his computer and try and organize his thoughts into the following short story which he would title, "Living Will."

"I may sit here all day and stare out the window at the sunshine. I feel a tug in my heart caused by this beautiful day. Every beautiful day reminds me of every other beautiful day I have ever known. So many beautiful days have come and gone now that sometimes they just paralyze me. I can't go outside or even do anything at all because of all the memories flooding back into my heart. I open the curtains and see the sun shining off the leaves in the walnut tree and I remember the sun shining off the water in Key West the first time Audrey and I were there. And that reminds me of our wedding in Key West two years later and how Mom made the trip even though she had stage-four kidney cancer. I am so glad she came. I am so glad I have her on video, even though I can't watch the video yet. I can't imagine what I might feel if I watch the DVD of Mom telling me not to quit my day job after I sang Audrey my rendition of 'Love Will Keep Us Together' at the reception at Blue Heaven. Serendipity. We were all in Heaven together that night. Blue Heaven. We'll be in Heaven again one day I hope. Regular Heaven.

"Mom passed away last month. I held her head in my hands as she took her final breath. I managed to squeak out a prayer at the final moment, the perfect moment, to my dad's amazement. He was a self-prescribed lump at that moment. He was in tears. So was Audrey. She was holding on to Mom's hand. I was also in tears, but I managed to say a prayer anyway. I can't remember what I said, but I believe it had everything to do with commending Mom's spirit to God's care. Not that I'm anyone to be commending anyone's spirit anywhere. I am not in a position to commend or command anything or anyone ever. A better word would be 'persuade.' I said a prayer of persuasion that Mom's spirit would go straight to heaven. 'Straight to Heaven on a rocket ship.' Those were my exact words now that I think about it.

"It was a beautiful sunny day that day. And it was leap day. Imagine that. February 29th. At the viewing, Mom's cousin Jack said, 'She played a trick on us, didn't she?' And that's what he meant. He meant we can only really experience the anniversary of her death every four years. I told Jack, 'She made the leap. You know? Leap day. She made the leap.'

"He said, 'The big leap.'

"My dad said, 'In a beautiful way on a beautiful day.'

"And so there's one more memory for me when I look out at the sunshine. The images of that morning. That beautiful day. The beautiful way. Flashes in my mind and my heart. Walking down the driveway with a phone in my hand calling Hospice and demanding someone come quick. 'We're having a crisis,' my dad said on the other receiver. 'We're having a crisis,' I repeated. I was supposed to wait at the edge of the driveway for the hospice nurse, but I didn't wait there. I went back inside. I wanted to be with Audrey and Dad. I wanted to be with Mom.

"That is just one episode. There were more that morning. More things happened one right after the other that morning than ever before in my life. I could write a short story or an essay about every one of them. I could write about church. I could write about Dad going outside after the sermon to call Audrey and give her his cell phone number in case something happened. Premonition. I could write about the sermon itself. But what was it? I can't remember. You would think I would remember that. It must hold some clue, some key to my grief and my recovery. What was the sermon the morning Mom passed away? Trivia for the heart.

"I could write a story about Donut Shop. I had been trying to go there with Audrey for breakfast for a month of Sundays. That was going to be the day. That Sunday was going to be Donut Shop day, finally. We got home from church, Dad and I, and I went in to get Audrey and we would be on our way to Donut Shop. I would just check in on Mom first. But there was black fluid coming out of her mouth. It might have been blood or bile. Her eyes were open, unblinking. Her breathing was difficult. 'Dad, I think something's wrong!'

"And then the next hour and a half.

"Call Cyndi in Dallas. 'If you're going to come, come today.'

" 'Is Mom all right?'

" 'Just get on a plane and come today.'

"Should I call Karen and Sheryl? Not yet. Where's the damn hospice nurse? Dad says Mom wants to go to Hospice if she's dying. Well, she's dying. This is it.

"When the nurse finally arrived, she let us know something. She let us know Mom wouldn't last in the ambulance. She wouldn't survive the trip to Hospice.

"Where are the DNR papers? They aren't in the file. Didn't the doctor sign them? Well, if there's no DNR, they have to resuscitate. They can't resuscitate, though. She doesn't want that. They will, though, if there's no DNR. We thought there was a DNR. Here's the Living Will. Isn't that good enough? The doctor told us that was good enough.

"It isn't good enough. Lesson learned. You really need a DNR. It needs to be official. Everybody had to cover his own ass around here.

"It's a beautiful day.

" 'You have a decision to make,' the hospice nurse told us. 'She'll die in the ambulance, and they'll have to resuscitate her and then they'll take her to emergency instead of Hospice.'

"She doesn't want to go to the emergency room.

" 'That's where they'll take her.'

"Call the ambulance.

" 'But she won't live long enough for the ambulance to get here. These are the last moments right now.'

"The last moments and we're arguing with the nurse about hypotheticals and DNRs.

" 'Call the ambulance, and we'll take our chances,' I told her. 'We have to honor our mother's wishes.'

"The nurse called for an ambulance. We went back into the room with Mom, and we all three held her. Dad, Audrey and I. We held Mom's hands and her head and we waited. And it happened. The nurse was right. The final moments were upon us. A beautiful way on a beautiful day. And I managed to squeak out a little prayer at the perfect time. The last breath. And I kept whispering to Mom, 'It's okay. It's okay. It's okay.' I wanted her to know it was okay. I just really wanted her to know that.

"But the ambulance never got to arrive. We called it off. And then I called Karen in Virginia and Sheryl in New Jersey, and then I called everybody else, Madonna, Delores, Ann—Mom's lifelong friends. I hated to do that. But I hated more for Dad to have to do it. So I did it. And I called the neighbors and Cousin Jack. And I called Aunt Dood. And Uncle Joe. But he was at the movies. So I called the Robinsons, Mom and Dad's former camping buddies. And Audrey and Dad tried their best to get it together.

"How do you do that? How do you get it together? That's the same thing I'm still wondering. It's the reason I just want to sit here, staring out the window at this beautiful day. How do I get it together? How do I go out there and make more memories? Don't I have enough yet? Aren't there enough echoes on a day like this? But the answer is 'No.' Never enough. Always more, and more. It's okay. It's okay. It's okay."

April 16, 2004
Carmel, Indiana

"Bernie," said Carmel Junior H.S. Latin teacher Betty Whittaker, "I'm not sure if the school will have you back again next year or not."

"What's going on?" asked Bernie who had just finished delivering three persona presentations of Fabius the Tribune to Carmel Junior H.S. foreign language students.

"They may be dropping the Latin program here. I just get so disgusted with the way things are going. I'm not sure how many more years I'm going to stick with it."

"Well, if you qualify for early retirement, I would encourage you to go for it," said Bernie.

"I'm thinking about it," said Betty as she walked around the room straightening out the chairs. "By the way, how's Lillian doing?"

"Lillian passed away in February," announced Bernie, glad that he was able to get that out without choking up.

"Oh, Bernie! I'm so sorry. I didn't know."

"We tried to contact as many people as possible, but you know how hectic everything is at a time like that."

"I'm just so sorry!"

"That's all right. It really was a blessing in the end. She was so uncomfortable."

"Did she suffer a lot?"

"Lillian wasn't really one to complain, but all during the night before she died, she just could not get comfortable no matter how I would turn her or scoot her up in her bed. And once in a while she would confide that she really was tired of hurting all the time."

And Bernie managed to have the whole conversation without loosing his composure.

As he would learn later while attending a Bereavement Support Group sponsored by the St. Vincent Hospice program, he would only have to tell his story about Lillian's passing away 99 more times before he could do so with total composure.

April 19, 2004
Broad Ripple, Indianapolis

"Do you think you can get up there?" asked Bernie as Lillian's high school friend, Delores, climbed up the cinder blocks that Bernie had staked outside the front door to the new house.

"Oh, yah," said Delores, "these old bones will just have to do their thing."

Delores had wanted to be present when the house was installed on its foundation, but with all the delays and her work schedule, she had missed it.

Now she had come over to see the inside, complete with the recently installed laminate floors.

"Oh, the floor is beautiful," exclaimed Delores.

"Lillian picked the color," said Bernie. "At first I thought that a cherry color would be too light, but now that I see it installed, it's just perfect."

Bernie was doing pretty well, keeping an upbeat countenance as he talked about Lillian. But that was about to change.

"Oh, Lillian," said Delores unexpectedly, "why couldn't you have just hung in there a little longer?"

That did it. Bernie's eyes welled up, and he had to focus on his breathing as he struggled to remain composed.

Finally, after an awkward silence, he managed a feeble reply.

"Well, she hung in there as long as she could, but she was really hurting toward the end. I think it was all for the best."

In the weeks and months that followed, Lillian's other long-time friends, Ann Berkeley, Madonna Bouwkamp and Pat and Bill Robinson, would stop by to see the home that their friend had helped plan but which she had not gotten to see completed.

The author believes the visits helped provide some closure for each of them.

April 24, 2004
Broad Ripple, Indianapolis

"Do you think it will fit?" asked Phil as he helped his dad carry the antique carved walnut mantel from the storage barn into the new house.

"Yup. I had to pour a couple of small concrete hearth extensions for the two ends, but I think it should fit perfectly."

Bernie and Lillian had bought the mantel from an antique dealer in Zionsville, Indiana, before they were even married. It was one of their first jointly decided-upon purchases. At that time, Bernie had just bought his small river house at 6544 Ferguson and had hired a mason to build a fireplace into the front room of the house. He had always wanted a fireplace and, more especially, he had always wanted a very elegant mantel.

This was now the third home in which the antique carved walnut mantel would rest.

It fit perfectly and looked beautiful!

May 19, 2004
St. Vincent Hospital, Indianapolis

"Ann, I really appreciate you driving me today," said Bernie. "I'm not sure how long this will take, so why don't I just call you at home when I'm done."

"I don't mind waiting."

"No, that's all right. It might take several hours."

Although Bernie always kidded Lillian that he really had the easier job taking care of her than she had going through all the various cancer treatments, the stress had taken its toll on him too.

Back in November, while Cyndi was visiting for Thanksgiving, she had had to drive him to the hospital because he suddenly became so dizzy that he couldn't take two steps across the floor without holding on to something. Of course, Lillian had insisted on coming along and sat patiently as Bernie was prodded and examined and Ct-scanned. No brain tumor. No nothing. In fact, the whole episode was blamed on an accidental misalignment of the three little stones in Bernie's inner ear that he brought on himself by tossing his head side to side while exercising.

Then in December, while Bernie was recording the traumatic episodes of his mother's care in Indianapolis for **THAT'S NOT THE WAY I REMEMBER IT**, he suddenly broke out in a cold sweat, doubled over with pain and became horribly nauseous. It was all he could do to catch his breath and successfully save his work on the computer before turning it off so he could hunch his way to the basement bathroom.

"My God," Bernie thought to himself, "I'm going to die in the basement, and I won't even be able to call up to Lillian to get help."

By this time, he was too far from the basement phone to dial 9-1-1 himself. But Bernie, of course, didn't die in the basement. He had his second very ugly, very black bowel movement of the day, and when he was finally able to walk again, he made it upstairs, called Dr. Youngblood and told her that he was going to go to the emergency room immediately.

And lucky for him that he did. After he was admitted, they pumped a quart or so of blood out of his stomach before telling him that he was suffering from a bleeding ulcer.

This diagnosis, of course, had been followed by five months of strict dietary restrictions—no chocolate, no caffeine, no tomato sauce, no black pepper, no carbonated drinks, no orange juice, no wine, no, no. no.

Today was the day that Bernie was scheduled to have his follow up endoscopy to learn whether or not he could resume his normal eating habits.

When the test was over, Bernie learned that his stomach ulcer had completely healed. He was, however, doomed to be struck by one more stress-related catastrophe. This time it would be—*horribile dictu*—a kidney stone.

As others who have suffered through a kidney stone attack can testify, the pain when it leaves the kidney and enters the tract down to the ureter is unbelievable.

May 21, 2004
Broad Ripple, Indianapolis

"Bernie, we've gone ahead and scheduled the closing for Wednesday, the 26th. Will that be okay?" said Tucker Realty agent Pegg Kennedy who had finally located a buyer for Bernie and Lillian's old house, and all parties had agreed on the sale price.

"Okay," said Bernie. "Now don't forget, I don't want to let them have possession until I can move into the new house."

"I guess I forgot to tell you," said Pegg, "the buyer wants possession upon signing."

"I don't think I can do that, Pegg. I'm not supposed to move into the new house until Bob Young has had his final draw from the bank."

"Do you think you could talk to him and get him to let you move in?"

"I could try, but I'm really not ready to move yet. I don't have the kitchen packed up, and that's going to be a job."

"How about if I come over tomorrow and help you?" offered Pegg.

"No, that's all right. I've got some friends I can call. I'll let you know what I learn from Bob Young."

So that was it. After months of showings—some of which were very brief walk-throughs by realtors who were looking for who knows what—the house was sold and Bernie had four days to be out.

In fact, if it weren't for the help of his son Phil, his wife Audrey and her parents (Bob and Joanne Liphard who drove down from Lafayette), there's no telling what other stress-related maladies Bernie would have had to suffer to pull it off.

On Tuesday, May 25, the day before the scheduled closing, Bernie and Lillian's dog, Rudy, spent the first night in the home that he and Lillian had so carefully planned.

Or, as Bernie's neighbor from across the street, John Patten, observed to his wife one day, "Bernie and his wife built a little love nest, but then, poor guy, she died before they could move in together."

As a finishing touch, the author installed a small door to cover an opening under the south porch. On the door he painted the little settlement of La Mattina in Italy where his dad had been born before christening his new house:

CASA DI CORAGGIO

With all the challenges surrounding the recording of the lots, the clearing of the trees, the proper installment of the two modular sections and the hurried move in, it had taken all the courage he could muster.

6020 Indianola was definitely THE HOUSE OF COURAGE.

June 25-27, 2004
Dallas, Texas

"Hey, Cyn," said Bernie when his daughter answered the phone at her desk at work. "Guess where I am."

"Where?"

"I'm sitting at an umbrella table in your pool area having lunch."

"I guess you found the apartment alright."

"No problem. Came right to it. So just take your time. No need to leave work early. Rudy and I will just hang out here and relax until you get here."

In fact, Bernie had had a little bit of a problem since he decided to enter Dallas from a different direction than Cyndi had indicated on the map she had sent him. Then, to make matters worse, he missed the exit that would have put him right next to her apartment and got off on the next one. The street name on the exit was the same street he was looking for, but it turned out that the exit put him several miles away from where he was supposed to be. At any rate, he kept his cool and got a nice tour of areas of Dallas not normally seen by visitors. Then, suddenly, there it was before him. He couldn't believe it. The little street that Cyndi had said to turn into to find the entrance to her complex! And there were the golf carts partially blocking the entrance as they sat plugged in to recharge their batteries. Bernie simply drove up to the keypad before the gate, punched in the code he had written on his sheet of directions, and, *voilà*, the gate slowly began to role open. He was home free!

Cyndi, of course, did leave work early, and hurried home to rescue her dad from some of the questionable male sunbathers that she knew frequented the pool area.

Once Rudy was encouraged to climb the 30 or so open steps up to the second level on which Cyndi's apartment was located, they all went in to cool off a little before unloading the back of the truck.

Bernie was impressed. Cyndi had a really neat apartment. It was nicely equipped with comfortable furniture and decorated with stylish appointments. Cat toys and a cat gym were casually located around the living room, but no cats could be seen. They had heard the tags on Rudy's collar and had retreated to their favorite hiding places before the door was ever opened. They would not re-emerge until much later when Bernie took Rudy out for his first walk.

Bernie stayed with Cyndi for the next two days before leaving Monday morning to drive down to Houston to deliver some heirloom pieces of furniture that he had promised Mary and Bernie, his niece and nephew, and visit with his brother and all the other members of the family that had made Houston their home.

Cyndi pretty much let her dad select the kind of food he wanted to eat, and each evening she would take him to the restaurant where the best selections could be found.

Without realizing it, Bernie quickly tired Cyndi out—she was used to taking it easy on weekends—by suggesting a variety of sights he would like to visit in Dallas.

Of course, they would have to go see the book depository from the sixth floor of which Kennedy had supposedly been shot. And the grassy knoll! And the railroad bridge and the sewer openings along that street that Dave (who had been in the Special Forces during Operation Sandstorm) had suggested would have made excellent hiding places for sharp shooters.

Then it was off to the "West Side" where every kind of quaint restaurant, shop and antique store could be found.

"This is where we all ate lunch when Phil and Audrey visited," said Cyndi, as they enjoyed pizza while watching the rain pour down outside.

On Sunday morning, they attended Mass at the Polish church which Cyndi was in the habit of attending with Troy, a very personable—albeit gay—friend who lived across the walkway from her. And, boy, was it Polish! The priest was obviously a recent immigrant from Poland, and his accent plucked strings in Bernie's memory from the Masses he used to attend as a youth at the Polish Holy Family Parish in Cudahy.

Bernie would later meet "Come-Up-For-A-Spot-Of-Tea-Sometime" Dan, another of Cyndi's gay friends who lived on the third floor, and an older lady friend, a Grandma Hacker look-alike, who lived on the ground floor. In fact, on his return from Houston, they would all go out for lunch and ice cream together. They seemed to be fun-loving, and Bernie was glad Cyndi had such a support group right in her complex. It was unfortunate that Troy, the young man with whom Cyndi was most *simpatico*, was preparing to move to Louisiana to live with his sister and her family.

Later that afternoon, Cyndi and Bernie drove out to visit the ranch that served as a backdrop for the J.R. Ewing series, "Dallas." Like all such locations, the TV cameras had created an illusion of greater size than was actually the case. In fact, the ranch was only leased for exterior shots and for those scenes shot on the outside breakfast patio and pool area. All interior scenes were shot on sets recreated in a studio. And, of course, there were a few token long-horn cattle grazing on the property—cattle cared for by students under the supervision of a local university.

"What else would you like to see in Dallas," asked Cyndi Sunday night as they sat watching "Trading Spaces" (one of Cyndi's favorite shows along with other remodeling and redecorating shows featured on TLC such as "While You Were Out," "Clean Sweep" and "In A Fix").

"You know that old fashioned trolley we saw today?" asked Bernie.

"Ye-es," said Cyndi in her hesitating, suspicious tone that she loves to adopt when she's not sure where the conversation is leading.

"Why don't you look into where it goes and how we can ride it."

"Okay. Anything else?"

"Not really. We've seen quite a bit. Of course, we'll be visiting your office when I get back next Friday so I can meet everyone that works with you."

"If they're all in," said Cyndi.

"Oh, there is one more thing," added Bernie.

"What?"

"While we were eating breakfast, I noticed in the paper that there is an exhibit of Dali's work at the Museum of Art. Think we could stop in and see it?"

"I'll check the times they're open," said Cyndi, as Bernie prepared, once more, to usher Rudy down the long staircase so he could do his business before being shut up in the kitchen for the night.

June 28, 2004
Houston, Texas

On Monday morning, Bernie got up early and packed his stuff into the truck. He fed Rudy his breakfast, took him back down the stairs for his morning walk, and then coaxed the weary little dog—who had to stop halfway up to catch his breath—back up the stairs to the apartment.

"So you don't think they'll mind your coming home to let Rudy out midmorning and mid-afternoon?"

"No," said Cyndi. "It's only five minutes away from work. Besides, I have to leave a lot of times to run errands and pick things up for the office. No one will probably even notice."

Now, anyone who has ever driven in Texas can appreciate just how big the state is. While a six-hour drive can take a person all the way through Indiana—driving from Louisville, Kentucky, to Chicago—it takes six hours just to drive from Dallas to Houston. And, of course, there are no roadside restrooms. All that's offered are picnic areas, trash containers and secluded bushes.

The weather was as clear as the directions Bernie was following so he had no trouble pulling into his brother's driveway early in the afternoon.

He was greeted by a large, colorful, computer-generated banner.

WELCOME TO HOUSTON, UNCLE BERNIE.
MI CASA, SU CASA. THE COFFEE POT IS ON!

And there, hurrying out to give him big welcoming hugs, were his brother Joe and his sister-in-law, Liz.

Home is good!

"Come in out of the heat," they invited, and Bernie was more than willing to comply.

Inside, Liz served up refreshments and they sat down to get caught up.

It was the first major trip Bernie had taken since Lillian had passed away, and it was a little weird to be solo after having spent the last 37 years as a couple. But he was adjusting.

"I've had some problems with dizziness and back pain, that, I think, is all stress related," explained Bernie. "But when I get back, I'm scheduled to take part in a six-week Bereavement Group. Hopefully that will help."

Delicious aromas filled the living room as Liz simmered a large pot of tomato sauce—or "*sugo*" as she sometimes refers to it—for the evening meal.

"Joey and Alisha will be joining us, along with Anthony," said Liz.

"And Mary and Gabriel intend to bring Xavier over too," added Joe.

"How about Liz and Bernie?"

"Liz and Chris will join us, but Bernie and Michelle can't make it down tonight. They live way on the other side of Houston. It's more than an hour's drive."

"Wanna give me a hand unloading the furniture from the back of the truck before anyone gets here?" asked Bernie.

So, back out into the heat of the afternoon went the two brothers, once again on a mission as they had often shared when they were younger.

"Bernie said he could use Ma's dresser and mirror, so I brought that down for him. I refinished it, and it looks pretty good."

Once the dresser and mirror were carefully situated off to one side of the two-car garage, they went to work putting the legs back on their mother's cedar chest.

"Wow!" said Joe. "That cedar smell is still powerful, isn't it?"

"It is amazing. And after more than 60 years! Now, Liz," continued Bernie, "if Mary can't use the afghans and blankets that are in there, tell her to feel free to do with them as she likes."

"Are they hand made?" asked Liz.

"I think one of them was made by Lillian, but I'm not sure about the others."

Before long, the extended family began to arrive. Hugs and happy greetings all around!

After things settled down before dinner, little Anthony began to chat with his great-uncle Bernie.

"Are you in shape?" asked little Anthony.

"Oh, sure. A guy's gotta stay in shape. How about you?"

"I'm in shape," boasted little Anthony as he began to stretch and squat with one hand resting on Joe's easy chair.

"Can you do pushups?" asked Bernie who quickly hit the floor and began to demonstrate.

"Look at that," said Joe from the behind the kitchen counter. "Uncle Bernie and Anthony are doing pushups!"

"Let's show Uncle Bernie the video Mary sent to try and get selected on Donald Trump's Apprentice show," suggested Liz.

Now this was something! Bernie knew his niece to be a talented, ambitious and aggressive competitor, and this only confirmed it. Following some film production advice from their cousin Phil, Mary's husband, brothers and in-laws had all helped in the filming and editing. After watching the presentation, Bernie saw no reason why his niece wouldn't have a fighting chance to get on the program.

"Have you heard anything yet?" asked Bernie.

"It's very competitive," said Liz.

"We still haven't heard anything," added Mary.

Now, there is no meal as good for the soul of an Italian as an Italian meal cooked by a full-blooded Italian wife in an Italian home. To paraphrase the beer-loving Benjamin Franklin, "The proof that God wants us to be happy is that he gave us spaghetti!"

After dinner, Mary, Gabriel and Xavier had to leave early. Joey and Alisha also had to get home to be sure little Anthony got to bed on time.

"I want to see your new house," said the author.

"I'll give you a tour," volunteered little Anthony.

"Why don't you all plan to come over for dinner Wednesday night?" invited Joey. "Alisha makes great fajitas."

"Alisha fajitas," repeated Bernie.

"Now," laughed Joey, "that's the first time anyone ever called them that. Clever!"

Later, Bernie and his niece Liz Marie spent a good deal of time hunched over albums of family pictures that he had made up several years ago and shared with his brother.

She was moved by so many early pictures of her parents and grandparents that she had never seen before.

"Oh, wow!," exclaimed Bernie. "I was wondering what had happened to that. It ended up in one of your albums."

"What's that?" asked Joe.

"It's the picture card of the church of Santa Maria that's on the main floor of the *palazzo* that the *Padrone* lived in at San Marco."

Everyone gathered around to look at the picture. This was the church where little Tirigi Barci, the father of Joe and Bernie and the grandfather of Liz Marie, had served as an altar boy when he was still living in Italy.

"And look how they spell "Matina," said Bernie. "Only one 't' instead of two. Can I borrow a piece of paper and a pen? I need to write that down so I can get it correct in the book. You know, when I was teaching, I always had a pen or two in my pocket, but not anymore."

As Liz Marie was getting ready to leave, she insisted that her Uncle Bernie be brought over to see all the work she and Chris had done fixing up her house that was just a couple blocks away.

"We'll try and come over tomorrow evening after we tour the Space Center," suggested Joe.

"That'll work," confirmed Chris.

June 29, 2004
Johnson Space Center, Houston, Texas

"Do any of you have any weapons or pocket knives?" asked the guard as they passed through a security check point.

"Man," thought Bernie to himself. "There I go causing a problem again." He had in his pocket the small pocketknife that he always carried, and it would have to be addressed.

Inside, the welcoming and orientation area was already teeming with visitors. Both children and adults were trying their skills at a great variety of hands-on educational exhibits as air hissed and large mechanical arms moved high above the crowd.

"Bern, why don't you and Liz wait here while I go get our badges and lunch passes."

Lunch! Not only were they going to be treated to a VIP Level 9 Tour of the Johnson Space Center by its most esteemed guide, but they would also get a free lunch in the Space Center cafeteria.

Before too long, they were all joined by Joey who was able to take off work to join the tour group that is limited to only 12 participants because of some sensitive areas it visits.

"I tell you what," suggested Joe, "I've got some things I need to do before we start the tour, so why don't you folks watch the orientation film in the auditorium. After that, Chris should be getting here and we can all go to lunch before we start."

So once again the author was transported back to the sixties as he and his sister-in-law and nephew watched clips of many of the events that he had witnessed live on a variety of black and white TV's owned by other people.

As they headed for the cafeteria, Joe was beginning to be concerned that Chris, Liz Marie's fiancé who worked in another of the many buildings at the Space Center, had not yet joined them.

"Here's his lunch ticket," said Joe. "Keep an eye out for him while I go through the cafeteria line."

Although Joey had worked for a company which served as a subcontractor on a number of NASA projects, and Chris actually worked for NASA monitoring and evaluating the stability-recovery rates of astronauts returning from space (both in the U.S.A. and in Russia), neither of them had ever been treated to the $65 per head tour that they were all about to enjoy.

"This is Pernille Houken," said Joe as he introduced the young lady from Denmark who would be driving the VIP Tour Van. "If everyone's ready, we'll load up and get started."

The Johnson Space Center campus is huge, and everywhere are displays of rockets and equipment used in the space program. And the buildings! And the politics and complexities behind the construction of the buildings—resulting in the complete omission of a Building #13, although the numbers go as high as the 400's.

The tour took the group, which by now included Chris, through a mockup of a Shuttle cockpit as well as providing close-up examinations of a number of the landing capsules used in the earlier missions. Talk about tight quarters! Bernie could not even imagine what would have happened if an astronaut got a cramp while stuffed into his small seat!

Then came the visits to the various Mission Control Centers.

As Joe led his elite group past a larger tour group that would be viewing the Historic Mission Control Center from behind the glass windows of a public viewing gallery, he advised them to pass in silence and move quickly to a small door located down a side hallway.

Once the group had all entered through the door, Joe began in a hushed and respectful voice.

"You are privileged to be standing on the floor of the Historic Mission Control Center. It was from this Control Center that the early space missions were run and the manned mission to the moon was coordinated. There is where Gene Kranz, the flight director of the Lunar Mission, stood. On these large screens were projected the images and data that were being sent back from the Lunar Lander."

The explanations continued with Joe pointing out the various plaques and flags and mission insignia that were proudly displayed on the sidewalls.

And, unobtrusively mounted on the right side of the front of the room, was a replica of the plaque that had been left on the moon proclaiming that men had "come in peace" from earth.

Not many months later, the author would fully appreciate how fortunate he was to visit the floor of the Historic Mission Control Center when any further access to that portion of the facility was suddenly denied to VIP tour groups by NASA.

Next, in the public viewing gallery of NASA's operational control center, the group watched in awe as a score of technicians and space scientists sat glued to their PC screens and watched the giant projection screens at the front of the room to monitor the position of the Sky Lab.

"That red light on the large screen," explained Joe, "shows that the Sky Lab is currently out of communication in a 'dead zone.' The light will turn green as soon as it passes into an area when it can once again communicate with the Control Center."

"See that little image on the map that shows where the Space Station is?" asked Joey.

"Ye-es," said Bernie.

"Well, they didn't used to have that. The scientists had to look at a screen full of numbers and try to determine the exact location of vehicles in space in relation to earth landmasses. What I did when our company was given a contract by NASA was to create a program that converts all those numbers into an actual image like you're seeing on the screen up there."

"Now, that's impressive, Joey," said the author. "I always knew you were a genius!"

"If anyone has trouble with stairs," advised Joe when they got to another location, "let me know and we can use the elevator."

Since no one spoke up, the small group began to make their way up the long narrow stairway that led to a catwalk around the outer walls of a huge training center.

"What you are looking at down there," pointed out Joe, "are full-sized replicas of all of the current and proposed sections of the Space Station. And there is a full-sized replica of a shuttle. Astronauts train here to become thoroughly familiar with all facets of the equipment, both inside and out."

The group moved slowly along the catwalk, watching those working below and reading the explanatory signboards mounted here and there.

At the far end of the huge hanger-type room was a replica of the shuttle with its upper bay doors open. Placed around that portion of the room were large pieces of cargo that astronauts would practice—seated behind a wall that only let them see what they were doing by watching a TV monitor—using the giant shuttle retrieval arm to pick up items and place them precisely into the shuttle bay.

Then, once again, it was back to the van and another long ride, this time to a humongous indoor pool. This was the Neutral Buoyancy Lab. When they entered the facility and took turns riding an elevator up to the observation walkway, Joe was thrilled by what he saw.

"Look, there are two astronauts being trained under the water! You can look down there or look on the TV screens to see what they're doing."

Not only where there two astronauts dressed in space-walk outfits being guided about under water by a troop of scuba divers, but there, under the water were, once again, complete replicas of a space shuttle and sections of the Space Station.

"Ok, everybody," Joe suddenly announced. "You're in for a very special treat. Look! They're getting ready to lift one of the astronauts out of the water!"

The group stood mesmerized, some with foreheads pressed against the glass observation windows, and some in front of the TV monitors as a giant lift slowly raised from the pool the cage on which the astronaut was standing. After communicating a while with a nearby young man and woman equipped with headphones, they began to remove his helmet. They then talked normally until the young man finally offered the astronaut a bit of what appeared to be a candy bar.

A rare treat, indeed! But even greater things were yet to come.

At the next building the group visited, they were confronted by a spectacularly huge round steel door mounted on two gargantuan hinges.

"First of all," cautioned Joe who had quickly taken his place with his back to the door, "no one is allowed to touch the door. Believe it or not, as large and heavy as it is, this 40-ton door moves with the touch of a finger."

The door led to an even larger vacuum compartment in which all equipment and apparatuses to be sent into outer space need first to be tested.

"They can also create extreme temperatures in there—either hot or cold— to be sure that the equipment won't malfunction once it is in space," explained Joe.

Then there were photo ops as folks took turns posing before the giant door. The building also contained a smaller vacuum chamber that could be used more economically as well as a display of the next generation of astronaut space-walk suits which, believe it or not, closely resemble outfits worn by Storm Troopers in the **Star Wars** movies.

"Joe," said Chris Miller (Liz Marie's fiancé) when they had all re-boarded the VIP van, "if you like, I can take you over to my lab and show you the equipment we use to test the physical stability of astronauts when they return from space."

"O.K., folks," said Joe immediately. "You're in for a special treat today. This is not part of the VIP tour, but my future son-in-law, Chris Miller, who is joining us today as my treat, is offering to show us the lab in which he works here at NASA. Would you all like to see it?"

Boy, would they! Everyone was most enthusiastic in anticipation.

"It's going to be a bit of a ride," said Chris, "since our building is way out on the outskirts of the Space Center."

No problem. Everyone just settled down and enjoyed the sights.

It was a non-imposing one-floor building that they all finally entered. The lab itself was a real eye-opener. Its layout and equipment provided a special insight into the very human and inventive way that many phases of the whole space program are worked out.

"When an astronaut returns from space," began Chris, "he finds that the time he spent in a weightless environment has caused him to lose—almost completely—his sense of balance and coordination. Our assignment was to figure out a way to determine when he had regained his balance and coordination to a sufficient degree that he could be trusted to get around on his own and drive safely once again."

Now this was something most in the group had never even considered!

"We've pretty much had to invent our own equipment," explained Chris as he pointed to a variety of computer monitors, a treadmill, a very unusual-looking pair of glasses that had a tiny camera mounted in front of one of its lenses, and an exercise bike.

"We hook monitoring wires up to an astronaut's legs as he walks on the treadmill," explained Chris. "Since walking is simply a series of controlled falls—that is, each time we begin to fall forward, we need to break our fall by moving the next leg out, and so on—if the astronaut is anyway uneasy about loosing his balance or falling, the pupil of his eye will reflect that uneasiness, and we can pick that up on our monitor."

The floor at the opposite end of the room was covered with a very thick, and very spongy, foam pad.

"We have to take our shoes off when we walk on this pad," explained Chris. "The pad has a special seal on it designed to keep the pad soft and we don't want to tear the seal."

Here and there on the pad were obstacles that the astronaut being tested would have to step over. Hanging from the ceiling were foam tubes—such as are sold as pool floatation devices—suspended by string. Clipped to each string were simple clothespins that could be used to raise or lower the tubes.

"An astronaut has to be able to maneuver this obstacle course without loosing his balance or giving any indication that he's uncomfortable before we can sign off on his recovery," explained Chris.

"And, believe me! It's hard even for me to walk around on here unless I'm very careful. If any of you want to try it, you'll have to take your shoes off first."

Several in the group did remove their shoes to give it a go. In the meantime, Joe took out his digital camera again and began to take some pictures of Chris helping the visitors on the pad.

"Joe," asked one of the guests on the tour, "would you please take a picture of me with my camera?" Joe agreed and set his own camera down.

As they all settled down in the van for the long ride back, Joe advised his tour group that if any of them were interested, there were several additional areas and special exhibits that they should feel free to visit before leaving the Space Center.

Now, the author must confess, that on occasion over the many years since the first lunar landing was televised, he had harbored suspicions that man had not, in fact, ever traveled to the moon. That it had all been contrived in a studio somewhere to dupe the American public into believing that we were superior to the Russians and their little Sputnik. But now that he had seen the tremendously complex and expensive equipment and facilities, and the astronauts training, he had to admit that there was no way it could be a hoax.

If only it were possible to look up at the moon with a telescope and actually see some of the pieces of equipment or the little flag that had been left up there!

Back in the orientation center, Joey and Chris said their goodbyes, as they each had to return to their places of work.

"Bern, would you wait here with Liz while I go turn in our badges and fill out some forms?" asked Joe.

When Joe returned, Liz looked quizzically at his shoulder.

"Dad, where's your camera?"

It was gone! Not only was it a very expensive digital camera, but it also had all the special photos that Joe had taken during the tour. Since the author had been asked, off and on, during the tour to hang onto the camera in its case, he immediately began to consider whether or not he had mislaid it himself.

"When was the last time you used it," asked Liz.

"I think it was in Chris' lab. In fact, I think I set it down on a cabinet when I was asked to take a picture of one of the guests with her camera."

"Why don't you use your cell phone and call Chris right away. He's probably back in his office by now," suggested Liz.

"And I'll go out to see if it's in the van," suggested Bernie.

On the way out to the van, Bernie met their driver and explained the lost camera.

"I always check the van out before I park it," explained Pernille, "and I didn't see a camera."

"Can we look again?" asked Bernie.

So they walked back out to the van and checked. There was no camera on the seats where Joe had been sitting at the front of the van, nor was anything under the floor of the front seats.

"Any luck at the lab?" asked Bernie when he returned.

"Nope. Chris looked everywhere!"

Before they headed out to the parking lot, Joe went over and picked up copies of the photo that had been taken of the three of them and Joey before boarding the van. It was a way for the Space Center to provide a souvenir photo to visitors and also keep a photographic record of all visitors to the buildings on the campus.

The loss of Joe's digital camera had certainly put a damper on what otherwise had been a spectacular day. Now the three of them, aware for the first time of their weariness after a long day of touring, slowly made their way back to the parking lot.

"I'm sure it will show up, Dad," comforted Liz. "Someone will surely turn it in at Lost and Found."

"Boy," observed Bernie, "you would hate to think that any of the special guests on the tour would stoop to stealing it."

After dinner, before it got too dark out, they headed over for Liz Marie's house. Chris was there relaxing in his stocking feet, and he said that he had given his office a second thorough going over. No camera. They would just have to hope for the best.

Now, Liz Marie and Chris had been very busy doing some very creative things both with the landscaping and to the interior of the house in which they planned to live after they would be married in November.

"This is our master bath," explained Liz Marie. "You should have seen it before it was remodeled!"

It was gorgeous. Large, airy and bright. And it featured a comfortable Jacuzzi surrounded by picture windows that looked out onto a cozy privacy patio that resembled a small Japanese garden.

"Very nice," exclaimed the author.

The rest of the house was nicely decorated and furnished, although Chris explained that they would probably be getting new living room furniture after they were married.

"Wanna see the rest of the back yard," asked Liz Marie. "It's big!"

And it was. Right outside the sliding glass doors that opened onto a nice patio, was an adjoining wooden deck that had been built by a previous owner."

"That's neat," remarked the author.

"Well," observed Chris, "it needs a lot of work. Some of the boards are going bad."

"We think we may just take it out later," added Liz Marie.

All in all, it was a great day. It was too bad that the camera had been lost.

"We'll check Lost and Found in the morning on our way out to Kemah," said Joe after they had returned home.

Liz was tired, understandably, and she soon excused herself to turn in for the night.

Bernie and Joe sat in the living room until late, enjoying a good heart-to-heart such as they had not had an opportunity to do for many years.

June 30, 2004
Houston, Texas

"Uncle Bernie," asked Liz after they had had their morning coffee and doughnuts and were waiting to begin a new adventure. "Do you think you and Joe could put in a small piece of molding that never got put in when the carpet was installed?"

"Why, sure. I'll bet we could do that in no time."

"I've got the molding leaning against the wall in the garage."

In fact, the job was so easy that Bernie had it done before Joe was done shaving.

When he was growing up, Bernie had always admired his great-uncle Frank Bufano. As has been already mentioned earlier in this book, Frank was a factotum. He never visited anyone without taking time to help them fix whatever needed tending to in the house, be it plumbing, carpentry or electrical work.

Bernie had already helped his brother glue back together a large decorative letter B that their dad had made years earlier. While the author had always hung his indoors, Joe had hung his on the outside of his house, and it had cracked.

"You know what else?" asked Liz.

"What's that?" asked Bernie.

"Would you be able to help Joe clean out the vent hose for our clothes dryer? We're afraid it may be clogged and could be a fire hazard."

That, too, proved to be a quick and easy job for the facile author who had just spent months installing appliances and getting his new modular home up and running.

Joe was amazed when his brother pulled an old soda can out of the dryer vent.

"A disgruntled workman must have shoved that in there just for spite before the vent cover was put on," observed the author.

"You know," said Joe, "I'd like to have you look at the downspouts at the back of our house. We've got to find some way to divert the rain water toward the front of the house so the backyard doesn't flood when we get a heavy rain."

For that problem, too, the author proposed a fairly simple solution that Joe said he would consider in the near future.

This day's adventure would take the trio out to the Kemah Boardwalk located on the coast at Kemah, Texas.

On the way, they drove by the Johnson Space Center so Joe could check the Lost and Found for his camera while Bernie and Liz toured the gift shop.

Unfortunately for the author, he would once again have to go through security even to enter the gift shop, and, once again, his little pocketknife would be called into question. Now, is this a slow learner, or what?

"Should have left it in the car," thought the author to himself.

The camera had not been turned in. But Joe did run into another person who sometimes drove the van they had used the day before, and that driver assured Joe that he would keep an eye out for the camera.

In fact, so as not to keep the reader in any more suspense than necessary, it was this driver who would later locate the camera on the floor way at the back of the van. It had apparently slid there after Joe had set it down upon re-entering the van when leaving Chris' lab, and both the author and Pernille had missed spotting it during their searches. The author was greatly relieved to learn this a couple weeks after returning to Indianapolis, and he was even more pleased to receive copies of a number of the photos that Joe had taken during the tour.

"Can we ride the train, Daddy?" asked Liz playfully when they got there.

And, of course, they did. The train was one of those miniature railroad setups that are frequently found in zoos and other attractions around the country. This one ran around the outskirts of the amusement park which catered primarily to younger children. The thing that would make this train ride memorable was the fact that whenever the train passed through each of the several tunnels along its route, a recorded voice would encourage all the young people on board to scream at the top of their lungs. And they did. And did again. And did once more.

But it was still fun.

As the trio toured the boardwalk area, it began to drizzle and they decided to go indoors for lunch.

"Let's go to that restaurant we like so much on the upper level," suggested Liz.

"You'll like this, Bern," said Joe. "It's called the Saltgrass Steakhouse, and it has a western motif. The food is great."

"Now," said the author when they had been seated, "this is going to be my treat!"

"Oh, my," said Liz, "you sound so authoritative!"

"Well, I really appreciate your taking me around, and the great tour yesterday that I know wasn't cheap, and I want to do something to show my appreciation."

"O.K. then. We won't argue," agreed Joe.

After lunch it was still drizzling a little, so they stopped in an ice cream shop for dessert.

As the rain slowed to light mist, they returned to the boardwalk.

"Oh, look. We should try those remote control boats," suggested Joe.

"They look like fun," agreed the author.

"Maybe on our way back, Dad" said Liz.

The moment, however, was lost, as they did not return the same way at the end of their walk.

"Hey," said Joe when they rounded the next corner, "We should all ride The Beast! What do you say?"

"Oh, I don't know, Daddy," said Liz hesitatingly. "You know I get seasick."

"Come on. Let's look into it."

As Joe stood in the ticket line, Bernie and Liz read the list of disclaimers that was posted on a nearby wall. It was advised that no one with a weak heart should take the ride.

"Ah, Daddy," called Liz, "I think I'm going to sit this one out. You and your brother go, and I'll wait for you here."

So, while Liz went off to find a restroom, Bernie and his brother boarded The Beast. It was a long-keeled speedboat and looked like it could really move once it got cranked up. There probably was a very good reason why it was called "The Beast."

"You know," suggested Bernie, "once this thing gets going, all the water is going to splash on the people sitting toward the rear. I suggest we sit up front."

As they made their way to their seats, loud and raucous music blared through the boat's loudspeakers. Bernie figured that was just to keep the hype going until they left the dock.

Boy, was he wrong.

As they prepared to shove off, a shapely young girl in cutoffs took her place at the bow of the boat and began to advise passengers to remove and secure their hats and to hang on to their seats because they were in for the ride of their lives.

The music was turned back up while ropes were cast off, and The Beast headed for open water. The shapely young girl in cutoffs immediately assumed a cage-dancer's pose and began to wildly gyrate to the music—a feat she kept up without holding on to anything for support—song after endless song—until the boat reached its farthest destination in the bay.

The author personally felt that they could have all enjoyed the ride a lot more and paid closer attention to the sights in the bay if the music had been turned off and the cage dancer had taken a seat at the back of the boat.

As the boat began to turn around for the return trip, a new song blasted their ears as a replacement girl took up the gyrations in the bow. It was kind of like watching strip tease dancers who never actually took anything off!

As far as the author could make out, his brother, seated on the outside seat of the boat, was pretty well managing to ignore the girls—a harder task for the author who was seated in the aisle seat.

Definitely a memorable boat ride!

Tragically, the entire theme park at Kemah was seriously damaged on September 13, 2008, when it was struck by Hurricane Ike. By 2013, however, it had been completely rebuilt and was back in business.

Before returning to Houston, Liz Marie and Chris had insisted that her folks take Uncle Bernie out to Maas Nursery located just a little north of Seabrook, Texas.

"You'll love the place, Uncle Bernie," Liz Marie had said. "They have hundreds of classical statues and fountains and exotic plants. It's awesome!"

And it was. Not only were there many very expensive life-sized classical reproductions, but there was also a variety of exotic animals on display here and there throughout the nursery.

Unfortunately, there was also such an ample supply of mosquitoes on hand that Liz had to retreat to an indoor setting while Joe and Bernie continued their tour of the nursery.

On the way home, they all began to look forward to dinner at Joey's house.

"Are Bernie and Michelle going to be able to join us?" asked the author.

"I don't think so," said Liz. "Dad, why don't we call them just to be sure?"

On the cell phone, the author's nephew confirmed that, unfortunately, he and his family would not be able to make the drive to Joey's house that evening. Michelle wasn't home yet, and it would be very hard on them to get the kids ready and be there for dinner.

"Let me say 'Hi' to him before you hang up," said the author.

"Hey, Bernie," began the author, "I'm sorry I won't get to see you all this time. I brought Grandma's dresser for you, and you can pick it up the next time you're at your dad's house. I guess I'll see you all at Liz and Chris' wedding."

Now Joey and Alisha had just moved into a newly constructed, two-story house in a very nice neighborhood—most impressive next to the one-floor modular home into which the author had recently moved.

"You win the New House Contest," said the author as he sat on the couch talking with his nephew.

"Oh, I don't think so," said Alisha. "You haven't seen Bernie and Michelle's house yet. They have an in-ground swimming pool."

As little Anthony passed through the room, the author reminded him that he had promised to provide a tour of the house for him.

"Yes," said Liz Marie who had just arrived with Chris. "We want the tour!"

The tour began at the front door.

"This is the foyer," announced little Anthony. "A foyer is a large open area."

What amazing confidence and poise for a little guy!

Then there was the room where Alisha did her handicrafts and Joey's office—where a number of laptop computers ran constantly, serving as drones being run by a distant program as it made millions of very complex computations.

Little Anthony next led them upstairs to point out bedrooms and a play area. As they passed a balcony overlooking the living room below, the call for dinner was heard.

The tour ended and Liz Marie and the author each slipped little Anthony a quarter to thank him for his wonderful guided tour.

The surprise of the evening came, however, when in walked Bernie and Michelle and their two children, Regina and Aaron Bernard. Regina was too cute by half in a little cheerleader's outfit that her mom had got her for school.

The author sincerely enjoyed this visit by Bernie and Michelle, as he got to listen to them tell of some very complicated and humorous developments in their lives, both with the ongoing Enron investigations and with Michelle's experiences as an intern earlier in her career. In fact, it was one of the few times that the author could remember Michelle being so relaxed and comfortable sharing her thoughts and experiences.

It was a special time!

Being the eldest of the children, Regina would later coordinate all the children's games. All the little ones except Xavier tried to keep up with her. Xavier just sort of sat back in amazement at his cousin's energy.

It was another great evening in Houston, but the author's mind was already beginning to think of the long drive back to Dallas in the morning.

July 1-2, 2004
Dallas, Texas

"So, how did the Rudester do while I was gone?" asked Bernie after he had re-climbed the stairs to Cyndi's apartment.

Since the author's brother, Joe, was suffering from allergies and wasn't sure if he could host a visit by Rudy, Cyndi had volunteered to dog-sit while her dad drove down to Houston for a few days.

"Just fine. In fact, Naven and Shadow are just now beginning to stay in the same room with him. They'll even come up and sniff him when they think they can get away with it."

"What did you find out about the trolley?"

"It's free, and we can catch it right across the highway from the apartment," said Cyndi.

"And the Museum of Art?"

"Actually, the trolley's last stop is right across the street from the Art Museum."

So they had their Friday afternoon all planned. They would ride the trolley, see the works of Dali and catch lunch at a quaint restaurant on their way back.

The next day, they visited the ACS Consumer Loan Services buildings where Cyndi worked. She had taken the day off to spend it sightseeing with her dad.

Most of Cyndi's coworkers were in except for Cyndi's immediate supervisor—the one man Bernie was most interested in meeting.

C'est la vie!

Although it was very hot standing in the sun waiting for the trolley, once they were on board, the ride in the old open-sided wooden car was quite comfortable.

"This old car was built in Australia back in the 20's," informed the conductor as he incessantly rang a warning bell with his foot while guiding the car along the tracks through the streets of Dallas.

At the museum, Bernie bought entrance tickets while Cyndi hit the restroom.

"Where's the exhibit of Dali's work?" asked Bernie of the lady at the information desk.

"Right down the hall there."

Bernie looked but could see nothing but a number of small frames hanging along one side of the hall in the distance.

"Cyndi," said Bernie after he had studied the display of drawings and sketches, "these are just sketches that Dali made in preparation for his actual paintings. What a rook! I was hoping to see some actual paintings, you know, like the drooping watch or the glorious painting he did of the crucifixion."

"And where's the only authenticated Caravaggio in America that's supposed to be in the museum?" asked Bernie as they returned to the information desk.

"Oh, that's not at this museum. That's in a different museum in Dallas," informed the gentleman now manning the counter.

Oh, well! At least the trolley ride was pleasant, and Cyndi had selected a very neat place—albeit a little off the beaten track—where they could stop for lunch on the way back.

Later that evening, Bernie rested out on the balcony for a bit after lighting the bug candle while Cyndi wondered whether or not she could catch an episode of FBI Files, New Detectives or Court TV.

The next morning, Bernie would pack up and drive back to Indianapolis to spend the Fourth of July with Phillip and Audrey who were planning a cookout on the unique patio that Phil was designing and laying in behind their house.

And after the cookout, they would watch the fireworks, both those being officially fired from the roof of the Bank One building in downtown Indianapolis, and the ones being exploded recklessly and cavalierly in the middle of the street and all around them by scores of Spanish speaking residents who also lived in Phil and Audrey's neighborhood.

"LOOK OUT!" warned Huey, a friend of Phil and Audrey, who, along with his fiancée, had joined them. "That Roman candle hit your leg, didn't it?"

Huey brushed the ash off his fiancée's leg and headed right across the street to complain to the parents of the little Spanish boy who had recklessly lit the firework.

"A lot of good that did," said Huey when he returned. "They don't even speak English!"

July 23, 2004
Paris, France

Kathy Nudi was in Paris, France. It was going to take a little while to sink in. She had willingly put her dream on hold for eleven years to return to her childhood home in Lynwood, Illinois, to oversee the care of her ailing mother. She had had to put all belongings from her Virginia apartment into storage, transfer to a new job in Army Intelligence in downtown Chicago and selflessly care for the woman who had been divorced by her father and who was no longer able to care for herself.

But now all that was over. It had been a year since her mother, the author's Aunt Rose, had passed away, and Kathy had transferred back to Virginia to pick up the path of her dreams. Then it had come, quickly and almost unexpectedly. There was an opening in the American Embassy in Paris for which she could apply.

"Thanks, Bernie," Kathy had written in an e-mail to the author on July 21. "I was very touched that you and Phil drove all the way up and back just to have lunch with me in Lynwood and give me a great send off. I will be leaving tomorrow and will arrive in Paris 23 July. My job title is Office Manager Specialist."

Kathy Nudi, the granddaughter of Helen Posanska Fusic who had had to enter America as a stowaway back in 1912, was now affiliated with the American Embassy in Paris.

So sometimes good things do happen to good people!

August 1, 2004
Indianapolis

"Hi, Aunt Dood. How are you doing?" asked Bernie as he entered the room in The Waters Nursing Home where Lillian's aunt was now staying.

"Oh, pretty good."

"You look a lot better than you did when Phil and I visited you in the hospital a couple weeks ago."

"Well, they've been giving me therapy every day. I think it's working. I can get out of bed, climb into my wheelchair and make it to the bathroom by myself."

"That's great, Aunt Dood."

Although Lillian's aunt hadn't really wanted to leave the home that had been built by her husband, John Kemp, and which she had been recently sharing with her son, Butch, she had had no choice. Her health had taken a turn for the worse, and her daughter Nancy had to have her mother taken to St. Francis Hospital. There they were told that Aunt Dood would not be able to return to her home again, but would have to have nursing home care from then on.

As fate would have it, Aunt Dood was now occupying a room in the same nursing home, handily located just across the street from her house, in which her husband John had spent his final days.

"Well," said Bernie after the two had visited for a while, "I've got to get going. I'm headed to Karen's house to pick up my canoe so Phil and Audrey and I can go canoeing this afternoon at Lake Indy."

"Where's that?"

"Oh, it's just a wide spot in the White River a little south of 30th Street."

"If you can stay a minute longer, Nancy's on her way over with doughnuts," suggested Aunt Dood.

"I hope you brought an extra one," challenged Bernie as Nancy entered the room.

"Sure did! In fact I brought a few extras," perked Nancy.

Now that Nancy had arrived, the visiting continued, and the conversation soon turned to earlier days when Lillian had lived with her aunt off and on.

"Did you know," asked Nancy, "that Lillian was best friends with Hoagie Carmichael's niece when they were at Shortridge High School?"

And so it goes. Family stories, as it seems, are endless. The more a person talks to different members, the more new and fascinating stories a person hears. And, of course, if a person shares these new stories with other family members, the inevitable "That's not the way I remember it!" will eventually be thrown into the mix.

August 1, 2004
Broad Ripple, Indianapolis

"Well, Audrey, what do you think of my dad's outdoor fireplace?" asked Phil.

Audrey, Phil and Bernie had just passed the afternoon canoeing in Lake Indy. It was a beautiful day and they were celebrating Phil and Audrey's pending purchase of a second fixer-upper home. This house was located at 924 Prospect St., right across the street from their primary residence near Fountain Square in Indianapolis.

"I built it out of Indiana granite that I bought with the $100 gift certificate that Cyndi and Phil gave me for Father's Day," said Bernie.

"It's beautiful," said Audrey.

Later, after cooking Italian sausage and veggie burgers and veggie hotdogs and roasting un-husked ears of corn on the new grill, everyone helped carry the dishes and cooler back into the house.

"Before you leave, Audrey," said Bernie, "you have to see the new addition to my model railroad layout."

"It's awesome!" said Phil. "You'll love it!"

Bernie had just finished adding an upper level to the layout into which the merry-go-round and Ferris wheel music boxes that he had given Lillian as Christmas presents had been incorporated. The rotating lights from the music boxes reflected pleasantly in a large mirror-lake that he had also built into the layout. Running around the outside of the upper level was the new Lionel train set that Bernie had purchased from a National Geographic catalog—just in case the engine of the original set ever quit working.

With all the lights on the layout turned on and the other lights in the room turned off, Audrey, Phil and Bernie gazed at the expanded imaginary scenery before them.

"See Santa circling the house that my dad used to live in in Norfolk?" asked Phil.

"And there I am," said Bernie pointing to a tiny figure huddled on all fours under a small bush next to the house. "I used to get in trouble and spent a lot of time hiding under a trumpet vine that grew next to our house. There's my brother sitting on the porch steps. That's my mom and there's my dad standing next to our car. That's a model of a maroon 1949 four-door ford just like we used to own."

"It's all so interesting," said Audrey who, being an artist, was impressed by the many models and careful details that covered the layout.

"Let me turn on the overhead light so you can see everything better," said Bernie.

He and Phil then fired up the engines, and, before long, the room was filled with the sounds of trains rumbling along their tracks and whistles blaring warnings to the model cars waiting at all the crossings.

Life was slowly beginning to return to normal for Bernie and his family.

August 5, 2004
Broad Ripple, Indianapolis

"I'm done!" thought Bernie to himself as he stored the last box on a newly built shelf in the storage barn.

Even though Bernie had moved into his new home, now known as 6020 Indianola Ave, in May, there had remained many major jobs that needed completing. He and Phil had to install a large carport (which they finally managed to get to stay up after two unsuccessful tries that were casually observed by Scott, the son of neighbor John Patten who lived across the street), lay out the garden areas, rebuild a swing/patio area, and install a cedar picket fence that had been ordered from Canada. Canada was also where Bernie had had to look to buy six bridal wreath bushes for the front of the house. No local garden shops seemed even to be aware of these wonderful little bushes that were so popular during the 1930's after having been introduced to America in the late 1800's.

Bernie was "done," but, unfortunately, the house still had one job still unfinished by one of Bob Young's subcontractors.

"Hi, this is Bernie Barcio in Broad Ripple, 255-0589," said Bernie as he left yet another message on the subcontractor's answering machine. "You assured me last Friday that the porch railings were ready for you to pick up on Monday and that you would be installing them on Tuesday or Wednesday. Then on Monday you told me you hadn't been able to pick them up because your trailer broke down but that you would be getting them Tuesday and getting them installed by Wednesday. Well, it's Thursday today, and no one has shown up to finish the job. I really would like to have them installed this week. Please do not put the job off until next week again. This has gone on for too many months already the way it is."

Bernie hoped he sounded just a little upset. All Bob Young, Jr., could do was continue to apologize for the unreliability of the subcontractor and assure Bernie that Young Homes would not be using them again.

"I wonder if I can sue them if I accidentally fall off the porch because there's no railing?" thought Bernie to himself. "Probably not. Probably can't even take them to small claims court for failing to complete their job in a timely manner."

Oh well, at least Bernie was done with his jobs. He would just have to keep after the subcontractor and continue being very careful every time he went out the laundry room or kitchen side door.

Bad enough Lillian couldn't join him in their "love nest," it would be just too ironic if he fell and hurt himself while he was living there!

August 13, 2004
South Chicago, Illinois

"If you take the 87th Street exit off of 94," said Uncle Charlie, "you can go to the cemetery where your folks are buried."

"St. Mary's, right?" asked Bernie.

"That's right. Did you know that Nonno had the headstone imported from Italy?" asked Uncle Charlie.

Bernie knew that both his parents and his grandparents on his mother's side all shared the same gravestone, but he had not known that his grandfather had had it imported specially from Italy.

Soon they reached the 95th Street exit and Bernie turned off so his Uncle could revisit the neighborhood where he had grown up and gone to school as a boy.

Three days earlier, Bernie had driven up to Dunewood National Campground to do some camping with his dog, Rudy, before attending the 8th Annual Car and Bike Show at Ryan's Tavern run by his Cousin Evy's sons. The original plan was to pick up his Uncle Charlie at the show and then bring him back to Indianapolis for a few days to see the new house and some of the sights. But when Bernie learned that his uncle did not have a ride to the bar from Cudahy, he volunteered to leave the campground early that morning and drive up to Cudahy to pick him up.

On the way back through the north side of Chicago, they had stopped in at the Lutheran Home in Arlington Heights to visit Aunt Angeline whom Charlie had not seen for years.

"The old neighborhood doesn't look so bad," observed Charlie as Bernie pulled his truck into the alley behind 9506 Commercial where Charlie had grown up.

"They took out the grapevine," observed Bernie.

"But the garage that we built with the old paving bricks is still standing," said Charlie. "I used to have a clubhouse up in the attic."

"And Uncle Leonard used to raise racing pigeons up there too," said Bernie. "And there's Mussolini's house," said Bernie referring to an eccentric old Italian who used to shoot his gun from his second floor back porch at kids making too much noise in the alley.

"There's the narrow space on the south side of our house where Uncle Gusty climbed out of the bathroom window to go out with his friends," said Bernie.

"That's the yard where our neighbor used to put on his dead wife's nightgown and walk around at night."

"Yeah, Mom told me about him," said Bernie.

"And there's the passageway where Maggie's husband, Tony, died," said Charlie.

"Didn't they have to do an autopsy on him to see why he died so suddenly?" asked Bernie, already knowing the answer. "And they've moved Brown's Mortuary to a new building across the alley."

"Yeah, it used to be there in that house. See that room up there on the second floor?" asked Charlie.

"Uh-huh," said Bernie.

"I used to work up there and clean up after school when the mortuary was in that house. But I never went downstairs where the dead bodies were."

After the author's dog had a chance to do his business behind the old house, Bernie and his uncle got back into the truck to drive around to the front of the house.

As they rounded the corner, Charlie pointed to a large hall on the right.

"That's where your folks had their wedding reception when they were married, and there's where the broom maker used to live," said Charlie as they passed a house on the corner of 96th and Commercial Ave. "And there's where the Orlando's used to live."

"You mean they just lived two houses south of you?" asked Bernie. "Those were the people that your mother was living with before Nonno married her, weren't they?"

This was incredible. The author had been spending the last two years recording stories about all the colorful people in South Chicago without really knowing for sure where they all lived and how they all fit into the picture.

Uncle Charlie was now playing the role of Vergil as he conducted Bernie through the Inferno of those early days.

"And back in there is where Aunt Maggie lived for a while. That little house in the back there," said Bernie pointing.

"You remember that house?"

"Sure. Anthony and I used to wrestle and have a great time there," said Bernie.

They drove past what used to be St. Patrick's Catholic Church (now a Baptist Community Center for the Spanish population) and came to the corner where the bar in which Nonno and Leonard Leo used to hang out.

"There used to be a candy store right next to the bar," said Bernie. "We walked down there to buy penny candies."

As they drove under the viaduct, the two reminisced about the time that an unlucky thug had tried to mug Florence there, only to get the tar beat out of him.

"And that two-story house on the left is where Fred and Ida Mosacchio used to live," said Charlie. "Turn left there and we'll go by the bar that Nonno used to own."

And sure enough, just a few more blocks and there they were parked across the street from Tony Nudo's bar, in the second story flat of which Bernie's cousin, Rudy Strano, had been born just a few brief months after his father was shot to death.

"Let's go see where the shooting took place," suggested Bernie.

Bernie remembered that his Cousin Rudy had said that the shooting had taken place behind what is now known as 9545 Marquette Ave.

This was before the author had found the July 29, 1924, **Daily Calumet Newspaper** article that described the actual details and location of the shooting.

"What do you want to see that place for?" insisted Charlie. "It's way down there and out of the way. Turn left at the railroad tracks instead, and I'll show you my grade school."

And sure enough, there it was, big as life.

"It looks just like it did when I went there," said Charlie. "They even have the same out buildings for extra classes that they had way back then."

"That's not Phil Sheridan Grade School that Ma attended, is it?" asked Bernie.

"No," said Charlie. "That's up north farther. This is Marsh Grammar School. Gusty went to school here, too."

When the author would return home, he would come across a certificate issued by the Chicago Board of Education documenting his Uncle Gusty's school attendance. The certificate showed that a student named Augustine Nudo, Gust Nudo, Gust Nudi and Augustine Nudi attended L. Sheridan School during the 1930-1931 school year, Marsh School during the 1931-1932 school year and J.N. Thorp School until June 9, 1933.

Before the impromptu tour would end, Charlie told Bernie to drive down a street where his old school chum, Butch, used to live.

"There. That's the house," said Charlie as he beamed with recognition.

Once again, Bernie walked Rudy while Charlie climbed the steps and knocked on the door. For a long while there was no answer.

"There's probably no one home," Charlie had just said when the front door opened a crack.

A little old lady appeared who glared suspiciously at the large hulk who had been knocking on her door.

"You don't know me, but I know you," announced Charlie with a wide grin on his face.

It took a while, but before too long, Butch's sister, who still lived in the old family home, finally recognized her brother's old school chum and invited him in.

As they got back into the truck to continue their trip to Ryan's Bar, Bernie felt really glad that he was able to provide this opportunity to his uncle and to have him serve as his guide to so many of the places that he had heard of over the years but could not remember having seen.

As they drove over to get on the Skyway, Charlie pointed out facilities, now closed, that had once served as area steel mills. The South Chicago power plant, however, was still in operation. It still generates power using coal and, in fact, Bernie and his uncle had to turn off the engine and wait a good fifteen minutes while a coal barge passed between the raised halves of one of the many signature raising bridges located along the Chicago River.

"Boy, they have really cleaned that river up," observed Charlie as they finally made their way over the lowered bridge. "The water used to be rust colored when I was living here."

August 19, 2004
Lansing, Illinois

Not many days later, the author found himself back in the Chicago area, this time not for a nostalgic visit but to attend the funeral of John Sulek, the husband of his cousin Carmella—one of his Aunt Maggie's many children.

Of course, almost everyone was in attendance. Bernie was especially pleased to see his cousin Anthony again and to meet Carmella's two daughters, Carla and Marilyn, and her son, Little John, none of whom he could remember ever having met before.

When Jimmie Miresso announced that he was going outside for a smoke, Bernie went with him to talk over old times.

"You know," said Jimmie, "I still remember your ma's favorite saying."

"What was that?" asked Bernie.

"Now you're cooking with gas!" said Jimmie. "She always used to say that to me whenever she heard I had done something good."

As usual, whenever Jimmie talks to someone in the family, he quickly announced how he spends his time.

"I gamble."

"I know," said Bernie.

"I play Texas poker."

"How is that different from regular poker?" asked Bernie.

"It's too hard to explain. Know what I remember most about that time I visited you in Nebraska?"

"Was it our trip to the circus?" suggested Bernie.

"No. It was when you took me to the slaughter house to watch those guys kill the cows."

"Yeah," said Bernie. "They used to shoot them in the head with a .22 rifle."

"No," countered Jimmy. "That's not how I remember it."

"It's not?"

"No. They hit them in the head with a hammer."

Back inside the funeral home, Bernie sat in an alcove next to his cousin, Rudy Strano.

"Did you ever visit us when we lived in Nebraska?" asked Bernie.

At first Rudy said that he never did but then he did recall one visit that he had made.

"Back in 1950," began Rudy, "I had just bought a brand new Chevy when Dickie and a friend of his said we should all take a ride out to California. We were going to drive straight through, taking turns behind the wheel. You know, Bernie, the first night on the road I was sleeping in the back seat when all of a sudden the car bounced into the air. 'What the hell!' I said and jumped up. Hell, Dickie's friend was going 90 mph. 'Stop the damn car!' I yelled. 'What the hell do you think you're doing?' After that, Bernie, I drove myself. Couldn't trust those idiots."

Rudy looked around the funeral parlor a little, and then continued.

"When we got to California, we took a motel room, and I decided to go to a movie. Dickie and his friend had other plans. When I got back to the room and opened the door, two cops were waiting for me in the room, and, hell, Bernie, they accused me of trying to rob a jewelry store. 'Two guys just tried to rob a jewelry store. One got away, but the one we caught had a key to this room in his pocket.' Bernie, I told them that I had been at the movie and that, if they wanted, they could take me in and let the jewelry store owner try and identify me. Of course, he couldn't so they let me go. Since I had no idea what had happened to Dickie, I packed up the next morning and headed for Vegas for a few days."

Once again Rudy paused to look over recent arrivals coming in to express their condolences to Carmella and her family.

"Did you win any money?" asked Bernie.

"No. In fact I lost most of what I had left. On my way back to Chicago I ran out of money. All I could think of to do was to stop in Norfolk. Your dad gave me some money to get back home. That was the only time I was ever at your house in Nebraska."

Bernie listened even more closely as his cousin Rudy next began to tell Uncle Gusty, who had taken the third chair in the little alcove, about how his half-sister, Florence, had recently been mugged by two "shines" (his slang reference for blacks) who jumped her in the hallway of her apartment building while she was opening her mail box.

"Florence," said Bernie when he got a chance to talk with his cousin alone, "I hear you got mugged again."

"Yeah, Bernie. Ya know, I'll never forget the face of the guy who grabbed me. He hit me in the ribs and then put one hand over my mouth while he cut the strap of my purse with his other hand. I tell you, if I ever see him again, I'll know who he is."

"He was just lucky you weren't a few years younger," consoled Bernie. "Remember what you did to that guy who tried to mug you under the viaduct on Commercial Ave.?"

Florence remembered. She also shared that after 14 years of cooking for five priests at the rectory of Annunciata Catholic Church at 112 Ave. G in South Chicago, she was going to retire and move to Schererville, Indiana, to live with her daughter, Carla.

"They have a separate little apartment in their home, and they want me to live with them."

"You'll be safer there," observed Bernie.

Cousin Florence, of course, has a wealth of stories that she could share if one had occasion to spend some time visiting with her.

August 22, 2004
Indianapolis

"2502 Cold Spring Road, 2502 Cold Spring Road," said Bernie to himself as he tried to impress on his mind the address. He was on his bike, and he didn't have a pencil and paper to jot the address down.

"Let's see," said Bernie to himself, "I used to rent that room up there in the north east corner of the second floor when I first moved to Indianapolis."

It was a Sunday afternoon, and, as usual of late, Bernie was out for a ride on his bike. He had already ridden all of the other Indianapolis Greenway Trails and had decided to check out a small portion of one of the trails that ran along the west side of the White River south of 38th Street. The trail didn't go far, just down to 30th Street where there was a neat little riverside restaurant run by the city. Bernie had once eaten lunch there with Lillian and Phil. On this day, the parking lot sported a temporary altar and wedding decorations that were slowly being dismantled.

So Bernie turned around and rode back until he came to a side trail that led over to a skateboard arena and a bicycle velodrome that the city had built alongside Cold Spring Road.

Once there, he decided to ride down Cold Spring Road a little and revisit the old Park School buildings in which he had taught when he first moved to Indianapolis.

After Park School had moved to its new campus in the Lilly Orchard, its old buildings had been taken over by Marian College. The building in which Bernie's Latin classes used to meet was now used for Admissions. Amazingly, the exteriors of the old buildings had hardly been changed at all. There were some landscaping differences, but the old Headmaster's house, the Lower School wing and the Middle School and science buildings still looked the same.

Pedaling off his old stomping grounds where he had built and fired his first national-publicity attracting catapult, the Mars I, Bernie continued south to revisit the Carmelite Monastery where he used to attend Sunday Mass while living in the area. He was surprised to see a plethora of new churches representing a variety of denominations being built along this stretch of Cold Spring Road and had a moment of unease as he wondered whether the Carmelite Monastery had, in fact, been shut down and sold to a different denomination. The monastery buildings weren't where he initially expected them to be. He kept riding, past the Iron Skillet Restaurant where he and Lillian sometimes took the kids to eat on Sunday afternoons—home-style food served family-style in big platters. More future building sites for new congregations! At last he recognized the low brownstone wall that he remembered lined the street in front of the monastery. He rode in and felt comfortable among the familiar sights.

"Now, let's see," thought Bernie to himself. "If I'm not mistaken, the house where I first rented a room before I moved out to the Orchard with the art teacher Bill Hopper bordered the south side of the monastery grounds."

So Bernie pedaled back out onto Cold Spring Road, and, sure enough, there was the house. 2502 Cold Spring Road.

"2502 Cold Spring Road," said Bernie to himself. "Gotta remember that and put it in my book. 2502 Cold Spring Road."

August 25, 2004
Broad Ripple, Indianapolis

Bernie was just beginning to work on the Nudi family genealogy and was quickly beginning to realize that it would be no easy task. He decided to begin by making a few phone calls, one of the first of which was to his cousin Florence.

After he had gotten as many birth- and death-dates from her as she could remember, they began to chat.

"How's Lillian doing?" asked Florence.

"Oh, I'm sorry. I guess we didn't let you know," said Bernie. "Lillian died in February from kidney cancer."

"That's what Rosie died from too," said Florence.

"Yes. Rosie was sure a fighter," said Bernie.

"You know," began Florence, "when Rosie first got sick, I took her to see Fr. Rookie at the Basilica. He blesses people. I got blessed too. When you stand before him for his blessing, another person stands behind you to catch you. I tell you, Bernie, it's like a hot flash shoots through your body! I didn't believe it when people told me about it, but it happened to me. As soon as Father blessed me, the next thing I knew I was down on my knees being helped up by the man behind me."

"That's incredible," said Bernie. "What's the name of the basilica?"

"Oh, I don't know. I just always call it the Basilica. Anyway, after I took Rosie there to get blessed, all signs of her cancer disappeared."

"You're kidding!"

"No, I'm not. When she went to see her doctor, he couldn't find any trace of cancer anywhere in her body. In fact, he finally asked her if she had gone to get blessed by Fr. Rookie."

"That's amazing!"

"And you know, Bernie, she was cancer-free for seven years after that. But when it came back, it was kidney cancer, and there wasn't anything they could do about it."

"Same thing with Lillian," said Bernie. "There's no cure for kidney cancer."

August 26, 2004
Fountain Square, Indianapolis

"Look what came in the mail, Sweetie," said Phil.

"What's that, Hon?"

"Elizabeth Marie and Christopher Andrew with the support of their parents, Joseph and Elizabeth Barcio and Leonard and Janet Miller, invite us to share in a celebration of love on Saturday, the thirteenth of November, 2004, in Nassau Bay, Texas."

"Did you say Saturday, November 13th?" asked Audrey.

"Why? Is that going be a problem?"

"Well, yeah! I'll be teaching my class at Herron on Saturdays. I won't be able to go."

Audrey, in fact, had been receiving great recognition for her work as an artist while attending the Herron School of Art in Indianapolis. She also had a small studio in a converted warehouse near their home in Fountain Square where she was producing impressive large and small abstract works of art that led to her being hired to teach a Saturday class at Herron in the fall.

"You wouldn't mind if I went down to Texas with my dad for the wedding, would you, Hon?" asked Phil.

"Of course not. I can stay and teach and take care of Eli and Pico," offered Audrey.

Eli was Audrey's dog that had been her pet since she lived at home. He's a collie-golden retriever mix. Pico was Phil's cat that had become part of his life when he was working in Houston. Since Pico is the offspring of a housecat crossbred with a bobcat, she is a bob-tailed fluff ball with a full set of claws.

Audrey's dedication and talent as an artist would also find her invited to have a booth at a special invitation-only interactive experience of art and music in Indianapolis called ORANJE to be held on September 18, 2004. She would also have one of her canvases featured in a prestigious exhibit sponsored by the Young Friends of the Arts (the YFA) in the fall.

"Guess what, Hon," said Audrey.

"What?"

"Remember the owner of that gallery that I showed my photo album to?"

"The one who said he wasn't interested?"

"Yeah, him. Well, now he wants to visit my studio and pick out four canvases to show in his gallery. How about that?"

"Well, I guess he finally saw the light," said Phil.

Phil was very glad that he had encouraged Audrey to resign her position as a flight attendant with American Trans Air airlines (ATA)—which, by the way, was filing for bankruptcy in August 2004—and pursue her dream of becoming an artist and a teacher. Her talent was definitely shining through.

August 27, 2004
Old Broad Ripple, Indianapolis

Bernie checked his watch as he sat with a modesty sheet wrapped around his waist.

8:45 a.m.

Yup, his appointment for his annual physical with Dr. Lisa Youngblood had been scheduled for 8:00 a.m. He had gotten up early, showered and put on a new pair of maroon boxer shorts especially for the occasion before finishing his usual morning routine.

After the nurse had invited him back into the examining area to check his weight and height and get his blood pressure (which was great: 126 over 80), she asked if the doctor usually had him get undressed right away.

She was filling in for the regular nurse.

"I think I'll wait a bit," Bernie had said. "I don't want to freeze to death while I'm waiting."

"Probably a good idea," said the sub. "Doctor's not even in yet."

When Dr. Youngblood finally arrived to interrupt Bernie's perusal of an outdated **PEOPLE** magazine that had the doctor's home address blacked out with a magic marker, they had chatted a bit and then she had told him to go ahead and get undressed but to leave his underwear on. Hmmm. That was a good ten minutes ago.

Bernie sat on the edge of the examining table and waited, admiring his not too shabby shape in a mirror on the opposite wall.

"Okay, take a deep breath," said the doctor as she finally began her examination.

She continued by running the tips of her fingers down his back, pressing on his neck and looking into his ears.

"Any wax buildup in there?" asked Bernie.

"No, they look pretty clear. Open your mouth and say 'Ah.' "

The doctor made some notes on her clipboard.

"Now," she instructed, "lie on your left side and I'll check your prostate."

Rather than focus on what his lady doctor was doing back there, Bernie continued to chat nonchalantly.

"Okay. You can sit up now. Did you have something to eat this morning?"

"Yup," said Bernie. "My usual oatmeal, toast and orange juice."

"Well then, I'll write you an order to get a blood test at the lab."

"That will also indicate if there's any problem with the old prostate, won't it?" asked Bernie.

"Yeah, as well as show us how the cholesterol levels are doing and blood sugars."

More notations on the clipboard.

"How's Lillian doing?" asked the doctor without looking up.

Bernie was stunned briefly. He had suspected that Dr. Youngblood did not know that Lillian had passed away since she had not referred to her death the last couple of times he had visited her office. Now he knew it was true. Her staff must have really dropped the ball.

"Lillian passed away in February," said Bernie, now able to share that information with composure since his participation in the six-week bereavement program sponsored by the St. Vincent Hospice.

"Oh, really," said the doctor. "I thought I just saw her fairly recently."

"I don't think so," said Bernie. "She passed away on February 29. Kidney cancer."

"Oh. I'm sorry. Are you still taking the pills for your stomach ulcer?"

"No. I had an endoscopy in May and was told I could go back to my normal diet. At the moment, the only pills I'm taking are Centrum Silver vitamins."

"Pretty healthy for a 65-year-old," observed the doctor.

"Knock on wood," said Bernie, first looking around for some wood on which to knock, and then, finding none, rapping his knuckles against his own skull. "I think all those problems I was having with dizziness, back pain, kidney stones and a bleeding ulcer were all brought on by the stress surrounding Lillian's illness and death."

"Hmm. Could be. You can get dressed now, and I'll go write up my order for your blood test."

"Poor Dr. Youngblood," thought Bernie to himself. "She really doesn't keep very close tabs on her patients. Maybe I ought to consider switching doctors at some point."

November 28, 2004
Arlington Heights, Illinois

Angeline Barcio Santostefano passed away at the Luthern Home where she was living after her health had declined. The author was sincerely sorry that a personal health crisis of his own prevented his attending her funeral. His Aunt Angeline had provided such a wealth of family lore after he and his wife broke the ice of the 30-year family rift that had followed the settlement of the estate of her mother, Vrigita Barcio.

He was glad, however, that he and his Uncle Charlie had stopped to visit her at the Luthern Home on August 13, four months before her death.

January, 2005
The Oaks Academy, Indianapolis

When Andrew Hart, the Head of School at the Oaks Academy phoned the author, he was in dire need of a Latin teacher to replace Jeannette Wilson who had resigned at Thanksgiving.

"I understand you might be able to help us find a replacement Latin teacher," said Mr. Hart.

"I'm on vacation in Texas right now," replied the author, "but when I get back, I'll make some calls."

"Would you be willing to take over the Latin program for us?" asked Mr. Hart.

"Only if you can't find anyone else," replied the author, realizing immediately that this was the wrong thing to say.

Once Mr. Hart knew the author could be counted on, he simply stopped looking. Why bother?

So, at the beginning of the second semester of the 2004-2005 school year, the author came out of retirement once again, insisting, however, that he would only help them out for the spring semester. He would definitely not be available to continue teaching Latin for them in the fall.

April, 2005
Broad Ripple, Indianapolis

Lillian's dog, Rudy, was getting weaker by the day. He still ate well, but had trouble sitting up and using steps. Ever resourceful, the author quickly built a little ramp at the north side door so Rudy could be let out and back in on his own.

The day finally came, however, when the author knew the end was near. He had no intention, however, of rushing Rudy off to the vet to be put to sleep. Rudy did not seem to be suffering. He just preferred to lie still and sleep. So the author comforted him with words and petting before leaving to teach his classes at The Oaks Academy.

On returning one day, he found that Rudy had made the trip to the Big Doggy Park in the sky while lying on the rug near the door.

A large hole had already been prepared in the garden, so gently wrapping his buff companion of 14 ½ years in the rug on which he had passed, the author added this latest deceased family pet to the many others already resting in peace in their private pet cemetery.

The author then prepared the following IN MEMORIAM to share with family and friends.

"Rudolph (Rudy) Barcio, a buff and white AKC Registered Cocker Spaniel, born October 31, 1990, to Sire Steoger Spook and Dam Douglas Sally Joe, in Williamsville, Missouri, has passed away leaving no descendents. After moving to Indiana as a pup (the smallest of the litter), his first home was at Uncle Bill's pet Center, 8252 E. Washington Ave. in Indianapolis.

"On December 19, 1990, Rose Ammons, his new owner while living at Uncle Bill's, transferred ownership to Bernard Barcio.

"Rudolph was subsequently presented as a Christmas present (complete with stuffed reindeer horns which suggested his being named afer the fictional reindeer) to Lillian Barcio.

"Following the death of Lillian, Rudolph has continued to live with Bernard Barcio at their new home at 6020 Indianola.

"Rudolph was adept not only at ball retrieval but also enjoyed standing at the head of the basement stairway, catching (either in his mouth or by leaping on it with both front paws) a blue handball that was tossed to him from the base of the stairs and throwing (spitting) it back to his game partner. He could play this game for as much time as a game partner had to spare.

"On walks, Rudy was fearlessly protective—challenging any and all other dogs regardless of their size or ferocity (or lack thereof).

"During his long life, he traveled extensively both in cars and even in a motor home. He enjoyed both motel stays and overnights at campgrounds.

"Like many Cockers, Rudy's ears needed regular medication, the application of which may have eventually led to his developing a bad case of 'selective hearing' for the last two years of his life. Also, like many Cockers, the tendons in both of his back knees failed and needed to be surgically repaired when he was approximately ten years old. Following these surgeries, he took daily arthritis pills for the rest of his life.

"Not only was Rudy a 'treat-a-holic' (frequently getting bored and forcing his caregivers to change brands often), but he also insisted on being treated to a small piece of banana nightly before retiring to his buff & white blanket to curl up for the night on the kitchen floor.

"The family is requesting no flowers or memorials—only occasional warm thoughts of remembrance. Since Rudy is irreplaceable, there are absolutely no plans for a new family pet in the near future. Any offers to provide such a replacement will be kindly, but forcibly, refused.

"REQUIESCAT IN PACE!"

June, 2005
Mammoth Cave National Park, Kentucky

The author had submitted his resignation to the Oaks Academy, insisting that he had firmly determined to embrace his retirement, which he had first tried to do by retiring early from Carmel H.S. in June of 1995. He had, however, already been contacted by Butler University and implored to teach Advanced Latin, Latin Comedy, Latin Satire and Roman Civilization during the 2005-2006 School Year while they tried to replace the Head of the Department of Classical Studies, Dr. Bert Steiner, whose Parkinson's Disease would not allow him to teach his final year before being eligible to retire.

Since one of the author's retirement goals was to visit all of the National Parks, he decided to start his travel plans this summer with a camping trip to Mammoth Cave.

September 13, 2005
Saline, Michigan

"Dear Mr. Barcio,
"It was a bittersweet moment when I saw your letter in the current issue of REMINISCE. I was saddened to learn of Mrs. Barcio's passing, but some good memories were awakened."

The author had received a letter from Michael Hausner who had grown up in Broad Ripple and had fond memories of Lillian's VILLAGE SAMPLER.

The letter (reproduced below) that Michael saw had been submitted by the author to the REMINISCE magazine, and he was very pleased it had been selected for publication in its September/October 2005 issue.

"Laura's Theme was Lillian's Too

"One of the first movies that my fiancée, Lillian, and I saw together was *Doctor Zhivago* in the mid-1960's. The epic so impressed us that *Lara's Theme* remained our own special song during our 37 years of marriage.

"I was able to locate and have framed a poster from the movie, and our son later found another while studying in England. Both are framed and hanging in our master bedroom.

"After having been single for 28 years, I married Lillian and was immediately swept into the lives of three stepdaughters and, later, two of our own children.

"Over the years, Lillian and I collected several music boxes playing *Lara's Theme*, and it brought tears to our eyes when we wound them up.

"When Lillian succumbed to cancer, our son-in-law, Mike Pence, brought tears to all our eyes when he quoted the lyrics from Lillian's favorite song [as part of the eulogy he delivered at her funeral].

"*—Bernard Barcio*"

January 7, 2006
Suffix, Wisconsin

Esther Barcio Duga passed away after being taken to the Emergency Room in Suffix. She had suffered an aneurysm while living in the new apartment where her daughter Eileen had moved her to be closer to her own home.

Esther was buried beside her husband George at Arlington Cemetery in Milwaukee.

It was the author's priviledge to deliver the following eulogy for his aunt.

"Those who knew Aunt Esther, realize she was a good student. She attended St. Mary's Academy here in Milwaukee where, among other things, she studied bookkeeping.

"At home, Aunt Esther shared the same bedroom with her two younger sisters, Aunt Ida and Aunt Yolanda. Having all three girls share the same bedroom worked out fairly well, except that one night when Aunt Esther returned home later than she was supposed to from a dance, she couldn't escape being noticed by her sisters when she crawled into the bedroom window to avoid getting in trouble with Papa.

"Aunt Esther's knowledge of bookkeeping turned out to be very handy for her since she was asked to take over railroad record keeping responsibilities for Papa and several other Italian railroad relatives after my dad, who had been helping everyone with that job, moved his family to Nebraska.

"But the really good thing about her new bookkeeping responsibilities was that they got her out of doing the dishes at night, a job that had to be handled by Aunt Ida and Aunt Yolanda.

"One of my first memories of Aunt Esther has to do with the way we were all raised to show our love and respect by kissing all of our older relatives whenever we met them. Well, I have to say, that Aunt Esther was not someone who believed in returning any traditional gentle peck on the cheek. When you were kissed by Aunt Esther, you knew you had been kissed!

"I also noticed early that Aunt Esther was not the traditional stay-at-home, cook-a the pasta and clean-a the house Italian mother. She was a trendsetter, one of the new breed of housewives who dared to enter the world of work. As you know, Aunt Esther worked for the company that built Nash automobiles here in Milwaukee and also for Ladish Dropforge in Cudahy.

"She and Uncle George encouraged Eileen and Henry to follow their interests, even if one of those interests was racing Go Carts! Interests, by the way, that have led Eileen into the world of publications and Henry into the world of motorcycle racing, which, in turn, I'm sure, inspired her grandson Scotty to build and successfully race his own Monte Carlo racecar, Number19!

"Her nephew Joe remembers how Aunt Esther always greeted him with a positive, happy smile. She had a way of letting him know that she was glad to see him. She encouraged him in his studies and in his career. And if she had something flattering to say, like telling Joe that he looked like Gregory Peck, she didn't hesitate to share the compliment.

"Aunt Esther was also a great family historian. Along with Uncle Gene and Aunt Angeline (who shared her childhood memories of growing up in Italy) Aunt Esther helped tremendously with the writing of **THAT'S NOT THE WAY I REMEMBER IT**—stories like how Papa accidentally hooked bumpers with a car parked behind him and pulled it half a block down the street before he noticed it.

"I was also privileged to be able to talk to her on New Year's Day [this year] and was glad to hear that she had successfully avoided any dangerous falls this New Year's Eve. And, you know, somehow I believe that her soul is going to have a much happier New Year in her new home than we're going to have here without her."

August 17, 2006
Methodist Hospital, Indianapolis

Bob Liphard, the father of the author's daughter-in-law, Audrey, worked as a chemical technician at Eli Lilly Pharmaceuticals in Lafayette, Indiana. It was a job he enjoyed because it was close enough to his home in the country that he could ride his motorcycle to work and back.

Bob, however, was not one to shy away from risks. He did not believe in wearing a helmet. Thus, on August 16, when a car, driven by a man who violated his parole by driving, heedlessly turned into a driveway right in front of Bob's motorcycle. Travelling about 50 mph, Bob's cycle hit the side of the car and sent him flying. When he hit the pavement, he suffered broken bones and massive head injuries.

After being medevaced via helicopter to Methodist Hospital in Indianapolis, he spent the night in intensive care as doctors watched and waited to see what might be done first, if at all, to try and save his life.

By the morning of the 17th, it was clear there was nothing that could be done, and Bob was moved into a private glass-enclosed room in the cardiology ward.

"Is Father George on duty?" asked the author at the nurses' station.

"No. He doesn't come in until noon."

"Can you call Sts. Peter and Paul Cathedral and ask them to send a priest for Mr. Liphard?" asked the author.

The nurse was very cooperative and made the call.

"They want to know who his parish priest is," she said.

"He and his family live in Lafayette," said the author. "That's why they need a local priest."

After passing the information along, the nurse said, "They say they can send a priest in a couple hours."

"That won't work," insisted the author. "Tell them we need a priest within the hour."

An hour later, at a time when Bob's wife Joanne and her children had just stepped down the hall for a minute, a tall, slim, slightly graying Fr. Don walked up to the Nurses' Station.

"Oh, Father! You're here," said the author. "Great! Let me go get Mrs. Liphard and her family."

"You do that," said Father Don. "I'll be back in two minutes."

Joanne, her children and other family members all re-assembled around Bob's bed.

"Do you know where Father Don went?" the author asked the nurse.

She didn't.

"Could you call his cell phone?"

She did. She had to leave a message.

"Can you page him on the overhead speakers?"

She did, but he did not respond.

Bob Liphard passed away.

September 1, 2006
Fountain Square, Indianapolis

The author's son Phil and daughter-in-law Audrey had bought a large two-story home at 925 Prospect, and while Lillian was still alive, he had helped them and Mr. and Mrs. Liphard rehab and paint it so they could use it as their primary residence.

Phil and Audrey also bought a little one-story "shotgun" house right across the street, 924 Prospect, as an investment property to be rehabbed later.

During the late summer and fall of 2006, Phil, Audrey and the author were hard at work gutting and rehabbing a second one-story "shotgun" investment house at 958 Lexington in Fountain Square.

Audrey was still having a hard time dealing with the tragic death of her father, but when Phillip told her he and his dad were about to refinish the floor, she insisted that they wait and let her do that. She needed a positive project to help get her back on her feet.

September 29, 2006
Cudahy, Wisconsin

At the end of Butler's school year, the author was adamant that he would not be willing to continue teaching the Classical courses at Butler. This was it! He was now permanently retired.

"I'm about to celebrate my 69th birthday," he had told the Dean. "And I don't want to die grading papers!"

To be absolutely sure that he could not be cajoled back into the classroom, the author planned a road trip to California that would keep him out of town until the school year was underway.

To make the excursion more memorable he had invited his 90-year old Uncle Gusty and his 85-year old Uncle Charlie, both of whom lived in Wisconsin, to travel with him.

On September 29th he had driven to Cudahy Wisconsin to pick them both up.

They would visit the author's brother Joe in Friendswood, Texas, the author's cousins Hank Santostefano and Rose Aloia in Phoenix, Arizona, and the author's cousins Mary Leo in San Diego (where the author's daughter Cyndi would join them) and Gloria Leo in Las Vegas, before returning to Cudahy on October 15.

Because the author still enjoyed delivering his Roman Persona performances, he needed to leave Indianapolis on the 16th to drive to the University of South Carolina in Columbia.

October 20, 2006
Broad Ripple, Indianapolis

After attending his usual 8 a.m. morning communion service at Christ the King, the author was enjoying his walk back home. The air was crisp and clear. The sun was shining. Autumn leaves were bright with color. Suddenly, he was almost overcome by a feeling of absolute euphoria!

His travels were done for a while. He had pulled off a six thousand mile trip to the West Coast with two elderly uncles, and had just successfully completed another fifteen-hundred-mile round trip to South Carolina—coast to coast in twenty-one days.

He was home. He was safe. And he was about to deposit his healthy fee for his Columbia performance. It was as if his body had just run a self-diagnosis, and, after discovering that all was well, gave itself a little pat on the back.

"Permission granted for all parts to feel good!"

December, 2007
Indianapolis-Marion County Public Library

Because Bernie had kept several complete sets of all the **Village Sampler** newspapers and magazines published by both Lillian and Phillip, he and Phillip decided to make one set available to the community by donating it to The Nina Mason Pulliam Indianapolis Special Collections Room at the Central Library.

Two other complete sets were set aside by the author to be given to Phil and Cyndi when they are ready to accept them.

January, 2008
Chicago, Illinois

The Pompeiiana **NEWSLETTER** had been created and edited by the author, Bernard Barcio, and ran from 1974 through 2003. The **NEWSLETTER** offered a place for Latin students to publish comics, stories, games, and articles, and was a beloved resource for Latin teachers. In 2008, the author granted Bolchazy-Carducci Publishers the rights for all material contained in the Pompeiiana Newsletters. Bolchazy-Carducci subsequently announced that in a special blog (www.pompeiiana.blogspot.com) it would make all 229 issues freely available to Latin teachers, students, and others interested in Classics, one issue per day.

In 2009, Bolchazy-Carducci published **WHEN IN ROME**, a collection of the Best Cartoons selected from the Pompeiiana **NEWSLETTER**.

In the AFTERWORD to **WHEN IN ROME**, the author wrote:

> "When Pompeiiana, Inc., closed its doors at the end of the 2002-2003 school year, we were proud to have introduced Latin teachers and students across the nation to The National Catapult Contest, National Chariathons for Latin, Latin Weekender Conferences, A Persona-Presenters Speakers Bureau, an annual Textbook Giveaway Program, a Ferias Agamus: Let's Celebrate a Roman Festival booklet, a publication of Roman Games (that includes both ancient games and classroom learning games), a set of Latin Cultural Drill Tapes and Accompanying Study Sheets, The Life and Training of a Roman Legionnaire video, a set of Roman Emperor Posters, and the Pompeiiana **NEWSLETTER**, the only national monthly publication in the world for secondary school students of Latin."

Because Phil had worked closely with the author by writing for and helping to digitally publish the **NEWSLETTER** once its printer would no longer accept paste-up layout boards, the author also reserved a complete set of the Pompeiiana **NEWSLETTER** for him.

February 12, 2008
Joy's House, Broad Ripple, Indianapolis

Since beginning his retirement travels in 2005, Bernie had travelled widely and camped in many of Indiana's State Parks. And he had written a story about each of his adventures which he compiled in a scrapbook entitled, **Ubinam Gentium Sumus?** On the cover of the scrapbook he placed the following notice:

> "You are invited to ride this
> river of words to share
> my thoughts and reflections
> corroborated by the flotsam of memorabilia."

He was now at Joy's House, an adult day care center in Broad Ripple, where he had volunteered to read his stories aloud to the residents for an hour on Tuesdays and Thursdays. The staff and residents so enjoyed his adventures that he not only continued reading until December 9, 2008, but was also invited back to read weekly from March 3, 2009 through March 30, 2010.

February 29, 2008
Fountain Square, Indianapolis

Audrey Barcio was now managing the Big Car Art Gallery housed in the Murphy Art Center. As part of a special exhibit, she invited Phil to install banks of T.V. monitors which would flash individual pages of a limited publication, hand-crafted book he wrote entitled **TELEVISION HATES ITSELF**.

Phil's display was so well received that he later published it commercially under the aegis of Caprice Books.

March 25, 2008
DePauw University, Greencastle, Indiana

> "Dear Bernie, Please find enclosed two copies of a sales agreement for the purchase of your collection of realia [costumes, weapons, musical instruments, etc.] from the Classical world. ... Our [Classical Studies] department is very excited that your collection will reside here at DePauw and that both our students, as well as high school students in Indiana, will continue to benefit from it. Rebecca K. Schindler, Associate Professor and Chair of Classical Studies"

The author had finally decided to hang up his buskins, and, after advertising the availability of all his performance gear, agreed to sell/donate the collection to DePauw University when their Professor of Classical Studies, Pedar Foss, indicated his interest.

September 26, 2008
Winston-Salem, North Carolina

After Eugene Barcio retired, concluding a 42-year career, from his position of Post Master in South Milwaukee, Wisconsin, he took a "retirement" job with the Italian Community Center in Milwaukee. For 14 years he worked as their Parking Lot Manager. In this capacity, he was able to obtain discount tickets for the annual *Festa Italiana* sponsored by the I.C.C. and make them available to family and friends.

On September 26, 2008, Eugene passed away peacefully at home in the apartment which he and his wife Mary had rented after moving, for the second time, from Cudahy, Wisconsin.

Because of his father's declining health, their son David had insisted that they sell their house in Cudahy and move near him so he could help if needed.

After their first move, however, Eugene and Mary were not happy being away from friends and other family members they left behind, so they moved back, renting an apartment in South Milwaukee.

When, however, Eugene's health took another turn for the worse, David put his foot down, insisting that they return to Winston-Salem, where he continues to visit his mother Mary every day to see if there is anything she needs.

Because Eugene and Mary had earlier purchased side-by-side burial vaults in Holy Sepulcher Cemetery in Cudahy, his body was returned to Wisconsin for his funeral Mass and intombment.

November 1, 2008
San Francisco, California

The author's son Phil and his wife Audrey had rented out their rehabbed houses on Prospect and Lexington in Fountain Square so they could move to San Francisco. Once they would establish residency, it was Audrey's goal to take advantage of California's free college tuition and work toward an M.A. in art so she could teach at the university level.

In the interim she accepted a job in San Francisco managing an up-scale Italian restaurant called S.P.Q.R., and Phillip was hired to manage the famous Clock Bar at the Weston Hotel. S.P.Q.R. featured wines imported from small vineyards in Italy.

Unfortunately, before the year was over, California was bankrupt, and one of the first programs cut was free college tuition for residents.

August 5, 2009
The Domiciliary, Indianapolis

> "Hi, Bernie,
> "I was out of the office on your last Wednesday morning at the Domiciliary last week (8/5/09). I wanted to send you a message thanking you for your volunteer service to the Domiciliary residents. It was a pleasure meeting you and learning about your book. I know that many residents enjoyed your reading—you kept being voted to return each month! We wish you all the best in your future endeavors. Take care!
> >Laura V. Otis-Miles, Ph.D., CPRP
> >Domiciliary Chief/Psychologist.
> >Richard L. Roudebush VA Medical Center"

The author had arranged to share all the stories in the first edition of **That's Not the Way I Remember It** by reading them aloud to the veteran residents of the Domiciliary for one hour a week, beginning in 2008. The book was so well received that he even held a drawing on his last day to award copies to lucky vets.

August 21, 2009
Auburn, Indiana

The first time Bernie had seen a SmartCar in Paris in 2006, he knew he wanted to own one. It took a while, but as soon as a dealership finally opened on the north side of Indianapolis in 2008, he placed his order for a white SmartCar with black trim. He had had to wait 14 months for his car to be delivered from Germany, but he was now driving it north to Auburn, Indiana.

Because of his work for the railroad during his college summers, Bernie had become immediately fascinated when he learned that there were groups who organized motor car ventures on seldom used railroad rightaways throughout the United States.

After contacting Mike Ford with the North American Railcar Ooperators Association, Bernie had arranged to join a roundtrip excursion Mike's group would be making from Auburn, Indiana, to Coldwater, Michigan.

To get to Auburn, Bernie was now driving a little car that was actually not much bigger than the small two-man motorcar on which he would be riding with Mike.

His 2009 SmartCar was a basic model. No power steering, no frills. Which was great! It meant that during the three years he drove this car, it averaged 48 miles per gallon!

Three years later, when Bernie learned that 2012 SmartCars came with built-in Navigational Systems, he quickly traded up to a silver 2012 Smart Car with black trim.

In addition to the Navigational System (that could be programmed to give spoken directions in Italian, French, German and Spanish), his new car came with powersteering (not really necessary with such a small car) and heated seats. The 2012 also had a little smoother ride than the 2009 model.

The trade off, however, was that the 2012 SmartCar averaged only 38 miles per gallon.

Bernie hopes that by 2016, when he intends to trade in his 2012 SmartCar at the end of its 4-year warranty, that there will be 4-wheel drive vehicles on the market that will deliver at least 40 miles per gallon.

August 24, 2010
Munster, Indiana

Frank Strano, Jr., better known to friends and family as Rudy, passed away. He suffered much from cancer during the final years of his life, but remained tough to the end. Rudy had always been a special cousin to the author, not only because of the many colorful stories relating to the murder of Rudy's father, but also because he found Rudy's macho image fascinating. Rudy knew the importance of family, as was shown by the time and energy he spent helping, guiding, cajoling, financing and even burying those he loved.

With the help of men and materials from the Carpenters Union for which he worked as a no-nonsense Business Manager, Rudy had built a beautiful home in Munster, Indiana, where he lived with his wife, Helen, and her three children from a previous marriage. After Helen died on October 13, 1995, Rudy lived by himself in the house. To the end, he remained involved in the lives of his stepchildren and kept in touch with his siblings, cousins and uncles.

November 17, 2010
Broad Ripple, Indianapolis

In addition to his travels, his writing and readings, the author also enjoyed building children's furniture and toys in a woodshop he and his son Phil had built on the back of his property in 1992. Having constructed nearly 30 antique children's desks, he now waited for the Disabled American Veterans truck to arrive so they could be donated and distributed to poor children for Christmas.

In subsequent years, the author donated more than 20 small Adirondack chairs he built from walnut he had cured after cutting down one of his black walnut trees.

He would later turn to making and donating scores of different wooden toys made from walnut, maple and oak he had also cut and dried.

These were activities that definitely fit his retirement goals, and he completely enjoyed his daily freedom to pursue his own goals, no longer needing to further the agendas of others.

November 24, 2010
San Anselmo, California

After leaving Park School in 1970, the author had no further contact with the Headmaster, Bill McCluskey, whom he had liked so well upon joining the faculty in 1965. Later, however, he learned that Bill and his wife Betsy had been hired by George Lucas, of Star Wars fame, to help found a private school in San Anselmo and, with that challenge complete, they were still living there. So, while visiting his son Phil and daughter-in-law Audrey in San Francisco for Thanksgiving in 2010, he asked if they could drive over the Golden Gate Bridge and pay a visit to his old Headmaster.

Bill and Betsy were thrilled to see the author and to meet Phil and Audrey.

"Your dad stole one of the best secretaries I ever had," Bill told Phil, who was amused by this insight into the early life of his parents.

On a Christmas card received by the author in 2013, Betsy said she was still doing well, but that Bill was beginning to suffer from dementia.

Over the course of his teaching career, the author worked under one Headmaster and six different principals. Of all these, Bill was the only one still alive in 2014.

December 12, 2010
Dallas, Texas

As the author was settling the final estate of his mother, he had come across hundreds of her hand-written recipes, which he offered to his daughter Cyndi.

"Sure," said Cyndi. "I'll take them. Maybe someday I'll be able to publish them to share with the family."

Working with Bookemon Publishing in 2010, Cyndi produced **Grandma's Still in the Kitchen, Recipes from Stella Barcio** in time to mail copies as Christmas presents to her cousins and other family members.

January, 2011
American Village Retirement Home, Indianapolis
The author had now volunteered to read his travel stories, essays and poems to the Independent Living Residents at American Village. Once again the readings were so well received that, as of 2014 he continues to read weekly to folks gathered in the library of Lincoln Lodge. Since he still travels and writes there is no shortage of stories to share.

July 2, 2011
Yosemite National Park
When the author set out from Indianapolis to visit Yosemite with Phil and Audrey who now lived in San Francisco, he decided to add a special flair to the trip. He bought a roundtrip ticket on Greyhound.

Travelling by Greyhound one experiences the "underbelly of America," as the author likes to say—bus travel being basically the next step up from hitchhiking or riding the rails. Especially travelling west from Indianapolis. Greyhound uses some of its oldest equipment on this route, equipment that broke down several times along the way. And the author's fellow passengers seemed to be primarily ex-convicts hoping to start new lives in the west, abused women escaping from dangerous relationships, and young men planning to go into business growing legal marijuana. And the drivers, fully aware of their clientele, were often brusque or downright hostile!

Travelling by Greyhound east from Indianapolis is, however, a different story. Later the same summer, when travelling roundtrip on Greyhound to visit Acadia National Park in Maine, the author got to ride on Greyhound's 2010 buses, complete with recharging plugs for cellphones and Wi-Fi connections! And the passengers were completely different, mostly young college students or folks travelling with family or friends.

Nevertheless, riding Greyhound is always a challenging experience, no matter how nice the buses, the drivers and the passengers. There are always middle of night connections that require everyone to take their things into terminals and line up to board their next bus.

But, as the author also likes to say, once you are on a Greyhound, the seats are as comfortable as firstclass on an airplane, and, unless the bus is unusually crowded, you generally have two seats to yourself.

October 29, 2012
Santa Monica, California

"It certainly wasn't the easiest place for [crocuses] to grow. It would be nice if they could live in better surroundings. It would be nice if their contributions were welcomed with more open arms, in a yard that showed signs of appreciation.
"Crocuses, however, simply
Bloom where they are!

"And if they're helpless to change their world, they're happy to make it a little brighter."

This excerpt from a short essay entitled, "Bloom Where You Are" was included in Caprice Reader #2, called **PowerlessPoint**, published by Phillip Barcio. He had solicited entries from writers and artists across the nation, and the author was lucky enough to have his short entry accepted.

November 23, 2012
Los Angeles, California
"Are you going to walk under it?" the author asked his daughter-in-law, Audrey.
"Sure."
"But what if it falls?" he worried.
"It won't fall!"
"What if there's an earthquake right when you're under it?"
"There won't be an earthquake. The whole point of having a sidewalk under it is so people can see it from underneath."
"Well," said the author. "I'm gonna walk over to the side up here and take a picture of it."
Since his son Phil had to work on the Friday after Thanksgiving, the author and Audrey were visiting the Los Angeles County Museum grounds to see the famous La Brea Tar Pits, which are still bubbling away. After studying a 2009 excavation still in progress, they walked over to the monstrous 340-ton boulder installed nearby as a combination curiosity and pseudo work-of-art.
Audrey and Phil had moved to Santa Monica on May 17, 2012, so Audrey could hopefully work her way into a promised lucrative position managing The Tasting Kitchen in nearby Venice Beach.

January 12, 2013
J.W. Marriott Hotel, Indianapolis
Congressman Mike Pence had resigned his seat in Washington to make a bid to become the 50th Governor of Indiana. And he had won. Now, two months later, after his acceptance speech given in Lucus Oil Stadium in November, 2012, he and the First Lady-elect of Indiana, Karen, were enjoying a dance following the lavish dinner sponsored as part of their Inaugural Ball held at the Marriott.
The author and his daughter Cyndi were both honored to be in attendance, along with most of Mike's family.
On Sunday, January 13, the author and Cyndi were also invited to join the First Family-elect at a Prayer and Worship service sponsored by soon-to-be-sworn-in Governor Pence for family and friends. The service was held in a room in the Indianapolis Convention Center and featured speakers, singers and performers representing almost all of the counties in Indiana.
Because it was very cold on Monday, January 14, and Mike had insisted that he be sworn into office on the west outdoor balcony of the State House,

Karen arranged for her staff to distribute hand warmers and provide hot chocolate for those in attendance.

Even though the author and Cyndi had seats in the sunshine, it was still very chilly and Karen's thoughtfulness was sincerely appreciated.

February 4, 2013
Chicago, Illinois

Things did not go well for Audrey in Venice Beach. The owners of The Tasting Kitchen, violating a California law, had reneged on the position they had promised when they asked her and Phil to move from San Francisco to Santa Monica.

Audrey, of course, had perfect grounds for a lawsuit, which she filed and won.

As they waited for their settlement, however, they decided it would be less expensive to sublease an apartment in Chicago from a friend rather than continue to pay the higher rent being charged for their beautiful Malibu apartment.

August 17, 2013
Las Vegas, Nevada

Audrey's wish had come true. She had been accepted for a three-year Teaching Fellowship leading to a Master's Degree in Art at the University of Las Vegas.

While living in Chicago, she and Phillip had driven to Nebraska to rescue a tiny black Brussels Griffon puppy that they named Rocky, and he was now sharing their lucky #711 apartment on Bonneville Avenue in Las Vegas.

December 1, 2013
Broad Ripple, Indianapolis

After spending years having his manuscript about the early years of Jesus rejected by agents and publishers, the author finally decided to ask Phil to publish it under the aegis of his publishing venture called The Constance Book Project.

This small 143-page book, titled **Raising Jesus—The Early Years,** is a fictional story about how Jesus, the Son of Mary, came to know and prepare for his life as the Messiah.

The publication of **Raising Jesus—The Early Years** was timed so that the author could include a selection about the birth of Jesus in his 2014 Christmas greeting to friends and family while indicating how they might purchase a copy of the book from Lulu.com.

December 5, 2013
Las Vegas, Nevada

After once again soliciting entries from writers and artists, this time reaching out to Canada as well, Phil Barcio published Caprice Reader #3, entitled **THE DUST NEVER SETTLES**. This time the author's submission was entitled "Comin' or Goin," an essay explaining why we are all, indeed, co-eternal with the universe.

December 19, 2013
Broad Ripple, Indianapolis

"I just mailed my last extra copy of **That's Not the Way I Remember It** to a cousin," announced the author to his son Phil who had arrived early with Audrey and Rockie to spend Christmas with the family.

"Well," said Phil, "Why don't we publish a 2nd Edition."

And that spontaneous suggestion is what led the author to revisit his earlier work, make corrections and additions, and cooperate with Phil to produce this expanded and hopefully improved version for family and friends to enjoy.

Phil undertook to publish the revised text with a new ISBN number under the aegis of his publishing venture, The Constance Book Project.

December 23, 2013
Talkeetkna, Alaska

Rick Leo, the cousin that had inspired Mary Leo (cf. January 8, 2004), died on this date. He was 61 years old. Rick and two of his sled dogs riding in the car with him were killed tragically in an auto accident near Talkeetna, Alaska.

In 1981, Rick had claimed an Alaskan homestead in Trapper Creek near Talkeetna, he and his first wife leaving a lucrative profession in advertising in New York City to head for the wilderness. For more than 30 years Rick chaired the local community council, worked on numerous environmental issues, including the campaign opposing the state's proposal to build the Watana Dam on the Susitna River.

A Harvard graduate, Rick wrote "**Edges of the Earth: A Man, a Woman, a Child in the Alaskan Wilderness**" a novel about his young family's move to Alaska. He also spent about six years during the 1980's writing a column for the "We Alaskans" magazine, a Sunday supplement to the **Anchorage Daily News**. His columns focused on life in Trapper Creek, where he had built a cabin in which he raised and homeschooled his sons Janus, Krister and Forrest, and shared his strong opinions on stewardship issues in his community.

Trapper Creek was a far cry from his earlier life spent in Chicago, where he had been born on February 21, 1952, and an even farther cry from New York City, where he and his wife Michelle had been well employed in the advertising industry. According to a December 23, 2013 article in the **Anchorage Daily News**, written by Zaz Hollander and Devin Kelley, Rick occasionally recalled life in New York City in his columns, a time when subway riders still knew which line they were using—IRT, BMT or IND, nostalgic names that are all but forgotten now.

Rick's second book, titled "**Way Out Here: Modern Life in Ice-Age Alaska**," included the following observation:

"Our genetic dispositions have a basis here—dispositions to dominate and to herd together for the sake of survival, to wander alone in hope of revelation, instinctively to seek more in order to allay fear of scarcity, and to stand silently, if only for a moment, in humility, and awe at all that exists beyond ourselves."

During the summer of 2013, Rick invited his three sons to return to the homestead near Trapper Creek to help build a new log cabin with lumber harvested from their own woods, the sleigh dogs being used to drag the trimmed logs to the building site.

When the author visited Talkeetna in 2007, it was his privilege to meet Rick, his youngest son, Forrest, and the two dogs with which Rick travelled when leaving the homestead.

Monday, January 6, 1014
American Village Senior Care Center, Indianapolis
Bill Donnella, the father-in-law of the author's step-daughter, Sheryl, passed away after spending a year trying to recover from a bad fall he suffered in December 2012 while walking his large, beloved dog, Buddy.

Bill had been a well-known and respected radio announcer in the community for years, retiring in 1992 from a career spent reporting for Channels 8 & 13 in Indianapolis, as well as for WIFE, WIBC and WXIR radio.

Because Bill had been both an announcer at, and an avid fan of, the Indianapolis 500, he and his second wife, Maggie, seldom missed a race.

Before Bill's Final Services began on Wednesday, January 15, the author got to express his condolences to Bill's younger brother and to three of his children, Jerry, Jill and Jane.

During the services held at Tabernacle Presbyterian Church, three very touching eulogies were delivered by fellow announcers Bill Batt, Gary Lee (whom Bill had trained to follow in his footsteps) and Don Hein.

January 10, 2014
Indianapolis Hilton North
It had been 28 years since Bernie had been honored as Indiana Teacher of the Year. As a result, he was a little surprised to be invited by the Indiana State Department of Education to attend the 2014 Teacher of the Year Banquet given to honor Steve Perkins, teacher of Latin at North Central H.S.

Bernie was glad that Steve had won, not only because he was a fellow Latin teacher, but also because, in 1986, the Runner Up for Teacher of the Year, Richard Dick, had been from North Central H.S. The school would finally have its moment in the spotlight.

Attending the banquet with the author were Phil and Audrey, the First Lady of Indiana, Karen, and Governor Pence, who would use the occasion to present Steve with Indiana's prestigious Sagamore of the Wabash Award.

What a surprise the author received when he opened the banquet program and read the following tribute to himself.

> "For many years Dr. Barcio taught Latin at the high school and university levels, furthered the cause of Classics through Pompeiiana, and introduced countless audiences to 'the grandeur that was Rome' through such characters as tribune [Fabius] Loreius Tiburtinus. I owe Dr. Barcio quite a debt of gratitude for his gracious help as I began the process of re-enactment. To this I would add that I owe him thanks as well for the position I have at North Central High School. When my wife and I had decided to move back to Indiana from Texas, my first call was to Bernie to see if he would keep an eye out for any Latin positions. Thanks to him a connection was made at NC, and my life is the better for it."

To top it off, the author was honored once more when he was given special recognition, along with Steve Perkins, by Brian Bosma, Speaker of the House, during Governor Pence's State of State Address delivered in the Chamber of the House of Representatives at the State Capitol building on Tuesday, January 14.

January 14, 2014
Indianapolis

At 10:15 a.m., the author began his second year of reading to the Day Care Residents at The Caring Place by treating them to a story about his visit to the Abe Martin Lodge in Brown County State Park. Since he had a little extra time left, he also shared one of the many personalized birthday stories that he writes for his grandniece and nephews in Texas. This story was entitled, "Michael Grows a Pumpkin."

At 1:30 p.m., the author began his third year of reading to the residents at American Village with a story entitled, "Camp American Legion, Lake Tomahawk, Wisconsin." This story introduced the listeners to more of the many adventures the author has had with his 97-year old Uncle Gusty and his 92-year old Uncle Charlie.

April 15, 2014
Cudahy, Wisonsin

Yolanda Barcio Kowalski, the last surviving member of the original Barcio family, passed away on Friday, April 11, and was interred on this date next to her husband, Louis Kowalski, at Holy Sepulcher Cemetery in Cudahy, Wisconsin.

"Since every story has to end," the author, has chosen this to be his final entry in this updated and expanded second edition of **That's Not the Way I Remember It.**

Lillian Barcio's Ford Pinto Wagon at 6026 Indianola Ave. Broad Ripple, 1972

Phillip Barcio cavorts in Trafalgar Square during his Ball State Univ. session in London, Sept. 23, 1990

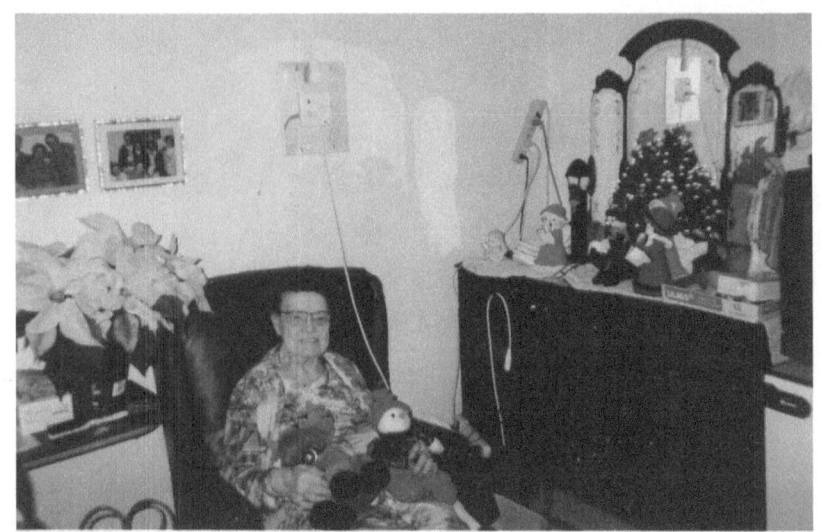
Stella Barcio at the Indianapolis Retirement Home, 2000

(L to R): Gusty Nudi, the Author, Stella Barcio, Charles Nudi, April 29, 2000

Basswood stump carving of Pomona by the Author, 1997

(L to R) Liz and Joe, Lillian and Bernie pose with walnut stump carving of Vertumnus by the author, Sept., 2003

North College Ave. median
2003

Patches (L) and Heathcliff

Brother Joe (L) and the author examing the Lionel layout dating from 1950 after it was set up again at 6026 Indianola, Sept., 2003

Joe Barcio with his HO model RR layout, Friendswood, TX, 2012

The author's Lionel Layout
at 6020 Indianola, 2013

Phillip and his mom in the Cruise America Camper
rented by the author to travel to perform
in Maryland, July 10, 2001

Phil sets the picnic table to celebrate his mom's 70th birthday

The author and Lillian show off newly purchased burial vault to daughter Cyndi (dressed as the Grim Reaper), Our Lady of Peace Cemetery, October 31, 2000

Phil Barcio gets tossed into the Atlantic Ocean on the day of his marriage to Audrey, Bahia Honda State Park, the Florida Keys, May 17, 2003

The foundation is laid for the modular home to be installed on extra lots owned by the author and Lillian, 6020 Indianola Ave., February, 2004

Author watches the two halves of his modular home being installed, March 2004

Walnut mantle reinstalled at 6020 Indianola Ave. May, 2004

Rudy
October 31, 1990—April, 2005

The completed modular house, named
Casa di Coraggio (House of Courage)
6020 Indianola Ave., April, 2013

Painted by the author, the scene portrays the little settlement of La Mattina where his dad was born in Italy.

Author in his garden at 6026 Indianola Ave., August, 2002

Mike Pence with his family as he wins a Congressional seat representing Indiana's 6th District in Washington, November, 2000. Mike was in Congress from 2001 to 2013, serving as the Chairman of the House of the Republican Conference from 2009 to 2011.

Author's gardens and their harvest at 6020 Indianola Ave., August, 2013

Phillip and Audrey harvest their Christmas tree, Stoney Creek Farms, Noblesville, Dec., 2009

Phillip and Audrey Barcio's renovated house, 925 Prospect, Fountain Square, Indianapolis, 2005

Congressman Mike and Karen Pence with Laura and George W. Bush, 2007.

Congressman Mike Pence with his family as he wins the Governorship of Indiana, November, 2012

Karen and Governor Pence, Inaugural Ball, Indianapolis, January 12, 2013

First Lady of Indiana, Karen Pence, State House, Indianapolis, 2013

Phillip Barcio's artistic contributions to the Fountain Square Mural Project he sponsored during the summer of 2008

Phillip Barcio paints the exterior of his investment property, 924 Prospect, Fountain Square, Indianapolis, Summer, 2013

Cyndi Barcio at Zion National Park
August 2012

Cyndi with her Xerox coworkers
Austin, August 2012

(L to R) Ren, Liz Alma, Elyse, Cyndi and Carla
Austin Put Put, August 2012

Model planes representing the hundreds of hand-crafted toys the author has made with hard woods to be given away at Christmas to needy Children, 2012.

Old fashioned children's desks made by the author.

Small Adirondack chairs made by the author to give away to needy children.

Author reading his travel stories to Adult Day Care participants, The Caring Place, Indianapolis, 2013

The author (L) and Steve Perkins,
2014 Indiana Teacher of the Year
January 10, 2014

The extended family of the author's Brother Joe and his wife Liz, Friendswood, TX, 2013

1. Papa Joe Barcio, black shirt, Grandma Elizabeth, white jacket with black polka dots.

2. The Chris Miller family, in black, far left, top down, Chris, Elizabeth, and Jacob (6).

3. The Bernie Barcio family, in purples, top down, Bernie, Dr. Michelle, Regina (15), and Aaron (8).

4. The Joey Barcio family, in beige, top down, Joey, Alisha, Anthony (12), and Michael (8).

5. The Gabriel Fuzat family, in blue, far right, top down, Gabriel, Mary, Xavier (11), and Isaac (8).

Closure

Since every story has to end, September, 2004, was chosen to start working with a publisher to produce the first edition of this book. That way, copies of **THAT'S NOT THE WAY I REMEMBER IT** could be presented to family members in lieu of the usual Christmas gifts, thereby helping to offset the cost of their production.

Just a few brief parting notes about the principal survivors of the original Nudi and Barcio families.

At the time of the publication of the 2nd Edition in 2014, Tony Nudi's sons, Charlie and Gusty, are both still alive and doing well. Charlie (92 in 2013) is a widower in Cudahy, Wisconsin, living in the house in which he has lived all his married life, and Gusty (97 in 2013) continues to live in the trailer he and his second wife, Netti, bought when they moved to Necedah, Wisconsin.

Mary Barcio, the widow of Giuseppe's son Eugene, lives near her retired-postmaster son, David, in Winston-Salem, North Carolina.

Epilogue

There are those who say that when a person begins looking back on his life, it's because he has nothing left to look forward to. This author does not agree with that opinion. Those who make that statement have surely not come across the observation by the Greek philosopher Socrates that "an unexamined life is not worth living." Besides, if a person values and appreciates the life he has been privileged to live, he should be allowed to document its most memorable moments—both good and bad. He should be permitted to write his own history, as it were; for as anyone knows who has studied history, "what" is done is often not as important as "how it is reported."

The great Julius Caesar knew this well and thus chose to send his own personal reports back to the Senate in Rome that was funding his campaigns in Gaul, Germany and Britain.

Caesar's adopted son, Octavianus Augustus, also knew this and, for this reason, hired Rome's greatest epic poet, Publius Vergilius Maro, to "create" a history of Rome that would glorify Augustus' goals and accomplishments.

Not to be outdone by his predecessors, the Roman emperor, Vespasian, had the historian Polybius in his employ to guarantee that his achievements were recorded with the proper "spin."

In view of such precedents, it is hoped that this author, with his extensive training and long career in Classical Studies, will not be judged negatively for having put his own personal spin on the stories that he has chosen to record.

By the Same Author

After having researched and published the first edition of **That's Not the Way I Remember It** in 2004, Bernard F. Barcio, L.H.D., began to consider just how all the details surrounding the birth of Jesus may have been communicated to the writers of the New Testament Gospels.

Since some of the most interesting family stories pertain to a person's younger years, he was disappointed that the Gospel writers made little or no reference to all the things Jesus was experiencing between the time he was twelve and when he began his public life at age 30.

He therefore attempted to bring those early years to life with hundreds of warm and realistic details and family scenes by writing and publishing **Raising Jesus—The Early Years**. In this book of religious fiction, the author tries to show how Jesus, the Son of Mary, may have come to know and prepare for His life as the Messiah.

Raising Jesus—The Early Years
is available from Lulu.com, ISBN: 978-0-9849159-4-1

Following his retirement in May, 2005, from a full-time teaching position in the Department of Religion and Philosophy at Butler University in Indianapolis, the author continued to write, composing short stories about his travels by car, Greyhound Bus and plane, and about his camping experiences. In addition, he wrote essays, poems and personalized children's birthday stories for his great-niece and great-nephews.

The following titles completed at the time of this publication are contained in two private collections called **Ubinam Gentium Sumus?** One is a text-only collection, while the second is corroborated with memorabilia and photos.

Index of **Ubinam Gentium Sumus?**
The writings of Bernard F. Barcio, A.B., M.A., L.H.D.
Traveler, Essayist, Story Teller and Occasional Poet

6's & 7's, A Clockwise Poem (March 21, 2013)
6026 Indianola (April 2012)
A 4th of July Gone Sad (July 3-8, 2008)
Aaron's First Decade (August 5, 2012)
Aaron Meets the Sneezle (August 5, 2010)
Abe Martin Lodge, Brown County State Park (October 9-11, 2012)
Acadia National Park (August 7-11, 2011)
American Art & Artists at the IMA (July 27, 2010)
An Apician Adventure (June 15, 2007)
An Early Surprise Party (April 18-21, 2008)
An Easter Getaway (April 4-8, 2012)
Anthony and the JARIX (February 6, 2011)
Anthony Barcio's 9th Birthday Story (February 6, 2010)

Anthony Meets Mr. Twelve (February 6, 2013)
Are You a Writer? (January 1, 2010)
Arlington, Virginia (June 6-8, 2006)
Atheist Evangelism and a Personal Apologia (February 2008)
Audrey's Graduation (June 6-12, 2009)
Back to Camp American Legion (June 30-July 10, 2013)
Back to St. Meinrad's (March 19-22, 2008)
Baltimore Maryland (June 24-29, 2006)
A Barcio Family Thanksgiving (Nov. 27-Dec. 1, 2013)
Benny's Funeral (April 24-25, 2009)
The Big Box, A Special 12th Birthday Story for Xavier (June 28, 2011)
Bloom Where You Are (March 15, 2009)
Breakin' In My New SmartCar (March 29, 2012)
C'e La Luna, Camping at Brown County State Park
    (September 1-3, 2009)
California to South Carolina (September 29-October 19, 2006)
A Call From Rosina (October 26-27, 2009)
Camp American Legion (June 3-10, 2012)
Camping at Clifty Falls (May 26-28, 2010)
Camping at Whitewater (August 5-8, 2009)
Camping Shakamak (July 20-23, 2010)
Cent' Anni! A "Toast" with a "Twist" (September 26, 2010)
Chain O' Lakes (August 12-15, 2008)
Change of Plans (May 20-24, 2010)
Charlestown State Park (June 1-3, 2011)
Charlotte's Eighth Grade Graduation (June 10, 2008)
Charlotte's Eighth Grade Graduation (June 10, 2008),
    "A Special 2009 Edition for Charlotte Rose Pence"
Christianity, Are We Finally Getting It Right? (December 29, 2009)
The Class of '68 (May 3, 2008)
Contemplata Aliis Tradere (April 1-4, 2010)
Cyndi's 4th of July Visit (July 2-6, 2011)
Don Barcio (April 20, 2012)
Do You Live in Wannabe, U.S.A.? (November 14, 2010)
"Dr. Livingstone, I Presume" (March 14, 2011)
Drum Roll, Please (June 6-12, 2009)
An Easter Getaway (April 4-8, 2012)
The Empire Builder (January 9-13, 2007)
Enjoy Every Minute, (June 18, 2009)
Enrico Mastronardi, 100th Memorial Birthday Celebration
    (April 30, 2011)
An Eternal Consciousness (December 18, 2012)
Fatima Retreat House (December 1-3, 2006)
A February to Remember 2007
Festa Italiana, Canton, Ohio (July 7-9, 2006)
Fifty-Fifth H. S. Reunion, Sparta High School (August 19-21, 2011)

First Significant Kiss (2008)
Fishin' for Walleye (May 18-29, 2007)
Fort Harrison State Park (October 9-11, 2011)
Fourth Time's Charm (August 15-16, 2009)
French Lick and west Baden Springs Hotels (March 27-31, 2013)
Gettysburg National Park Trip (July 9-18, 2005)
Giant City and Superman (April 16-18, 2007)
The Goblins Will Get Ya (October 31, 2008)
A Graduation Party (July 27-28, 2013)
The Grand Hotel (May 2-6, 2009)
Grand Teton & Yellowstone (June 6-14, 2010)
Grave Matters (July 24-25, 2008)
The Great Meltdown (Anthony's 10th Birthday: January 28, 2011)
The Great Orpheus (Michael Barcio's 8th Birthday: November 16, 2013)
Hanging Up the Buskins (June 20-27, 2008)
Happy New Year 2007
Harmonie State Park (July 13-15, 2011)
Having Fun with American History (November 6, 2012)
A Hawaiian Adventure (11th Birthday Story for Aaron Barcio, August 5, 2013)
Hebdomadal Apex (October 2006)
The Hurting, The Recovering and The Dead (November 10, 2007)
I Find Stuff (April 22, 2011)
Il Cavalière (November 16, 2011)
Il Mammalucco (July 1-5, 2009)
I'm 5 Today (Birthday story for Jacob Miller, November 8, 2012)
Indiana Live Steamers (July 16, 2009)
Indian State Fair (August 14, 2007)
The Indiana State Museum (March 4, 2010)
Infatuation (June, 2007)
I Seldom Write Fiction (April 1, 2009)
"I Saw a Calf Being Born!" (November 20-22, 2010)
Is There a Bigger Picture? (February 2, 2009)
Isaac, a Name Heard Round the World (7th Birthday Story, September 15, 2012)
Isaac Joseph's Birthday Story (September 15, 2009)
Isaac's Upside Down Birthday (September 15, 2011)
Isaac Sets a World Record (8th Birthday Story, September 15, 2013)
Isle Royale National Park (August 6-14, 2005)
It Really is a Wonderful Life (November 3, 2009)
It's My Art (March 29, 2009)
"It's Not Fair!" (Michael's 9th Birthday: November 16, 2010)
It's Only Money! Or, as my brother Joe likes to say, "It's All About Economics!" (January 14, 2009)
It's the Day After Christmas (December 26, 2010)
It's the Message, Not the Messenger! (2006)

I Wish Everyday Was My Birthday (Isaac's 5th: September 15, 2010)
Jacob's Thanksgiving Friend (Jacob's 3rd Birthday: November 8, 2010)
John McCormick's Creek (August 31-September 2, 2010)
Joseph Barcio (Giuseppe Barci) Italian Home Winemaker
 (February 13, 2013)
"Labor Day at the Lake" (August 28-September 2, 2008)
La Famiglia (May 3, 2006)
La Festa del Reingraziamento (November 17-24, 2007)
La Musica (May 19, 2009)
The Last Arlington Graduation (June 18-21, 2012)
The Last Camping Trip of the Season, Leiber Recreational Area
 (September 23-26, 2005)
The Last Shall Be First (February 2008)
Le Case dei Cugini (March 16-18, 2007)
The Leo's, La Jolla to Alaska (August 26-September 2, 2007)
License Renewal (August 7, 2006)
Lillian Rose Barcio, Broad Ripple Author, Publisher, Editor
 (March 14, 2008)
Lincoln State Park (May 18-20, 2011)
Little Green (July 9-14, 2006)
A Little "Trip" to Necedah (May 5-10, 2011)
The Lost Art of Culinary Foreplay (December 31, 2010)
Madison Wisconsin Persona-Performance Trip (March 1-4, 2006)
Mammoth Cave National Park, KY (June 9-11, 2005)
Mary Leo's Visit (July 1-5, 2010)
May It Be So! (August 23-25, 2008)
Mere Roman Catholicism (January 25-27, 2007)
Mezz' Agosto **(Anniversaries!)** (August 15-19, 2006)
Michael Dean's Fourth Birthday Story (November 16, 2009)
Michael Grows a Pumpkin (Michael Dean's 7th Birthday Story,
 November 16, 2012)
Michael J's H.S. Graduation (June 24-25, 2010)
Milwaukee *Festa Italiana* (July 19-21, 2007)
A Moral with a Story (2008)
Motorcar Weekend (August 21-23, 2009)
Mounds State Park (September 21-23, 2012)
The New AAU President (Xavier Fuzat 11th Birthday Story,
 June 28, 2013)
New Year's Eve (December 31, 2007)
New Year's Eve MMVIII, "Following the Star"
 (December 31, 2008-January 1, 2009)
New Year's Eve 2011
NJCL Convention, Bloomington, IN (July 31-August 3, 2006)
Ode to a Loon (2008)
Oklahoma & Texas Trip (November 20-27, 2005)
One of a Kind (6th Birthday Story for Jacob Miller, November 1, 2013)

On Reading The Search for the Historical Jesus, by Albert Schweitzer (December 12, 2012)
On Reading Being and Time, by Martin Heidegger (January 3, 2014)
On Reading the Qur'an (September 21, 2013)
Ouabache State Park (September 23-25, 2012)
Out of Control Robot (13 Birthday Story for Anthony Barcio, February 6, 2014)
Paris (May 25-June 2, 2006)
Pence Edgewater Dinner (August 2, 2008)
The Perfect Campsite, Versailles State Park (June 24-26, 2009)
The Perfect Question (April 16, 2008)
Pokagon State Park (August 31-Sepember 2, 2011)
Pompeii Revisited (February 7-9, 2010)
Potato Creek State Park (May 9-11, 2012)
The Problem With Euphoria (2006)
Quakertown SRS, Brookville Lake, Indiana (May 15-17, 2013)
Quid Est Veritas? (January 10, 2010)
RACCOON State Recreational Area (October 1-3, 2013)
Raymond, The Unwritten Story (February 23, 2011)
Regina's Big Adventure—A Birthday Story (December 4, 2009)
Regina's Secret (Regina's 12th Birthday: December 4, 2010)
"The Road is Life"—Cuyahoga Valley National Park (October 13-14, 2010)
Robert Browning's "Pied Piper of Hamelin" (November 3, 2006)
The Rock (April 11-13, 2009)
The "Roman" Catholic Church, A Friendly Look at the Ancient Roman Origins of its Structure, Rituals and Customs (2008)
Rosina's Party (July 14-17, 2006)
Run, turkey, Run (10 Birthday Story for Xavier Fuzat—June 28, 2012)
Samuel Johnson, Blustery Bore or Talented Genius? (May 30, 2011)
A San Francisco Thanksgiving (November 24-26, 2010)
A Santa Monica Thanksgiving (November 21-24, 2012)
"Seek and You Shall Find" (November 13, 2009)
Shades of Camping (July 10-12, 2008)
Shenandoah National Park (May 6-10, 2010)
A Small Achievement and a Little Story (October 2006)
Small Problem, Big Solution (September 8-9, 2006)
"So, are we talking about ghosts now?" (January 26, 2009)
So, Someone Doesn't Like You! (2006)
Somatopsychism (2006)
Spaghetti Day (July 27, 2006)
Spring Mill State Park, Indiana (August 3-5, 2007)
St. Anselm's College, Manchester, NH (May 9-13, 2006)
Summit Lake State Park (June 25-27, 2007)
Surprise Birthday Party, Houston Trip (April 28-May 1, 2006)
Tempus fugit, A 75th Birthday Photo Essay (October 10, 2013)

The Terrible Two's, Jacob Christopher Birthday Story
   (November 8, 2009)
Thanksgiving at Bernie's (November 25-28, 2009)
Thanksgiving at Mary's House (November 20-30, 2011)
"That's None of Your Business!"—Phil's 40th Birthday
   (October 16-18, 2009)
The Third Funeral (August 7-8, 2008)
There Are Stories and There Are Stories (2008)
Tippecanoe River State Park (August 29-31, 2012)
A Touching Instinct for Survival (January 7, 2011)
A Trip Delayed, Milwaukee, Wisconsin (January 12-14, 2006)
Turkey Run State Park (August 10-13, 2010)
The Ultimate Rejection Letter (November 11, 2011)
Uncle Charlie Turns 90, March 25, 2011 (April 2, 2011)
Uncle Gene's Memorial Service (October 17-19, 2008)
University of Oklahoma Performance Trip (November 19-22, 2006)
Up, Up and Away…(May 7, 2007)
Verdi Club Rendezvous (May 31-June2, 2013)
A Very Special Cello (Aaron's 9th Birthday Story, August 5, 2011)
A Visit with the Widow of Simon Peter (January 26, 2010)
"We'll Stop and See Rudy" (August 26-29, 2010)
We The Sober (November 1, 2007)
Why We Are Coeternal With the Universe (January 13, 2012)
A Wild and Wonderful Boy, A Special 4th Birthday Story for Jacob
   (November 8, 2011)
Who, Me? Worry? (January 2-9, 2010)
Worth Ten Sermons (April 17, 2010)
Writers vs Authors (April 7, 2011)
Xavier Fuzat's 8th Birthday Story (June 28, 2010)
Yellowwood State Forest (June 19-21, 2013)
Yosemite National Park (July 2-6, 2011)
You Hear Me Talkin'? (2008)
You Just Might Get It (March 2, 2009)
You're Not My Valentine (2008)
Zebedee and Sons, "Fresh Fish Daily" (January 26, 2012)
Zion and Great Basin National Parks (July 1-13, 2012)

www.ingramcontent.com/pod-product-compliance
Lightning Source LLC
Chambersburg PA
CBHW021129230426
43667CB00005B/68